Business

Essentials

197 - 205
285 - 317

Library of Congress Cataloging-in-Publication Data

Ebert, Ronald J.
 Business essentials / Ronald J. Ebert, Ricky W. Griffin.—6th ed.
  p. cm.
 Includes bibliographical references and index.
 ISBN 0-13-228785-4
  1. Industrial management—United States. 2. Business enterprises United States. I. Griffin,
Ricky W. II. Title.
 HD70.U5E2 2007
 658—dc22

                                                              2006049823

AVP/Executive Editor: Jodi McPherson
VP/Editorial Director: Jeff Shelstad
Product Development Manager: Ashley
 Santora
Assistant Editor: Denise Vaughn
Development Editor:
 Shannon K. LeMay-Finn
Assistant Editor for Media: Ashley Lulling
Marketing Manager: Anne Howard
Marketing Assistant: Susan Osterlitz
Associate Director, Production Editorial:
 Judy Leale
Production Editor: Kevin H. Holm
Permissions Coordinator: Charles Morris
Associate Director, Manufacturing:
 Vinnie Scelta
Manufacturing Buyer: Diane Peirano
Design/Formatting Manager: Christy
 Mahon
Composition Liaison: Suzanne Duda

Art Director: Steve Frim
Interior Design: Kevin Kall
Cover Design: Steve Frim
Cover Illustration/Photo: iStockphoto
Director, Image Resource Center:
 Melinda Patelli
Manager, Rights and Permissions:
 Zina Arabia
Manager, Visual Research: Beth Brenzel
Manager, Cover Visual Research &
 Permissions: Karen Sanatar [If applicable]
Image Permission Coordinator:
 Rob Farrell
Photo Researcher: Melinda Alexander
Composition: Integra Software Services, Inc.
Full-Service Project Management:
 BookMasters, Inc.
Printer/Binder: R. R. Donnelley &
 Sons/Lehigh Press
Typeface: 10/13 Janson Text

Credits and acknowledgments borrowed from other sources and reproduced, with permission, in
this textbook appear on appropriate page within text (or on page 569).

Pearson Education LTD.
Pearson Education Singapore, Pte. Ltd
Pearson Education, Canada, Ltd
Pearson Education–Japan

Pearson Education Australia PTY, Limited
Pearson Education North Asia Ltd
Pearson Educación de Mexico, S.A. de C.V.
Pearson Education Malaysia, Pte. Ltd.

10 9 8 7 6 5 4 3 2 1
ISBN: 0-13-228785-4

SIXTH EDITION

Business

Essentials

RONALD J. EBERT

University of Missouri–Columbia

RICKY W. GRIFFIN

Texas A&M University

PEARSON

Prentice
Hall

Upper Saddle River, New Jersey 07458

CONTENTS

PART **1**  THE CONTEMPORARY
BUSINESS WORLD

PART 5 MANAGING INFORMATION

PART 3 PEOPLE IN ORGANIZATIONS

PART 4 PRINCIPLES OF MARKETING

CHAPTER 11: MARKETING PROCESSES AND CONSUMER BEHAVIOR 326

CHAPTER 12: PRICING, DISTRIBUTING, AND PROMOTING PRODUCTS 362

PART 6   FINANCIAL ISSUES

CHAPTER 15: MONEY AND BANKING   460

CHAPTER OPENING CASE
Going with the Currency   460

CHAPTER 16: SECURITIES AND INVESTMENTS   490

CHAPTER OPENING CASE
Wanna Bet (on a Sure Thing)?   490

RON EBERT and RICKY GRIFFIN

Businesses today face constant change—change in their competitive landscape, change in their workforce, change in governmental regulation, change in the economy, change in technology, change in . . . well, you get the idea. As we began to plan this revision, we too recognized the need for change. Changing demands from instructors, changing needs and preferences by students, and changing views on what material to cover in this course and how to cover it have all affected how we planned and revised the book. This time, though, we took change to a whole new level.

A new team of reviewers gave us great ideas about content changes we needed to make. A new editorial team was assembled to guide and shape the creation and development of the book. The business world itself provided us with dozens of new examples, new challenges, new success stories, and new perspectives on what they must do to remain competitive. And a new dedication to relevance guided our work from beginning to end. For example, we know that some business students will go to work for big companies. Others will work for small firms. Some will start their own business. Still, others may join a family business. So, we accepted the challenge of striving to make the book as relevant as possible to all students, regardless of their personal and career goals and objectives.

How did we meet this challenge? To start, we open the book with an exciting new feature—the business prologue. This prologue does two things. First, it creates a framework within which the study of business can be most logically discussed. This framework establishes the four basic perspectives from which you as a learner may approach business—as an employee, as an owner or boss, as a customer, and as an investor. Second, the prologue introduces you to a variety of people from a cross-section of businesses—large, small, successful, unsuccessful, new, old, and so on. Later in the book, at relevant spots, we relate topics and material back to some of these stories. We think these introductions and the subsequent stories and examples will help make the material seem even more alive and personal for you.

We also carefully reviewed the existing book line by line. Extraneous material was removed, and new material was added. Examples were updated or replaced with newer ones. We worked extra hard to make our writing as clear and as crisp as possible. A whole new chapter on leadership and decision making was added, and the Information Technology chapter was completely rewritten to reflect all the changes that have taken place in IT and business over the past few years. We've also introduced a new feature to the book—each chapter now opens with the question "What's in It for Me?" We then answer that question by identifying the key elements in the chapter that are most central to your future career in business. And because so much work in modern organizations is performed by teams, we added a special team ethics exercise at the end of each chapter to complement the individual ethics exercises that have been so popular in previous editions.

These are just some of the many changes, additions, and improvements we've made to the book.

We are proud of what we have accomplished and believe that we have taken this book to a higher level of excellence. Its content is stronger, its learning framework is better, its design is more accessible, and its support materials are the best in the market. We hope that you enjoy reading and learning from this book as much as we enjoyed creating it. And who knows? Perhaps one day we can tell your story of business success to other students.

Ronald J. Ebert is Emeritus Professor at the University of Missouri-Columbia where he lectures in the Management Department and serves as advisor to students and student organizations. Dr. Ebert draws upon more than 30 years of teaching experience at such schools as Sinclair College, University of Washington, University of Missouri, Lucian Blaga University of Sibiu (Romania), and Consortium International University (Italy). His consulting alliances include such firms as Mobay Corporation, Kraft Foods, Oscar Mayer, Atlas Powder, and John Deere. He has designed and conducted management development programs for such diverse clients as the American Public Power Association, the United States Savings and Loan League, and the Central Missouri Manufacturing Training Consortium.

His experience as a practitioner has fostered an advocacy for integrating concepts with best business practices in business education. The five business books he has written have been translated into Spanish, Chinese, Malaysian, and Romanian.

Dr. Ebert has served as the editor of the *Journal of Operations Management*. He is a past-president and fellow of the Decision Sciences Institute. He has served as consultant and external evaluator for *Quantitative Reasoning for Business Studies*, an introduction-to-business project sponsored by the National Science Foundation.

Ricky W. Griffin is Distinguished Professor of Management and holds the Blocker Chair in Business in the Mays School of Business at Texas A&M University. Dr. Griffin currently serves as executive associate dean. He previously served as head of the Department of Management and as director of the Center for Human Resource Management at Texas A&M. His research interests include workplace aggression and violence, executive skills and decision making, and workplace culture. Dr. Griffin's research has been published in such journals as *Academy of Management Review*, *Academy of Management Journal*, *Administrative Science Quarterly*, and *Journal of Management*. He has also served as editor of *Journal of Management*. Dr. Griffin has consulted with such organizations as Texas Instruments, Tenneco, Amoco, Compaq Computer, and Continental Airlines.

Dr. Griffin has served the Academy of Management as chair of the organizational behavior division. He also has served as president of the southwest division of the Academy of Management and on the board of directors of the Southern Management Association. He is a fellow of both the Academy of Management and the Southern Management Association. He is also the author of several successful textbooks, each of which is a market leader. In addition, they are widely used in dozens of countries and have been translated into numerous foreign languages, including Spanish, Polish, Malaysian, and Russian.

CONTENTS

PART 1

THE CONTEMPORARY
BUSINESS WORLD

CHAPTER 1: THE U.S. BUSINESS ENVIRONMENT   2

CHAPTER 2: BUSINESS ETHICS AND SOCIAL RESPONSIBILITY   36

New!

"INFORMATION TECHNOLOGY FOR BUSINESS" CHAPTER

Information Technology has completely changed the business landscape, and this completely new chapter on business IT reflects those changes. We discuss not only the impacts IT has had on the business world, but also the many IT resources businesses have at their disposal, the threats information technology poses on businesses, and the ways in which businesses protect themselves from these threats.

New!

"WHAT'S IN IT FOR ME?" FEATURES

Each chapter now opens with a section called "What's in It for Me?" In this section, we answer that question by identifying the key elements in the chapter that are most central to students' future careers in business— making it clear why each chapter really matters.

> **WHAT'S IN IT FOR ME?**
>
> Growth in the cruise industry exemplifies a growing issue in the business world today: the economic imperatives (real or imagined) facing managers versus pressures to function as good world citizens. By understanding the material in this chapter, you'll be better able to assess ethical and socially responsible issues facing you as an employee and as a boss or business owner and understand the ethical and socially responsible actions of businesses you deal with as a consumer and as an investor.
>
> In this chapter, we'll look at ethics and social responsibility—what they mean and how they apply to environmental issues and to a firm's relationships with customers, employees, and investors. Along the way, we look at general approaches to social responsibility, the steps businesses must take to implement social responsibility programs, and how issues of social responsibility and ethics affect small businesses. But first, we begin this chapter by discussing ethics in the workplace—individual, business, and managerial.

New!

"EXERCISING YOUR ETHICS: TEAM EXERCISE" ACTIVITIES

> **INDIVIDUAL ETHICS**
>
> Because ethics are based on both individual beliefs and social concepts, they vary from person to person, from situation to situation, and from culture to culture. Social standards are broad enough to support differences in beliefs. Without violating general standards, people may develop personal codes of ethics reflecting a wide range of attitudes and beliefs.
>
> Thus, ethical and unethical behaviors are determined partly by the individual and partly by the culture. For instance, virtually everyone would agree that if you see someone drop $20, it would be ethical to return it to the owner. But there'll be less agreement if you find $20 and don't know who dropped it. Should you turn it in to the lost-and-found department? Or, since the rightful owner isn't likely to claim it, can you just keep it?
>
> **BUSINESS ETHICS** ethical or unethical behaviors by employees in the context of their jobs

Each chapter now contains a team ethics exercise to complement the already popular individual ethics exercise. These new exercises ask students to take on the role of employee, owner, customer, or investor and examine a chapter-related business ethics dilemma through the perspective of that role. By working together as a team, students decide what outcome is ultimately best in each situation, learn how to cooperate with each other, and see an ethical dilemma from various points of view.

PART 2

THE BUSINESS OF MANAGING

CHAPTER 5: BUSINESS MANAGEMENT   140

CHAPTER 6: ORGANIZING THE BUSINESS   172

BUSINESS PLAN PROJECT

The book now features a completely rewritten business plan project, tailor-made to match and reinforce book content. This new business plan project is software-independent and provides students with an easy-to-understand template that they work from as they create their business plans. Based on reviewer feedback, we've divided the business plan project into logical sections, placing each part of the project at the end of each main part of the book. With six parts in all, students can slowly apply the concepts they've learned in the chapters to their business plans throughout the course.

LOOK AND FEEL

The book's new design and improved art helps students who are visual learners better process and understand chapter content.

TWO-PART CHAPTER CASE VIGNETTES

We've updated or completely replaced the chapter-opening cases, keeping them fresh, relevant, and up-to-date. Covering companies from Coach to Mercedes to Royal Caribbean, these chapter case vignettes pique students' interest at the beginning of the chapter and reinforce concepts they've learned throughout the chapter at the end.

Updated!

"ENTREPRENEURSHIP AND NEW VENTURES" FEATURES

Whether working for a large corporation or starting their own business, students need to be both entrepreneurial and intrapreneurial. These now updated popular boxed features touch on entrepreneurs who have really made a difference.

Updated!

"SAY WHAT YOU MEAN" FEATURES

Updated "Say What You Mean" boxed features sensitize students to cultural differences and teach them to communicate more effectively, both orally and in writing.

*We've also maintained all
the features that you've always
loved about the text.*

- **Self-Check Questions** help students review their understanding of the core concepts presented before moving on to study further materials. These special self-check assessment exercises are introduced at three points in the chapter. Answers to these questions in the back of the book reference textbook pages to ensure complete mastery of the concepts.

- **Extensive End-of-Chapter Materials** help students review, apply chapter concepts, and build skills.

- **Key Terms** with page references help students reinforce chapter concepts.

- **Building Your Business Skills** activities allow students to apply their knowledge and critical thinking skills to an extended problem drawn from a wide range of realistic business experiences.

- **Exercising Your Ethics Individual Exercises** ask students to examine an ethical dilemma and think critically about how they would approach and resolve it.

- **Video Exercises** help students see how real-life businesses and the people who run them apply fundamental business principles on a daily basis.

Teaching Tools for Instructors

. . . Everything You Need for a Course That Gets Students Excited and Involved!

New!

FOUR-COLOR *INSTRUCTOR'S EDITION*

The new and most important addition to the instructor support package is the *Instructor's Edition* (IE). Four-color, three-holed punched, and containing shrunk-down pages of the textbook, the IE includes fully explained In-Class Activities, Homework Assignments, Teaching Tips, Quick Questions, Lecture and Chapter Outlines, Supplemental Case Studies, and Handouts. The *Instructor's Edtion* fully integrates all the materials you use to prepare for your class in one easy-to-use visual guide with links to extra materials.

Updated and Expanded!

TEST ITEM FILE

The new Test Item File has been updated and expanded to include 200 questions per chapter. Each question is fully referenced to corresponding learning objectives, chapter heads, page references, and difficulty level.

INSTRUCTOR'S RESOURCE CENTER

At www.prenhall.com/irc, instructors can access a variety of print, digital, and presentation resources available with this text in a downloadable format. Registration is simple, giving you immediate access to new titles and new editions. As a registered faculty member, you can download resource files and receive immediate access and instructions for installing course management content on your campus server.

If you ever need assistance, our dedicated technical support team is ready to help with the media supplements that accompany this text. Visit www.247.prenhall.com for answers to frequently asked questions and toll-free user support phone numbers.

The following supplements are available to adopting instructors (for detailed descriptions, please visit **www.prenhall.com/irc**):

- Instructor's Resource Center (IRC) on CD-ROM
- Printed Instructor's Edition
- Printed Test Item File
- Printed Study Guide
- The Business Plan Project
- Transparency Package
- All of the art files from the text
- Current, exciting, and relevant custom videos that expand upon themes discussed in the chapters
- A second set of topically oriented videos that reinforce fundamental business concepts
- TestGen Test Generating Software—Available at the IRC (online or on CD-ROM).
- PowerPoint Slides—Available at the IRC (online or on CD-ROM).
- Classroom Response Systems (CRS)—Available at the IRC (both online and on CD-ROM), and you can learn more at **www.prenhall.com/crs**.

ONEKEY ONLINE COURSES: CONVENIENCE, SIMPLICITY, AND SUCCESS

OneKey offers complete teaching and learning online resources all in one place. OneKey is all that instructors need to plan and administer courses, and OneKey is all that students need for anytime, anywhere access to online course material. Conveniently organized by textbook chapter, these resources save time and help students reinforce and apply what they have learned. OneKey is available in three course management platforms: Blackboard, CourseCompass, and WebCT.

OneKey resources include the following:

- Learning modules (Each section within each chapter offers a 5-question pretest, a summary for review, an online learning activity, and a 10-question post test.)

- Student PowerPoints

- Access to Research Navigator helps your students make the most of their research time. From finding the right articles and journals, to citing sources, drafting and writing effective papers, and completing research assignments, this site simplifies and streamlines the entire process.

OneKey requires an access code, which can be shrink-wrapped with new copies of this text. Please contact your local sales representative for the correct ISBN. Codes may also be purchased separately at **www.prenhall.com/management**.

COMPANION WEBSITE

This text's Companion Website at **www.prenhall.com/ebert** contains valuable resources for both students and professors, including access to a student version of the PowerPoint package and an online Study Guide.

SAFARIX ETEXTBOOKS ONLINE

Developed for students looking to save on required or recommended textbooks, SafariX eTextbooks Online saves students money off the suggested list price of the print text. Students simply select their eText by title or author and purchase immediate access to the content for the duration of the course using any major credit card. With a SafariX eText, students can search for specific keywords or page numbers, take notes online, print out reading assignments that incorporate lecture notes, and bookmark important passages for later review. For more information, or to purchase a SafariX eTextbook, visit **www.safarix.com.**

VANGONOTES IN MP3 FORMAT

Students can study on the go with VangoNotes, chapter reviews in downloadable MP3 format that offer brief audio segments for each chapter:

- Big Ideas: The vital ideas in each chapter
- Practice Test: Lets students know if they need to keep studying
- Key Terms: Audio "flashcards" that review key concepts and terms
- Rapid Review: A quick drill session—helpful right before tests

Students can learn more at **www.vangonotes.com.**

In partnership with **Audible** Education

Hear it. Get It.

Study on the go with VangoNotes.

Just download chapter reviews from your text and listen to them on any mp3 player. Now wherever you are-- whatever you're doing--you can study by listening to the following for each chapter of your textbook:

Big Ideas: Your "need to know" for each chapter

Practice Test: A gut check for the Big Ideas--tells you if you need to keep studying

Key Terms: Audio "flashcards" to help you review key concepts and terms

Rapid Review: A quick drill session--use it right before your test

VangoNotes.com

Preface

Acknowledgments

Although two names appear on the cover of the book, we could never have completed the sixth edition without the assistance of many fine individuals. Everyone who worked on the book was committed to making it the best that it could be. Quality and closeness to the customer are things that we read a lot about today. Both we and the people who worked with us took these concepts to heart in this book and made quality our watchword by listening to our users and trying to provide what they want. First, we would like to thank all the professionals who took time from their busy schedules to review materials for *Business Essentials*:

We'd like to thank the reviewers of the sixth edition:

Kari Anderson
University of Nebraska

Ellen Benowitz
Mercer Community College

Bonnie S. Bolinger
Ivy Tech State College

Chuck Bowles
Pikes Peak Community College

Kate Demarest
Carroll Community College

Gary M. Donnelly
Casper College

Glenda Eckert
Oklahoma State University-Okmulgee

Badie Farah
Eastern Michigan University

Rusty Freed
Tarleton State University

James P. Hess
Ivy Tech State College

Gokhan Karahan
Nicholls State University

Pam Janson
Stark State College of Technology

Jerry A. Kozlowski
Genesee Community College

Martha Laham
Diablo Valley College

Bill Logan
Middle Georgia College

Monty Lynn
Abilene Christian University

Susan D. McClaren
Mt. Hood Community College

Tatyana Pashnyak
Bainbridge College

Paul C. Rogers
Community College of Beaver County

Jean Rose
Southeast Tech

Bert Sanchez
Pierce College

Jana Schrenkler
Rasmussen College

John R Schrieber
NorthWest Arkansas Community College

Marcianne Schusler
Prairie State College

Phyllis Shafer
Brookdale Community College

Linda Shul
Albuquerque TVI Community College

Peter Stone
Spartanburg Technical College

what's in it for you?

If you're like many students, you may be starting this semester with some questions about why you're here. Whether you're taking this course at a two-year college, at a four-year university, or at a technical school, in a traditional classroom setting or online, you may be wondering just what you're supposed to get from this course and how it will benefit you. In short, you may be wondering, "What's in it for me?"

First, regardless of what it may be called at your school, this is a survey course designed to introduce you to the many exciting and challenging facets of business, both in the United States and elsewhere. The course is designed to fit the needs of a wide variety of students. You may be taking this course as the first step toward earning a degree in business, you may be thinking about business and want to know more about it, or you may know you want to study business but are unsure of the area you want to pursue. You may plan to major in another field but want some basic business background and are taking this course as an elective. Or you may be here because, frankly, this course is required or is a prerequisite to another course.

For those of you with little work experience, you may be uncertain as to what the business world is all about. If you have a lot of work experience, you may even be a bit skeptical as to what you can actually learn about business from an introductory course. One of our biggest challenges as authors is to write a book that meets the needs of such a diverse student population, especially when we acknowledge the legitimacy of your right to ask "What's in it for me?" We also want to do our best to ensure that you find the course challenging, interesting, and useful. To help lay the foundation for meeting these challenges, let's look at the various "hats" that you may wear, both now and in the future.

WEARING THE HATS

There's an old adage that refers to people wearing different "hats." In general, this is based on the idea that any given person usually has different roles to play in different settings. For example, your roles may include student, child, spouse, employee, friend, and/or parent. You could think of each of these roles as needing a different hat—when you play the role of a student, for example, you wear one hat, but when you leave campus and go to your part-time job, you put on a different hat. From the perspective of studying and interfacing with the world of *business*, there are at least four distinct "hats" that you might wear:

Margie Flores-Vance
Drury University

Candace Vogelsong
Cecil Community College

William Woomer
Delaware County Community College

Daniel Wubbena
Western Iowa Tech Community College

We'd like to thank reviewers of the Test Item File:

Bill McPherson
Eberly College of Business

Dave Murphy
Madisonville Community College

Dan Pacheco
Kansas City Kansas Community College

We'd like to thank reviewers of our previous editions:

Roanne Angiello
Bergen Community College

Michael Baldigo
Sonoma State University

Ed Belvins
DeVry Institute of Technology

Mary Jo Boehms
Jackson State Community College

Harvey Bronstein
Oakland Community

Ronald Cereola
James Madison University

Gary Christiansen
North Iowa Area Community College

Michael Cicero
Highline Community College

Karen Collins
Lehigh University

James Darnell
Ivy Tech-Kokomo

Richard Drury
Northern Virginia Community College

Pat Ellebracht
Truman State University

John Gubbay
Moraine Valley Community College

Dr. Shiv Gupta
University of Findlay

Karen W. Harris
Montgomery College

Jeff Harper
Texas Tech University

Edward M. Henn
Broward Community College

Jim Hess
Ivy Tech-Fort Wayne

Jerry Hufnagel Horry
Georgetown Technical College

Robert W. James
DeVry University

Jeffrey Jones
Community College of Southern Nevada

James H. Kennedy
Angelina College

Betty Ann Kirk
Tallahassee Community College

Sofia B. Klopp
Palm Beach Community College

Kenneth J. Lacho
University of New Orleans

Keith Leibham
Columbia Gorge Community College

Robert Markus
Babson College

John F. Mastriani
El Paso Community College

William E. Matthews
William Paterson University

Bronna McNeeley
Midwestern State University

Thomas J. Morrisey
Buffalo State College

William Morrison
San Jose State

David William
Murphy Madisonville Community College

Scott Norwood
San Jose State University

Joseph R. Novak
Blinn College

Mark Nygren
Brigham Young University-Idaho

Glenn Perser
Houston Community College System

Constantine Petrides
Borough of Manhattan Community College

Roy R. Pipitone
Eric Community College

William D. Raffield
University of St. Thomas

Richard Randall
Nassau Community College

Betsy Ray
Indiana Business College

Richard Reed
Washington State University

Christopher Rogers
Miami-Dade Community College

Phyllis Schafer
Brookdale Community College

Lewis Schlossinger
Community College of Aurora

David Sollars
Auburn University-Montgomery

Robert N. Stern
Cornell University

Arlene Strawn
Tallahassee Community College

Peggy Takahashi
University of San Francisco

Jane A. Treptow
Broward Community College

Janna P. Vice
Eastern Kentucky University

Patricia R. Ward
Upper Iowa University

Phillip A Weatherford
Embry-Riddle Aeronautical University

Jerry E. Wheat
Indiana University Southeast

Lynne Spellman White
Trinity Christian College

JoAnn Wiggins
Walla Walla College

Pamela J. Winslow
Berkeley College of Business

Gerrit Wolf
SUNY-Stony Brook

A number of other professionals also made substantive contributions to the text. We are most indebted to two people. Jodi McPherson became our executive editor with this edition. From day one, she was committed to elevating the quality and profile of this book. Just as businesses want to be number one in their markets, Jodi has been steadfast in her efforts to help us maintain and enhance our leadership position in this highly competitive market. Shannon LeMay-Finn also joined us as our development editor. Shannon consistently pushed us, challenged us, guided us, and encouraged us to enhance our writing, our relevance, and our timeliness. The book you hold is truly a team effort.

Of course, this edition also builds on past successes. Hence, we would be remiss not to acknowledge Ron Librach, our development editor on our previous editions. Other people at Prentice Hall who made important contributions include Judy Leale, associate director, production; Kevin Holm and Suzanne Grappi, production editors; Diane Peirano, manufacturing buyer; Melinda Alexander, photo researcher; Steve Frim, art director; and Denise Vaughn, assistant editor. We also want to acknowledge the contributions of the entire team at Prentice Hall Business Publishing, including Jeff Shelstad, editorial director; Anne Howard, marketing manager; and Steve Deitmer, director of development.

The supplements package for *Business Essentials, Sixth Edition,* also benefited from the able contributions of several individuals, including Jim Hess (Instructor's Edition and Test Item File), Mark King (Business Plan Project), Patricia M. Bernson (Student Study Guide), and Charles Cook (PowerPoints). We would like to thank those people for developing the finest set of instructional and learning materials for this field.

Our colleagues at the University of Missouri-Columbia and Texas A&M University also deserve recognition. Each of us has the good fortune to be a part of a community of scholars who enrich our lives and challenge our ideas. Without their intellectual stimulation and support, our work would suffer greatly. Finally, we want to acknowledge the people who are the foundation of our lives. We take pride in the accomplishments of our wives, Mary and Glenda, and draw strength from the knowledge that they are there for us to lean on. And we take joy from our children, Matt and Kristen, and Ashley, Dustin, and Matt. Sometimes in the late hours when we're ready for sleep but have to get one or two more pages written, looking at your pictures keeps us going. Thanks to all of you for making us what we are.

Ronald J. Ebert
Ricky W. Griffin

- *The Employee Hat.* One business hat is as an employee working for a business. Many people wear this hat during the early stages of their career. To wear the hat successfully, you will need to understand your "place" in the organization—your job duties and responsibilities, how to get along with others, how to work with your boss, what your organization is all about, and so on. You'll begin to see how to best wear this hat as you learn more about organizing business enterprises in Chapter 6 and how organizations manage their human resources in Chapter 10, as well as in several other places in this book.

- *The Employer or Boss Hat.* Another business hat that many people wear is as an employer or boss. Whether you start your own business or get promoted within someone else's business, one day people will be working for you. You'll still need to know your job duties and responsibilities. But you'll now also need to understand how to manage other people—how to motivate and reward them, how to lead them, how to deal with conflict among them, and the legal parameters that may affect how you treat them. Chapters 3, 5, 8, and 9 provide a lot of information about how you can best wear this hat, although the role of employer runs throughout the entire book.

- *The Consumer Hat.* Even if you don't work for a business, you will still wear the hat of a consumer. Whenever you fill your car with Shell gasoline, bid for something on eBay, buy clothes at Urban Outfitters, or download a song from iTunes, you're consuming products or services created by business. To wear this hat effectively, you need to understand how to assess the value of what you're buying, your rights as a consumer, and so on. We discuss how you can best wear this hat in Chapters 4, 11, and 12.

- *The Investor Hat.* The final business hat many people wear is that of an investor. You may buy your own business or work for a company that allows you to buy its own stock. You may also invest in other companies through the purchase of stocks or shares of a mutual fund. In order for you to invest wisely, you must understand some basics, such as financial markets, business earnings, and the basic costs of investment. Chapters 4, 14, 16, and an appendix will help you learn how to best wear this hat.

Many people wear more than one of these hats at the same time. Regardless of how many hats you wear or when you may be putting them on, it should be clear that you have in the past, do now, and will in the future interface with many businesses in different ways. Knowing how to best wear all of these hats is what this book is all about.

The Stories of Business

How do businesses work? How do they get started? Why do some grow and others fail? How do they affect us regardless of the hats we may be wearing? These are the questions we'll discuss throughout this book. But first, let's "meet" a few people and see how these questions have affected them.

Let's Google It

Sergey Brin and Larry Page decided they were tired of Internet search engines that yielded an over-whelming mess of random returns so, about 10 years ago they decided to do something about it— create their own. Today, their creation, Google, has become the world's most popular Web search engine, conducting upward of 200 million searches everyday. The word "google" has become virtually synonymous with the word search among many computer users.

But Brin and Page are not resting on their laurels as they push and expand Google into more corners of our daily lives. Google now offers Google Talk (instant messaging), Google Maps, Gmail, and Google Desktop, all rapidly growing products. Google also generates more than one-quarter of its revenues from foreign markets and has been trans-lated into 97 languages. And when Google began selling its stock to the public in 2004, it generated over $1.6 billion that it plans to use for even faster expansion. We'll discuss how Google used information technology on its path to success, how companies like it create their lineup of products (their so-called "product mix"), as well as how companies like Google's public stock offerings affect a company's balance sheet in Chapters 11, 13, and 14.

Google founders Sergey Brin and Larry Page.

Hip Hop Hoops

When most people think of athletic footwear, global brands, such as Nike and Adidas, come to mind. But a small upstart company called And1 is fast making a name for itself as well. Founded by Jay Coen Gilbert, Seth Berger, and Tom Austin, And1 takes a decided "streetball" approach to basketball. At the core of its business is a growing line of tapes highlighting the skills—and swagger— of playground legends showing incredible moves and turning basketball purists on their heads.

But if the tapes are the catalyst, And1's shoes and shirts are the drivers. Indeed, And1 now trails only Nike in terms of NBA player endorsements. The counterculture firm has 165 employees, generates $180 million in annual revenues, and sells its products in over 125 countries. Among its more recent activities was a smash summer tour showcasing the talents—and footwear—of more than 15 top streetball players. And to help keep itself fresh, And1 hires mostly younger staffers and pays close attention to their advice. And1 is successful because it knows, hires, and promotes to its target market. You'll learn more about these factors in Chapters 3, 10, and 12.

The Price of Pasta

Maureen Jenkins, a Chicago-based professional writer, longed to live in Italy. A few years ago, she decided that, with some careful budgeting, she could indeed move to Italy and support herself, working as a freelance writer for clients back home. So, she packed up and moved to Florence, rented a small apartment, kept busy with her writing, and enjoyed the gorgeous Tuscany countryside. She found that she could indeed live a nice, comfortable life. But then things took a turn for the worse.

As a result of economic shifts and international trading patterns, the value of the dollar gradually began to decline relative to the local currency (the euro). For instance, over one six-month period, the price of a dinner at Maureen's favorite restaurant jumped from less than $50 to over $60, even though the menu price (in local currency) didn't change at all—the jump was totally attributable to changes in the value of the dollar relative to the euro. Similarly, the price of a pair of shoes at Maureen's favorite shop almost doubled in price.

Coupled with increasing bank and credit card fees for exchanging one currency for another, the cost of living in Italy simply became too much for Maureen to bear. So, she packed up and moved back to Chicago. While she was disappointed in how things turned out, she also took a pragmatic view, commenting, "It's one thing to go on vacation for a week and you suck it up. But it's another thing for every single thing you buy to cost one-third more.

You feel like you're digging yourself into a hole, and at some point you have to stop digging." You'll learn more about how and why the world of global business affects both individuals and businesses alike, as well as what motivates people like Maureen, in Chapters 2, 7, 8, and 15.

Maureen Jenkins

A Boy and His Computer

When Michael Dell was 13, he ran a successful mail-order stamp trading business out of his bedroom, grossing over $2,000 a month. When he entered college in 1983 as a pre-med student, he had already been bitten by the entrepreneurial bug. At the time, personal computers were just making their entrance into mainstream America, and Michael saw them as the wave of the future. During his freshman year, he realized he could buy computer parts direct from manufacturers, assemble the computers himself, and then sell them directly to consumers for 40 percent below retail. By the second semester of his freshman year, Michael was grossing $80,000 from his dorm room. At the end of the semester, he decided to drop out of school and launch a mail-order computer business.

He named his business Dell Computer, and the rest is history. Over the next two decades, Dell has mushroomed to become a dominant firm in the industry and has established a true global presence. Annual revenues have surpassed $41 billion, and the company employs 46,000 people. Dell owns manufacturing plants in the United States, China, Brazil, and Ireland, and the firm has now expanded into other product lines, such as printers, M3P players, and LCD televisions. Why and how did a business like Dell prosper? How can you make your own business successful? Chapters 1, 3, 7, and 11 will help you better understand its reasons for success.

Dell Computer founder Michael Dell

A Good Cup of Java

Starbucks has become a ubiquitous part of the urban landscape in most major cities. In less than 30 years, the firm has grown to become the largest retailer in the world. It's actually difficult to provide an accurate count of the number of Starbucks outlets because the firm opens a new one somewhere in the world almost every day! But in mid-2006 there were 7,661 Starbucks shops in the United States and another 3,140 abroad.

The three people who founded Starbucks did not have ambitious retail plans for the firm, but were primarily interested in wholesaling high-quality beans to independent coffeehouses. However, a former employee, Howard Schultz, bought the company from its three original owners in 1987 and began an aggressive expansion campaign across the country.

By combining tight quality control with an uncanny sense of consumer tastes and preferences, Starbucks has become one of the strongest brand names in the country. The firm has also become a surprisingly important force in the music industry. Managers determined that many premium coffee drinkers also share a passion for music, so the company started selling a small number of hand-picked CDs in its store. As a result, music company executives now line up to try and get their latest offerings on the Starbucks play list. What are the secrets behind Starbucks' success, and how do savvy Starbucks marketers apply their skills to understand Starbucks' customers' preferences? You'll learn about this and more in Chapters 3, 5, 10, and 11.

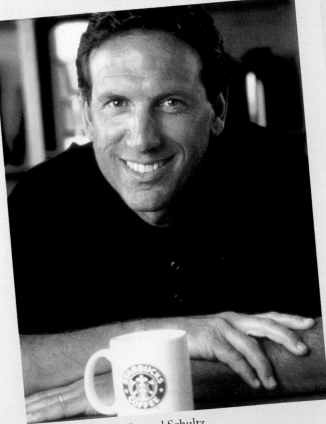

Starbucks founder Howard Schultz

The Hard-Headed Executive

For the first half of the twentieth century, Sears and Wards battled tooth-and-nail for retailing supremacy in the United States. But in the years following World War II, Sears flourished and pulled away from its chief rival, whereas Wards withered and died.

What accounted for such a turn in fortunes? Managers at Sears correctly forecasted a population shift to the suburbs after the war and started aggressively opening new stores in suburban retailing centers. But Wards' CEO, Sewell Avery, thought the suburbs were a "fad." He repeatedly predicted that Sears would fail and that Wards would then be positioned to buy its rival at a bargain-basement price. From 1941 to 1957, Wards did not open a single new store as Avery clung to his position and refused to admit that he might be wrong.

While fortunes at Sears have waned in recent years and it can only look up at industry giant Wal-Mart, it nevertheless remains an important force in the retailing industry. Wards, meanwhile, continues to operate a small Internet and catalog-based retail business but is only a shell of its former self. Much of its problems can be laid at the feet of a single hardheaded executive. How do managers and leaders—and organizations' structures themselves—affect the success of a business? You'll learn more in Chapters 5, 6, 9, and 10.

Planting the Seeds

During the heady days of the dot-com boom, new Web-based businesses were popping up left and right. Garden.com was founded in 1996 by three friends, Cliff and Lisa Sharples and Jamie O'Neill. In early 2000, their company employed over 200 people, and Garden.com was acclaimed by *Fortune*, *Forbes*, and *Inc.* as one of the best Internet-based retailers in the world. The company also had more cash than it needed and was in the enviable position of being able to turn down investment proposals from venture capitalists.

But by the end of that very same year, the business environment had made a quantum shift. Venture capital dried up, operating costs escalated, and investors sought lower risk. These forces combined to drive many of the dot-com darlings under. Cliff, Lisa, and Jamie were sufficiently realistic to see the fate of their business and shut down their operations in a relatively orderly manner. They managed to pay off all of their obligations and still have a tidy nest egg left over to explore future opportunities. We'll discuss how and why some businesses succeed and others fail, as well as some of the underlying forces for successes and failures, in Chapters 3, 5, and 14.

Changing the Urban Landscape

Urban Outfitters does not have the widespread specialty retailing presence of Express or Old Navy, but the hip retailer nevertheless is a real success story. Urban Outfitters sells clothes, accessories, gifts, housewares, and shoes to young metropolitan customers seeking affordable but fashionable lifestyle brands. The more than 60 Urban Outfitters locations are located in fashion centers in or near large cities; the firm plans to open 20 or more stores a year.

The company also owns Anthropologie, a similarly focused store that targets consumers in the 30- to 45-year-old range. Its newest venture, called Free People, will offer similar merchandise as Urban Outfitters and Anthropologie, but at slightly lower prices. Free People will also offer a wider range of houseware merchandise geared toward apartment dwellers. Urban Outfitters is also picking up its international expansion. It currently owns a handful of stores in Canada and the United Kingdom, but plans to increase its presence both in the United Kingdom as well as continental Europe. How is one company able to open different kinds or retail stores and operate at different "price points," not just in the United States but also abroad? You'll learn more about this in Chapters 1, 3, and 12.

so what *is* in it for you?

We hope that these business stories have piqued your interest about what lies ahead in this book—we'll revisit many of these people and companies later in the text. The world today is populated with a breathtaking array of businesses and business opportunities. Big and small business, established and new businesses, broad-based and niche business, successful unsuccessful businesses, global and domestic businesses—regardless of where your future plans take you, we hope that you look back on this course as one of your first steps.

Going forward, we also urge you to consider that what you get out of this course—what's in it for you—is shaped by at least three factors. One factor is this book and the various learning aids that accompany it. Another factor is your instructor. He or she is a dedicated professional who wants nothing more than to help you grow and develop intellectually and academically.

The third factor? You. Learning is an active process that requires you to be a major participant. Simply memorizing the key terms and concepts in this book may help you achieve an acceptable course grade. But true learning requires that you read, study, discuss, question, review, experience, evaluate—wear the four hats-as you go along. While tests and homework may be a "necessary evil," we believe we will have done our part if you finish this course with new knowledge and increased enthusiasm for the world of business. We know your instructor will do his or her best to facilitate your learning. The rest, then, is up to you. We wish you success.

BUSINESS ESSENTIALS

PART I:
THE CONTEMPORARY BUSINESS WORLD

After reading this chapter, you should be able to:

1   Define the nature of U.S. business and identify its main goals and functions.

2   Describe the external environments of business and discuss how these environments affect the success or failure of any organization.

3   Describe the different types of global economic systems according to the means by which they control the factors of production.

4   Show how markets, demand, and supply affect resource distribution in the United States.

5   Identify the elements of private enterprise and explain the various degrees of competition in the U.S. economic system.

6   Explain the importance of the economic environment to business and identify the factors used to evaluate the performance of an economic system.

WHAT GOES UP . . . CAN GO EVEN HIGHER!

The sign in front of a Florida Shell gasoline station summed it up nicely: The "prices" for the three grades of gasoline sold at the station were listed as "an arm," "a leg," and "your first born." While the sign no doubt led to a few smiles from motorists, its

THE U.S. BUSINESS ENVIRONMENT

sentiments were far from a laughing matter. The stark reality was that in mid-2005, retail gasoline prices in the United States were at an all-time high, hovering around $3 per gallon in most places. While prices dropped a bit in late 2005 and early 2006, by mid-2006 they had surged again to record levels. Indeed, while gasoline prices have often fluctuated up and down, the upward price spiral that began in mid-2004 left consumers, government officials, and business leaders struggling to find answers.

What made this gas crisis unusual was that it began with an unusual mix of supply, demand, and global forces. In the past, gas prices generally increased only when the supply was reduced. For example, an Arab embargo on petroleum exports to the United States in 1973 to 1974 led to major price jumps. But these higher prices spurred new exploration, and as new oil fields came on line, prices eventually dropped again.

Higher energy costs flow into every nook and cranny of the economy.

—Daniel Yergin, chairman, Cambridge Energy Research Associates

Subsequent supply disruptions due to political problems in Venezuela, Nigeria, and Iraq have also contributed to reduced supplies and higher prices at different times.

But the circumstances underlying the increases that started in 2004 were much more complex. First, the supply of domestically produced gasoline in the United States has dropped steadily since 1972 due to the rapid depletion of domestic oil fields currently in production, along with new sources being identified in many other parts of the world. Hence, global supplies have been increasing at a rate that has more than offset the declines in U.S. domestic production. As a result, the United States has being relying more on foreign producers and is, therefore, subject to whatever prices those producers want to charge. And as prices escalated, fears grew that there could be major economic damage. In the words of one expert, "Higher energy costs flow into every nook and cranny of the economy."

Second, demand for gasoline in the United States has continued to rise. A growing population, the increased popularity of gas-guzzling SUVs and other big vehicles, and strong demand for other products (plastics, for instance) that require petroleum as a raw material have all contributed to increased demand. For example, in 2005, the United States consumed approximately 20 million barrels of oil per day. This total was greater than the combined consumption of Germany, Russia, China, and Japan.

Another major piece of the puzzle, surprisingly enough, has been a surging global economy. As nation after nation started to recover from the global downturn that had slowed economic growth, the demand for oil and gasoline also surged. More people were buying cars, and petroleum refiners worked around the clock to help meet the unprecedented demand for gasoline. China, in particular, has become a major consumer of petroleum, passing Japan in 2005 to trail only the United States in total consumption.

Adding to the mix was the disastrous fallout of hurricanes Katrina and Rita in 2005. These natural disasters caused extensive damage to oil drilling platforms and refineries all along the Gulf Coast. Although supplies had actually been reasonably strong up to that point, fears quickly grew regarding potential impending shortages and overall economic fallout. These fears, in turn, led to yet another upsurge in prices.

So, the initial surge in gas prices that started in 2004 was fueled by strong global demand. Conditions worsened when supplies actually did begin to drop in late 2005. And the price increases were leading to a wide array of consequences. Automobile manufacturers stepped up their commitment to making more fuel-efficient cars. Refiners posted record profits (indeed, some critics charged that the energy companies were guilty of price gouging). And even local police officers were kept busy combating a surge in gasoline theft, yet another indication that gas was becoming an increasingly valuable commodity! ■

Our opening story continues on page 27.

WHAT'S IN IT FOR ME?

The forces that have caused jumps in gas prices reflect both the opportunities and challenges you'll find in today's business world. All businesses are subject to the influences of economic forces. But these same economic forces also provide astute managers and entrepreneurs with opportunities for profits and growth. By understanding these economic forces and how they interact, you'll be better able to (1) appreciate how managers must contend with the challenges and opportunities resulting from economic forces from the standpoint of an employee and a manager or business owner, and (2) understand why prices fluctuate from the perspective of a consumer.

In this chapter, we'll look at some basic elements of economic systems and describe the economics of market systems. We'll also introduce and discuss several indicators that are used to gauge the vitality of our domestic economic system. But first, let's start with some business basics.

THE CONCEPT OF BUSINESS AND THE CONCEPT OF PROFIT

What do you think of when you hear the word *business*? Does it conjure up images of successful corporations, such as Shell Oil and IBM? Or of less successful companies, such as Enron and Kmart? Are you reminded of smaller firms, such as your local supermarket or favorite restaurant? Or do you think of even smaller family-owned operations, such as your neighborhood pizzeria or the florist down the street?

All these organizations are **businesses**—organizations that provide goods or services that are then sold to earn profits. Indeed, the prospect of earning **profits**—the difference between a business's revenues and its expenses—is what encourages people to open and expand businesses. After all, profits are the rewards owners get for risking their money and time. The right to pursue profits distinguishes a business from those organizations—such as most universities, hospitals, and government agencies—that run in much the same way but that generally don't seek profits.[1]

BUSINESS organization that provides goods or services to earn profits

PROFITS difference between a business's revenues and its expenses

Consumer Choice and Demand In a capitalistic system, such as that in the United States, businesses exist to earn profits for owners; an owner is free to set up a new business, grow that business, sell it, or even shut it down. But consumers also have freedom of choice. In choosing how to pursue profits, businesses must take into account what consumers want and/or need. No matter how efficient a business is, it won't survive if there is no demand for its goods or services. Neither a snowblower shop in Florida nor a beach-umbrella store in Alaska is likely to do well.

Opportunity and Enterprise If enterprising businesspeople can identify either unmet consumer needs or better ways of satisfying consumer needs, they can be successful. In other words, someone who can spot a promising opportunity and then develop a good plan for capitalizing on it can succeed. The opportunity always involves goods or services that consumers need and/or want—especially if no one else is supplying them or if existing businesses are doing so inefficiently or incompletely.

The Benefits of Business So what are the benefits of businesses? Businesses produce most of the goods and services we consume, and they employ most working people. They create most new innovations and provide a vast range of opportunities for new businesses, which serve as their suppliers. A healthy business climate also contributes to the quality of life and standard of living of people in a society. Business profits enhance the personal incomes of millions of owners and stockholders, and business taxes help to support governments at all levels. Many businesses support charities and provide community leadership. However, some businesses also harm the environment, and their decision makers sometimes resort to unacceptable practices for their own personal benefit.

In this chapter, we begin our introduction to business by examining the environment in which businesses operate. This provides a foundation for our subsequent discussions dealing with economic forces that play a major role in the success and failure of businesses everywhere.

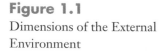

Figure 1.1
Dimensions of the External
Environment

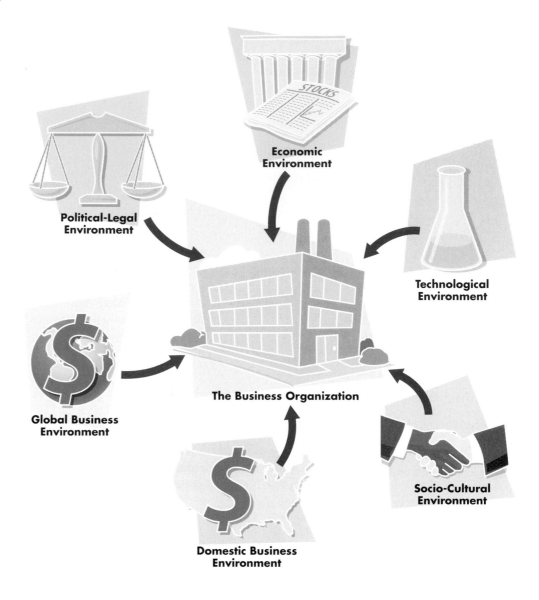

THE EXTERNAL ENVIRONMENTS OF BUSINESS

EXTERNAL ENVIRONMENT
everything outside an
organization's boundaries that
might affect it

All businesses, regardless of their size, location, or mission, operate within a larger external environment. This **external environment** consists of everything outside an organization's boundaries that might affect it. (Businesses also have an *internal environment*, more commonly called *corporate culture*; we discuss this in Chapter 5.) Not surprisingly, the external environment plays a major role in determining the success or failure of any organization. Managers must, therefore, have a complete and accurate understanding of their environment and then strive to operate and compete within it. Businesses can also influence their environments.

Figure 1.1 shows the major dimensions and elements of the external environment as it affects businesses today. As you can see, these include the *domestic business environment*, the *global business environment*, the *technological environment*, the *political-legal environment*, the *sociocultural environment*, and the *economic environment*.

▪▪▪ DOMESTIC BUSINESS ENVIRONMENT

The **domestic business environment** refers to the environment in which a firm conducts its operations and derives its revenues. In general, businesses seek to be close to their customers, to establish strong relationships with their suppliers, and to distinguish themselves from their competitors. Take Urban Outfitters, for example. The firm initially located its stores near urban college campuses; it now also locates stores in other, often more upscale, areas as well. The company also has a strong network of suppliers and is itself a wholesale supplier to other retailers through its Free People division. And it has established a clear identity for itself within the domestic business environment that enables it to compete alongside such competitors as Aeropostale and dELiA*s.

DOMESTIC BUSINESS ENVIRONMENT the environment in which a firm conducts its operations and derives its revenues

▪▪▪ GLOBAL BUSINESS ENVIRONMENT

The **global business environment** refers to the international forces that affect a business. Factors affecting the global environment at a general level include international trade agreements, international economic conditions, political unrest, and so forth. At a more immediate level, any given business is likely to be affected by international market opportunities, suppliers, cultures, competitors, and currency values. For instance, Urban Outfitters currently has stores in Canada and the United Kingdom, but as it expands into other parts of the world, it will have to contend with different languages, more diverse cultures, and so forth. Even now, many of its suppliers are foreign companies.

GLOBAL BUSINESS ENVIRONMENT the international forces that affect a business

▪▪▪ TECHNOLOGICAL ENVIRONMENT

The **technological environment** generally includes all the ways by which firms create value for their constituents. Technology includes human knowledge, work methods, physical equipment, electronics and telecommunications, and various processing systems that are used to perform business activities. For instance, Urban Outfitters relies on a sophisticated information system that tracks sales and inventory levels in order to be highly responsive to its customers. The firm also enjoys considerable success with its e-commerce Web sites.

TECHNOLOGICAL ENVIRONMENT all the ways by which firms create value for their constituents

▪▪▪ POLITICAL-LEGAL ENVIRONMENT

The **political-legal environment** reflects the relationship between business and government, usually in the form of government regulation of business. It is important for several reasons. First, the legal system defines in part what an organization can and can't do. For instance, Urban Outfitters is subject to a variety of political and legal forces, including product identification laws and local zoning requirements. Likewise, various government agencies regulate important areas, such as advertising practices, safety and health considerations, and acceptable standards of business conduct. Pro- or anti-business sentiment in government and political stability are also important considerations, especially for international firms.

POLITICAL-LEGAL ENVIRONMENT the relationship between business and government

SOCIOCULTURAL ENVIRONMENT

SOCIOCULTURAL ENVIRONMENT the customs, mores, values, and demographic characteristics of the society in which an organization functions

The **sociocultural environment** includes the customs, mores, values, and demographic characteristics of the society in which an organization functions. Sociocultural processes also determine the goods and services, as well as the standards of business conduct, that a society is likely to value and accept. For example, a couple of years ago, Urban Outfitters introduced a Monopoly-like game called Ghettopoly. The company received a lot of unfavorable publicity about the game, based on critics' charges that it made light of poverty and other social problems. In response, Urban Outfitters pulled it from shelves and discontinued its sale.

ECONOMIC ENVIRONMENT

ECONOMIC ENVIRONMENT relevant conditions that exist in the economic system in which a company operates

The **economic environment** refers to relevant conditions that exist in the economic system in which a a company operates. For example, if an economy is doing well enough that most people have jobs, a growing company may find it necessary to pay higher wages and offer more benefits in order to attract workers from other companies. But if many people in an economy are looking for jobs, a firm may be able to pay less and offer fewer benefits.

The rest of this chapter is devoted to the economic environment; the other environments of business are covered throughout the rest of the book.

ECONOMIC SYSTEMS

ECONOMIC SYSTEM a nation's system for allocating its resources among its citizens

A U.S. business operates differently from a business in France or the People's Republic of China, and businesses in these countries differ from those in Japan or Brazil. A key factor in these differences is the economic system of a firm's *home country*—the nation in which it does most of its business. An **economic system** is a nation's system for allocating its resources among its citizens, both individuals and organizations.

FACTORS OF PRODUCTION

FACTORS OF PRODUCTION resources used in the production of goods and services—labor, capital, entrepreneurs, physical resources, and information resources

A basic difference between economic systems is the way in which a system manages its **factors of production**—the resources that a country's businesses use to produce goods and services. Economists have long focused on four factors of production: *labor*, *capital*, *entrepreneurs*, and *physical resources*. In addition to these classic four factors, *information resources* are now considered as well. Note that the concept of factors of production can also be applied to the resources that an individual organization *manages* to produce goods and services.

LABOR (HUMAN RESOURCES) physical and mental capabilities of people as they contribute to economic production

Labor People who work for businesses provide labor. **Labor**, sometimes called **human resources**, includes the physical and intellectual contributions people make while engaged in economic production. Starbucks, for example, employs over 75,000 people. The firm's workforce includes the baristas who prepare coffees for customers, store managers, regional managers, coffee tasters, quality control experts, coffee buyers, marketing experts, financial specialists, and other specialized workers and managers.

CAPITAL funds needed to create and operate a business enterprise

Capital Obtaining and using labor and other resources requires **capital**—the financial resources needed to operate a business. You need capital to start a new business and then to keep it running and growing. For example, when Howard Schultz decided to buy the fledgling Starbucks coffee outfit back in 1987, he used personal savings and a loan to finance his acquisition. As Starbucks grew, he came to rely more on Starbucks' profits. Eventually, the firm sold stock to other investors to raise even more money. Today, Starbucks continues to rely on a blend of current earnings and both short- and long-term debt to finance its operations and fuel its growth.

Entrepreneurs An **entrepreneur** is a person who accepts the risks and opportunities entailed in creating and operating a new business. As we noted in the Prologue, three individuals first founded Starbucks. However, they lacked either the interest or the vision to see the retail potential for coffee, instead choosing to focus on their wholesaling operation. But Howard Schultz was willing to accept the risks associated with retail growth and, after buying the company, he capitalized on the market opportunities for rapid growth. Had his original venture failed, Schultz would have lost most of his savings. Most economic systems encourage entrepreneurs, both to start new businesses and to make the decisions that allow them to create new jobs and make more profits for their owners.

ENTREPRENEUR individual who accepts the risks and opportunities involved in creating and operating a new business venture

(a)

(b)

Starbucks uses various factors of production, including (a) labor, such as this Starbucks barrista; (b) entrepreneurs, such as CEO Howard Schultz; and (c) physical resources, including coffee beans.

(c)

PHYSICAL RESOURCES tangible items organizations use in the conduct of their businesses

Physical Resources **Physical resources** are the tangible things that organizations use to conduct their business. They include natural resources and raw materials, offices, storage and production facilities, parts and supplies, computers and peripherals, and a variety of other equipment. For example, Starbucks relies on coffee beans and other food products, the equipment it uses to make its coffee drinks, paper products for packaging, other retail equipment, as well as office equipment and storage facilities for running its business at the corporate level.

INFORMATION RESOURCES data and other information used by businesses

Information Resources The production of tangible goods once dominated most economic systems. Today, **information resources**—data and other information used by businesses—play a major role. Information resources that businesses rely on include market forecasts, the specialized knowledge of people, and economic data. In turn, much of what they do results either in the creation of new information or the repackaging of existing information for new users. For example, Starbucks uses various economic

say what you mean

The Culture of Risk

Risk taking has been a defining feature of U.S. business culture for a long time. From the early pioneers and prospectors heading west to the would-be dot-com billionaires of the 1990s, Americans are known not only for their readiness to try out new ideas, but also for their willingness to risk everything for the chance to make it big. You can still hear Texans talking about how the spirit of the nineteenth century "wildcatters" spurred local traditions in oil drilling. Risk taking has become an important part of California's business culture, especially in the entertainment and high-tech industries, and New York is home to high rollers in the world of finance.

In contrast, many foreign cultures inhibit risk taking by businesses. In Japan, for example, business failure carries with it significant social stigma—a loss of "face." As a result, entrepreneurs there are slow to expand their businesses until they are certain they will succeed. Likewise, in countries like Russia and Poland, where up until a few years ago most businesses were government-owned, many managers today remain cautious and are reluctant to go too far out on a limb.

Risk taking in the United States differs by industry and size of company. Small companies are more likely to make risky decisions than large companies are, where elaborate approval processes may slow things down. Likewise, publicly traded companies whose stockholders usually keep a close eye on investments are less likely to take big risks than are privately held firms.

Americans' propensity to take risks is one of the reasons that the so-called "New Economy" took root

here more firmly than it did elsewhere. In fact, risk taking can be seen in the attitudes of U.S. lawmakers and regulators as well as in the entrepreneurial spirit of American businesspeople, particularly when it comes to tax policies and the financial market systems. For example, the U.S. airline industry was heavily regulated by the government for decades. Fares were set and routes were determined purely by Washington bureaucrats. After the industry was deregulated, fares dropped dramatically, and literally hundreds of new routes were created. At the same time, some airlines also failed. So, the net result has been reductions in fares and improvements in airline service coupled with losses by some investors (those who owned stock in failed airlines) and profits by others (those who owned stock in more successful airlines).

Why is America such a hotbed for risk taking? Easier access to capital encourages entrepreneurship, as does the American attitude toward those who fail in business. For people who lose their bets and end up going bankrupt, systems are in place to help them get solvent again. It's not uncommon for an American business to start up again under a new name and resume operations right on the heels of a failed venture. Even if failure is an accepted, almost time-honored tradition in this country, that's not to say that bankruptcy is taken lightly. Businesspeople who stumble can pick themselves up again, but they usually have some rehabbing to do, both to strengthen their reputations and to restore the trust once shared with former customers and associates.

statistics to decide where to open new outlets. It also uses sophisticated forecasting models to predict the future prices of coffee beans. And consumer taste tests help the firm decide when to introduce new products.

▦▦■ TYPES OF ECONOMIC SYSTEMS

Different types of economic systems manage these factors of production differently. In some systems, all ownership is private; in others, all factors of production are owned or controlled by the government. Most systems, however, fall between these extremes.

Economic systems also differ in the ways decisions are made about production and allocation. A **planned economy** relies on a centralized government to control all or most factors of production and to make all or most production and allocation decisions. In a **market economy**, individual producers and consumers control production and allocation by creating combinations of supply and demand. Let's look at each of these types of economic systems as well as mixed market economies in more detail.

PLANNED ECONOMY economy that relies on a centralized government to control all or most factors of production and to make all or most production and allocation decisions

Planned Economies There are two basic forms of planned economies: *communism* (discussed here) and *socialism* (discussed as a mixed market economy). As envisioned by nineteenth-century German economist Karl Marx, **communism** is a system in which the government owns and operates all factors of production. Under such a system, the government would assign people to jobs; it would also own all business and control business decisions—what to make, how much to charge, and so forth. Marx proposed that individuals would contribute according to their abilities and receive benefits according to their needs. He also expected government ownership of production factors to be temporary: Once society had matured, government would wither away, and workers would take direct ownership of the factors of production.

MARKET ECONOMY economy in which individuals control production and allocation decisions through supply and demand

The former Soviet Union and many Eastern European countries embraced communism until the end of the twentieth century. In the early 1990s, one country after another renounced communism as both an economic and a political system. Today, North Korea, Vietnam, and the People's Republic of China are among the few nations with openly communist systems. Even in these countries, however, planned economic systems are making room for features of the free enterprise system.

COMMUNISM political system in which the government owns and operates all factors of production

Market Economies A **market** is a mechanism for exchange between the buyers and sellers of a particular good or service. (Like *capital*, the term *market* can have multiple meanings.) Market economies rely on capitalism and free enterprise to create an environment in which producers and consumers are free to sell and buy what they choose (within certain limits). As a result, items produced and prices paid are largely determined by supply and demand.

MARKET mechanism for exchange between buyers and sellers of a particular good or service

To understand how a market economy works, consider what happens when you go to a fruit market to buy apples. While one vendor is selling apples for $1 per pound, another is charging $1.50. Both vendors are free to charge what they want, and you are free to buy what you choose. If both vendors' apples are of the same quality, you will buy the cheaper ones. If the $1.50 apples are fresher, you may buy them instead. In short, both buyers and sellers enjoy freedom of choice.

Taken to a more general level of discussion, individuals in a market system are free to not only buy what they want but also to work where they want and to invest, save, or spend their money in whatever manner they choose. Likewise, businesses are free to decide what products to make, where to sell them, and what prices to charge. This process contrasts markedly with that of a planned economy, in which individuals

CAPITALISM system that sanctions the private ownership of the factors of production and encourages entrepreneurship by offering profits as an incentive

may be told where they can and cannot work, companies may be told what they can and cannot make, and consumers may have little or no choice in what they purchase or how much they pay. The political basis of market processes is called **capitalism**, which allows the private ownership of the factors of production and encourages entrepreneurship by offering profits as an incentive. The economic basis of market processes is the operation of demand and supply, which we discuss in the next section.

Mixed Market Economies In reality, there are really no "pure" planned or "pure" market economies. Most countries rely on some form of **mixed market economy** that features characteristics of both planned and market economies. Even a market economy that strives to be as free and open as possible, such as the U.S. economy, restricts certain activities. Some products can't be sold legally, others can be sold only to people of a certain age, advertising must be truthful, and so forth. And the People's Republic of China, the world's most important planned economy, is increasingly allowing certain forms of private ownership and entrepreneurship (although with government oversight).

MIXED MARKET ECONOMY economic system featuring characteristics of both planned and market economies

PRIVATIZATION process of converting government enterprises into privately owned companies

When a government is making a change from a planned economy to a market economy, it usually begins to adopt market mechanisms through **privatization**—the process of converting government enterprises into privately owned companies. In Poland, for example, the national airline was sold to a group of private investors. In recent years, this practice has spread to many other countries as well. For example, the postal system in many countries is government-owned and government-managed. The Netherlands, however, is privatizing its TNT Post Group N.V., already among the world's most efficient post-office operations. Canada has also privatized its air traffic control system. In each case, the new enterprise reduced its payroll, boosted efficiency and productivity, and quickly became profitable.

SOCIALISM planned economic system in which the government owns and operates only selected major sources of production

In the partially planned system called **socialism**, the government owns and operates selected major industries. In such mixed market economies, the government may control banking, transportation, or industries producing such basic goods as oil and steel. Smaller businesses, such as clothing stores and restaurants, are privately owned. Many Western European countries, including England and France, allow free market operations in most economic areas but keep government control of others, such as health care.

As the People's Republic of China opens its doors to private enterprise, many businesses are seeking to tap into this increasingly lucrative market. Walt Disney, for example, recently opened a theme park near Hong Kong. To help promote the park's opening, the company began to aggressively market Disney-themed apparel, like these t-shirts, throughout the region.

SELF-CHECK QUESTIONS 1–3

You should now be able to answer Self-Check Questions 1–3.*

1 **Multiple Choice** Suppose a business finds that newly developed equipment available from one of its suppliers allows it to make its products much faster and less expensively than in the past. Which part of its external environment has allowed this to happen?
   (a) domestic business environment
   (b) political-legal environment
   (c) technological environment
   (d) sociocultural environment

2 **Multiple Choice** Which of the following is **not** considered one of the main categories of factors of production?
   (a) labor
   (b) government regulations and controls
   (c) capital
   (d) entrepreneurs

3 **True/False** If 18 percent of its total production and 16 percent of its total employment are created by its government, which also collects 30 percent of its total income in taxes, a nation does not really have a free market economy.

***Answers to Self-Check Questions 1–3 can be found on p. 563.**

THE ECONOMICS OF MARKET SYSTEMS

Understanding the complex nature of the U.S. economic system is essential to understanding the environment in which U.S. businesses operate. In this section, we describe the workings of the U.S. market economy. Specifically, we examine the nature of *demand and supply*, *private enterprise*, and *degrees of competition*.

▪▪▪ DEMAND AND SUPPLY IN A MARKET ECONOMY

A market economy consists of many different markets that function within that economy. As a consumer, for instance, the choices you have and the prices you pay for gas, food, clothing, and entertainment are all governed by different sets of market forces. Businesses also have many different choices about buying and selling their products. Dell Computer, for instance, can purchase keyboards from literally hundreds of different manufacturers. Its managers also have to decide what inventory levels should be, at what prices they should sell their goods, and how they will distribute these goods. Literally billions of exchanges take place every day between businesses and individuals; between businesses; and among individuals, businesses, and governments. Moreover, exchanges conducted in one area often affect exchanges elsewhere. For instance, the high cost of gas may also lead to prices going up for other products, ranging from food to clothing to delivery services. Why? Because each of these businesses relies heavily on gas to transport products.

The Laws of Demand and Supply On all economic levels, decisions about what to buy and what to sell are determined primarily by the forces of demand and supply.[2] **Demand** is the willingness and ability of buyers to purchase a product (a good or a

DEMAND the willingness and ability of buyers to purchase a good or service

SUPPLY the willingness and ability of producers to offer a good or service for sale

LAW OF DEMAND principle that buyers will purchase (demand) more of a product as its price drops and less as its price increases

LAW OF SUPPLY principle that producers will offer (supply) more of a product for sale as its price rises and less as its price drops

DEMAND AND SUPPLY SCHEDULE assessment of the relationships among different levels of demand and supply at different price levels

DEMAND CURVE graph showing how many units of a product will be demanded (bought) at different prices

SUPPLY CURVE graph showing how many units of a product will be supplied (offered for sale) at different prices

MARKET PRICE (EQUILIBRIUM PRICE) profit-maximizing price at which the quantity of goods demanded and the quantity of goods supplied are equal

SURPLUS situation in which quantity supplied exceeds quantity demanded

SHORTAGE situation in which quantity demanded exceeds quantity supplied

service). **Supply** is the willingness and ability of producers to offer a good or service for sale. Generally speaking, demand and supply follow basic laws:

- The **law of demand:** Buyers will purchase (demand) *more* of a product as its price *drops* and *less* of a product as its price *increases*.
- The **law of supply:** Producers will offer (supply) *more* of a product for sale as its price *rises* and *less* of a product as its price *drops*.

The Demand and Supply Schedule To appreciate these laws in action, consider the market for pizza in your town (or neighborhood). If everyone is willing to pay $25 for a pizza (a relatively high price), the town's only pizzeria will produce a large supply. But if everyone is willing to pay only $5 (a relatively low price), it will make fewer pizzas. Through careful analysis, we can determine how many pizzas will be sold at different prices. These results, called a **demand and supply schedule**, are obtained from marketing research, historical data, and other studies of the market. Properly applied, they reveal the relationships among different levels of demand and supply at different price levels.

Demand and Supply Curves The demand and supply schedule can be used to construct demand and supply curves for pizza in your town. A **demand curve** shows how many products—in this case, pizzas—will be demanded (bought) at different prices. A **supply curve** shows how many pizzas will be supplied (baked or offered for sale) at different prices.

Figure 1.2 shows demand and supply curves for pizzas. As you can see, demand increases as price decreases; supply increases as price increases. When demand and supply curves are plotted on the same graph, the point at which they intersect is the **market price** (also called the **equilibrium price**)—the price at which the quantity of goods demanded and the quantity of goods supplied are equal. In Figure 1.2, the equilibrium price for pizzas in our example is $10. At this point, the quantity of pizzas demanded and the quantity of pizzas supplied are the same: 1,000 pizzas per week.

Surpluses and Shortages What if the pizzeria decides to make some other number of pizzas? For example, what would happen if the owner tried to increase profits by making *more* pizzas to sell? Or what if the owner wanted to lower overhead, cut back on store hours, and *reduce* the number of pizzas offered for sale? In either case, the result would be an inefficient use of resources and lower profits. For instance, if the pizzeria supplies 1,200 pizzas and tries to sell them for $10 each, 200 pizzas will not be bought. Our demand schedule shows that only 1,000 pizzas will be demanded at this price. The pizzeria will therefore have a **surplus**—a situation in which the quantity supplied exceeds the quantity demanded. It will lose the money that it spent making those extra 200 pizzas.

Conversely, if the pizzeria supplies only 800 pizzas, a **shortage** will result. The quantity demanded will be greater than the quantity supplied. The pizzeria will "lose" the extra profit that it could have made by producing 200 more pizzas. Even though consumers may pay more for pizzas because of the shortage, the pizzeria will still earn lower total profits than if it had made 1,000 pizzas. It will also risk angering customers who cannot buy pizzas and encourage other entrepreneurs to set up competing pizzerias to satisfy unmet demand. Businesses should seek the ideal combination of price charged and quantity supplied so as to maximize profits, maintain goodwill among customers, and discourage competition. This ideal combination is found at the equilibrium point.

Our example involves only one company, one product, and a few buyers. The U.S. economy—indeed, any market economy—is far more complex. Thousands of companies sell hundreds of thousands of products to millions of buyers every day. In the end, however, the result is much the same: Companies try to supply the quantity and selection of goods that will earn them the largest profits.

Figure 1.2
Demand and Supply

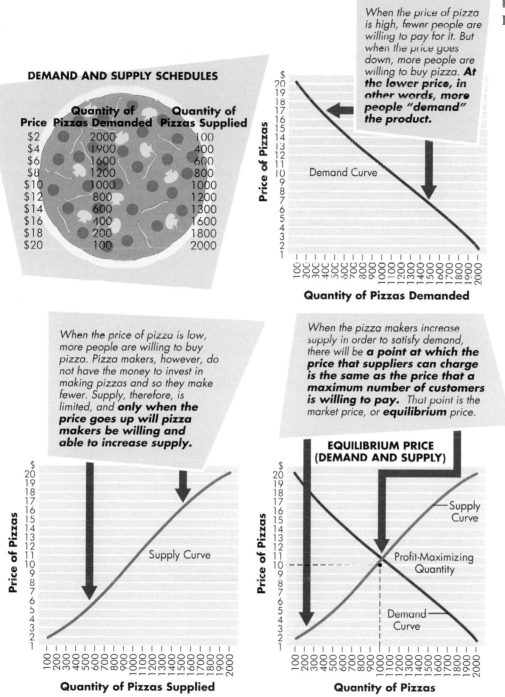

DEMAND AND SUPPLY SCHEDULES

Price	Quantity of Pizzas Demanded	Quantity of Pizzas Supplied
$2	2000	100
$4	1900	400
$6	1600	600
$8	1200	800
$10	1000	1000
$12	800	1200
$14	600	1300
$16	400	1600
$18	200	1800
$20	100	2000

When the price of pizza is high, fewer people are willing to pay for it. But when the price goes down, more people are willing to buy pizza. **At the lower price, in other words, more people "demand" the product.**

Demand Curve

Quantity of Pizzas Demanded

When the price of pizza is low, more people are willing to buy pizza. Pizza makers, however, do not have the money to invest in making pizzas and so they make fewer. Supply, therefore, is limited, and **only when the price goes up will pizza makers be willing and able to increase supply.**

Supply Curve

Quantity of Pizzas Supplied

When the pizza makers increase supply in order to satisfy demand, there will be **a point at which the price that suppliers can charge is the same as the price that a maximum number of customers is willing to pay.** That point is the market price, or **equilibrium** price.

EQUILIBRIUM PRICE (DEMAND AND SUPPLY)

Supply Curve

Profit-Maximizing Quantity

Demand Curve

Quantity of Pizzas

■■■■ PRIVATE ENTERPRISE AND COMPETITION IN A MARKET ECONOMY

Market economies rely on a **private enterprise** system—one that allows individuals to pursue their own interests with minimal government restriction. In turn, private enterprise requires the presence of four elements: private property rights, freedom of choice, profits, and competition.

PRIVATE ENTERPRISE economic system that allows individuals to pursue their own interests without undue governmental restriction

1 *Private property rights.* Ownership of the resources used to create wealth is in the hands of individuals.

2 *Freedom of choice.* You can sell your labor to any employer you choose. You can also choose which products to buy, and producers can usually choose whom to hire and what to produce.

3 *Profits.* The lure of profits (and freedom) leads some people to abandon the security of working for someone else and to assume the risks of entrepreneurship. Anticipated profits also influence individuals' choices of which goods or services to produce.

4 *Competition.* If profits motivate individuals to start businesses, competition motivates them to operate those businesses efficiently. **Competition** occurs when two or more businesses vie for the same resources or customers. To gain an advantage over competitors, a business must produce its goods or services efficiently and be able to sell at a reasonable profit. To achieve these goals, it must convince customers that its products are either better or less expensive than those of its competitors. Competition, therefore, forces all businesses to make products better or cheaper. A company that produces inferior, expensive products is likely to fail.

COMPETITION vying among businesses for the same resources or customers

Degrees of Competition Even in a free enterprise system, not all industries are equally competitive. Economists have identified four degrees of competition in a private enterprise system: *perfect competition*, *monopolistic competition*, *oligopoly*, and *monopoly*. Note that these are not always truly distinct categories but actually tend to fall along a continuum; perfect competition and monopoly anchor the ends of the continuum, with monopolistic competition and oligopoly falling in between. Table 1.1 summarizes the features of these four degrees of competition.

PERFECT COMPETITION market or industry characterized by numerous small firms producing an identical product

Perfect Competition For **perfect competition** to exist, two conditions must prevail: (1) all firms in an industry must be small and (2) the number of firms in the industry must be large. Under these conditions, no single firm is powerful enough to influence the price of its product. Prices are, therefore, determined by such market forces as supply and demand.

In addition, these two conditions also reflect four principles:

1 The products of each firm are so similar that buyers view them as identical to those of other firms.

2 Both buyers and sellers know the prices that others are paying and receiving in the marketplace.

TABLE 1.1 DEGREES OF COMPETITION

CHARACTERISTIC	PERFECT COMPETITION	MONOPOLISTIC COMPETITION	OLIGOPOLY	MONOPOLY
Example	Local farmer	Stationery store	Steel industry	Public utility
Number of competitors	Many	Many, but fewer than in pure competition	Few	None
Ease of entry into industry	Relatively easy	Fairly easy	Difficult	Regulated by government
Similarity of goods or services offered by competing firms	Identical	Similar	Can be similar or different	No directly competing goods or services
Level of control over price by individual firms	None	Some	Some	Considerable

3 Because each firm is small, it is easy for firms to enter or leave the market.
4 Going prices are set exclusively by supply and demand and accepted by both sellers and buyers.

U.S. agriculture is a good example of perfect competition. The wheat produced on one farm is the same as that from another. Both producers and buyers are aware of prevailing market prices. It is relatively easy to start producing wheat and relatively easy to stop when it's no longer profitable.

Monopolistic Competition In **monopolistic competition**, there are numerous sellers trying to make their products at least seem to be different from those of competitors. While there are many sellers involved in monopolistic competition, there tend to be fewer than in pure competition. Differentiating strategies include brand names (Tide versus Cheer), design or styling (Diesel versus Lucky jeans), and advertising (Coke versus Pepsi). For example, in an effort to attract health-conscious consumers, the Kraft Foods division of Philip Morris promotes such differentiated products as low-fat Cool Whip, low-calorie Jell-O, and sugar-free Kool-Aid.

Monopolistically competitive businesses may be large or small, but they can still enter or leave the market easily. For example, many small clothing stores compete successfully with large apparel retailers, such as Abercrombie & Fitch, Banana Republic, and J. Crew. A good case in point is bebe stores. The small clothing chain controls its own manufacturing facilities and can respond just as quickly as firms like the Gap to changes in fashion tastes. Likewise, many single-store clothing businesses in college towns compete by developing their own T-shirt and cap designs with copyrighted slogans and logos.

Product differentiation also gives sellers some control over prices. For instance, even though Target shirts may have similar styling and other features, Ralph Lauren Polo shirts can be priced with little regard for lower Target prices. But the large number of buyers relative to sellers applies potential limits to prices: Although Polo might be able to sell shirts for $20 more than a comparable Target shirt, it could not sell as many shirts if they were priced at $200 more.

Oligopoly When an industry has only a handful of sellers, an **oligopoly** exists. As a general rule, these sellers are quite large. The entry of new competitors is hard because large capital investment is needed. Thus, oligopolistic industries (the automobile, airline, and steel industries) tend to stay that way. Only two companies make large commercial aircraft: Boeing (a U.S. company) and Airbus (a European consortium). Furthermore, as the trend toward globalization continues, most experts believe that oligopolies will become increasingly prevalent.

Oligopolists have more control over their strategies than do monopolistically competitive firms, but the actions of one firm can significantly affect the sales of every other firm in the industry. For example, when one firm cuts prices or offers incentives to increase sales, the others usually protect sales by doing the same. Likewise, when one firm raises prices, others generally follow suit. Therefore, the prices of comparable products are usually similar. When an airline announces new fare discounts, others adopt the same strategy almost immediately. Just as quickly, when discounts end for one airline, they usually end for everyone else.

Monopoly A **monopoly** exists when an industry or market has only one producer (or else is so dominated by one producer that other firms cannot compete with it). A sole supplier enjoys complete control over the prices of its products. Its only constraint is a decrease in consumer demand due to increased prices. In the United States, laws, such as the

MONOPOLISTIC COMPETITION market or industry characterized by numerous buyers and relatively numerous sellers trying to differentiate their products from those of competitors

OLIGOPOLY market or industry characterized by a handful of (generally large) sellers with the power to influence the prices of their products

Global oligopolies are as inevitable as the sunrise.

—Louis Galambos, business historian

MONOPOLY market or industry in which there is only one producer that can therefore set the prices of its products

NATURAL MONOPOLY industry in which one company can most efficiently supply all needed goods or services

Sherman Antitrust Act (1890) and the Clayton Act (1914), forbid many monopolies and regulate prices charged by **natural monopolies**—industries in which one company can most efficiently supply all needed goods or services.[3] Many electric companies are natural monopolies because they can supply all the power needed in a local area. Duplicate facilities—such as two power plants and two sets of powerlines—would be wasteful.

SELF-CHECK QUESTIONS 4–6

You should now be able to answer Self-Check Questions 4–6.*

4 Multiple Choice Pierre discovered that when he lowered the price of his paintings, more people commissioned portraits from him. Pierre is experiencing which of the following?

(a) discounting
(b) the law of supply
(c) a supply shortage
(d) the law of demand

5 Multiple Choice According to the principle of demand and supply, which of the following should happen if the price of eggs goes up?

(a) Government regulators will step in and require that egg prices be lowered
(b) Producers will produce fewer eggs
(c) Shoppers will buy fewer eggs
(d) Shoppers will buy more eggs

6 True/False In an oligopoly, if one firm raises its prices, its competitors will likely lower theirs in order to attract new business.

*Answers to Self-Check Questions 4–6 can be found on p. 563.

ECONOMIC INDICATORS

Because economic forces are so volatile and can be affected by so many things, the performance of a country's economic system varies over time. Sometimes it gains strength and brings new prosperity to its members; other times it weakens and damages the fortunes of its members. But knowing how an economy is performing is useful for both business owners and investors alike. Most experts look to various economic indicators to help assess the performance of an economy. **Economic indicators** are statistics that show whether an economic system is strengthening, weakening, or remaining stable.

ECONOMIC INDICATOR a statistic that helps assess the performance of an economy

Given the importance of the economic environment to U.S. business, we will closely examine the two key goals of the U.S. economic system: *economic growth* and *economic stability*. We begin by focusing on the economic indicators with which we measure economic growth, including *aggregate output*, *standard of living*, *gross domestic product*, and *productivity*. We then discuss indicators of the main threats to economic stability—namely, *inflation* and *unemployment*. We conclude this section by discussing government attempts to manage the U.S. economy in the interest of meeting national economic goals.

ECONOMIC GROWTH, AGGREGATE OUTPUT, AND STANDARD OF LIVING

At one time, about half the population of this country was involved in producing the food that we needed. Today, less than 2.5 percent of the U.S. population works in agriculture. But agricultural efficiency has improved because better ways of producing products have been devised, and better technology has been invented for getting the job done. We can

Want a MacBrioche with That MacEspresso?

McDonald's has become an international icon of the fast-food industry. With 30,000 restaurants in over 100 countries, the golden arches have become synonymous with American culture. Yet in recent years, McDonald's seems to have lost its competitive edge both at home and abroad. In the United States, for example, its stores are outdated and its customer service skills seem to be slipping. Moreover, concerns about health (as dramatized in the recent documentary *Supersize Me*) have driven many customers away from Big Macs and French fries. McDonald's no longer leads in technology, with rivals inventing new processing and cooking technologies. The firm's traditional markets, children and young men, are spending less on food while markets McDonald's doesn't target, notably women and older consumers, spend more. Profits have dropped and Starbucks has replaced McDonald's as the food industry's success story.

To grow, McDonald's has had to expand aggressively into foreign markets, especially in Europe and Asia. However, consumers in many of those countries do not always like McDonald's "Americanized" look and products. So the burger maker has had to cater to local tastes. That means serving brioche and espresso in France, salmon sandwiches in Scandinavia, and beer in Germany. McDonald's is also customizing the look of its stores. In France, for example, some stores have ski-chalet décor—hardwood floors, televisions, and armchairs—while others feature 1950s-style booths with their own CD players.

So far, the new menu items and appearance are paying off. U.S. sales continue their downward trend, but French sales increased after the makeover. Ken Clement, a franchisee and former McDonald's vice president, claims the changes are not necessary in the United States. "People are not coming in to swoon over the décor," he says. "They are coming in and getting out of here. They don't give a rip what is inside." However, if the French market continues to improve, the innovations may make it to the United States, where the risk and the return could be great. The change could alienate McDonald's traditional customers or it could revitalize the firm and spark a renaissance for the entire fast-food industry.

---

say that agricultural productivity has increased because we have been able to increase total output in the agricultural sector.

We can apply the same concepts to a nation's economic system, although the computations are more complex. A fundamental question is: How do we know whether an economic system is growing or not? Experts call the pattern of short-term ups and downs (or, better, expansions and contractions) in an economy the **business cycle**. The primary measure of growth in the business cycle is **aggregate output**: the total quantity of goods and services produced by an economic system during a given period.[4]

To put it simply, an increase in aggregate output is growth (or economic growth). When output grows more quickly than the population, two things usually follow: Output per capita—the quantity of goods and services per person—goes up, and the system provides more of the goods and services that people want. And when these two things occur, people living in an economic system benefit from a higher **standard of living**, which refers to the total quantity and quality of goods and services that they can purchase with the currency used in their economic system.

Among other things, growth makes possible higher standards of living. In order to know how much your standard of living is improving, you need to know how much your nation's economic system is growing. Let's start to address this question by considering the data in Table 1.2.

BUSINESS CYCLE short-term pattern of economic expansions and contractions

AGGREGATE OUTPUT the total quantity of goods and services produced by an economic system during a given period

STANDARD OF LIVING the total quantity and quality of goods and services people can purchase with the currency used in their economic system

TABLE 1.2 U.S. GDP AND GDP PER CAPITA

GROSS DOMESTIC PRODUCT (GDP) ($ BILLION)	GDP: REAL GROWTH RATE (%)	GDP PER CAPITA: PURCHASING POWER PARITY
$11,750	4.4	$40,100

GROSS DOMESTIC PRODUCT (GDP) total value of all goods and services produced within a given period by a national economy through domestic factors of production

Gross Domestic Product The first number, **gross domestic product (GDP)**, refers to the total value of all goods and services produced within a given period by a national economy through domestic factors of production. Obviously, GDP is a measure of aggregate output. Generally speaking, if GDP is going up, aggregate output is going up; if aggregate output is going up, the nation is experiencing *economic growth*.

Sometimes, economists also use the term **gross national product (GNP)**, which refers to the total value of all goods and services produced by a national economy within a given period regardless of where the factors of production are located. What, precisely, is the difference between GDP and GNP? Consider a U.S.-owned automobile plant in Brazil. The profits earned by the factory are included in U.S. GNP—but not in GDP—because its output is not produced domestically (that is, in the United States). Conversely, those profits are included in Brazil's GDP—but not GNP—because they are produced domestically (that is, in Brazil). Calculations quickly become complex because of different factors of production. The labor, for example, will be mostly Brazilian but the capital mostly American. Thus, wages paid to Brazilian workers are part of Brazil's GNP even though profits are not.

GROSS NATIONAL PRODUCT (GNP) total value of all goods and services produced by a national economy within a given period regardless of where the factors of production are located

Real Growth Rate GDP and GNP usually differ by less than 1 percent, but economists argue that GDP is a more accurate indicator of domestic economic performance because it focuses only on domestic factors of production. With that in mind, let's look at the middle column in Table 1.2. Here we find that the real growth rate of U.S. GDP—the growth rate of GDP *adjusted for inflation and changes in the value of the country's currency*— is 4.4 percent. How good is that rate? Remember that *growth depends on output increasing at a faster rate than population*. The U.S. population is growing at a rate of 0.91 percent per year. The *real growth rate* of the U.S. economic system, therefore, seems quite healthy, and the U.S. standard of living should be improving.

GDP per Capita The number in the third column of Table 1.2 is a reflection of the standard of living: *GDP per capita* means GDP per person. We get this figure by dividing total GDP ($11.75 trillion) by total population, which happens to be about 293 million. In a given period (usually calculated on an annual basis), the United States produces goods and services equal in value to $40,100 for every person in the country. Figure 1.3 shows both GDP and GDP per capita in the United States between 1950 and 2004. GDP per capita is a better measure than GDP itself of the economic well-being of the average person.

REAL GDP gross domestic product (GDP) adjusted to account for changes in currency values and price changes

Real GDP **Real GDP** means that GDP has been adjusted to account for changes in currency values and price changes. To understand why adjustments are necessary, assume that pizza is the only product in a hypothetical economy. In 2005, a pizza cost $10; in 2006, a pizza cost $11. In both years, exactly 1,000 pizzas were produced. In 2005, the local GDP was $10,000 ($10 × 1,000); in 2006, the local GDP was $11,000 ($11 × 1,000). Has the economy grown? No. Because 1,000 pizzas were produced in both years, *aggregate output* remained the same. The point is to not be misled into believing that an economy is doing better than it is. If it is not adjusted, local GDP for 2006 is **nominal GDP**: GDP measured in current dollars or with all components valued at current prices.[5]

NOMINAL GDP gross domestic product (GDP) measured in current dollars or with all components valued at current prices

Purchasing Power Parity In the example, *current prices* would be 2006 prices. On the other hand, we calculate real GDP when we adjust GDP to account for changes in *currency values and price changes*. When we make this adjustment, we account for both GDP and **purchasing power parity**—the principle that exchange rates are set so that the prices of similar products in different countries are about the same. Purchasing power parity gives us a much better idea of *what people can actually buy with the financial*

PURCHASING POWER PARITY the principle that exchange rates are set so that the prices of similar products in different countries are about the same

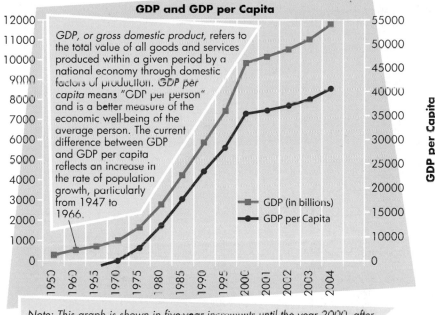

GDP and GDP per Capita

GDP, or gross domestic product, refers to the total value of all goods and services produced within a given period by a national economy through domestic factors of production. GDP per capita means "GDP per person" and is a better measure of the economic well-being of the average person. The current difference between GDP and GDP per capita reflects an increase in the rate of population growth, particularly from 1947 to 1966.

- ■ GDP (in billions)
- ● GDP per Capita

Note: This graph is shown in five-year increments until the year 2000, after which it is shown in one-year increments so as to provide more detail for recent periods. Hence, the curve artificially "flattens" after 2000.

Figure 1.3
GDP and GDP per Capita

resources allocated to them by their respective economic systems. In other words, it gives us a better sense of standards of living across the globe. Figure 1.4 illustrates a popular approach to see how purchasing power parity works in relation to a Big Mac. For instance, the figure pegs the price of a Big Mac in the United States at $3.15. Based on currency exchange rates, a Big Mac would cost $4.93 in Switzerland and $4.28 in Sweden. But the same burger would cost only $2.44 in Australia and $1.30 in China.

Productivity A major factor in the growth of an economic system is **productivity**, which is a measure of economic growth that compares how much a system produces with the resources needed to produce it. Let's say that it takes 1 U.S. worker and $1 (in U.S. dollars) to make 10 soccer balls in an 8-hour workday. Let's also say that it takes 1.2 Saudi workers and the equivalent of $1.2 (in riyals, the currency of Saudi Arabia) to make 10 soccer balls in the same 8-hour workday. We can say that the U.S. soccer-ball industry is more productive than the Saudi soccer-ball industry. The two factors of production in this extremely simple case are labor and capital.

Now let's look at productivity from a different perspective. If more products are being produced with fewer factors of production, what happens to the prices of these products? They go down. As a consumer, therefore, you would need less of your currency to purchase the same quantity of these products. In short, your standard of living—at least with regard to these products—has improved. If your entire economic system increases its productivity, then your overall standard of living improves. In fact, *standard of living improves only through increases in productivity.*[6] Real growth in GDP reflects growth in productivity.

Productivity in the United States is increasing, and as a result, so are GDP and GDP per capita. Ultimately, increases in these measures of growth mean an improvement in the standard of living. However, things don't always proceed so smoothly. What factors can inhibit the growth of an economic system? There are several such factors, but we'll focus on two of them: *balance of trade* and the *national debt.*

PRODUCTIVITY a measure of economic growth that compares how much a system produces with the resources needed to produce it

Figure 1.4

One interesting method for comparing purchasing power in different countries is the Big Mac Index—a comparison of the costs of a McDonald's hamburger in different countries.

Local currency under (−)/over (+) valuation against the dollar, %

Country	Big Mac Price*, $
Switzerland	4.93
Denmark	4.49
Sweden	4.28
Euro area	3.51†
Britain	3.32
United States	3.15‡
New Zealand	3.08
Turkey	3.07
Canada	3.01
Chile	2.98
Brazil	2.74
Hungary	2.71
Mexico	2.66
Czech Republic	2.60
South Korea	2.56
Australia	2.44
Taiwan	2.35
South Africa	2.29
Singapore	2.20
Japan	2.19
Poland	2.09
Egypt	1.61
Russia	1.60
Philippines	1.56
Argentina	1.55
Hong Kong	1.55
Indonesia	1.54
Thailand	1.51
Malaysia	1.47
China	1.30

Scale: 60 40 20 −0 +20 40 60

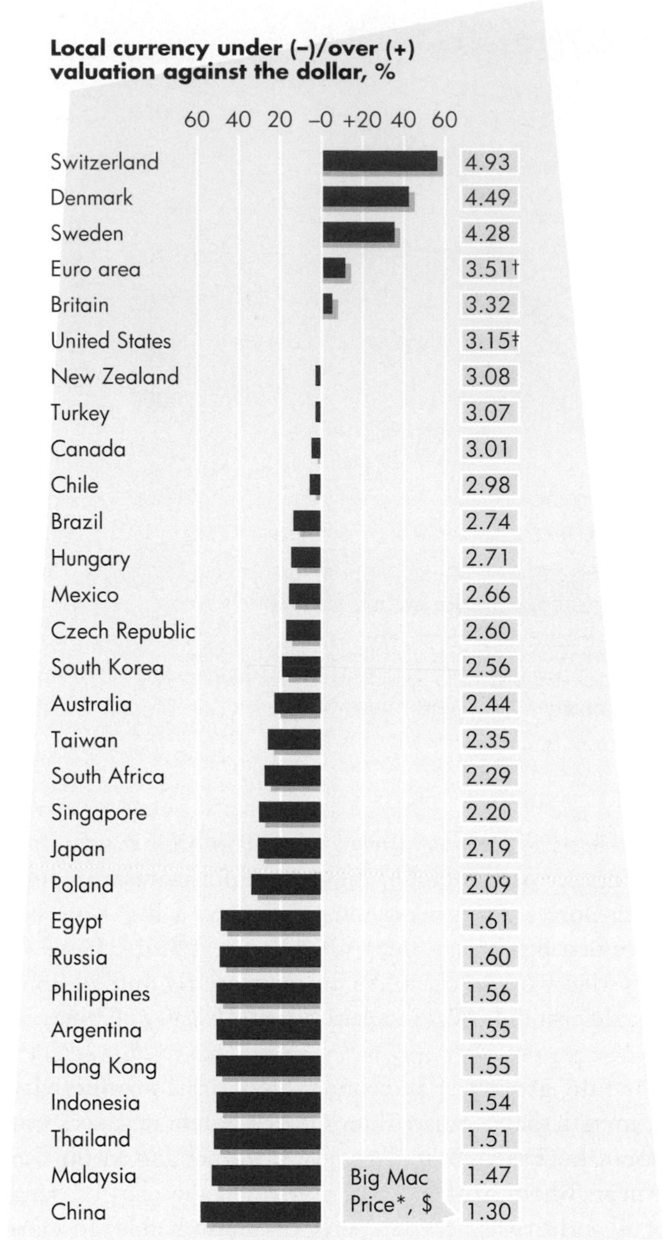

Note: *At market exchange rate (January 9, 2006).

† Weighted average of member countries.

‡ Average of four cities

BALANCE OF TRADE the economic value of all the products that a country exports minus the economic value of all the products it imports

Balance of Trade A country's **balance of trade** is the economic value of all the products that it exports minus the economic value of its imported products. The principle here is quite simple:

- A *positive* balance of trade results when a country exports (sells to other countries) more than it imports (buys from other countries).
- A *negative* balance of trade results when a country imports more than it exports.

Figure 1.5
Balance of Trade

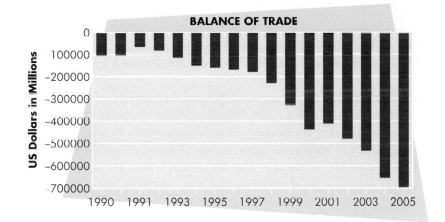

A negative balance of trade is commonly called a *trade deficit*. In 2005, the U.S. trade deficit exceeded $700 billion. The United States is a *debtor nation* rather than a *creditor nation*. Recent trends in the U.S. balance of trade are shown in Figure 1.5.

How does a trade deficit affect economic growth? The deficit exists because the amount of money spent on foreign products has not been paid in full. In effect, therefore, it is borrowed money, and borrowed money costs more money in the form of interest. The money that flows out of the country to pay off the deficit can't be used to invest in productive enterprises, either at home or overseas.

National Debt Its **national debt** is the amount of money that the government owes its creditors. As of this writing, the U.S. national debt is over $7.9 trillion. (You can find out the national debt on any given day by going to any one of several Internet sources, including the U.S. National Debt Clock at www.brillig.com/debt_clock.)

How does the national debt affect economic growth? While taxes are the most obvious way the government raises money, it also sells *bonds*—securities through which it promises to pay buyers certain amounts of money by specified future dates. (In a sense, a bond is an IOU with interest.) The government sells bonds to individuals, households, banks, insurance companies, industrial corporations, nonprofit organizations, and government agencies, both at home and overseas.[7] These bonds are attractive investments because they are extremely safe: The U.S. government is not going to default on them (that is, fail to make payments when due). Even so, they must also offer a decent return on the buyer's investment, and they do this by paying interest at a competitive rate. By selling bonds, therefore, the U.S. government competes with every other potential borrower—individuals, households, businesses, and other organizations—for the available supply of loanable money. The more money the government borrows, the less money is available for the private borrowing and investment that increases productivity.

NATIONAL DEBT the amount of money the government owes its creditors

▪▪▪ ECONOMIC STABILITY

We have now explored a great deal about economic systems and the ways in which they allocate resources among their citizens. We know, for example, that business production and pricing decisions are influenced by the laws of demand and supply. We also know that the laws of demand and supply result in equilibrium prices when the quantity of goods demanded and the quantity of goods supplied are equal. We know that we can measure growth and productivity in terms of GDP and standard of living in terms of the purchasing power parity of a system's currency: Living standards are stable when purchasing power parity remains stable.[8]

STABILITY condition in which the amount of money available in an economic system and the quantity of goods and services produced in it are growing at about the same rate

So, we can conclude that a chief goal of an economic system is **stability**: a condition in which the amount of money available in an economic system and the quantity of goods and services produced in it are growing at about the same rate. Now we can focus on certain factors that threaten stability—namely, inflation and unemployment.

Inflation **Inflation** occurs when widespread price increases occur throughout an economic system. How does it threaten stability? Inflation occurs when the amount of money injected into an economy exceeds the increase in actual output. When this happens, people will have more money to spend, but there will still be the same quantity of products available for them to buy. So, as supply and demand principles tell us, as they compete with one another to buy available products, prices go up. Before long, high prices will erase the increase in the amount of money injected into the economy. However, these processes are imperfect—the additional money will not be distributed proportionately to all people, and price increases often continue beyond what is really necessary. As a result, purchasing power for many people declines.

INFLATION occurs when widespread prices increases occur throughout an economic system

Inflation can also hurt you as a consumer because your primary concern when deciding whether to purchase a product is often price. In other words, you will probably decide to make a purchase if the value of the product justifies the price that you'll have to pay. Now look at Table 1.3, which reduces a hypothetical purchase decision to three bare essentials:

1 Your household income over a three-year period
2 The price of a hamburger over a three-year period
3 The rates of increase for both over a three-year period

In which year did the cost of a hamburger go up? At first glance, you might say in both YR2 and YR3 (to $4.00 and to $7.50). In YR2, your income kept pace: Although a hamburger cost twice as much, you had twice as much money to spend. In effect, the price to you was actually the same. In YR3, however, your income increased by 250 percent while the price of a hamburger increased by 275 percent. In YR3, therefore, you got hit by inflation (how hard depends on your fondness for hamburgers). This ratio—the comparison of your increased income to the increased price of a hamburger—is all that counts if you want to consider inflation when you're making a buying decision. Inflation, therefore, can be harmful to you as a consumer because *inflation decreases the purchasing power of your money*.

Measuring Inflation: The CPI How do we measure inflation? Remember that our definition of inflation is the occurrence of widespread price increases throughout an economic system. It stands to reason, therefore, that we can measure inflation by measuring price increases. To do this, we can turn to such price indexes as the **consumer price index** (CPI): a measure of the prices of typical products purchased by consumers living in urban areas.[9]

CONSUMER PRICE INDEX (CPI) a measure of the prices of typical products purchased by consumers living in urban areas

TABLE 1.3 HAMBURGER INFLATION

YR1 INCOME	YR2 INCOME	YR2 % INCREASE OVER YR1 BASE	YR3 INCOME	YR3 % INCREASE OVER YR1 BASE
$5,000	$10,000	100	$17,500	250
YR1 HAMBURGER PRICE	**YR2 HAMBURGER PRICE**	**YR2 % INCREASE OVER YR1 BASE**	**YR3 HAMBURGER PRICE**	**YR3 % INCREASE OVER YR1 BASE**
$2	$4	100	$7.50	275

Here's how the CPI works. First we need a base period—an arbitrarily selected time period against which other time periods are compared. The CPI base period used by the federal government is 1982 to 1984, which has been given an average value of 100. Table 1.4 gives CPI values computed for selected years. The CPI value for 1951, for instance, is 26. This means that $1 worth of typical purchases in 1982 to 1984 would have cost $0.26 in 1951. Conversely, you would have needed $1.95 to purchase the same $1 worth of typical goods in 2005. The difference registers the effect of inflation. In fact, that's what an *inflation rate* is—*the percentage change in a price index*.

We can calculate the CPI rate of inflation by using the data in Table 1.4. To find the inflation rate between, say, 2004 and 2005, we need to know the change from one year to the next. To find this change, we simply subtract the value of 2004 from the value of 2005: 195.3 − 188.8 = 6.5.

Now apply the following formula:

$$\text{Inflation rate} = \frac{\text{Change in price index}}{\text{Initial price index}} \times 100$$

or

$$\frac{6.50}{188.8} \times 100 = 3.40\%$$

Thus, the inflation rate between 2004 and 2005 was 3.40 percent. This rate was the highest in years, largely due to the dramatic increases in the prices of gas and health care.

TABLE 1.4	SELECTED CPI VALUES
YEAR	**CPI**
1951	26.0
1961	29.9
1971	40.6
1981	90.9
1989	124.0
1990	130.7
1991	136.2
1992	140.3
1993	144.5
1994	148.2
1995	152.4
1996	156.9
1997	160.5
1998	163.0
1999	166.6
2000	172.2
2001	177.1
2002	179.9
2003	184.0
2004	188.9
2005	195.3

Unemployment Finally, we need to consider the effect of unemployment on economic stability. **Unemployment** is the level of joblessness among people actively seeking work in an economic system. When unemployment is low, there is a shortage of labor available for businesses to hire. As businesses compete with one another for the available supply of labor, they raise the wages they are willing to pay. Then, because higher labor costs eat into profit margins, they raise the prices of their products. Although consumers have more money to inject into the economy, this increase is soon erased by higher prices. Purchasing power declines.

There are at least two related problems. If wage rates get too high, businesses will respond by hiring fewer workers and unemployment will go up. Businesses could raise prices to counter increased labor costs, but if they charge higher prices, they won't be able to sell as much of their products. Because of reduced sales, they will cut back on hiring and, once again, unemployment will go up. What if the government tries to correct this situation by injecting more money into the economic system—say by cutting taxes or spending more money? Prices in general may go up because of increased consumer demand. Again, purchasing power declines and inflation may set in.[10]

Recessions and Depressions Finally, unemployment is sometimes a symptom of a systemwide disorder in the economy. During a downturn in the business cycle, people in different sectors may lose their jobs at the same time. As a result, overall income and spending may drop. Feeling the pinch of reduced revenues, businesses may cut spending on the factors of production—including labor. Yet more people will be put out of work and unemployment will only increase further. Unemployment that results from this vicious cycle is called *cyclical unemployment*.

UNEMPLOYMENT the level of joblessness among people actively seeking work in an economic system

If we look at the relationship between unemployment and economic stability, we are reminded that when prices get high enough, consumer demand for goods and services goes down. We are also reminded that when demand for products goes down, producers cut back on hiring and, not surprisingly, eventually start producing less. Consequently, aggregate output decreases. When we go through a period during which aggregate output declines, we have a recession. During a *recession*, producers need fewer employees—less labor—to produce products. Unemployment, therefore, goes up.

How do we know whether we're in a recession? We start by measuring aggregate output. Recall that this is the function of real GDP, which we find by making necessary adjustments to the total value of all goods and services produced within a given period by a national economy through domestic factors of production. A **recession** is more precisely defined as a period during which aggregate output, as measured by real GDP, declines. A prolonged and deep recession is a **depression**.

RECESSION a period during which aggregate output, as measured by GDP, declines

DEPRESSION a prolonged and deep recession

▪▪▪ MANAGING THE U.S. ECONOMY

The government acts to manage the U.S. economic system through two sets of policies: fiscal and monetary. It manages the collection and spending of its revenues through **fiscal policies**. Tax rates, for example, can play an important role in fiscal policies helping to manage the economy. For example, throughout his administration, President George W. Bush has advocated lower taxes. His arguments are predicated on the idea that if people pay lower taxes, they will have more money for investment. More investment, in turn, is a key driver of economic growth. For instance, as more investors buy a firm's stock, its prices go up; higher stock prices, in turn, allow the firm to expand, hiring more employees, building new facilities, and so forth.

FISCAL POLICIES policies used by a government regarding how it collects and spends revenue

Monetary policies focus on controlling the size of the nation's money supply. Working primarily through the Federal Reserve System (the nation's central bank, often referred to simply as "the Fed"), the government can influence the ability and willingness of banks throughout the country to lend money.[11] It can also influence the supply of money by prompting interest rates to go up or down. For instance, in one recent year alone, the Fed cut interest rates six times. Why? Because it saw signs of an economy threatened by both inflation (rising prices) and recession (a slowing growth rate). The power of the Fed to make changes in the supply of money is the centerpiece of the U.S. government's monetary policy. The principle is fairly simple:

MONETARY POLICIES policies used by a government to control the size of its money supply

The U.S. government uses the Federal Reserve System to implement its monetary policies. The Chairman of "the Fed" is Ben Bernanke. He is shown here listening to opening remarks before the U.S. Senate Banking Committee in Washington, D.C.

■ Higher interest rates make money more expensive to borrow and thereby reduce spending by those who produce goods and services. When the Fed restricts the money supply, we say that it is practicing a *tight monetary policy*.

■ Lower interest rates make money less expensive to borrow and thereby increase spending by those who produce goods and services. When the Fed loosens the money supply—and stimulates the economy—we say that it is practicing an *easy (or loose) monetary policy*.

In short, the Fed can influence the aggregate market for products by influencing the supply of money. Taken together, fiscal policy and monetary policy make up **stabilization policy:** government economic policy whose goal is to smooth out fluctuations in output and unemployment and to stabilize prices.

STABILIZATION POLICY
government economic policy intended to smooth out fluctuations in output and unemployment and to stabilize prices

---

SELF-CHECK QUESTIONS 7–9

You should now be able to answer Self-Check Questions 7–9.*

7 Multiple Choice Which of the following is **not** generally used as a measure of economic growth?
(a) standard of living
(b) inflation
(c) aggregate output
(d) productivity

8 Multiple Choice Which of the following statements about GDP and GNP is true?

(a) They mean the same thing
(b) They mean different things and are usually very different values
(c) They mean different things but are usually close in value
(d) They both lead directly to inflation

9 True or False When the Fed tightens interest rates, the government is exercising fiscal policy.

*Answers to Self-Check Questions 7–9 can be found on p. 563.

CONTINUED FROM PAGE 4

HITTING THE PEAK

While surging oil and gas prices occupied the thoughts of consumers in 2006, government officials began to worry about the bigger picture. The surging global demand for gasoline has been forcing experts to face a stark reality—the global supply of petroleum will soon peak and then slowly begin to decline. While no one can pinpoint when this will happen, virtually all the experts agree that it will happen well before the middle of this century.

So then what? The laws of supply and demand will continue to work, but in perhaps different ways. First, just because the supply of oil will decline doesn't mean that it will disappear immediately. While there may be gradual reductions in supply, oil and gas will remain available for at least another century—but at prices that may make those of today seem like a bargain. New technology may also allow businesses to extract petroleum from locations that are not currently accessible, such as from the deepest areas under the oceans.

Second, and more significantly, there will be market incentives for businesses everywhere to figure out how to replace today's dependence on oil and gas with alternatives. For instance, automobile manufacturers are already seeing increased demand for their hybrid products—cars and trucks that use a combination of gasoline and electrical power. Hence, firms that can produce alternative sources of energy will spring up, and those who find viable answers will prosper. And companies that can figure out how to replace today's plastic products with new products that don't rely on petroleum will also find willing buyers.

QUESTIONS FOR DISCUSSION

1 What were the basic factors of production in the petroleum industry? What do you think the factors of production might be in the future?

2 Explain how the concepts of the demand and supply of petroleum combine to determine market prices.

3 What are the economic indicators most directly affected by energy prices?

4 Does the global energy situation increase or decrease your confidence in a capitalistic system based on private enterprise?

5 Should there be more government intervention in the exploration for and pricing of petroleum products? Why or why not?

SUMMARY OF LEARNING OBJECTIVES

1 Define the nature of U.S. business and identify its main goals and functions.

A *business* is an organization that provides goods or services to earn profits. The prospect of earning *profits*—the difference between a business's revenues and expenses—encourages people to open and expand businesses. Businesses produce most of the goods and services that Americans consume and employ most working people. New forms of technology, service businesses, and international opportunities promise to keep production, consumption, and employment growing indefinitely.

2 Describe the external environments of business and discuss how these environments affect the success or failure of any organization.

The *external environment* of business refers to everything outside its boundaries that might affect it. Both the *domestic* and the *global business environment* affect virtually all businesses. The *technological*, *political-legal*, *sociocultural*, and *economic environments* are also important.

3 Describe the different types of global economic systems according to the means by which they control the factors of production.

Economic systems differ in the ways in which they manage the five *factors of production* (1) *labor*, or *human resources*, (2) *capital*, (3) *entrepreneurship*, (4) *physical resources*, and (5) *information resources*. A *planned economy* relies on a centralized government to control factors of production and make decisions. Under *communism*, the government owns and operates all sources of production. In a *market economy*, individuals—producers and consumers—control production and allocation decisions through supply and demand. A *market* is a mechanism for exchange between the buyers and sellers of a particular product or service. Sellers can charge what they want, and customers can buy what they choose. The political basis of market processes is *capitalism*, which fosters private ownership of the factors of production and encourages entrepreneurship by offering profits as an incentive. Most countries rely on some form of *mixed market economy*—a system featuring characteristics of both planned and market economies.

4 Show how markets, demand, and supply affect resource distribution in the United States.

Decisions about what to buy and what to sell are determined by the forces of demand and supply. *Demand* is the willingness and ability of buyers to purchase a product or service. *Supply* is the willingness and ability of producers to offer a product or service for sale. A *demand and supply schedule* reveals the relationships among different levels of demand and supply at different price levels.

5 Identify the elements of private enterprise and explain the various degrees of competition in the U.S. economic system.

Market economies reflect the operation of a *private enterprise system*—a system that allows individuals to pursue their own interests without government restriction. Private enterprise works according to four principles: (1) private property rights, (2) freedom of choice, (3) profits, and (4) competition. Economists have identified four degrees of competition in a private enterprise system: (1) *perfect competition*, (2) *monopolistic competition*, (3) *oligopoly*, and (4) *monopoly*.

6 Explain the importance of the economic environment to business and identify the factors used to evaluate the performance of an economic system.

Economic indicators are statistics that show whether an economic system is strengthening, weakening, or remaining stable. The overall health of the economic environment—the economic system in which they operate—affects organizations. The two key goals of the U.S. system are *economic growth* and *economic stability*. Growth is assessed by *aggregate output*. Among the factors that can inhibit growth, two of the most important are *balance of trade* and the *national debt*. *Economic stability* means that the amount of money available in an economic system and the quantity of goods and services produced in it are growing at about the same rate. There are two key threats to stability: *inflation* and *unemployment*. The government manages the economy through two sets of policies: *fiscal policies* (such as tax increases) and *monetary policies* that focus on controlling the size of the nation's money supply.

KEY TERMS

aggregate output (p. 19)

balance of trade (p. 22)

business (p. 5)

business cycle (p. 19)

capital (p. 8)

capitalism (p. 12)

communism (p. 11)

competition (p. 16)

consumer price index (p. 24)

demand (p. 13)

demand and supply schedule (p. 14)

demand curve (p. 14)

depression (p. 26)

domestic business environment (p. 7)

economic environment (p. 8)

economic indicators (p. 18)

economic system (p. 8)

entrepreneur (p. 9)

external environment (p. 6)

factors of production (p. 8)

fiscal policies (p. 26)

global business environment (p. 7)

gross domestic product (GDP) (p. 20)

gross national product (GNP) (p. 20)

inflation (p. 24)

information resources (p. 10)

labor (human resources) (p. 8)

law of demand (p. 14)

law of supply (p. 14)

market (p. 11)

market economy (p. 11)

market price (equilibrium price) (p. 14)

mixed market economy (p. 12)

monetary policies (p. 26)

monopolistic competition (p. 17)

monopoly (p. 17)

national debt (p. 23)

natural monopoly (p. 18)

nominal GDP (p. 20)

oligopoly (p. 17)

perfect competition (p. 16)

physical resources (p. 10)

planned economy (p. 11)

political-legal environment (p. 7)

private enterprise (p. 15)

privatization (p. 12)

productivity (p. 21)

profits (p. 5)

purchasing power parity (p. 20)

real GDP (p. 20)

recession (p. 26)

shortage (p. 14)

socialism (p. 12)

sociocultural environment (p. 8)

stability (p. 24)

stabilization policy (p. 27)

standard of living (p. 19)

supply (p. 14)

supply curve (p. 14)

surplus (p. 14)

technological environment (p. 7)

unemployment (p. 25)

QUESTIONS AND EXERCISES

Questions for Review

1 What are the factors of production? Is one factor more important than the others? If so, which one? Why?

2 What is a demand curve? A supply curve? What is the term for the point at which they intersect?

3 What is GDP? Real GDP? What does each measure?

4 Why is inflation both good and bad? How does the government try to control it?

Questions for Analysis

5 In recent years, many countries that previously used planned economies have moved to market economies. Why do you think this has occurred? Can you envision a situation that would cause a resurgence of planned economies?

6 Cite an instance in which a surplus of a product led to decreased prices. Cite an instance in which a shortage led to increased prices. What eventually happened in each case? Why?

7 Explain how current economic indicators, such as inflation and unemployment, affect you personally. Explain how they may affect you as a manager.

8 At first glance, it might seem as though the goals of economic growth and stability are inconsistent with one another. How can you reconcile this apparent inconsistency?

Application Exercises

9 Visit a local shopping mall or shopping area. List each store that you see and determine what degree of competition it faces in its immediate environment. For example, if there is only one store in the mall that sells shoes, that store represents a monopoly. Note those businesses with direct competitors (two jewelry stores) and show how they compete with one another.

10 Interview a business owner or senior manager. Ask this individual to describe for you the following things: (1) how demand and supply affect the business, (2) what essential factors of production are most central to the firm's operations, and (3) how fluctuations in economic indicators affect his or her business.

PAYING THE PRICE OF DOING E-BUSINESS

Goal

To help you understand how the economic environment affects a product's price.

Background Information

Assume that you own a local business that provides Internet access to individuals and businesses. Yours is one of four such businesses in the local market. Each one charges the same price: $12 per month for unlimited dial-up service. You also provide e-mail service, as do two of your competitors. Two competitors give users free personal Web pages. One competitor just dropped its price to $10 per month, and the other two have announced that they'll follow suit. Your breakeven price is $7 per customer—that is, you must charge $7 for your service package in order to cover your costs. You are concerned about getting into a price war that may destroy your business.

Method

Step 1

Divide into groups of four or five people. Each group should develop a general strategy for responding to competitors' price changes. Be sure to consider the following factors:

- How demand for your product is affected by price changes
- The number of competitors selling the same or a similar product
- The methods you can use—other than price—to attract new customers and retain current customers

Step 2

Develop specific pricing strategies based on each of the following situations:

- A month after dropping the price to $10, one of your competitors raises it back to $12.
- Two of your competitors drop their prices even further—to $8 a month. As a result, your business falls off by 25 percent.
- One of the competitors who offers free Web pages announces that the service will become optional for an extra $2 a month.
- Two competitors announce that they will charge individual users $8 a month but will charge a higher price (not yet announced) for businesses.
- All four providers (including you) are charging $8 a month. One goes out of business, and you know that another is in poor financial health.

FOLLOW-UP QUESTIONS

1 Discuss the role that various inducements other than price might play in affecting demand and supply in this market.

2 Is it always in a company's best interest to feature the lowest prices?

3 Eventually, what form of competition is likely to characterize this market?

PRESCRIBING A DOSE OF COMPETITIVE MEDICINE

The Situation

You are a businessperson in a small town, where you run one of two local pharmacies. The population and economic base are fairly stable. Each pharmacy controls about 50 percent of the market. Each is reasonably profitable, generating solid if unspectacular revenues.

The Dilemma

You have just been approached by the owner of the other pharmacy. He has indicated an interest either in buying your pharmacy or in selling his to you. He argues that neither of you can substantially increase your profits and complains that if one pharmacy raises its prices, customers will simply go to the other one. He tells you outright that if you sell to him, he plans to raise prices by 10 percent. He believes that the local market will have to accept the increase for two reasons: (1) The town is too small to attract national competitors, such as Walgreens, and (2) local customers can't go elsewhere to shop because the nearest town with a pharmacy is 40 miles away.

QUESTIONS TO ADDRESS

1 What are the roles of supply and demand in this scenario?
2 What are the underlying ethical issues?
3 What would you do if you were actually faced with this situation?

MAKING THE RIGHT DECISION

The Situation

Hotel S is a large hotel in the heart of a southern city. The hotel is a franchise operation run by an international hotel chain. The primary source of revenue for the hotel is convention business. A major tropical storm is about to hit the city, which in the past has been prone to heavy flooding.

The Dilemma

Because Hotel S is a licensed operation, it must maintain numerous quality standards in order to keep its license. This license is important because the international management company handles advertising, reservations, and so on. If it were to lose its license, it is almost certain that the hotel would have to reduce its staff.

For the past few years, members of the Hotel S team have been lobbying the investors who own the hotel to undertake a major renovation. They fear that without such a renovation, the hotel will lose its license when it comes up for renewal in a few months. The owners, however, have balked at investing more of their funds in the hotel itself but have indicated that hotel management can use revenues earned above a specified level for upgrades.

The tropical storm approaching the city has cut off most major transportation avenues, and telephone service is also down. The Hotel S staff is unable to reach the general manager, who has been traveling on business. Because the city is full of conventioneers, hotel rooms are in high demand. Unfortunately, because of the disrepair at the hotel, it only has about 50 percent occupancy. Hotel S staff have been discussing what to do and have identified three basic options:

1 The hotel can reduce room rates in order to help both local citizens as well as out-of-town visitors. The hotel can also provide meals at reduced rates. A few other hotels are also doing this.

2 The hotel can maintain its present pricing policies. Most of the city's hotels are adopting this course of action.

3 The hotel can raise its rates by approximately 15 percent without attracting too much attention. It can also start charging for certain things it has been providing for free, such as local telephone calls, parking, and morning coffee. None of the staff members favors this option out of greed, but instead see it as a way to generate extra profits for renovation and to protect jobs.

Team Activity

Assemble a group of four students and assign each group member to one of the following roles:

■ A member of the hotel staff
■ The Hotel S manager
■ A customer at the hotel
■ A Hotel S investor

ACTION STEPS

1 Before hearing any of your group's comments on this situation, and from the perspective of your assigned role, which of the three options do you think is the best choice? Write down the reasons for your position.

2 Before hearing any of your group's comments on this situation, and from the perspective of your assigned role, what are the underlying ethical issues, if any, in this situation? Write down the issues.

3 Gather your group together and reveal, in turn, each member's comments on the best choice of the three options. Next, reveal the ethical issues listed by each member.

4 Appoint someone to record main points of agreement and disagreement within the group. How do you explain the results? What accounts for any disagreement?

5 From an ethical standpoint, what does your group conclude is the most appropriate action that should have been taken by the hotel in this situation?

6 Develop a group response to the following question: Can your team identify other solutions that might help satisfy both extreme views?

□□□□□□□□□□   **VIDEO EXERCISE**

HELPING BUSINESSES DO BUSINESS: U.S. DEPARTMENT OF COMMERCE

Learning Objectives

The purpose of this video is to help you:

1 Understand world economic systems and their effect on competition.
2 Identify the factors of production.
3 Discuss ways in which supply and demand affect a product's price.

Synopsis

The U.S. Department of Commerce (DOC) (www. commerce.gov) seeks to support U.S. economic stability and help U.S.-based companies do business in other countries. In contrast to the planned economy of the People's Republic of China, the United States features a market economy in which firms are free to set their own missions and transact business with any other company or individual. They do, however, face some constraints. U.S. firms must comply with governmental regulations that set such standards as minimum safety requirements. When doing business in other countries, they must consider tariffs and other restrictions that govern imports to those markets. In addition, supply and demand affect a company's ability to set prices and generate profits.

DISCUSSION QUESTIONS

1 **For analysis:** If a U.S. company must pay more for factors of production, such as human resources, what is the likely effect on its competitiveness in world markets?

2 **For analysis:** Is the equilibrium price for a company's product likely to be the same in every country? Explain your answer.
3 **For application:** To which factors of production might a small U.S. company have the easiest access? How would this access affect the company's competitive position?
4 **For application:** Is a company likely to see more competitors enter a market when supply exceeds demand or when demand exceeds supply?
5 **For debate:** Should the U.S. Department of Commerce, which is funded by tax money, be providing advice and guidance to U.S. companies that want to profit by doing business elsewhere? Support the position you take.

Online Exploration

Visit the U.S. Department of Commerce Web site (www.commerce.gov) and follow some of the links from the home page in order to identify some of the agency's resources for business. Also, follow the link inviting you to read about the DOC, including its mission and history. What assistance can a U.S. business expect from the DOC? Why would the agency include environmental management on its list of resources for businesses? How do the agency's offerings fulfill its stated mission?

1 Explain how individuals develop their personal codes of ethics and why ethics are important in the workplace.

2 Distinguish social responsibility from ethics, identify organizational stakeholders, and characterize social consciousness today.

3 Show how the concept of social responsibility applies both to environmental issues and to a firm's relationships with customers, employees, and investors.

4 Identify four general approaches to social responsibility and describe the four steps that a firm must take to implement a social responsibility program.

5 Explain how issues of social responsibility and ethics affect small business.

HIGH SEAS DUMPING

Cruising has become a very popular vacation. More than eight million passengers take an ocean voyage each year, cruising many areas of the world's oceans in search of pristine beaches and clear tropical waters. The Caribbean Sea, the Mediterranean Sea, and the coast of Alaska are among the most popular destinations, while Hawaii and the coasts of

BUSINESS ETHICS AND SOCIAL RESPONSIBILITY

Europe and Asia are also growing in popularity. While tourists and the giant ships that carry them are usually welcome for the revenues that they bring, unfortunately, the ships also bring something much less desirable—pollution and other environmental problems.

A modern cruise ship carries an average of 2,000 passengers and 1,000 crew members. This many people generate a lot of waste. On a typical day, a ship of this size can produce 7 tons of solid garbage, which is incinerated and then dumped; 15 gallons of highly toxic chemical waste; 30,000 gallons of sewage; 7,000 gallons of bilge water containing oil; and 225,000 gallons of "gray" water from sinks and laundries. Cruise ships also pick up ballast water whenever and wherever it's needed and then discharge it later, releasing animals and pollution from other parts of the world. Multiply this problem by more than 167 ships worldwide, cruising 50 weeks per year, and the scope of the potential environmental damage is staggering.

Environmental groups see the top pollution-related problem as the death—and, potentially, the ultimate extinction—of marine life. Foreign animals bring parasites and diseases, and in some cases, replace native species entirely. Bacteria that are harmless to

> *Recent cases document continuing [pollution] violations both by cruise ships and the much larger shipping industry.*
>
> —*Prosecutor Richard Udell, Justice Department senior trial attorney for environmental crimes*

human beings can kill coral reefs that provide food and habitat for many species. Oil and toxic chemicals are deadly to wildlife even in minute quantities. Turtles swallow plastic bags, thinking they are jellyfish, and starve, while seals and birds become entangled in the plastic rings that hold beverage cans and drown.

Other problems include the habitat destruction or disease that affects U.S. industries, costing $137 billion each year. For example, cholera, picked up in ships' ballast water off the coast of Peru, caused a devastating loss to fish and shrimp harvesters in the Gulf of Mexico in the 1990s when infected catches had to be destroyed. Heavy metal poisoning of fish is rising, and concern is on the rise that the poisons are moving up the food chain from microscopic animals, to fish, and ultimately to humans. Phosphorus, found in detergents, causes an overgrowth of algae, which then consume all the available oxygen in the water, making it incapable of supporting any flora or fauna. One such "dead zone" occurs each summer in the Gulf of Mexico at the mouth of the Mississippi River. The area, caused by pollution and warm water, is about the size of Massachusetts—8,000 square miles of lifelessness.

Lack of regulation is the biggest obstacle to solving the problem. By international law, countries may regulate oceans for three miles off their shores. International treaties provide some additional regulation up to 25 miles offshore. Beyond the 25-mile point, however, ships are allowed free rein. Also, each country's laws and enforcement policies vary considerably, and even when laws are strict, enforcement may be limited. The U.S. Coast Guard enforces regulations off the U.S. coast, but it is spread thinly. Only about 1 percent of the Coast Guard's annual budget is spent on environmental oversight. Regulation aside, however, one would think that cruise lines would remain cognizant of the importance of clean and safe seas for their own economic well-being. Sadly, however, this is often not the case. ■

Our opening story continues on page 63.

WHAT'S IN IT FOR ME?

Growth in the cruise industry exemplifies a growing issue in the business world today: the economic imperatives (real or imagined) facing managers versus pressures to function as good world citizens. By understanding the material in this chapter, you'll be better able to assess ethical and socially responsible issues facing you as an employee and as a boss or business owner and understand the ethical and socially responsible actions of businesses you deal with as a consumer and as an investor.

In this chapter, we'll look at ethics and social responsibility—what they mean and how they apply to environmental issues and to a firm's relationships with customers, employees, and investors. Along the way, we look at general approaches to social responsibility, the steps businesses must take to implement social responsibility programs, and how issues of social responsibility and ethics affect small businesses. But first, we begin this chapter by discussing ethics in the workplace—individual, business, and managerial.

ETHICS IN THE WORKPLACE

ETHICS beliefs about what is right and wrong or good and bad in actions that affect others

Just what is ethical behavior? **Ethics** are beliefs about what's right and wrong or good and bad. An individual's values and morals, plus the social context in which his or her behavior occurs, determine whether behavior is regarded as ethical or unethical.

In other words, **ethical behavior** conforms to individual beliefs and social norms about what's right and good. **Unethical behavior** is behavior that conforms to individual beliefs and social norms about what is defined as wrong and bad. **Business ethics** is a term often used to refer to ethical or unethical behaviors by employees in the context of their jobs.

ETHICAL BEHAVIOR behavior conforming to generally accepted social norms concerning beneficial and harmful actions

UNETHICAL BEHAVIOR behavior that does not conform to generally accepted social norms concerning beneficial and harmful actions

BUSINESS ETHICS ethical or unethical behaviors by employees in the context of their jobs

■■■ INDIVIDUAL ETHICS

Because ethics are based on both individual beliefs and social concepts, they vary from person to person, from situation to situation, and from culture to culture. Social standards are broad enough to support differences in beliefs. Without violating general standards, people may develop personal codes of ethics reflecting a wide range of attitudes and beliefs.

Thus, ethical and unethical behaviors are determined partly by the individual and partly by the culture. For instance, virtually everyone would agree that if you see someone drop $20, it would be ethical to return it to the owner. But there'll be less agreement if you find $20 and don't know who dropped it. Should you turn it in to the lost-and-found department? Or, since the rightful owner isn't likely to claim it, can you just keep it?

Ambiguity, the Law, and the Real World Societies generally adopt formal laws that reflect prevailing ethical standards or social norms. For example, because most people regard theft as unethical, we have laws against such behavior and ways of punishing those who steal. We try to make unambiguous laws, but interpreting and applying them can still lead to ethical ambiguities. Real-world situations can often be interpreted in different ways, and it isn't always easy to apply statutory standards to real-life behavior. For instance, during the aftermath of Hurricane Katrina, desperate survivors in New Orleans looted grocery stores for food. While few people criticized this behavior, such actions were technically against the law.

Unfortunately, the epidemic of scandals ranging from Enron and Arthur Andersen to Tyco, Martha Stewart, and WorldCom that dominated business news over the past few years only serves to show how willing people can be to take advantage of potentially ambiguous situations—indeed, to create them. In 1997, Tyco effectively sold itself in a merger with a firm called ADT Ltd. ADT was smaller than Tyco, but because its new parent company was based in the tax haven of Bermuda, Tyco no longer had to pay U.S. taxes on its non-U.S. income. In 2000 and 2001, Tyco's subsidiaries in such tax-friendly nations doubled from 75 to 150, and the company slashed its 2001 U.S. tax bill by $600 million. "Tyco," complained a U.S. congressman, "has raised tax avoidance to an art," but one tax expert replies that Tyco's schemes "are very consistent with the [U.S.] tax code."[1] Even in the face of blistering criticism and the indictment of its former CEO, Tyco made the business decision to retain its offshore ownership structure.[2]

Individual Values and Codes How should we deal with business behavior that we regard as unethical, especially when it's legally ambiguous? No doubt we have to start with the individuals in a business—its managers, employees, and other legal representatives. Each person's personal code of ethics is determined by a combination of factors. We start to form ethical standards as children in response to our perceptions of the behavior of parents and other adults. Soon, we enter school, where we're influenced by peers, and as we grow into adulthood, experience shapes our lives and contributes to our ethical beliefs and our behavior. We also develop values and morals that contribute to ethical standards. If you put financial gain at the top of your priority list, you may develop a code of ethics that supports the pursuit of material comfort. If you set family and friends as a priority, you'll no doubt adopt different standards.

Recent ethics scandals in several high-profile businesses has focused new attention on the need for managers to develop, maintain, and enforce high standards of ethical conduct within their organizations. Ex-Enron executives Kenneth Lay (left, recently deceased) and Jeff Skilling became two of the most recognized faces in the United States during their high-profile trials. Both were indicted on multiple counts of fraud.

■■■ BUSINESS AND MANAGERIAL ETHICS

MANAGERIAL ETHICS standards of behavior that guide individual managers in their work

Managerial ethics are the standards of behavior that guide individual managers in their work.[3] Although your ethics can affect your work in any number of ways, it's helpful to classify them in terms of three broad categories.

Behavior Toward Employees This category covers such matters as hiring and firing, wages and working conditions, and privacy and respect. Ethical and legal guidelines suggest that hiring and firing decisions should be based solely on the ability to perform a job. A manager who discriminates against African Americans or women in hiring exhibits both unethical and illegal behavior. But what about the manager who hires a friend or relative when someone else might be more qualified? Although such decisions may not be illegal, they may be objectionable on ethical grounds.

Wages and working conditions, while regulated by law, are also areas for controversy. Consider a manager who pays a worker less than he deserves because the manager knows that the employee can't afford to quit or risk his job by complaining. While some people will see the behavior as unethical, others will see it as smart business. Cases such as these are hard enough to judge, but consider the behavior of Enron management toward company employees. It encouraged employees to invest retirement funds in company stock and then, when financial problems began to surface, refused to permit them to sell the stock (even though top officials were allowed to sell). Ultimately, the firm's demise cost thousands of these very employees to lose their jobs and much of their pensions.

Behavior Toward the Organization Ethical issues also arise from employee behavior toward employers, especially in such areas as conflict of interest, confidentiality, and honesty. A *conflict of interest* occurs when an activity may benefit the individual to the detriment of his or her employer. Most companies have policies that forbid buyers from accepting gifts from suppliers since such gifts might be construed as a bribe or an attempt to induce favoritism. Businesses in highly competitive industries—software and fashion apparel, for example—have safeguards against designers selling company secrets to competitors.

Relatively common problems in the general area of honesty include such behavior as stealing supplies, padding expense accounts, and using a business phone to make personal long-distance calls. Most employees are honest, but many organizations are nevertheless vigilant. Again, Enron is a good example of employees' unethical behavior toward an organization: Top managers not only misused corporate assets, but they often committed the company to risky ventures in order to further their own personal interests.

Behavior Toward Other Economic Agents Ethics also comes into play in the relationship of a business and its employees with so-called *primary agents of interest*—mainly customers, competitors, stockholders, suppliers, dealers, and unions. In dealing with such agents, there is room for ethical ambiguity in just about every activity—advertising, financial disclosure, ordering and purchasing, bargaining and negotiation, and other business relationships.

For example, businesses in the pharmaceutical industry are under criticism because of the rising prices of drugs. Critics argue that pharmaceutical companies reap huge profits at the expense of the average consumer. In its defense, the pharmaceutical industry argues that prices must be set high in order to cover the costs of research and development programs to develop new drugs. The solution to such problems seems obvious: Find the right balance between reasonable pricing and price gouging (responding to increased demand with overly steep price increases). But like so many questions involving ethics, there are significant differences of opinion about the proper balance.

Another area of concern is financial reporting, especially by high-tech firms like WorldCom. Some of these companies have been very aggressive in presenting their financial positions in a positive light, and in a few cases they have overstated earnings projections in order to entice more investment. This practice played a key role in the legal problems encountered by Enron:

■ Senior officials there continued to mislead investors into thinking that the firm was solvent long after they knew that it was in serious trouble.
■ The company violated numerous state regulations during the California energy crisis, causing millions of consumers hardship and inconvenience.
■ Many of its partnerships with other firms violated terms of full disclosure and honesty, resulting in losses for other firms and their employees.

Another problem is global variations in business practices. In many countries, bribes are a normal part of doing business. U.S. law, however, forbids bribes, even if rivals from other countries are paying them. A U.S. power-generating company recently lost a $320 million contract in the Middle East because it refused to pay bribes that a Japanese firm used to get the job. We'll discuss some of the ways in which social, cultural, and legal differences among nations affect international business in Chapter 4.

▪▪▪ ASSESSING ETHICAL BEHAVIOR

What distinguishes ethical from unethical behavior is often subjective and subject to differences of opinion. So how can we decide whether a particular action or decision is ethical? The following three steps set a simplified course for applying ethical judgments to situations that may arise during the course of business activities:

1 Gather the relevant factual information.
2 Analyze the facts to determine the most appropriate moral values.
3 Make an ethical judgment based on the rightness or wrongness of the proposed activity or policy.

Unfortunately, the process doesn't always work as smoothly as these three steps suggest. What if the facts aren't clear-cut? What if there are no agreed-upon moral values? Nevertheless, a judgment and a decision must be made. Experts point out that, otherwise, trust is impossible. And trust is indispensable in any business transaction.

The Ethical Soft Shoe

To bribe or not to bribe? That is the question. Well, actually, it's not really a question at all because the textbook answer is a non-negotiable no. No matter what business environment you're in, whatever culture or country you're in, the answer is always no.

In reality, it's a little more complicated than that. Business dealings that ignore the strict letter of the law happen all the time—more so in some countries than in others. Not just bribes, but offering or accepting incentives to get things done or extracting a personal favor or two. We do it all the time in the United States—using the power and influence of people we know to get things done the way we want. Granted, American business practices overseas are subject to certain constraints, such as those embodied in the Foreign Corrupt Practices Act.

Elsewhere, however, the answer to the question is not necessarily no. A hallmark of Brazilian business culture, for example, is a creative approach to problem solving known as *jeitinho*. *Jeitinho* means "to find a way." For Brazilians, there's always another way to get something done. If you need some kind of official document, for instance, you might set out on the straight and narrow path, determined to take all the proper bureaucratic steps to get it. Unfortunately, you may soon find yourself in a maze of rules and regulations from which it's impossible to extricate yourself. That's when you're most likely to resort to *jeitinho*—using personal connections, bending the rules, making a "contribution," or simply approaching the problem from a different angle.

The focus of *jeitinho* appears to be on the goal—in this case, obtaining a document. For Brazilians, however, it's really on *the process of accomplishing it*—on being willing and able to find another way, no matter what the obstacle. After all, every obstacle forces you in another direction, and during the process of negotiating the maze, you may be forced to change your original destination. *Jeitinho* almost never involves butting heads with authority. Rather, it's a complex dance that enables individuals to go around problems instead of having to go through them. It's a philosophy in which ends sometimes justify a complicated web of means.

Even if you're operating in a country (like Brazil) in which sidestepping the rules is business as usual, you don't *have* to do an ethical soft-shoe. Many global companies have strict ethical guidelines for doing business, and the steps generally don't change just because you're dancing with a foreign partner. The key is understanding the culture of the host country—observing the way business is conducted and preparing yourself for any challenges—before you get out on the dance floor.

"From a purely business viewpoint, taking what doesn't belong to you is usually the cheapest way to go."

To assess more fully the ethics of specific behavior, we need a more complex perspective. Consider a common dilemma faced by managers with expense accounts. Companies routinely provide managers with accounts to cover work-related expenses—hotel bills, meals, rental cars, or taxis—when they're traveling on company business or entertaining clients for business purposes. They expect employees to claim only work-related expenses.

If a manager takes a client to dinner and spends $100, submitting a $100 reimbursement receipt for that dinner is accurate and appropriate. But suppose that this manager has a $100 dinner the next night with a good friend for purely social purposes. Submitting that receipt for reimbursement would be unethical, but some managers rationalize that it's okay to submit a receipt for dinner with a friend. Perhaps they'll tell themselves that they're underpaid and just "recovering" income due to them.

Ethical *norms* also come into play in a case like this. Consider four such norms and the issues they entail:[4]

1 *Utility.* Does a particular act optimize the benefits to those who are affected by it? (That is, do all relevant parties receive "fair" benefits?)
2 *Rights.* Does it respect the rights of all individuals involved?
3 *Justice.* Is it consistent with what's fair?
4 *Caring.* Is it consistent with people's responsibilities to each other?

Figure 2.1 incorporates the consideration of these ethical norms into a model of ethical judgment making.

Now let's return to our case of the inflated expense account. While the utility norm acknowledges that the manager benefits from a padded account, others, such as coworkers and owners, don't. Most experts would also agree that the act doesn't respect the rights of others (such as investors, who have to foot the bill). Moreover, it's clearly unfair and compromises the manager's responsibilities to others. This particular act, then, appears to be clearly unethical.

Figure 2.1, however, also provides mechanisms for dealing with unique circumstances—those that apply only in limited situations. Suppose, for example, that our manager loses the receipt for the legitimate dinner but retains the receipt for the social dinner. Some people will now argue that it's okay to submit the illegitimate receipt because the manager is only doing so to get proper reimbursement. Others, however, will reply that submitting the alternative receipt is wrong under any circumstances. We won't pretend to arbitrate the case, and we will simply make the following point: Changes in most situations can make ethical issues either more or less clear-cut.

■■■ COMPANY PRACTICES AND BUSINESS ETHICS

As unethical and even illegal activities by both managers and employees plague more companies, many firms have taken additional steps to encourage ethical behavior in the workplace. Many set up codes of conduct and develop clear ethical positions on how the firm and its employees will conduct business. An increasingly controversial area regarding business ethics and company practices involves the privacy of e-mail and other communications that take place inside an organization. For instance, some companies monitor the Web searches conducted by their employees; the appearance of certain key words may trigger a closer review of how an employee is using the company's computer network. While some companies argue they do this for business reaons, some employees claim that it violates their privacy.[5]

Perhaps the single most effective step that a company can take is to demonstrate top management support of ethical standards. This policy contributes to a corporate culture

Figure 2.1
Model of Ethical Judgment
Making

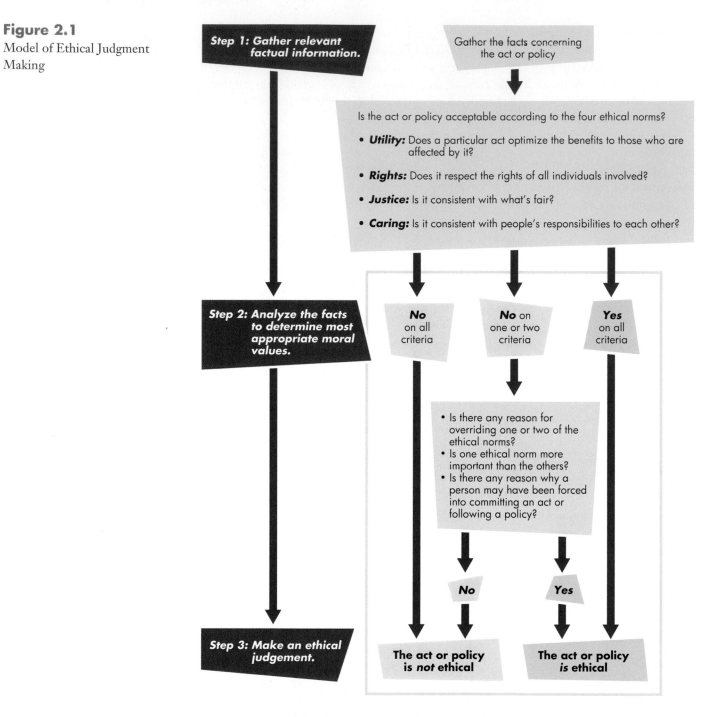

that values ethical standards and announces that the firm is as concerned with good citizenship as with profits. For example, when United Technologies (UT), a Connecticut-based industrial conglomerate, published its 21-page code of ethics, it also named a vice president for business practices to see that UT conducted business ethically and responsibly. With a detailed code of ethics and a senior official to enforce it, the firm sends a signal that it expects ethical conduct from its employees.

Two of the most common approaches to formalizing top management commitment to ethical business practices are *adopting written codes* and *instituting ethics programs*.

Adopting Written Codes Many companies, like UT, have written codes that formally announce their intent to do business in an ethical manner. The number of such companies has risen dramatically in the last three decades, and today almost all major

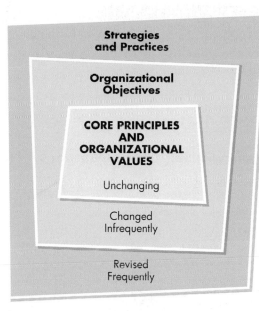

Figure 2.2
Core Principles and
Organizational Values

corporations have written codes of ethics. Even Enron had a code of ethics, but managers must follow the code if it's going to work. On one occasion, Enron's board of directors voted to set aside the code in order to complete a deal that would violate it; after the deal was completed, they then voted to reinstate it!

Figure 2.2 illustrates the role that corporate ethics and values should play in corporate policy. You can use it to see how a good ethics statement might be structured. Basically, the figure suggests that although strategies and practices can change frequently and objectives can change occasionally, an organization's core principles and values should remain steadfast. Hewlett-Packard, for example, has had the same written code of ethics, called *The HP Way*, since 1957. Its essential elements are these:

- We have trust and respect for individuals.
- We focus on a high level of achievement and contribution.
- We conduct our business with uncompromising integrity.
- We achieve our common objectives through teamwork.
- We encourage flexibility and innovation.

Instituting Ethics Programs Many examples suggest that ethical responses can be learned through experience. For instance, in a classic case several years ago, a corporate saboteur poisoned Tylenol capsules, resulting in the deaths of several consumers. Employees at Johnson & Johnson, the maker of Tylenol, all knew that, without waiting for instructions or a company directive, they should get to retailers' shelves and pull the product as quickly as possible. In retrospect, they reported simply knowing that this was what the company would want them to do. But can business ethics be taught, either in the workplace or in schools? Not surprisingly, business schools have become important players in the debate about ethics education. Most analysts agree that even though business schools must address the issue of ethics in the workplace, companies must take the chief responsibility for educating employees. In fact, more and more firms are doing so.

For example, both ExxonMobil and Boeing have major ethics programs. All managers must go through periodic ethics training to remind them of the importance of ethical decision making and to update them on the most current laws and regulations that might be particularly relevant to their firms. Interestingly, some of the more popular ethics training programs today are taught by former executives who have spent time in prison for their own ethical transgressions.[6] Others, such as Texas Instruments, have ethical hotlines—numbers that an employee can call, either to discuss the ethics of a particular problem or situation or to report unethical behavior or activities by others.

SELF-CHECK QUESTIONS 1–3

You should now be able to answer Self-Check Questions 1–3.*

1 **Multiple Choice** Suppose a manager cheats on an expense account. Into which of the following areas of managerial ethics does this behavior fall?
   (a) organizational behavior toward other economic agents
   (b) employee behavior toward the organization
   (c) organizational behavior toward the employee
   (d) other economic agents' behavior toward the organization

2 **Multiple Choice** Which of the following is **not** one of the norms for assessing ethical behavior discussed in this section?
   (a) utility
   (b) rights
   (c) justice
   (d) regulation

3 **True/False** Every business is legally required to develop and publish a corporate code of ethics.

*Answers to Self-Check Questions 1–3 can be found on p. 563.

SOCIAL RESPONSIBILITY

SOCIAL RESPONSIBILITY the attempt of a business to balance its commitments to groups and individuals in its environment, including customers, other businesses, employees, investors, and local communities

ORGANIZATIONAL STAKEHOLDERS those groups, individuals, and organizations that are directly affected by the practices of an organization and who therefore have a stake in its performance

Ethics affect individual behavior in the workplace. **Social responsibility** is a related concept, but it refers to the overall way in which a business attempts to balance its commitments to relevant groups and individuals in its social environment. These groups and individuals are often called **organizational stakeholders**—those groups, individuals, and organizations that are directly affected by the practices of an organization and, therefore, have a stake in its performance.[7] Major corporate stakeholders are identified in Figure 2.3.

■■■ THE STAKEHOLDER MODEL OF RESPONSIBILITY

Most companies that strive to be responsible to their stakeholders concentrate first and foremost on five main groups: *customers, employees, investors, suppliers,* and the *local communities* where they do business. They may then select other stakeholders that are particularly relevant or important to the organization and try to address their needs and expectations as well.

Customers Businesses that are responsible to their customers strive to treat them fairly and honestly. They also seek to charge fair prices, honor warranties, meet delivery commitments, and stand behind the quality of the products they sell. L.L.Bean, Lands' End, Dell Computer, and Johnson & Johnson are among those companies with excellent reputations in this area. In recent years, many small banks have increased their profits by offering much stronger customer service than the large national banks (such as Wells Fargo and Bank of America). For instance, some offer their customers free coffee and childcare while they're in the bank conducting

Big banks just don't get it.

—Gordon Goetzmann, a leading financial services executive, on why service-oriented small banks are growing faster

entrepreneurship and new ventures

The Electronic Equivalent of Paper Shredding

In virtually every major corporate scandal of the last few years, the best-laid plans of managerial miscreants have come unraveled, at least in part, when supposedly private e-mail surfaced as a key piece of evidence. At Citigroup, for example, analyst Jack Grubman changed stock recommendations in exchange for favors from CEO Sandy Weill and then sent an e-mail to confirm the arrangement. Investigators found that David Duncan, Arthur Andersen's head Enron auditor, had deleted incriminating e-mails shortly after the start of the Justice Department's investigation. After Tim Newington, an analyst for Credit Suisse First Boston, refused to give in to pressure to change a client's credit rating, an e-mail circulated on the problem of Newington's troublesome integrity: "Bigger issue," warned an upper manager, "is what to do about Newington in general. I'm not sure he's salvageable at this point."

Many corporations are nervous about the potential liability that employee e-mail may incur, but some entrepreneurs detect an opportunity in this same concern. A few software-development houses are busily designing programs to meet the needs of cautious corporate customers.

One such software house is Omniva Policy Systems. E-mail senders using Omniva's e-mail software can send encrypted messages and specify an expiration date after which encrypted e-mail messages can no longer be decrypted—the electronic equivalent of paper shredding. In addition, Omniva software can also prevent resending or printing, and users cannot unilaterally delete their own e-mail on their own initiative. In the event of a lawsuit or investigation, administrators can hit a "red button" that prevents all deletions.

"Our goal," says Omniva CEO Kumar Sreekanti, "is to keep the honest people honest. . . . We help organizations comply with regulations automatically so they don't have to rely on people to do it." Removing responsibility (and temptation) has become an increasingly popular strategy among executives who, like those at Metropolitan Life, the CIA, Eli Lilly, and many other organizations, are looking to e-mail-security systems to help them avoid the kind of exposure encountered by Citigroup, Arthur Andersen, and Credit Suisse.

business. According to Gordon Goetzmann, a leading financial services executive, "Big banks just don't get it" when it comes to understanding what customers want. As a result, for the past few years, small bank profits have been growing at a faster rate than profits at larger chain banks.

Employees Businesses that are socially responsible in their dealings with employees treat workers fairly, make them a part of the team, and respect their dignity and basic human needs. Organizations, such as The Container Store, Starbucks, Microsoft, FedEx, and American Express, have established strong reputations in this area. In addition, many of the same firms also go to great lengths to find, hire, train, and promote qualified minorities. Each year, *Fortune* magazine publishes lists of the "Best Companies to Work for in America" and the "Best Companies for Minorities." These lists attract more individuals who are eager to work for such highly regarded employers.[8]

Investors To maintain a socially responsible stance toward investors, managers should follow proper accounting procedures, provide appropriate information to shareholders about financial performance, and manage the organization to protect shareholder rights and investments. These managers should be accurate and candid in assessing future growth and profitability, and they should avoid even the appearance of impropriety in such sensitive areas as insider trading, stock-price manipulation, and the withholding of financial data.

In 2002, for example, WorldCom, a giant telecommunications business and owner of MCI, announced that it had overstated previous years' earnings by as much as $6 billion.

Figure 2.3 Major Corporate Stakeholders

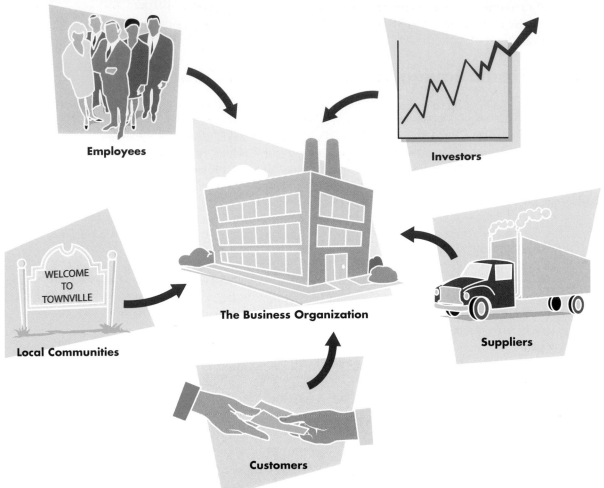

The SEC also announced that it was investigating the firm's accounting practices, and investors learned that the firm had lent CEO Bernard Ebbers $366 million that he might not be able to repay. On the heels of these problems, WorldCom's stock price dropped by more than 43 percent, and the company eventually had to seek bankruptcy protection

Most companies strive to be responsible to their primary stakeholders. FedEx has an exceptionally strong reputation for its social responsibility regarding it customers, employees, investors, suppliers, and the communities where it does business.

as it attempted to dig out of the hole it had created for itself. As for Ebbers, he was subsequently indicted on several charges related to the accounting scandal. In 2005, he was found guilty and sentenced to 25 years in prison (as of this writing, he is appealing the conviction).[9]

Suppliers Relations with suppliers should also be managed with care. For example, it might be easy for a large corporation to take advantage of suppliers by imposing unrealistic delivery schedules and reducing profit margins by constantly pushing for lower prices. Many firms now recognize the importance of mutually beneficial partnership arrangements with suppliers. Thus, they keep them informed about future plans, negotiate delivery schedules and prices that are acceptable to both firms, and so forth. Toyota and Amazon.com are among the firms acknowledged to have excellent relationships with their suppliers.

Local and International Communities Most businesses try to be socially responsible to their local communities. They may contribute to local programs, such as Little League baseball, get actively involved in charitable programs, such as the United Way, and strive to simply be good corporate citizens by minimizing their negative impact on communities. Target, for example, donates a percentage of sales to the local communities where it does business. The company says it gives over $2 million each week to neighborhoods, programs, and schools across the country.[10]

The stakeholder model can also provide some helpful insights into the conduct of managers in international business. In particular, to the extent that an organization acknowledges its commitments to its stakeholders, it should also recognize that it has multiple sets of stakeholders in each country where it does business. DaimlerChrysler, for example, has investors not only in Germany but also in the United States, Japan, and other countries where its shares are publicly traded. It also has suppliers, employees, and customers in multiple countries, and its actions affect many different communities in dozens of different countries. Similarly, international businesses must also address their responsibilities in areas, such as wages, working conditions, and environmental protection, across different countries that have varying laws and norms regulating such responsibilities. ExxonMobil, for instance, has helped build hospitals and expand schools in the west African nation of Angola, where it has established a growing oil business.[11]

The growth in international businesses poses new and complex social responsibility challenges for businesses today. For instance, a clothing manufacturer might boost its profits (and hence benefit its investors) by making its products in low-wage foreign countries. However, if it takes things too far it may end up exploiting poor laborers who have no other employment opportunities.

■■■ CONTEMPORARY SOCIAL CONSCIOUSNESS

Social consciousness and views toward social responsibility continue to evolve. The business practices of such entrepreneurs as John D. Rockefeller, J. P. Morgan, and Cornelius Vanderbilt raised concerns about abuses of power and led to the nation's first laws regulating basic business practices. In the 1930s, many people blamed the Great Depression on a climate of business greed and lack of restraint. Out of this economic turmoil emerged new laws that dictated an expanded role for business in protecting and enhancing the general welfare of society. Hence, the concept of *accountability* was formalized.

In the 1960s and 1970s, business was again characterized as a negative social force. Some critics even charged that defense contractors had helped to promote the Vietnam War to spur their own profits. Eventually, increased social activism prompted increased government regulation in a variety of areas. Health warnings were placed on cigarettes, for instance, and stricter environmental protection laws were enacted.

During the 1980s and 1990s, the general economic prosperity enjoyed in most sectors of the economy led to another period of laissez-faire attitudes toward business. While the occasional scandal or major business failure occurred, people for the most part seemed to view business as a positive force in society and one that was generally able to police itself through self-control and free-market forces. Many businesses continue to operate in enlightened and socially responsible ways. For example, retailers such as Sears and Target have policies against selling handguns and other weapons. Likewise, national toy retailers KayBee and Toys "R" Us refuse to sell toy guns that look too realistic, and Anheuser-Busch promotes the concept of responsible drinking in some of its advertising.

Firms in numerous other industries have also integrated socially conscious thinking into their production plans and marketing efforts. The production of environmentally safe products has become a potential boom area as many companies introduce products designed to be environmentally friendly. Electrolux, a Swedish appliance maker, has developed a line of water-efficient washing machines, a solar-powered lawn mower, and ozone-free refrigerators. Ford is aggressively studying and testing ways to develop and market low-pollution vehicles fueled by electricity, hydrogen, and other alternative energy sources.[12]

Unfortunately, the spate of corporate scandals and incredible revelations in the last few years may revive negative attitudes and skepticism toward business. As just a single illustration, widespread moral outrage erupted when some of the perquisites provided to former Tyco International CEO Dennis Kozlowski were made public. These perks included such extravagances as a $50 million mansion in Florida and an $18 million apartment in New York, along with $11 million for antiques and furnishings (including a $6,000 shower curtain). The firm even paid for a $2.1 million birthday party in Italy for Kozlowski's wife. It's not as though Kozlowski was a pauper—he earned almost $300 million between 1998 and 2001 in salary, bonuses, and stock proceeds. In late 2005, Kozlowski was sentenced to 25 years in prison.[13]

In Washington, critics and government officials alike are calling for tighter standards for business practices and increased control on accounting procedures. And to the extent that society begins to see economic problems as stemming from irresponsible business activities and unethical executive conduct, there may indeed be a return to the mindset of the 1930s. Such a shift could result in business being seen as less capable of controlling itself and thus requiring increased control and constraint by the government.[14]

SELF-CHECK QUESTIONS 4–6

You should now be able to answer Self-Check Questions 4–6.*

4 True/False Though closely related, ethics and social responsibility do not mean the same thing.

5 Multiple Choice The stakeholder model of social responsibility generally includes which of the following?

(a) customers
(b) employees
(c) suppliers
(d) All of these

6 Multiple Choice Contemporary social consciousness toward business currently reflects which of the following?

(a) universal admiration
(b) calls for higher taxes
(c) growing skepticism and concern regarding responsible corporate governance
(d) a laissez-faire philosophy

*Answers to Self-Check Questions 4–6 can be found on p. 563.

AREAS OF SOCIAL RESPONSIBILITY

When defining its sense of social responsibility, a firm typically confronts four areas of concern: responsibilities toward the *environment*, its *customers*, its *employees*, and its *investors*.

■■■ RESPONSIBILITY TOWARD THE ENVIRONMENT

During the first few years of his administration, some of the harshest criticism directed at President George W. Bush was leveled at his environmental policies. For example, he openly championed proposals for oil exploration in protected areas of Alaska, and he has steadfastly rejected the proposals of the 1997 Kyoto Protocol dealing with global warming. Most of the world's major countries endorsed that agreement, designed to slow global warming, but the United States has been condemned for its refusal to participate. "We know the surface temperature of the earth is rising," admits Bush, but he argues that his policies reflect a sound combination of free market expansion and exploration balanced against environmental protection and conservation.

Contrary to President Bush's assertions, however, Figure 2.4 tells a troubling story. The chart shows atmospheric carbon dioxide (CO_2) levels for the period between 1750 and 2000, and it offers three possible scenarios for future levels under different sets of conditions. The three projections—lowest, middle, highest—were developed by the Intergovernmental Panel on Climate Change, which calculated likely changes in the atmosphere during the twenty-first century if no efforts were made to reduce so-called greenhouse emissions—waste industrial gases that trap heat in the atmosphere. The criteria for estimating changes are population, economic growth, energy supplies, and technologies: The less pressure exerted by these conditions, the less the increase in CO_2 levels. Energy supplies are measured in exajoules—roughly the annual energy consumption of the New York Metropolitan area.

Under the lowest, or best-case, scenario, by 2100 the population would only grow to 6.4 billion people, economic growth would be no more than 1.2 to 2.0 percent a year, and energy supplies would require only 8,000 exajoules of conventional oil. However, under the highest, or worst-case, scenario, the population would increase to 11.3 billion people,

Figure 2.4
CO$_2$ Emissions, Past and Future

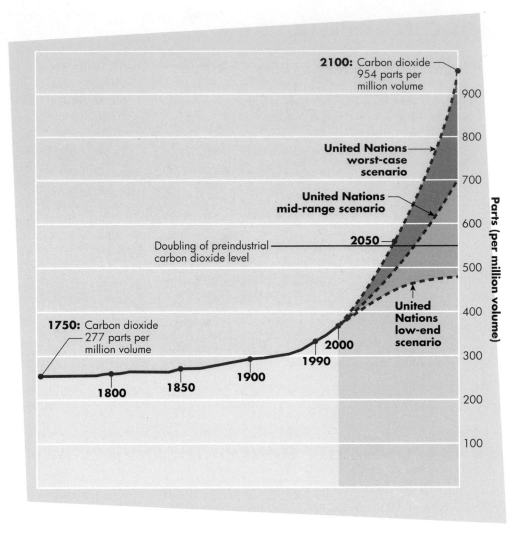

annual economic growth would be between 3.0 and 3.5 percent, and energy supplies would require as much as 18,400 exajoules of conventional oil.

The resulting changes in climate would be relatively mild; we would experience hardly any day-to-day changes in the weather. We would, however, increase the likelihood of having troublesome weather around the globe—droughts, hurricanes, winter sieges, and so forth. The charges leveled against greenhouse emissions are disputed, but as one researcher puts it, "The only way to prove them for sure is to hang around 10, 20, or 30 more years, when the evidence would be overwhelming. But in the meantime, we're conducting a global experiment. And we're all in the test tube." The movie *The Day After Tomorrow* portrayed one possible scenario of rapid climate changes wrought by environmental damage.

Controlling *pollution*—the injection of harmful substances into the environment—is a significant challenge for contemporary business. Although noise pollution is now attracting increased concern, air, water, and land pollution remain the greatest problems in need of solutions from governments and businesses alike. In the following sections, we focus on the nature of the problems in these areas and on some of the current efforts to address them.

Air Pollution Air pollution results when several factors combine to lower air quality. Carbon monoxide emitted by cars contributes to air pollution, as do smoke and other

The U.S.-based environmental group Nature Conservancy has recently teamed up with Indonesian logging company Sumalindo Lestari Jaya to help local villagers log a forest in a remote area of Indonesia. Why? The group believes that by working together with the company, it can better enforce sustainable practices.

chemicals produced by manufacturing plants. Air quality is usually worst in certain geographic locations, such as the Denver area and the Los Angeles basin, where pollutants tend to get trapped in the atmosphere. For this very reason, the air around Mexico City is generally considered to be the most polluted in the entire world.

Legislation has gone a long way toward controlling air pollution. Under new laws, many companies must now install special devices to limit the pollutants they expel into the air, and such efforts are costly. Air pollution is compounded by such problems as acid rain, which occurs when sulfur is pumped into the atmosphere, mixes with natural moisture, and falls to the ground as rain. Much of the damage to forests and streams in the eastern United States and Canada has been attributed to acid rain originating in sulfur from manufacturing and power plants in the midwestern United States. The North American Free Trade Agreement (NAFTA) also includes provisions that call for increased controls on air pollution, especially targeting areas that affect more than one member nation.

Water Pollution Water becomes polluted primarily from chemical and waste dumping. For years, businesses and cities dumped waste into rivers, streams, and lakes with little regard for the consequences. Cleveland's Cuyahoga River was once so polluted that it literally burst into flames one hot summer day. After an oil spill, a Houston ship channel burned for days.

Thanks to new legislation and increased awareness, water quality in many areas of the United States is improving. The Cuyahoga River now boasts fish and is even used for recreation. Laws in New York and Florida forbidding dumping of phosphates (an ingredient found in many detergents) have helped to make Lake Erie and other major waters safe again for fishing and swimming. Both the Passaic River in New Jersey and the Hudson River in New York are much cleaner now than they were just a few years ago.

Land Pollution Two key issues characterize land pollution. The first is how to restore the quality of land that has already been damaged. Land and water damaged by toxic waste, for example, must be cleaned up for the simple reason that people still need to use them. The second problem is the prevention of future contamination. New forms of solid-waste disposal constitute one response to these problems. Combustible wastes can be separated and used as fuels in industrial boilers, and decomposition can be accelerated by exposing waste matter to certain microorganisms.

Toxic Waste Disposal An especially controversial problem in land pollution is toxic waste disposal. Toxic wastes are dangerous chemical or radioactive byproducts of manufacturing processes. U.S. manufacturers produce between 40 and 60 million tons of such material each year. As a rule, toxic waste must be stored; it cannot be destroyed or processed into harmless material. Few people, however, want toxic waste storage sites in their backyards. A few years ago, American Airlines pled guilty—and became the first major airline to gain a criminal record—to a felony charge that it had mishandled some hazardous materials packed as cargo in passenger airplanes. While fully acknowledging the firm's guilt, Anne McNamara, American's general counsel, argued that "this is an incredibly complicated area with many layers of regulation. It's very easy to inadvertently step over the line."

Recycling Recycling is another controversial area in land pollution. Recycling—the reconversion of waste materials into useful products—has become an issue not only for municipal and state governments but also for many companies engaged in high-waste activities. Certain products, such as aluminum cans and glass, can be very efficiently recycled. Others, such as plastics, are more troublesome. For example, brightly colored plastics, such as some detergent and juice bottles, must be recycled separately from clear plastics, such as milk jugs. Most plastic bottle caps, meanwhile, contain a vinyl lining that can spoil a normal recycling batch. Nevertheless, many local communities actively support various recycling programs, including curbside pickup of aluminum, plastics, glass, and pulp paper. Unfortunately, consumer awareness and interest in this area—and the policy priorities of businesses—are more acute at some times than at others.

■■■ RESPONSIBILITY TOWARD CUSTOMERS

A company that does not act responsibly toward its customers will ultimately lose their trust—and their business. Moreover, the government controls or regulates many aspects of what businesses can and cannot do regarding consumers. The Federal Trade Commission (FTC) regulates advertising and pricing practices. The Food and Drug Administration (FDA) enforces guidelines for labeling food products.

Unethical and irresponsible business practices toward customers can result in government-imposed penalties and expensive civil litigation. For example, Abbott Laboratories agreed to pay $100 million to settle accusations that the firm failed to meet federal quality standards when it made hundreds of different medical test kits. The FDA indicated that it was, at the time, the largest fine the agency had ever levied.

Social responsibility toward customers generally falls into two categories: providing quality products and pricing products fairly. Naturally, firms differ as much in their level of concern about their responsibility toward customers as in their approaches to environmental responsibility. Yet unlike environmental problems, many customer problems do not require expensive solutions. Most problems can be avoided if companies simply adhere to regulated practices and heed laws regarding consumer rights.

Consumer Rights Much of the current interest in business responsibility toward customers can be traced to the rise of **consumerism**—social activism dedicated to protecting the rights of consumers in their dealings with businesses. The first formal declaration of consumer rights protection came in the early 1960s when President John F. Kennedy identified four basic consumer rights. Since that time, general agreement on

CONSUMERISM form of social activism dedicated to protecting the rights of consumers in their dealings with businesses

two additional rights has also emerged; these rights are also backed by numerous federal and state laws:

1 *Consumers have a right to safe products.* Businesses can't knowingly sell products that they suspect of being defective. For example, Philip Morris has been marketing a brand of cigarettes, Merit, on the basis that they are safer and less likely to cause a fire if left unattended. However, recent evidence suggests that the firm ignored research by one of its own scientists showing just the opposite—that Merit cigarettes are actually more prone to causing fires than are conventional cigarettes.[15]

2 *Consumers have a right to be informed about all relevant aspects of a product.* For example, apparel manufacturers are now required to provide full disclosure on all fabrics used (cotton, silk, polyester, and so forth) and instructions for care (dry clean, machine wash, hand wash).

3 *Consumers have a right to be heard.* Labels on most products sold today have either a telephone number or address through which customers can file complaints or make inquiries.

4 *Consumers have a right to choose what they buy.* For example, customers getting auto-repair service are allowed to know and make choices about pricing and warranties on new versus used parts. Similarly, with the consent of their doctors, people have the right to choose between name-brand medications versus generic products that might be cheaper.

5 *Consumers have a right to be educated about purchases.* For example, all prescription drugs now come with detailed information regarding dosage, possible side effects, and potential interactions with other medications.

6 *Consumers have a right to courteous service.* This right is hard to legislate. But as consumers become increasingly knowledgeable, they're more willing to complain about bad service. Consumer hotlines can also be used to voice service-related issues.

American Home Products provides an instructive example of what can happen to a firm that violates one or more of these consumer rights. For several years the firm aggressively marketed the drug Pondimin, a diet pill containing fenfluramine. During its heyday, doctors were writing 18 million prescriptions a year for Pondimin and other medications containing fenfluramine. The FDA subsequently discovered a link between the pills and heart-valve disease. A class-action lawsuit against the firm charged that the drug was unsafe and that users had not been provided with complete information about possible side effects. American Home Products eventually agreed to pay $3.75 billion to individuals who had used the drug.

Unfair Pricing Interfering with competition can take the form of illegal pricing practices. **Collusion** occurs when two or more firms agree to collaborate on such wrongful acts as price fixing. The U.S. Justice Department charged three international pharmaceutical firms with illegally controlling worldwide supplies and prices of vitamins. France's Rhone-Poulenc cooperated with the investigation, helped break the case several months earlier than expected, and was not fined. Switzerland's F. Hoffmann-LaRoche was fined $500 million and one of its senior executives was sentenced to four months in a U.S. prison. Germany's BASF was fined $225 million. Similarly, Dow Chemical and DuPont (U.S. firms) and Bayer (a German company) are under investigation for widespread price fixing.[16]

Under some circumstances, firms can also come under attack for *price gouging*—responding to increased demand with overly steep (and often unwarranted) price increases. For example, when residents of a coastal area are warned of a possible hurricane, they often flock to retailers to stock up on bottled water and batteries. Unfortunately, some retailers take advantage of this pattern by marking up their prices. Reports were widespread of

COLLUSION illegal agreement between two or more companies to commit a wrongful act

gasoline retailers doubling or even tripling prices immediately after the events of September 11, 2001, and following the U.S. invasion of Iraq in 2003. Similar problems arose in the wake of hurricanes Katrina and Rita after they damaged oil refineries along the Gulf Coast in late 2005. Critics charge that petroleum retailers were counting on consumer panic in response to fear and uncertainty.

Ethics in Advertising In recent years, increased attention has been given to ethics in advertising and product information. Because of controversies surrounding the potential misinterpretation of words and phrases, such as *light*, *reduced calorie*, *diet*, and *low fat*, food producers are now required to use a standardized format for listing ingredients on product packages. Similarly, controversy arose when it was discovered that Sony had literally created a movie critic who happened to be particularly fond of movies released by Sony's Columbia Pictures. When advertising its newest theatrical releases, the studio had been routinely using glowing quotes from a fictitious critic. After *Newsweek* magazine reported what was going on, Sony hastily stopped the practice and apologized.

Another issue concerns advertising that some consumers consider morally objectionable. Examples include advertising for products such as underwear, condoms, alcohol, tobacco products, and firearms. Laws regulate some of this advertising (for instance, tobacco can no longer be promoted in television commercials but can be featured in print ads in magazines), and many advertisers use common sense and discretion in their promotions. But some companies, such as Calvin Klein and Victoria's Secret, have come under fire for being overly explicit in their advertising. Likewise, consumer advocates are paying close attention to advertising for erectile dysfunction drugs such as Viagra and Levitra.

Advertising guidelines are set and monitored by the FTC. If a firm is found guilty of deceptive advertising, it may even be required to subsequently run additional ads correcting its previous deceptions. Kraft recently decided to ban some of its own food ads in media targeted toward kids. Part of the reason for this unusual step was to head off critics charging food companies with contributing to growing rates of obesity by promoting unhealthy foods.[17]

In 2003, London-based Sotheby's and New York-based Christie's paid a $537 million settlement to former customers after the U.S. Justice Department began investigating whether the two auction houses secretly agreed to charge the same rates for all sales.

■■■ RESPONSIBILITY TOWARD EMPLOYEES

In Chapter 10, we show how a number of human resource management activities are essential to a smoothly functioning business. These activities—recruiting, hiring, training, promoting, and compensating—are also the basis for social responsibility toward employees.

Legal and Social Commitments Socially responsible behavior toward employees has both legal and social components. By law, businesses cannot practice numerous forms of illegal discrimination against people in any facet of the employment relationship. For example, a company cannot refuse to hire someone because of ethnicity or pay someone a lower salary than someone else on the basis of gender. Such actions must be taken for job-related purposes only. A company that provides its employees with equal opportunities for rewards and advancement without regard to race, sex, or other irrelevant factors is meeting both its legal and its social responsibilities. Firms that ignore these responsibilities run the risk of losing productive, highly motivated employees. They also leave themselves open to lawsuits.

In the opinion of many people, however, social responsibility toward employees goes beyond equal opportunity. According to popular opinion, an organization should strive to ensure that the workplace is physically and socially safe. It should also recognize its obligations to help protect the health of its employees by providing opportunities to balance work and life pressures and preferences. From this point of view, social responsibility toward workers would also include helping them maintain proper job skills and, when terminations or layoffs are necessary, treating them with respect and compassion.

Ethical Commitments: The Special Case of Whistle-Blowers Respecting employees as people also means respecting their behavior as ethically responsible individuals. Suppose, for instance, an employee discovers that a business has been engaging in practices that are illegal, unethical, or socially irresponsible. Ideally, this employee should be able to report the problem to higher-level management, confident that managers will stop the questionable practices. Enron's Sherron Watkins reported concerns about the company's accounting practices well before the company's problems were made public, warning top management that Enron would "implode in a wave of accounting scandals." CEO

Enron's Sherron Watkins (right) reported concerns about the company's accounting practices well before the company's problems were made public, warning top management that Enron would "implode in a wave of accounting scandals."

Kenneth Lay commissioned a legal review of the firm's finances but told his investigators not to "second-guess" decisions by Enron's auditor, accounting firm Arthur Andersen.[18]

Too often, people who try to act ethically on the job find themselves in trouble with their employers. If no one in the organization will take action, the employee might elect to drop the matter. Occasionally, however, the individual will inform a regulatory agency or perhaps the media. At this point, he or she becomes a **whistle-blower**—an employee who discovers and tries to put an end to a company's unethical, illegal, or socially irresponsible actions by publicizing them.[19] The 1999 Al Pacino–Russell Crowe movie *The Insider* told the true story of a tobacco-industry whistle-blower named Jeffrey Wigand.

Unfortunately, whistle-blowers are sometimes demoted—and even fired—when they take their accusations public. Jeffrey Wigand was fired. "I went from making $300,000 a year," he reports, "plus stock options, plus, plus, plus—to making $30,000. Yes, there is a price I've paid." Even if they retain their jobs, they may still be treated as outsiders and suffer resentment or hostility from coworkers. Many coworkers see whistle-blowers as people who simply can't be trusted. One recent study suggests that about half of all whistle-blowers eventually get fired, and about half of those who get fired subsequently lose their homes and/or families.[20]

The law does offer some recourse to employees who take action. The current whistle-blower law stems from the False Claims Act of 1863, which was designed to prevent contractors from selling defective supplies to the Union Army during the Civil War. With 1986 revisions to the law, the government can recover triple damages from fraudulent contractors. If the Justice Department does not intervene, a whistle-blower can proceed with a civil suit. In that case, the whistle-blower receives 25 to 30 percent of any money recovered.[21]

When Phillip Adams worked in the computer industry, he discovered a flaw in the chip-making process that, under certain circumstances, could lead to data being randomly deleted or altered. He reported the flaw to manufacturers, but several years later, he found that one company, Toshiba, had ignored the problem and continued to make flawed chips for 12 years. He went on to report the problem and became actively involved in a class-action lawsuit based heavily on his research. Toshiba eventually agreed to a $2.1 billion settlement. Adams's share was kept confidential, but he did receive a substantial reward for his efforts. Unfortunately, however, the prospect of large cash rewards has also generated a spate of false or questionable accusations.

▪▪▪ RESPONSIBILITY TOWARD INVESTORS

Because shareholders are the owners of a company, it may sound odd to say that a firm can act irresponsibly toward its investors. But managers can abuse their responsibilities to investors in several ways. As a rule, irresponsible behavior toward shareholders means abuse of a firm's financial resources. In such cases, the ultimate losers are indeed the shareholder-owners who do not receive their due earnings or dividends. Companies can also act irresponsibly toward shareholder-owners by misrepresenting company resources.

Improper Financial Management Occasionally, organizations or their officers are guilty of blatant financial mismanagement—offenses that are unethical but not necessarily illegal. Some firms, for example, have been accused of paying excessive salaries to senior managers, of sending them on extravagant "retreats" to exotic and expensive resorts, and of providing frivolous perks, including ready access to corporate jets, lavish expense accounts, and memberships at plush country clubs.

In such situations, creditors can often do little, and stockholders have few options. Trying to force a management changeover is a difficult process that can drive down stock prices—a penalty that shareholders are usually unwilling to impose on themselves.

WHISTLE-BLOWER employee who detects and tries to put an end to a company's unethical, illegal, or socially irresponsible actions by publicizing them

I went from making $300,000 a year plus stock options, plus, plus, plus—to making $30,000. Yes, there is a price I've paid.

—Jeffrey Wigand, tobacco-industry whistle-blower

Insider Trading When someone uses confidential information to gain from the purchase or sale of stocks, that person is practicing **insider trading**. Suppose, for example, that a small firm's stock is currently trading at $50 a share. If a larger firm is going to buy the smaller one, it might have to pay as much as $75 a share for a controlling interest. Individuals who are aware of the impending acquisition before it is publicly announced might, therefore, be able to gain by buying the stock at $50 in anticipation of selling it for $75 after the proposed acquisition is announced. Individuals in a position to take advantage of such a situation generally include managers of the two firms and key individuals at banking firms working on the financial arrangements.

At the other extreme, informed executives can avoid financial loss by selling stock that's about to drop in value. Selling stock is not illegal, but, legally, you can sell only on the basis of public information that's available to all investors. Potential violations of this regulation were at the heart of the Martha Stewart scandal. The original case involved the pharmaceutical company ImClone, its president Samuel Waksal, and Martha Stewart, a close friend of Waksal. Waksal learned that ImClone stock was going to drop in value when it became known that the FDA had rejected ImClone's new "miracle" drug Erbitux. Waksal hastily tried to sell his own stock; he also made a telephone call to Stewart, who subsequently sold her stock as well. Stewart, though, argued that she never received Waksal's call but sold her stock only because she wanted to use the funds elsewhere. She eventually pled guilty to other charges (lying to investigators) and served time in prison. Waksal, meanwhile, received a much stiffer sentence because his own attempts to dump his stock were well documented.

Misrepresentation of Finances Certain behaviors regarding financial representation are also illegal. In maintaining and reporting its financial status, every corporation must conform to generally accepted accounting principles (GAAP) (see Chapter 14). Sometimes, however, unethical managers project profits far in excess of what they actually expect to earn; others go so far as to hide losses and/or expenses in order to boost paper profits. They may also slant their financial reports so as to make their firm seem much stronger than is really the case. When the truth comes out, however, the damage is often substantial.

Various issues involving the misrepresentation of finances were central in the Enron case. One review, for example, called Enron's accounting practices "creative and aggressive." It seems that CFO Andrew Fastow had set up a complex network of partnerships that were often used to hide losses. Enron, for instance, could report all of the earnings from a partnership as its own while transferring all or most of the costs and losses to the partnership. Inflated profits would then support increased stock prices.

In partial response to such problems, the U.S. Congress passed the *Sarbanes-Oxley Act* in 2002. This law requires that an organization's chief financial officer personally guarantee the accuracy of all financial reporting. We discuss Sarbanes-Oxley in more detail in Chapter 14.

IMPLEMENTING SOCIAL RESPONSIBILITY PROGRAMS

So far, we have discussed social responsibility as if there were some agreement on how organizations should behave. Opinions differ dramatically concerning the role of social responsibility as a business goal. Some people oppose any business activity that threatens profits. Others argue that social responsibility must take precedence over profits.

Even businesspeople who agree on the importance of social responsibility will cite different reasons for their views. Some skeptics of business-sponsored social projects fear that if businesses become too active, they will gain too much control over the ways in which those projects are addressed by society as a whole. These critics point to the influence that many businesses have been able to exert on the government agencies that are supposed to regulate their industries. Other critics claim that business organizations lack the expertise needed to address social issues. They argue, for instance, that technical experts, not businesses, should decide how to clean up polluted rivers.

Proponents of socially responsible business believe that corporations are citizens and should, therefore, help to improve the lives of fellow citizens. Still others point to the vast resources controlled by businesses and note that they help to create many of the problems social programs are designed to alleviate.

▪▪▪ APPROACHES TO SOCIAL RESPONSIBILITY

Given these differences of opinion, it is little wonder that corporations have adopted a variety of approaches to social responsibility. Not surprisingly, organizations themselves adopt a wide range of positions on social responsibility. As Figure 2.5 illustrates, the four stances that an organization can take concerning its obligations to society fall along a continuum ranging from the lowest to the highest degree of socially responsible practices.

Obstructionist Stance The few organizations that take what might be called an **obstructionist stance** to social responsibility usually do as little as possible to solve social or environmental problems. When they cross the ethical or legal line that separates acceptable from unacceptable practices, their typical response is to deny or cover up their actions. Firms that adopt this position have little regard for ethical conduct and will generally go to great lengths to hide wrongdoing. For example, IBP, a leading meat-processing firm, has a long (and undistinguished) record of breaking environmental protection, labor, and food processing laws and then trying to cover up its offenses. Enron would fall into this category as well.

OBSTRUCTIONIST STANCE approach to social responsibility that involves doing as little as possible and may involve attempts to deny or cover up violations

Defensive Stance One step removed from the obstructionist stance is the **defensive stance**, whereby the organization will do everything that is required of it legally but nothing more. This approach is most consistent with arguments against corporate social responsibility. Managers who take a defensive stance insist that their job is to generate profits. Such a firm, for example, would install pollution-control equipment dictated by law but would not install higher-quality equipment even though it might further limit pollution.

DEFENSIVE STANCE approach to social responsibility by which a company meets only minimum legal requirements in its commitments to groups and individuals in its social environment

Tobacco companies generally take this position in their marketing efforts. In the United States, they are legally required to include warnings to smokers on their products and to limit advertising to prescribed media. Domestically, they follow these rules to the letter of the law but use more aggressive marketing methods in countries that have no such rules. In many Asian and African countries, cigarettes are heavily promoted, contain higher levels of tar and nicotine than those sold in the United States, and carry few or no health warning labels. Firms that take this position are also unlikely to cover up wrongdoing, will generally admit to mistakes, and will take appropriate corrective actions.

Figure 2.5
Spectrum of Approaches to Corporate Social Responsibility

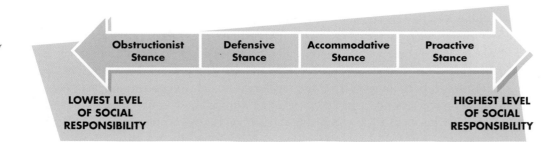

Accommodative Stance A firm that adopts an **accommodative stance** meets its legal and ethical requirements but will also go further in certain cases. Such firms voluntarily agree to participate in social programs, but solicitors must convince them that given programs are worthy of their support. Both Shell and IBM, for example, will match contributions made by their employees to selected charitable causes. Many organizations respond to requests for donations to Little League, Girl Scouts, youth soccer programs, and so forth. The point is, however, that someone has to knock on the door and ask. Accommodative organizations do not necessarily or proactively seek avenues for contributing.

Proactive Stance The highest degree of social responsibility that a firm can exhibit is the **proactive stance**. Firms that adopt this approach take to heart the arguments in favor of social responsibility. They view themselves as citizens in a society and proactively seek opportunities to contribute. The most common—and direct—way to implement this stance is to set up a foundation for providing direct financial support for various social programs.

An excellent example of a different kind of proactive stance is the Ronald McDonald House program undertaken by the McDonald's Corporation. These houses, located close to major medical centers, can be used for minimal cost by families while their sick children are receiving medical treatment nearby. Similarly, some firms, such as UPS, Home Depot, and USWest, employ individuals who hope to compete in the Olympics and support them in various ways. UPS, for instance, underwrites the training and travel costs of four employees competing for Olympic berths and allows them to maintain flexible work schedules. These and related programs exceed the accommodative stance—they indicate a sincere commitment to improving the general social welfare—and represent a proactive stance to social responsibility.

Remember, however, that these categories are not sharply distinct: They merely label stages along a continuum of approaches. Organizations do not always fit neatly into one category or another. The Ronald McDonald House program has been widely applauded, but McDonald's has also come under fire for allegedly misleading consumers about the nutritional value of its food products. Likewise, while UPS has sincere motives for helping Olympic athletes, the company will also benefit by featuring the athletes' photos on its envelopes and otherwise promoting its own benevolence. And even though Enron may have taken an obstructionist stance in the past, many individual employees and managers at the firm no doubt made substantial contributions to society in a number of different ways.

ACCOMMODATIVE STANCE approach to social responsibility by which a company, if specifically asked to do so, exceeds legal minimums in its commitments to groups and individuals in its social environment

PROACTIVE STANCE approach to social responsibility by which a company actively seeks opportunities to contribute to the well-being of groups and individuals in its social environment

TABLE 2.1 TOP 15 CORPORATE FOUNDATIONS

FOUNDATION	STATE	TOTAL GIVING	FISCAL DATE
1. Wal-Mart Foundation	AR	$154,537,406	01/31/05
2. Aventis Pharmaceuticals Health Care Foundation	NJ	114,668,984	12/31/04
3. The Bank of America Charitable Foundation, Inc.	NC	80,734,705	12/31/04
4. Ford Motor Company Fund	MI	77,916,903	12/31/04
5. The Wells Fargo Foundation	CA	64,747,007	12/31/04
6. ExxonMobil Foundation	TX	63,660,965	12/31/05
7. Citigroup Foundation	NY	57,720,957	12/31/03
8. Verizon Foundation	NJ	56,968,636	12/31/04
9. The JPMorgan Chase Foundation	NY	56,786,083	12/31/04
10. GE Foundation	CT	49,177,477	12/31/04
11. AT&T Foundation	TX	48,159,537	12/31/04
12. Fannie Mae Foundation	DC	47,742,454	12/31/04
13. Avon Foundation	NY	45,974,681	12/31/05
14. Johnson & Johnson Family of Companies Contribution Fund	NJ	42,871,365	12/31/04
15. The Merck Company Foundation	NJ	41,736,724	12/31/04

Figure 2.6
Establishing a Social
Responsibility Program

MANAGING SOCIAL RESPONSIBILITY PROGRAMS

Making a company socially responsible in the full sense of the social response approach takes a carefully organized and managed program. In particular, managers must take steps to foster a companywide sense of social responsibility.[22] Figure 2.6 summarizes these steps.

1 *Social responsibility must start at the top and be considered as a factor in strategic planning.* Without the support of top management, no program can succeed. Thus, top management must embrace a strong stand on social responsibility and develop a policy statement outlining that commitment.

2 *A committee of top managers must develop a plan detailing the level of management support.* Some companies set aside percentages of profits for social programs. Levi Strauss, for example, earmarks 2.4 percent of pretax earnings for worthy projects. Managers must also set specific priorities. For instance, should the firm train the hard-core unemployed or support the arts?

3 *One executive must be put in charge of the firm's agenda.* Whether the role is created as a separate job or added to an existing one, the selected individual must monitor the program and ensure that its implementation is consistent with the firm's policy statement and strategic plan.

4 *The organization must conduct occasional* **social audits**—*systematic analyses of its success in using funds earmarked for its social responsibility goals.* Consider the case of a company whose strategic plan calls for spending $100,000 to train 200 hard-core unemployed people and to place 180 of them in jobs. If, at the end of a year, the firm has spent $98,000, trained 210 people, and filled 175 jobs, a social audit will confirm the program's success. But if the program has cost $150,000, trained only 90 people, and placed only 10 of them, the audit will reveal the program's failure. Such failure should prompt a rethinking of the program's implementation and its priorities.

SOCIAL AUDIT systematic analysis of a firm's success in using funds earmarked for meeting its social responsibility goals

SOCIAL RESPONSIBILITY AND THE SMALL BUSINESS

As the owner of a garden supply store, how would you respond to a building inspector's suggestion that a cash payment will speed your application for a building permit? As the manager of a liquor store, would you call the police, refuse to sell, or sell to a customer whose identification card looks forged? As the owner of a small laboratory, would you call the state board of health to make sure that it has licensed the company with whom you want to contract to dispose of medical waste? Who will really be harmed if a small firm pads its income statement to help it get a much-needed bank loan?

Many of the examples in this chapter illustrate big-business responses to ethical and social responsibility issues. Such examples, however, show quite clearly that small businesses must answer many of the same questions. Differences are primarily differences of scale.

At the same time, these are largely questions of *individual* ethics. What about questions of social responsibility? Can a small business, for example, afford a social agenda? Should it sponsor Little League baseball teams, make donations to the United Way, and buy light bulbs from the Lion's Club? Do joining the chamber of commerce and supporting the Better Business Bureau cost too much? Clearly, ethics and social responsibility are decisions faced by all managers in all organizations, regardless of rank or size. One key to business success is to decide in advance how to respond to the issues that underlie all questions of ethical and social responsibility.

SELF-CHECK QUESTIONS 7–9

You should now be able to answer Self-Check Questions 7–9.*

7 Multiple Choice Which of the following is **not** an area of social responsibility?
(a) responsibility toward the board of directors
(b) responsibility toward the environment
(c) responsibility toward customers
(d) responsibility toward employees

8 Multiple Choice General approaches to social responsibility include which of the following?

(a) obstructionist
(b) defensive
(c) accommodative
(d) All of these

9 True/False Because of their size and limited financial resources, small businesses do **not** need to be concerned with social responsibility.

*Answers to Self-Check Questions 7–9 can be found on p. 563.

CONTINUED FROM PAGE 38

ROYAL FLUSHES

While some polluting by cruise ships can be expected, intentional illegal dumping may also be growing in scope. Over the last decade, for instance, as enforcement has tightened, 10 cruise lines have collectively paid $48.5 million in fines related to illegal dumping. In the largest settlement to date, Royal Caribbean paid $27 million for making illegal alterations to facilities, falsifying records, lying to the Coast Guard, and deliberately destroying evidence. The fine may seem high, but it covers 30 different charges and 10 years of violations and seems small compared to the firm's 2001 profits of almost $1 billion. Observers agree that Royal Caribbean's fine was less than what the firm would have paid to dispose of the waste properly over a decade. In addition, a lawsuit is pending regarding the firing of a whistle-blower, the firm's former vice president for safety and environment. "This [case] is like the Enron of the seas," says attorney William Amlong, who represents the whistle-blower.

Many feel that the fines haven't been steep enough. Norwegian Cruise Lines recently paid just $1 million for falsifying records in a case that included "some of the worst [violations] we've ever seen," according to Rick Langlois, an EPA investigator. Langlois and others are outspoken against the cruise lines' profiteering from an environment that they are destroying, but the critics note that the companies won't stop as long as the profits continue. Technology exists to make the waste safe, but industry experts estimate that dumping can save a firm millions of dollars annually. From that perspective, Norwegian's actions were just a "brilliant business decision," says Langlois.

QUESTION FOR DISCUSSION

1 What are the major ethical issues in this case?

2 Aside from personal greed, what factors might lead a cruise line to illegally dump waste into the ocean?

3 Which approach to social responsibility do cruise lines appear to be taking?

4 Distinguish between ethical issues and social responsibility issues as they apply to this problem.

SUMMARY OF LEARNING OBJECTIVES

1 Explain how individuals develop their personal codes of ethics and why ethics are important in the workplace.

Ethics are beliefs about what's right and wrong or good and bad. *Ethical behavior* conforms to individual beliefs and social norms about what's right and good. *Unethical behavior* is behavior that individual beliefs and social norms define as wrong and bad. *Managerial ethics* are standards of behavior that guide managers. There are three broad categories of ways in which managerial ethics can affect people's work: (1) *behavior toward employees,* (2) *behavior toward the organization,* and (3) *behavior toward other economic agents.*

One model for applying ethical judgments to business situations recommends the following three steps: (1) Gather relevant factual information, (2) analyze the facts to determine the most appropriate moral values, and (3) make an ethical judgment based on the rightness or wrongness of the proposed activity or policy. Perhaps the single most effective step that a company can take is to *demonstrate top management support.* In addition to promoting attitudes of honesty and openness, firms can also take specific steps to formalize their commitment: (1) *adopting written codes* and (2) *instituting ethics programs.*

2 Distinguish social responsibility from ethics, identify organizational stakeholders, and characterize social consciousness today.

Ethics affect individuals. *Social responsibility* refers to the way a firm attempts to balance its commitments to organizational stakeholders—those groups, individuals, and organizations that are directly affected by the practices of an organization and, therefore, have a stake in its performance. Many companies concentrate on five main groups: (1) *customers,* (2) *employees,* (3) *investors,* (4) *suppliers,* and (5) *local communities.*

Attitudes toward social responsibility have changed. The late nineteenth century, though characterized by the entrepreneurial spirit and the laissez-faire philosophy, also featured labor strife and predatory business practices. Concern about unbridled business activity was soon translated into laws regulating business practices. Out of the economic turmoil of the 1930s, when greed was blamed for business failures and the loss of jobs, came new laws protecting and enhancing social well-being. During the 1960s and 1970s, activism prompted increased government regulation in many areas of business. Today's attitudes stress a greater social role for business. This view, combined with the economic prosperity of the 1980s and 1990s, marked a return to the laissez-faire philosophy, but the recent epidemic of corporate scandals threatens to revive the 1930s call for more regulation and oversight.

3 Show how the concept of social responsibility applies both to environmental issues and to a firm's relationships with customers, employees, and investors.

A firm confronts four areas of concern: (1) *responsibility toward the environment,* (2) *responsibility toward customers,* (3) *responsibility toward employees,* and (4) *responsibility toward investors.* Organizations and managers may be guilty of *financial mismanagement*—offenses that are unethical but not necessarily illegal. Certain unethical practices are illegal. Using confidential information to gain from a stock transaction is *insider trading.* Certain behavior regarding financial representation is also unlawful.

4 Identify four general approaches to social responsibility and describe the four steps that a firm must take to implement a social responsibility program.

A business can take one of four stances concerning its social obligations to society: (1) *obstructionist stance,* (2) *defensive stance,* (3) *accommodative stance,* or (4) *proactive stance.* One model suggests a four-step approach to fostering a company-wide sense of social responsibility: (1) Social responsibility must start at the top and be included in strategic planning. (2) Top managers must develop a plan detailing the level of management support. (3) One executive must be put in charge of the agenda. (4) The organization must conduct occasional social audits—analyses of its success in using funds earmarked for social responsibility goals.

5 Explain how issues of social responsibility and ethics affect small business.

For small businesspeople, ethical issues are questions of individual ethics. But in questions of social responsibility, they must ask themselves if they can afford a social agenda, such as sponsoring Little League baseball teams or making donations to the United Way. They should also realize that managers in *all* organizations face issues of ethics and social responsibility.

accommodative stance (p. 61)

business ethics (p. 39)

collusion (p. 55)

consumerism (p. 54)

defensive stance (p. 60)

ethical behavior (p. 39)

ethics (p. 38)

insider trading (p. 59)

managerial ethics (p. 40)

obstructionist stance (p. 60)

organizational stakeholders (p. 46)

proactive stance (p. 61)

social audit (p. 61)

social responsibility (p. 46)

unethical behavior (p. 39)

whistle-blower (p. 58)

Questions for Review

1 What basic factors should be considered in any ethical decision?

2 Who are an organization's stakeholders? Who are the major stakeholders with which most businesses must be concerned?

3 What are the major areas of social responsibility with which businesses should be concerned?

4 What are the four basic approaches to social responsibility?

5 In what ways do you think your personal code of ethics might clash with the operations of some companies? How might you try to resolve these differences?

Questions for Analysis

6 What kind of wrongdoing would most likely prompt you to be a whistle-blower? What kind of wrongdoing would be least likely? Why?

7 In your opinion, which area of social responsibility is most important? Why? Are there areas other than those noted in the chapter that you consider important?

8 Identify some specific ethical or social responsibility issues that might be faced by small-business managers and employees in each of the following areas: environment, customers, employees, and investors.

Application Exercises

9 Develop a list of the major stakeholders of your college or university. How do you think the school prioritizes these stakeholders? Do you agree or disagree with this prioritization?

10 Using newspapers, magazines, and other business references, identify and describe at least three companies that take a defensive stance to social responsibility, three that take an accommodative stance, and three that take a proactive stance.

TO LIE OR NOT TO LIE: THAT IS THE QUESTION

Goal

To encourage you to apply general concepts of business ethics to specific situations.

Background Information

It seems workplace lying has become business as usual. According to one survey, one-quarter of working adults in the United States said that they had been asked to do something illegal or unethical on the job. Four in 10 did what they were told. Another survey of more than 2,000 secretaries showed that many employees face ethical dilemmas in their day-to-day work.

Method

Step 1

Working with a small group of other students, discuss ways in which you would respond to the following ethical dilemmas. When there is a difference of opinion among group members, try to determine the specific factors that influence different responses.

■ Would you lie about your supervisor's whereabouts to someone on the phone? Would it depend on what the supervisor was doing?

■ Would you lie about who was responsible for a business decision that cost your company thousands of dollars to protect your own or your supervisor's job?

■ Would you inflate sales and revenue data on official company accounting statements to increase stock value? Would you do so if your boss ordered it?

■ Would you say that you witnessed a signature when you did not if you were acting in the role of a notary?

■ Would you keep silent if you knew that the official minutes of a corporate meeting had been changed? Would the nature of the change matter?

■ Would you destroy or remove information that could hurt your company if it fell into the wrong hands?

Step 2

Research the commitment to business ethics at Johnson & Johnson (www.jnj.com) and Texas Instruments (www.ti.com/corp/docs/cthics/home.htm) by checking out their respective Web sites. As a group, discuss ways in which these statements are likely to affect the specific behaviors mentioned in step 1.

Step 3

Working with group members, draft a corporate code of ethics that would discourage the specific behaviors mentioned in step 1. Limit your code to a single printed page, but make it sufficiently broad to cover different ethical dilemmas.

FOLLOW-UP QUESTIONS

1 What personal, social, and cultural factors do you think contribute to lying in the workplace?

2 Do you agree or disagree with the statement "The term business ethics is an oxymoron." Support your answer with examples from your own work experience or that of someone you know.

3 If you were your company's director of human resources, how would you make your code of ethics a "living document"?

4 If you were faced with any of the ethical dilemmas described in step 1, how would you handle them? How far would you go to maintain your personal ethical standards?

TAKING A STANCE

The Situation

A perpetual debate revolves around the roles and activities of business owners in contributing to the greater social good. Promoting the so-called proactive stance, some people argue that businesses should be socially responsible by seeking opportunities to benefit the society in which they are permitted to conduct their affairs. Others promoting the defensive stance maintain that because businesses exist to make profits for owners, they have no further obligation to society.

The Dilemma

Assume that you are the manager of a restaurant near a major manufacturing plant. Many of your customers are employees at the plant. Due to inflation, you are about to raise your prices 10 to 15 percent. You have had new menus created and updated your posters. You have been planning to implement the higher prices in about three weeks.

You have just heard that another plant owned by the same company has been shut down for two weeks due to an explosion. The plant near you will be expected to make up the slack by asking workers to put in longer hours, adding a new shift, and so forth. You anticipate a substantial jump in your business immediately. You are now trying to make a quick decision about your pricing. One option is to go ahead and roll out your higher prices now. Combined with the big jump in traffic, your profits would skyrocket. The other option is to follow your original timetable and wait three weeks to increase your prices. You will have then passed up the opportunity to capitalize on the temporary jump in business.

QUESTION TO ADDRESS

1 Which course of action is easier to defend? Why?
2 What is your personal opinion about the appropriate stance that a business should take regarding social responsibility?
3 To what extent is the concept of social responsibility relevant to nonbusiness organizations such as universities, government units, health care organizations, and so forth?

FINDING THE BALANCE

The Situation

Managers often find it necessary to find the right balance among the interests of different stakeholders. For instance, paying employees the lowest possible wages can enhance profits, but paying a living wage might better serve the interests of workers. As more businesses outsource production to other countries, these trade-offs become even more complicated.

The Dilemma

The Delta Company currently uses three different suppliers in Southeast Asia for most of its outsourced production. Due to increased demand for its products, it needs to double the amount of business it currently subcontracts to one of these suppliers. (For purposes of this exercise, assume that the company must award the new supplier contract to a single firm, and that it must be one of these three. You can also assume that the quality provided is about the same for all three companies.)

Subcontractor A provides a spartan but clean work environment for its workers; even though the local weather conditions are hot and humid much of the year, the plant is not air conditioned. Delta Company safety experts have verified, though, that the conditions are not dangerous, simply a bit uncomfortable at times. The firm pays its workers the same prevailing wage rate that is paid by its local competitors. While it has never had a legal issue with its workforce, it does push its employees to meet production quotas and it has a very tough policy regarding discipline for tardiness. For instance, an employee who is late gets put on probation; a second infraction within three months results in termination. This supplier provides production to Delta Company at a level such that Delta can attach a 25 percent markup.

Subcontractor B also provides a spartan work environment. It pays its workers about 5 percent above local wage levels and hence is an attractive employer. Because of its higher pay, this firm is actually quite ruthless with some of its policies, however. For instance, any employee who reports to work more than 15 minutes late without a medical excuse is automatically terminated. This supplier's costs are such that Delta Company can achieve a 20 percent markup.

Subcontractor C runs a much nicer factory; the plant is air conditioned, for instance. It also pays its workers about 10 percent above local wage levels. The company also operates an on-site school for the children of its employees, and provides additional training for its workers so they can improve their skills. Due to its higher costs, Delta Company's markup on this firm's products is only around 15 percent.

Team Activity

Assemble a group of four students and assign each group member to one of the following roles:
- Delta Company executive
- Delta Company employee
- Delta Company customer
- Delta Company investor

ACTION STEPS

1 Before hearing any of your group's comments on this situation, and from the perspective of your assigned role, which firm do you think should get the additional business? Which firm is your second choice? Write down the reasons for your position.

2 Before hearing any of your group's comments on this situation, and from the perspective of your assigned role, what are the underlying ethical issues in this situation? Write down the issues.

3 Gather your group together and reveal, in turn, each member's comments on their choices. Next, reveal the ethical issues listed by each member.

4 Appoint someone to record main points of agreement and disagreement within the group. How do you explain the results? What accounts for any disagreement?

5 From an ethical standpoint, what does your group conclude is the most appropriate choice for the company in this situation?

6 Develop a group response to the following question: Would your decision have been any different if you were able to break up the new contract across different suppliers? Why?

DOING THE RIGHT THING: AMERICAN RED CROSS

Learning Objectives

The purpose of this video is to help you:

1 Identify some of the social responsibility and ethics challenges faced by a nonprofit organization.
2 Discuss the purpose of an organizational code of ethics.
3 Understand the potential conflicts that can emerge between an organization and its stakeholders.

Synopsis

Founded in 1881 by Clara Barton, the American Red Cross is a nonprofit organization dedicated to helping victims of war, natural disasters, and other catastrophes. The organization's chapters are governed by volunteer boards of directors who oversee local activities and enforce ethical standards in line with community norms and the Red Cross's own code of ethics. Over the years, the Red Cross has been guided in its use of donations by honoring donor intent. This policy helped the organization deal with a major ethical challenge after the terrorist attacks of September 11, 2001. The Red Cross received more than $1 billion in donations and initially diverted some money to ancillary operations, such as creating a strategic blood reserve. After donors objected, however, the organization reversed its decision and—honoring donor intent—used the contributions to directly benefit people affected by the tragedy.

DISCUSSION QUESTIONS

1 **For analysis**: What are the social responsibility implications of the decision to avoid accepting donations of goods for many local relief efforts?

2 **For analysis**: What kinds of ethical conflicts might arise because the American Red Cross relies so heavily on volunteers?
3 **For application**: What can the American Red Cross do to ensure that local chapters are properly applying its code of ethics?
4 **For application**: How might a nonprofit, such as the American Red Cross, gain a better understanding of its stakeholders' needs and preferences?
5 **For debate**: Should the American Red Cross have reversed its initial decision to divert some of the money donated for September 11 relief efforts to pressing but ancillary operations? Support your chosen position.

Online Exploration

Visit the American Red Cross Web site (www.redcross.org) and scan the headlines referring to the organization's response to recent disasters. Also look at the educational information available through links to news stories, feature articles, and other material. Next, carefully examine the variety of links addressing the needs and involvement of different stakeholder groups. What kinds of stakeholders does the American Red Cross expect to visit its Web site? Why are these stakeholders important to the organization? Do you think the organization should post its code of ethics prominently on this site? Explain your answer.

1   Define *small business*, discuss its importance to the U.S. economy, and explain popular areas of small business.

2   Explain entrepreneurship and describe some key characteristics of entrepreneurial personalities and activities.

3   Describe the business plan and the start-up decisions made by small businesses and identify sources of financial aid available to such enterprises.

4   Discuss the trends in small business start-ups and identify the main reasons for success and failure among small businesses.

5   Explain sole proprietorships, partnerships, and cooperatives and discuss the advantages and disadvantages of each.

6   Describe corporations, discuss their advantages and disadvantages, and identify different kinds of corporations.

7   Explain the basic issues involved in managing a corporation and discuss special issues related to corporate ownership.

THE COMPETITOR FROM OUT OF THE BLUE

For years now, Southwest Airlines has been flying high in the short-haul, low-fare market. Its emphasis on reliability and customer service, combined with a dedication to cost control and a corporate culture that attracts only the best employees, has allowed

ENTREPRENEURSHIP, NEW VENTURES, AND BUSINESS OWNERSHIP

Southwest to remain virtually unchallenged. Literally dozens of upstarts and spin-offs from existing airlines have attempted to achieve Southwest's level of success, but few of them have ever managed to get off the ground.

Why has it been so hard for start-up airlines to copy the operational success of Southwest? For one thing, the airline industry is challenging for managers. An airline needs people skilled in scheduling, purchasing, customer service, and mechanical maintenance. Teams of individuals performing a wide variety of jobs, from piloting planes to handling baggage, must be coordinated. In addition, costs are high and revenues are subject to unexpected fluctuations. Last but not least, competition is intense. In this hostile environment, few companies survive—United, Delta, and US Airways have recently spent time under protection of bankruptcy. Indeed, of the 27 carriers that have gone public since 1980, only 8 are still in the air.

Then along came JetBlue. Since its founding in 1999, the airline has become one of the most profitable start-up carriers in the United States, and it has done so in large part by learning and applying many of the lessons professed by Southwest. How has JetBlue managed to do what no other carrier has managed to do? First and foremost, the credit goes to CEO David Neeleman's creativity as a manager and marketer. In 1984, Neeleman founded Morris Air, a discount carrier based in Salt Lake City, which he sold to Southwest in 1993 for $128 million. When he was fired after a brief stint at Southwest, Neeleman

JetBlue is not merely a clone of Southwest Airlines; it is the new gold standard among low-cost carriers.

—James Craun, airline industry consultant

set out to play his own hand in his former employer's own game. He consulted—and in some cases, hired—experienced managers from competitors. He copied elements of Southwest's discount strategy, such as point-to-point scheduling, reliance on a single type of aircraft, and use of nonunion employees. Then, he added some extras: reserved seats, upscale snacks, leather chairs, and seat-back televisions with 24 channels of DIRECTV. "JetBlue," reports one industry consultant, "is not merely a clone of Southwest Airlines; it is the new gold standard among low-cost carriers."

Relying on his extensive industry experience, Neeleman focused most of his energy on a few key factors that he felt would make or break his company. By hiring younger, more productive workers and giving them stock options in lieu of high wages, JetBlue kept labor expenses down to 25 percent of revenues (compared to Southwest's 33 percent and Delta's 44 percent). JetBlue fills planes to capacity, gets more flying hours out of each aircraft, and saves on maintenance costs because its fleet is new. Even the luxurious leather seats are cost-effective—they're easier to clean. Because Neeleman regards on-time arrival as a critical element in customer service, his pager (which he wears to bed) beeps whenever a JetBlue flight touches down more than one minute late. ■

Our opening story continues on page 97.

WHAT'S IN IT FOR ME?

JetBlue has been successful because its founder, entrepreneur David Neeleman, has adhered to sound business practices and made effective decisions. Neeleman has also maintained a clear focus on what it takes to succeed in the highly competitive airline industry. By understanding the material discussed in this chapter, you'll be better prepared to (1) understand the challenges and opportunities provided in new venture start-ups, (2) assess the risks and benefits of working in a new business, and (3) evaluate the investment potential inherent in a new enterprise.

In this chapter, we look at the key characteristics of both small businesses and entrepreneurial personalities. We also examine business plans, sources of financial aid available to small businesses, and reasons for success and failure in small businesses. Finally, we discuss sole proprietorships, types of corporations, and then conclude with a discussion of the basic issues involved in creating and managing a corporation. But first, let's define what small businesses are, and discuss the importance they have on the U.S. economy.

WHAT IS A "SMALL" BUSINESS?

The term *small business* defies easy definition. Locally owned and operated restaurants, dry cleaners, and hair salons are obviously small businesses, and giant corporations, such as Dell, Starbucks, and Best Buy, are clearly big businesses. Between these two extremes, though, fall thousands of companies that cannot be easily categorized.

SMALL BUSINESS ADMINISTRATION (SBA) government agency charged with assisting small businesses

The U.S. Department of Commerce considers a business "small" if it has fewer than 500 employees. The U.S. **Small Business Administration (SBA)**, a government agency that assists small businesses, regards some companies with as many as 1,500 employees as small, but only if the business has relatively low annual revenues. Because strict numerical terms sometimes lead to contradictory classifications, we will consider a **small business** to be one that is independent (that is, not part of a larger business) and that has relatively little influence in its market. A small neighborhood grocer would be small, assuming it is not part of a chain and that the prices it pays to wholesalers and that it can charge its

SMALL BUSINESS independently owned business that has relatively little influence in its market

customers are largely set by market forces. Dell Computer was a small business when founded by Michael Dell in 1984, but today it's number one in the personal computer market and is not small in any sense of the term. Hence, it can negotiate from a position of strength with its suppliers and can set its prices with less consideration for what other computer firms are charging.

▪▪▪ THE IMPORTANCE OF SMALL BUSINESS IN THE U.S. ECONOMY

As Figure 3.1 shows, most U.S. businesses employ fewer than 100 people, and most U.S. workers are employed by small firms. Figure 3.1(a) shows that 89.02 percent of all businesses employ 20 or fewer people. Another 9.16 percent employ between 20 and 99 people, and 1.5 percent employ between 100 and 499. Only about two-tenths of 1 percent employ 1,000 or more people. Figure 3.1(b) also shows that 25.60 percent of all workers are employed by firms with fewer than 20 people, and 29.10 percent are employed by firms with between 20 and 99 people. Another 25.50 percent are employed by firms with between 100 and 499 people. Only 19.80 percent of all workers are employed by firms with 500 or more employees.

We can measure the contribution of small business in terms of its impact on key aspects of the U.S. economic system, including *job creation*, *innovation*, and their *contributions to big business*.

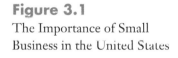

Figure 3.1

The Importance of Small Business in the United States

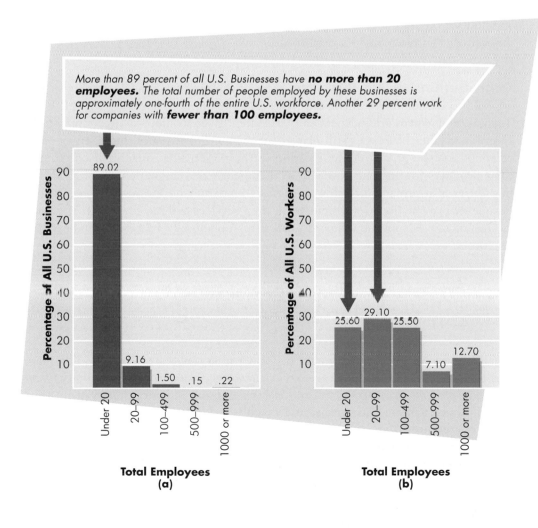

More than 89 percent of all U.S. Businesses have **no more than 20 employees.** The total number of people employed by these businesses is approximately one-fourth of the entire U.S. workforce. Another 29 percent work for companies with **fewer than 100 employees.**

Total Employees
(a)

Total Employees
(b)

Job Creation Small businesses—especially in certain industries—are an important source of new (and often well-paid) jobs. In recent years, small businesses have accounted for 38 percent of all new jobs in high-technology sectors of the economy.[1] Jobs are created by companies of all sizes, all of which hire and lay off workers. Although small firms often hire at a faster rate, they also tend to cut jobs at a higher rate. They are generally the first to hire in times of economic recovery, while big firms are generally the last to lay off workers during downswings.

However, relative job growth among businesses of different sizes is not easy to determine. For one thing, when a successful small business starts adding employees at a rapid clip, it may quickly cease being small. For example, Dell Computer had 1 employee in 1984 (Michael Dell himself). But the payroll grew to 100 employees in 1986, to 2,000 in 1992, and to more than 39,000 in 2004. While there was no precise point at which Dell turned from "small" into "large," some of the jobs it created should be counted in the small business sector and some in the large.

Innovation History reminds us that major innovations are as likely to come from small businesses (or individuals) as from big ones. Small firms and individuals invented the personal computer, the stainless-steel razor blade, the photocopier, the jet engine, and the self-developing photograph. The device recently used to repair Vice President Dick Cheney's ailing heart was developed by a small business, as was the battery-powered, one-person vehicle called the Segway Human Transporter.

Innovations are not always new products. Michael Dell didn't invent the PC. He did, however, develop an innovative way to build it (buy finished components and then assemble them) and an innovative way to sell it (directly to consumers, first by telephone and now via the Internet). Today, says the SBA, small business supplies 55 percent of all innovations that reach the U.S. marketplace.[2]

Contributions to Big Business Most of the products made by big businesses are sold to consumers by small ones. For example, most dealerships that sell Fords, Toyotas, and Volvos are independently operated. Even as more shoppers turn to the Internet, smaller businesses still play critical roles. For instance, most larger online retailers actually outsource the creation of their Web sites and the distribution of their products to other firms, many of them small or regional companies. Smaller businesses also provide data storage services for larger businesses. Moreover, small businesses provide big ones with many of their services and raw materials. Microsoft, for instance, relies on hundreds of small firms for most of its routine code-writing functions.

■■■ POPULAR AREAS OF SMALL-BUSINESS ENTERPRISE

Small businesses are more common in some industries than in others. The major small-business industry groups are *services*, *retailing*, *construction*, *wholesaling*, *finance and insurance*, *manufacturing*, and *transportation*. Each industry differs in its needs for employees, money, materials, and machines, but as a general rule, the more resources required, the harder it is to start a business and the less likely an industry is dominated by small firms. Remember, too, that small is a relative term. The criteria (number of employees and total annual sales) differ from industry to industry and are often meaningful only when compared with truly large businesses. Figure 3.2 shows

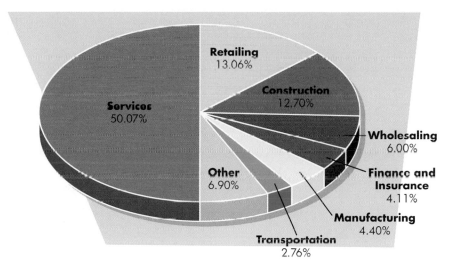

Figure 3.2
Small Business by Industry

the distribution of all U.S. businesses employing fewer than 20 people across industry groups.[3]

Services About 50 percent of businesses with fewer than 20 employees are involved in the service industry. Small-business services range from marriage counseling to computer software, from management consulting to professional dog walking. Partly because they require few resources, service providers are the fastest-growing segment of small business.

Retailing Retailers account for about 13 percent of all firms with fewer than 20 employees. A retailer sells products made by other firms directly to consumers. Usually, people who start small retail businesses favor specialty shops—big men's clothing or gourmet coffees—that let them focus limited resources on narrow market segments.

Construction About 13 percent of businesses with fewer than 20 employees are involved in construction. Because many construction jobs are small local projects, local contractors are often best suited to handle these projects. For instance, a homeowner who wants to add a garage or remodel a room will almost always contract with a small local firm to get the work done.

Wholesaling Small-business owners often do well in wholesaling; about 6 percent of businesses with fewer than 20 employees are wholesalers. Wholesalers buy products from manufacturers or other producers and sell them to retailers. They usually purchase goods in bulk and store them in quantities at locations convenient for retailers. For a given volume of business, therefore, they need fewer employees than manufacturers, retailers, or service providers.

Finance and Insurance Financial and insurance firms also account for about 4 percent of all firms with fewer than 20 employees. Most of these businesses are affiliates of or agents for larger national firms. For instance, local State Farm Insurance offices fall into this category.

Manufacturing More than any other industry, manufacturing lends itself to big business, but this doesn't mean that no small businesses do well in manufacturing; rather,

There are many areas in which small businesses excel. This enterprising entrepreneur, for example, has a lucrative business as a dog walker. A small business is much more likely than a large business to succeed in such a venture.

about 4 percent of firms with fewer than 20 employees are involved in manufacturing. Indeed, small manufacturers sometimes outperform big ones in such innovation-driven industries as electronics, toys, and computer software.

Transportation About 3 percent of all companies with fewer than 20 employees are in transportation and related businesses. These include many taxi and limousine companies, charter airplane services, and tour operators.

Other The remaining 7 percent or so of small businesses with fewer than 20 employees are in other industries. Examples of these "other" firms include small research and development laboratories and some independent media companies, such as small-town newspapers and radio broadcasters.

say what you mean

The Wide World of Risk

One reason why globalization has become such a factor in everyday business life is the expanded reach and power of multinational companies. Many large corporations have actually become engines for innovation as well as growth, adapting to new markets and new economic circumstances. In a highly interconnected world, however, it's often hard to figure out the complex ownership and organizational structures of many global corporations. Sometimes, for example, their branding strategies and management structures lead people to think that they're local companies when, in fact, the real source of corporate power may lie thousands of miles away on another continent. One thing's for sure: If you're going to be dealing with a company overseas, you'd better have a good idea of where and how decisions are made, and who has the real power to make them.

Remember, too, that different cultures have different attitudes when it comes to entrepreneurship. In some countries and cultures, like that of the United States, there's a lively entrepreneurial spirit. Businesspeople are open to taking risks, and if they fail, they tend to pick themselves up and move on to something else. In some Asian countries, the entrepreneurial spirit is often tempered by the need for consensus and getting everyone on board. This approach requires a lot of patience and the ability to compromise. Knowing the cultural forces that shape both a business organization and people's attitudes toward risk, success, and failure is an elementary but important component of international business.

ENTREPRENEURSHIP

We noted earlier that Dell Computer started as a one-person operation and grew into a giant corporation. Dell's growth was spurred by the imagination and skill of Michael Dell, the entrepreneur who founded the company. **Entrepreneurs** are people, like Michael Dell, who assume the risk of business ownership. **Entrepreneurship** is the process of seeking businesses opportunities under conditions of risk. However, not all entrepreneurs have the same goals.

For instance, many entrepreneurs seek to launch a new business with the goal of independence—independence from working for someone else coupled with some reasonable degree of financial security. Such entrepreneurs want to achieve a safe and secure financial future for themselves and their families but do not aspire to grow their business beyond their capacity to run it. Consider Jack Matz, a former corporate executive in Houston who lost his job when his firm merged with another. Rather than look for another management position, Matz opened a photocopying business near a local university. His goal is to earn enough money to lead a comfortable life until he retires in 10 years. The term *small business* is most closely associated with these kinds of enterprises.

Other entrepreneurs, however, launch new businesses with the goal of growth and expansion—that is, to transform their venture into a large business. This was Michael Dell's vision when he started his business; likewise, when Howard Schultz took over Starbucks, he too had plans to grow and develop the fledging coffee company into a much larger enterprise. Terms such as *new ventures* and *start-ups* are often used to refer to these kinds of businesses.

In some cases, the goals of an entrepreneur may not always be clear in the early stages of business development. For instance, one entrepreneur might launch a business with little or no expectation that it will have huge growth potential but then find that it can grow dramatically. The founders of Google, for example, had no idea that their firm would grow to its present size. Another entrepreneur might start out with ambitious growth plans but find that expected opportunities cannot be realized—perhaps there really is no large market or another firm establishes dominance over that market first.

ENTREPRENEUR businessperson who accepts both the risks and the opportunities involved in creating and operating a new business venture

ENTREPRENEURSHIP the process of seeking businesses opportunities under conditions of risk

■■■ ENTREPRENEURIAL CHARACTERISTICS

Regardless of their goals, many successful entrepreneurs share certain characteristics—for example, resourcefulness and a concern for good, often personal, customer relations. Most of them also have a strong desire to be their own bosses. Many express a need to "gain control over my life" or "build for the family" and believe that building successful businesses will help them do it. They can also deal with uncertainty and risk.

Yesterday's entrepreneur was often stereotyped as "the boss"—self-reliant, male, and able to make quick, firm decisions. Today's entrepreneur is seen more often as an open-minded leader who relies on networks, business plans, and consensus. Although today's entrepreneur may be male, she is just as likely to be female. Past and present entrepreneurs also have different views on such topics as how to succeed, how to automate business, and when to rely on experience in the trade or on basic business acumen.[4]

Consider Patrick Byrne. Byrne runs Overstock.com, an e-commerce firm that buys excess inventory from makers of clothing, electronics, and other products, and then offers the merchandise for resale on the Internet at deeply discounted prices. Byrne started out by creating a personal-investment fund named High Plains. After amassing a $100 million portfolio, he bought Overstock.com. Along the way, he earned a Ph.D. in philosophy from Stanford and a black belt in Tae Kwon Do. He bicycled across the United States three times, studied more philosophy at Cambridge, and learned five languages. He discovered Overstock.com when its owners came to High Plains seeking capital. "The financials," admits Byrne, "were a joke. But buried in all that was this billion-dollar idea." And so instead of investing in the business, Byrne bought it. Unlike many Internet ventures, Overstock.com has prospered.[5]

Among other things, Byrne's story illustrates the role of *risk* in entrepreneurship. Assuming risk is almost always a key element in entrepreneurship. Interestingly, most successful entrepreneurs seldom see what they do as risky. Whereas others may focus on possibilities for failure and balk at gambling everything on a new venture, most entrepreneurs are so passionate about their ideas and plans that they see little or no likelihood of failure. Byrne, for example, detected major problems in Overstock.com's financial outlook but believed so strongly in its promise that he took an enormous gamble on the company's prospects for success.

SELF-CHECK QUESTIONS 1–3

You should now be able to answer Self-Check Questions 1–3.*

1 Multiple Choice Which of the following is the *best* definition of *small business*?
(a) one that employs fewer than 25 people
(b) one that operates out of a single location
(c) one with annual revenues of less than $100,000
(d) one that is independently owned and managed and cannot strongly influence its market

2 Multiple Choice Which area of small business is likely to be the most difficult to enter?
(a) services
(b) manufacturing
(c) construction
(d) wholesaling

3 True/False Entrepreneurs typically see their new ventures as being highly risky.

*Answers to Self-Check Questions 1–3 can be found on p. 563.

STARTING AND OPERATING A NEW BUSINESS

The Internet has changed the rules for starting and operating a small business. Setting up is easier and faster than ever, there are more potential opportunities than at any other time, and the ability to gather and assess information is at an all-time high. Today, for example, many one-person retailers do most of their business—both buying and selling—on Internet auction sites, such as eBay.

Even so, would-be entrepreneurs must make the right start-up decisions. They must decide how to get into business—should they buy an existing business or build from the ground up? They must know when to seek expert advice and where to find sources of financing. If, for example, a new firm needs financial backing from investors or a line of credit from vendors or distributors, the entrepreneur must have in place a comprehensive, well-crafted business plan.

BUSINESS PLAN document in which the entrepreneur summarizes her or his business strategy for the proposed new venture and how that strategy will be implemented

■■■ CRAFTING A BUSINESS PLAN

The starting point for virtually every new business is a **business plan** in which the entrepreneur describes her or his business strategy for the new venture and demonstrates how it will be implemented.[6] A real benefit of a business plan is the fact that in the act of preparing it, the would-be entrepreneur must develop the business idea on paper and firm up his or her thinking about how to launch it before investing time and money in it. The idea of the business plan isn't new. What is new is the use of specialized business plans, mostly because creditors and investors demand them as tools for deciding whether to finance or invest.

Setting Goals and Objectives A business plan describes the match between the entrepreneur's abilities and experiences and the requirements for producing and/or marketing a particular product. It also defines strategies for production and marketing, legal elements and organization, and accounting and finance. In particular, a business plan should answer three questions: (1) What are the entrepreneur's goals and objectives? (2) What strategies will be used to obtain them? (3) How will these strategies be implemented?

Sales Forecasting While a key element of any business plan is sales forecasts, plans must carefully build an argument for likely business success based on sound logic and research. Entrepreneurs, for example, can't forecast sales revenues without first researching markets. Simply asserting that the new venture will sell 100,000 units per month is not credible. Instead, the entrepreneur must demonstrate an understanding of the current market, of the strengths and weaknesses of existing firms, and of the means by which the new venture will compete. Without the sales forecast, no one can estimate the required size of a plant, store, or office or decide how much inventory to carry and how many employees to hire.

Financial Planning Financial planning refers to the entrepreneur's plan for turning all other activities into dollars. It generally includes a cash budget, an income statement, balance sheets, and a breakeven chart. The cash budget shows how much money you need before you open for business and how much you need to keep the business going before it starts earning a profit.[7]

■■■ STARTING THE SMALL BUSINESS

An old Chinese proverb says that a journey of a thousand miles begins with a single step. This is also true of a new business. The first step is the individual's commitment to becoming a business owner. In preparing a business plan, the entrepreneur must choose the industry and market in which he or she plans to compete. This choice means assessing not only industry conditions and trends but also one's own abilities and interests. Like big-business managers, small-business owners must understand the nature of the enterprises in which they are engaged.

Buying an Existing Business Next, the entrepreneur must decide whether to buy an existing business or start from scratch. Many experts recommend the first approach because, quite simply, the odds are better: If it's successful, an existing business has already proven its ability to attract customers and generate profit. It has also established relationships with lenders, suppliers, and other stakeholders. Moreover, an existing track record gives potential buyers a much clearer picture of what to expect than any estimate of a start-up's prospects.

Ray Kroc bought McDonald's as an existing business, added entrepreneurial vision and business insight, and produced a multinational giant. Both Southwest Airlines and Starbucks were small but struggling operations when entrepreneurs took over and made them successful. About 35 percent of all new businesses that were started in the past decade were bought from someone else.

Franchising Most McDonald's, Subway, 7-Eleven, RE/Max, Ramada, and Blockbuster outlets are franchises operating under licenses issued by parent companies to local owners.

FRANCHISE arrangement in which a buyer (franchisee) purchases the right to sell the good or service of the seller (franchiser)

A **franchise** agreement involves two parties, a *franchisee* (the local owner) and a *franchiser* (the parent company).

Franchisees benefit from the parent corporation's experience and expertise, and the franchiser may even supply financing. It may pick the store location, negotiate the lease, design the store, and purchase equipment. It may train the first set of employees and managers and issue standard policies and procedures. Once the business is open, the franchiser may offer savings by allowing the franchisee to purchase from a central location. Marketing strategy (especially advertising) may also be handled by the franchiser. In short, franchisees receive—that is, invest in—not only their own ready-made businesses but also expert help in running them.

Franchises have advantages for both sellers and buyers. Franchises can grow rapidly by using the investment money provided by franchisees. The franchisee gets to own a business and has access to big-business management skills. The franchisee does not have to build a business step by step, and because each franchise outlet is probably a carbon copy of every other outlet, failure is less likely. Recent statistics show that franchising increased 11 percent between 2004 and 2005, more than triple the rate from the previous year.[8]

Perhaps the most significant disadvantage in owning a franchise is start-up cost. Franchise prices vary widely. The fee for a Fantastic Sam's hair salon is $30,000, but a McDonald's franchise costs $650,000 to $750,000, and professional sports teams (which are also franchises) can cost several hundred million dollars. Franchisees may also be obligated to contribute a percentage of sales to parent corporations. From the perspective of the parent company, some firms choose not to franchise in order to retain more control over quality and earn more profits for themselves. Starbucks, for instance, does not franchise its coffee shops.

Starting from Scratch Despite the odds, some people seek the satisfaction that comes from planting an idea and growing it into a healthy business. There are also practical reasons to start from scratch. A new business doesn't suffer the ill effects of a prior owner's

"Eventually I'd like to have a business where the money rolls in and I wouldn't have to be there much."

errors, and the start-up owner is free to choose lenders, equipment, inventories, locations, suppliers, and workers. Of all new businesses begun in the past decade, 64 percent were started from scratch. Dell Computer, Wal-Mart, and Microsoft are among today's most successful businesses that were started from scratch by an entrepreneur.

But as we have already noted, the risks of starting a business from scratch are greater than those of buying an existing firm. New-business founders can only make projections about their prospects. Success or failure depends on identifying a genuine opportunity, such as a product for which many customers will pay well but which is currently unavailable. To find openings, entrepreneurs must study markets and answer the following questions:

- Who and where are my customers?
- How much will those customers pay for my product?
- How much of my product can I expect to sell?
- Who are my competitors?
- Why will customers buy my product rather than the product of my competitors?

▪▪▪▪ FINANCING THE SMALL BUSINESS

Although the choice of how to start a business is obviously important, it's meaningless unless you can get the money. Among the more common sources for funding are family and friends, personal savings, lending institutions, investors, and governmental agencies. Lending institutions are more likely to help finance the purchase of an existing business because the risks are better understood. Individuals starting new businesses will probably have to rely on personal resources.

According to the National Federation of Independent Business, personal resources, not loans, are the most important sources of money. Including money borrowed from friends and relatives, personal resources account for over two-thirds of all money invested in new small businesses, and one-half of that is used to purchase existing businesses. Getting money from banks, independent investors, and government loans requires extra effort. At a minimum, banks and private investors will want to review business plans, and government loans have strict eligibility guidelines.

Other Sources of Investment Venture capital companies are groups of small investors seeking to make profits on companies with rapid growth potential. Most of these firms do not lend money. They invest it, supplying capital in return for partial ownership (like stocks, discussed later in this chapter). They may also demand representation on boards of directors. In some cases, managers need approval from the venture capital company before making major decisions. In most cases, venture capitalists do not provide money to start a new business; instead, once a business has been successfully launched and its growth potential established, they provide the funds to fuel expansion. Of all venture capital currently committed in the United States, about 30 percent comes from true venture capital firms.

VENTURE CAPITAL COMPANY group of small investors who invest money in companies with rapid growth potential

Small-business investment companies (SBICs) also invest in companies with potential for rapid growth. They are federally licensed to borrow money from the SBA and to invest it in or lend it to small businesses, and they are themselves investments for their shareholders. Past beneficiaries of SBIC capital include Apple Computer, Intel, and FedEx. The government also sponsors *minority enterprise small-business investment companies (MESBICs)*. As the name suggests, MESBICs target minority-owned businesses.

SMALL-BUSINESS INVESTMENT COMPANY (SBIC) government-regulated investment company that borrows money from the SBA to invest in or lend to a small business

SBA Financial Programs Since its founding in 1953, the SBA has sponsored financing programs for small businesses that meet standards in size and independence. Eligible firms must be unable to get private financing at reasonable terms. Under the SBA's *guaranteed loans*

The ability of an entrepreneur to obtain adequate financing is a critical component in the potential success of a new venture. Many entrepreneurs rely on SBA financial programs, venture capital companies, or small-business investment companies to launch their businesses.

program, for example, small businesses can borrow from commercial lenders. The SBA guarantees to repay 75 to 85 percent of the loan up to $750,000. Through the *immediate participation loans program*, the SBA and a bank each put up portions of the amount to be loaned.

Under the *local development companies (LDCs) program*, the SBA works with a local corporation devoted to boosting the local economy. For instance, some communities support what are called *business incubators*—facilities that fledgling businesses share at low costs until they become sufficiently solvent to go out on their own. The SBA may provide funds to help the operators of the incubator provide support to the new businesses they are hosting.

Spurred in large part by the boom in Internet businesses, both venture capital and loans are becoming easier to get. Most small businesses report that it has generally gotten easier to obtain loans in the last few years.

Other SBA Programs   Even more important than its financing role is the SBA's role in helping entrepreneurs improve their management skills. It's easy for entrepreneurs to spend money; SBA programs show them how to spend it wisely. The SBA offers management counseling programs at virtually no cost. For example, an entrepreneur who needs help in starting a new business can get it free through the Service Corps of Retired Executives (SCORE). All SCORE members are retired executives, and all are volunteers.

Another of the SBA's management counseling projects is its **Small Business Development Center (SBDC)** program. Begun in 1976, SBDCs are designed to consolidate information from various disciplines and institutions, including technical and professional schools. Then they make this knowledge available to new and existing small businesses.

SMALL BUSINESS DEVELOPMENT CENTER (SBDC)
SBA program designed to consolidate information from various disciplines and make it available to small businesses

TRENDS, SUCCESSES, AND FAILURES IN NEW VENTURES

For every Henry Ford, Walt Disney, Mary Kay Ash, or Bill Gates—entrepreneurs who transformed small businesses into big ones—there are many entrepreneurs who fail. Each year there are generally between 150,000 and 190,000 new businesses launched in the United States. On the other hand, there are also between 50,000 and

100,000 failures each year as well. In this section, we look first at a few key trends in small-business start-ups. Then we examine some of the reasons for success and failure in small-business undertakings.

■■■ TRENDS IN SMALL-BUSINESS START-UPS

As noted previously, thousands of new businesses are started in the United States every year. Several factors account for this trend, and in this section, we focus on five of them.

Emergence of E-Commerce The most significant recent trend is the rapid emergence of electronic commerce. Because the Internet provides fundamentally new ways of doing business, savvy entrepreneurs have created and expanded new businesses faster and easier than ever before. Such leading-edge firms as Google, America Online, Amazon.com, E*Trade, and eBay owe their very existence to the Internet. Figure 3.3 underscores this point by summarizing the growth in online commerce from 1997 through 2004.

Crossovers from Big Business More businesses are being started by people who have opted to leave big corporations and put their experience to work for themselves.[9] In some cases, they see great new ideas that they want to develop. Others get burned out in the corporate world. Some have lost their jobs, only to discover that

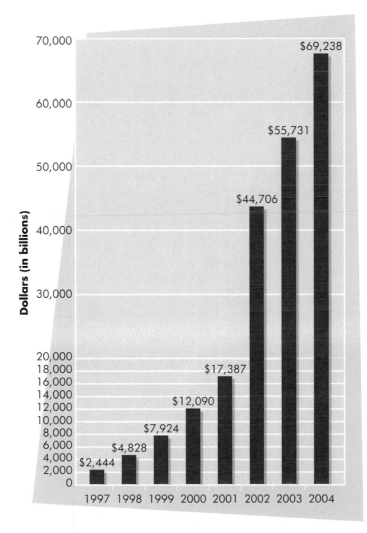

Figure 3.3
Growth of Online Commerce

working for themselves was a better idea anyway. John Chambers spent several years working at IBM and Wang Laboratories/GLOBAL before he decided to try his hand at entrepreneurship. After resigning from Wang, he signed on to help Cisco, then a small and struggling firm. Under his leadership and entrepreneurial guidance, Cisco has become one of the largest and most important technology companies in the world.

Opportunities for Minorities and Women   More small businesses are also being started by minorities and women.[10] The number of businesses owned by African Americans increased by 48 percent during the most recent five-year period for which data are available and now totals about 635,000. Hispanic-owned businesses have grown at the even faster rate of 75 percent and now number about 860,000. Ownership among Asians and Pacific Islanders has increased 56 percent, to over 600,000. Although ownership among Native Americans and Alaskan natives is still modest, at slightly over 100,000, the total represents a five-year increase of 93 percent.

Over 10 million businesses are now owned by women—40 percent of all businesses in the United States. Combined, they generate over $4 trillion in revenue a year—an increase of 132 percent since 1992. Since 1992, the number of people that they employ has grown to around 29.5 million—an increase of 115 percent.[11]

Figure 3.4 summarizes the corporate backgrounds of women entrepreneurs and provides some insight into what they like about running their own businesses. Corporate

Figure 3.4   Profiles of Women Entrepreneurs

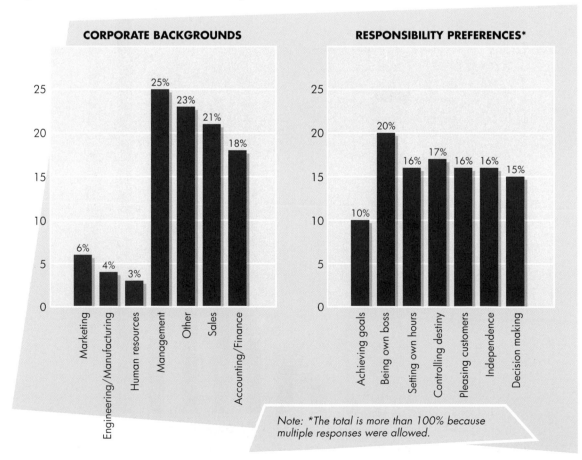

positions in general management (25 percent), sales (21 percent), and accounting and finance (18 percent) account for almost two-thirds of the women who start their own businesses. Once in charge of their own businesses, women also report that they like being their own bosses, setting their own hours, controlling their own destinies, relating to customers, making decisions, and achieving goals.

Global Opportunities Many entrepreneurs are also finding new opportunities in foreign markets. Doug Mellinger is founder and CEO of PRT Group, a software development company. One of Mellinger's biggest problems was finding trained programmers. There aren't enough U.S.-based programmers to go around, and foreign born programmers face strict immigration quotas. So Mellinger set up shop on Barbados, a Caribbean island where the government helps him attract foreign programmers and does everything it can to make things easier. Today, PRT, which is a part of enherent, has customers and suppliers from dozens of nations.

Better Survival Rates More people are encouraged to test their skills as entrepreneurs because the small-business failure rate has declined. During the 1960s and 1970s, less than half of all new start-ups survived more than 18 months; only one in five lasted 10 years. Now, however, new businesses have a better chance. Of all those started in the 1980s, over 77 percent remained in operation for at least three years. The SBA now estimates that 40 percent can expect to survive for at least six years.

> *Women-owned businesses are the largest emerging segment of the small-business market. Women-owned businesses are an economic force that no bank can afford to overlook.*
>
> —Teresa Cavanaugh, director of the Women Entrepreneur's Connection at BankBoston

■■■ REASONS FOR FAILURE

Unfortunately, well over half of all new businesses will not enjoy long-term success. Why do some succeed and others fail? Although no set pattern has been established, four general factors contribute to failure:

1 *Managerial incompetence or inexperience.* Some entrepreneurs put too much faith in common sense, overestimate their own managerial skills, or believe that hard work alone ensures success. If managers don't know how to make basic business decisions or don't understand basic management principles, they aren't likely to succeed in the long run.

2 *Neglect.* Some entrepreneurs try to launch ventures in their spare time, and others devote only limited time to new businesses. But starting a small business demands an overwhelming time commitment. If you aren't willing to put in the time and effort that a business requires, you aren't likely to survive.

3 *Weak control systems.* Effective control systems keep a business on track and alert managers to potential trouble. If your control systems don't signal impending problems, you may be in serious trouble before you spot more obvious difficulties. For instance, some businesses fail because they do a poor job of managing their credit collection policies—anxious to grow, they may be too liberal in extending credit to their customers and then end up not being able to collect all the money that is owed to them.

4 *Insufficient capital.* Some entrepreneurs are overly optimistic about how soon they'll start earning profits. In most cases, it takes months or even years. Amazon.com didn't earn a profit for 10 years but obviously still required capital to pay employees and to cover other expenses. Experts say you need enough capital to operate at least six months without earning a profit; some recommend enough to last a year.[12]

▪▪▪ REASONS FOR SUCCESS

Four basic factors are also typically cited to explain small-business success:

1. *Hard work, drive, and dedication.* Small-business owners must be committed to succeeding and willing to spend the time and effort to make it happen. Gladys Edmunds, a single mother in Pittsburgh, wanted to open a travel agency but did not have enough money to get started. So, she washed laundry, made chicken dinners to sell to cab drivers, and sold fire extinguishers door to door to earn start-up money. Today, Edmunds Travel Consultants employs eight people and earns about $6 million a year.

2. *Market demand for the products or services being provided.* Careful analysis of market conditions can help small-business owners assess the probable reception of their products. Attempts to expand restaurants specializing in baked potatoes, muffins, and gelato have largely failed, but hamburger and pizza chains continue to expand.

3. *Managerial competence.* Successful owners may acquire competence through training or experience or by drawing on the expertise of others. Few, however, succeed alone or straight out of college. Most spend time in successful companies or partner with others to bring expertise to a new business.[13]

4. *Luck.* After Alan McKim started Clean Harbors, an environmental cleanup firm in New England, he struggled to keep his business afloat. Then the U.S. government committed $1.6 billion to toxic waste cleanup—McKim's specialty. He landed several large government contracts and put his business on solid financial footing. Had the government fund not been created at just the right time, McKim might well have failed.

SELF-CHECK QUESTIONS 4–6

You should now be able to answer Self-Check Questions 4–6.*

4. **True/False** Preparing a business plan is usually an optional step for a would-be entrepreneur.

5. **Multiple Choice** Which of the following is usually the most important source of financing for a new business?
   (a) banks
   (b) investors
   (c) government agencies, such as the SBA
   (d) personal resources

6. **Multiple Choice** Which of the following is **not** a common cause of business failure?
   (a) managerial incompetence and inexperience
   (b) neglect
   (c) employee theft or sabotage
   (d) insufficient capital

***Answers to Self-Check Questions 4–6 can be found on p. 563.**

NONCORPORATE BUSINESS OWNERSHIP

Whether they intend to launch a small local business or a new venture projected to grow rapidly, all entrepreneurs must decide which form of legal ownership best suits their goals: *sole proprietorship*, *partnership*, or *corporation*. Because this choice affects a host of managerial and financial issues, few decisions are more critical. Entrepreneurs must consider their own preferences, their immediate and long-range needs, and the advantages and disadvantages of each form. Table 3.1 compares the most important differences among the three major ownership forms.

Food for Thought

Once upon a time, dot-com start-ups were all the rage. One of the highest profiles belonged to WebVan, a firm that sold food on the Internet for home delivery. In 2001, however, WebVan went spectacularly bankrupt—to the tune of $1 billion. Many similar businesses also failed, but a new firm called FreshDirect is building a successful online grocery business by downplaying online and emphasizing grocery. The firm's motto: "It's all about the food."

A few online food sellers have achieved modest success by partnering with traditional groceries. Most of them work through "personal shoppers" who push carts around the store and select purchases to be delivered to customers. This method, unfortunately, is not very efficient and requires the store to charge a 35-percent markup. FreshDirect uses a unique, low-cost business model. For starters, CEO Joe Fedele is a grocery expert who has already founded one thriving traditional store. Fedele likes to say, "This is a company based on food people, not dot-com people."

At FreshDirect, most of the inventory is purchased directly from suppliers rather than from intermediaries. This strategy not only cuts costs by 25 percent but also increases freshness. (FreshDirect is capitalizing on changing consumer tastes: In 1970, 30 percent of food dollars were spent on fresh—not packaged—food; now 70 percent is spent on fresh food.) The firm doesn't own a store. Instead, it's located in a state-of-the-art 300,000-square-foot warehouse on Long Island, near Manhattan. FreshDirect offers baked goods, prepared meals, fresh pasta, deli salads, and more, all prepared by chefs trained at top restaurants. The company delivers to 22 zip codes, all in Manhattan, Queens, and Long Island, and to

"depots" set up at large corporations, where employees can get groceries delivered at the end of the day. The delivery charge is a flat $3.95, the minimum order is $40, and there is no tipping. Deliveries are scheduled only for evening and weekend hours, when Manhattan traffic is lighter. All these policies allow FreshDirect to offer unique and tempting goods for a lower price than the corner market, plus the convenience of home delivery.

Information technology is integrated throughout the Long Island warehouse, with nine climate-controlled rooms providing optimal conditions for everything from avocados to smoked salmon. Equipment is linked to controls in a central room, where alarms sound if a conveyer belt stops or a freezer warms up. To ensure food safety, the entire plant is automatically hosed down nightly with antiseptic foam and then sprayed with an antibacterial coating.

In its most ambitious move yet, FreshDirect has asked each of its chefs to develop recipes to be programmed by artificial intelligence software. If, during the preparation process, an ingredient's barcode readout, electronic-scale reading, or computer-controlled oven setting is not correct, the equipment shuts down. Because this practice ensures that hourly workers follow recipes exactly, FreshDirect controls quality while using less-expensive labor.

Some users have reported problems—overripe grapes, mixed-up deliveries. Some people worry about the lack of direct contact, especially those who want to sniff the melons or squeeze the bread. A few cite online commerce in general when bemoaning the impersonal nature of contemporary society. Most shoppers, however, seem to find online grocery shopping a liberating experience.

TABLE 3.1 COMPARATIVE SUMMARY: THREE FORMS OF BUSINESS

Business Form	Liability	Continuity	Management	Sources of Investment
Proprietorship	Personal, unlimited	Ends with death or decision of owner	Personal, unrestricted	Personal
General Partnership	Personal, unlimited	Ends with death or decision of any partner	Unrestricted or depends on partnership agreement	Personal by partner(s)
Corporation	Capital invested	As stated in charter, perpetual or for specified period of years	Under control of board of directors, which is selected by stockholders	Purchase of stock

▪▪▪▪ SOLE PROPRIETORSHIPS

SOLE PROPRIETORSHIP
business owned and usually
operated by one person who is
responsible for all of its debts

The **sole proprietorship** is owned and usually operated by one person. About 73 percent of all U.S. businesses are sole proprietorships; however, they account for only about 5 percent of total business revenues.[14] Though usually small, they may be as large as steel mills or department stores.

Advantages of Sole Proprietorships Freedom may be the most important benefit of sole proprietorships. Because they own their businesses, sole proprietors answer to no one but themselves. Sole proprietorships are also easy to form. Sometimes, you can go into business simply by putting a sign on the door. The simplicity of legal setup procedures makes this form appealing to self-starters and independent spirits, as do low start-up costs.

Another attractive feature is the tax benefits extended to businesses that are likely to suffer losses in their early stages. Tax laws permit owners to treat sales revenues and operating expenses as part of their personal finances, paying taxes based on their personal tax rate. They can cut taxes by deducting business losses from income earned from personal sources other than the business.

UNLIMITED LIABILITY legal
principle holding owners
responsible for paying off all debts
of a business

Disadvantages of Sole Proprietorships A major drawback is **unlimited liability**: A sole proprietor is personally liable for all debts incurred by the business. If it fails to generate enough cash, bills must be paid out of the owner's pocket. Another disadvantage is lack of continuity: A sole proprietorship legally dissolves when the owner dies. Although the business can be reorganized by a successor, executors or heirs must otherwise sell its assets.

Finally, a sole proprietorship depends on the resources of one person whose managerial and financial limitations may constrain the business. Sole proprietors often find it hard to borrow money to start up or expand. Many bankers fear that they won't be able to recover loans if owners become disabled or insolvent.

▪▪▪▪ PARTNERSHIPS

GENERAL PARTNERSHIP
business with two or more owners
who share in both the operation
of the firm and the financial
responsibility for its debts

The partnership is frequently used by professionals. The most common type, the **general partnership**, is a sole proprietorship multiplied by the number of partner-owners. There is no legal limit to the number of parties, but the average is slightly under 10. Partners may invest equal or unequal sums of money and may earn profits that bear no relation to their investments. Thus, a partner with no financial investment in a two-person partnership could receive 50 percent or more of the profits if he or she has made some other contribution—say, a well-known name or special expertise.

Advantages of Partnerships The most striking advantage of general partnerships is the ability to grow by adding new talent and money. Because banks prefer to make loans to enterprises that are not dependent on single individuals, partnerships find it easier to borrow than sole proprietorships. They can also invite new partners to join by investing money.

Like a sole proprietorship, a partnership can be organized by meeting only a few legal requirements. Even so, all partnerships must begin with an agreement of some kind. In all but two states, the Revised Uniform Limited Partnership Act requires the filing of specific information about the business and its partners. Partners may also agree to bind themselves in ways not specified by law. In any case, an agreement should answer questions such as the following:

- Who invested what sums?
- Who will receive what share of the profits?
- Who does what, and who reports to whom?
- How may the partnership be dissolved? In the event of dissolution, how will assets be distributed?
- How will surviving partners be protected from claims made by a deceased partner's heirs?

The partnership agreement is strictly a private document. No laws require partners to file agreements with any government agency. Nor are partnerships regarded as legal entities. In the eyes of the law, a partnership is just two or more people working together. Because partnerships have no independent legal standing, the Internal Revenue Service (IRS) taxes partners as individuals.

Disadvantages of Partnerships For general partnerships as for sole proprietorships, unlimited liability is the greatest drawback. Each partner may be liable for all debts incurred by the partnership. If any partner incurs a business debt, all partners may be liable, even if some of them did not know about or agree to the new debt.

Partnerships also share with sole proprietorships the potential lack of continuity. When one partner dies or leaves, the original partnership dissolves, even if one or more of the other partners want it to continue. But dissolution need not mean a loss of sales revenues. Survivors may form a new partnership to retain the old firm's business.

A related disadvantage is difficulty in transferring ownership. No partner may sell out without the consent of the others. A partner who wants to retire or to transfer interest to a son or daughter must have the other partners' consent.

Alternatives to General Partnerships Because of these disadvantages, general partnerships are among the least popular forms of business. Roughly 1.79 million U.S. partnerships generate only 5.8 percent of total sales revenues.[15] To resolve some of the problems inherent in general partnerships, especially unlimited liability, some partners have tried alternative agreements. The **limited partnership** allows for **limited partners** who invest money but are liable for debts only to the extent of their investments. They cannot, however, take active roles in business operations. A limited partnership must have at least one **general (or active) partner**, mostly for liability purposes. This is usually the person who runs the business and is responsible for its survival and growth.

Under a **master limited partnership**, an organization sells shares (partnership interests) to investors on public markets such as the New York Stock Exchange. Investors are paid back from profits. The master partner retains at least 50 percent ownership and runs the business, while minority partners have no management voice. (The master partner differs from a general partner, who has no such ownership restriction.) The master partner must regularly provide minority partners with detailed operating and financial reports.

▪▪▪ COOPERATIVES

Sometimes, groups of sole proprietorships or partnerships agree to work together for their common benefit by forming cooperatives. **Cooperatives** combine the freedom of sole proprietorships with the financial power of corporations. They give members greater production power, greater marketing power, or both. On the other hand, they are

LIMITED PARTNERSHIP type of partnership consisting of limited partners and a general (or managing) partner

LIMITED PARTNER partner who does not share in a firm's management and is liable for its debts only to the limits of said partner's investment

GENERAL (OR ACTIVE) PARTNER partner who actively manages a firm and who has unlimited liability for its debts

MASTER LIMITED PARTNERSHIP form of ownership that sells shares to investors who receive profits and that pays taxes on income from profits

COOPERATIVE form of ownership in which a group of sole proprietorships and/or partnerships agree to work together for common benefits limited to serving the specific needs of their members. Although cooperatives make up only a minor segment of the U.S. economy, their role is still important in agriculture. Ocean Spray, the Florida Citrus Growers, Riceland, and Cabot Cheese are among the best-known cooperatives.

CORPORATIONS

There are about 4.93 million corporations in the United States. As you can see from Figure 3.5, they account for about 19 percent of all U.S. businesses but generate about 90 percent of all sales revenues.[16] Almost all large businesses use this form, and corporations dominate global business. As we will see, corporations need not be large—indeed, many small businesses also elect to operate as corporations.

According to the most recent data, Wal-Mart, the world's largest corporation, posted annual revenue of over $287 billion, with total profits of over $10 billion. Even "smaller" large corporations post huge sales figures. The New York Times Co., though five-hundredth in size among U.S. corporations, posted a profit of $475 million on annual sales of $3.23 billion. Given the size and influence of this form of ownership, we devote a great deal of attention to various aspects of corporations.

▪▪▪ THE CORPORATE ENTITY

CORPORATION business that is legally considered an entity separate from its owners and is liable for its own debts; owners' liability extends to the limits of their investments

When you think of corporations, you probably think of giant operations such as General Motors and IBM. The very word *corporation* inspires images of size and power. In reality, however, your corner newsstand has as much right to incorporate as a giant automaker. Moreover, the newsstand and GM would share the characteristics of all **corporations**: legal status as separate entities, property rights and obligations, and indefinite life spans.

In 1819, the U.S. Supreme Court defined a corporation as "an artificial being, invisible, intangible, and existing only in contemplation of the law." The court

Figure 3.5   Proportions of U.S. Firms in Terms of Organization Type and Sales Revenue

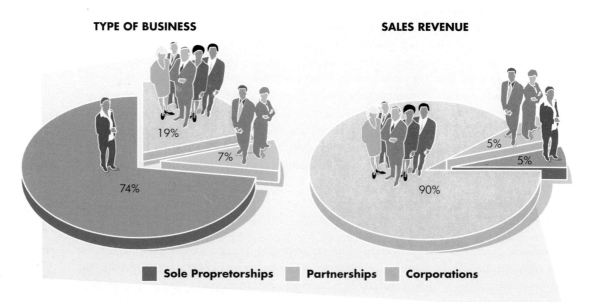

TYPE OF BUSINESS

SALES REVENUE

19%

7%

74%

5%

5%

90%

■ **Sole Propretorships**   ■ **Partnerships**   ■ **Corporations**

defined the corporation as a legal person. Corporations may, therefore, perform the following activities:

- Sue and be sued
- Buy, hold, and sell property
- Make and sell products
- Commit crimes and be tried and punished for them

Advantages of Incorporation The biggest advantage of corporations is **limited liability**: Investor liability is limited to personal investment (through stock ownership, covered later) in the corporation. In the event of failure, the courts may seize and sell a corporation's assets but cannot touch the investors' personal possessions. If, for example, you invest $1,000 in stock in a corporation that ends up failing, you may lose your $1,000, but no more. In other words, your liability is limited to the $1,000 you invested.

Another advantage is continuity. Because it has a legal life independent of founders and owners, a corporation can, at least in theory, continue forever. Shares of stock may be sold or passed on to heirs, and most corporations also benefit from the continuity provided by professional management. Finally, corporations have advantages in raising money. By selling stock, they expand the number of investors and the amount of available funds. Continuity and legal status tend to make lenders more willing to grant loans.

Disadvantages of Incorporation Although a chief attraction is ease of transferring ownership, this same feature can create complications. For example, using a legal process called a **tender offer**—an offer to buy shares made by a prospective buyer directly to a corporation's shareholders—a corporation can be taken over against the will of its managers. Another disadvantage is start up cost. Corporations are heavily regulated, and incorporation entails meeting the complex legal requirements of the state in which the firm is chartered.

The biggest disadvantage of incorporation, however, is **double taxation**. First, a corporation pays income taxes on company profits. In addition, stockholders then pay taxes on income returned by their investments in the corporation. Thus, the profits earned by corporations are taxed twice—once at the corporate level and then again at the ownership level. Because profits are treated as owners' personal income, sole proprietorships and partnerships are taxed only once.

The advantages and disadvantages of corporate ownership have inspired laws establishing different kinds of corporations. Most are intended to help businesses take advantage of the benefits of the corporate model without assuming all the disadvantages. We discuss these corporate forms next.

■■■ TYPES OF CORPORATIONS

We can classify corporations as either *public* or *private*. But within these broad categories, we can identify several specific types of corporations, some of which are summarized in Table 3.2.

- The most common form of U.S. corporation is the **closely held (or private) corporation**. Stock is held by only a few people and is not available for sale to the public. The controlling group of stockholders may be a family, a management group, or even the firm's employees. Most smaller corporations fit this profile.[17]
- When shares are publicly issued, the firm becomes a **publicly held (or public) corporation**. Stock is widely held and available for sale to the public. Many large businesses are of this type.

LIMITED LIABILITY legal principle holding investors liable for a firm's debts only to the limits of their personal investments in it

TENDER OFFER offer to buy shares made by a prospective buyer directly to a target corporation's shareholders, who then make individual decisions about whether to sell

DOUBLE TAXATION situation in which taxes may be payable both by a corporation on its profits and by shareholders on dividend incomes

CLOSELY HELD (OR **PRIVATE**) **CORPORATION** corporation whose stock is held by only a few people and is not available for sale to the general public

PUBLICLY HELD (OR **PUBLIC**) **CORPORATION** corporation whose stock is widely held and available for sale to the general public

TABLE 3.2 TYPES OF CORPORATIONS

TYPE	DISTINGUISHING FEATURES	EXAMPLES
Closely Held	Stock held by only a few people Subject to corporate taxation	Blue Cross/Blue Shield MasterCard Primestar
Publicly Held	Stock widely held among many investors Subject to corporate taxation	Dell Computer Starbucks Texas Instruments
Subchapter S	Organized much like a closely held corporation Subject to additional regulation Subject to partnership taxation	Minglewood Associates Entech Pest Systems Frontier Bank
Limited Liability	Organized much like a publicly held corporation Subject to additional regulation Subject to partnership taxation	Pacific Northwest Associates Global Ground Support Ritz Carlton
Professional	Subject to partnership taxation Limited business liability Unlimited professional liability	Norman Hui, DDS & Associates B & H Engineering Anderson, McCoy & Oria
Multinational	Spans national boundaries Subject to regulation in multiple countries	Toyota Nestlé General Electric

S CORPORATION hybrid of a closely held corporation and a partnership, organized and operated like a corporation but treated as a partnership for tax purposes

LIMITED LIABILITY CORPORATION (LLC) hybrid of a publicly held corporation and a partnership in which owners are taxed as partners but enjoy the benefits of limited liability

PROFESSIONAL CORPORATION form of ownership allowing professionals to take advantage of corporate benefits while granting them limited business liability and unlimited professional liability

MULTINATIONAL (OR TRANSNATIONAL) CORPORATION form of corporation spanning national boundaries

CORPORATE GOVERNANCE roles of shareholders, directors, and other managers in corporate decision making and accountability

- The **S corporation** (more fully called the *Subchapter S corporation*) is a hybrid of a closely held corporation and a partnership. It is organized and operates like a corporation, but it is treated like a partnership for tax purposes. To qualify, firms must meet stringent legal conditions. For instance, stockholders must be individual U.S. citizens.

- Another hybrid is the **limited liability corporation (LLC)**. Owners are taxed like partners, each paying personal taxes only. However, they also enjoy the benefits of limited liability accorded to publicly held corporations. LLCs have grown in popularity in recent years, partially because of IRS rulings that allow corporations, partnerships, and foreign investors to be partial owners.

- **Professional corporations** are most likely composed of doctors, lawyers, accountants, or other professionals. While the corporate structure protects from unlimited financial liability, members are not immune from unlimited liability. Professional negligence by a member can entail personal liability on the individual's part.

- As the term implies, the **multinational (or transnational) corporation** spans national boundaries. Stock may be traded on the exchanges of several countries, and managers are likely to be of different nationalities.

▪▪▪ MANAGING A CORPORATION

Creating any type of corporation can be complicated, due to the various legal conditions that must be met. In addition, once the corporate entity comes into existence, it must be managed by people who understand the principles of **corporate governance**—the roles of shareholders, directors, and other managers in corporate decision making and accountability. In this section, we discuss the principles of *stock ownership* and *stockholders' rights* and describe the role of *boards of directors*. We then examine some special issues related to corporate ownership.

Corporate Governance Corporate governance is established by the firm's bylaws and usually involves three distinct bodies. **Stockholders (or shareholders)** are the owners of a corporation—investors who buy ownership shares in the form of stock. The *board of directors* is a group elected by stockholders to oversee corporate management. Corporate *officers* are top managers hired by the board to run the corporation on a day-to-day basis.

Stock Ownership and Stockholders' Rights Corporations sell shares, called *stock*, to investors who then become stockholders, or shareholders. Profits are distributed among stockholders in the form of *dividends*, and corporate managers serve at stockholders' discretion. In a closely held corporation, only a few people own stock. Shares of publicly held corporations are widely held.

Boards of Directors The governing body of a corporation is its **board of directors**. Boards communicate with stockholders and other stakeholders through such channels as an annual report—a summary of a firm's financial health. They also set policy on dividends, major spending, and executive compensation. They are legally responsible and accountable for corporate actions and are increasingly being held personally liable for them.

Officers Although board members oversee operations, most do not participate in day-to-day management. Rather, they hire a team of managers to run the firm. This team, called **officers**, is usually headed by the firm's **chief executive officer (CEO)**, who is responsible for overall performance. Other officers typically include a *president*, who is responsible for internal management, and *vice presidents*, who oversee various functional areas such as marketing and operations.

One of the outgrowths of the Enron debacle is heightened criticism of corporate governance in the United States.[18] Many Enron-related lawsuits target the firm's officers and directors. In a classic example of how governing bodies can fail shareholders, Enron's board of directors formally voted in at least one instance to set aside the company's code of ethics because its members wanted to approve an action that violated it. Other corporations whose boards have come in for ethical scrutiny include Disney, Bank of America, Eastman Kodak, Lucent, Xerox, and ICN Pharmaceuticals.[19] Many other boards continue to function very effectively, including those at Texas Instruments, Intel, Pfizer, Target, and Coca-Cola.

STOCKHOLDER (OR SHAREHOLDER) owner of shares of stock in a corporation

BOARD OF DIRECTORS governing body of a corporation that reports to its shareholders and delegates power to run its day-to-day operations while remaining responsible for sustaining its assets

OFFICERS top management team of a corporation

CHIEF EXECUTIVE OFFICER (CEO) top manager who is responsible for the overall performance of a corporation

Recent controversies surrounding corporate governance have led some social activists to become more aggressive in their criticisms of big business. These protestors, for example, are picketing a recent meeting of the board of directors of Coca-Cola.

▪▪▪ SPECIAL ISSUES IN CORPORATE OWNERSHIP

In recent years, several issues have grown in importance in the area of corporate owner-ship, including *joint ventures and strategic alliances*, *employee stock ownership plans*, and *institutional ownership*. Other important issues in contemporary corporate ownership involve *mergers*, *acquisitions*, *divestitures*, and *spin-offs*.

Joint Ventures and Strategic Alliances In a **strategic alliance**, two or more organizations collaborate on a project for mutual gain. When partners share ownership of what is essentially a new enterprise, it is called a **joint venture**. The number of strategic alliances has increased rapidly in recent years on both domestic and international fronts.

Employee Stock Ownership Plans An **employee stock ownership plan (ESOP)** allows employees to own a significant share of the corporation through trusts established on their behalf. Current estimates count about 11,500 ESOPs in the United States. The growth rate in new ESOPs has slowed a bit in recent years, but they still are an important part of corporate ownership patterns in the United States.[20]

Institutional Ownership Most individual investors don't own enough stock to exert influence on corporate managers. In recent years, however, more stock has been purchased by **institutional investors**. Because they control enormous resources, these investors—especially mutual and pension funds—can buy huge blocks of stock. The national teachers' retirement system (TIAA-CREF) has assets of over $255 billion, much of it invested in stocks. Institutional investors own almost 40 percent of all the stock issued in the United States.

Mergers, Acquisitions, Divestitures, and Spin-Offs Another important set of issues includes mergers, acquisitions, divestitures, and spin-offs. Mergers and acquisitions involve the legal joining of two or more corporations. A divestiture occurs when a corporation sells a business operation to another corporation; with a spin-off, it creates a new operation.

Mergers and Acquisitions (M&As) A **merger** occurs when two firms combine to create a new company. In an **acquisition**, one firm buys another outright. Many deals that are loosely called mergers are really acquisitions. Why? Because one of the two firms will usu-ally control the newly combined ownership. In general, when the two firms are roughly the same size, the combination is usually called a merger even if one firm is taking control of the other. When the acquiring firm is substantially larger than the acquired firm, the deal is really an acquisition. So-called M&As are an important form of corporate strategy. They let firms increase product lines, expand operations, go international, and create new enterprises.

Divestitures and Spin-Offs Sometimes, a corporation decides to sell a part of its existing business operations or set it up as a new and independent corporation. There may be sev-eral reasons for such a step. A firm might decide, for example, that it should focus more specifically on its core businesses, and thus it will sell off unrelated and/or underper-forming businesses. Such a sale is called a **divestiture**. When a firm sells part of itself to raise capital, the strategy is known as a **spin-off**. A spin-off may also mean that a firm deems a business unit more valuable as a separate company. The Limited, for example, spun off three of its subsidiaries—Victoria's Secret, Bath & Body Works, and White Barn Candle Co.—to create a new firm, Intimate Brands, which it then offered through an Initial Public Offering (IPO). The Limited retained 84 percent ownership of Intimate Brands while getting an infusion of new capital.

STRATEGIC ALLIANCE strategy in which two or more organizations collaborate on a project for mutual gain

JOINT VENTURE strategic alliance in which the collaboration involves joint ownership of the new venture

EMPLOYEE STOCK OWNERSHIP PLAN (ESOP) arrangement in which a corporation holds its own stock in trust for its employees, who gradually receive ownership of the stock and control its voting rights

INSTITUTIONAL INVESTOR large investor, such as a mutual fund or a pension fund, that purchases large blocks of corporate stock

MERGER the union of two corporations to form a new corporation

ACQUISITION the purchase of one company by another

DIVESTITURE strategy whereby a firm sells one or more of its business units

SPIN-OFF strategy of setting up one or more corporate units as new, independent corporations

SELF-CHECK QUESTIONS 7–9

You should now be able to answer Self-Check Questions 7–9.*

7 Multiple Choice The sole proprietorship enjoys which of the following advantages?
(a) freedom
(b) simplicity
(c) tax benefits
(d) all of the above

8 True/False A general partnership is a sole proprietorship multiplied by the number of partner-owners.

9 Multiple Choice Which of the following is **not** a kind of corporation?
(a) public corporation
(b) private corporation
(c) limited liability corporation
(d) All of the above are corporations

*Answers to Self-Check Questions 7–9 can be found on p. 563.

CONTINUED FROM PAGE 74

HOW HIGH CAN AN AIRLINE FLY?

David Neeleman's dedication to monitoring JetBlue's performance is matched by his passion for feedback. He jumps on a plane once a week or so, and not just to ride: He loads baggage and serves drinks. Along the way, he smiles politely when passengers tell him how well he's doing, but he prefers to hear their complaints. No concern is too small or too large, whether a desire for better biscotti or a request for more flights to Chicago. Customers' suggestions are taken seriously. In response to customer input, for example, Neeleman instituted a frequent-flyer program in July 2002. He also gives employees the authority to make immediate customer-service decisions. "Employees at other airlines," he explains, "get so caught up in procedure—rules, rules, rules—that they often forget there is a paying customer there." JetBlue passengers get discount coupons and free accommodations if their flight is diverted, compensation that rival airlines don't always provide.

JetBlue is clearly a successful enterprise. But this question remains: Can success be sustained? Expansion, for example, is the trap that ensnared many now-failed airline ventures, and Neeleman intends to expand. "I can't believe how quickly we got out of the gate and how profitable we became," he says. "Now I don't think there's a limit to how big JetBlue can get." Many observers, however, think that successful expansion will be a big challenge for the company. "It's easy for JetBlue to be golden with 30 airplanes," observes one industry expert, "but it doesn't mean it can manage 100." As increasing size leads to increasing complexity, Neeleman will have to guard against inefficiencies and too much bureaucracy. In addition, costs will undoubtedly rise, as planes age and skilled workers demand raises, and unionization (which will also increase labor costs) is probably on the horizon.

There is some room for growth. "In a lot of places now," says Neeleman, "there's no low-fare nonstop service. That creates some opportunities for us." In the future, however, JetBlue will have a harder time finding opportunities to foster growth. At present, funds for expansion are cheap because JetBlue raised start-up capital from outside investors. But to buy more planes, the firm will have to borrow money, and that will increase debt expense.

QUESTIONS FOR DISCUSSION

1 Why do you think JetBlue has succeeded where so many other start-up airlines have failed?

2 JetBlue is a corporation. Why do you think the firm uses this form of ownership?

3 Do you think JetBlue's success could be emulated in the same way that JetBlue has emulated Southwest? Why or why not?

4 JetBlue recently announced plans to begin using a second type of aircraft (it previously has used only Boeing 737s, a practice Southwest strictly follows). Do you think this is a good or bad idea? Why?

1 Define *small business*, discuss its importance to the U.S. economy, and explain popular areas of small business.

A *small business* is independently owned and managed and has relatively little influence in its market. The importance of small business includes (1) *job creation*, (2) *innovation*, and (3) *contributions to big business*. The major small-business industry groups are (1) *services*, (2) *retailing*, (3) *construction*, (4) *wholesaling*, (5) *finance and insurance*, (6) *transportation*, and (7) *manufacturing*.

2 Explain entrepreneurship and describe some key characteristics of entrepreneurial personalities and activities.

Entrepreneurs are people who assume the risk of business ownership. *Entrepreneurship* is the process of seeking businesses opportunities under conditions of risk. Some entrepreneurs have a goal of independence and financial security, while others want to launch a new venture that can be grown into a large business. Most successful entrepreneurs are resourceful and concerned for customer relations. They have a strong desire to be their own bosses and can handle ambiguity and surprises. Today's entrepreneur is often an open-minded leader who relies on networks, business plans, and consensus and is just as likely to be female as male. Finally, although successful entrepreneurs understand the role of risk, they do not necessarily regard what they do as being risky.

3 Describe the business plan and the start-up decisions made by small businesses and identify sources of financial aid available to such enterprises.

The starting point for virtually every new business is a *business plan*, in which the entrepreneur summarizes business strategy for the new venture and shows how it will be implemented. Business plans are increasingly important because creditors and investors demand them as tools for deciding whether to finance or invest. Entrepreneurs must also decide whether to buy an existing business, operate a franchise, or start from scratch.

Common funding sources include personal funds, family and friends, savings, lenders, investors, and governmental agencies. *Venture capital companies* are groups of small investors seeking to make profits on companies with rapid growth potential. Most of these firms do not lend money but rather invest it, supplying capital in return for partial ownership. Lending institutions are more likely to finance an existing business than a new business because the risks are better understood.

4 Discuss the trends in small business start-ups and identify the main reasons for success and failure among small businesses.

Five factors account for the fact that thousands of new businesses are started in the United States every year: (1) *the emergence of e-commerce*; (2) *entrepreneurs who cross over from big business*; (3) *increased opportunities for minorities and women*; (4) *new opportunities in global enterprise*; and (5) *improved rates of survival among small businesses*.

Four factors contribute to most small-business failure: (1) *managerial incompetence or inexperience*; (2) *neglect*; (3) *weak control systems*; and (4) *insufficient capital*. Likewise, four basic factors explain most small-business success: (1) *hard work, drive, and dedication*; (2) *market demand for the products or services being provided*; (3) *managerial competence*; and (4) *luck*.

5 Explain sole proprietorships and partnerships and discuss the advantages and disadvantages of each.

The *sole proprietorship* is owned and usually operated by one person. There are tax benefits for new businesses that are likely to suffer losses in early stages. A major drawback is *unlimited liability*. Another disadvantage is lack of continuity. Finally, a sole proprietorship depends on the resources of a single individual. The *general partnership* is a sole proprietorship multiplied by the number of partner-owners. The biggest advantage is its ability to grow by adding new talent and money. A partnership is not a legal entity. It is just two or more people working together. Partners are taxed as individuals, and *unlimited liability* is a drawback. Partnerships may lack continuity, and transferring ownership may be hard. No partner may sell out without the consent of the others. *Cooperatives* combine the freedom of sole proprietorships with the financial power of corporations.

6 Describe corporations, discuss their advantages and disadvantages, and identify different kinds of corporations.

All *corporations* share certain characteristics: legal status as separate entities, property rights and obligations, and indefinite life spans. They may sue and be sued; buy, hold, and sell property; make and sell products; and commit crimes and be tried and punished for them. The biggest advantage of incorporation is *limited liability*: Investor liability is limited to one's personal investments in the corporation. Another advantage is continuity. Finally, corporations have advantages in raising money. By selling stock, they expand the number of investors and the amount of available funds. Legal protections tend to make lenders more willing to grant loans.

One disadvantage is that a corporation can be taken over against the will of its managers. Another disadvantage is start-up cost. Corporations are heavily regulated and must meet complex legal requirements in the states in which they're chartered. The greatest potential drawback to incorporation is *double taxation*. Different kinds of corporations help businesses take advantage of incorporation without assuming all of the disadvantages.

7 Explain the basic issues involved in managing a corporation and special issues in corporate ownership.

Corporations sell shares, called *stock*, to investors who then become *stockholders* (or shareholders) and the real owners. Profits are distributed among stockholders in the form of *dividends*, and managers serve at their discretion. The governing body of a corporation is its *board of directors*. Most board members do not participate in day-to-day management but rather hire a team of managers. This team, called *officers*, is usually headed by a *chief executive officer (CEO)* who is responsible for overall performance. Several issues have grown in importance in the area of corporate ownership. In a *strategic alliance*, two or more organizations collaborate on a project for mutual gain. When partners share ownership of a new enterprise, the arrangement is called a *joint venture*. The *employee stock ownership plan (ESOP)* allows employees to own a significant share of the corporation through trusts established on their behalf. More stock is now being purchased by institutional investors. A *merger* occurs when two firms combine to create a new company. In an *acquisition*, one firm buys another outright. A *divestiture* occurs when a corporation sells a part of its existing business operations or sets it up as a new and independent corporation. When a firm sells part of itself to raise capital, the strategy is known as a *spin-off*.

KEY TERMS

acquisition (p. 96)

board of directors (p. 95)

business plan (p. 80)

chief executive officer
(CEO) (p. 95)

closely held (or private)
corporation (p. 93)

cooperative (p. 91)

corporate governance (p. 94)

corporation (p. 92)

divestiture (p. 96)

double taxation (p. 93)

employee stock ownership
plan (ESOP) (p. 96)

entrepreneur (p. 79)

entrepreneurship (p. 79)

franchise (p. 82)

general (or active) partner (p. 91)

general partnership (p. 90)

institutional investor (p. 96)

joint venture (p. 96)

limited liability (p. 93)

limited liability corporation
(LLC) (p. 94)

limited partner (p. 91)

limited partnership (p. 91)

master limited partnership (p. 91)

merger (p. 96)

multinational (or transnational)
corporation (p. 94)

officers (p. 95)

professional corporation (p. 94)

publicly held (or public)
corporation (p. 93)

S corporation (p. 94)

small business (p. 74)

Small Business Administration
(SBA) (p. 74)

Small Business Development
Center (SBDC) (p. 84)

small-business investment
company (SBIC) (p. 83)

sole proprietorship (p. 90)

spin-off (p. 96)

stockholder (or shareholder) (p. 95)

strategic alliance (p. 96)

tender offer (p. 93)

unlimited liability (p. 90)

venture capital company (p. 83)

QUESTIONS AND EXERCISES

Questions for Review

1 Why are small businesses important to the U.S. economy?
2 Which industries are easiest for start-ups to enter? Which are hardest? Why?
3 What are the primary reasons for new business failure and success?
4 What are the basic forms of noncorporate business ownership? What are the key advantages and disadvantages of each?

Questions for Analysis

5 Why might a closely held corporation choose to remain private? Why might it choose to be publicly traded?
6 If you were going to open a new business, what type would it be? Why?

7 Would you prefer to buy an existing business or start from scratch? Why?
8 Under what circumstances might it be wise for an entrepreneur to reject venture capital? Under what circumstances might it be advisable to take more venture capital than he or she actually needs?

Application Exercises

9 Interview the owner/manager of a sole proprietorship or a general partnership. What characteristics of that business form led the owner to choose it? Does he or she ever contemplate changing the form of the business?
10 Identify two or three of the fastest growing businesses in the United States during the last year. What role has entrepreneurship played in the growth of these firms?

WORKING THE INTERNET

Goal

To encourage you to define the opportunities and problems for new companies doing business on the Internet.

Background Information

Let's say that you and two partners plan to launch a new business. Using a virtual storefront on the Internet, you intend to offer local delivery services for books and magazines. Customers can select books and magazines after perusing any online retailer's listings. But rather than placing an order with that retailer, which then entails paying postage and waiting several days for delivery, customers can place their order with your local company. You will purchase the desired item from a local discounter, deliver it within two hours, and collect a full retail price from the customer. Your profit margin will be the difference between the discount price you pay and the full retail price you collect from your customers.

Method

Step 1

Join with two other students and assume the role of business partners. Start by discussing this idea among yourselves.

Identify as many strengths and weaknesses as possible for your potential new venture.

Step 2

Based on your assessment, now determine the importance of the following new business issues:

■ Analyzing your competitive marketplace and how you should go about promoting your service
■ Identifying sources of management advice as expansion proceeds
■ The role of technology consultants in launching and maintaining a Web site
■ Customer-service policies and costs in a virtual environment
■ The primary pitfalls that could derail your business

FOLLOW-UP QUESTIONS

1 Do you think this business would be successful? Why or why not?
2 Based on your analysis, what future developments could most affect your business? How might you best prepare yourself for these developments?
3 Do you think that operating a virtual storefront will be harder or easier than doing business from a traditional brick-and-mortar operation? Explain your answer.

BREAKING UP IS HARD TO DO

The Situation

Connie and Mark began a 25-year friendship after finishing college and discovering their mutual interest in owning a business. Established as a general partnership, their home furnishings center is a successful business sustained for 20 years by a share-and-share-alike relationship. Start-up cash, daily responsibilities, and profits have all been shared equally. The partners both work four days each week except when busy seasons require both of them to be in the store. Shared goals and compatible personalities have led to a solid give-and-take relationship that helps them overcome business problems while maintaining a happy interpersonal relationship.

The division of work is a natural match and successful combination because of the partners' different but complementary interests. Mark buys the merchandise and maintains up-to-date contacts with suppliers; he also handles personnel matters (hiring and training employees). Connie manages the inventory, buys shipping supplies, keeps the books, and manages the finances. Mark does more selling, with Connie helping out only during busy seasons. Both partners share in decisions about advertising and promotions.

The Dilemma

Things began changing two years ago, when Connie became less interested in the business and got more involved in other activities. Whereas Mark's enthusiasm remained high, Connie's time was increasingly consumed by travel, recreation, and community-service activities. At first, she reduced her work commitment from four to three days a week. Then she indicated that she wanted to cut back further, to just two days. "In that case," Mark replied, "we'll have to make some changes."

Mark insisted that profit sharing be adjusted to reflect his larger role in running the business. He proposed that Connie's monthly salary be cut in half (from $4,000 to $2,000). Connie agreed. He recommended that the $2,000 savings be shifted to his salary because of his increased workload, but this time Connie balked, arguing that Mark's current $4,000 salary already compensated him for his contributions. She proposed to split the difference, with Mark getting a $1,000 increase and the other $1,000 going into the firm's cash account. Mark said no and insisted on a full $2,000 raise. To avoid a complete falling out, Connie finally gave in, even though she thought it unfair for Mark's salary to jump from $4,000 per month to $6,000. At that point, she made a promise to herself: "To even things out, I'll find a way to get $2,000 worth of inventory for personal use each month."

QUESTIONS TO ADDRESS

1 Identify the ethical issues, if any, regarding Mark's and Connie's respective positions on Mark's proposed $2,000 salary increase.

2 What kind of salary adjustments do you think would be fair in this situation? Explain why.

3 There is another way for Mark and Connie to solve their differences: Because the terms of participation have changed, it might make sense to dissolve the existing partnership. What do you recommend in this regard?

PUBLIC OR PRIVATE? THAT IS THE QUESTION

The Situation

The Thomas Corporation is a very well-financed, private corporation with a solid and growing product line, little debt, and a stable workforce. However, in the past few months, there has been a growing rift among the board of directors that has created considerable differences of opinion as to the future directions of the firm.

The Dilemma

Some board members believe the firm should "go public" with a stock offering. Since each board member owns a large block of corporate stock, each would make a considerable amount of money if the company went public.

Other board members want to maintain the status quo as a private corporation. The biggest advantage of this approach is that the firm maintains its current ability to remain autonomous in its operations.

The third faction of the board also wants to remain private, but clearly has a different agenda. Those board members have identified a small public corporation that is currently one of the company's key suppliers. Their idea is to buy the supplying company, shift its assets to the parent firm, sell all of its remaining operations, terminate employees, and then outsource the production of the parts it currently buys from the firm. Their logic is that the firm would gain significant assets and lower its costs.

Team Activity

Assemble a group of four students and assign each group member to one of the following roles:

- An employee at the Thomas Corporation
- A customer of the Thomas Corporation
- An investor in the Thomas Corporation
- A board member who has not yet decided which option is best

ACTION STEPS

1 Before hearing any of your group's comments on this situation, and from the perspective of your assigned role, which option do you think is best? Write down the reasons for your position.

2 Before hearing any of your group's comments on this situation, and from the perspective of your assigned role, what are the underlying ethical issues, if any, in this situation? Write down the issues.

3 Gather your group together and reveal, in turn, each member's comments on the situation. Next, reveal the ethical issues listed by each member.

4 Appoint someone to record main points of agreement and disagreement within the group. How do you explain the results? What accounts for any disagreement?

5 From an ethical standpoint, what does your group conclude is the most appropriate action that should have been taken by the Thomas Corporation in this situation?

6 Develop a group response to the following question: What do you think most people would do in this situation?

VIDEO EXERCISE

DOING BUSINESS PRIVATELY: AMY'S ICE CREAM

Learning Objectives

The purpose of this video is to help you:

1 Distinguish among types of corporations.
2 Consider the advantages and disadvantages of incorporation.
3 Understand the role that shareholders play in a privately held corporation.

Synopsis

Amy's Ice Cream, based in Austin, Texas, is a privately held corporation formed in 1984 by Amy Miller and owned by Miller and a small group of family members and friends. At the outset, one of the most important decisions Miller faced was choosing an appropriate legal ownership structure for the new business. Fueled by the founder's dedication to creating happy ice cream memories for customers, Amy's has continued to evolve and grow. The company now operates nine stores and rings up close to $3.5 million in annual sales. Applying for a job is an adventure in creativity, and Miller welcomes employees' suggestions for new flavors and new promotions.

DISCUSSION QUESTIONS

1 **For analysis**: How does Amy's Ice Cream differ from a publicly held corporation?
2 **For analysis**: What are some of the particular advantages of corporate ownership for a firm such as Amy's Ice Cream?
3 **For application**: How well do you think Amy's is working to ensure its continued survival and success? Looking ahead to future growth, what marketing, financial, or other suggestions would you make?
4 **For application**: What are some of the issues that Amy Miller may have to confront because her 22 investors are family members and friends?
5 **For debate**: Should Amy's Ice Cream become a publicly held corporation? Support your chosen position.

Online Exploration

Find out what's required to incorporate a business in your state. You might begin by searching the CCH Business Owner's Toolkit site at www.toolkit.cch.com. If you were going to start a small business, would you choose incorporation or a different form of legal organization? List the pros and cons that incorporation presents for the type of business that you would consider.

After reading this chapter, you should be able to:

1 Discuss the rise of international business and describe the major world marketplaces and trade agreements and alliances.

2 Explain how differences in import-export balances, exchange rates, and foreign competition determine the ways in which countries and businesses respond to the international environment.

3 Discuss the factors involved in deciding to do business internationally and in selecting the appropriate levels of international involvement and international organizational structure.

4 Describe some of the ways in which social, cultural, economic, legal, and political differences among nations affect international business.

WHERE DOES MANAGEMENT STAND ON BEER BREAKS?

What's left to be said about an enormous retailer that has become the most profitable corporation on earth? Wal-Mart is gigantic, by any measure. It has 1.6 million workers in 5,300 worldwide stores that are visited by more than 138 million customers every week.

THE GLOBAL CONTEXT OF BUSINESS

Total sales in 2004 exceeded $285 billion, and in 2002, Wal-Mart topped the *Fortune* 500 list of the world's largest companies—the first time that a nonmanufacturing firm had ever occupied that position.

But with U.S. sales flat and the domestic discount market approaching saturation, Wal-Mart has set its sights on new ways to grow. For instance, it is already invading the markets of specialty retailers, such as Toys "R" Us and Best Buy, and it continues to introduce new products into existing stores. "Wal-Mart's aggressive roll-out of retail gas stations," speculates one retail consultant, "could be followed closely with the company selling used cars, financial services, home improvement, and food service." But even with all this domestic activity, Wal-Mart still finds expansion into international markets its most appealing option.

Germans are skeptical. They don't want to be paying the salary of that guy at the door.

—Analyst at Deutsche Bank on the German attitude toward Wal-Mart greeters

Wal-Mart's international expansion began in 1991, when a Sam's Club opened near Mexico City. The firm's international division operates over 1,100 overseas outlets, with stores in Argentina, Brazil, Canada, China, Germany, Korea, Mexico, Puerto Rico, and the United Kingdom. In each of these markets, acquisitions have played as important a role as expansion from within. In Canada, for example, Wal-Mart entered the market by buying 122 Woolco stores. German operations began with the acquisition of 21 Wertkauf hypermarkets and 74 Interspar stores. Most ambitious to date, however, have been the company's activities in Britain, where it has bought 230 ASDA stores.

The process for integrating acquired stores into Wal-Mart operations involves changing names, renovating facilities, bringing in American store managers, and altering product mixes.

Wal-Mart is still learning how to deal effectively with international differences in culture and business practices, however. An initial problem was the relatively small size of the acquired stores, most of which had only one-third the floor space of a typical U.S. Wal-Mart. Wal-Mart's "one-stop" strategy depends, in part, on size—having everything under one roof—but European customers don't like the impersonal feel of very large stores. In addition, because they typically shop more frequently than Americans and buy less at each visit, they see no reason to be pushing large carts around. Thus, the dilemma for Wal-Mart management: Although smaller carts would allow it to cram more products into limited store space, small carts don't encourage large purchases. Finally, Europeans don't care for greeters or other superfluous employees. "Germans are skeptical," explains an analyst at Deutsche Bank. "They don't want to be paying the salary of that guy at the door."

Regulation creates yet another set of hurdles. In England and Germany, 24-hour stores are banned. A German court upheld employees' rights to wear earrings and sport facial hair, and when the company tried to forbid English employees from drinking beer during lunch breaks, English labor unions threatened to go to court. European laws are also quite strict about the sale of "loss leaders"—popular products that are sold below cost in order to bring customers into the store. Negotiations with suppliers are also heavily regulated. In Mexico, for example, Wal-Mart ran afoul of local authorities when it demanded deep discounts from many suppliers, a common practice in the United States. ∎

Our opening story continues on page 131.

WHAT'S IN IT FOR ME?

Regardless of whether you see yourself living abroad, working for a big company, or starting your own business, the global economy will affect you in some way. Exchange rates for different currencies and global markets for buying and selling are all of major importance to everyone, regardless of their role or perspective. As a result, this chapter will better enable you to (1) understand how global forces affect you as a customer, (2) understand how globalization affects you as an employee, and (3) assess how global opportunities and challenges can affect you as a business owner and as an investor.

This chapter explores the global context of business. We begin with an exploration of the major world marketplaces and trade agreements that affect international business. Next, we examine several factors that help determine how countries and businesses respond to international opportunities and challenges. We then direct our attention to some of the decisions managers must make if they intend to compete in international markets. Finally, we conclude with a discussion of some of the social, cultural, economic, legal, and political factors that affect international business.

THE CONTEMPORARY GLOBAL ECONOMY

GLOBALIZATION process by which the world economy is becoming a single interdependent system

The total volume of world trade is immense—over $9 trillion in merchandise trade each year (see Figure 4.1). Foreign investment in the United States is approaching $100 billion, and U.S. investment abroad exceeds $300 billion.[1] As more firms engage in international business, the world economy is fast becoming an interdependent system—a process called **globalization**.

Figure 4.1
Annual Global Imports and Exports

We often take for granted the diversity of products we can buy as a result of international trade. Your television, your shoes, and even your morning coffee or juice are probably **imports**—products made or grown abroad and sold domestically in the United States. At the same time, the success of many U.S. firms depends on **exports**—products made or grown here, such as machinery, electronic equipment, and grains, and shipped for sale abroad.

Our opening case discussed Wal-Mart's entrance into international markets. Firms like Starbucks and Urban Outfitters are also finding international markets to be a fruitful area for growth. But as Wal-Mart has found, as these companies expand into other countries, they must also be mindful of different regulations imposed on them by their host countries as well as differences in consumer tastes. And the impact of globalization doesn't stop with firms looking to open locations abroad. Small firms with no international operations (such as an independent coffee shop) may still buy from international suppliers, and even individual contractors or self-employed people can be affected by fluctuations in exchange rates.

Indeed, international trade is becoming increasingly important to most nations and their businesses. Many countries that once followed strict policies to protect domestic business now encourage trade just as aggressively. They are opening borders to foreign business, offering incentives for domestic businesses to expand internationally, and making it easier for foreign firms to partner with local firms. Likewise, as more industries and markets become global, so, too, are the firms that compete in them.

Several forces have combined to spark and sustain globalization. For one thing, governments and businesses are more aware of the benefits of globalization to businesses and shareholders. These benefits include the potential for higher standards of living and improved business profitability. New technologies have made international travel, communication, and commerce faster and cheaper than ever before. Finally, there are competitive pressures: Sometimes a firm must expand into foreign markets simply to keep up with competitors.

Globalization is not without its detractors. Some critics charge that globalization allows businesses to exploit workers in less developed countries and bypass domestic environmental and tax regulations. They also charge that globalization leads to the loss of cultural heritages and often benefits the rich more than the poor. As a result, many international gatherings of global economic leaders are marked by protests and demonstrations.

IMPORT product made or grown abroad but sold domestically

EXPORT product made or grown domestically but shipped and sold abroad

■■■ THE MAJOR WORLD MARKETPLACES

Managers involved with international businesses need to have a solid understanding of the global economy, including the major world marketplaces. This section examines some fundamental economic distinctions between countries based on wealth and then looks at some of the world's major international marketplaces.

Distinctions Based on Wealth   The World Bank, an agency of the United Nations, uses per-capita income—average income per person—to make distinctions among countries. Its current classification method consists of four different categories of countries.[2]

1   *High-income countries.* Those with annual per-capita income greater than $10,065. These include the United States, Canada, most countries in Europe, Australia, New Zealand, Japan, South Korea, Kuwait, the United Arab Emirates, Israel, Singapore, and Taiwan.

2   *Upper middle-income countries.* Those with annual per-capita income of $10,065 or less but more than $3,255. This group includes, among others, the Czech Republic, Greece, Hungary, Poland, most of the countries of the former Soviet bloc, Turkey, Mexico, Argentina, and South Africa.

3   *Low middle-income countries.* Those with annual per-capita income of $3,255 or lower but more than $825. Among the countries in this group are Colombia, Guatemala, Samoa, and Thailand.

4   *Low-income countries* (often called *developing countries*). Those with annual per-capita income of $825 or less. Cambodia, Ethiopia, Haiti, and Vietnam are among the countries in this group. These countries often suffer from low literacy rates, weak infrastructures, and unstable governments; these factors, in turn, make these countries relatively unattractive to international businesses. For example, the East African nation of Somalia, plagued by drought, starvation, and internal strife, plays virtually no role in the world economy.

Geographic Clusters   The world economy revolves around three major marketplaces: North America, Europe, and Asia. In general, these clusters include relatively more of the upper-middle and high-income nations, but relatively few low- and low middle-income countries. For instance, because Africa consists primarily of low- and low middle-income countries, it is not generally seen as a major marketplace. The three geographic regions that do warrant this designation are home to most of the world's largest economies, biggest corporations, most influential financial markets, and highest-income consumers.

North America   As the world's largest marketplace and most stable economy, the United States dominates the North American market. Canada also plays a major role in the international economy, and the United States and Canada are each other's largest trading

Globalization has become a source of debate in many countries today. Advocates of globalization argue that increased international commerce benefits all sectors of society and should be actively encouraged. But critics like these protestors argue that globalization benefits only big business and that it is eroding distinctive national cultures.

partners. Many U.S. firms, such as General Motors and Procter & Gamble, have maintained successful Canadian operations for years, and many Canadian firms, such as Northern Telecom and Alcan Aluminum, are also major international competitors.

Mexico has become a major manufacturing center, especially along the U.S. border, where cheap labor and low transportation costs have encouraged many firms from the United States and other countries to build factories. The auto industry has been especially active, with DaimlerChrysler, General Motors, Volkswagen, Nissan, and Ford all running large assembly plants in the region. Several major suppliers have also built facilities in the area. Interestingly, however, Mexico's role as a low-cost manufacturing center may have peaked. The emergence of China as a low-cost manufacturing center may lead companies to begin to shift their production from Mexico to China.[3]

Europe Europe is often regarded as two regions—Western and Eastern. Western Europe, dominated by Germany, the United Kingdom, France, Spain, and Italy, has long been a mature but fragmented marketplace. But the transformation of this region via the European Union (discussed later) into an integrated economic system has further increased its importance. Major international firms, such as Unilever, Renault, Royal Dutch/Shell, Michelin, Siemens, and Nestlé, are all headquartered in Western Europe. E-commerce and technology have also become increasingly important in this region. There has been a surge in Internet start-ups in southeastern England, the Netherlands, and the Scandinavian countries; and Ireland is now one of the world's largest exporters of software. Strasbourg, France, is a major center for biotech start-ups, Barcelona, Spain, has many flourishing software and Internet companies, and the Frankfurt region of Germany is dotted with both software and biotech start-ups.

Eastern Europe, once primarily communist, has also gained in importance, both as a marketplace and as a producer. Such multinational corporations as Daewoo, Nestlé, General Motors, and ABB Asea Brown Boveri have all set up operations in Poland. Ford, General Motors, Suzuki, and Volkswagen have all built new factories in Hungary. On the other hand, governmental instability has hampered development in parts of Russia, Bulgaria, Albania, Romania, and other countries.

The growth in international commerce has led to the emergence of several major marketplaces. Much of the international commerce in these marketplaces, in turn, is generally managed from major cities. Traditional centers of international commerce include New York, London, Paris, Brussels, and Tokyo. In recent years, though, cities like Shanghai, Beijing, Hong Kong, Dubai, Vancouver, Bangladore, and Kuala Lumpur have taken on increased importance. For example, the glittering skyline of Shanghai has become defined by international business.

Pacific Asia Pacific Asia consists of Japan, China, Thailand, Malaysia, Singapore, Indonesia, South Korea, Taiwan, the Philippines, and Australia. (While Australia is not in Asia, we include it here because of its proximity to the region.) Some experts still distinguish Hong Kong, though now part of China, as a part of the region, and others include Vietnam. Fueled by strong entries in the automobile, electronics, and banking industries, the economies of these countries grew rapidly in the 1970s and 1980s. Unfortunately, a currency crisis in the late 1990s slowed growth in virtually every country of the region. That crisis, though, has essentially run its course, and most countries in this region, especially Japan and China, are showing clear signs of revitalization.

Pacific Asia is an important force in the world economy and a major source of competition for North American firms. Led by firms such as Toyota, Toshiba, and Nippon Steel, Japan dominates the region. South Korea (home to such firms as Samsung and Hyundai), Taiwan (owner of Chinese Petroleum and the manufacturing home of many foreign firms), and Hong Kong (a major financial center) are also successful players in the international economy. China, the world's most densely populated country, has emerged as an important market and now boasts the world's third-largest economy behind that of the United States and only slightly behind that of Japan. While its per-capita income remains low, the sheer number of potential consumers there makes it an important market. India, though not part of Pacific Asia, is also rapidly emerging as one of the globe's most important economies.

As in North America and Europe, technology promises to play an increasingly important role in the future of this region. In some parts of Asia, however, the emergence of technology firms has been hampered by poorly developed electronic infrastructures, slower adoption of computers and information technology, and a higher percentage of lower-income consumers. Although the future looks promising, technology companies are facing several obstacles as they work to keep pace with foreign competitors.

■■■ TRADE AGREEMENTS AND ALLIANCES

Various legal agreements have sparked international trade and shaped the global business environment. Indeed, virtually every nation has formal trade treaties with other nations. A *treaty* is a legal agreement that specifies areas in which nations will cooperate with one another. Among the most significant treaties is the *North American Free Trade Agreement*. The *European Union*, the *Association of Southeast Asian Nations*, and the *World Trade Organization*, all governed by treaties, are also instrumental in promoting international business activity.

NORTH AMERICAN FREE TRADE AGREEMENT (NAFTA) agreement to gradually eliminate tariffs and other trade barriers among the United States, Canada, and Mexico

North American Free Trade Agreement The **North American Free Trade Agreement (NAFTA)** (see Figure 4.2) removes most tariffs and other trade barriers among the United States, Canada, and Mexico and includes agreements on environmental issues and labor abuses. Some barriers came down on January 1, 1994; others were removed in 1999, and still others in 2004; most remaining barriers will follow in 2009.

Most observers agree that NAFTA is achieving its basic purpose—to create a more active North American market. The following are representative of its impact:

■ Direct foreign investment increased substantially. U.S. and Canadian firms accounted for 55 percent of all foreign investment in Mexico, with $2.4 billion in the first year alone. Companies from other nations—for instance, Japan's Toyota—also have made investments to take advantage of the freer movement of goods.

Figure 4.2
The Nations of NAFTA

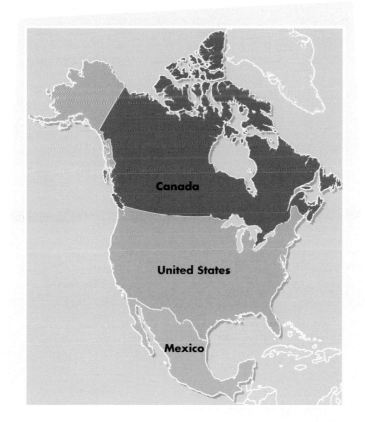

- U.S. exports to Mexico have increased significantly (20 percent in the first year alone). Procter & Gamble, for example, enjoyed an increase of nearly 75 percent, and the giant agribusiness firm Archer Daniels Midland tripled exports to Mexico. Mexico has passed Japan as the second-largest buyer of U.S. goods, and trade with Canada has also increased significantly.

- U.S. imports from Mexico and Canada rose even faster than rates in the opposite direction, setting records of $48 billion and $120 billion, respectively, in the first year of NAFTA. In particular, electronics, computers, and communications products came into the United States twice as fast as they went out.

- NAFTA has created several hundred thousand new jobs, although this number is smaller than NAFTA proponents had hoped. One thing is clear, though—the flood of U.S. jobs lost to Mexico predicted by NAFTA critics, especially labor unions, has not occurred. For instance, Ford Motor Co.'s Mexican division created jobs in both countries. Ford's exports of Mexican-made vehicles to the United States has risen 30 percent, but 80 percent of all components in those cars are U.S. made. Ford also reports that its exports of U.S.-made cars to Mexico rose from 1,200 to 30,000 in a recent one-year period.

The European Union Originally called the *Common Market*, the **European Union (EU)** includes most European nations, as shown in Figure 4.3. These nations have eliminated most quotas and set uniform tariff levels on products imported and exported within their group. In 1992, virtually all internal trade barriers went down, making the EU the largest free market-place in the world.

EUROPEAN UNION (EU) agreement among major European nations to eliminate or make uniform most trade barriers affecting group members

Figure 4.3

The Nations of the European Union

ASSOCIATION OF SOUTHEAST ASIAN NATIONS (ASEAN) organization for economic, political, social, and cultural cooperation among Southeast Asian nations

The Association of Southeast Asian Nations (ASEAN) The **Association of Southeast Asian Nations (ASEAN)** was founded in 1967 as an organization for economic, political, social, and cultural cooperation. In 1995, Vietnam became the group's first communist member. Today, the ASEAN group has a population of over 575 million and a GDP of approximately $2.6 billion.[4] Figure 4.4 shows a map of the ASEAN countries. Because of its relative size, ASEAN does not have the same global economic significance as NAFTA and the EU.

GENERAL AGREEMENT ON TARIFFS AND TRADE (GATT) international trade agreement to encourage the multilateral reduction or elimination of trade barriers

WORLD TRADE ORGANIZATION (WTO) organization through which member nations negotiate trading agreements and resolve disputes about trade policies and practices

The World Trade Organization The **General Agreement on Tariffs and Trade (GATT)** was signed after World War II. Its purpose was to reduce or eliminate trade barriers, such as tariffs and quotas. It did so by encouraging nations to protect domestic industries within agreed-upon limits and to engage in multilateral negotiations. The GATT proved to be relatively successful. So, to further promote globalization, most of the world's countries joined to create the **World Trade Organization (WTO)**, which began on January 1, 1995. (The GATT is the actual treaty that governs the WTO). The 149 member countries are required to open markets to international trade, and the WTO is empowered to pursue three goals:

1 Promote trade by encouraging members to adopt fair trade practices.
2 Reduce trade barriers by promoting multilateral negotiations.
3 Establish fair procedures for resolving disputes among members.

Figure 4.4
The Nations of the Association of Southeast Asian Nations (ASEAN)

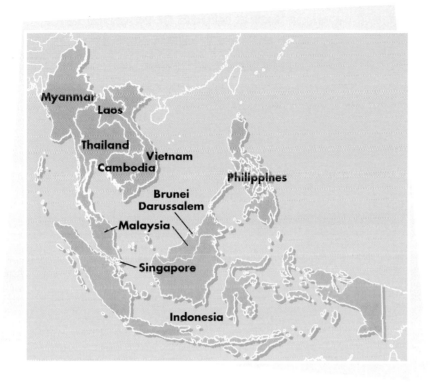

▪▪▪ IMPORT-EXPORT BALANCES

Although international trade has many advantages, it can also pose problems if a country's imports and exports don't maintain an acceptable balance. Table 4.1 lists the major trading partners of the United States. The top part of the table shows the 10 largest markets for exports from the United States, while the bottom part of the table shows the 10 largest markets that import to the United States. Note that many countries are on both lists (indeed, Canada is at the top of both). The United States does business with many more countries. For instance, in 2004, the United States exported $3.2 billion to Egypt, $1.4 billion to Kuwait, $790 million to Poland, and $32 million to Zambia; imports from those same countries were $1.22 billion, $1.77 billion, $1.17 billion, and $8.4 million, respectively.

In deciding whether an overall balance exists, economists use two measures: *balance of trade* and *balance of payments*.

Balance of Trade As you'll recall from Chapter 1, a country's **balance of trade** is the total economic value of all the products that it exports minus the economic value of all the products that it imports. A *positive balance of trade* results when a country exports (sells to other countries) more than it imports (buys from other countries). A *negative balance of trade* results when a country imports more than it exports.

Relatively small trade imbalances are common and are unimportant. Large imbalances, however, are another matter. In 2004, for example, the United States had a negative balance in merchandise trade of $666.2 billion and a positive balance in service trade of $4.2 billion. The result was an overall negative balance of $662 billion—large enough to be a concern for U.S. business and political leaders. The biggest concern about trade balances involves the flow of currency. When U.S. consumers and businesses buy foreign

BALANCE OF TRADE economic value of all products a country exports minus the economic value of all products it imports

TABLE 4.1 THE MAJOR TRADING PARTNERS OF THE UNITED STATES

TOP 10 U.S. SUPPLIER COUNTRIES		
RANK	**COUNTRY**	**2005 EXPORTS (IN $ BILLIONS)**
1	Canada	194.0
2	Mexico	109.8
3	Japan	50.5
4	China	37.6
5	United Kingdom	35.5
6	Federal Republic of Germany	31.1
7	South Korea	25.1
8	Netherlands	24.1
9	France	20.4
10	Taiwan	20.1

TOP 10 U.S. EXPORT MARKETS		
RANK	**COUNTRY**	**2005 IMPORTS (IN $ BILLIONS)**
1	Canada	262.3
2	China	222.9
3	Mexico	155.7
4	Japan	126.4
5	Federal Republic of Germany	77.3
6	United Kingdom	46.7
7	South Korea	40.1
8	Taiwan	31.9
9	Venezuela	30.9
10	France	30.8

products, dollars flow from the U.S. to other countries; when U.S. businesses are selling to foreign consumers and businesses, dollars flow back into the United States. A large negative balance of trade means that many dollars are controlled by interests outside the United States.

Trade Deficits and Surpluses When a country's imports exceed its exports—that is, when it has a negative balance of trade—it suffers a **trade deficit**. In short, more money is flowing out than flowing in. A positive balance occurs when exports exceed imports, and then the nation enjoys a **trade surplus**: More money is flowing in than flowing out. Trade deficits and surpluses are influenced by several factors, such as general economic conditions and the effect of trade agreements. For example, higher domestic costs, greater international competition, and continuing economic problems among some of its regional trading partners have slowed the tremendous growth in exports that Japan once enjoyed. But rising prosperity in China and India has led to strong increases in both exports from and imports to those countries.

In general, the United States suffers from large deficits with Japan ($75.6 billion), China ($185 billion), Germany ($46 billion), Canada ($68 billion), Mexico ($45 billion), and Taiwan ($12 billion). In any given year, the United States may also have smaller deficits with other countries. On the other hand, we enjoy healthy surpluses with many countries. For instance, we have a $10 billion surplus with the Netherlands, $8 billion with Australia, $6 billion with Belgium–Luxembourg, and $1 billion with Egypt. The United States has surpluses with other countries as well.

TRADE DEFICIT situation in which a country's imports exceed its exports, creating a negative balance of trade

TRADE SURPLUS situation in which a country's exports exceed its imports, creating a positive balance of trade

Figure 4.5
U.S. Imports and Exports

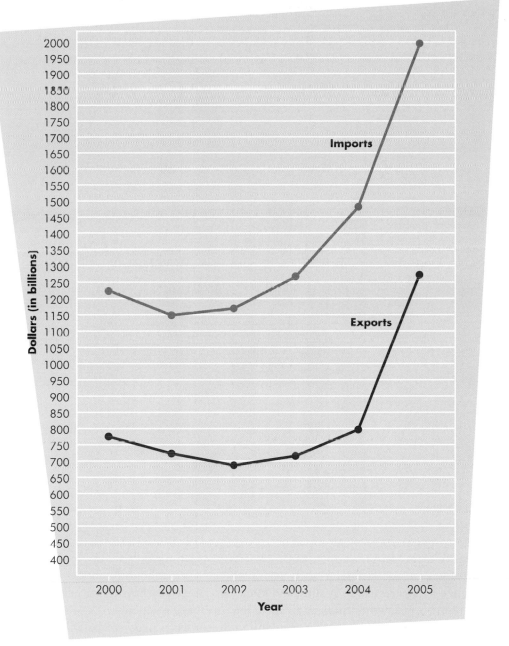

Figures 4.5 and 4.6 highlight two series of events: (1) recent trends in U.S. exports and imports and (2) the resulting trade deficit. As Figure 4.5 shows, both U.S. imports and U.S. exports have, with minor variations, increased over the past six years—a trend that's projected to continue.

In 2005, the United States exported $1,271.1 billion in goods and services. In the same year, the United States imported $1,996.0 billion in goods and services. Because imports exceeded exports, the United States had a *trade deficit* of $727.8 billion (the difference between exports and imports).[5] Trade deficits between 2000 and 2005 are shown in Figure 4.6: There was a deficit in each of these years because more money flowed out to pay for foreign imports than flowed in to pay for U.S. exports.

Balance of Payments The **balance of payments** refers to the flow of *money* into or out of a country. The money that a country pays for imports and receives for exports—its balance of trade—accounts for much of its balance of payments. Other financial

BALANCE OF PAYMENTS flow of all money into or out of a country

Figure 4.6
U.S. Trade Deficit

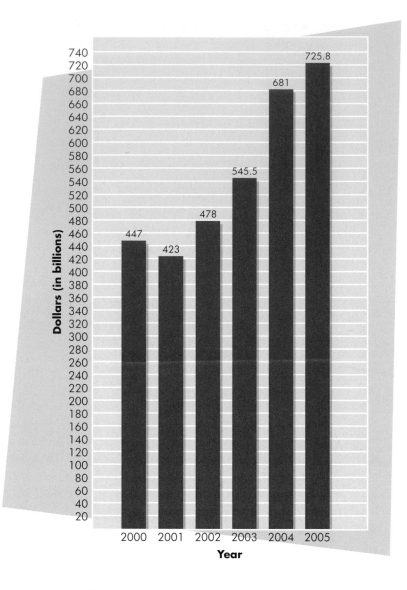

exchanges are also factors. Money spent by tourists in our country, money spent by our country on foreign-aid programs, and money exchanged by buying and selling currency on international money markets all affect the balance of payments.

For instance, suppose that the United States has a negative balance of trade of $1 million dollars. Now, suppose that this year, U.S. citizens travel abroad as tourists and spend a total of $200,000 in other countries (that is, they take those dollars out of the U.S. and "leave" them in other countries). This amount gets added to the balance of trade to form the balance of payments. So, the balance of payments is now a negative $1.2 million dollars. But further suppose that tourists from other countries come to the United States and spend the equivalent of $300,000 while they are here. This has the effect of reducing the negative balance of payments to $900,000 ($1.2 million–$300,000). Now further suppose that the United States then sends $600,000 in "aid" to help the victims of a tsunami-ravaged country in Asia. Because this represents additional dollars also leaving the United States, the balance of payments is now a negative $1.5 million ($900,000 + $600,000).

For many years, the United States enjoyed a positive balance of payments (more inflows than outflows). Recently, however, the overall balance has become negative and is currently approximately $200 billion.[6] While there are myriad contributing factors, the war in Iraq is one major cause of the growing negative balance of payments. Some U.S.

industries have positive balances, whereas others have negative balances. Such firms as Dow Chemical and Monsanto are among world leaders in chemical exports. The cigarette, truck, and industrial-equipment industries also have positive balances. Conversely, the metalworking-machinery, airplane-parts, and auto industries suffer negative balances because more of the products these industries use are imported than exported.

■■■ EXCHANGE RATES

The balance of imports and exports between two countries is affected by the rate of exchange between their currencies. An **exchange rate** is the rate at which the currency of one nation can be exchanged for that of another. The exchange rate between U.S. dollars and British pounds is usually about $1.5 to £1. This means that it costs £1 to "buy" $1.5 or $1 to "buy" £0.67. Stated differently, it also means that £1 and $1.5 have the same purchasing power.

At the end of World War II, the major nations of the world agreed to set *fixed exchange rates*. The value of any country's currency relative to that of another would remain constant. The goal was to allow the global economy to stabilize. Today, however, *floating exchange rates* are the norm, and the value of one country's currency relative to that of another varies with market conditions. For example, when many British citizens want to spend pounds to buy U.S. dollars (or goods), the value of the dollar relative to the pound increases. Demand for the dollar is high, and a currency is strong when demand for it is high. It's also strong when there's high demand for the goods manufactured with that currency. On a daily basis, exchange rates fluctuate very little. Significant variations usually occur over longer time spans.

Exchange-rate fluctuation can have an important impact on balance of trade. Suppose you want to buy some English tea for £10 per box. At an exchange rate of $1.5 to £1, a box will cost you $15 (£10 × 1.5 = 15). But what if the pound is weaker? At an exchange rate of, say, $1.25 to £1, the same box would cost you only $12.50 (£10 × 1.25 = 12.50).

If the dollar is strong in relation to the pound, the prices of all U.S.-made products will rise in England and the prices of all English-made products will fall in the United States. The English would buy fewer U.S.-made products, and Americans would be prompted to spend more on English-made products. The result would probably be a U.S. trade deficit with England.

One of the most significant developments in foreign exchange has been the introduction of the **euro**—a common currency among most of the members of the European Union (Denmark, Sweden, and the United Kingdom do not participate). The euro was officially introduced in 2002 and has replaced other currencies, such as the German deutsche mark and the French franc. The EU anticipates that the euro will become as important as the dollar and the yen in international commerce. When the euro was first introduced, its value was pegged as being equivalent to the dollar: €1 = $1. But because the dollar has been relatively weak, its value eroded relative to that of the euro. While the dollar has been gaining strength, as of this writing, $1 was still worth somewhat less than €1.

Companies with international operations must watch exchange-rate fluctuations closely because changes affect overseas demand for their products and can be a major factor in competition. In general, when the value of a country's currency rises—becomes stronger—companies based there find it harder to export products to foreign markets and easier for foreign companies to enter local markets. It also makes it more cost-efficient for domestic companies to move operations to lower-cost foreign sites. When the value of a currency declines—becomes weaker—the opposite occurs. As the value of a country's currency falls, its balance of trade should improve because domestic companies should experience a boost in exports. There should also be less reason

EXCHANGE RATE rate at which the currency of one nation can be exchanged for the currency of another nation

EURO a common currency shared among most of the members of the European Union (excluding Denmark, Sweden, and the United Kingdom)

for foreign companies to ship products into the domestic market and less reason to establish operations in other countries.

■■■ FORMS OF COMPETITIVE ADVANTAGE

We are now almost ready to discuss the fundamental issues involved in international business management. But first, we should consider one last factor, forms of *competitive advantage*. Managers need to understand these concepts when making decisions about international competition. This understanding can help them better assess their potential for success in different markets.

Because no country can produce everything that it needs, countries tend to export what they can produce better or less expensively than other countries and use the proceeds to import what they can't produce as effectively. This principle doesn't fully explain why nations export and import what they do. Such decisions hinge partly on the advantages that a particular country enjoys regarding its abilities to create and/or sell certain products and resources.[7] Economists traditionally focused on absolute and comparative advantage to explain international trade. But because this approach focuses narrowly on such factors as natural resources and labor costs, the more contemporary view of national competitive advantage has emerged.

ABSOLUTE ADVANTAGE the ability to produce something more efficiently than any other country can

Absolute Advantage An **absolute advantage** exists when a country can produce something that is cheaper and/or of higher quality than any other country. Saudi oil, Brazilian coffee beans, and Canadian timber come close (because these countries have such abundant supplies of these resources), but examples of true absolute advantage are rare. In reality, "absolute" advantages are always relative. For example, many experts say that the vineyards of France produce the world's finest wines. But the burgeoning wine business in California demonstrates that producers there can also make very good wine—wines that rival those from France but come in more varieties and at lower prices.

COMPARATIVE ADVANTAGE the ability to produce some products more efficiently than others

Comparative Advantage A country has a **comparative advantage** in goods that it can produce more efficiently or better than other goods. If businesses in a given country can make computers more efficiently than they can make automobiles, then that nation has a comparative advantage in computer manufacturing.

In general, both absolute and comparative advantage translate into competitive advantage. Brazil, for instance, can produce and market coffee beans knowing full well that there are few other countries with the right mix of climate, terrain, and altitude to enter the coffee bean market. The United States has comparative advantages in the computer industry (because of technological sophistication) and in farming (because of fertile land and a temperate climate). South Korea has a comparative advantage in electronics manufacturing because of efficient operations and cheap labor. As a result, U.S. firms export computers and grain to South Korea and import DVD players from South Korea. South Korea can produce food, and the United States can build DVD players, but each nation imports certain products because the other holds a comparative advantage in the relevant industry.

NATIONAL COMPETITIVE ADVANTAGE international competitive advantage stemming from a combination of factor conditions, demand conditions, related and supporting industries, and firm strategies, structures, and rivalries

National Competitive Advantage In recent years, a theory of national competitive advantage has become a widely accepted model of why nations engage in international trade.[8] **National competitive advantage** derives from four conditions:

1 *Factor conditions* are the factors of production we discussed in Chapter 1—*labor*, *capital*, *entrepreneurs*, *physical resources*, and *information resources*.

2 *Demand conditions* reflect a large domestic consumer base that promotes strong demand for innovative products.

3 *Related and supporting industries* include strong local or regional suppliers and/or industrial customers.

4 *Strategies, structures, and rivalries* refer to firms and industries that stress cost reduction, product quality, higher productivity, and innovative products.

When all attributes of national competitive advantage exist, a nation is likely to be heavily involved in international business. Japan, for instance, has an abundance of natural resources and strong domestic demand for automobiles. Its carmakers have well-oiled supplier networks, and domestic firms have competed intensely with each other for decades. These circumstances explain why Japanese car companies like Toyota, Honda, Nissan, and Mazda are successful in foreign markets.

SELF-CHECK QUESTIONS 1–3

You should now be able to answer Self-Check Questions 1–3.*

1 True/False The balance of payments refers to the total economic value of all the products that a country exports minus the economic value of all the products that it imports.

2 True/False When a country's imports exceed its exports, it suffers a trade deficit.

3 Multiple Choice An absolute advantage exists when

(a) a business stresses cost reduction and product quality

(b) a country can produce something that is cheaper and/or of higher quality than any other country

(c) a country can produce some goods more efficiently or better than other goods

(d) a business stresses cost, higher productivity, and innovative products

*Answers to Self-Check Questions 1–3 can be found on p. 563.

INTERNATIONAL BUSINESS MANAGEMENT

Wherever a firm is located, its success depends largely on how well it's managed. International business is so challenging because basic management tasks—planning, organizing, directing, and controlling—are much more difficult when a firm operates in markets scattered around the globe.

Managing means making decisions. In this section, we examine the three basic decisions that a company must make when considering globalization. The first decision is whether to go international at all. Once that decision has been made, managers must decide on the level of international involvement and on the organizational structure that will best meet the firm's global needs.

■■■ GOING INTERNATIONAL

As the world economy becomes globalized, more firms are conducting international operations. U.S. firms are aggressively expanding abroad, while foreign companies such as BP and Nestlé continue to expand into foreign markets as well, including the U.S. market.

Rolling in the Worldwide Dough

Is any business more confined to a local market than a bakery? Breads and pastries get stale quickly, and even the largest operations, such as those that make buns for McDonald's, only move products over short distances. But a baker in Paris has refused to accept geographic limitations and is now selling his famous bread in global markets.

When Lionel Poilâne took over the family business about 30 years ago, he was determined to return breadmaking to its roots. As a result of studying the craft of breadmaking, Poilâne built clay ovens based on sixteenth-century plans and technology. Then, he trained his breadmakers in ancient techniques and soon began selling old-style dark bread known for a thick, chewy, fire-tinged flavor. It quickly became a favorite in Parisian bistros and demand soared.

To help meet demand, Poilâne built two more bakeries in Paris, and today he sells 15,000 loaves of bread a day—about 2.5 percent of all the bread sold in Paris. Poilâne

opened a bakery in London, but his efforts to expand to Japan were stymied: Local ordinances prohibited wood-burning ovens, and Poilâne refused to compromise. During the negotiation process, however, he realized that he didn't really *want* to build new bakeries all over the world.

Instead, he turned to modern technology to expand his old-fashioned business. The key was the big FedEx hub at Roissy-Charles-de-Gaulle Airport near Poilâne's largest Paris bakery. After launching a Web site with minimal marketing support, Poilâne started taking international orders. New orders are packaged as the bread cools and then picked up by FedEx. At about 4 pounds, the basic loaf travels well, and a quick warm-up in the customer's oven gives it the same taste as it had when it came out of Poilâne's oven. Today, a loaf of bread baked in Paris in the morning can easily be reheated for tomorrow night's dinner in more than 20 countries.

This route, however, isn't appropriate for every company. If you buy and sell fresh fish, you'll find it more profitable to confine your activities to limited geographic areas because storage and transport costs may be too high to make international operations worthwhile. As Figure 4.7 shows, several factors affect the decision to go international.

Gauging International Demand In considering international expansion, a company must consider whether there is a demand for its products abroad. Products that are successful in one country may be useless in another. Snowmobiles are popular

Figure 4.7
Going International

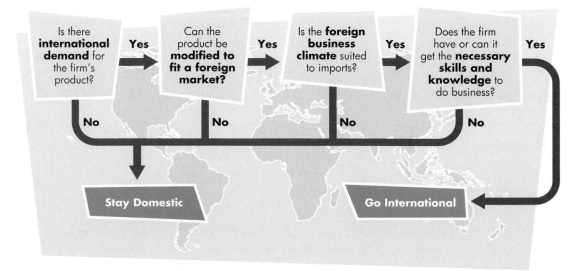

Quotas, tariffs, and subsidies are common techniques used by governments to affect international business. These U.S. customs officials, for instance, are carefully examining a shipment of goods being imported into the country. Their purpose is to make sure that (1) no banned or outlawed items are being shipped in and (2) the shipper pays the appropriate tariff that has been levied on the goods.

per year. Quotas are often determined by treaties. Better terms are often given to friendly trading partners, and quotas are typically adjusted to protect domestic producers.

The ultimate quota is an **embargo**: a government order forbidding exportation and/or importation of a particular product—or even all products—from a specific country. Many nations control bacteria and disease by banning certain agricultural products. Because the United States has embargoes against Cuba and Libya, American firms can't invest in these countries, and their products can't legally be sold on American markets.

Tariffs are taxes on imported products. They raise the prices of imports by making consumers pay not only for the products but also for tariff fees. Tariffs take two forms. Revenue tariffs are imposed to raise money for governments, but most tariffs, called protectionist tariffs, are meant to discourage particular imports. Did you know that firms that import ironing-board covers into the United States pay a 7-percent tariff on the price of the product? Firms that import women's athletic shoes pay a flat rate of $0.90 per pair plus 20 percent of the product price. Such figures are determined through a complicated process designed to put foreign and domestic firms on competitive footing (that is, to make the foreign goods about the same cost as the domestic goods).

Quotas and tariffs are imposed for numerous reasons. The U.S. government aids domestic automakers by restricting the number of Japanese cars imported into this country. Because of national security concerns, we limit the export of technology (for example, computer and nuclear technology to China). The United States isn't the only country that uses tariffs and quotas. To protect domestic firms, Italy imposes high tariffs on electronic goods. As a result, CD players are prohibitively expensive.

A **subsidy** is a government payment to help a domestic business compete with foreign firms. They're actually indirect tariffs that lower the prices of domestic goods rather than raise the prices of foreign goods. For example, many European governments subsidize farmers to help them compete against U.S. grain imports.

The Protectionism Debate In the United States, **protectionism**—the practice of protecting domestic business at the expense of free market competition—is controversial. Supporters argue that tariffs and quotas protect domestic firms and jobs as well as shelter new industries until they're able to compete internationally. They contend that we need such measures to counter steps taken by other nations. Other advocates justify protectionism in the name of national security. A nation, they argue, must be able to produce efficiently the goods needed for survival in case of war. Thus, the U.S. government requires the Air Force to buy planes only from U.S. manufacturers.

EMBARGO government order banning exportation and/or importation of a particular product or all products from a particular country

TARIFF tax levied on imported products

SUBSIDY government payment to help a domestic business compete with foreign firms

PROTECTIONISM practice of protecting domestic business against foreign competition

Critics cite protectionism as a source of friction between nations. They also charge that it drives up prices by reducing competition. They maintain that although jobs in some industries would be lost as a result of free trade, jobs in other industries (for example, electronics and automobiles) would be created if all nations abandoned protectionist tactics.

Protectionism sometimes takes on almost comic proportions. Neither Europe nor the United States grows bananas, but both European and U.S. firms buy and sell bananas in foreign markets. Problems arose when the EU put a quota on bananas imported from Latin America—a market dominated by two U.S. firms, Chiquita and Dole—in order to help firms based in current and former European colonies in the Caribbean. To retaliate, the United States imposed a 100-percent tariff on certain luxury products imported from Europe, including Louis Vuitton handbags, Scottish cashmere sweaters, and Parma ham.

LOCAL CONTENT LAW law requiring that products sold in a particular country be at least partly made there

Local Content Laws Many countries, including the United States, have **local content laws**—requirements that products sold in a country be at least partly made there. Firms seeking to do business in a country must either invest there directly or take on a domestic partner. In this way, some of the profits from doing business in a foreign country stay there rather than flow out to another nation. In some cases, the partnership arrangement is optional but wise. In Mexico, for instance, Radio Shack de México is a joint venture owned by Tandy Corp. (49 percent) and Mexico's Grupo Gigante (51 percent). This allows the retailer to promote a strong Mexican identity; it also makes it easier to address certain import regulations that are easier for Mexican than for U.S. firms. Both China and India currently require that when a foreign firm enters into a joint venture with a local firm, the local partner must have the controlling ownership stake.

BUSINESS PRACTICE LAW law or regulation governing business practices in given countries

Business Practice Laws Many businesses entering new markets encounter problems in complying with stringent regulations and bureaucratic obstacles. Such practices are affected by the **business practice laws** by which host countries govern business practices within their jurisdictions. As part of its entry strategy in Germany, Wal-Mart has had to buy existing retailers rather than open brand-new stores. Why? Because the German government is not currently issuing new licenses to sell food products. Wal-Mart also had to stop refunding price differences on items sold for less by other stores because the practice is illegal in Germany. Finally, Wal-Mart must comply with business-hour restrictions: Stores can't open before 7:00 A.M., must close by 8:00 P.M. on weeknights and 4:00 P.M. on Saturday, and must remain closed on Sunday.

CARTEL association of producers whose purpose is to control supply and prices

Cartels and Dumping Sometimes, a legal—even an accepted—practice in one country is illegal in another. In some South American countries, for example, it is sometimes legal to bribe business and government officials. The existence of **cartels**—associations of producers that control supply and prices—gives tremendous power to some nations, such as those belonging to the Organization of Petroleum Exporting Countries (OPEC). U.S. law forbids both bribery and cartels.

DUMPING practice of selling a product abroad for less than the cost of production

Finally, many (but not all) countries forbid **dumping**—selling a product abroad for less than the cost of production at home. U.S. antidumping legislation sets two conditions for determining whether dumping is being practiced:

1 Products are being priced at "less than fair value."
2 The result unfairly harms domestic industry.

Just a few years ago, the United States charged Japan and Brazil with dumping steel at prices 70 percent below normal value. To protect local manufacturers, the U.S. government imposed a significant tariff on steel imported from those countries.

SELF-CHECK QUESTIONS 7–9

You should now be able to answer Self-Check Questions 7–9.*

7 Multiple Choice Which of the following does **not** serve as a barrier to international trade?
(a) social differences
(b) legal differences
(c) economic differences
(d) transportation differences

8 Multiple Choice Which of the following is **not** a legal barrier to international trade:

(a) quotas and tariffs
(b) exchange rate parameters
(c) local content laws
(d) business practice laws

9 True/False Protectionism refers to the practice of hiring local mobsters to protect a foreign company from local competitors.

*Answers to Self-Check Questions 7–9 can be found on p. 564.

CONTINUED FROM PAGE 108

MARIACHI BANDS AND OTHER WEAPONS OF THE RETAIL WARS

In mid-2006 Wal-Mart took a careful look at its international efforts. Company officials decided that the firm's operations in Germany and South Korea were simply losing too much money and announced plans to close them. In Germany, for example, Wal-Mart had never really been able to learn what makes customers choose to shop at one store over another; the company had also underestimated the competitiveness of other retailers in Germany. But not all the news was bad. Wal-Mart's joint venture in China was doing well, and its newest operation in India is showing considerable potential. And it is still the market leader in the United States, Canada, and Mexico, and has a solidly profitable operation in the United Kingdom.

QUESTIONS FOR DISCUSSION

Wal-Mart's entry into a new market is a nightmare for a lot of retailers.

—Retail consultant
Michael P. Godliman

1 What are some of the advantages that Wal-Mart hopes to gain by globalization? What are some of the challenges that it faces in its efforts to globalize?

2 What methods has Wal-Mart used to globalize? Are they the most appropriate methods for the firm? Why or why not?

3 In an effort to reduce trade barriers, nations are entering into more international agreements. In your opinion, will this trend help or hurt Wal-Mart?

SUMMARY OF LEARNING OBJECTIVES

1 Discuss the rise of international business and describe the major world marketplaces and trade agreements and alliances.

Several forces combine to sustain *globalization*: (1) Governments and businesses are more aware of the benefits of globalization; (2) new technologies make international travel, communication, and commerce faster and cheaper; (3) competitive pressures sometimes force firms to expand into foreign markets just to keep up with competitors; (4) treaties and trade agreements also play a major role. The most important influences are (1) the *North American Free Trade Agreement* (*NAFTA*); (2) the *European Union* (*EU*); and (3) the *General Agreement on Tariffs and Trade* (*GATT*) and the *World Trade Organization* (*WTO*). The contemporary world economy revolves around three major marketplaces: North America, Europe, and Asia.

2 Explain how differences in import-export balances, exchange rates, and foreign competition determine the ways in which countries and businesses respond to the international environment.

A nation's *balance of trade* is the total economic value of all products that it exports minus the total economic value of all products that it imports. When a country's imports exceed its exports—when it has a *negative balance of trade*—it suffers a *trade deficit*; a *positive balance of trade* occurs when exports exceed imports, resulting in a *trade surplus*. The *balance of payments* refers to the flow of money into or out of a country.

An *exchange rate* is the rate at which one nation's currency can be exchanged for that of another. Under *floating exchange rates*, the value of one currency relative to that of another varies with market conditions.

Countries *export* what they can produce better or less expensively than other countries and use the proceeds to *import* what they can't produce as effectively. Economists once focused on two forms of advantage to explain international trade: *absolute advantage* and *comparative advantage*. Today, the theory of *national competitive advantage* is a widely accepted model of why nations engage in international trade.

3 Discuss the factors involved in deciding to do business internationally and in selecting the appropriate levels of international involvement and international organizational structure.

Several factors enter into the decision to go international. One overriding factor is the *business climate* in other nations. A company should also consider at least two other issues: (1) Is there a *demand* for its products abroad? (2) If so, must it *adapt* those products for international consumption?

After deciding to go international, a firm must decide on its level of involvement. Several levels are possible: (1) *exporters and importers*; (2) *international firms*; and (3) *multinational firms*. Different levels of involvement require different kinds of organizational structure. The spectrum of international organizational strategies includes the following: (1) *independent agents*; (2) *licensing arrangements*; (3) *branch offices*; (4) *strategic alliances* (or *joint ventures*); and (5) *foreign direct investment* (*FDI*).

4 Describe some of the ways in which social, cultural, economic, legal, and political differences among nations affect international business.

Some social and cultural differences, like language, are obvious, but a wide range of subtle value differences can also affect operations. Economic differences can be fairly pronounced. Common legal and political issues in international business include *quotas, tariffs, subsidies, local content laws,* and *business practice laws*.

KEY TERMS

absolute advantage (p. 120)

Association of Southeast Asian Nations (ASEAN) (p. 114)

balance of payments (p. 117)

balance of trade (p. 115)

branch office (p. 126)

business practice law (p. 130)

cartel (p. 130)

comparative advantage (p. 120)

dumping (p. 130)

embargo (p. 129)

euro (p. 119)

European Union (EU) (p. 113)

exchange rate (p. 119)

export (p. 109)

exporter (p. 124)

foreign direct investment (FDI) (p. 126)

General Agreement on Tariffs and Trade (GATT) (p. 114)

globalization (p. 108)

import (p. 109)

importer (p. 124)

independent agent (p. 125)

international firm (p. 124)

licensing arrangement (p. 125)

local content law (p. 130)

multinational firm (p. 124)

national competitive advantage (p. 120)

North American Free Trade Agreement (NAFTA) (p. 112)

offshoring (p. 124)

outsourcing (p. 123)

protectionism (p. 129)

quota (p. 127)

strategic alliances (p. 126)

subsidy (p. 129)

tariff (p. 129)

trade deficit (p. 116)

trade surplus (p. 116)

World Trade Organization (WTO) (p. 114)

QUESTIONS AND EXERCISES

Questions for Review

1 How does the balance of trade differ from the balance of payments?

2 What are the three possible levels of involvement in international business? Give examples of each.

3 How does a country's economic system affect the decisions of foreign firms interested in doing business there?

4 What aspects of the culture in your state or region would be of particular interest to a foreign firm thinking about locating there?

Questions for Analysis

5 List all the major items in your bedroom, including furnishings. Try to identify the country in which each item was made. Offer possible reasons why a given nation might have a comparative advantage in producing a given good.

6 Suppose that you're the manager of a small firm seeking to enter the international arena. What basic information would you need about the market that you're thinking of entering?

7 Do you support protectionist tariffs for the United States? If so, in what instances and for what reasons? If not, why not?

8 Do you think that a firm operating internationally is better advised to adopt a single standard of ethical conduct or to adapt to local conditions? Under what kinds of conditions might each approach be preferable?

Application Exercises

9 Interview the manager of a local firm that does at least some business internationally. Why did the company decide to go international? Describe the level of the firm's international involvement and the organizational structure(s) it uses for international operations.

10 Select a product familiar to you. Using library reference works to gain some insight into the culture of India, identify the problems that might arise in trying to market this product to Indian consumers.

FINDING YOUR PLACE

Goal

To encourage you to apply global business strategies to a small-business situation.

Background Information

Some people might say that Yolanda Lang is a bit too confident. Others might say that she needs confidence—and more—to succeed in the business she's chosen. But one thing is certain: Lang is determined to grow INDE, her handbag design company, into a global enterprise. At only 28 years of age, she has time on her side—if she makes the right business moves now.

These days, Lang spends most of her time in Milan, Italy. Backed by $50,000 of her parents' personal savings, she is trying to compete with Gucci, Fendi, and other high-end handbag makers. Her target market is American women willing to spend $200 on a purse. Ironically, Lang was forced to set up shop in Italy because of the snobbishness of these customers, who buy high-end bags only if they're European-made. "Strangely enough," she muses, "I need to be in Europe to sell in America."

To succeed, she must first find ways to keep production costs down—a tough task for a woman in a male-dominated business culture. Her fluent Italian is an advantage, but she's often forced to turn down inappropriate dinner invitations. She also has to figure out how to get her 22-bag collection into stores worldwide. Retailers are showing her bags in Italy and Japan, but she's had little luck in the United States. "I intend to be a global company," says Lang. The question is how to succeed first as a small business.

Method

Step 1

Join together with three or four other students to discuss the steps that Lang has taken so far to break into the U.S. retail market. These steps include:

- Buying a mailing list of 5,000 shoppers from high-end department store Neiman Marcus and selling directly to these customers.

- Linking with a manufacturer's representative to sell her line in major U.S. cities while she herself concentrates on Europe.

Step 2

Based on what you learned in this chapter, suggest other strategies that might help Lang grow her business. Working with group members, consider whether the following options would help or hurt Lang's business. Explain why a strategy is likely to work or likely to fail.

- Lang could relocate to the United States and sell abroad through an independent agent.
- Lang could relocate to the United States and set up a branch office in Italy.
- Lang could find a partner in Italy and form a strategic alliance that would allow her to build her business on both continents.

FOLLOW-UP QUESTIONS

1 What are the most promising steps that Lang can take to grow her business? What are the least promising?

2 Lang thinks that her trouble breaking into the U.S. retail market stems from the fact that her company is unknown. How would this circumstance affect the strategies suggested in Steps 1 and 2?

3 When Lang deals with Italian manufacturers, she is a young woman in a man's world. Often she must convince men that her purpose is business and nothing else. How should Lang handle personal invitations that get in the way of business? How can she say no while still maintaining business relationships? Why is it often difficult for American women to do business in male-dominated cultures?

4 The American consulate has given Lang little business help because her products are made in Italy. Do you think the consulate's treatment of an American businessperson is fair or unfair? Explain your answer.

5 Do you think Lang's relocation to Italy will pay off? Why or why not?

6 With Lang's goals of creating a global company, can INDE continue to be a one-person operation?

PAYING HEED TO FOREIGN PRACTICES

The Situation

Assume that you're an up-and-coming manager in a regional U.S. distribution company. Firms in your industry are just beginning to enter foreign markets, and you've been assigned to head up your company's new operations in a Latin American country. Because at least two of your competitors are also trying to enter this same market, your boss wants you to move as quickly as possible. You also sense that your success in this assignment will likely determine your future with the company.

You have just completed meetings with local government officials, and you're pessimistic about your ability to get things moving quickly. You've learned, for example, that it will take 10 months to get a building permit for a needed facility. Moreover, once the building's up, it will take another 6 months to get utilities. Finally, the phone company says that it may take up to two years to install the phone lines that you need for high-speed Internet access.

The Dilemma

Various officials have indicated that time frames could be considerably shortened if you were willing to pay special "fees." You realize that these "fees" are bribes, and you're well aware that the practice of paying such "fees" is both unethical and illegal in the United States. In this foreign country, however, it's not illegal and not even considered unethical. Moreover, if you don't pay and one of your competitors does, you'll be at a major competitive disadvantage. In any case, your boss isn't likely to understand the long lead times necessary to get the operation running. Fortunately, you have access to a source of funds that you could spend without the knowledge of anyone in the home office.

QUESTIONS TO ADDRESS

1 What are the key ethical issues in this situation?
2 What do you think most managers would do in this situation?
3 What would you do?

WEIGHING THE TRADEOFFS

The Situation

A medium-size regional banking corporation has its headquarters in a small city in the Midwestern United States. The firm is privately owned; all managers own stock in the bank corporation. The company's senior managers (and majority owners) have decided to sell the bank to a major international banking company within the next two to three years. First, though, the bank corporation needs to trim its expenses in order to make it more attractive to a potential buyer.

The Dilemma

Because the bank corporation has been a locally owned and operated enterprise, it has maintained a full slate of operations within the local market. For instance, its corporate offices, many banking outlets, and all of its support activities are housed locally. The latter category includes a large call center—a staff of 300 people who handle most customer calls with questions about their accounts.

There has been a growing trend in banking, though, to outsource call centers to foreign countries, most notably India. Such markets have an abundance of potential English-speaking employees, excellent technology, and low wages. One senior manager has argued that the bank corporation should outsource its call center immediately. This would enable the firm to lower its costs, thus making it even more attractive to a potential buyer. When confronted with the prospect of cutting 300 jobs, the manager acknowledges that that will be tough but is certain that any buyer will eventually do the same anyway.

Another vocal senior manager, though, is opposed to this idea. This person argues that because the bank corporation was started locally and has longstanding ties throughout the local community, it should maintain its current operations until the bank is sold. Then, this manager argues, if a new owner decides to cut jobs, "it will be on their conscience, not ours."

Team Activity

Assemble a group of four students and assign each group member to one of the following roles:
- Senior manager (majority owner) of the bank
- Call center employee
- Bank customer
- Bank corporation investor

ACTION STEPS

1 Before hearing any of your group's comments on this situation, and from the perspective of your assigned role, do you think that the call center should be outsourced immediately? Write down the reasons for your position.

2 Before hearing any of your group's comments on this situation, and from the perspective of your assigned role, what are the underlying ethical issues, if any, in this situation? Write down the issues.

3 Gather your group together and reveal, in turn, each member's comments on whether the call center should be outsourced immediately. Next, reveal the ethical issues listed by each member.

4 Appoint someone to record main points of agreement and disagreement within the group. How do you explain the results? What accounts for any disagreement?

5 From an ethical standpoint, what does your group conclude is the most appropriate action for the bank to take in this situation?

6 Develop a group response to the following question: Can your team identify other solutions that might help satisfy both senior managers' views?

PART 1: THE CONTEMPORARY BUSINESS ENVIRONMENT

Goal of the Exercise

In Chapter 3 we discussed how the starting point for virtually every new business is a *business plan*. Business plans describe the business strategy for any new business and demonstrate how that strategy will be implemented. One benefit of a business plan is that in preparing it, would be entrepreneurs must develop their idea on paper and firm up their thinking about how to launch their business before investing time and money in it. In this exercise, you'll get started on creating your own business plan.

Exercise Background: Part 1 of the Business Plan

The starting point for any business plan is coming up with a "great idea." This might be a business that you've already considered setting up. If you don't have ideas for a business already, look around. What are some businesses that you come into contact with on a regular basis? Restaurants, childcare services, and specialty stores are a few examples you might consider. You may also wish to create a business that is connected with a talent or interest you have, such as crafts, cooking, or car repair. It's important that you create a company from "scratch" rather than use a company that already exists. You'll learn more if you use your own ideas.

Once you have your business idea, your next step is to create an "identity" for your business. This includes determining a name for your business and an idea of what your business will do. It also includes identifying the type of ownership your business will take, topics we discussed in Chapter 3. The first part of the plan also briefly looks at who your ideal customers are as well as how your business will stand out from the crowd. Part 1 of the plan also looks at how the business will interact with the community and demonstrate social responsibility, topics we discussed in Chapter 2. Finally, almost all business plans today include a perspective on the impact of global business.

Your Assignment

Step 1

To complete this assignment, you first need to download the *Business Plan Student Template* file from the book's Companion Website at www.prenhall.com/ebert. This is a Microsoft Word file you can use to complete you business plan. For this assignment, you will fill in "Part 1" of the plan.

Step 2

Once you have the *Business Plan Student Template* file, you can begin to answer the following questions in "Part 1: The Contemporary Business Environment."

1 What is the name of your business?
   Hint: When you think of the name of your business, make sure that it captures the spirit of the business you're creating.

2 What will your business do?
   Hint: Imagine that you are explaining your idea to a family member or a friend. Keep your description to 30 words or less.

3 What form of business ownership (sole proprietorship, partnership, or corporation) will your business take? Why did you choose this form?
   Hint: For more information on types of business ownership, refer to the discussion in Chapter 3.

4 Briefly describe your ideal customer. What are they like in terms of age, income level, and so on?
   Hint: You don't have to give too much detail in this part of the plan; you'll provide more details about customers and marketing in later parts of the plan.

5 Why will customers choose to buy from your business instead of your competition?
   Hint: In this section, describe what will be unique about your business. For example, is the product special or will you offer the product at a lower price?

6 All businesses have to deal with ethical issues. One way to address these issues is to create a code of ethics. List three core principles your business will follow.
   Hint: To help you consider the ethical issues that your business might face, refer to the discussion in Chapter 2.

7 A business shows social responsibility by respecting all of its stakeholders. What steps will you take to create a socially responsible business?
   Hint: Refer to the discussion of social responsibility in Chapter 2. What steps can you take to be a "good citizen" in the community? Consider also how you may need to be socially responsible toward your customers and, if applicable, investors, employees, and suppliers.

8 Will you sell your product in another country? If so, what countries and why? What challenges will you face?
   Hint: To help you consider issues of global business, refer to Chapter 4. Consider how you will expand internationally (i.e., independent agent, licensing, etc.). Do you expect global competition for your product? What advantages will foreign competitors have?

Note: Once you have answered the questions, save your Word document. You'll be answering additional questions in later chapters.

VIDEO EXERCISE

GLOBALIZING THE LONG ARM OF THE LAW: PRINTRAK

Learning Objectives

The purpose of this video is to help you:

1 Understand how and why a company adapts to the needs of foreign customers.
2 Identify the levels of international involvement that are available to companies.
3 Discuss the differences that can affect a company's international operations.

Synopsis

Scotland Yard and the Canadian Mounties are only two of the many organizations around the world that use security technology from Printrak, a Motorola company. Starting with a computerized fingerprint-management system, Printrak has added a number of security and criminal information products as it has expanded from its California headquarters to serve customers around the globe. General Manager Darren Reilly and his management team study each country's legal, political, economic, and cultural differences and analyze local demand and customer needs. Rather than invest in local plants and equipment, Printrak works through local sales agents to ensure that products are marketed in a culturally savvy way. Despite country-by-country differences in business customs and ethics, the decisions and actions of Printrak employees are guided by Motorola's code of conduct.

DISCUSSION QUESTIONS

1 **For analysis**: What are some of the barriers that affect Printrak's ability to do business in foreign markets?
2 **For analysis**: From Printrak's perspective, what are the advantages and disadvantages of hiring and training local sales agents to work with customers in each foreign market?
3 **For application**: In addition to establishing user committees, what else should Printrak do to track changing customer needs in other countries?
4 **For application**: How would you suggest that Printrak build on its relations with "beachhead customers" to expand in particular regions?
5 **For debate**: Printrak employees and managers must comply with Motorola's global ethics policy. Should local sales agents be allowed to take any actions they deem necessary to make sales in local markets, regardless of Motorola's policy? Support your chosen position.

Online Exploration

Use a search engine, such as Google, to research security technologies, such as computerized fingerprint-management systems. Who are Printrak's main global competitors? Who may the main global customers be? Are you able to find any news releases about security companies, such as Printrak, with international operations? Finally, do you think companies like Printrak should translate some or all of their Web site to accommodate foreign customers? Explain your response.

PART II:
THE BUSINESS OF MANAGING

After reading this chapter, you should be able to:

1 Describe the nature of management and identify the four basic functions that constitute the management process.

2 Identify different types of managers likely to be found in an organization by level and area.

3 Describe the basic skills required of managers.

4 Explain the importance of strategic management and effective goal setting in organizational success.

5 Discuss contingency planning and crisis management in today's business world.

6 Describe the development and explain the importance of corporate culture.

THE BUSINESS OF BAGGING CUSTOMERS

Fickle customers and rapid changes make planning difficult in the high-end fashion industry. Most fashion designers—Ralph Lauren, Donna Karan, Prada, Gucci, Fendi—have adopted a design-driven business model, in which the designer dictates style to the customers. Coach, however, has taken a different approach. The company asks the customers what they want

BUSINESS MANAGEMENT

and then provides it. Coach's customer focus has created a competitive advantage for the firm, which annually sells $865 of merchandise for every square foot of store space, compared to an industry average of $200 to $300.

Coach started out in 1941 making virtually indestructible, high-quality handbags. In the 1970s it was bought by Sara Lee Corporation, a big company pursuing a strategy of diversification. However, Coach's products were not stylish, and sales languished. Because it was just one of literally dozens of businesses owned by Sara Lee at the time, the company suffered from the lack of focused management attention. CEO Lew Frankfort knew the company was failing and said, "We were about to hit a wall." Frankfort also knew that the company's success depended on finding the right industry niche. Finally, in 2000, he convinced Sara Lee to spin off Coach as an independent company, and he wanted the job of turning it around.

To be successful you need to live your business. You have to understand it organically and thoroughly.

—Coach CEO Lew Frankfort

Frankfort wanted to attract high-end fashion's elite customers but remain an affordable luxury for customers who must save for a $200 bag. But how could Coach find and maintain that delicate balance? For help, he first turned to planning and forecasting. He said, "To be successful you need to live your business. You have to understand it organically and thoroughly."

He introduced many new analytical tools for tracking market trends, evaluating effectiveness, and managing risk. The firm's leaders look at sales data for each store and each product type on a daily basis, and several times daily during busy seasons. But extensive and intensive customer research remains the cornerstone of his planning. The company spends $2 million per year on surveys. The surveys are supplemented with one-on-one interviews with customers from locations around the world, to quiz them on everything from appearance and quality to the correct length for a shoulder strap.

"The tremendous amount of testing they do differentiates them from a lot of other fashion companies," says industry analyst Robert Ohmes. Analyst Bob Drbul says, "Their execution and business planning is in the league of a Wal-Mart or a Target" (two much larger firms known for their effective business planning). To test new products, they are first shown to selected buyers in 12 worldwide markets, to gauge initial customer reaction. An initial demand forecast is then made, and six months before introduction, they are tested in another 12 markets. At launch time, sales are monitored closely and adjustments made quickly.

For example, an unexpected spike in sales was investigated, and managers found that buying by Hispanic customers was increasing. Within a week, the firm had moved up the opening date of a South Miami store and begun advertising in Spanish for the first time. Frankfort understands that, to be effective, plans must be translated into appropriate actions. "Not only do you need to know your business and your customers . . . you also need to be nimble to adapt," he claims. ■

Our opening story continues on page 164.

WHAT'S IN IT FOR ME?

Lew Frankfort is clearly an effective manager, and he understands how to carry out his responsibilities to help Coach continue to grow and prosper. After reading this chapter, you'll be better positioned to carry out various management responsibilities yourself. And from the perspective of a consumer or investor, you'll be able to more effectively assess and appreciate the quality of management in various companies.

In this chapter, we explore the importance of strategic management and effective goal setting to organizational success. We also examine the functions that constitute the management process and identify different types of managers likely to be found in an organization by level and area. Along the way, we look at basic management skills and explain the importance of corporate culture. But first, let's look at some profiles of some well-known managers.

WHO ARE MANAGERS?

All corporations depend on effective management. Regardless of whether they run a growing business like Coach or a small local fashion boutique, managers perform many of the same functions, are responsible for many of the same tasks, and have many of the same responsibilities. The work of all managers involves developing strategic and tactical plans. Along with numerous other activities, they must analyze their competitive environments and plan, organize, direct, and control day-to-day operations.

Although our focus is on managers in business settings, remember that the principles of management apply to all kinds of organizations. Managers work in charities, churches, social organizations, educational institutions, and government agencies. The prime minister of Canada, curators at the Museum of Modern Art, the dean of your college, and the chief administrator of your local hospital are all managers. Remember, too, that managers bring to small organizations much the same kinds of skills—the ability to make decisions and respond to a variety of challenges—that they bring to large ones.

Regardless of the nature and size of an organization, managers are among its most important resources. Consider the profiles of the following three managers:

■ Texas native Marjorie Scardino runs Pearson PLC, a huge British media company. When she was named CEO, Pearson was considered a stodgy company that had diversified into too many different areas. Scardino set about systematically pruning unrelated businesses and sharpening the firm's focus into three basic business groups. One group is heavily involved in educational publishing; the second operates the *Financial Times*, a leading business newspaper; and the third consists of the Penguin publishing group. The current economic climate has limited her ability to look for new acquisitions. Instead, she is looking for ways to increase efficiency and lower costs. If she is successful, Pearson will be well positioned for new growth when economic conditions improve. The high marks she receives from analysts have her firmly in control of the media giant, and she is routinely placed among the most powerful women executives in the world.[1]

■ Kenneth Chenault is considered one of the best senior managers around. He joined American Express (AmEx) in 1981 as a marketing specialist and then worked his way up to become president in 1997. During the next two years, Chenault presided over a major overhaul at AmEx as the firm sought to undo an ill-fated diversification strategy undertaken by a previous CEO. So impressive was Chenault's performance

(a)

(b)

As top managers, (a) Marjorie Scardino (Pearson PLC), (b) Kenneth Chenault (American Express), and (c) Steve Reinemund (Pepsi) are important resources for their companies. In particular, they set the strategic direction for their companies and provide leadership to others. They are also accountable to shareholders, employees, customers, and other key constituents for the performance and effectiveness of their businesses.

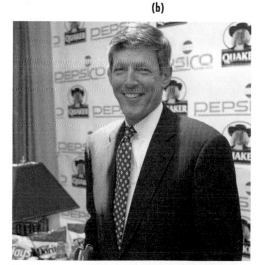

(c)

that in 2001 he was named chairman and CEO of the company. Having reorganized a huge number of services at AmEx into four core businesses, Chenault has AmEx on solid footing and a set a path of consistent growth and expansion.[2]

■ Steve Reinemund is CEO of Pepsi. Perhaps more significantly, he is also the manager who did what many experts thought was impossible—he has (at least for the moment) led Pepsi to levels of revenue and profit that exceed those of its archrival Coca-Cola. Well, that's not entirely true. Coca-Cola still sells more soda than Pepsi; but Pepsi is also a giant in other markets as well—bottled water (Aquafina), for instance, as well as sports drinks (Gatorade) and snack foods (Frito-Lay). Reinemund, an ex-marine, credits his success to detail—he understands the importance of setting clear goals, setting his expectations in precise language, and outlining exactly when things need to get done. Moreover, Reinemund has shown an uncanny knack for leading his company to the forefront of just about every twist and turn in consumer tastes. Most recently, for instance, Pepsi bought Sobe, a rapidly growing enterprise in the so-called New Age beverage business and established a lucrative partnership with Starbucks to distribute bottled-coffee products like Frappuccinos.[3]

Although Marjorie Scardino, Kenneth Chenault, and Steve Reinemund are clearly different people who work in different kinds of organizations and have different approaches to what they do, they also share one thing in common with other high-level managers: responsibility for the performance and effectiveness of the businesses for which they work. They are accountable to shareholders, employees, customers, and other key constituents. Now let's take a look at the actual process of management.

THE MANAGEMENT PROCESS

MANAGEMENT process of planning, organizing, leading, and controlling an organization's resources to achieve its goals

Management is the process of planning, organizing, leading, and controlling an organization's financial, physical, human, and information resources to achieve its goals. Managers oversee the use of all these resources in their respective firms. All aspects of a manager's job are interrelated. Any given manager is likely to be engaged in each of these activities during the course of any given day.

■■■ PLANNING

PLANNING management process of determining what an organization needs to do and how best to get it done

Determining what the organization needs to do and how best to get it done requires planning. **Planning** has three main components. It begins when managers determine the firm's goals. Next, they develop a comprehensive *strategy* for achieving those goals. After a strategy is developed, they design *tactical and operational plans* for implementing the strategy. We discuss these three components in more detail later in this chapter.

When Yahoo! was created, for example, the firm's top managers set a strategic goal of becoming a top firm in the then-emerging market for Internet search engines. But then came the hard part—figuring out how to do it. The company started by assessing the ways in which people actually use the Web and concluded that users wanted to be able to satisfy a wide array of needs, preferences, and priorities by going to as few sites as possible to find what they were looking for. One key component of Yahoo!'s strategy was to foster partnerships and relationships with other companies so that potential Web surfers could draw upon several sources through a single site, or portal—which would be Yahoo!. The goal of partnering emerged as one set of *tactical plans* for moving forward.

Yahoo! managers then began fashioning alliances with such diverse partners as Reuters, Standard & Poor's, and the Associated Press (for news coverage), RE/Max (for real estate information), and a wide array of information providers specializing in sports, weather, entertainment, shopping, and travel. The creation of individual partnership agreements with each of these partners represents a form of *operational planning*.

▪▪▪ ORGANIZING

Managers must also organize people and resources. For example, some businesses prepare charts that diagram the various jobs within the company and how those jobs relate to one another. These so-called *organization charts* help everyone understand roles and reporting relationships, key parts of the organizing function. Some businesses go so far as to post their organization chart on a office wall. But in most larger businesses, roles and reporting relationships, while important, may be too complex to draw as a simple box-and-line diagram. To better appreciate the complexities and importance of organizing in a big business, let's consider the following example.

Once one of the leading-edge, high-tech firms in the world, Hewlett-Packard (HP) began to lose some of its luster a few years ago. Ironically, one of the major reasons for its slide could be traced back to what had once been a major strength. Specifically, HP had long prided itself on being little more than a corporate confederation of individual businesses. Sometimes, these businesses even ended up competing among themselves. This approach had been beneficial for much of the firm's history: It was easier for each business to make its own decisions quickly and efficiently, and the competition kept each unit on its toes. By the late 1990s, however, problems had become apparent, and no one could quite figure out what was going on.

Enter Ann Livermore, then head of the firm's software and services business. Livermore realized that the structure that had served so well in the past was now holding the firm back. To regain its competitive edge, HP needed an integrated, organizationwide strategy. Unfortunately, the company's highly decentralized organization made that impossible. Livermore led the charge to create one organization united behind one strategic plan. "I felt we could be the most powerful company in the industry," she said, "if we could get our hardware, software, and services aligned." Eventually, a new team of top managers was handed control of the company, and every major component of the firm's structure was reorganized. As a result, while the firm still has a long way to go, it appears to be back on solid footing and set to regain its place as one of the world's preeminent technology businesses.[4] The process that was used to revive HP—determining the best way to arrange a business's resources and activities into a coherent structure—is called **organizing**. We explore organizing in more detail in Chapter 6.

ORGANIZING management process of determining how best to arrange an organization's resources and activities into a coherent structure

▪▪▪ LEADING

Managers have the power to give orders and demand results. Leading, however, involves more complex activities. When **leading**, a manager works to guide and motivate employees to meet the firm's objectives. Legendary management figures like Walt Disney, Sam Walton (of Wal-Mart), and Herb Kelleher (of Southwestern Airlines) had the capacity to unite their employees in a clear and targeted manner and motivate them to work in the best interests of their employer. Their employees respected them, trusted them, and believed that by working together, both the firm and themselves as individuals would benefit. Today, Steve Reinemund is a master at motivating his employees. For example, while on a ski vacation recently he was picking up supplies at a convenience store when he noticed a Frito-Lay truck driver pulling up to unload a delivery of chips. Reinemund put his own purchases aside and helped the driver with his job.

LEADING management process of guiding and motivating employees to meet an organization's objectives

eBay CEO Meg Whitman understands the importance of human relations in a business. At conventions where 10,000 of eBay's 28 million customers gather to communicate without the medium of cyberspace, Whitman autographs (collectible) eBay trading cards of herself, and depends on ordinary users to tell her what works and what doesn't work at the online auction company.

On the other hand, other managers have been noticeably lacking in their ability to lead others. As detailed in our Prologue, former Montgomery Ward CEO Avery Sewell was by any measure a poor leader. In more recent times, many of the top managers at the Federal Emergency Management Agency (FEMA) came under fire for their poor leadership and decision making after Hurricane Katrina. We discuss leadership and decision making more fully in Chapter 9.

■■■ CONTROLLING

CONTROLLING management process of monitoring an organization's performance to ensure that it is meeting its goals

Controlling is the process of monitoring a firm's performance to make sure that it is meeting its goals. All CEOs must pay close attention to costs and performance. Managers at Continental Airlines, for example, focus almost relentlessly on numerous indicators of performance that they can constantly measure and adjust. Everything from on-time arrivals to baggage-handling errors to the number of empty seats on an airplane to surveys of employee and customer satisfaction are regularly and routinely monitored. If on-time arrivals start to slip, managers focus on the problem and get it fixed. If customers complain too much about the food, catering managers figure out how to improve. As a result, no single element of the firm's performance can slip too far before it's noticed and fixed.

Figure 5.1 illustrates the control process that begins when management establishes standards, often for financial performance. If, for example, a company sets a goal of increasing its sales by 20 percent over the next 10 years, an appropriate standard to assess progress toward the 20-percent goal might be an increase of about 2 percent a year.

Managers then measure actual performance each year against standards. If the two amounts agree, the organization continues along its present course. If they vary significantly, however, one or the other needs adjustment. If sales have increased 2.1 percent by the end of the first year, things are probably fine. If sales have dropped 1 percent, some revision in plans may be needed. Perhaps the original goal should be lowered or more money should be spent on advertising.

Control can also show where performance is running better than expected and can serve as a basis for providing rewards or reducing costs. For example, when Chevrolet recently introduced the Super Sport Roadster (a classic, late-1940s pickup-style vehicle with a two-seat roadster design), the firm thought it had a major hit on its hands. But

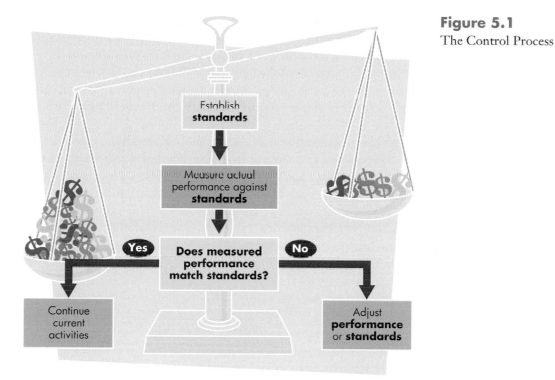

Figure 5.1
The Control Process

poor sales led to Chevrolet's decision to suspend production of the vehicle. On the other hand, after the distributor of the surprise 2005 hit movie *The March of the Penguins* saw how popular the movie was becoming, the firm was able to increase advertising and distribution even more, making the niche movie into a major commercial success.

TYPES OF MANAGERS

Although all managers plan, organize, lead, and control, not all managers have the same degree of responsibility for these activities. It is helpful to classify managers according to levels and areas of responsibility.

■■■ LEVELS OF MANAGEMENT

The three basic levels of management are *top*, *middle*, and *first-line* management. Most firms have more middle managers than top managers and more first-line managers than middle managers. Both the power of managers and the complexity of their duties increase as they move up the ladder.

Top Managers Like Marjorie Scardino, Kenneth Chenault, and Steve Reinemund, the fairly small number of executives who get the chance to guide the fortunes of most companies are top managers. Common titles for top managers include *president, vice president, treasurer, chief executive officer* (CEO), and *chief financial officer* (CFO). **Top managers** are responsible for the overall performance and effectiveness of the firm. They set general policies, formulate strategies, approve all significant decisions, and represent the company in dealings with other firms and with government bodies.

TOP MANAGER manager responsible for a firm's overall performance and effectiveness

Middle Managers Just below the ranks of top managers is another group of managers who also occupy positions of considerable autonomy and importance and who are called middle managers. Titles such as *plant manager, operations manager*, and *division*

MIDDLE MANAGER manager responsible for implementing the strategies and working toward the goals set by top managers

manager designate middle-management slots. In general, **middle managers** are responsible for implementing the strategies and working toward the goals set by top managers. For example, if top management decides to introduce a new product in 12 months or to cut costs by 5 percent in the next quarter, middle management must decide how to meet these goals. The manager of an AmEx service center, a Pearson distribution center, or a regional sales manager of Frito-Lay snack products will likely be a middle manager.

First-Line Managers Those who hold such titles as *supervisor*, *office manager*, *project manager*, and *group leader* are **first-line managers**. Although they spend most of their time working with and supervising the employees who report to them, first-line managers' activities are not limited to that arena. At a building site, for example, the project manager not only ensures that workers are carrying out construction as specified by the architect, but also interacts extensively with materials suppliers, community officials, and middle- and upper-level managers at the home office. A sales manager for Pearson's Educational Publishing Group and the supervisor of delivery drivers for Frito-Lay products in a city would also be considered first-line managers.

FIRST-LINE MANAGER manager responsible for supervising the work of employees

■■■ AREAS OF MANAGEMENT

In any large company, top, middle, and first-line managers work in a variety of areas, including human resources, operations, marketing, information, and finance. For the most part, these areas correspond to the types of basic management skills described later in this chapter and to the wide range of business principles and activities discussed in the rest of this book.

Human Resource Managers Most companies have *human resource managers* who hire and train employees, evaluate performance, and determine compensation. At large firms, separate departments deal with recruiting and hiring, wage and salary levels, and labor relations. A smaller firm may have a single department—or a single person—responsible for all human resource activities. (We discuss some key issues in human resource management in Chapter 10.)

Operations Managers As we will see in Chapter 7, the term *operations* refers to the systems by which a firm produces goods and services. Among other duties, *operations managers* are responsible for production, inventory, and quality control. Manufacturing companies such as Texas Instruments, Ford, and Caterpillar have a strong need for operations managers at many levels. Such firms typically have a *vice president for operations* (top manager), *plant managers* (middle managers), and *production supervisors* (first-line managers). In recent years, sound operations management practices have become increasingly important to a variety of service organizations.

Marketing Managers As we will see in Chapter 11, marketing encompasses the development, pricing, promotion, and distribution of goods and services. *Marketing managers* are responsible for getting products from producers to consumers. Marketing is especially important for firms that manufacture consumer products, such as Procter & Gamble, Coca-Cola, and Levi Strauss. Such firms often have large numbers of marketing managers at several levels. For example, a large consumer products firm is likely to have a *vice president for marketing* (top manager), several *regional marketing managers* (middle managers), and several *district sales managers* (first-line managers).

Information Managers Occupying a fairly new managerial position in many firms, *information managers* design and implement systems to gather, organize, and distribute

Japanese organizations usually don't like radical restructuring, but when Senichi Hoshino took over the hapless Hanshin Tigers, he axed 24 of the team's 70 players and replaced them with free agents. He tracked performance daily and made individual coaches responsible for seeing that players executed certain skills. After 18 years, the Tigers finally won the pennant—a particularly important achievement because superstition says that when the Tigers win, Japan will soon enjoy a period of prolonged prosperity.

information. Huge increases in both the sheer volume of information and the ability to manage it have led to the emergence of this important function.

Although relatively few in number, the ranks of information managers are growing at all levels. Some firms have a top-management position for a *chief information officer* (*CIO*). Middle managers help design information systems for divisions or plants. Computer systems managers within smaller businesses are usually first-line managers. We'll discuss information management in more detail in Chapter 13.

Financial Managers Nearly every company has *financial managers* to plan and oversee its accounting functions and financial resources. Levels of financial management may include *CFO* or *vice president for finance* (top), a *division controller* (middle), and an *accounting supervisor* (first-line manager). Some institutions—NationsBank and Prudential, for example—have even made effective financial management the company's reason for being. We'll discuss financial management in more detail in Chapters 14 and 15.

Other Managers Some firms also employ other specialized managers. Many companies, for example, have public relations managers. Chemical and pharmaceutical companies such as Monsanto and Merck have research and development managers. The range of possibilities is wide, and the areas of management are limited only by the needs and imagination of the firm.

SELF-CHECK QUESTIONS 1–3

You should now be able to answer Self-Check Questions 1–3.*

1 **True/False** Organizing is the process of monitoring a firm's performance to make sure that it is meeting its goals.

2 **True/False** In general, there are three basic levels of management in most organizations.

3 **Multiple Choice** Which of the following is responsible for production, inventory, and quality control?
(a) human resources
(b) operations
(c) marketing
(d) finance

*Answers to Self-Check Questions 1–3 can be found on p. 564.

BASIC MANAGEMENT SKILLS

Although the range of managerial positions is almost limitless, the success that people enjoy in those positions is often limited by their skills and abilities. Effective managers must develop *technical*, *human relations*, *conceptual*, *decision-making*, and *time management skills*. Unfortunately, these skills are quite complex, and it is the rare manager who excels in every area.

■■■ TECHNICAL SKILLS

TECHNICAL SKILLS skills needed to perform specialized tasks

The skills needed to perform specialized tasks are called **technical skills**. A programmer's ability to write code, an animator's ability to draw, and an accountant's ability to audit a company's records are all examples of technical skills. People develop technical skills through a combination of education and experience. Technical skills are especially important for first-line managers. Many of these managers spend considerable time helping employees solve work-related problems, training them in more efficient procedures, and monitoring performance.

■■■ HUMAN RELATIONS SKILLS

HUMAN RELATIONS SKILLS skills in understanding and getting along with people

Effective managers also generally have good **human relations skills**—skills that enable them to understand and get along with other people. A manager with poor human relations skills may have trouble getting along with subordinates, cause valuable employees to quit or transfer, and contribute to poor morale.

Although human relations skills are important at all levels, they are probably most important for middle managers, who must often act as bridges between top managers, first-line managers, and managers from other areas of the organization. Managers should possess good communication skills. Many managers have found that being able both to understand others and to get others to understand them can go a long way toward maintaining good relations in an organization.

"I like to think of myself as a nice guy. Naturally, sometimes you have to step on a few faces."

▪▪▪ CONCEPTUAL SKILLS

Conceptual skills refer to a person's ability to think in the abstract, to diagnose and analyze different situations, and to see beyond the present situation. Conceptual skills help managers recognize new market opportunities and threats. They can also help managers analyze the probable outcomes of their decisions. The need for conceptual skills differs at various management levels. Top managers depend most on conceptual skills, first-line managers least. Although the purposes and everyday needs of various jobs differ, conceptual skills are needed in almost any job-related activity.

In many ways, conceptual skills may be the most important ingredient in the success of executives in e-commerce businesses. For example, the ability to foresee how a particular business application will be affected by or can be translated to the Internet is clearly conceptual in nature.

CONCEPTUAL SKILLS abilities to think in the abstract, diagnose and analyze different situations, and see beyond the present situation

▪▪▪ DECISION-MAKING SKILLS

Decision-making skills include the ability to define problems and to select the best course of action. These skills involve gathering facts, identifying solutions, evaluating alternatives, and implementing the chosen alternative. Periodically following up and evaluating the effectiveness of the choice are also part of the decision-making process. These skills allow some managers to identify effective strategies for their firm, such as Michael Dell's commitment to direct marketing as the firm's distribution model. But poor decision-making skills can also lead a failure to ruin, as was the case with Avery Sewell at Montgomery Ward. We'll discuss decision making more fully in Chapter 9.

DECISION-MAKING SKILLS skills in defining problems and selecting the best courses of action

▪▪▪ TIME MANAGEMENT SKILLS

Time management skills refer to the productive use that managers make of their time. In 2005, for example, Lew Frankfort at Coach was paid $2 million in base salary. Assuming that he worked 50 hours a week and took two weeks' vacation, Frankfort earned $800 an hour—a little more than $13 per minute. Any amount of time that Frankfort wastes clearly represents a large cost to Coach and its stockholders. Most managers receive much smaller salaries than Frankfort. Their time, however, is valuable, and poor use of it still translates into costs and wasted productivity.

To manage time effectively, managers must address four leading causes of wasted time:

TIME MANAGEMENT SKILLS skills associated with the productive use of time

1 *Paperwork.* Some managers spend too much time deciding what to do with letters and reports. Most documents of this sort are routine and can be handled quickly. Managers must learn to recognize those documents that require more attention.
2 *Telephone calls.* Experts estimate that managers get interrupted by the telephone every five minutes. To manage this time more effectively, they suggest having an assistant screen all calls and setting aside a certain block of time each day to return the important ones. Unfortunately, the explosive use of cell phones seems to be making this problem even worse for many managers.

3 *Meetings.* Many managers spend as much as four hours a day in meetings. To help keep this time productive, the person handling the meeting should specify a clear agenda, start on time, keep everyone focused on the agenda, and end on time.

4 *E-mail.* Increasingly, managers are relying heavily on e-mail and other forms of electronic communication. Time is wasted when managers have to sort through spam and a variety of electronic folders, in-boxes, and archives.

▪▪▪ MANAGEMENT SKILLS FOR THE TWENTY-FIRST CENTURY

Although the skills discussed in this chapter have long been important parts of every successful manager's career, new skill requirements continue to emerge. Today, most experts point to the growing importance of skills involving *global management* and *technology.*

Global Management Skills Tomorrow's managers must equip themselves with the special tools, techniques, and skills needed to compete in a global environment. They will need to understand foreign markets, cultural differences, and the motives and practices of foreign rivals. They also need to understand how to collaborate with others around the world on a real-time basis.

On a more practical level, businesses will need more managers who are capable of understanding international operations. In the past, most U.S. businesses hired local managers to run their operations in the various countries in which they operated. More recently, however, the trend has been to transfer U.S. managers to foreign locations. This practice helps firms transfer their corporate cultures to foreign operations. In addition, foreign assignments help managers become better prepared for international competition as they advance within the organization. The top management teams of large corporations today are also likely to include directors from other countries.

To run its operations in China, MTV needed someone who understood both conservative Chinese television regulators and China's young urban elite. The company chose Li Yifei, a former Baylor University student, U.N. intern, and tai chi champion. She brought the Chinese MTV awards to state-owned TV, receiving a 7.9 percent rating—a whopping 150 million viewers.

Management and Technology Skills Another significant issue facing tomorrow's managers is technology, especially as it relates to communication. Managers have always had to deal with information. In today's world, however, the amount of information has reached staggering proportions. In the United States alone, people exchange hundreds of millions of e-mail messages every day. New forms of technology have added to a manager's ability to process information while simultaneously making it even more important to organize and interpret an ever-increasing wealth of input.

Technology has also begun to change the way the interaction of managers shapes corporate structures. Elaborate computer networks control the flow of a firm's lifeblood—information. This information no longer flows strictly up and down through hierarchies. It now flows to everyone simultaneously. As a result, decisions are made quicker, and more people are directly involved. With e-mail, videoconferencing, and other forms of communication, neither time nor distance—nor such corporate boundaries as departments and divisions—can prevent people from working more closely together. More than ever, bureaucracies are breaking down, while planning, decision making, and other activities are beginning to benefit from group building and teamwork. We discuss the effects technology has on business in more detail in Chapter 13.

SELF-CHECK QUESTIONS 4–6

You should now be able to answer Self-Check Questions 4–6.*

4 Multiple Choice The ability to think in the abstract reflects which of the following managerial skills?
(a) technical skills
(b) human relations skills
(c) conceptual skills
(d) decision-making skills

5 Multiple Choice Which of the following identifies two emerging new skill sets that managers need to master?

(a) interpersonal and global
(b) global and technology
(c) time management and conceptual
(d) conceptual and technology

6 True/False All managers have to be highly proficient with all skills in order to be successful.

***Answers to Self-Check Questions 4–6 can be found on p. 564.**

STRATEGIC MANAGEMENT: SETTING GOALS AND FORMULATING STRATEGY

As we noted earlier, planning is a critical part of the manager's job. Managers today are increasingly being called on to think and act strategically. **Strategic management** is the process of helping an organization maintain an effective alignment with its environment. For instance, if a firm's business environment is heading toward fiercer competition, the business may need to start cutting its costs and developing more products and services before the competition really starts to heat up. Likewise, if an industry is globalizing,

STRATEGIC MANAGEMENT
process of helping an organization maintain an effective alignment with its environment

entrepreneurship and new ventures

Samuel Adams Makes Headway

In the mid-1980s, James Koch was a high-flying management consultant pulling in over $250,000 a year. To the surprise of his family and friends, however, he quit this job and invested his life's savings to start a business from scratch and go head-to-head with international competitors in a market that had not had a truly successful specialty product in decades. To everyone's even greater surprise, he succeeded.

Koch's company is Boston Beer, and its flagship product is a premium beer called Samuel Adams. The Koch family had actually been brewing beer for generations, and James started with a recipe developed by his great-great-grandfather, who had sold the beer in St. Louis in the 1870s under the name Louis Koch Lager. To fund his start-up, James Koch put up $100,000 in personal savings and another $300,000 invested by his friends.

He set up shop in an old warehouse in Boston, bought some surplus equipment from a large brewery, and started operations. Because he used only the highest-quality ingredients, Koch had to price his product at about $1 more per case than such premium imports as Heineken. Boston-area distributors, meanwhile, doubted that consumers would pay $6 per six-pack for an American beer, and most refused to carry it. So Koch began selling his beer directly to retailers and bars.

His big break came when he entered Samuel Adams Lager in the Great American Beer Festival, where it won the consumer preference poll—the industry's equivalent of an Oscar. Koch quickly turned this victory into an advertising mantra, proclaiming Samuel Adams "The Best Beer in America." As sales took off, national distributors came calling, and in order to meet surging demand, Koch contracted part of his brewing operations to a nearly defunct Stroh's facility in Pittsburgh.

During the early 1990s, sales of Samuel Adams products grew at an annual rate of over 50 percent and today exceed $275 million per year. Boston Beer even exports Samuel Adams to Germany, where it's become quite popular among finicky beer drinkers. Koch, who retains controlling interest in the business, still oversees day-to-day brewing operations. Indeed, he claims that he has sampled at least one of the firm's products every day, primarily as a way of monitoring quality.

Koch's success has not gone unnoticed, especially by industry giant Anheuser-Busch (AB). AB and other national brewers have seen their sales take a hit from so-called microbreweries like Samuel Adams—small regional or local companies that sell esoteric brews made in small quantities and that derive cachet from their scarcity. The Boston Beer Co. was the first microbrewery to make it big, and most of the others are trying to follow in Koch's footsteps. AB wants to keep small start-ups from gaining too much market share, most of which would come at its own expense.

Recently, for example, Koch learned that AB had made inquiries about buying his entire crop from a German hops farmer who has an exclusive arrangement with Boston Beer. Had AB succeeded, Koch admits, he would have been out of business. AB has also complained that Samuel Adams labeling is misleading because it neglects the fact that its Pittsburgh-made beer is actually produced under contract by Stroh's. The industry giant has even tried to convince wholesalers, who are highly dependent on such AB products as Budweiser, to stop selling specialty beers.

Koch, meanwhile, simply sees all this attention as a clear sign that he's made an impact on the market. Moreover, his business continues to thrive. Recently, for instance, he expanded the firm's Cincinnati brewery to a capacity of 600,000 barrels per year.

---

a firm's managers may need to start entering new markets, developing international partnerships, and so forth during the early stages of globalization rather than waiting for its full effects.

GOAL objective that a business hopes and plans to achieve

The starting point in effective strategic management is setting **goals**—objectives that a business hopes and plans to achieve. Every business needs goals. Remember, however, that deciding what it intends to do is only the first step for an organization. Managers must also make decisions about what actions will and will not achieve company goals. Decisions cannot be made on a problem-by-problem basis or merely to meet needs as they arise. In most companies, a broad program underlies those decisions. That program

STRATEGY broad set of organizational plans for implementing the decisions made for achieving organizational goals

is called a **strategy**, which is a broad set of organizational plans for implementing the decisions made for achieving organizational goals. Let's begin by examining business goals more closely.

▪▪▪ SETTING BUSINESS GOALS

Goals are performance targets—the means by which organizations and their managers measure success or failure at every level. For example, Marjorie Scardino's goals at Pearson are currently tied to cost reductions and improved profitability; in the future, she will likely focus more on growth. At AmEx, however, Kenneth Chenault is focusing more on revenue growth and the firm's stock price. Steve Reinemund's goals at Pepsi include keeping abreast of changing consumer tastes and leveraging the firm's current products into new markets.

Purposes of Goal Setting An organization functions systematically because it sets goals and plans accordingly. An organization commits its resources on all levels to achieve its goals. Specifically, we can identify four main purposes in organizational goal setting:

1 *Goal setting provides direction and guidance for managers at all levels.* If managers know precisely where the company is headed, there is less potential for error in the different units of the company. Starbucks, for example, has a goal of increasing capital spending by 15 percent, with all additional expenditures devoted to opening new stores. This goal clearly informs everyone in the firm that expansion into new territories is a high priority for the firm.

2 *Goal setting helps firms allocate resources.* Areas that are expected to grow will get first priority. The company allocates more resources to new projects with large sales potential than it allocates to mature products with established but stagnant sales potential. Thus, Starbucks is primarily emphasizing new store expansion, while its e-commerce initiatives are currently given a lower priority. "Our management team," says CEO Howard Schultz, "is 100 percent focused on growing our core business without distraction . . . from any other initiative."

3 *Goal setting helps to define corporate culture.* For years, the goal at General Electric has been to push each of its divisions to first or second in its industry. The result is a competitive (and often stressful) environment and a corporate culture that rewards success and has little tolerance for failure. At the same time, however, GE's appliance business, television network (NBC), aircraft engine unit, and financial services business are each among the very best in their respective industries. Eventually, the firm's CEO set an even higher companywide standard—to make the firm the most valuable in the world.

4 *Goal setting helps managers assess performance.* If a unit sets a goal of increasing sales by 10 percent in a given year, managers in that unit who attain or exceed the goal can be rewarded. Units failing to reach the goal will also be compensated accordingly. GE has a long-standing reputation for evaluating managerial performance, richly rewarding those who excel—and getting rid of those who do not. Each year, the lower 10 percent of GE's managerial force are informed that either they make dramatic improvements in performance or consider alternative directions for their careers.

Kinds of Goals Goals differ from company to company, depending on the firm's purpose and mission. Every enterprise has a purpose, or a reason for being. Businesses seek profits, universities seek to discover and transmit new knowledge, and government agencies seek to set and enforce public policy. Many enterprises also have missions and **mission statements**—statements of how they will achieve their purposes in the environments in which they conduct their businesses.

MISSION STATEMENT
organization's statement of how it will achieve its purpose in the environment in which it conducts its business

A company's mission is usually easy to identify, at least at a basic level. Starbucks sums up its mission very succinctly: the firm intends to "establish Starbucks as the premier purveyor of the finest coffee in the world while maintaining our uncompromising

Our management team is 100 percent focused on growing our core business without distraction . . . from any other initiative.

—Howard Schultz, Starbucks CEO

LONG-TERM GOAL goal set for an extended time, typically five years or more into the future

INTERMEDIATE GOAL goal set for a period of one to five years into the future

SHORT-TERM GOAL goal set for the very near future

CORPORATE STRATEGY strategy for determining the firm's overall attitude toward growth and the way it will manage its businesses or product lines

principles while we grow." But businesses sometimes have to rethink their strategies and mission as the competitive environment changes. A few years ago, for example, Starbucks announced that Internet marketing and sales were going to become core business initiatives. Managers subsequently realized, however, that this initiative did not fit the firm as well as they first thought. As a result, they scaled back this effort and made a clear recommitment to their existing retail business. The demands of change force many companies to rethink their missions and revise their statements of what they are and what they do.

In addition to its mission, every firm also has long-term, intermediate, and short-term goals:

- **Long-term goals** relate to extended periods of time, typically five years or more. For example, AmEx might set a long-term goal of doubling the number of participating merchants during the next 10 years. Kodak might adopt a long-term goal of increasing its share of the digital picture processing market by 10 percent during the next eight years.
- **Intermediate goals** are set for a period of one to five years. Companies usually set intermediate goals in several areas. For example, the marketing department's goal might be to increase sales by 3 percent in two years. The production department might want to reduce expenses by 6 percent in four years. Human resources might seek to cut turnover by 10 percent in two years. Finance might aim for a 3-percent increase in return on investment in three years.
- **Short-term goals** are set for perhaps one year and are developed for several different areas. Increasing sales by 2 percent this year, cutting costs by 1 percent next quarter, and reducing turnover by 4 percent over the next six months are examples of short-term goals.

After a firm has set its goals, it then focuses attention on strategies to accomplish them.

■ ■ ■ TYPES OF STRATEGY

Figure 5.2 shows the relationship among the three types of strategy that are usually considered by a company: *corporate stategy*, *business* (or *competitive*) *strategy*, and *functional strategy*.

Corporate Strategy   The purpose of **corporate strategy** is to determine what business or businesses a company will own and operate. Some corporations own and operate only a single business. The makers of WD-40, for example, concentrate solely on that

Figure 5.2
Hierarchy of Strategy

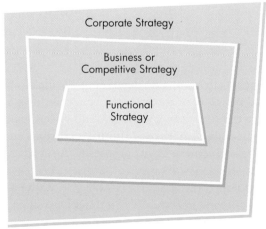

Corporate Strategy

Business or Competitive Strategy

Functional Strategy

brand. Other corporations own and operate many businesses. A company may decide to *grow* by increasing its activities or investment or to *retrench* by reducing them.

Sometimes a corporation buys and operates multiple businesses in compatible industries as part of its corporate strategy. For example, the restaurant chains operated by YUM! (KFC, Pizza Hut, Taco Bell, and Long John Silver's) are clearly related to one another. This strategy is called *related diversification*. However, if the businesses are not similar, the strategy is called *unrelated diversification*. When Pearson ran such unrelated businesses as publishing and a wax museum, it was following this approach. Under Kenneth Chenault, AmEx corporate strategy calls for strengthening operations through a principle of growth called *e-partnering*—buying shares of small companies that can provide technology that AmEx itself does not have.

Business (or Competitive) Strategy When a corporation owns and operates multiple businesses, it must develop strategies for each one. **Business (or competitive) strategy**, then, takes place at the level of the business unit or product line and focuses on improving the company's competitive position. For example, at this level, AmEx makes decisions about how best to compete in an industry that includes Visa, MasterCard, and other credit card companies. In this respect, the company has committed heavily to expanding its product offerings and serving customers through new technology. Pepsi, meanwhile, has one strategy for its soft drink business as it competes with Coca-Cola and a different strategy for its sports drink business and yet another strategy for its New Age beverage company.

BUSINESS (OR COMPETITIVE) STRATEGY strategy, at the business-unit or product-line level, focusing on improving a firm's competitive position

Functional Strategy At the level of **functional strategy**, managers in specific areas such as marketing, finance, and operations decide how best to achieve corporate goals by performing their functional activities most effectively. At AmEx, for example, each business unit has considerable autonomy in deciding how to use the single Web site at which the company has located its entire range of services. Pearson, meanwhile, develops functional strategies for marketing its books and operations strategies for distributing them. The real challenges—and opportunities—lie in successfully creating these strategies. Therefore, we now turn our attention to the basic steps in strategy formulation.

FUNCTIONAL STRATEGY strategy by which managers in specific areas decide how best to achieve corporate goals through productivity

■ ■ ■ FORMULATING STRATEGY

Planning is often concerned with the nuts and bolts of setting goals, choosing tactics, and establishing schedules. In contrast, *strategy* tends to have a wider scope. By definition, it is a broad concept that describes an organization's intentions. Further, a strategy outlines how the business intends to meet its goals and includes the organization's responsiveness to new challenges and new needs. Because a well-formulated strategy is so vital to a business's success, most top managers devote substantial attention and creativity to this process. **Strategy formulation** involves the three basic steps summarized in Figure 5.3 and discussed next.

STRATEGY FORMULATION creation of a broad program for defining and meeting an organization's goals

Step 1: Setting Strategic Goals **Strategic goals** are derived directly from a firm's mission statement. For example, Bernd Pischets, CEO of Volkswagen, has clear strategic goals for the European carmaker. When he took over, Volkswagen was only marginally profitable, was regarded as an also-ran in the industry, and was thinking about pulling out of the U.S. market altogether because its sales were so poor. Over the next few years, however, Pischets totally revamped the firm and has it making big profits. Volkswagen is now a much more formidable force in the global automobile industry.[5]

STRATEGIC GOAL goal derived directly from a firm's mission statement

Figure 5.3   Strategy Formulation

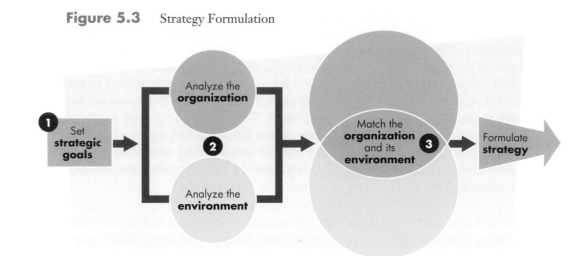

SWOT ANALYSIS identification and analysis of organizational strengths and weaknesses and environmental opportunities and threats as part of strategy formulation

ENVIRONMENTAL ANALYSIS process of scanning the business environment for threats and opportunities

ORGANIZATIONAL ANALYSIS process of analyzing a firm's strengths and weaknesses

Step 2: Analyzing the Organization and the Environment: SWOT Analysis After strategic goals have been established, managers usually attempt to assess both their organization and its environment. A common framework for this assessment is called a **SWOT analysis**. This process involves assessing organizational strengths and weaknesses (the **S** and **W**) and environmental opportunities and threats (the **O** and **T**). In formulating strategy, managers attempt to capitalize on organizational strengths and take advantage of environmental opportunities. During this same process, they may seek ways to overcome or offset organizational weaknesses and avoid or counter environmental threats.

Scanning the business environment for threats and opportunities is often called **environmental analysis**. Changing consumer tastes and hostile takeover offers are threats, as are new government regulations that will limit a firm's opportunities. Even more important threats come from new products and new competitors. For example, online music services like iTunes are a major threat to manufacturers of CDs and CD players. Likewise, the emergence of digital photography poses a threat to companies tied to print photography. Opportunities, meanwhile, are areas in which the firm can potentially expand, grow, or take advantage of existing strengths. For example, when Pepsi managers recognized the growing market potential for bottled water, they moved quickly to launch their Aquafina brand and to position it for rapid growth.

In addition to analyzing external factors by performing an environmental analysis, managers must also examine internal factors. The purpose of such an **organizational analysis** is to better understand a company's strengths and weaknesses. Strengths might include surplus cash, a dedicated workforce, an ample supply of managerial talent, technical expertise, or little competition. For example, Pepsi's strength in beverage distribution through its network of soft drink distributors was successfully extended to distribution of bottled water. A cash shortage, aging factories, a heavily unionized workforce, and a poor public image can all be important weaknesses. Garden.com's total reliance on the emerging Internet-based retailing model became its downfall when the dot-com bubble burst, and poor decision making at Montgomery Ward clearly led to that firm's demise.

Step 3: Matching the Organization and Its Environment The final step in strategy formulation is matching environmental threats and opportunities against corporate strengths and weaknesses. This matching process is at the heart of strategy formulation.

That is, a firm should attempt to leverage its strengths so as to capitalize on opportunities and counteract threats; it should also attempt to shield its weaknesses, or at least not allow them to derail other activities. For instance, knowing how to distribute consumer products (a strength) allows Pepsi to add new businesses and extend existing ones that use the same distribution models. But a firm that lacked a strong understanding of consumer product distribution would be foolish to add new products whose success relied heavily on efficient distribution.

Understanding strengths and weaknesses may also determine whether a firm typically takes risks or behaves more conservatively. Either approach can be successful. Blue Bell, for example, is one of the most profitable ice-cream makers in the world, even though it sells its products in only about a dozen states. Based in Brenham, Texas, Blue Bell controls more than 50 percent of the market in each state where it does business. The firm, however, has resisted the temptation to expand too quickly. Its success is based on product freshness and frequent deliveries—strengths that may suffer if the company grows too large.

▪▪▪ A HIERARCHY OF PLANS

The final step in formulating strategy is translating the strategy into more operational language. This process generally involves the creation of actual plans. Plans can be viewed on three levels: strategic, tactical, and operational. Managerial responsibilities are defined at each level. The levels constitute a hierarchy because implementing plans is practical only when there is a logical flow from one level to the next.

- **Strategic plans** reflect decisions about resource allocations, company priorities, and the steps needed to meet strategic goals. They are usually created by the firm's top management team but, as noted earlier, often rely on input from others in the organization. So, the fundamental outcome of the strategic planning process is the creation of a strategic plan. General Electric's decision that viable businesses must rank first or second within their respective markets is a matter of strategic planning.

- **Tactical plans** are shorter-term plans for implementing specific aspects of the company's strategic plans. That is, after a strategic plan has been created, managers then develop shorter-term plans to guide decisions so they are consistent with the strategic plan. They typically involve upper and middle management. Dell's efforts to extend its distribution expertise into the markets for televisions and other home electronics is an example of tactical planning.

- **Operational plans**, which are developed by mid-level and lower-level managers, set short-term targets for daily, weekly, or monthly performance. Starbucks, for instance, has operational plans dealing with how its stores must buy, store, and brew coffee.

STRATEGIC PLAN plan reflecting decisions about resource allocations, company priorities, and steps needed to meet strategic goals

TACTICAL PLAN generally short-term plan concerned with implementing specific aspects of a company's strategic plans

OPERATIONAL PLAN plan setting short-term targets for daily, weekly, or monthly performance

CONTINGENCY PLANNING AND CRISIS MANAGEMENT

Because business environments are often difficult to predict and because the unexpected can create major problems, most managers recognize that even the best-laid plans sometimes simply do not work out. For instance, when Walt Disney announced plans to launch a cruise line replete with familiar Disney characters and themes, managers also began aggressively developing and marketing packages linking three- and four-day cruises with visits to Disney World in Florida. The inaugural sailing was sold out more than a year in advance, and the first year was booked solid six months before the ship was launched. Three months before the first sailing, however, the shipyard constructing Disney's first ship (the *Disney Magic*) notified the company that it was behind schedule and that delivery would be several weeks late. When similar problems befall other cruise lines, they can offer to rebook passengers on alternative itineraries. But because Disney had no other ship, it had no choice but to refund the money it had collected as prebooking deposits for its first 15 cruises.

The 20,000 displaced customers were offered big discounts if they rebooked on a later cruise. Many of them, however, could not rearrange their schedules and requested full refunds. Moreover, quite a few blamed Disney for the problem, and a few expressed outrage at what they saw as poor planning by the entertainment giant. Fortunately for Disney, however, the *Disney Magic* was eventually launched and has now become very popular and very profitable.

Because managers know such things can happen, they often develop alternative plans in case things go awry. Two common methods of dealing with the unknown and unforeseen are *contingency planning* and *crisis management*.

▪▪▪ CONTINGENCY PLANNING

Contingency planning recognizes the need to find solutions to specific aspects of a problem. By its very nature, a contingency plan is a hedge against changes that might occur. **Contingency planning**, then, is planning for change: It seeks to identify in advance important aspects of a business or its market that might change. It also identifies the ways in which a company will respond to changes. Today, many companies use computer forecasts for contingency planning.

CONTINGENCY PLANNING
identifying aspects of a business or its environment that might entail changes in strategy

Suppose, for example, that a company develops a plan to create a new division. It expects sales to increase at an annual rate of 10 percent for the next five years, and it develops a marketing strategy for maintaining that level. But suppose that sales have increased by only 5 percent by the end of the first year. Does the firm (1) abandon the venture, (2) invest more in advertising, or (3) wait to see what happens in the second year? Any of these alternatives is possible. Regardless of the firm's choice, however, its efforts will be more efficient if managers decide in advance what to do in case sales fall below planned levels.

Contingency planning helps them do exactly that. Disney learned from its mistake with its first ship, and when the second (the *Disney Wonder*) was launched a year later, managers did several things differently. For one thing, they allowed for an extra two weeks between when the ship was supposed to be ready for sailing and its first scheduled cruise. They also held open a few cabins on the *Disney Magic* as a backup for any especially disgruntled customers who might need accommodations if there were unexpected delays in the launching of the *Disney Wonder*.

▪▪▪ CRISIS MANAGEMENT

A crisis is an unexpected emergency requiring immediate response. **Crisis management** involves an organization's methods for dealing with emergencies. The devastating hurricanes that hit the Gulf Coast in 2005—Katrina and Rita—dramatically underscored the importance of effective crisis management. For example, inadequate and ineffective responses by FEMA illustrated to many people that organization's weaknesses in coping with crisis situations.

CRISIS MANAGEMENT
organization's methods for dealing with emergencies

Crisis management involves an organization's methods for dealing with emergencies. Here, Red Cross volunteers organize and file paperwork submitted by Hurricane Katrina victims in Texas. Hundreds of businesses affected by the hurricane also had to respond quickly to events they had never anticipated. But today, most of those same businesses have much clearer crisis management plans in the event any disaster strikes.

On the other hand, some organizations responded much more effectively. Wal-Mart began ramping up its emergency preparedness on the same day that Katrina was upgraded from a tropical depression to a tropical storm. In the days before the storm struck, Wal-Mart stores in the region were supplied with powerful generators and large supplies of dry ice so they could reopen as quickly as possible after the storm had passed. The firm also had scores of trucks standing by in neighboring states crammed with both emergency-related inventory for its stores and emergency supplies it was prepared to donate—bottled water, medical supplies, and so forth. And Wal-Mart often beat FEMA by several days in getting those supplies delivered.[6]

Seeing the consequences of poor crisis management after the terrorist attacks of September 11, 2001, and the 2005 hurricanes, many firms today are actively working to create new and better crisis management plans and procedures. For example, both Reliant Energy and Duke Energy rely on computer trading centers where trading managers actively buy and sell energy-related commodities. If a terrorist attack or natural disaster, such as a hurricane, were to strike their trading centers, they would essentially be out of business. Prior to September 11, each firm had relatively vague and superficial crisis plans. But now they, and most other companies, have much more detailed and comprehensive plans in the event of another crisis. Both Reliant and Duke, for example, have created secondary trading centers at other locations. In the event of a shutdown at their main trading centers, these firms can quickly transfer virtually all their core trading activities to their secondary centers within 30 minutes or less.[7] Unfortunately, however, because it is impossible to forecast the future precisely, no organization can ever be perfectly prepared for every eventuality.

MANAGEMENT AND THE CORPORATE CULTURE

Every organization—big or small, more successful or less successful—has an unmistakable "feel" to it. Just as every individual has a unique personality, every company has a unique identity, a **corporate culture**: the shared experiences, stories, beliefs, and norms that characterize an organization. This culture helps define the work and business climate that exists in an organization.

CORPORATE CULTURE the shared experiences, stories, beliefs, and norms that characterize an organization

A strong corporate culture serves several purposes. For one thing, it directs employees' efforts and helps everyone work toward the same goals. Some cultures, for example, stress financial success to the extreme, whereas others focus more on quality of life. In addition, corporate culture helps newcomers learn accepted behaviors. If financial success is the key to a culture, newcomers quickly learn that they are expected to work long, hard hours and that the "winner" is the one who brings in the most revenue. But if quality of life is more fundamental, newcomers learn that it's more acceptable to spend less time at work and that balancing work and nonwork is encouraged.

Where does a business's culture come from? In some cases, it emanates from the days of an organization's founder. Firms such as the Walt Disney, Hewlett-Packard, Wal-Mart, and J. C. Penney, for example, still bear the imprint of their founders. In other cases, an organization's culture is forged over a long period of time by a constant and focused business strategy. Pepsi, for example, has an achievement-oriented culture tied to its long-standing goal of catching its biggest competitor, Coca-Cola. Similarly, Apple Computer has a sort of "counterculture" culture stemming from its self-styled image as the alternative to the staid IBM corporate model for computer makers.

▪▪▪ COMMUNICATING THE CULTURE AND MANAGING CHANGE

Corporate culture influences management philosophy, style, and behavior. Managers, therefore, must carefully consider the kind of culture they want for their organizations and then work to nourish that culture by communicating with everyone who works there. Continental Airlines' CEO delivers weekly messages for all Continental employees to update them on what's going on in the firm; the employees can either listen to it on a closed-circuit broadcast or call a toll-free telephone number and hear a recorded version at their own convenience.

Communicating the Culture To use a firm's culture to its advantage, managers must accomplish several tasks, all of which hinge on effective communication. First, managers themselves must have a clear understanding of the culture. Second, they must transmit the culture to others in the organization. Thus, training and orientation for newcomers in an organization often includes information about the firm's culture. A clear and meaningful statement of the organization's mission is also a valuable communication tool. Finally, managers can maintain the culture by rewarding and promoting those who understand it and work toward maintaining it.

Managing Change Organizations must sometimes change their cultures. In such cases, they must also communicate the nature of the change to both employees and customers. According to the CEOs of several companies that have undergone radical change in the last decade or so, the process usually goes through three stages:

1 *At the highest level, analysis of the company's environment highlights extensive change as the most effective response to its problems.* This period is typically characterized by conflict and resistance.

A business's founder or CEO plays a major role in shaping the company's culture. For example, Apple co-founder and CEO Steve Jobs helped establish an informal and laid-back culture at the company. Casual business attire and an open open-door policy help him maintain that same culture today. And that culture, in turn, helps Apple continue to attract and retain talented people.

2 *Top management begins to formulate a vision of a new company.* Whatever that vision, it must include renewed focus on the activities of competitors and the needs of customers.

3 *The firm sets up new systems for appraising and compensating employees who enforce the firm's new values.* The purpose is to give the new culture solid shape from within the firm.

While some firms like to build on their legacies, others know better. When Gordon Bethune first took over Continental Airlines in the early 1990s, the firm was nearing its third bankruptcy and was ranked last in its industry on virtually all major indicators. Hence, when Bethune announced his rebuilding plans at Continental, he dubbed it the "Go Forward" program. He stressed that the firm had little to look back on with pride, and he wanted everyone to look only to the future.

SELF-CHECK QUESTIONS 7–9

You should now be able to answer Self-Check Questions 7–9.*

7 Multiple Choice Which of the following is **not** a basic purpose served by goal setting?
  (a) Goals show the government what the firm hopes to achieve
  (b) Goals set direction and guidance
  (c) Goals help direct resource allocation
  (d) Goals help managers assess performance

8 Multiple Choice Which of these is a contingency plan?

  (a) setting guidelines for when supplies will be ordered
  (b) placing an ad to hire new employees
  (c) deciding which division to sell if a firm runs short of cash
  (d) All of these are contingency plans

9 True/False Corporate culture refers to the shared experiences, stories, beliefs, and norms that characterize an organization.

*Answers to Self-Check Questions 7–9 can be found on p. 564.

Communicating the Corporate Message

The business environment is in a constant state of change, sometimes providing a company with major opportunities, sometimes presenting it with serious challenges, sometimes both at once. The most successful companies take change for granted, continually adapting to ensure the best possible business outcomes. Being adaptable means communicating effectively, not only with stakeholders but also with the public at large.

Corporate communications—the means by which a company communicates to its stakeholders—is an increasingly important business activity. Many major companies now maintain corporate communications teams whose members are skilled in the art of public relations, who understand the media, and who can communicate a company's mission. They're also responsible for dealing with problems that may affect the relationship between the company and the larger environment in which it operates.

In recent years, the pace of corporate change has been unprecedented: mergers, acquisitions, corporate failures, and the emergence of new names and brands—all have caused profound shifts in the business landscape. In addition, one of the biggest ongoing challenges to any company is effectively communicating what it does and where it stands on the major issues in the public mind, including social responsibility, the environment, human rights, and diversity, to name just a few.

The most successful companies control their communications activities by making clear mission statements, remaining open about both internal policies and external relationships, and making sure that the public knows that they are ready to respond to environmental change. The process varies from company to company. In some instances, top managers become spokespeople, attracting media attention and providing the organization with a face. In other cases, groups of people interact on a daily basis with the media, interest groups, politicians, and the general public to project a company's image and respond to concerns.

One thing is certain: The ever-increasing pace of change makes it harder for companies to stay ahead of the curve. They can't afford to be perceived as outdated and unresponsive and must project images of dynamic, up-to-date organizations that know how to get engaged with the larger community.

CONTINUED FROM PAGE 142

THE IMAGE COACH

In addition to CEO Lew Frankfort, a host of other changes have aided Coach in its rapid rise. Frankfort hired a former Tommy Hilfiger designer, Reed Krakoff, to update the firm's classic but clunky styles. "Coach was an American icon, but something was missing," says Krakoff. "I had to take these ideas and make them fun—young in spirit." Instead of introducing new products twice a year, a common practice in the fashion industry, Coach releases new styles monthly. Customers now have a reason to visit the stores more often. Outsourcing the production function allowed the company to increase gross profit margins by 24 percent over five years. The firm has diversified into many other related lines of business, including shoes, jewelry, furniture, and more. There is even a Coach car, a cobranded Lexus, with a Coach leather interior.

Frankfort's approach to managing Coach seems to be paying big dividends. In addition, Coach has become a standard fixture on various lists of "best managed" companies. *Women's Wear Daily*, the bible of the fashion industry, recently named Coach as the "most splurge-worthy luxury brand." Customers agree. Since the firm was spun off, its revenues have doubled and profits have grown at an average annual compound rate of 55 percent. Investors, too, like Coach. The firm's share price rose an astonishing 900 percent during its first four years as an independent firm. Krakoff gives the credit for the firm's achievements to Frankfort's planning skills, saying, "The key to Lew's success . . . is his ability to orchestrate a decision-making process that is both inclusive and incisive."

QUESTIONS FOR DISCUSSION

1 Describe examples of each of the management functions illustrated in this case.
2 Which management skills seem to be most exemplified in Lew Frankfort?
3 What role have goals and strategy played in the success of Coach?
4 What corporate culture issues might exist when a former division of a big company is spun off?

I had to take these ideas and make them fun— young in spirit.

—Designer Reed Krakoff, on the strategy of modernizing the Coach image

1 Describe the nature of management and identify the four basic functions that constitute the management process.

Management is the process of planning, organizing, leading, and controlling all of a firm's resources to achieve its goals. *Planning* is determining what the organization needs to do and how best to get it done. The process of arranging resources and activities into a coherent structure is called *organizing*. When *leading*, a manager guides and motivates employees to meet the firm's objectives. *Controlling* is the process of monitoring performance to make sure that a firm is meeting its goals.

2 Identify different types of managers likely to be found in an organization by level and area.

There are three levels of management. The few executives who are responsible for the overall performance of large companies are *top managers*. Just below top managers are *middle managers*, including plant, operations, and division managers, who implement strategies, policies, and decisions made by top managers. Supervisors and office managers are the *first-line managers* who work with and supervise the employees who report to them.

In any large company, most managers work in one of five areas. *Human resource managers* hire and train employees, assess performance, and fix compensation. *Operations managers* are responsible for production, inventory, and quality control. *Marketing managers* are responsible for getting products from producers to consumers. *Information managers* design and implement systems to gather, organize, and distribute information. Some firms have a top manager called a *chief information officer (CIO)*. *Financial managers*, including the chief financial officer (top), division controllers (middle), and accounting supervisors (first-line), oversee accounting functions and financial resources.

3 Describe the basic skills required of managers.

Effective managers must develop a number of important skills. *Technical skills* are skills needed to perform specialized tasks. *Human relations skills* are skills in understanding and getting along with other people. *Conceptual skills* refer to the ability to think abstractly as well as diagnose and analyze different situations.

Decision-making skills include the ability to define problems and select the best courses of action. *Time management skills* refer to the productive use of time. *Global management skills* include understanding foreign markets, cultural differences, and the motives and practices of foreign rivals. *Technology management skills* include the ability to process, organize, and interpret an ever-increasing amount of information.

4 Explain the importance of strategic management and effective goal setting in organizational success.

Strategic management is the process of helping an organization maintain an effective alignment with its environment. It starts with setting *goals*—objectives that a business hopes (and plans) to achieve. Determined by the board and top management, *strategies* reflect decisions about resource allocations, company priorities, and plans. The three types of strategy that are usually considered by a company are *corporate stategy*, *business (or competitive) strategy*, and *functional strategy*.

5 Discuss contingency planning and crisis management in today's business world.

Companies often develop alternative plans in case things go awry. There are two common methods of dealing with the unforeseen, *contingency planning* and *crisis management*. Contingency planning is planning for change: It seeks to identify in advance important aspects of a business or its market that might change. It also identifies the ways in which a company will respond to changes. Crisis management involves an organization's methods for dealing with emergencies.

6 Describe the development and explain the importance of corporate culture.

Every company has a unique identity called *corporate culture*: its shared experiences, stories, beliefs, and norms. It helps define the work and business climate of an organization. A strong corporate culture directs efforts and helps everyone work toward the same goals. If an organization must change its culture, it must communicate the nature of the change to both employees and customers.

KEY TERMS

business (or competitive) strategy (p. 157)

conceptual skills (p. 151)

contingency planning (p. 160)

controlling (p. 146)

corporate culture (p. 161)

corporate strategy (p. 156)

crisis management (p. 160)

decision-making skills (p. 151)

environmental analysis (p. 158)

first-line manager (p. 148)

functional strategy (p. 157)

goal (p. 154)

human relations skills (p. 150)

intermediate goal (p. 156)

leading (p. 145)

long-term goal (p. 156)

management (p. 144)

middle manager (p. 148)

mission statement (p. 155)

operational plan (p. 159)

organizational analysis (p. 158)

organizing (p. 145)

planning (p. 144)

short-term goal (p. 156)

strategic goal (p. 157)

strategic management (p. 153)

strategic plan (p. 159)

strategy (p. 154)

strategy formulation (p. 157)

SWOT analysis (p. 158)

tactical plan (p. 159)

technical skills (p. 150)

time management skills (p. 151)

top manager (p. 147)

QUESTIONS AND EXERCISES

Questions for Review

1 Relate the five basic management skills (technical, human relations, conceptual, decision-making, and time management) to the four activities in the management process (planning, organizing, leading, and controlling). For example, which skills are most important in leading?

2 What are the four main purposes of setting goals in an organization?

3 Identify and explain the three basic steps in strategy formulation.

4 What is corporate culture? How is it formed? How is it sustained?

Questions for Analysis

5 Select any group of which you are a member (your company, your family, or a club or organization, for example). Explain how planning, organizing, leading, and controlling are practiced in that group.

6 Identify managers by level and area at your school, college, or university.

7 In what kind of company would the technical skills of top managers be more important than human relations or conceptual skills? Are there organizations in which conceptual skills are not important?

8 What differences might you expect to find in the corporate cultures of a 100-year-old manufacturing firm based in the Northeast and a 1-year-old e-commerce firm based in Silicon Valley?

Application Exercises

9 Interview the manager at any level of a local company. Identify that manager's job according to level and area. Show how planning, organizing, leading, and controlling are part of this person's job. Inquire about the manager's education and work experience. Which management skills are most important for this manager's job?

10 Compare and contrast the corporate cultures of two companies that do business in your community. Be sure to choose two companies in the same industry—for example, a Sears department store and a Wal-Mart discount store.

SPEAKING WITH POWER

Goal

To encourage you to appreciate effective speaking as a critical human relations skill.

Background Information

A manager's ability to understand and get along with supervisors, peers, and subordinates is a critical human relations skill. At the heart of this skill, says Harvard University Professor of Education Sarah McGinty, is the ability to speak with power and control. McGinty defines "powerful speech" in terms of the following characteristics:

■ The ability to speak at length and in complete sentences
■ The ability to set a conversational agenda
■ The ability to deter interruptions
■ The ability to argue openly and to express strong opinions about ideas, not people
■ The ability to make statements that offer solutions rather than pose questions
■ The ability to express humor

Taken together, says McGinty, "all this creates a sense of confidence in listeners."

Method

Step 1

Working alone, compare your own personal speaking style with McGinty's description of powerful speech by taping yourself as you speak during a meeting with classmates or during a phone conversation. (Tape both sides of the conversation only if the person to whom you are speaking gives permission.) Listen for the following problems:

■ Unfinished sentences
■ An absence of solutions
■ Too many disclaimers ("I'm not sure I have enough information to say this, but . . .")
■ The habit of seeking support from others instead of making definitive statements of personal conviction (saying,

"I recommend consolidating the medical and fitness functions," instead of, "As Emily stated in her report, I recommend consolidating the medical and fitness functions")
■ Language fillers (saying, "you know," "like," and "um" when you are unsure of your facts or uneasy about expressing your opinion)

Step 2

Join with three or four other classmates to evaluate each other's speaking styles. Finally,

■ Have a 10-minute group discussion on the importance of human relations skills in business.
■ Listen to other group members, and take notes on the "power" content of what you hear.
■ Offer constructive criticism by focusing on what speakers say rather than on personal characteristics (say, "Bob, you sympathized with Paul's position, but I still don't know what you think," instead of, "Bob, you sounded like a weakling").

FOLLOW-UP QUESTIONS

1 How do you think the power content of speech affects a manager's ability to communicate? Evaluate some of the ways in which effects may differ among supervisors, peers, and subordinates.
2 How do you evaluate yourself and group members in terms of powerful and powerless speech? List the strengths and weaknesses of the group.
3 Do you agree or disagree with McGinty that business success depends on gaining insight into your own language habits? Explain your answer.
4 In our age of computers and e-mail, why do you think personal presentation continues to be important in management?
5 McGinty believes that power language differs from company to company and that it is linked to the corporate culture. Do you agree, or do you believe that people express themselves in similar ways no matter where they are?

MAKING ROOM FOR ALTERNATIVE ACTIONS

The Situation

Assume that you are the manager of a large hotel adjacent to a medical center in a major city. The medical center itself consists of 10 major hospitals and research institutes. Two of the hospitals are affiliated with large universities and two with churches. Three are public and three are private. The center has an international reputation and attracts patients from around the world.

Because so many patients and their families travel great distances to visit the medical center and often stay for days or weeks, there are also eight large hotels in the area, including three new ones. The hotel that you manage is one of the older ones and, frankly, is looking a bit shabby. Corporate headquarters has told you that the hotel will either be closed or undergo a major remodeling in about two years. In the meantime, you are expected to wring every last cent of profit out of the hotel.

The Dilemma

A tropical storm has just struck the area and brought with it major flooding and power outages. Three of the medical center hospitals have been shut down indefinitely, as have six of the nearby hotels. Fortunately, your hotel sustained only minor damage and is fully functional. You have just called a meeting with your two assistant managers to discuss what actions, if any, you should take.

One assistant manager has urged you to cut room rates immediately for humanitarian reasons. This manager also wants you to open the hotel kitchens 24 hours a day to prepare free food for rescue workers and meals to donate to the hospitals, whose own food-service operations have been disrupted. The other assistant manager, meanwhile, has urged just the opposite approach: raise room rates by at least 20 percent and sell food to rescue workers and hospitals at a premium price. You can also choose to follow the advice of neither and continue doing business as usual.

QUESTIONS TO ADDRESS

1 What are the ethical issues in this situation?
2 What do you think most managers would do in this situation?
3 What would you do?

CLEAN UP NOW, OR CLEAN UP LATER?

The Situation

The top management team of a medium-sized manufacturing company is on a strategic planning "retreat" where it is formulating ideas and plans for spurring new growth in the company. As one part of this activity, the team, working with the assistance of a consultant, has conducted a SWOT analysis. During this activity, an interesting and complex situation has been identified. Next year, the Environmental Protection Agency (EPA) will be issuing new—and much more stringent—pollution standards for the company's industry. The management team sees this as a potential "threat" in that the company will have to buy new equipment and change some of its manufacturing methods in order to comply with the new standards.

The Dilemma

One member of the team, James Smith, has posed an interesting option—not complying. His logic can be summarized as follows:

1 The firm has already developed its capital budgets for the next two years. Any additional capital expenditures will cause major problems with the company's cash flow and budget allocations.

2 The company has a large uncommitted capital budget entry available in three years; those funds could be used to upgrade pollution control systems at that time.

3 Because the company has a spotless environmental record, James Smith argues that if the company does not buy the equipment for three years, the most likely outcomes will be (a) a warning in year 1; (b) a small fine in year 2; and (c) a substantial fine in year 3. However, the total amounts of the years 2 and 3 fines will be much

lower than the cost of redoing the company budgets and complying with the new law next year.

Team Activity

Assemble a group of four students and assign each group member to one of the following roles:
- Management team member
- Lower-level employee at the company
- Company customer
- Company investor

ACTION STEPS

1 Before hearing any of your group's comments on this situation, and from the perspective of your assigned role, do you think that James Smith's suggestion regarding ignoring pollution standards is a good one? Write down the reasons for your position.

2 Before hearing any of your group's comments on this situation, and from the perspective of your assigned role, what are the underlying ethical issues in this situation? Write down the issues.

3 Gather your group together and reveal, in turn, each member's comments on James Smith's suggestion. Next, reveal the ethical issues listed by each member.

4 Appoint someone to record main points of agreement and disagreement within the group. How do you explain the results? What accounts for any disagreement?

5 From an ethical standpoint, what does your group conclude is the most appropriate action that should be taken by the company in this situation?

6 Develop a group response to the following question: What are the respective roles of profits, obligations to customers, and obligations to the community for the firm in this situation?

☐☐☐☐☐☐☐☐☐☐ | **VIDEO EXERCISE**

IMAGINATIVE MANAGEMENT: CREATIVE AGE PUBLICATIONS

Learning Objectives

The purpose of this video is to help you:

1 Understand how and why managers set organizational goals.
2 Identify the basic skills that managers need to be effective.
3 Discuss ways in which corporate culture can affect an organization.

Synopsis

Creative Age Publications uses creativity in managing its beauty-industry publications. With offices or franchised operations in Europe, Japan, Russia, and other areas of the world, the company has expanded rapidly—thanks to sound management practices. One of the company's goals is to avoid overtaxing its management team by growing more slowly in the future. The CEO is working toward delegating most or all decisions to her management team, and as Creative Age managers move up through the ranks, they hone both their technical skills and their skills in working with others. "Having heart" is a major part of the company's culture—an important element that, in the CEO's opinion, many companies lack.

DISCUSSION QUESTIONS

1 **For analysis**: How does global growth affect Creative Age's emphasis on the management skill of interacting well with other people?
2 **For analysis**: How does moving managers up through the ranks help them develop conceptual skills?
3 **For application**: How would you suggest that the CEO spread the Creative Age culture throughout its global offices?
4 **For application**: How might the CEO manage growth through the process of controlling?
5 **For debate**: Do you agree with the CEO's policy of allowing managers and employees to work on any company magazine they choose? Support your position.

Online Exploration

Visit the Creative Age Web site at (www.creativeage.com) and follow the link to *Day Spa* magazine. Scan the magazine's home page and then click on "About Us" to read more about the magazine and its parent company. Why would Creative Age call attention to each magazine's goals and market rather than focusing on the parent company? How might Creative Age use a corporate Web site to communicate with other people and organizations that affect its ability to achieve its goals?

After reading this chapter, you should be able to:

1 Discuss the factors that influence a firm's organizational structure.

2 Explain specialization and departmentalization as two of the building blocks of organizational structure.

3 Describe centralization and decentralization, delegation, and authority as the key ingredients in establishing the decision-making hierarchy.

4 Explain the differences among functional, divisional, matrix, and international organizational structures and describe the most popular new forms of organizational design.

5 Describe the informal organization and discuss intrapreneuring.

COOKING UP A NEW STRUCTURE

For years, the Sara Lee Corporation grew by buying an amalgam of different businesses and piecing them together under its corporate umbrella. And for years, the firm's senior managers have struggled with how best to structure the various Sara Lee holdings. One former long-term CEO, John Bryan, presided over growth that took Sara Lee far beyond

ORGANIZING
THE BUSINESS

its foundation in food products to encompass dozens of business lines—everything from cake mixes to insecticide to lingerie. The various businesses were acquisitions, but their original managers still controlled each one as if it were a separate company. Hence, each business retained its own legal department, human resource staff, administrative units, accounting departments, and so forth. Calculating the cost of all this duplication, Bryan reached the conclusion that the company could not afford such high costs at a time when price competition was heating up.

In an effort to fix things, starting in 1997, Bryan sold or eliminated about one-quarter of the firm's 200 products. He cut redundant factories and the workforce, reduced the number of products, and standardized companywide processes. His goal was to remove Sara Lee from manufacturing while strengthening its focus and effectiveness as a marketer. In the meantime, though, he continued to acquire rival firms in order to sustain the company's growth. However, despite Bryan's efforts, Sara Lee still suffered from high costs and remained unfocused and inefficient. Said one industry analyst about Bryan's strategy: "Sometimes, the more chairs you move around, the more dust you see behind the chairs."

In 2000, Bryan retired and was replaced by C. Steven McMillan. McMillan knew that Bryan's moves had had little impact on the firm's performance and that he himself would need to start making some big changes. Borrowing a page from rival Kraft Foods, he began by merging the sales forces that specialized in various brands to create smaller,

> *Sometimes, the more chairs you move around, the more dust you see behind the chairs.*
>
> —Consumer-products analyst on one of the drawbacks of extensive reorganization

customer-focused teams. In meats alone, for instance, Sara Lee had 10 different brands, including Ball Park, Hillshire Farms, Bryan, and Jimmy Dean. "So if you're . . . a Kroger or a Safeway [supermarket]," explained McMillan, "you've got to deal with 10 different organizations and multiple invoices." The new customer-focused teams reduced duplication and were more convenient for buyers—a win-win situation. National retailers responded by increasing their orders for Sara Lee products.

McMillan also centralized decision making at the firm by shutting down 50 weaker regional brands and reorganizing the firm into three broad product categories: Food and Beverage, Intimates and Underwear, and Household Products. He abolished several layers of corporate hierarchy, including many of the middle managers the firm had inherited from its acquisitions. He created category managers to oversee related lines of business, and the flattened organizational structure led to improved accountability and more centralized control over Sara Lee's far-flung operations.

McMillan also borrowed some tactics from his predecessor, selling 15 businesses, including Coach leather goods, and laying off 10 percent of his workers. In another move that was widely questioned by industry observers, he paid $2.8 billion for breadmaker Earthgrains. The move increased Sara Lee's market share in baked goods, but many observers felt that McMillan paid too much for a small potential return. ■

Our opening story continues on page 194.

WHAT'S IN IT FOR ME?

Sara Lee has been undergoing changes over the past several years, most of them aimed at improving the organization's structure. As a result, people who work for Sara Lee have had to continually work to understand their "place" in the organization. By understanding the material in this chapter, you'll also be prepared to understand your "place" in the organization that employs you. Similarly, as a boss or owner, you'll be better equipped to create the optimal structure for your own organization.

This chapter examines factors that influence a firm's organizational structure. We discuss the building blocks of organizational structure as well as the differences between decision making in different types of organizations. Along the way, we look at a variety of organizational structures and describe the most popular new forms of organizational design.

WHAT IS ORGANIZATIONAL STRUCTURE?

ORGANIZATIONAL STRUCTURE
specification of the jobs to be done within an organization and the ways in which they relate to one another

One key decision that business owners and managers must address is how best to structure their organization. Stated differently, they must decide on an appropriate organizational structure. We can define **organizational structure** as the specification of the jobs to be done within an organization and the ways in which those jobs relate to one another. Perhaps the easiest way to understand structure is in terms of an *organization chart*.

ORGANIZATION CHART
diagram depicting a company's structure and showing employees where they fit into its operations

▪▪■ ORGANIZATION CHARTS

Most businesses prepare **organization charts** to clarify structure and to show employees where they fit into a firm's operations. Figure 6.1 is an organization chart for Contemporary Landscape Services, a small but thriving business in Bryan, Texas. Each box in the chart represents a job. The solid lines define the **chain of command**,

CHAIN OF COMMAND
reporting relationships within a company

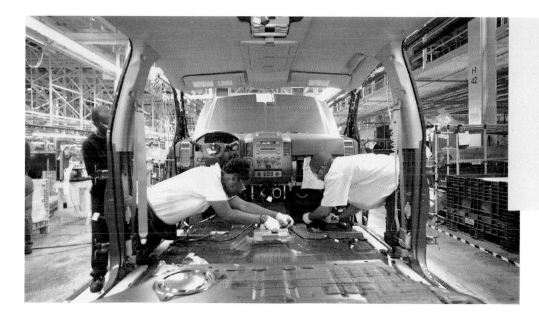

At plants like this one in Canton, Mississippi, Nissan has developed an assembly process so efficient that it can turn out a vehicle in up to 10 fewer hours than Ford. The key is the organization of the workstations. At this station, workers install just about everything that the driver touches inside the truck cab. Other stations take care of the whole vehicle frame, the entire electrical system, or completed doors.

Geographic Departmentalization Some firms opt for **geographic departmentalization**—meaning they are divided according to the areas of the country or the world that they serve. Levi Strauss, for instance, has one division for the United States, one for Europe, one for the Asia Pacific region, and one for Latin America. Within the United States, geographic departmentalization is common among utilities. For example, Pacific Power and Light is organized as four geographic departments—Southwestern, Columbia Basin, Mid-Oregon, and Wyoming.

GEOGRAPHIC DEPARTMENTALIZATION dividing an organization according to the areas of the country or the world served by a business

Multiple Forms of Departmentalization Because different forms of departmentalization have different advantages, larger companies tend to adopt different types of departmentalization for various levels. The company illustrated in Figure 6.2 uses functional departmentalization at the top level. At the middle level, production is divided along geographic lines. At a lower level, marketing is departmentalized by product group.

Figure 6.2   Multiple Forms of Departmentalization

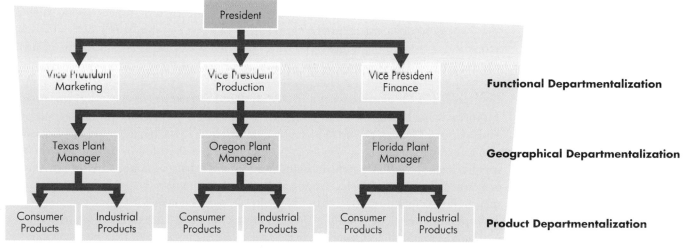

SELF-CHECK QUESTIONS 1–3

You should now be able to answer Self-Check Questions 1–3.*

1 True/False Organizations create a stable structure for themselves and then seldom have to change it.

2 Multiple Choice Which of the following jobs is likely to reflect the highest degree of specialization?
(a) chief executive officer
(b) sales representative
(c) assembly line worker
(d) human resources manager

3 Multiple Choice Which of the following is **not** a common basis for departmentalization?
(a) sequence
(b) function
(c) process
(d) product

*****Answers to Self-Check Questions 1–3 can be found on p. 564.**

ESTABLISHING THE DECISION-MAKING HIERARCHY

As we noted earlier, the third major building block of organizational structure is the establishment of a decision-making hierarchy. This is usually done by formalizing reporting relationships. When the focus is on the reporting relationships among individual managers and the people who report to them, it is most commonly referred to as *delegation*. However, when the focus is on the overall organization, it becomes a question of *decentralization* versus *centralization*. Given the overall importance of decisions about decentralization and centralization to organizational success, we will address these first.

DISTRIBUTING AUTHORITY: CENTRALIZATION AND DECENTRALIZATION

Some managers make the conscious decision to retain as much decision-making authority as possible at the higher levels of the organizational structure; others decide the push authority as far down the hierarchy as possible. While we can think of these two extremes as anchoring a continuum, most companies fall somewhere between the middle of such a continuum and one end point or the other.

CENTRALIZED ORGANIZATION
organization in which most decision-making authority is held by upper-level management

Centralized Organizations In a **centralized organization**, most decision-making authority is held by upper-level managers. Most lower-level decisions must be approved by upper management before they can be implemented.[3] McDonald's practices centralization as a way to maintain standardization. All restaurants must follow precise steps in buying products and making and packaging burgers and other menu items. Most advertising is handled at the corporate level, and any local advertising must be approved by a regional manager. Restaurants even have to follow prescribed schedules for facilities' maintenance and upgrades like floor polishing and parking lot cleaning. Centralized authority is most commonly found in companies that face relatively stable and predictable environments and is also typical of small businesses.

The oil-industry giant ExxonMobil owns vast reserves of natural gas, like this field in the former Soviet republic of Turkmenistan. In most respects, ExxonMobil is a highly centralized company, but in this less stable market, which tends to innovate rapidly, many experts are skeptical about the company's ability to decentralize the control that management exercises over corporate operations.

Decentralized Organizations As a company gets larger, more decisions must be made; thus, the company tends to adopt a more decentralized pattern. In a **decentralized organization**, much decision-making authority is delegated to levels of management at various points below the top. Decentralization is typical in firms that have complex and rapidly changing environmental conditions. The purpose of decentralization is to make a company more responsive to its environment by allowing managers more discretion to make decisions that affect their areas of responsibility as quickly as possible. For example, Urban Outfitters practices relative decentralization in that it allows individual store managers considerable discretion over how to create product displays, which products to display close to the door, and so forth.

Tall and Flat Organizations In addition to moving decision-making authority up or down the organization, centralization and decentralization also tend to influence the number of "layers" in an organizational structure. Decentralized firms tend to have relatively fewer layers of management, resulting in a **flat organizational structure** like that of the hypothetical law firm shown in Figure 6.3(a). In contrast, companies with centralized authority systems typically require multiple layers of management and thus **tall organizational structures**. As you can see from Figure 6.3(b), the U.S. Army is a good example. Because information, whether upward or downward bound, must pass through so many organizational layers, tall structures are prone to delays in information flow.

As organizations grow in size, it is both normal and necessary that they become at least somewhat taller. For instance, a small firm with only an owner-manager and a few employees is likely to have two layers—the owner-manager, and the employees who report to that person. As the firm grows, more layers will be needed. Born Information Services, for instance, is a small consulting firm created and run by Rick Born. At first, all his employees reported to him. But when the size of his firm had grown to more than 20 people, Born knew that he needed help in supervising and coordinating projects. As a result, he added a layer of management, consisting of what he termed staff managers, to serve as project coordinators. This move freed up time for Born to seek new business clients. Like other managers, however, Born must ensure that he has only the number of layers his firm needs. Too few layers can create chaos and inefficiency, whereas too many layers can create rigidity and bureaucracy.

DECENTRALIZED ORGANIZATION organization in which a great deal of decision-making authority is delegated to levels of management at points below the top

If you don't let managers make their own decisions, you're never going to be anything more than a one-person business.

—Jack Welch, former CEO of General Electric

FLAT ORGANIZATIONAL STRUCTURE characteristic of decentralized companies with relatively few layers of management

TALL ORGANIZATIONAL STRUCTURE characteristic of centralized companies with multiple layers of management

Figure 6.3
Organizational Structure
and Span of Control

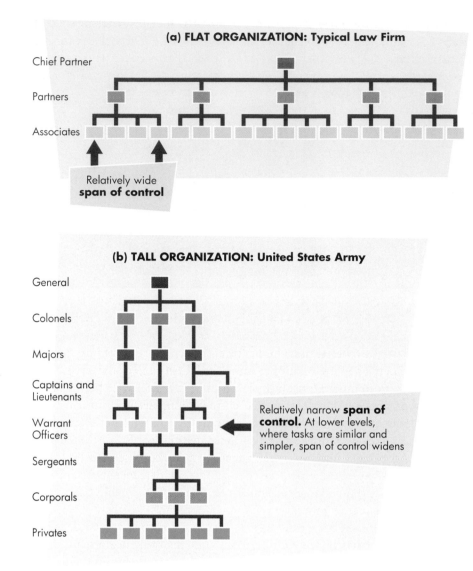

SPAN OF CONTROL number of
people supervised by one manager

Span of Control As you can see from Figure 6.3, the distribution of authority in an organization also affects the number of people who work for any individual manager. In a flat organizational structure, the number of people directly managed by one supervisor—the manager's **span of control**—is usually wide. In tall organizations, span of control tends to be relatively narrower. Span of control, however, depends on many factors. Employees' abilities and the supervisor's managerial skills help determine whether span of control is wide or narrow, as do the similarity and simplicity of those tasks performed under the manager's supervision and the extent to which they are interrelated.

If lower-level managers are given more decision-making authority, their supervisors will have less work to do because some of the decisions they previously made will be transferred to their subordinates. By the same token, these managers may then be able to oversee and coordinate the work of more subordinates, resulting in an increased span of control. Similarly, when several employees perform either the same simple task or a group of interrelated tasks, a wide span of control is possible and often desirable. For instance, because all the jobs are routine, one supervisor may well control an entire assembly line. Moreover, each task depends on another. If one station stops, everyone stops. Having one supervisor for all stations ensures that all stations receive equal attention and function equally well.

In contrast, when jobs are more diversified or prone to change, a narrow span of control is preferable. In Racine, Wisconsin, for example, the Case Corporation factory makes farm tractors exclusively to order in five to six weeks. Farmers can select from a wide array of options, including engines, tires, power trains, and even a CD player. A wide assortment of machines and processes is used to construct each tractor. Although workers are highly skilled operators of their assigned machines, each machine is different. In this kind of setup, the complexities of each machine and the advanced skills needed by each operator mean that one supervisor can oversee only a small number of employees.[4]

THE DELEGATION PROCESS

Delegation is the process through which a manager allocates work to subordinates. In general, the delegation process involves three steps: (1) the assignment of responsibility, (2) the granting of authority, and (3) the creation of accountability. **Responsibility** is the duty to perform an assigned task. **Authority** is the power to make the decisions necessary to complete the task. **Accountability** is the obligation employees have to their manager for the successful completion of the assigned task. For the delegation process to work smoothly, responsibility and authority must be equivalent.

For example, imagine a mid-level buyer for Macy's department store who encounters an unexpected opportunity to make a large purchase at an extremely good price. Assume that an immediate decision is absolutely necessary, but the buyer does not have the necessary authority to make the decision. In this instance, responsibility and authority are not equivalent, and so the firm misses a good opportunity. Now, though, consider a slight variation—the buyer does have the authority and decides to make the purchase. Now Macy's has benefited because of the attractive price it paid for new merchandise. If the purchase decision was actually a poor one, the buyer (because of accountability) will have to justify why it seemed like a good idea.

Unfortunately, many managers actually have trouble delegating tasks to others. There are several reasons for this problem:

- The fear that subordinates don't really know how to do the job
- The desire to keep as much control as possible over how things are done
- The fear that a subordinate might "show the manager up" in front of others by doing a superb job
- A simple lack of ability as to how to effectively delegate to others

Fortunately, there are some remedies if managers want to learn to delegate more effectively. First, managers should recognize that they can't do everything themselves. Second, if subordinates can't do a job, they should be trained so that they can assume more responsibility in the future. Third, managers should actually recognize that if a subordinate performs well, it also reflects favorably on the manager. Finally, a manager who simply doesn't know how to delegate might need specialized training in how to divide up and assign tasks to others.

THREE FORMS OF AUTHORITY

Whatever type of structure a company develops, it must decide who will have authority over whom. As individuals are delegated responsibility and authority in a firm, a complex web of interactions develops. These interactions may take one of three forms of

DELEGATION process through which a manager allocates work to subordinates

RESPONSIBILITY duty to perform an assigned task

AUTHORITY power to make the decisions necessary to complete a task

ACCOUNTABILITY obligation employees have to their manager for the successful completion of an assigned task

authority: *line*, *staff*, or *committee and team*. Like departmentalization, all three forms may be found in a given company, especially a large one.

Line Authority The type of authority that flows up and down the chain of command is **line authority**. Most companies rely heavily on **line departments**—those directly linked to the production and sales of specific products. For example, Clark Equipment has a division that produces forklifts and small earthmovers. In this division, line departments include purchasing, materials handling, fabrication, painting, and assembly (all of which are directly linked to production) along with sales and distribution (both of which are directly linked to sales).

Each line department is essential to an organization's success. Line employees are the doers and producers in a company. If any line department fails to complete its task, the company cannot sell and deliver finished goods. Thus, the authority delegated to line departments is important. A bad decision by the manager in one department can hold up production for an entire plant. For example, the painting department manager at Clark Equipment changes a paint application on a batch of forklifts, which then show signs of peeling paint. The batch will have to be repainted (and perhaps partially reassembled) before the machines can be shipped.

Staff Authority Some companies also rely on **staff authority**, which is based on special expertise and usually involves counseling and advising line managers. Common staff members include specialists in areas such as law, accounting, and human resource management. A corporate attorney, for example, may be asked to advise the marketing department as it prepares a new contract with the firm's advertising agency. Legal staff members, however, do not typically make decisions that affect how the marketing department does its job. **Staff members**, therefore, help line departments in making decisions but do not usually have the authority to make final decisions.

Typically, the separation between line authority and staff responsibility is clearly delineated. As Figure 6.4 shows, this separation is usually indicated in organization charts by solid lines (line authority) and dotted lines (staff responsibility). It may help to understand this separation by remembering that whereas *staff members* generally provide services to management, *line managers* are directly involved in producing the firm's products.

LINE AUTHORITY organizational structure in which authority flows in a direct chain of command from the top of the company to the bottom

LINE DEPARTMENT department directly linked to the production and sales of a specific product

STAFF AUTHORITY authority based on expertise that usually involves counseling and advising line managers

STAFF MEMBERS advisers and counselors who help line departments in making decisions but who do not have the authority to make final decisions

Figure 6.4
Line and Staff Organization

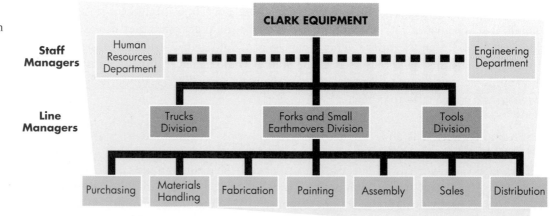

Committee and Team Authority Recently, more organizations have started to use **committee and team authority**—authority granted to committees or teams that play central roles in the firm's daily operations. A committee, for example, may consist of top managers from several major areas. If the work of the committee is especially important and if the committee members will be working together for an extended time, the organization may even grant it special authority as a decision-making body that goes beyond the individual authority possessed by each of its members.

At the operating level, many firms today are also using **work teams**—groups of operating employees who are empowered to plan and organize their own work and to perform that work with minimal supervision. As with permanent committees, the organization will usually find it beneficial to grant special authority to work teams so that they may function more effectively.

> **COMMITTEE AND TEAM AUTHORITY** authority granted to committees or teams involved in a firm's daily operations

> **WORK TEAM** groups of operating employees who are empowered to plan and organize their own work and to perform that work with a minimum of supervision

SELF-CHECK QUESTIONS 4–6

You should now be able to answer Self-Check Questions 4–6.*

4 **Multiple Choice** A tall organization usually has which of the following kinds of span of control?
  (a) wide
  (b) smooth
  (c) narrow
  (d) none of these

5 **Multiple Choice** The delegation process includes all but which of the following?

  (a) assigning responsibility
  (b) granting authority
  (c) creating accountability
  (d) all of these are part of the delegation process

6 **True/False** Organizations often have line authority, staff authority, and committee and team authority.

*__Answers to Self-Check Questions 4–6 can be found on p. 564.__

BASIC FORMS OF ORGANIZATIONAL STRUCTURE

Organizations can structure themselves in an almost infinite number of ways—according to specialization, for example, or departmentalization or the decision-making hierarchy. Nevertheless, it is possible to identify four basic forms of organizational structure that reflect the general trends followed by most firms: *functional, divisional, matrix,* and *international.*

▪▪▪ FUNCTIONAL STRUCTURE

Functional structure is a form of business organization in which authority is determined by the relationships between group functions and activities. It is based on the use of functional departmentalization at the highest level of the business and is used by most small to medium-sized firms. Such organizations are usually structured around basic business functions (marketing, operations, finance). Within the company, there is a marketing department, an operations department, and a finance department. The benefits of

> **FUNCTIONAL STRUCTURE** organization structure in which authority is determined by the relationships between group functions and activities

entrepreneurship and new ventures

Making the Grade

The story has become the stuff of business legend. In the mid 1960s, undistinguished Yale student Fred Smith wrote a paper describing how the adoption of automated technology necessitated a quicker, more reliable transportation system for repair parts. As legend has it, the paper received a poor grade. But Smith himself debunks the myth, saying, "It's become a well-known story because everybody likes to flout authority. But to be honest, I don't really remember what grade I got."

Whatever grade the paper earned, the idea was a winner. Smith joined the Marines and served in Vietnam before investing his own money to start up the air transport business he called Federal Express. FedEx was revolutionary in competing with the monopolistic U.S. Postal Service. In the first of what would prove to be many innovations, FedEx used a hub-and-spoke system for increased speed and efficiency. The company developed a reputation for high-quality, reliable, and fast service, albeit at a high price. The company pioneered the use of bar codes and handheld PDAs for drivers, and online, real-time package tracking for customers.

Then, in 2000, rival UPS decided to enter the air freight segment. This move forced FedEx to respond in some way. "The economics of airplanes are such that we couldn't just keep taking prices down," Smith says. "We finally realized that if we wanted to grow, we had to get into surface transportation." His firm acquired several key players in the ground transportation industry and renamed them to better capitalize on the FedEx brand name. Observers approve. "People say 'FedEx this' when they mean 'Get it someplace fast,'" says investor Timothy M. Ghriskey. "No one says 'UPS this.'" FedEx is unique in the industry with its system of independent, nonunion truckers.

One key to FedEx's success has been its commitment to decentralization. While the firm preaches and practices standardization in its day-to-day business activities, managers throughout the firm are encouraged to question, to challenge, and to develop new ideas. These ideas are always given serious consideration by upper management, and the company prides itself on rewarding what seem to be well-developed ideas, even if they are never used.

FedEx continues to innovate, developing a proprietary pocket-size PC in conjunction with Motorola and Microsoft. FedEx was the first shipper to send package information to customers' cell phones, and the firm is creating software products for small business's logistics. "Engage in constant change," is a mantra for CEO Smith, and he adds, "Companies that don't take risks—some of which are going to work and some of which aren't—are going to end up getting punched up by the marketplace."

> **Companies that don't take risks are going to end up getting punched up by the marketplace.**
>
> **—Fred Smith, founder and CEO, FedEx**

this approach include specialization within functional areas and smoother coordination among them. Experts with specialized training, for example, are hired to work in the marketing department, which handles all of the marketing for the firm.

In large firms, coordination across functional departments becomes more complicated. Functional structure also fosters centralization (which may possibly be desirable but is usually counter to what larger businesses want to do) and makes accountability more difficult. As organizations grow, therefore, they tend to shed this form and move toward one of the other three structures. Figure 6.5 illustrates a functional structure.

DIVISIONAL STRUCTURE
organizational structure in which corporate divisions operate as autonomous businesses under the larger corporate umbrella

DIVISION department that resembles a separate business in that it produces and markets its own products

■ ■ ■ DIVISIONAL STRUCTURE

A **divisional structure** relies on product departmentalization. The firm organizes itself around product-based divisions, each of which may then be managed as a separate enterprise. Organizations using this approach are typically structured around several **divisions**—departments that resemble separate businesses in that they produce and market their own products. The head of each division may be a corporate vice president or, if the organization is large enough, a divisional president. In addition, each division usually

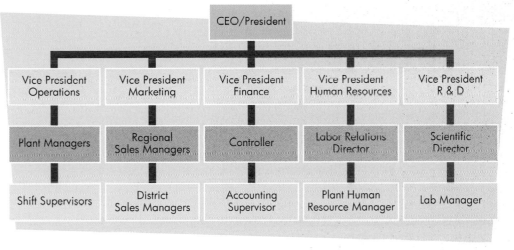

Figure 6.5
Functional Structure

has its own identity and operates as a relatively autonomous business under the larger corporate umbrella. Figure 6.6 illustrates a divisional structure.

H. J. Heinz is one of the world's largest food-processing companies. Heinz makes literally thousands of different products and markets them around the world. The firm is organized into seven basic divisions: food service (selling small packaged products, such as mustard and relish to restaurants), infant foods, condiments (Heinz ketchup, steak sauce, and tomato sauce), Star-Kist tuna, pet foods, frozen foods, and one division that handles miscellaneous products, including new lines being test marketed and soups, beans, and pasta products. Because of its divisional structure, Heinz can evaluate the performance of each division independently. Until recently, Heinz also had a division for its Weight Watchers business, but because this business was performing poorly, the company sold the Weight Watchers classroom program and folded its line of frozen foods into its existing frozen-foods division. Because divisions are relatively autonomous, a firm can take such action with minimal disruption to its remaining business operations.

Like Heinz, other divisionalized companies are free to buy, sell, create, and disband divisions without disrupting the rest of their operations. Unilever, for instance, bought the Weight Watchers business from Heinz and kept it functioning as a separate entity. Divisions can maintain healthy competition among themselves by sponsoring separate advertising campaigns, fostering different corporate identities, and so forth. They can also share certain corporate-level resources (such as market research data). If too much control is delegated to divisional managers, corporate managers may lose touch with

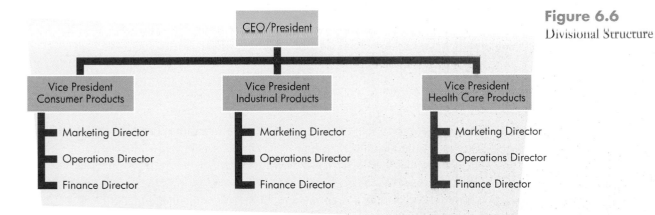

Figure 6.6
Divisional Structure

daily operations. Competition between divisions can also become disruptive, and efforts in one division may be duplicated by those of another.

■■■ MATRIX STRUCTURE

Sometimes a "combination" structure—one that combines two separate structures—works better than either simpler structure alone. A so-called **matrix structure** is organized along two dimensions, instead of just one, by combining, for example, a functional and a divisional structure. This structure gets its matrix-like appearance, when shown in a diagram, by using one underlying "permanent" organizational structure (say, the divisional structure flowing up-and-down in the diagram), and then superimposing a different organizing framework on top of it (e.g., the functional form flowing side-to-side in the diagram). This structure was pioneered by NASA for use in developing specific space programs. It is a highly flexible form that is readily adaptable to changing circumstances.

Suppose a company is using a functional structure. If, as a one-time special project, it wants to develop a new product, a common approach is to create a project team to be responsible for creating that product. The project team may draw members from existing functional departments, such as finance and marketing, so that all viewpoints are represented as the new product is being developed: The marketing member may provide ongoing information about product packaging and pricing issues, for instance, while the finance member may have useful information about when the funds will be available to pay for various things.

In some companies, the matrix organization is a temporary measure installed to complete a specific project and affecting only one part of the firm. In these firms, the end of the project usually means the end of the matrix—either a breakup of the team or a restructuring to fit it into the company's existing line-and-staff structure. Ford, for example, uses a matrix organization to design new models, such as the newest Mustang. A design team composed of people from engineering, marketing, operations, and finance was created to design the new car. After its work was done, the team members moved back to their permanent functional jobs.

In other settings, the matrix organization is a semipermanent fixture. Figure 6.7 shows how Omnimedia (the firm founded by Martha Stewart) has created a permanent matrix organization for its burgeoning lifestyle business. As you can see, the company is organized broadly into media and merchandising groups, each of which has specific product and product groups. For instance, there is an Internet group housed within the media group. Layered on top of this structure are teams of lifestyle experts led by area specialists organized into groups, such as cooking, entertainment, weddings, crafts, and so forth. Although each group targets specific customer needs, they all work, as necessary, across all product groups. An area specialist in weddings, for example, might contribute to an article on wedding planning for an Omnimedia magazine, contribute a story idea for an Omnimedia cable television program, and supply content for an Omnimedia site. This same individual might also help select fabrics suitable for wedding gowns that are to be retailed.

■■■ INTERNATIONAL STRUCTURE

As we saw in Chapter 4, many businesses today manufacture, purchase, and sell in the world market. Thus, several different **international organizational structures** have emerged. International organizational structures are developed in response to the need to manufacture, purchase, and sell in global markets.

For example, when Wal-Mart opened its first store outside the United States in 1992, it set up a special projects team to handle the logistics. As more stores were opened abroad in

Figure 6.7   Matrix Organization at Martha Stewart's Omnimedia

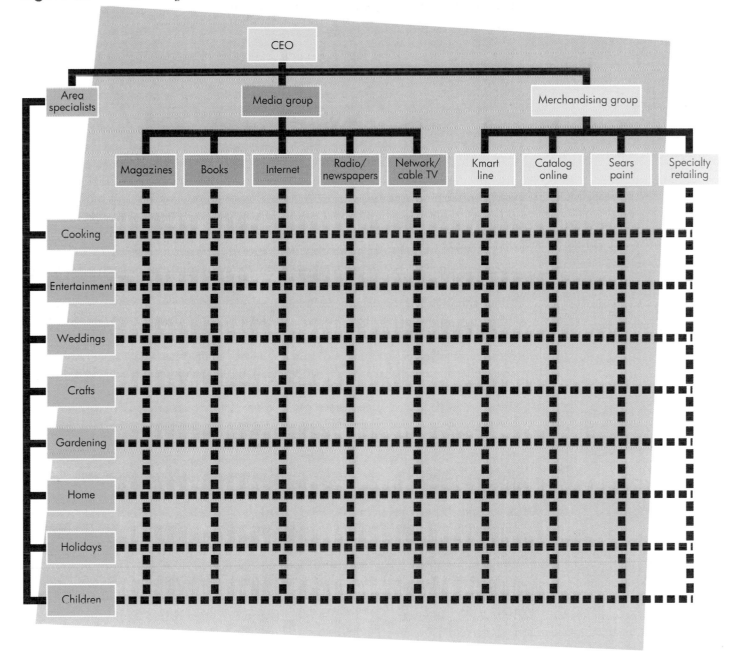

the mid-1990s, the firm created a small international department to handle overseas expansion. By 1999, however, international sales and expansion had become such a major part of Wal-Mart's operations that the firm created a separate international division headed up by a senior vice president. And by 2002, international operations had become so important to Wal-Mart that the international division was further divided into geographic areas where the firm does business, such as Mexico and Europe. And as the firm expands into more foreign markets, such as China and Brazil, new units are created to oversee those operations.[5]

Organizations with important international operations often begin with the form of organization outlined in Figure 6.8. Other firms have also developed a wide range of approaches to international organizational structure. The French food giant Danone Group, for instance, has three major product groups: dairy products (Danone yogurts),

Figure 6.8
International Division Structure

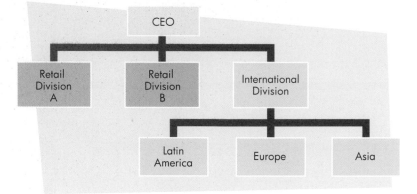

bottled water (Evian), and cookies (Pim's). Danone's structure does not differentiate internationally but rather integrates global operations within each product group.

Finally, some companies adopt a truly global structure in which they acquire resources (including capital), produce goods and services, engage in research and development, and sell products in whatever local market is appropriate, without any consideration of national boundaries. Until a few years ago, General Electric (GE) kept its international business operations as separate divisions. Now, however, the company functions as one integrated global organization. GE businesses around the world connect and interact with each other constantly, and managers freely move back and forth among them. This integration is also reflected in the top management team. The head of GE's audit team is French, the head of quality control is Dutch, and a German runs one of GE's core business groups.[6]

say what you mean

What to Call the Boss

One of the big reasons why global companies are organized in different ways is the culture of their home countries. Consequently, not only organizations but also culture influences the way decisions are made and communicated. In some companies, there's a big gap between senior management and those on the lower rungs, and communication across the gap is often quite formal. In other companies, because the vertical structure is less rigid, people tend to communicate in more familiar terms.

German companies, for example, tend to have fairly rigid structures, with jobs, authority, and responsibility clearly defined. Likewise, people in German organizations tend to respect status and titles. They're usually respectful of superiors and continue to use last names even when they're communicating with people they've known for years. Surprisingly, when it comes to decision making, German companies like to keep everyone in the loop and be sure that people at all levels know what's going on.

In contrast, U.S. companies tend to have formal organizational structures while fostering communication—even between senior managers and lower-level workers—that's often casual and easygoing, right down to the use of first names. Bosses command respect, but once they're outside the workplace, people from different levels tend to interact quite easily.

In many Latin American and South American cultures, bosses have a great deal of power and authority, and workers give them a corresponding degree of respect. Mexican workers sometimes call the boss *patrón*, and as the title suggests, the *patrón* is expected to provide employees with more than orders in the workplace: He's supposed to be a source of moral support and even material assistance and is a regular guest at weddings, funerals, and christenings (where he's often called on to serve as godfather).

Sensitivity to local workplace behavior and attitudes—to the ways in which information is communicated and authority exercised and accepted—is one of the most important qualities that a global company can bring to its relationships with foreign organizations.

▪▪▪ ORGANIZATIONAL DESIGN FOR THE TWENTY-FIRST CENTURY

As the world grows increasingly complex and fast-paced, organizations also continue to seek new forms of organization that permit them to compete effectively. Among the most popular of these new forms are the *team organization*, the *virtual organization*, and the *learning organization*.

Team Organization *Team organization* relies almost exclusively on project-type teams, with little or no underlying functional hierarchy. People float from project to project as dictated by their skills and the demands of those projects. As the term suggests, team authority is the underlying foundation of organizations that adopt the team organizational structure. At Cypress Semiconductor, CEO T. J. Rodgers refuses to allow the organization to grow so large that it can't function at that size. Whenever a unit or group starts getting too large, he simply splits it into smaller units. Therefore, the organization is composed entirely of small units. This strategy allows each unit to change direction, explore new ideas, and try new methods without having to deal with a rigid bureaucratic superstructure. Although few large organizations have actually reached this level of adaptability, Apple Computer and Xerox are among those moving toward it.

Virtual Organization Closely related to the team organization is the *virtual organization*. A virtual organization has little or no formal structure. Typically, it has only a handful of permanent employees, a very small staff, and a modest administrative facility. As the needs of the organization change, its managers bring in temporary workers, lease facilities, and outsource basic support services to meet the demands of each unique situation. As the situation changes, the temporary workforce changes in parallel, with some people leaving the organization and others entering. Facilities and the subcontracted services also change. In other words, the virtual organization exists only in response to its own needs.[7]

Global Research Consortium (GRC) is a virtual organization. GRC offers research and consulting services to firms doing business in Asia. As clients request various services, GRC's staff of three permanent employees subcontracts the work to an appropriate set of several dozen independent consultants and researchers with whom it has relationships. At any given time, therefore, GRC may have several projects underway with 20 or 30 people working on various projects. As the projects change, so too does the composition of the organization. Figure 6.9 illustrates a hypothetical virtual organization.

Learning Organization The so-called *learning organization* works to integrate continuous improvement with continuous employee learning and development. Specifically, a learning organization works to facilitate the lifelong learning and personal development of all of its employees while continually transforming itself to respond to changing demands and needs.

While managers might approach the concept of a learning organization from a variety of perspectives, the most frequent goals are improved quality, continuous improvement, and performance measurement. The idea is that the most consistent and logical strategy for achieving continuous improvement is to constantly upgrade employee talent, skill, and knowledge. For example, if each employee in an organization learns one new thing each day and can translate that knowledge into work-related practice, continuous improvement will logically follow. Indeed, organizations that wholeheartedly embrace

Figure 6.9
The Virtual Organization

this approach believe that only through constant employee learning can continuous improvement really occur.

In recent years, many different organizations have implemented this approach on various levels. Shell Oil, for example, recently purchased an executive conference center north of its headquarters in Houston. Called the Shell Learning Center, the facility boasts state-of-the-art classrooms and instructional technology, lodging facilities, a restaurant, and recreational amenities, such as a golf course, swimming pool, and tennis courts. Line managers at the firm rotate through the center and serve as teaching faculty. Teaching assignments last anywhere from a few days to several months. At the same time, all Shell employees routinely attend training programs, seminars, and related activities, all the while gathering the latest information they need to have to contribute more effectively to the firm. Recent seminar topics have included time management, implications of the Americans with Disabilities Act, balancing work and family demands, and international trade theory.

INFORMAL ORGANIZATION

INFORMAL ORGANIZATION
network, unrelated to the firm's formal authority structure, of everyday social interactions among company employees

The *formal organization* of a business is the part that can be seen and represented in chart form. The structure of a company, however, is by no means limited to the organization chart and the formal assignment of authority. Frequently, the **informal organization**— everyday social interactions among employees that transcend formal jobs and job interrelationships—effectively alters a company's formal structure.[8] This level of organization is sometimes just as powerful—if not more powerful—than the formal structure. For instance, Hewlett-Packard fired its CEO, Carly Fiorina, in mid-2005. Much of the discussion that led to her firing took place outside of formal structural arrangements in the organization—members of the board of directors, for example, held secret meetings and reached confidential agreements among themselves before Fiorina's future with the company was addressed in a formal manner.[9]

On the negative side, the informal organization can also reinforce office politics that put the interests of individuals ahead of those of the firm. Likewise, a great deal of harm can be caused by distorted or inaccurate information communicated without management input or review. For example, if the informal organization is highlighting false information about impending layoffs, valuable employees may act quickly (and unnecessarily) to seek other employment. Among the more important elements of the informal organization are informal groups and the organizational grapevine.

▪▪▪ INFORMAL GROUPS

Informal groups are simply groups of people who decide to interact among themselves. They may be people who work together in a formal sense or who just get together for lunch, during breaks, or after work. They may talk about business, the boss, or nonwork-related topics like families, movies, or sports. Their impact on the organization may be positive (if they work together to support the organization), negative (if they work together in ways that run counter to the organization's interests), or irrelevant (if what they do is unrelated to the organization).

▪▪▪ ORGANIZATIONAL GRAPEVINE

The **grapevine** is an informal communication network that can run through an entire organization. Grapevines are found in all organizations except the very smallest, but they do not always follow the same patterns as formal channels of authority and communication, nor do they necessarily coincide with them. Because the grapevine typically passes information orally, such information often becomes distorted in the process.

Attempts to eliminate the grapevine are fruitless, but, fortunately, managers do have some control over it. By maintaining open channels of communication and responding vigorously to inaccurate information, they can minimize the damage the grapevine can cause. The grapevine can actually be an asset. By getting to know the key people in the grapevine, for example, the manager can partially control the information they receive and use the grapevine to sound out employee reactions to new ideas (for example, a change in human resource policies or benefit packages). The manager can also get valuable information from the grapevine and use it to improve decision making.

GRAPEVINE informal communication network that runs through an organization

▪▪▪ INTRAPRENEURING

Sometimes, organizations actually take steps to encourage the informal organization. They do so for a variety of reasons, two of which we have already discussed. First, most experienced managers recognize that the informal organization exists whether they want it or not. Second, many managers know how to use the informal organization to reinforce the formal organization. Perhaps more important, however, the energy of the informal organization can be harnessed to improve productivity.

Many firms, including Rubbermaid, 3M, and Xerox, support a process called **intrapreneuring**: creating and maintaining the innovation and flexibility of a small-business environment within the confines of a large, bureaucratic structure. The concept is basically sound. Historically, most innovations have come from individuals in small businesses. As businesses increase in size, however, innovation and creativity tend to become casualties in the battle for more sales and profits. In some large companies, new ideas are even discouraged, and champions of innovation have been stalled in midcareer.

Compaq, now part of Hewlett-Packard, is an excellent example of how intrapreneuring works to counteract this trend. The firm has one major division, the New Business Group. When a manager or engineer has an idea for a new product or product application, the individual takes it to the New Business Group and "sells" it. The managers in the group itself are then encouraged to help the innovator develop the idea for field testing. If the product takes off and does well, it is then spun off into its own new business group or division. If it doesn't do as well as hoped, it may still be maintained as part of the New Business Group, or it may be phased out

INTRAPRENEURING process of creating and maintaining the innovation and flexibility of a small business environment within the confines of a large organization

SELF-CHECK QUESTIONS 7–9

You should now be able to answer Self-Check Questions 7–9.*

7 Multiple Choice Which of the following is **not** a basic form of organizational structure?
(a) functional structure
(b) process structure
(c) divisional structure
(d) matrix structure

8 True/False A virtual organization has little or no formal structure.

9 True/False Few large businesses have informal organizations because of their formal and rigid organization charts.

*Answers to Self-Check Questions 7–9 can be found on p. 564.

CONTINUED FROM PAGE 174

IS THERE SYNERGY AMONG BAKED GOODS, SHOE POLISH, AND UNDERWEAR?

Sara Lee's CEO, C. Steven McMillan, tried a number of new tricks to get Sara Lee back on track. One bold move was developing a chain of retail stores named Inner Self. Each store features a spa-like atmosphere in which to sell Sara Lee's Hanes, Playtex, Bali, and Wonderbra products. Susan Nedved, head of development for Inner Self, thinks that the company-owned stores provide a more realistic and comforting environment for making underwear purchases than do some specialty outlets. "There seems to be an open void for another specialty concept that complements Victoria's Secret," says Nedved. "There was a need for shopping alternatives that really cater to the aging population."

By 2005, though, it was clear that new perspectives were needed. So, Sara Lee's board of directors made a change at the top, promoting Brenda Barnes, a senior vice president, to run the company. Barnes initially maintained the same approach—more centralization, coordination, and focus—to get Sara Lee back on track. But many observers were not optimistic that this would work. As for Inner Self and underwear, one analyst points out that "even if you fix that business, it's still apparel, and it's not really viewed as a high-value-added business."

By 2006, Barnes realized that more drastic measures were needed. While the company was posting substantial profits at the corporate level, most of those profits came from only a few businesses, while more than half of the individual businesses were losing money. So, she and her executive team began drawing up plans to break the company into several smaller, more focused, more profitable companies. The firm also announced its intentions to sell perhaps as many as one-third of the businesses it owns.

QUESTIONS FOR DISCUSSION

1 Describe the basic structural components at Sara Lee.
2 What role does specialization play at Sara Lee?
3 What kinds of authority are reflected in this case?
4 What kind of organizational structure does Sara Lee seem to have?
5 What role may the informal organization have played in Sara Lee's various acquisitions and divestitures?

1 Discuss the factors that influence a firm's organizational structure.

Each organization must develop an appropriate *organizational structure*—the specification of the jobs to be done and the ways in which those jobs relate to one another. Most organizations change structures almost continuously. Firms prepare *organization charts* to clarify structure and to show employees where they fit into a firm's operations. Each box represents a job, and solid lines define the *chain of command*, or *reporting relationships*. The charts of large firms are complex and include individuals at many levels. Because size prevents them from charting every manager, they may create single organization charts for overall corporate structure and separate charts for divisions.

2 Explain specialization and departmentalization as two of the building blocks of organizational structure.

The process of identifying specific jobs and designating people to perform them leads to *job specialization*. After they're specialized, jobs are grouped into logical units—the process of *departmentalization*. Departmentalization follows one (or any combination) of five forms: (1) *product departmentalization*, (2) *process departmentalization*, (3) *functional departmentalization*, (4) *customer departmentalization*, or (5) *geographic departmentalization*. Larger companies take advantage of different types of departmentalization for various levels.

3 Describe centralization and decentralization, delegation, and authority as the key ingredients in establishing the decision-making hierarchy.

After jobs have been specialized and departmentalized, firms establish decision-making hierarchies. One major issue addressed through the creation of the decision-making hierarchy involves whether the firm will be relatively *centralized* or relatively *decentralized*. Centralized authority systems typically require multiple layers of management and thus *tall organizational structures*. Decentralized firms tend to have relatively fewer layers of management, resulting in a *flat organizational structure*. *Delegation* is the process through which a manager allocates work to subordinates. In general, the delegation process involves three steps: (1) the assignment of *responsibility*, (2) the granting of *authority*, and (3) the creation of *accountability*. As individuals are delegated responsibility and authority in a firm, a complex web of interactions develops. These interactions may take one of three forms of authority: *line*, *staff*, or *committee and team*.

4 Explain the differences among functional, divisional, matrix, and international organizational structures and describe the most popular new forms of organizational design.

Most firms rely on one of four basic forms of organizational structure: (1) *functional*, (2) *divisional*, (3) *matrix*, or (4) *international*. As global competition becomes more complex, companies may experiment with ways to respond. Some adopt truly global structures, acquiring resources and producing and selling products in local markets without consideration of national boundaries. Organizations also continue to seek new forms of organization that permit them to compete effectively. The most popular new forms include (1) *team organization*, (2) *virtual organization*, and (3) *learning organization*.

5 Describe the informal organization and discuss intrapreneuring.

The *formal organization* is the part that can be represented in chart form. The *informal organization*—everyday social interactions among employees that transcend formal jobs and job interrelationships—may alter formal structure. There are two important elements in most informal organizations. *Informal groups* consist of people who decide to interact among themselves. Their impact on a firm may be positive, negative, or irrelevant. The *grapevine* is an informal communication network that can run through an entire organization. Because it can be harnessed to improve productivity, some organizations encourage the informal organization. Many firms also support *intrapreneuring*—creating and maintaining the innovation and flexibility of a small business within the confines of a large, bureaucratic structure.

KEY TERMS

accountability (p. 183)

authority (p. 183)

centralized organization (p. 180)

chain of command (p. 174)

committee and team authority (p. 185)

customer departmentalization (p. 178)

decentralized organization (p. 181)

delegation (p. 183)

departmentalization (p. 177)

division (p. 186)

divisional structure (p. 186)

flat organizational structure (p. 181)

functional departmentalization (p. 178)

functional structure (p. 185)

geographic departmentalization (p. 179)

grapevine (p. 193)

informal organization (p. 192)

international organizational structures (p. 188)

intrapreneuring (p. 193)

job specialization (p. 176)

line authority (p. 184)

line department (p. 184)

matrix structure (p. 188)

organization chart (p. 174)

organizational structure (p. 174)

process departmentalization (p. 178)

product departmentalization (p. 178)

profit center (p. 177)

responsibility (p. 183)

span of control (p. 182)

staff authority (p. 184)

staff members (p. 184)

tall organizational structure (p. 181)

work team (p. 185)

QUESTIONS AND EXERCISES

Questions for Review

1 What is an organization chart? What purpose does it serve?

2 Explain the significance of size as it relates to organizational structure. Describe the changes that are likely to occur as an organization grows.

3 What is the difference between responsibility and authority?

4 Why do some managers have difficulties in delegating authority?

5 Why is a company's informal organization important?

Questions for Analysis

6 Draw up an organization chart for your college or university.

7 Describe a hypothetical organizational structure for a small printing firm. Describe changes that might be necessary as the business grows.

8 Compare and contrast the matrix and divisional approaches to organizational structure. How would you feel personally about working in a matrix organization in which you were assigned simultaneously to multiple units or groups?

Application Exercises

9 Interview the manager of a local service business, such as a fast-food restaurant. What types of tasks does this manager typically delegate? Is the appropriate authority also delegated in each case?

10 Using books, magazines, or personal interviews, identify a person who has succeeded as an intrapreneur. In what ways did the structure of the intrapreneur's company help this individual succeed? In what ways did the structure pose problems?

GETTING WITH THE PROGRAM

Goal

To encourage you to understand the relationship between organizational structure and a company's ability to attract and keep valued employees.

Background Information

You are the founder of a small but growing high-tech company that develops new computer software. With your current workload and new contracts in the pipeline, your business is thriving, except for one problem: You cannot find computer programmers for product development. Worse yet, current staff members are being lured away by other high-tech firms. After suffering a particularly discouraging personnel raid in which competitors captured three of your most valued employees, you schedule a meeting with your director of human resources to plan organizational changes designed to encourage worker loyalty. You already pay top dollar, but the continuing exodus tells you that programmers are looking for something more.

Method

Working with three or four classmates, identify some ways in which specific organizational changes might improve the working environment and encourage employee loyalty. As you analyze the following factors, ask yourself the obvious question:

If I were a programmer, what organizational changes would encourage me to stay?

- *Level of job specialization.* With many programmers describing their jobs as tedious because of the focus on detail in a narrow work area, what changes, if any, would you make in job specialization? Right now, for instance, few of your programmers have any say in product design.
- *Decision-making hierarchy.* What decision-making authority would encourage people to stay? Is expanding employee authority likely to work better in a centralized or decentralized organization?
- *Team authority.* Can team empowerment make a difference? Taking the point of view of the worker, describe the ideal team.
- *Intrapreneuring.* What can your company do to encourage and reward innovation?

FOLLOW-UP QUESTIONS

1 With the average computer programmer earning nearly $70,000, and with all competitive firms paying top dollar, why might organizational issues be critical in determining employee loyalty?

2 If you were a programmer, what organizational factors would make a difference to you? Why?

3 As the company founder, how willing would you be to make major organizational changes in light of the shortage of qualified programmers?

MINDING YOUR OWN BUSINESS

The Situation

Assume that you have recently gone to work for a large high-tech company. You have discovered an interesting arrangement in which one of your coworkers is engaging. Specifically, he blocks his schedule for the hour between 11:00 a.m. and 12:00 noon each day and does not take a lunch break. During this one-hour interval, he is actually running his own real estate business.

The Dilemma

You recently asked this employee how he manages to pull this off. "Well," he responded, "the boss and I never talked about it, but she knows what's going on. They know they can't replace me, and I always get my work done. I don't use any company resources. So, what's the harm?" Interestingly, you also have a business opportunity that could be pursued in the same way.

QUESTION TO ADDRESS

1 What are the ethical issues in this situation?
2 What do you think most people would do in this situation?
3 What would you do in this situation?

TO POACH, OR NOT TO POACH . . .

The Situation

The Hails Corporation, a manufacturing plant, has recently moved toward an all-team-based organization structure. That is, all workers are divided into teams. Each team has the autonomy to divide up the work assigned to it among its individual members. In addition, each team handles its own scheduling for members to take vacations and other time off. The teams also handle the interviews and hiring of new team members when the need arises. Team A has just lost one of its members who moved to another city to be closer to his ailing parents.

The Dilemma

Since moving to the team structure, every time a team has needed new members, it has advertised in the local newspaper and hired someone from outside the company. However, Team A is considering a different approach to fill its opening. Specifically, a key member of another team (Team B) has made it known that she would like to join Team A. She likes the team members, sees the team's work as being enjoyable, and is somewhat bored with her team's current assignment.

The concern is that if Team A chooses this individual to join the team, several problems may occur. For one thing, her current team will clearly be angry with the members of Team A. Further, "poaching" new team members from other teams inside the plant is likely to become a common occurrence. On the other hand, though, it seems reasonable that she should have the same opportunity to join Team A as an outsider would. Team A needs to decide how to proceed.

Team Activity

Assemble a group of four students and assign each group member to one of the following roles:

- Member of Team A
- Member of Team B
- Manager of both teams
- Hails investor

ACTION STEPS

1　Before hearing any of your group's comments on this situation, and from the perspective of your assigned role, do you think that the member of Team B should be allowed to join Team A? Write down the reasons for your position.

2　Before hearing any of your group's comments on this situation, and from the perspective of your assigned role, what are the underlying ethical issues, if any, in this situation? Write down the issues.

3　Gather your group together and reveal, in turn, each member's comments on the situation. Next, reveal the ethical issues listed by each member.

4　Appoint someone to record main points of agreement and disagreement within the group. How do you explain the results? What accounts for any disagreement?

5　From an ethical standpoint, what does your group conclude is the most appropriate action that should be taken by Hails in this situation? Should Team B's member be allowed to join Team A?

6　Develop a group response to the following questions: Assuming Team A asks the Team B member to join its team, how might it go about minimizing repercussions? Assuming Team A does not ask the Team B member to join its team, how might it go about minimizing repercussions?

JUICING UP THE ORGANIZATION: NANTUCKET NECTARS

Learning Objectives

The purpose of this video is to help you:

1 Recognize how growth affects an organization's structure.
2 Discuss the reasons why businesses departmentalize.
3 Understand how flat organizations operate.

Synopsis

Tom Scott and Tom First founded Nantucket Nectars in 1989 when they had an idea for a peach drink. In the early days, the two ran the entire operation from their boat. Now, Nantucket Nectars has more than 130 employees split between headquarters in Cambridge, Massachusetts, and several field offices. As a result, management has developed a more formal structure, and the company relies on cross-functional teams to handle special projects, such as the implementation of new accounting software. This and other strategies have helped Nantucket Nectars successfully manage rapid growth.

DISCUSSION QUESTIONS

1 **For analysis**: What type of organization is in place at Nantucket Nectars?
2 **For analysis**: How would you describe the top-level span of control at Nantucket Nectars?

3 **For application**: Nantucket Nectars may need to change its organizational structure as it expands into new products and new markets. Under what circumstances might some form of divisional organization be appropriate?
4 **For application**: Assume that Nantucket Nectars is purchasing a well-established beverage company with a tall structure stressing top-down control. What are some of the problems that management might face in integrating the acquired firm into the existing organizational structure of Nantucket Nectars?
5 **For debate**: Assume that someone who is newly promoted into a management position at Nantucket Nectars cannot adjust to the idea of delegating work to lower-level employees. Should this new manager be demoted? Support your chosen position.

Online Exploration

Visit the Nantucket Nectars site (www.juiceguys.com) and follow the links about the company and its products. Then use the Internet to search for the latest news about the company, which is formally known as Nantucket Allserve. Has it been acquired by a larger company, or has it acquired one or more smaller firms? What are the implications for the chain of command, the decision making, and the organizational structure of Nantucket Nectars?

1 Explain the meaning of the term *production* or *operations*.

2 Describe the three kinds of utility that operations processes provide for adding customer value.

3 Explain how companies with different business strategies are best served by having different operations capabilities.

4 Identify the major factors that are considered in operations planning.

5 Discuss the information contained in four kinds of operations schedules—the master production schedule, detailed schedule, staff schedule, and project schedule.

6 Identify the activities involved in operations control.

7 Identify the activities and underlying objectives involved in total quality management.

8 Explain how a supply chain strategy differs from traditional strategies for coordinating operations among firms.

KEEPING TRACK OF GERMAN ENGINEERING

For auto enthusiasts, the first faint signs of criticism seemed an anomaly, a false blip on the radar screen rather than the beginning of the full-scale trend that was to follow. Results of a secret European poll on car quality were leaked to the press in 2002, and Mercedes—for

OPERATIONS MANAGEMENT AND QUALITY

decades the pride of German engineering—was not at the top of the list. The poll, conducted by Europe's automakers, showed Mercedes quality and customer satisfaction slipping to levels even below Opel, the German-made General Motors brand with a not-so-good image in the European market. In a more recent German study of reliability during the first three years of ownership, customers rated six Toyota models and five other cars ahead of the MLK, the highest-rated Mercedes model. In the United States, too, the quality rankings for Mercedes were nose-diving: A 2004 J. D. Power & Associates study of vehicle dependability found Mercedes tumbling to twenty-ninth place among 37 U.S. industry brands.

"Being Mercedes, quality is absolutely the highest priority," said company spokeswoman Donna Boland. "It's what our brand is based on. We will use every resource at our disposal to bring those numbers up," she added at the time. But the J. D. Power numbers indicated that a challenging climb lies ahead for this industry icon. The survey of car owners reported that three-year-old Mercedes cars had 327 problems per 100 vehicles, versus just 285 for other luxury brands. When questioned about specific problem areas, drivers gave Mercedes the biggest markdown of all premium brands for quality of "transmission" and "features/controls," ranging from batteries to emergency lights.

The quality downslide started, industry analysts say, when Mercedes decided to shift away from its traditional emphasis on "making what the engineers want" to an emphasis

Being Mercedes, quality is absolutely the highest priority. . . . We will use every resource at our disposal to bring those numbers up.

—*Mercedes spokeswoman Donna Boland, on the automaker's slumping quality ratings*

on what executives wanted, which was to design cars to meet a certain price point, including smaller and less expensive models.

As the quality downslide continues, competitors are closing the gap on Mercedes' traditional market leadership. BMW, one of Mercedes' key competitors, gained customers with a 10-percent increase in sales for 2004, while the Mercedes Brand lost 3 percent. ■

Our opening story continues on page 226.

WHAT'S IN IT FOR ME?

Mercedes is learning a hard lesson—and paying a steep price—by shifting its primary emphasis from engineering to marketing, while allowing a downslide in its production and quality operations. By understanding this chapter's methods for managing operations and improving quality, you can benefit in two ways: (1) As an employee, you'll have a clearer picture of who your customers are, what they want, and how your job depends on the services they receive from you; and (2) you'll better understand how companies around you—even successful firms—have to change production methods whenever they adopt new business goals, to remain competitive.

In this chapter, we'll look at many aspects of operations management, including how businesses create value through operations, the many facets of operations planning and scheduling, as well as operations control. We'll also talk about quality—how businesses can improve and manage quality, and why it's important that they do so.

WHAT DOES *OPERATIONS* MEAN TODAY?

SERVICE OPERATIONS (SERVICE PRODUCTION) activities producing intangible and tangible products, such as entertainment, transportation, and education

GOODS OPERATIONS (GOODS PRODUCTION) activities producing tangible products, such as radios, newspapers, buses, and textbooks

OPERATIONS activities involved in making products—goods and services—for customers

Although you're not always aware of it, you're constantly involved in business activities that provide goods and services to customers. You wake up to the sound of your favorite radio station and pick up a newspaper on your way to the bus stop, where you catch your ride to work or school. Your instructors, the bus driver, the clerk at the 7-Eleven store, and the morning radio announcer all work in **service operations** (or **service production**). They provide intangible and tangible service products, such as entertainment, transportation, education, and food preparation. Firms that make only tangible products—radios, newspapers, buses, textbooks—are engaged in activities for **goods operations** (or **goods production**).

The term **operations** (or **production**) refers to all the activities involved in making products—goods and services—for customers. In modern societies, much of what we need or want, from health care to fast food, is produced by service operations. As a rule, managers in the service sector give more consideration to the human element in operations (as opposed to the equipment or technology involved) because success or failure depends often on provider-customer contact. Employees who deal directly with customers affect customer feelings about the service, and as we will see, a key difference between goods and service operations is the customer's involvement in the latter.

Although companies are typically classified as either goods producers or service providers, the distinction is often blurred. All businesses are service operations to some extent. Consider General Electric. When you think of GE, you most likely think of appliances and jet engines. However, GE is not just a goods producer. According to its annual report, GE's "growth engines"—its most vibrant business activities—are service

operations, including media and entertainment (NBC-Universal), consumer and commercial finance, investment, transportation services, health care information, and real estate, which account for over 80 percent of the company's revenues.[1]

CREATING VALUE THROUGH OPERATIONS

To understand a firm's production processes, we need to know what kinds of benefits its production provides, both for itself and for its customers. Production provides businesses with economic results: profits, wages, and goods purchased from other companies. At the same time, it adds customer value by providing **utility**—the ability of a product to satisfy a want or need—in terms of form, time, and place:

UTILITY a product's ability to satisfy a human want or need

- Production makes products available: By converting raw materials and human skills into finished goods and services, production creates *form utility*, as when an ornament maker combines glass, plastic, and other materials to create tree decorations for Christmas.
- When a company turns out ornaments in time for Christmas, it creates *time utility*; that is, it adds customer value by making products available when consumers want them.
- When a department store opens its annual Trim-a-Tree department, it creates *place utility*: It makes products available where they are convenient for consumers.

Creating a product that customers value, then, is no accident, but instead results from organized effort. **Operations (production) management** is the systematic direction and control of the processes that transform resources into finished services and goods that create value for and provide benefits to customers. In overseeing production, **operations (production) managers** are responsible for ensuring that operations processes create what customers want and need.

As Figure 7.1 shows, operations managers draw up plans to transform resources into products. First, they bring together basic resources: knowledge, physical materials, information, equipment, the customer, and human skills. Then they put them to effective use in a production facility. As demand for a product increases, they schedule and

OPERATIONS (PRODUCTION) MANAGEMENT systematic direction and control of the processes that transform resources into finished products that create value for and provide benefits to customers

OPERATIONS (PRODUCTION) MANAGERS managers responsible for ensuring that operations processes create value and provide benefits to customers

Figure 7.1
The Resource Transformation
Process

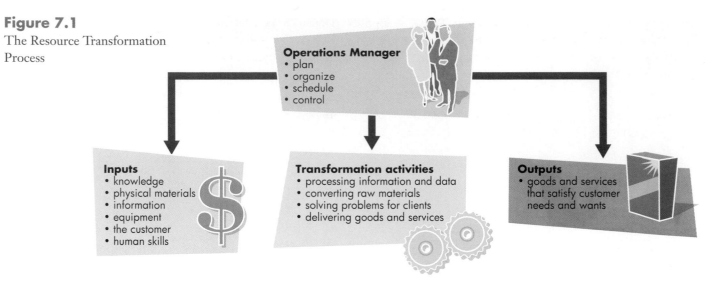

control work to produce the required amount. Finally, they control costs, quality levels, inventory, and facilities and equipment. In some businesses, the operations manager is one person. Typically, different employees work together to complete these different responsibilities.

Some operations managers work in factories; others work in offices and stores. Farmers are operations managers who create utility by transforming soil, seeds, fuel, and other inputs into soybeans, milk, and other outputs. They may hire crews of workers to plant and harvest, opt instead for automated machinery, or prefer some combination of workers and machinery. These decisions affect costs and determine the kinds of buildings and equipment in operations and the quality and quantity of goods produced.

■■■ DIFFERENCES BETWEEN SERVICE AND GOODS MANUFACTURING OPERATIONS

Both service and manufacturing operations transform raw materials into finished products. In service operations, however, the raw materials, or inputs, are not things like glass or steel. Rather, they are people who have either unsatisfied needs or possessions needing care or alteration. In service operations, finished products or outputs are people with needs met and possessions serviced.

Thus, there is at least one obvious difference between service and manufacturing operations. Whereas goods are *produced*, services are *performed*. Four aspects of service operations can make such operations more complicated than simple goods production. These include (1) interacting with consumers, (2) the intangible and unstorable nature of some services, (3) the customer's presence in the process, and (4) service quality considerations.

Interacting with Consumers Manufacturing operations emphasize outcomes in terms of physical goods—for example, a new jacket. But the products of most *service* operations are really combinations of goods and services—both making a pizza *and* delivering (serving) it. Service workers need different skills. For example, gas company employees may need interpersonal skills to calm frightened customers who have reported gas leaks. Thus, the job includes more than just repairing pipes. In contrast, factory workers who install gas pipes in manufactured homes without any customer contact don't need such skills.

Services Can Be Intangible and Unstorable Two prominent characteristics—*intangibility* and *unstorability*—set services apart from physical goods.

- *Intangibility*. Often, services can't be touched, tasted, smelled, or seen, but they're still there. An important satisfier for customers, therefore, is the *intangible* value they receive in the form of pleasure, gratification, or a feeling of safety. For example, when you hire an attorney, you purchase not only the intangible quality of legal expertise but also the equally intangible reassurance that help is at hand.
- *Unstorability*. Many services—such as trash collection, transportation, child care, and house cleaning—can't be produced ahead of time and then stored for high-demand periods. If a service isn't used when available, it's usually wasted. Services, then, are typically characterized by a high degree of *unstorability*.

Customer's Presence in the Operations Process Because service operations transform customers or their possessions, the customer is often present in the operations process. To get a haircut, for example, most of us have to go to the barbershop or hair salon. As physical participants in the operations process, consumers can affect it. As a customer, you expect the salon to be conveniently located (place utility), to be open for business at convenient times (time utility), to provide safe and comfortable facilities, and to offer quality grooming (form utility) at reasonable prices (value for money spent). Accordingly, the manager sets hours of operation, available services, and an appropriate number of employees to meet customer requirements. But what happens if a customer, scheduled to receive a haircut, also asks for additional services, such as highlights or a shave when they arrive? In this case, the service provider must balance customer satisfaction with a tight schedule. High customer contact has the potential to significantly affect the process.

Intangibles Count for Service Quality Consumers use different measures to judge services and goods because services include intangibles, not just physical objects. Most service managers know that quality of work and quality of service are not necessarily the same thing. Your car, for example, may have been flawlessly repaired (quality of work), but you'll probably be unhappy with the service if you're forced to pick it up a day later than promised (quality of service).

■■■ OPERATIONS PROCESSES

To better understand the diverse kinds of production in various firms and industries, it is helpful to classify production according to general differences in operations processes. An **operations process** is a set of methods and technologies used to produce a good or a service. We can classify goods production, for example, by asking whether its operations process has a "make-to-order" or a "make-to-stock" emphasis. We can classify services according to the extent of customer contact required.

OPERATIONS PROCESS set of methods and technologies used to produce a good or a service

Because service operations transform customers or their possessions, the customer is often present in the operations process.

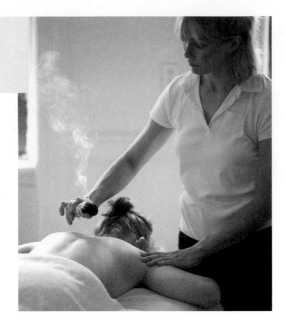

MAKE-TO-ORDER OPERATIONS activities for one-of-a-kind or custom-made production

MAKE-TO-STOCK OPERATIONS activities for producing standardized products for mass consumption

LOW-CONTACT SYSTEM level of customer contact in which the customer need not be part of the system to receive the service

HIGH-CONTACT SYSTEM level of customer contact in which the customer is part of the system during service delivery

Goods Production Processes: Make-to-Order Versus Make-to-Stock Processes Clothing, such as evening gowns, is available either "off-the-shelf" in department stores, or custom-made at a designer-tailor shop. The designer-tailor's **make-to-order operations** respond to one-of-a-kind gown requirements, including unique patterns, materials, sizes, and shapes, depending on customers' unique characteristics. **Make-to-stock operations**, in contrast, produce standard gowns in large quantities to be stocked on store shelves or in displays for mass consumption. The production processes are quite different for the two settings, including procedures for designing gowns; planning for materials purchases; methods for cutting, sewing, and assembling gowns; and employee skills for production.

Service Production Processes: Extent of Customer Contact In classifying services, we may ask whether a service can be provided without the customers being part of the production system. In answering this question, we classify services according to *extent of customer contact.*

Low-Contact Systems Consider the check-processing operations at your bank. Bank employees sort checks that have been cashed that day and send them to the banks on which they were drawn. This operation is a **low-contact system**: Customers are not in contact with the bank while the service is performed. They receive the service—funds are transferred to cover checks—without setting foot in the processing center. Gas and electric companies, auto repair shops, and lawn-care services are other examples of low-contact systems.

High-Contact Systems Think about your local public transit system. The service is transportation, and when you purchase transportation, you board a bus or train. For example, the Bay Area Rapid Transit (BART) system connects San Francisco with outlying suburbs and, like all public transit systems, is a **high-contact system**: To receive the service, the customer must be part of the system. Thus, managers must worry about the cleanliness of trains and the appearance of stations. By contrast, a firm that ships coal is not concerned with the appearance of its trains since no paying passengers are riding on them. It's a low-contact system.

SELF-CHECK QUESTIONS 1–3

You should now be able to answer Self-Check Questions 1–3.*

1 True/False Whereas the term *production* refers primarily to the creation of physical goods, the term *operations* refers to activities for providing services to customers.

2 Multiple Choice Which of the following is **not true** regarding operations processes?
(a) In high-contact service processes, the customer is a part of the process
(b) Make-to-stock operations are quite different than those for make-to-order production
(c) Skills for interacting with consumers are more important for service operations than for manufacturing operations
(d) Foot surgery is a good example of a low-contact operation

3 Multiple Choice Which of the following is **true** regarding the differences between service and manufacturing operations?
(a) Many services cannot be produced ahead of time and then stored
(b) The products offered by all service operations are intangible and don't involve physical goods
(c) Whereas all service operations are customized for customers, manufacturing operations focus on mass-production processes
(d) Customers generally use the same measures for judging the quality of service products and physical goods products

*Answers to Self-Check Questions 1–3 can be found on p. 564.

BUSINESS STRATEGY AS THE DRIVER OF OPERATIONS

The discussion to this point suggests that there is no one standard way for doing production. Rather, it is a flexible activity that can be molded into many shapes to give quite different production, or operations, capabilities for different purposes. How, then, do companies go about selecting the kind of production that is best for their company? Its design is best driven from above by the firm's larger business strategy.

■■■ THE MANY FACES OF PRODUCTION OPERATIONS

In this section we present examples of four firms—two in goods production and two in services—having contrasting business strategies and, as we shall see, that have chosen different operations capabilities. All four firms are successful, but they've taken quite different operations paths to get there. As shown in Table 7.1, each company has identified a business strategy that it can use for winning customer orders— that is, attracting customers—in its industry. For Toyota, *quality* was chosen as the strategy for competing in selling autos. Save-A-Lot grocery stores, in contrast to others in the grocery industry, offer customers *lower prices*. The *flexibility* strategy at 3M emphasizes new product development in an ever-changing line of products for home and office. FedEx captures the overnight delivery market by emphasizing delivery *dependability*, first and foremost.

entrepreneurship and new ventures

Can Table Scraps Become Fine Wine?

Norcal Waste Systems isn't a small company; it boasts 400,000 residential, industrial, and commercial customers in 50 California communities, including San Francisco. But size and 50 years of success aren't slowing the company's innovative approach to garbage collection and waste management. Its entrepreneurial spirit is propelling this 100-percent employee-owned firm into a new venture in creative recycling: turning food scraps into fine wine.

The transformation is not exactly direct. Norcal jumped at the opportunity to invest in a unique idea for turning organic waste—food trimmings from produce markets and food waste from restaurants—into a useful product. Instead of dumping it in a landfill, Norcal collects organic material to use in a process that converts waste into finished compost. The compost is then bagged and sold as a soil reconditioner, mostly to California vineyards. Always looking for better ways to grow stronger grapevines, vineyard managers in Sonoma–Napa Valley apply Norcal compost between rows of vines because it returns nitrogen and other

nutrients to the soil. It also aerates the soil and helps it retain water.

Norcal's composting process uses new technologies to separate, collect, and deliver incoming waste to a specially designed production facility. Compostable material is collected from over 1,400 food-related businesses and thousands of households in the San Francisco Bay Area. Every day, more than 300 tons of waste are removed from the standard waste-disposal stream and delivered to Norcal, where finished compost is produced in a three-month conversion cycle.

The various participants in and beneficiaries of the enterprise—customers, waste contributors, and communities—are enthusiastic about Norcal's profitable new twist on recycling. In addition to vineyards, participating businesses benefit because the venture reduces garbage bills. Bay Area officials like it because it reduces the need for landfills. "Innovative programs like Norcal's Composting Program," says Oakland Mayor Jerry Brown, "bring us closer to realizing our waste-reduction goals while providing cost savings for Oakland's businesses."

OPERATIONS CAPABILITY an activity or process that production does especially well with high proficiency

Business Strategy Determines Operations Capabilities Successful firms design their operations to support the company's business strategy.[2] In other words, production operations are adjusted to support the firms' target markets. Since our four firms use different business strategies, we should expect to see differences in their operations, too, so let's examine them. The top-priority **operations capability (production capability)**—the activity or process that production must do especially well, with high proficiency—is listed for each firm in Table 7.2, along with key operations characteristics for implementing that capability. Each company's operations capability matches up with its business strategy so that the firm's activities—from top to bottom—are focused in a particular direction.

As you can see in Table 7.2, Toyota's top priority focuses on quality—being best in the industry on that characteristic—so its operations—the resource inputs for production,

TABLE 7.1 BUSINESS STRATEGIES THAT WIN CUSTOMERS FOR FOUR COMPANIES

COMPANY	STRATEGY FOR ATTRACTING CUSTOMERS	WHAT THE COMPANY DOES TO IMPLEMENT ITS STRATEGY
Toyota	Quality	Cars perform reliably, have an appealing fit-and-finish, and consistently meet or exceed customer expectations at a competitive price
Save-A-Lot	Low Price	Foods and everyday items offered at savings up to 40 percent less than conventional food chains
3M	Flexibility	Innovation, with more than 55,000 products in a constantly changing line of convenience items for home and office
FedEx	Dependability	Every delivery is fast and on-time, as promised

TABLE 7.2 OPERATIONS CAPABILITIES AND CHARACTERISTICS FOR FOUR COMPANIES

OPERATIONS CAPABILITY	KEY OPERATIONS CHARACTERISTICS
Quality (Toyota)	• High-quality standards for materials suppliers • Just-in-time materials flow for lean manufacturing • Specialized, automated equipment for consistent product build-up • Operations personnel are experts on continuous improvement of product, work methods, and materials
Low Cost (Save-A-Lot)	• Avoids excessive overhead and costly inventory (no floral departments, sushi bars, or banks that drive up costs) • Limited assortment of products, staples, in one size only for low-cost restocking, lower inventories, and less paperwork • Many locations; small stores—less than half the size of conventional grocery stores—for low construction and maintenance costs • Reduces labor and shelving costs by receiving and selling merchandise out of custom shipping cartons
Flexibility (3M)	• Maintains some excess (expensive) production capacity available for fast startup on new products • Adaptable equipment/facilities for production changeovers from old to new products • Hires operations personnel who thrive on change • Many medium- to small-sized facilities in diverse locations, which enhances creativity
Dependability (FedEx)	• Customer automation: uses electronic and online tools with customers to shorten shipping time • Wireless information system for package scanning by courier, updating of package movement, and package tracking by customer • Maintains a company air force, global weather forecasting center, and ground transportation for pickup and delivery, with backup vehicles for emergencies • Each of 30 automated regional distribution hubs processes up to 45,000 packages per hour for next-day deliveries

the transformation activities, and the outputs from production—are devoted first and foremost to quality. Its car designs emphasize appearance, reliable performance, and desirable features at a reasonable price. All production processes, equipment, and training are designed to build better cars. The entire culture supports a quality emphasis among employees, suppliers, and dealerships. Had Toyota instead chosen to compete as the low price car in the industry, as some successful car companies do, then a cost-minimization focus would have been appropriate, giving Toyota's operations an altogether different form. Toyota's operations support its chosen business strategy, and do it successfully.

Expanding into Additional Capabilities Finally, it should be noted that excellent firms learn, over time, how to achieve more than just one competence. Our four example firms eventually became excellent in several capabilities. FedEx, for example, in addition to dependability, is noted for world-class service quality and cost containment, too. But in the earlier startup years, its primary and distinguishing capability—that set it apart from the competition—was dependability, the foundation upon which future success was built.

OPERATIONS PLANNING

Now that we've contrasted various kinds of production, let's turn to a discussion of production activities and resources that are considered in every business organization. Like all good managers, we start with planning. Managers from many departments

Figure 7.2
Operations Planning
and Control

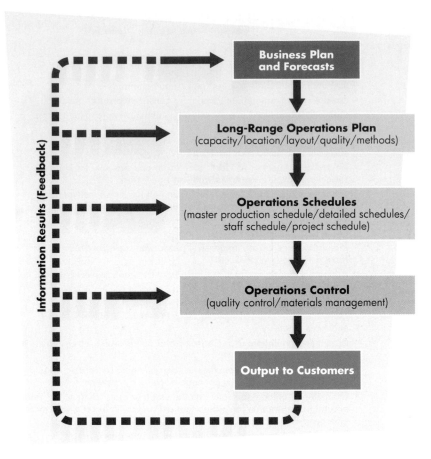

contribute to decisions about operations. As Figure 7.2 shows, however, no matter how many decision makers are involved, the process is a logical sequence of decisions.

The business plan and forecasts developed by top managers provide guidance for long-term operations plans. Covering a two-to-five-year period, the operations plan anticipates the number of plants or service facilities and the amount of labor, equipment, transportation, and storage needed to meet future demand for new and existing products. In this section, we survey long-term planning, discussing the planning activities that fall into its five categories: *capacity*, *location*, *layout*, *quality*, and *methods planning*.

■■■ CAPACITY PLANNING

CAPACITY amount of a product that a company can produce under normal conditions

The amount of a product that a company can produce under normal conditions is its **capacity**. A firm's capacity depends on how many people it employs and the number and size of its facilities. A supermarket's capacity for customer checkouts, for instance, depends on its number of checkout stations. A typical store has excess capacity—more cash registers than it needs—on an average day, but on Saturday morning or during the three days before Thanksgiving, they'll all be running at full capacity.

Long-range capacity planning considers both current and future requirements. If capacity is too small for demand, the company must turn away customers—a situation that cuts into profits and alienates both customers and salespeople. If capacity greatly exceeds demand, the firm is wasting money by maintaining facilities that are too large, by keeping excess machinery online, or by employing too many workers.

The stakes are high in capacity decisions: While expanding fast enough to meet future demand and to protect market share from competitors, firms must also weigh the costs of expanding. "We are constantly evaluating our business to make certain we're adding capacity in advance of demand to serve our markets, meet our customers' needs, and grow with them," says John Pagano, vice president of Owens Corning, North America. Corning reopened a previously shut down production line in Kansas City to increase capacity for fiberglass insulation products by 15 percent in 2004, and expanded its Fairburn, Georgia, plant by 20 percent in 2005.[3]

■■■ LOCATION PLANNING

Because location affects production costs and flexibility, sound location planning is crucial for factories, offices, and stores. Depending on its site, a company may be able to produce low-cost products or it may find itself at a cost disadvantage relative to its competitors.

Consider the reasons why Slovakia, with an existing Volkswagen plant producing 850,000 cars a year, is fast becoming the "Detroit" of Europe. Why did two more giant automakers—Peugeot Citroën (French) and Hyundai Motor Company (Korean)—open new plants in 2006? Located in Central Europe, Slovakia has a good railroad system and nearby access to the Danube River, meaning economical transportation for incoming materials and outgoing cars once auto factories are in operation. The area also has skilled workers, a good work ethic, and wages below those of the surrounding countries.[4] Therefore, in terms of its location, Slovakia is an ideal place to produce cars.

In contrast to manufacturing, consumer services concentrate on being located near customers. Thus, fast-food restaurants, such as Taco Bell and McDonald's, are located in areas with high traffic, such as dormitories, hospital cafeterias, and shopping malls. At retail giant Wal-Mart, managers of the company's huge distribution centers regard Wal-Mart outlets as their customers. To ensure that truckloads of merchandise flow quickly to stores, distribution centers are located near the hundreds of Wal-Mart stores that they supply, not near the companies that supply them.

■■■ LAYOUT PLANNING

Layout of machinery, equipment, and supplies determines whether a company can respond efficiently to demand for more and different products or whether it finds itself unable to match competitors' speed and convenience. Among the many layout possibilities, two well-known alternatives—*process layouts* and *product layouts*—are presented here to illustrate how different layouts serve different purposes for operations.

Process Layouts In a **process layout**, which is well suited to *make-to-order shops* (or *job shops*) specializing in custom work, equipment and people are grouped according to function. Kinko's Copy Centers, for example, use process layouts for custom jobs. Specific activities, such as photocopying, computing, binding, photography, and laminating, are performed in separate specialized areas of the store.

The main advantage of process layouts is flexibility—at any time, the shop can process individual customer orders, each requiring different kinds of work. One job,

PROCESS LAYOUT physical arrangement of production activities that groups equipment and people according to function

for example, calls for reproducing and binding 100 color copies of a 10-page document. Another requires making a collage from eight photos and superimposing it on a holiday background for a personalized greeting card. Depending on its work requirements, a job may flow through three activity areas, another through just one area, and still others through four or more work zones. Machining, woodworking, and dry cleaning shops, as well as health clinics, are among the many facilities using process layouts.

PRODUCT LAYOUT physical arrangement of production activities designed to make one type of product in a fixed sequence according to its production requirements

ASSEMBLY LINE product layout in which a product moves step by step through a plant on conveyor belts or other equipment until it is completed

Product Layouts A **product layout** is set up to make one type of product in a fixed sequence and is arranged according to its production requirements. It is efficient for large-volume make-to-stock operations that mass-produce products quickly, often using an **assembly line**: A partially finished product moves step by step through the plant on conveyor belts or other equipment, often in a straight line, as it passes through each stage until the product is completed. Automobile, food-processing, and television-assembly plants use product layouts. Mail-processing facilities, such as UPS or FedEx, look very much like a factory product layout. Machines and people are arranged in the order in which they help to mass-process mail and packages.

Product layouts are efficient because the work skill is built into the equipment, allowing unskilled labor to perform simple tasks. But they are often inflexible, especially where they use specialized equipment that's hard to rearrange for new applications.

■■■ QUALITY PLANNING

QUALITY the combination of "characteristics of a product or service that bear on its ability to satisfy stated or implied needs"

Every operations plan includes activities for ensuring that products meet the firm's and customers' quality standards. The American Society for Quality defines **quality** as the combination of "characteristics of a product or service that bear on its ability to satisfy stated or implied needs."[5] Such characteristics may include a reasonable price and dependability in delivering the benefits it promises.

PERFORMANCE (IN QUALITY) a dimension of quality that refers to how well a product does what it is supposed to do

Planning for quality begins when products are being designed. Early in the process, goals are established for both performance and consistency. **Performance** refers to how well the product does what it is supposed to do. For loyal buyers of Godiva premium chocolates, performance includes such sensory delights as aroma, flavor, and texture. "Truly fine chocolates," observes master chocolatier Thiery Muret, "are always fresh, contain high-quality ingredients like cocoa beans and butter . . . and feature unusual textures and natural flavors." The recipe was designed to provide these features. Superior performance helps Godiva remain one of the world's top brands.[6]

CONSISTENCY (IN QUALITY) a dimension of quality that refers to sameness of product quality from unit to unit

In addition to performance, quality also includes **consistency**—the sameness of product quality from unit to unit. Toyota automobile owners, for example, enjoy high consistency with every purchase, one reason the Camry is the best-selling car in the United States. It is achieved by monitoring for consistent raw materials, encouraging conscientious work, and maintaining equipment. All of Toyota's production processes—equipment, methods, worker skills, and materials—were planned and designed to provide product consistency.

In addition to product design, quality planning includes employees deciding what constitutes a high-quality product—for both goods and services—and determining how to measure these quality characteristics.

■■■ METHODS PLANNING

In designing operations systems, managers must identify each production step and the specific methods for performing it. They can then reduce waste and inefficiency by examining procedures on a step-by-step basis—an approach called *methods improvement*.

Improving Process Flows Improvements for operations begin by documenting current production practices. A detailed description, often using a diagram called a *process flowchart*, is helpful in organizing and recording information. The flowchart identifies the sequence of production activities, movements of materials, and work performed at each stage of the process. It can then be analyzed to isolate wasteful activities, sources of delay, and other inefficiencies in both goods and services operations. The final step is implementing improvements.

Improving Customer Service Consider, for example, the traditional checkout method at hotels. A process flowchart shows five stages of customer activities in Figure 7.3. As is widely known among guests and employees, hotel checkout can be time consuming for customers standing in line to pay. They become impatient and annoyed, especially during popular checkout times when lines are long. Other hotel tasks are disrupted, too, as employees, called to assist with surging checkout lines, are reassigned from their normal jobs that are left until later. An improved checkout method was developed that avoids wasting time in line for customers and reduces interruptions of other staff duties as well. Customers now scan their bills on television in the privacy of their rooms anytime before departure. If the bill is correct, no further checkout is required, and the hotel submits the charges against the credit card that the customer submitted during check-in. It saves time for customers by eliminating steps 1, 2, 3A, and 5 in the flowchart in Figure 7.3.

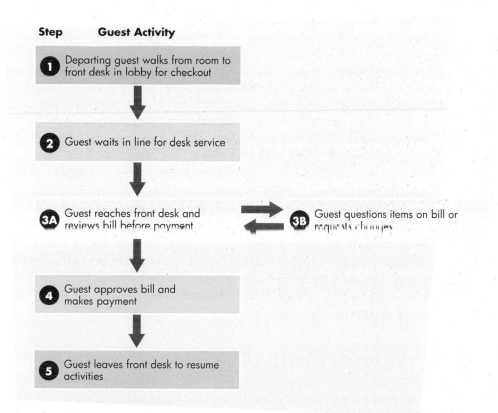

Figure 7.3
Flowchart of Traditional Guest Checkout Process

SELF-CHECK QUESTIONS 4–6

You should now be able to answer Self-Check Questions 4–6.*

4 True/False Each company's operations capabilities should be driven by the firm's business strategy.

5 Multiple Choice Which of the following is **true** about layout planning?
- (a) An assembly line is a good example of a product layout
- (b) Process layouts, also called assembly lines, are well suited for high-volume, continuous-flow operations
- (c) Process layouts are appropriate for manufacturing operations but not for service operations
- (d) Process layouts are usually arranged for a fixed sequence of operations, whereas the main advantage of product layouts is flexibility

6 Multiple Choice Which of the following is **not true** about operations planning?
- (a) Location planning for goods-producing facilities is influenced by proximity to suppliers
- (b) Methods improvements are possible in goods-producing operations but are usually impossible in service operations
- (c) Operations planning should ensure that products meet the firm's quality standards
- (d) The firm's overall business plan should provide guidance for operations planning

*Answers to Self-Check Questions 4–6 can be found on p. 564.

OPERATIONS SCHEDULING

Continuing with the flow of activities in Figure 7.2, once operations plans have been determined, managers then develop timetables for implementing them—causing the plans to become reality. This aspect of operations, called *operations scheduling*, identifies times when specific production activities will occur.

In this section we consider four general kinds of schedules. (1) The *master schedule* is "the game plan" for upcoming production. (2) *Detailed schedules* show day-to-day activities that will occur in production. (3) *Staff schedules* identify who and how many employees will be working, and when. (4) Finally, *project schedules* provide coordination for completing large-scale projects.

▪▪▪ THE MASTER PRODUCTION SCHEDULE

MASTER PRODUCTION SCHEDULE schedule showing which products will be produced, and when, in upcoming time periods

Scheduling of production occurs at different levels. First, a top-level **master production schedule** shows which products will be produced, and when, in upcoming time periods. Logan Aluminum, for example, makes coils of aluminum that it supplies to five customer companies that use it to make beverage cans. Logan's master schedule, with a format like the partial schedule shown in Figure 7.4, covers production for 60 weeks in which more than 300,000 tons will be produced. For various types of coils (products), it specifies how many tons will be produced each week. It helps managers determine the kinds of materials, equipment, and other resources that will be needed for each week's production.

▪▪▪ DETAILED SCHEDULES

DETAILED SCHEDULE a schedule showing daily work assignments with start and stop times for assigned jobs

While the master production schedule is the backbone for overall scheduling, additional information comes from **detailed schedules**—schedules showing daily work assignments

Figure 7.4
Example Partial Master
Production Schedule
(Tons of Each Product
to Be Produced)

Coil # (Product)	8/6/07	8/13/07	8/20/07	...	11/5/07	11/12/07
TC016	1,500	2,500			2,100	600
TC032	900		2,700		3,000	
TR020	300		2,600			1,600

with start and stop times for assigned jobs at each work station. Logan's production personnel need to know the locations of all coils in the plant and their various stages of completion. Start and stop times must be assigned, and employees need scheduled work assignments daily, not just weekly. Detailed short-term schedules fill in these blanks; they allow managers to use customer orders and information about equipment status to update sizes and the variety of coils to be made each day.

▪▪▪ STAFF SCHEDULES AND COMPUTER-BASED SCHEDULING

Scheduling is useful for employee staffing as well as for the work to be done. **Staff schedules**, in general, specify assigned working times in upcoming days—perhaps for as many as 30 days or more—for each employee on each work shift. They consider employees' needs and the company's efficiency and costs, including the ebbs and flows of demand for production.

Computer-based scheduling, using tools such as the ABS Visual Staff Scheduler PRO software, can easily handle multi-shift activities for many employees—both part-time and full-time. It accommodates vacation times, holiday adjustments, and daily adjustments in staffing for unplanned absences and changes in production schedules.

STAFF SCHEDULE assigned working times in upcoming days for each employee on each work shift

▪▪▪ PROJECT SCHEDULING WITH PERT

Special projects, such as new business construction or relocations, require close coordination and precise timing among many activities. In these cases, project management is facilitated by project scheduling tools, such as the *Program Evaluation and Review Technique* (*PERT*).

PERT charts break down large projects into steps to be performed and specify the time required to perform each one. The layout of the chart uses arrows to show the necessary sequence among activities, from start to finish, for completing the project. It also identifies the *critical path*—the most time-consuming set of activities—for completing the project.

Figure 7.5 shows a PERT chart for the renovation of a college classroom. The project's nine activities and the times required to complete them are identified. Each activity is represented by an arrow. The arrows are positioned to show the required sequence for performing the activities. For example, chairs and tables can't be returned to the classroom (H) until after they've been reworked (G) and after new floor tiles are installed (F). Accordingly, the diagram shows arrows for G and F coming before activity H. Similarly, funding approval (A) has to occur before anything else can get started.

PERT CHART production schedule specifying the sequence of activities, time requirements, and critical path for performing the steps in a project

Figure 7.5
PERT Chart

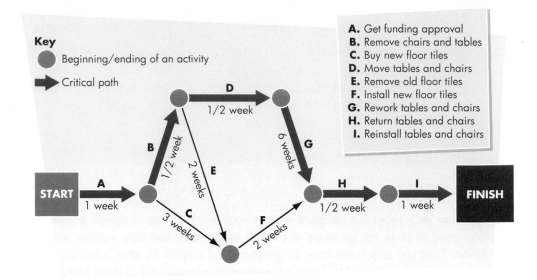

The critical path is informative because it reveals the most time-consuming path for project completion, and for most projects speed of completion is vital. The critical path for classroom renovation consists of activities A, B, D, G, H, and I, requiring 9.5 weeks. It's critical because a delay in completing any of those activities will cause corresponding lateness beyond the planned completion time (9.5 weeks after startup). Project managers will watch those activities and, if potential delays arise, take special action—by reassigning workers and equipment—to speed up late activities and stay on schedule.

Do You Really Have to Be on Time for that Meeting in Cairo?

We all use time to organize our lives, and in the United States, we're particularly avid clock watchers. In some cultures, however, people think a little differently about time, and the differences can have a big impact on the way business is conducted around the world. When we call a friend or business associate in the United States, we expect a quick reply. Not necessarily so in countries where different priorities can mean different time frames for doing things.

If you're supposed to be at an 8:00 A.M. meeting in the United States or northern Europe, you'd better be on time (or 8:05 at the latest). We expect people to be punctual, whether it's for a board meeting or a family picnic. Time is one of our ways of imposing order on our activities, and we regard regulated activity as something necessary to our workday productivity. But in some countries, thinking about time is, well, less timely. In Latin America, the Mediterranean, and the Middle East, for example, people generally do business according to relaxed timetables. They're likely to schedule a

number of things at once, and if this habit means that schedules get ignored and some "scheduled" activities get delayed, it doesn't really matter.

There are advantages as well as disadvantages to these relaxed timetables. Sometimes a more relaxed attitude toward making productive use of your time means taking time to develop relationships and getting to know someone instead of just achieving a specific goal in a specific time frame. Whatever the case, if you're operating in another country and culture, you need to know how people regard time and timeliness. Not only will you know when to show up at meetings and other events, but you may also have more luck in scheduling production and delivery dates. The most successful companies know their host cultures and are prepared to make allowances for local conditions.

And as for whether you really have to be on time for that meeting in Cairo, the answer is that being on time is always your best bet. But knowing that others may be late goes a long way toward understanding how to operate.

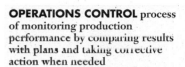

OPERATIONS CONTROL

Once long-range plans have been put into action and schedules have been drawn up, **operations control** requires managers to monitor performance by comparing results with detailed plans and schedules. If schedules or quality standards aren't met, managers can take corrective action. **Follow-up**—checking to ensure that production decisions are being implemented—is a key and ongoing facet of operations.

Operations control includes *materials management* and *quality control*, as we discuss in this section. Both activities ensure that schedules are met and products delivered, both in quantity and in quality.

▪▪▪ MATERIALS MANAGEMENT

Most of us have difficulty keeping track of personal items now and then—clothes, books, DVDs, and so on. Imagine keeping track of thousands or even millions of things at any one time. That's the challenge in **materials management**—the process by which managers plan, organize, and control the flow of materials from sources of supply through distribution of finished goods.

For manufacturing firms, typical materials costs make up 50 to 75 percent of total product costs. For service firms, too, the materials stakes are high. UPS delivers 13 million packages every day and promises that all of them will arrive on schedule. It keeps this promise by tracking the locations, schedules, and on-time performance of 500 aircraft and 88,000 vehicles as they carry packages through the delivery system. The company's performance depends on materials flowing reliably in, through, and out to customers at reasonable cost.

Materials Management Activities Once a product has been designed, successful materials flows depend on five activities. From selecting suppliers on through the distribution of finished goods, materials managers engage in the following areas that compose materials management:

- **Supplier selection** means finding and choosing suppliers of services and materials to buy from. It includes evaluating potential suppliers, negotiating terms of service, and maintaining positive buyer-seller relationships.
- **Purchasing** is the acquisition of all the raw materials and services that a company needs to produce its products; most large firms have purchasing departments to buy proper materials in the amounts needed.
- **Transportation** includes the means of transporting resources to the producer and finished goods to buyers.
- **Warehousing** is the storage of both incoming materials for production and finished goods for distribution to customers.
- **Inventory control** includes the receiving, storing, handling, and counting of all raw materials, partly finished goods, and finished goods. It ensures that enough materials inventories are available to meet production schedules while at the same time avoiding expensive excess inventories.

Lean Production Systems: Just-in-Time Operations **Lean production systems**, pioneered by Toyota, are designed for smooth production flows that avoid inefficiencies, eliminate unnecessary inventories, and continuously improve production processes. **Just-in-time (JIT) production**, a type of lean system, brings together all

---

OPERATIONS CONTROL process of monitoring production performance by comparing results with plans and taking corrective action when needed

FOLLOW-UP operations control activity for ensuring that production decisions are being implemented

MATERIALS MANAGEMENT planning, organizing, and controlling the flow of materials from sources of supply through distribution of finished goods

SUPPLIER SELECTION process of finding and choosing suppliers from whom to buy

PURCHASING acquisition of the materials and services that a firm needs to produce its products

TRANSPORTATION activities in transporting resources to the producer and finished goods to customers

WAREHOUSING storage of incoming materials for production and finished goods for distribution to customers

INVENTORY CONTROL receiving, storing, handling, and counting of all raw materials, partly finished goods, and finished goods

LEAN PRODUCTION SYSTEM a production system designed for smooth production flows that avoid inefficiencies, eliminate unnecessary inventories, and continuously improve production processes

JUST-IN-TIME (JIT) PRODUCTION a type of lean production system that brings together all materials at the precise time they are required at each production stage

needed materials at the precise moment they are required for each production stage, not before, thus creating fast and efficient responses to customer orders. All resources flow continuously—from arrival as raw materials to final assembly and shipment of finished products.

JIT production reduces to practically nothing the number of goods in process (goods not yet finished). It minimizes inventory costs, reduces storage space requirements for inventories, and saves money by replacing stop-and-go production with smooth movement. Once smooth flow is the norm, disruptions are more visible and get resolved more quickly. Finding and eliminating disruptions by the continuous improvement of production is a major objective of JIT.

▪▪▪ QUALITY CONTROL

QUALITY CONTROL taking action to ensure that operations produce products that meet specific quality standards

Quality control means taking action to ensure that operations produce products that meet specific quality standards. Consider, for example, service operations where customer satisfaction depends largely on the employees who provide the service. By monitoring services, mistakes can be detected and corrections made. First, however, managers must establish specific standards and measurements. At a bank, for example, quality control for teller services might require supervisors to observe employees periodically and evaluate their work according to a checklist. The results would then be reviewed with employees and would either confirm proper performance or indicate changes for bringing performance up to standards.

The quality of customer-employee interactions is no accident in firms that monitor customer encounters and provide training for employee-skills development. Many managers realize that without employees trained in customer-relationship skills, quality suffers, and businesses, such as airlines and hotels, can lose customers to better-prepared competitors.

Quality control means taking action to ensure that operations produce products that meet specific quality standards.

QUALITY IMPROVEMENT AND TOTAL QUALITY MANAGEMENT

It is not enough to *control* quality by inspecting products and monitoring service operations as they occur, like when a supervisor listens in on a catalog sales service representative's customer calls. Businesses must also consider *building* quality into products and services. In order to compete on a global scale, U.S. companies continue to emphasize a quality orientation. They are, for example, increasingly customer-driven—offering characteristics that customers want. All employees, not just managers, participate in quality efforts, and firms have embraced new methods to measure progress and to identify areas for improvement. In many organizations, quality improvement has become a way of life.

■■■ MANAGING FOR QUALITY

Total quality management (TQM) includes all of the activities necessary for getting high-quality goods and services into the marketplace. TQM begins with leadership and a desire for continuously improving both processes and products. It must consider all aspects of a business, including customers, suppliers, and employees. Says John Kay, director of Oxford University's School of Management, "You can't run a successful company if you don't care about customers and employees, or if you are systematically unpleasant to suppliers." To marshal the interests of all these stakeholders, TQM involves assigning and accepting responsibility for quality.

TOTAL QUALITY MANAGEMENT (TQM) the sum of all activities involved in getting high-quality goods and services into the marketplace

Quality Ownership: Taking Responsibility for Quality Producing high-quality goods and services requires an effort from all parts of an organization. A separate quality control department is no longer enough. With TQM, everyone—purchasers, engineers, janitors, marketers, machinists, suppliers, and others—must focus on quality. At St. Luke's Hospital of Kansas City, for example, every employee receives the hospital's "balanced scorecard" showing whether the hospital is meeting its goals: fast patient recovery for specific illnesses, 94 percent or better patient-satisfaction rating, every room cleaned when a patient is gone to X-ray, and the hospital's return on investment being good enough to get a good bond rating in the financial markets. Quarterly scores of green, yellow, or red show the achievement level reached for each goal. Every employee can recite where the hospital is excelling and where it needs improvement.[7]

At the same time, many firms assign responsibility for some aspects of TQM to specific departments or positions. These specialists and experts may be called in to assist with quality-related problems in any department, and they keep everyone informed about the latest developments in quality-related equipment and methods. They also monitor quality-control activities to identify areas for improvement.

The backbone of TQM, and its biggest challenge, is motivating employees throughout the company and its suppliers to achieve quality goals. Leaders of the quality movement use various methods and resources to foster a quality focus—training, verbal encouragement, teamwork, and tying compensation to work quality. When those efforts succeed, employees and suppliers will ultimately accept **quality ownership**—the idea that quality belongs to each person who creates it while performing a job.

QUALITY OWNERSHIP principle of total quality management that holds that quality belongs to each person who creates it while performing a job

▪▪▪ TOOLS FOR TOTAL QUALITY MANAGEMENT

COMPETITIVE PRODUCT ANALYSIS process by which a company analyzes a competitor's products to identify desirable improvements

Hundreds of tools have proven useful for quality improvement, ranging from statistical analysis of production data, to satisfaction surveys of customers, to **competitive product analysis**—a process by which a company analyzes a competitor's products to identify desirable improvements. Using competitive analysis, for example, Toshiba might take apart a Xerox copier and test each component. The results would help managers decide which Toshiba product features are satisfactory, which features should be upgraded, and which operations processes need improvement.

In this section, we survey five of the most commonly used tools for TQM: *value-added analysis*, *quality improvement teams*, *getting closer to the customer*, *the ISO series*, and *business process reengineering*.

VALUE-ADDED ANALYSIS process of evaluating all work activities, materials flows, and paperwork to determine the value that they add for customers

Value-Added Analysis **Value-added analysis** refers to the evaluation of all work activities, materials flows, and paperwork to determine the value that they add for customers. It often reveals wasteful or unnecessary activities that can be eliminated without jeopardizing customer service. The basic tenet is so important that Tootsie Roll Industries, the venerable candy company, employs it as a corporate principle: "We run a trim operation and continually strive to eliminate waste, minimize cost, and implement performance improvements."[8]

QUALITY IMPROVEMENT TEAM TQM tool in which collaborative groups of employees from various work areas work together to improve quality by solving common shared production problems

Quality Improvement Teams Companies throughout the world have adopted **quality improvement teams** patterned after the successful Japanese concept of *quality circles*: collaborative groups of employees from various work areas who meet regularly to define, analyze, and solve common production problems. Their goal is to improve both their own work methods and the products they make. Quality improvement teams organize their own work, select leaders, and address problems in the workplace. For years, Motorola has sponsored companywide team competitions to emphasize the value of the team approach, to recognize outstanding team performance, and to reaffirm the team's role in the company's continuous-improvement culture.

> *Customers are an economic asset. They're not on the balance sheet, but they should be.*
>
> —Claess Fornell, quality improvement advocate

Getting Closer to the Customer Says one advocate of quality improvement, "Customers are an economic asset. They're not on the balance sheet, but they should be." Struggling companies have often lost sight of customers as the driving force behind all business activity. Such companies waste resources by designing products that customers do not want. Sometimes, they ignore customer reactions to existing products or fail to keep up with changing tastes. Meanwhile, successful businesses take steps to know what their customers want in the products they consume.

Caterpillar Financial Services won a recent Malcolm Baldrige National Quality Award—the prestigious U.S. award for excellence in quality—for high ratings by its customers (that is, dealers and buyers of Caterpillar equipment). Buying and financing equipment from Cat Financial became easier as Cat moved its services increasingly online. Customers now have 24/7 access to information on how much they owe on equipment costing anywhere from $30,000 to $2 million, and they can make payments around the clock, too. In the past, the 60,000 customers had to phone a Cat representative, who was often unavailable, resulting in delays and wasted time. The improved online system is testimony to Cat Financial's dedication in knowing what customers want, and then providing it.[9]

Identifying Customers—Internal and External Improvement projects are undertaken not just for external customers, but for internal customers as well. Internal suppliers and internal customers exist wherever one employee or activity relies on others. Servers at the counter in a fast-food restaurant, for example, cannot deliver satisfying food to customers until it is received properly prepared from the kitchen. The internal suppliers, then, move the product from kitchen cooks to servers to eaters. Similarly, marketing managers rely on internal accounting information—costs for materials, supplies, and wages—for planning marketing activities for coming months. The marketing manager is a customer of the firm's accountants—the information user relies on the information supplier. Accountants in a TQM environment recognize this supplier-customer connection and take steps to improve information for marketing.

The ISO Series Perhaps you've driven past companies proudly displaying large banners announcing, "This Facility Is ISO Certified." The ISO label is a mark of quality achievement that is respected throughout the world and, in some countries, it's a requirement for doing business.

ISO 9000 **ISO 9000** is a certification program attesting that a factory, a laboratory, or an office has met the rigorous quality management requirements set by the International Organization for Standardization. ISO 9000 (pronounced ICE-o nine thousand) originated in Europe to standardize materials received from suppliers in such industries as electronics, chemicals, and aviation. Today, more than 140 countries have adopted ISO 9000 as a national standard. More than 400,000 certificates have been issued in 160 countries, 40,000 of those in the United States.

> **ISO 9000** program certifying that a factory, laboratory, or office has met the quality management standards set by the International Organization for Standardization

The revised standards of *ISO 9000:2000* (revised in the year 2000) allow firms to show that they follow documented procedures for testing products, training workers, keeping records, and fixing defects. It allows international companies to determine (or be assured of) quality of product (or the business) when shipping for/from/to suppliers across borders. To become certified, companies must document the procedures followed by workers during every stage of production. The purpose is to ensure that a company's processes can create products exactly the same today as it did yesterday and as it will be tomorrow.

ISO 14000 The **ISO 14000** program certifies improvements in environmental performance. Extending the ISO approach into the arena of environmental protection and hazardous waste management, ISO 14000 requires a firm to develop an *environmental management system*: a plan documenting how the company has acted to improve its performance in using resources (such as raw materials) and in managing pollution. A company must not only identify hazardous wastes that it expects to create, but it must also stipulate plans for treatment and disposal.

> **ISO 14000** certification program attesting to the fact that a factory, laboratory, or office has improved its environmental performance

Business Process Reengineering Every business consists of processes—activities that it performs regularly and routinely in conducting business. Examples abound: receiving and storing materials from suppliers, billing patients for medical treatment, filing insurance claims for auto accidents, inspecting property for termites, opening checking accounts for new customers, filling customer orders from Internet sales. Any business process can increase customer satisfaction by performing it well. By the same token, any business process can disappoint customers when it's poorly managed.

Business process reengineering focuses on improving a business process—rethinking each of its steps by starting from scratch. *Reengineering* is the fundamental rethinking and radical redesign of business processes to achieve dramatic improvements as measured by cost, quality, service, and speed. The discussion of Caterpillar's changeover to an online system for customers is an example. Cat reengineered the whole payments and financing process by improving equipment, retraining employees, and connecting customers to Cat's

> **BUSINESS PROCESS REENGINEERING** the rethinking and radical redesign of business processes to improve performance, quality, and productivity

databases. As the example illustrates, redesign is guided by a desire to improve operations and thereby provide higher-value services for the customer.

ADDING VALUE THROUGH SUPPLY CHAINS

SUPPLY CHAIN (VALUE CHAIN) flow of information, materials, and services that starts with raw-materials suppliers and continues adding value through other stages in the network of firms until the product reaches the end customer

Managers sometimes forget that a company belongs to a network of firms and must be coordinated with their activities. As each firm performs its transformation processes, it relies on others in the network. The term *supply chain* refers to the group of companies and stream of activities that work together to create a product. A **supply chain** (or **value chain**) for any product is the flow of information, materials, and services that starts with raw-materials suppliers and continues adding value through other stages in the network of firms until the product reaches the end customer.

Figure 7.6 shows the chain of activities for supplying baked goods to consumers. Each stage adds value for the final customer. This bakery example begins with raw materials (grain harvested from the farm). It also includes storage and transportation activities, factory operations for baking and wrapping, and distribution to retailers. Each stage depends on the others for success in getting fresh-baked goods to consumers.

■■■ THE SUPPLY CHAIN STRATEGY

Traditional strategies assume that companies are managed as individual firms rather than as members of a coordinated supply system. Supply chain strategy is based on the idea that members of the chain will gain competitive advantage by working as a coordinated unit. Although each company looks out for its own interests, it works closely with suppliers and customers throughout the chain. Everyone focuses on the entire chain of relationships rather than on just the next stage in the chain.

A traditionally managed bakery, for example, would focus simply on getting production inputs from flour millers and paper suppliers and supplying baked goods to distributors. Unfortunately, this approach limits the chain's performance and doesn't allow for possible improvements when activities are more carefully coordinated. Proper management and better coordination of the supply chain can provide fresher baked goods at lower prices.

Figure 7.6   Supply Chain for Baked Goods

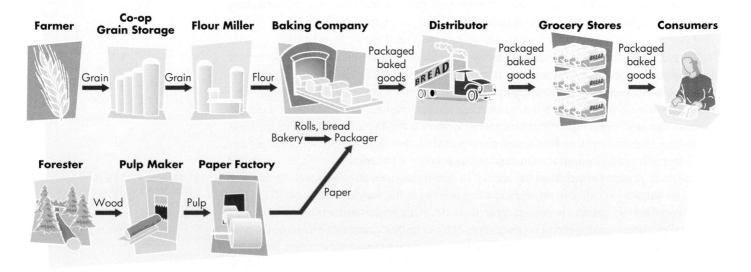

Supply Chain Management Supply chain management (SCM) looks at the chain as a whole to improve the overall flow through a system composed of companies working together. Because customers ultimately get better value, supply chain management gains competitive advantage for each of the chain's members.

SUPPLY CHAIN MANAGEMENT (SCM) principle of looking at the supply chain as a whole to improve the overall flow through the system

An innovative supply chain strategy was the heart of Michael Dell's vision when he established Dell Inc. Dell's concept improves performance by sharing information among chain members. Dell's long-term production plans and up-to-the-minute sales data are available to suppliers via the Internet. The process starts when customer orders are automatically translated into updated production schedules in the factory. These schedules are used not only by operations managers at Dell but also by such parts suppliers as Sony, which adjust their own production and shipping activities to better meet Dell's production needs. In turn, parts suppliers' updated schedules are transmitted to their materials suppliers, and so on up the chain. As Dell's requirements change, suppliers up and down the chain synchronize their schedules to produce only the right materials and parts. As a result, Dell's prices are low and turnaround time for shipping PCs to customers is reduced to a matter of hours instead of days.

Reengineering Supply Chains for Better Results Process improvements and reengineering often are applied in supply chains to lower costs, speed up service, and coordinate flows of information and material. Because the smoother flow of accurate information along the chain reduces unwanted inventories and transportation, avoids delays, and cuts supply times, materials move faster to business customers and individual consumers. For both, the efficiency of supply chain management means faster deliveries and lower costs than customers could get if each member acted only according to its own operations requirements.

▪▪▪ OUTSOURCING AND GLOBAL SUPPLY CHAINS

Outsourcing is the strategy of paying suppliers and distributors to perform certain business processes or to provide needed materials or services. The decision to outsource expands supply chains. The much-publicized movement of manufacturing and service operations from the United States to China, Mexico, and India reduces U.S. employment in traditional jobs. It also creates new operations jobs for supply chain management. Maytag, for example, had to develop its own internal global operations expertise before it could decide to open a new refrigerator factory in Mexico, import refrigerators from South Korea's Daewoo, and get laundry appliances from South Korea's Samsung Electronics. In departing from a long-standing practice of domestic production, Maytag adopted new supply chain skills for evaluating prospective outsourcing partners.

Skills for coordinating Maytag's domestic activities with those of its cross-border partners didn't end with the initial decision to get appliances from Mexico and Korea. Maytag personnel in their Newton, Iowa, headquarters have near-constant interaction with their partners on a host of continuing new operations issues. Product redesigns are transferred from the United States and adopted at remote manufacturing sites. Arrangements for cross-border materials flows require compliance with each country's commerce regulations. Production and global transportation scheduling are coordinated with U.S. market demand so that outsourced products arrive in the right amounts and on time without tarnishing Maytag's reputation for high quality.[10] Although manufacturing operations are located remotely, they are closely integrated with the firm's home-base activities. That tightness of integration demands on-site operations expertise on both sides of the outsourcing equation. Global communication technologies are essential. The result for outsourcers is a greater need of operations skills for integration among dispersed facilities.

SELF-CHECK QUESTIONS 7–9

You should now be able to answer Self-Check Questions 7–9.*

7 Multiple Choice Which of the following is **not true** for JIT operations and materials management?

(a) One purpose of JIT systems is to reduce inventories

(b) JIT production can create fast responses to customer orders

(c) JIT creates smooth materials movements by adding more storage space for inventories

(d) JIT production reduces to practically nothing the number of goods in process (goods not yet finished)

8 Multiple Choice Which of the following is **true** regarding quality management?

(a) TQM focuses only on suppliers, as they are the most important factor affecting quality

(b) In controlling for quality, managers should establish specific standards and measurements

(c) Because it sets the tone for everything that follows, planning for quality is the most important stage in quality management

(d) TQM is sometimes called quality insurance

9 Multiple Choice Which of the following is **not true** regarding supply chains and supply chain management?

(a) Supply chains involve the flow of information as well as materials and services

(b) A company using a supply chain strategy always focuses on the next stage (either incoming or outgoing) in the chain

(c) Efficiency in supply chains means faster on-time deliveries and lower costs

(d) Reengineering is used to improve supply chains

*Answers to Self-Check Questions 7–9 can be found on p. 564.

CONTINUED FROM PAGE 204

MERCEDES HITS THE LONG ROAD BACK

Customers willingly pay a premium price—up to $128,000 for a CL600 sedan—because Mercedes cars are engineered to higher standards, are on the forefront with advanced technology features, and are assembled with greater care than other cars. At least that has been the belief of luxury-car lovers—until recently. It seems that Mercedes' operations capabilities, and those of its supply chain partners, did not live up to traditional high-quality standards after the changeover to the new strategy of making more models, including smaller and less expensive ones, requiring new features and components. In addition to lost customers, Mercedes' quality downslide is having its effects on profitability, too: Mercedes' annual operating profits plummeted more than 40 percent for 2004, while profits for rivals BMW and Lexus increased. In contrast to a decade or more ago, when Mercedes was one of few genuinely fine products for luxury car fans, today's drivers are not so kind to any one brand. "The market is less and less forgiving," says Garel Rhys, director of the Center for Automotive Industry Research at the University of Cardiff in Wales. "People don't have to wait for Mercedes to sort itself out. They're going to buy a BMW or Lexus."

Mercedes is taking drastic steps to keep U.S. customers happy and restore confidence in the company's once-pristine reputation. To remedy one recent problem, nearly 2,000 owners were offered new E-class cars—at no charge—with factory-installed navigation systems to replace cars with failed navigation systems that had been installed after purchase. In a more strategic outreach for customer satisfaction, Mercedes executives are urging U.S. dealers to invest $500 million for expanded service facilities to handle complaints, including training for 1,000 new service technicians. Meanwhile, back at Mercedes headquarters in Stuttgart,

The market is less and less forgiving. People don't have to wait for Mercedes to sort itself out. They're going to buy a BMW or Lexus.

—Garel Rhys, director, center for Automotive Industry Research, on brand loyalty in the luxury-car business

Germany, executives are reorganizing the company's electronics engineering to prevent premature introduction of the latest technology in its high-end cars. In their haste to catch up with Asian automakers, over-eager engineers sometimes pushed for new gadgets, such as navigation, phone, radio, satellite, and computer diagnostics, without first testing them as a unified system to ensure they work together reliably.

Similarly, the smallest Mercedes model—the new A-class, with a short wheel base and high roof—needed expensive redesigning for the suspension system after the car failed a safety test conducted by a Swedish car magazine. These recent failures have revealed a recurring Mercedes problem: The company is unable to design a car right the first time, and that causes customer complaints, lower quality, confusion for supply chain partners, expensive repairs, and a tarnished image. But it also points to an area that, by rejuvenating its TQM commitment, could lead to the company's revival as the industry's quality leader.

QUESTIONS FOR DISCUSSION

1 How would you define *quality* and how is quality measured in this industry? Are some measurements more useful than others? Explain.
2 Think about Mercedes products, the company, and its customers. What are the basic causes that led to declining quality?
3 What are some advantages and disadvantages to a company when it lets the marketing/accounting departments dictate product design rather than the engineering department?
4 What further steps or actions (in addition to those listed in the case) would you recommend for restoring the quality stature of Mercedes? What priority ordering would you assign for those steps?
5 In hindsight, what actions could Mercedes have taken to maintain its top-quality position and prevent deterioration of quality? For each action you identify, tell how it would have prevented the company's quality downfall.

1 Explain the meaning of the term *production* or *operations*.

Operations (or *production*) refers to all the activities involved in making products—goods and services—for customers. Through their operations processes—using knowledge, physical materials, information, equipment, the customer, and human skills—firms provide benefits for themselves and for their customers. Production provides businesses with economic results: profits, wages, and goods purchased from other companies. At the same time, it adds value for customers by providing products that satisfy a want or need.

2 Describe the three kinds of utility that operations processes provide for adding customer value.

Production or operations adds customer value by providing *utility*—the ability of a product to satisfy a want or need—in terms of form, time, and place: (1) *Form utility*: By turning raw materials into finished goods, production makes products available. (2) *Time utility*: Production makes products available when consumers want them. (3) *Place utility*: Production makes products available where they are convenient for consumers.

3 Explain how companies with different business strategies are best served by having different operations capabilities.

Production is a flexible activity that can be molded into many shapes to give different operations capabilities (production capabilities) for different purposes. Its design is best driven from above by the firm's larger business strategy. When firms adopt different strategies for winning customers, they should also adjust their *operations capabilities*—what production must do especially well—to match the strategy. The operations capability that is appropriate for a low-cost strategy, for example, is different than the kind of competence for a firm that chooses a dependability strategy. Accordingly, the operations characteristics—such as number and size of production facilities, employee skills, kinds of equipment—will be different for the two firms, resulting in different operations capabilities that better support their different purposes.

4 Identify the major factors that are considered in operations planning.

Operations planning includes five major considerations: (1) *Capacity planning* considers current and future capacity requirements for meeting anticipated customer demand. The amount of a product that a company can produce under normal conditions is its *capacity*, and it depends on how many people it employs and the number and size of its facilities. (2) *Location planning* is crucial because a firm's location affects costs of production, ease of transporting, access to skilled workers, and convenient accessibility for customers. (3) *Layout planning* determines the spatial arrangement of machinery, equipment, and facilities and affects how efficiently a company can respond to customer demand. A *process layout* is effective for make-to-order production specializing in custom jobs. A *product layout*, such as assembly lines, is often used for large-volume, make-to-stock production. (4) *Quality planning* begins when products are being designed and extends into production operations for ensuring that the desired performance and consistency are built into products. (5) *Methods planning* considers each production step and the specific methods for performing it. The purpose is to reduce waste and inefficiency by improving process flows.

5 Discuss the information contained in four kinds of operations schedules—the master production schedule, detailed schedule, staff schedule, and project schedule.

Operations scheduling identifies times when specific production activities will occur. The *master production schedule*, the top-level schedule for upcoming production, shows how many of which products will be produced in each time period to meet upcoming customer demand. *Detailed schedules* take a shorter-range perspective by specifying daily work assignments with start and stop times for assigned jobs at each work station. *Staff schedules* identify who and how many employees will be working, and when, for each work shift. Finally, *project schedules* provide information for completing large-scale projects. Project scheduling tools such as *PERT* break down large projects into the sequence of steps to be performed and when to perform them.

6 Identify the activities involved in operations control.

Once plans and schedules have been drawn up, *operations control* requires managers to monitor performance by comparing results against those plans and schedules. If schedules or quality standards are not met, managers take corrective action. *Follow-up*—checking to ensure that decisions are being implemented—is an essential facet of operations control. *Materials management*—including supplier selection, purchasing, transportation, warehousing, and inventory control—facilitates the flow of materials. It may use lean production systems, such as *just-in-time operations*, for smooth production flows that avoid inefficiencies, comply with schedules, eliminate unnecessary inventories, and continuously improve production processes. *Quality control* means taking action to ensure that operations produce products that meet specific quality standards.

7 Identify the activities and underlying objectives involved in total quality management.

Total quality management (*TQM*) is a customer-driven culture for offering products with characteristics that customers want. It includes all of the activities necessary for getting customer-satisfying goods and services into the marketplace and, internally, getting every job to give better service to internal customers. TQM begins with leadership and a desire for continuously improving both processes and products. It considers all aspects of a business, including customers, suppliers, and employees. The TQM culture fosters an attitude of quality ownership among employees and suppliers—the idea that quality belongs to each person who creates it while performing a job—so that quality improvement becomes a continuous way of life.

8 Explain how a supply chain strategy differs from traditional strategies for coordinating operations among firms.

The supply chain strategy is based on the idea that members of the *supply chain*—the stream of all activities and companies that add value in creating a product—will gain competitive advantage by working together as a coordinated unit. In contrast, traditional strategies assume that companies are managed as individual firms, each acting in its own interest. By managing the chain as a whole—using *supply chain management*—companies can more closely coordinate activities throughout the chain. By sharing information, overall costs and inventories can be reduced, quality can be improved, overall flow through the system improves, and deliveries to customers can be faster.

KEY TERMS

assembly line (p. 214)

business process reengineering (p. 223)

capacity (p. 212)

competitive product analysis (p. 222)

consistency (in quality) (p. 214)

detailed schedule (p. 216)

follow-up (p. 219)

goods operations (goods production)
   (p. 204)

high-contact system (p. 208)

inventory control (p. 219)

ISO 14000 (p. 223)

ISO 9000 (p. 223)

just-in-time (JIT) production (p. 219)

lean production system (p. 219)

low-contact system (p. 208)

make-to-order operations (p. 208)

make-to-stock operations (p. 208)

master production schedule (MPS)
   (p. 216)

materials management (p. 219)

operations (production) (p. 204)

operations (production) management
   (p. 205)

operations (production) manager
   (p. 205)

operations capability (p. 210)

operations control (p. 219)

operations process (p. 207)

performance (in quality) (p. 214)

PERT chart (p. 217)

process layout (p. 213)

product layout (p. 214)

purchasing (p. 219)

quality (p. 214)

quality control (p. 220)

quality improvement team (p. 222)

quality ownership (p. 221)

service operations (service production)
   (p. 204)

staff schedule (p. 217)

supplier selection (p. 219)

supply chain (value chain) (p. 224)

supply chain management (SCM)
   (p. 225)

total quality management (TQM)
   (p. 221)

transportation (p. 219)

utility (p. 205)

value-added analysis (p. 222)

warehousing (p. 219)

QUESTIONS AND EXERCISES

Questions for Review

1 What are the major differences between goods-production operations and service operations?

2 What are the major differences between high-contact and low-contact service systems?

3 What are the five major categories of operations planning?

4 What activities are involved in total quality management?

5 What are the major activities in materials management?

Questions for Analysis

6 What are the input resources and finished products in the following services?
   ■ Real estate firm
   ■ Child care facility
   ■ Bank
   ■ Hotel

7 Choose a consumer item, such as an iPod, packaged food, or another everyday product, and trace its supply chain. Identify at least four upstream stages in the chain. Based on your familiarity with the product and the supply chain stages you identified, what recommendations would you make to improve the supply chain?

8 Find good examples of a make-to-order production process and a make-to-stock process in both goods operations and service operations. Explain your choices.

9 Develop a list of internal customers and internal suppliers for some business that you use frequently (or where you work), such as a cafeteria, a dormitory or hotel, or a movie theater. Identify areas of potential quality improvement in these internal customer-supplier activity relationships.

Application Exercises

10 Think of an everyday activity, either personal or professional, that you would like to streamline for faster performance or more convenience. It could be something like gassing up your car, going to work or school, enrolling in classes at school, or any other activity that involves several stages with which you are familiar. Describe how you would use methods planning as described in the chapter to improve the activity. Draw a process flowchart that shows the stages in the activity you chose, then tell how you would use it.

11 Interview the manager of a local service business, such as a laundry or dry-cleaning shop, movie theater, or catering business, or speak to a food service, bookstore, or other manager at your school. Identify the major decisions involved in planning its service operations.

BUILDING YOUR BUSINESS SKILLS

THE ONE-ON-ONE ENTREPRENEUR

Goal

To encourage you to apply the concept of customization to an entrepreneurial idea.

Background Information

You are an entrepreneur who wants to start your own service business. You are intrigued with the idea of creating some kind of customized one-on-one service that would appeal to baby boomers, who often like to be pampered, and working women, who have little time to get things done.

Method

Step 1

Get together with three or four other students to brainstorm ideas for services that would appeal to harried working people. Here are just a few:

- A concierge service in office buildings that would handle such personal and business services as arranging children's birthday parties and booking guest speakers for business luncheons.
- A personal-image consultation service aimed at helping clients improve appearance, etiquette, and presentation style.
- A mobile pet-care network through which vets and groomers make house calls.

Step 2

Choose one of these ideas or one that your team thinks of. Then write a memo explaining why you think your idea will succeed. Research may be necessary as you target any of the following:

- A specific demographic group or groups (Who are your customers, and why would they buy your service?)
- Features that make your service attractive to this group
- The social factors in your local community that would contribute to success

FOLLOW-UP QUESTIONS

1 Why is the customization of and easy access to personal services so desirable?

2 As services are personalized, do you think quality will become more or less important? Why?

3 Why does the trend toward personalized, one-on-one service present unique opportunities for entrepreneurs?

4 In a personal one-on-one business, how important are the human relations skills of those delivering the service? Can you make an argument that they are more important than the service itself?

PROMISES, PROMISES

The Situation

Unfortunately, false promises are not uncommon when managers feel pressure to pump up profits. Many operations managers no doubt recall times when excited marketing managers asked for unrealistic commitments from production to get a new customer contract. This exercise will introduce you to some ethical considerations pertaining to such promises and commitments.

The Dilemma

You are an operations manager for a factory that makes replacement car mufflers and tailpipes. Your products are distributed throughout the country to muffler-repair shops that install them on used vehicles. After several years of modest but steady growth, your company recently suffered a downturn and shut down 5 percent of the factory's production capacity. Two supervisors and 70 production workers were laid off.

After returning from lunch, you get a phone call from the general manager of King Kong Mufflers, one of the nation's top three muffler-repair chains, who says the following:

I suppose you know that we're about to sign a contract for your firm to supply us with replacement parts in large volumes, beginning two months from now. Your sales manager assures me that you can reliably meet my needs, and I just want to confirm that promise with you before I sign the contract.

This is the first you've heard about this contract. While your potential customer is talking, you realize that meeting his needs will require a 20-percent increase in your current production capacity. Two months, however, isn't enough time to add more equipment, acquire tools, hire and train workers, and contract for supplies. An increase this large might even require a bigger building (which would take considerably more than two months to arrange). On the other hand, you also know how much your firm needs the business. Your thoughts are interrupted when the caller says, "So what's your production situation insofar as meeting our needs?" The caller waits in silence while you gather your thoughts.

QUESTIONS TO ADDRESS

1 What are the underlying ethical issues in this situation?
2 From an ethical standpoint, what is an appropriate response to the customer's question? What steps should you take in responding to it? Explain.
3 What would you say on the phone at this time to this customer?

CALCULATING THE COST OF CONSCIENCE

The Situation

Product quality and cost affect every firm's reputation and profitability, as well as the satisfaction of customers. This exercise will expose you to some ethical considerations that pertain to certain cost and service decisions that must be made by operations managers.

The Dilemma

As director of quality for a major appliance manufacturer, Ruth was reporting to the executive committee on the results of a program for correcting problems with a newly redesigned compressor that the company had recently begun putting in its refrigerators. Following several customer complaints, the quality lab had determined that some of the new compressor units ran more loudly than expected. One corrective option was simply waiting until customers complained and responding to each complaint if and when it occurred. Ruth, however, decided that this approach was inconsistent with the company's policy of being the high-quality leader in the industry. Insisting on a proactive, "pro-quality" approach, Ruth initiated a program for contacting all customers who had purchased refrigerators containing the new compressor.

Unfortunately, her "quality-and-customers-first" policy was expensive. Service representatives nationwide had to phone every customer, make appointments for home visits, and replace original compressors with a newer model. Because replacement time was only 30 minutes, customers were hardly inconvenienced, and food stayed refrigerated without interruption. Customer response to the replacement program was overwhelmingly favorable.

Near the end of Ruth's report, an executive vice president was overheard to comment, "Ruth's program has cost this company $400 million in service expenses." Two weeks later, Ruth was fired.

Team Activity

Assemble a group of four students and assign each group member to one of the following roles:

- Ruth
- Ruth's boss
- customer
- company investor

ACTION STEPS

1 Before hearing any of your group's comments on this situation, and from the perspective of your assigned role, do you think that Ruth's firing is consistent with the company's desire for industry leadership in quality? Write down the reasons for your position.

2 Before hearing any of your group's comments on this situation, and from the perspective of your assigned role, what are the underlying ethical issues, if any, in this situation? Write down the issues.

3 Gather your group together and reveal, in turn, each member's comments on Ruth's firing. Next, reveal the ethical issues listed by each member.

4 Appoint someone to record main points of agreement and disagreement within the group. How do you explain the results? What accounts for any disagreement?

5 From an ethical standpoint, what does your group conclude is the most appropriate action that should have been taken by the company in this situation?

6 Develop a group response to the following question: What are the respective roles of profits, obligations to customers, and employee considerations for the firm in this situation?

PART 2: THE BUSINESS OF MANAGING

Goal of the Exercise

In Part 1 of the business plan project, you formulated a basic identity for your business. Part 2 of the business plan project asks you to think about the goals of your business, some internal and external factors affecting the business, as well as the organizational structure of the business.

Exercise Background: Part 2 of the Business Plan

As you learned in Chapter 5, every business sets goals. In this part of the plan, you'll define some of the goals for your business. Part 2 of the business plan also asks you to perform a basic SWOT analysis for your business. As you'll recall from Chapter 5, a SWOT analysis looks at the business's *strengths*, *weaknesses*, *opportunities*, and *threats*. The strengths and weaknesses are internal factors—things that the business can control. The opportunities and threats are generally external factors that affect the business:

Sociocultural forces	Will changes in population or culture help your business or hurt it?
Economic forces	Will changes in the economy help your business or hurt it?
Technological forces	Will changes in technology help your business or hurt it?
Competitive forces	Does your business face much competition or very little?
Political-legal forces	Will changes in laws help your business or hurt it?

Each of these forces will affect different businesses in different ways, and some of these may not apply to your business at all.

Part 2 of the business plan also asks you to determine how the business is to be run. Part of this will require you to create an organizational chart to get you thinking about the different tasks needed for a successful business. You'll also examine various factors relating to operating your business.

Your Assignment

Step 1

Open the saved *Business Plan* file you began working on in Part 1. You will continue to work from the same file you started working on in Part 1.

Step 2

For the purposes of this assignment, you will answer the questions in "Part 2: The Business of Managing:"

1 Provide a brief mission statement for your business.

Hint: Refer to the discussion of mission statements in Chapter 5. Be sure to include the name of your business, how you will stand out from your competition, and why a customer will buy from you.

2 Consider the goals for your business. What are three of your business goals for the first year? What are two intermediate to long-term goals?

Hint: Refer to the discussion of goal setting in Chapter 5. Be as specific and realistic as possible with the goals you set. For example, if you plan on selling a service, how many customers do you want by the end of the first year, and how much do you want each customer to spend?

3 Perform a basic SWOT analysis for your business, listing its main strengths, weaknesses, opportunities, and threats.

Hint: We explained previously what factors you should consider in your basic SWOT analysis. Look around at your world, talk to classmates, or talk to your instructor for other ideas in performing your SWOT analysis.

4 Who will manage the business?

Hint: Refer to the discussion of managers in Chapter 5. Think about how many *levels* of management as well as what *kinds* of managers your business needs.

5 Show how the "team" fits together by creating a simple organizational chart for your business. Your chart should indicate who will work for each manager as well as each person's job title.

Hint: As you create your organizational chart, consider the different tasks involved in the business. Whom will each person report to? Refer to the discussion of organizational structure in Chapter 6 for information to get you started.

6 Create a floor plan of the business. What does it look like when you walk through the door?

Hint: When sketching your floor plan, consider where equipment, supplies, and furniture will be located.

7 Explain what types of raw materials and supplies you will need to run your business. How will you produce your good or service? What equipment do you need? What hours will you operate?

Hint: Refer to the discussion of operations in this chapter for information to get you started.

8 What steps will you take to ensure that the quality of the product or service stays at a high level? Who will be responsible for maintaining quality standards?

Hint: Refer to the discussion of quality improvement and TQM in this chapter for information to get you started.

Note: Once you have answered the questions, save your Word document. You'll be answering additional questions in later chapters.

MANAGING GLOBAL PRODUCTION: BODY GLOVE

Learning Objectives

The purpose of this video is to help you:

1 Recognize some of the operations challenges faced by a growing company.
2 Understand the importance of quality in operations processes.
3 Discuss how and why a company may shift production operations to other countries and other companies.

Synopsis

Riding the wave of public interest in water sports, Body Glove began manufacturing wetsuits in the 1950s. The founders, dedicated surfers and divers, came up with the idea of making the wetsuits from neoprene, which offered more comfortable insulation than the rubber wetsuits of the time. The high costs of both neoprene and labor were major considerations in Body Glove's eventual decision to do its manufacturing in Thailand. The company's constant drive for higher quality was also a factor. Now company management can focus on building Body Glove's image as a California-lifestyle brand without worrying about inventory and other production issues. In licensing its brand for a wide range of goods and services—from cell-phone cases and footwear to flotation devices and vacation resorts—Body Glove has also created a network of partners around the world.

DISCUSSION QUESTIONS

1 **For analysis:** Even though Body Glove makes its products in Thailand, why must managers continually research the ways in which U.S. customers use them?
2 **For analysis:** With which aspects of product quality are wetsuit buyers most likely to be concerned?
3 **For application:** When deciding whether to license its name for a new product, what production issues might Body Glove managers research in advance?
4 **For application:** How might Body Glove's Thailand facility use forecasts of seasonal demand to plan production?
5 **For debate:** Should the products that Body Glove does not manufacture be labeled to alert buyers that they are produced under license? Support your position.

Online Exploration

Visit the Body Glove Web site at (www.bodyglove.com), and look over the variety of products sold under the Body Glove brand. Then, browse the site to find out which U.S. and international companies have licensed the Body Glove brand. How do various licensed products fit with the Body Glove brand image? What challenges might Body Glove face in coordinating its operations with so many different companies and licensed products?

PART III:
PEOPLE IN ORGANIZATIONS

After reading this chapter, you should be able to:

1. Identify and discuss the basic forms of behaviors that employees exhibit in organizations.

2. Describe the nature and importance of individual differences among employees.

3. Explain the meaning and importance of psychological contracts and the person-job fit in the workplace.

4. Identify and summarize the most important models and concepts of employee motivation.

5. Describe some of the strategies and techniques used by organizations to improve employee motivation.

WHAT'S THE DEAL ABOUT WORK?

The "plight" of the American worker is common subject matter for television shows, movies, and stand-up comedians. The stereotypic image often shows people overworked, underpaid, and generally unhappy about their work life. Unfortunately, this stereotype is all too often a true reflection of what some workers face. Increased competition, longer

EMPLOYEE BEHAVIOR AND MOTIVATION

working hours, heightened pressures to do more with less, economic uncertainty, and technology that "allows" workers to be on call 24/7 are all culprits. Some employees of video game maker Electronic Arts, for example, claim they routinely work between 65 and 85 hours a week without overtime pay; this claim has led to some unhappy workers and at least one lawsuit. Some managers at both Taco Bell and Radio Shack have made similar arguments—they are expected to run a business but must then also do a lot of other chores as well.

The consequences for businesses, in terms of increased employee turnover, lost efficiency, low morale, and so on, are high, and the consequences for workers are even worse. Although statistics are inconclusive, observers report that white-collar injuries, illnesses, and even suicides related to work have risen recently. For instance, one recent study found that 23 percent of male stockbrokers were clinically depressed, three times the national average for U.S. men. Other studies find that many workers feel overworked and constantly worry about both their job security and financial stability.

Yet there are also many individuals who find happiness and fulfillment at work. One study describes 40 percent of U.S. workers as excited about their jobs, eager to begin work on Monday mornings, and loving what they do. In many cases, happy workers have jobs that are easy to love. Sandor Zombori was working as an engineer but always longed to cook. He walked away from his job, invested his savings in a

As the parent of a toddler, it's exciting to have the coolest job at preschool.

—*Robert Sunday, Cheerios associate marketing manager, General Mills*

237

restaurant, and 20 years later is the owner and chef of an award-winning restaurant. "All the time, I am soaking it up, like a sponge, trying to learn as much as I can," Zombori explains.

For others, traditional careers hold rewards. Robert Sunday, associate marketing manager of Cheerios brand at General Mills, says about his job, "I truly love it! As the parent of a toddler, it's exciting to have the coolest job at preschool." For college professors, nurses, bank loan officers, and others, job happiness often comes from satisfying intellectual curiosity, helping others, giving back to the community, and feeling needed.

Sometimes jobholders can change or define their work in ways that bring them more satisfaction. Richard Karlgaard is the publisher of *Forbes* magazine. At first, his job primarily involved assessing and managing the reporting of financial data, a task he quickly decided was mundane and unexciting. So, he created a new set of responsibilities for himself, serving as an editor-at-large and writing about technology, while leaving most of the financial reporting to others.

Unfortunately, other individuals don't find their jobs rewarding but also cannot change the work they are doing. In these cases, looking elsewhere may be the best option. Mary Lou Quinlan was the CEO of a New York advertising agency, the pinnacle of her profession, but chose to quit and start a small consulting business. The pay is less, but she is happier. "Finally, I'm doing something I can picture doing for a long, long time," Quinlan says. ■

Our opening story continues on page 258.

WHAT'S IN IT FOR ME?

The connections that people have with their jobs can go a long way toward determining how happy employees are with their work. At the extremes, some people truly love their jobs, while others just as truly hate them. Most people, however, fall somewhere in between. By understanding the basic elements of this chapter, you'll be better able to (1) understand your own feelings toward your work from the perspective of an employee and (2) understand the feelings of others toward their work from the perspective of a boss or owner.

So, what causes one employee to work hard and have a positive attitude and another worker to do just enough to get by while constantly grumbling about how awful things are? Successful managers usually have at least a fundamental understanding of what accounts for such differences. To start developing your understanding, let's begin by describing the different forms of behaviors that employees can exhibit at work. Later in the chapter, we'll look at some important models and concepts of employee motivation, as well as some strategies and techniques used by organizations to improve employee motivation.

FORMS OF EMPLOYEE BEHAVIOR

EMPLOYEE BEHAVIOR the pattern of actions by the members of an organization that directly or indirectly influences the organization's effectiveness

Employee behavior is the pattern of actions by the members of an organization that directly or indirectly influences the organization's effectiveness. Some employee behaviors, called *performance behaviors*, directly contribute to productivity and performance. Other behaviors, referred to as *organizational citizenship*, provide positive benefits to the organization but in more indirect ways. *Counterproductive behaviors* detract from performance and actually cost the organization. Let's look at each of these types of behavior in a bit more detail.

PERFORMANCE BEHAVIORS

Performance behaviors are the total set of work-related behaviors that the organization expects employees to display. Essentially, these are the behaviors directly targeted at performing a job. For some jobs, performance behaviors can be narrowly defined and easily measured. For example, an assembly-line worker who sits by a moving conveyor and attaches parts to a product as it passes by has relatively few performance behaviors. He or she is expected to remain at the workstation for a predetermined number of hours and correctly attach the parts. Such performance can often be assessed quantitatively by counting the percentage of parts correctly attached.

For many other jobs, however, performance behaviors are more diverse and difficult to assess. For example, consider the case of a research-and-development scientist at Merck Pharmaceuticals. The scientist works in a lab trying to find new scientific breakthroughs that have commercial potential. The scientist must apply knowledge and experience gained from previous research. Intuition and creativity are also important. But even with all the scientist's abilities and effort, a desired breakthrough may take months or even years to accomplish.

PERFORMANCE BEHAVIORS
the total set of work-related behaviors that the organization expects employees to display

ORGANIZATIONAL CITIZENSHIP

Employees can also engage in positive behaviors that do not directly contribute to the bottom line. Such behaviors are often called **organizational citizenship**. Organizational citizenship refers to the behavior of individuals who make a positive overall contribution to the organization.[1] Consider, for example, an employee who does work that is highly acceptable in terms of both quantity and quality. However, she refuses to work overtime, won't help newcomers learn the ropes, and is generally unwilling to make any contribution beyond the strict performance requirements of her job. This person may be seen as a good performer, but she is not likely to be seen as a good organizational citizen. Another employee may exhibit a comparable level of performance. In addition, however, she always works late when the boss asks her to, she takes time to help newcomers learn their way around, and she is perceived as being helpful and committed to the organization's success. She is likely to be seen as a better organizational citizen.

ORGANIZATIONAL CITIZENSHIP positive behaviors that do not directly contribute to the bottom line

For some jobs, performance behaviors can be narrowly defined and easily measured. For many other jobs, such as those held by scientists or doctors however, performance behaviors are less objective, more diverse, and more difficult to assess.

A number of factors, including individual, social, and organizational variables, play roles in promoting or minimizing organizational citizenship behaviors. For example, the personality, attitudes, and needs of the individual may cause some people to be more helpful than others. Similarly, the individual's work group may encourage or discourage such behaviors. And the organization itself, especially its corporate culture, may or may not promote, recognize, and reward these types of behaviors.

■■■ COUNTERPRODUCTIVE BEHAVIORS

COUNTERPRODUCTIVE BEHAVIORS behaviors that detract from organizational performance

ABSENTEEISM when an employee does not show up for work

TURNOVER annual percentage of an organization's workforce that leaves and must be replaced

Still other work-related behaviors are counterproductive. **Counterproductive behaviors** are those that detract from, rather than contribute to, organizational performance. **Absenteeism** occurs when an employee does not show up for work. Some absenteeism has a legitimate cause, such as illness, jury duty, or death or illness in the family. Other times, the employee may report a feigned legitimate cause that's actually just an excuse to stay home. When an employee is absent, legitimately or not, his or her work does not get done at all, a substitute must be hired to do it, or others in the organization must pick up the slack, In any event, though, absenteeism results in direct costs to a business.

Turnover occurs when people quit their jobs. An organization usually incurs costs in replacing workers who have quit—lost productivity while seeking a replacement, training someone new, etc. Turnover results from a number of factors, including aspects of the job, the organization, the individual, the labor market, and family influences. In general, a poor person-job fit (which we'll discuss later in the chapter) is also a likely cause of turnover. There are some employees whose turnover doesn't hurt the business; however, when productive employees leave an organization, it does reflect counterproductive behavior.

Other forms of counterproductive behavior may be even more costly for an organization. *Theft and sabotage*, for example, result in direct financial costs for an organization. *Sexual and racial harassment* also cost an organization, both indirectly (by lowering morale, producing fear, and driving off valuable employees) and directly (through financial liability if the organization responds inappropriately). *Workplace aggression and violence* are also a growing concern in some organizations.

INDIVIDUAL DIFFERENCES AMONG EMPLOYEES

INDIVIDUAL DIFFERENCES personal attributes that vary from one person to another

What causes some employees to be more productive than others, to be better citizens than others, or to be more counterproductive than others? As we already noted, every individual is unique. **Individual differences** are personal attributes that vary from one person to another. Individual differences may be physical, psychological, and emotional. The individual differences that characterize a specific person make that person unique. As we see in the sections that follow, basic categories of individual differences include *personality* and *attitudes*.

■■■ PERSONALITY AT WORK

PERSONALITY the relatively stable set of psychological attributes that distinguish one person from another

Personality is the relatively stable set of psychological attributes that distinguish one person from another. In recent years, researchers have identified five fundamental traits that are especially relevant to organizations. These are commonly called the *"big five" personality traits*. *Emotional intelligence*, while not part of the "big five," also plays a large role in employee personality.

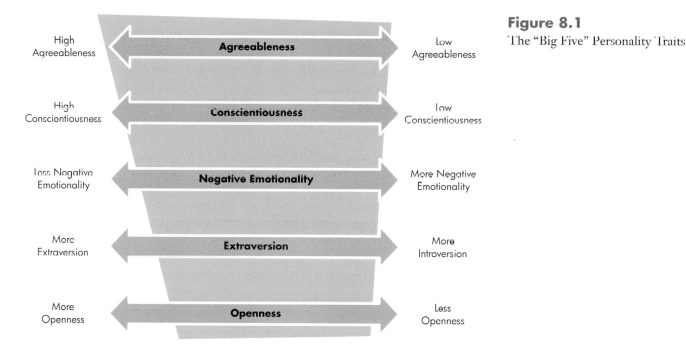

Figure 8.1
The "Big Five" Personality Traits

The "Big Five" Personality Traits

The **"big five" personality traits** are shown in Figure 8.1 and can be summarized as follows.

"BIG FIVE" PERSONALITY TRAITS five fundamental personality traits especially relevant to organizations

- *Agreeableness* is a person's ability to get along with others. A person with a *high* level of agreeableness is gentle, cooperative, forgiving, understanding, and good-natured in their dealings with others. A person with a *low* level of agreeableness is often irritable, short-tempered, uncooperative, and generally antagonistic toward other people. Highly agreeable people are better at developing good working relationships with coworkers, whereas less agreeable people are not likely to have particularly good working relationships.

- *Conscientiousness* in this context is a reflection of the number of things a person tries to accomplish. *Highly conscientious* people tend to focus on relatively few tasks at one time; as a result, they are likely to be organized, systematic, careful, thorough, responsible, and self-disciplined. *Less conscientious* people tend to pursue a wider array of tasks; as a result, they are often more disorganized, irresponsible, as well as less thorough and self-disciplined. Highly conscientious people tend to be relatively higher performers in a variety of different jobs.

- *Emotionality* refers to the degree to which people tend to be positive or negative in their outlook and behaviors toward others. People with *positive* emotionality are relatively poised, calm, resilient, and secure; people with negative emotionality are more excitable, insecure, reactive, and subject to mood swings. People with positive emotionality might be expected to better handle job stress, pressure, and tension. Their stability might also lead them to be seen as being more reliable than their less-stable counterparts.

- *Extraversion* refers to a person's comfort level with relationships. *Extroverts* are sociable, talkative, assertive, and open to establishing new relationships. *Introverts* are much less sociable, talkative, and assertive, and more reluctant to begin new relationships. Extroverts tend to be higher overall job performers than introverts and are more likely to be attracted to jobs based on personal relationships, such as sales and marketing positions.

■ *Openness* reflects how open or rigid a person is in terms of his or her beliefs. People with *high* levels of openness are curious and willing to listen to new ideas and to change their own ideas, beliefs, and attitudes in response to new information. People with *low* levels of openness tend to be less receptive to new ideas and less willing to change their minds. People with more openness are often better performers due to their flexibility and the likelihood that they will be better accepted by others in the organization.

The "big five" framework continues to attract the attention of both researchers and managers. The potential value of this framework is that it encompasses an integrated set of traits that appear to be valid predictors of certain behaviors in certain situations. Thus, managers who can both understand the framework and assess these traits in their employees are in a good position to understand how and why they behave as they do.[2]

Emotional Intelligence The concept of emotional intelligence has also been identified in recent years and provides some interesting insights into personality. **Emotional intelligence**, or **emotional quotient (EQ)**, refers to the extent to which people are self-aware, can manage their emotions, can motivate themselves, express empathy for others, and possess social skills.[3] These various dimensions can be described as follows:

EMOTIONAL INTELLIGENCE (EMOTIONAL QUOTIENT, EQ) the extent to which people are self-aware, can manage their emotions, can motivate themselves, express empathy for others, and possess social skills

■ *Self-awareness* refers to a person's capacity for being aware of how they are feeling. In general, more self-awareness allows people to more effectively guide their own lives and behaviors.
■ *Managing emotions* refers to a person's capacities to balance anxiety, fear, and anger so that they do not overly interfere with getting things accomplished.
■ *Motivating oneself* refers to a person's ability to remain optimistic and to continue striving in the face of setbacks, barriers, and failure.
■ *Empathy* refers to a person's ability to understand how others are feeling even without being explicitly told.
■ *Social skills* refers to a person's ability to get along with others and to establish positive relationships.

Preliminary research suggests that people with high EQs may perform better than others, especially in jobs that require a high degree of interpersonal interaction and that involve influencing or directing the work of others. Moreover, EQ appears to be something that isn't biologically based but which can be developed.[4]

■■■ ATTITUDES AT WORK

ATTITUDES a person's beliefs and feelings about specific ideas, situations, or people

People's attitudes also affect their behavior in organizations. **Attitudes** reflect our beliefs and feelings about specific ideas, situations, or other people. Attitudes are important because they are the mechanism through which we express our feelings. An employee's comment that he feels underpaid by the organization reflects his feelings about his pay. Similarly, when a manager says that she likes the new advertising campaign, she is expressing her feelings about the organization's marketing efforts.

People in an organization form attitudes about many different things. Employees are likely to have attitudes about their salary, their promotion possibilities, their boss, employee benefits, and so on. Especially important attitudes are *job satisfaction* and *organizational commitment*.

■ **Job satisfaction** reflects the extent to which people have positive attitudes toward their jobs. (Some people use the word *morale* instead of job satisfaction.) A satisfied employee tends to be absent less often, to be a good organizational citizen, and to stay with the organization. Dissatisfied employees may be absent more often, may experience stress that disrupts coworkers, and may be continually looking for another job. Contrary to what a lot of managers believe, however, high levels of job satisfaction do not necessarily lead to higher levels of productivity.

■ **Organizational commitment**, sometimes called *job commitment*, reflects an individual's identification with the organization and its mission. A highly committed person will probably see herself as a true member of the firm (for example, referring to the organization in personal terms, such as "we make high-quality products"), overlook minor sources of dissatisfaction, and see herself remaining a member of the organization. A less committed person is more likely to see himself as an outsider (for example, referring to the organization in less personal terms, such as "they don't pay their employees very well"), to express more dissatisfaction about things, and to not see himself as a long-term member of the organization.

There are a few critical things managers can do to promote satisfaction and commitment. For one thing, if the organization treats its employees fairly and provides reasonable rewards and job security, its employees are more likely to be satisfied and committed. Allowing employees to have a say in how things are done can also promote these attitudes. Designing jobs so that they are stimulating can enhance both satisfaction and commitment. Another key element is understanding and respecting what experts call *psychological contracts*, which we will discuss in the next section.

JOB SATISFACTION degree of enjoyment that people derive from performing their jobs

ORGANIZATIONAL COMMITMENT an individual's identification with the organization and its mission

MATCHING PEOPLE AND JOBS

Given the array of individual differences that exists across people and the many different forms of employee behaviors that can occur in organizations, it stands to reason that managers would like to have a good match between people and the jobs they are performing. Two key methods for helping to understand how this match can be better understood are *psychological contracts* and the *person-job fit*.

PSYCHOLOGICAL CONTRACTS

A **psychological contract** is the overall set of expectations held by employees and the organization regarding what employees will contribute to the organization and what the organization will provide in return. Unlike a business contract, a psychological contract is not written on paper, nor are all of its terms explicitly negotiated.

Figure 8.2 illustrates the essential nature of a psychological contract. The individual makes a variety of *contributions* to the organization—such things as effort, ability, loyalty, skills, and time. These contributions satisfy their obligation under the contract. For example, Jill Henderson, a branch manager for Merrill Lynch, uses her knowledge of financial markets and investment opportunities to help her clients make profitable investments. Her MBA in finance, coupled with hard work and motivation, have led her to become one of the firm's most promising young managers. The firm believed she had these attributes when it hired her and expected that she would do well.

PSYCHOLOGICAL CONTRACT set of expectations held by an employee concerning what he or she will contribute to an organization (referred to as contributions) and what the organization will in return provide the employee (referred to as inducements)

Figure 8.2
The Psychological Contract

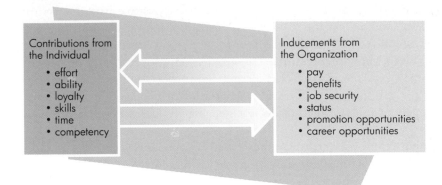

In return for these contributions, the organization provides *inducements* to the individual. These inducements satisfy the organization's contract obligation. Some inducements, such as pay and career opportunities, are tangible rewards. Others, such as job security and status, are more intangible. Jill Henderson started at Merrill Lynch at a very competitive salary and has received a salary increase each of the six years she has been with the firm. She has also been promoted twice and expects another promotion in the near future.

In this instance, both Jill Henderson and Merrill Lynch apparently perceive that the psychological contract is fair and equitable. Both will be satisfied with the relationship and will do what they can to continue it. Henderson is likely to continue to work hard and effectively, and Merrill Lynch is likely to continue to increase her salary and give her promotions. In other situations, however, things might not work out as well. If either party sees an inequity in the contract, that party may initiate a change. The employee might ask for a pay raise or promotion, put forth less effort, or look for a better job elsewhere. The organization can also initiate change by training the worker to improve his skills, transferring him to another job, or by firing him.

All organizations face the basic challenge of managing psychological contracts. They want value from their employees, and they need to give employees the right inducements. For instance, underpaid employees may perform poorly or leave for better jobs elsewhere. Similarly, an employee may even occasionally start to steal from the company as a way to balance the psychological contract.

Recent trends in downsizing and cutbacks have complicated the process of managing psychological contracts. For example, many organizations used to offer at least reasonable assurances of job permanence as a fundamental inducement to employees. Now, however, job permanence is less likely so alternative inducements may be needed. Among the new forms of inducements, some companies are providing additional training opportunities and increased flexibility in working schedules.

■ ■ ■ THE PERSON-JOB FIT

PERSON-JOB FIT the extent
to which a person's contributions
and the organization's
inducements match one another

The **person-job fit** refers to the extent to which a person's contributions and the organization's inducements match one another. A good person-job fit is one in which the employee's contributions match the inducements the organization offers. In theory, each employee has a specific set of needs that she wants fulfilled and a set of job-related behaviors and abilities to contribute. If the organization can take perfect advantage of those behaviors and abilities and exactly fulfill her needs, it will have achieved a perfect person-job fit. Good person-job fit, in turn, can result in higher performance and more positive attitudes. A poor person-job fit, though, can have just the opposite effects.

SELF-CHECK QUESTIONS 1–3

You should now be able to answer Self-Check Questions 1–3.*

1 Multiple Choice The "big five" personality traits include:
(a) self-awareness
(h) empathy
(c) agreeableness
(d) all of these

2 True/False A psychological contract consists of employee contributions and organizational inducements.

3 True/False A good person-job fit is one in which the employee's contributions match the inducements the organization offers.

Answers to Self-Check Questions 1–3 can be found on pp. 564–565.

BASIC MOTIVATION CONCEPTS AND THEORIES

Broadly defined, **motivation** is the set of forces that cause people to behave in certain ways.[5] One worker may be motivated to work hard to produce as much as possible, whereas another may be motivated to do just enough to survive. Managers must understand these differences in behavior and the reasons for them.

Over the years, a steady progression of theories and studies has attempted to address these issues. In this section, we survey the major studies and theories of employee motivation. In particular, we focus on three approaches to human relations in the workplace that reflect a basic chronology of thinking in the area: (1) *classical theory* and *scientific management*, (2) *early behavioral theory*, and (3) *contemporary motivational theories*.

MOTIVATION the set of forces that cause people to behave in certain ways

CLASSICAL THEORY

According to the so-called **classical theory of motivation**, workers are motivated solely by money. In his 1911 book, *The Principles of Scientific Management*, industrial engineer Frederick Taylor proposed a way for both companies and workers to benefit from this widely accepted view of life in the workplace. If workers are motivated by money, Taylor reasoned, paying them more should prompt them to produce more. Meanwhile, the firm that analyzed jobs and found better ways to perform them would be able to produce goods more cheaply, make higher profits, and pay and motivate workers better than its competitors.

Taylor's approach is known as *scientific management*. His ideas captured the imagination of many managers in the early twentieth century. Soon, manufacturing plants across the United States were hiring experts to perform time-and-motion studies: Industrial engineering techniques were applied to each facet of a job to determine how to perform it most efficiently. These studies were the first scientific attempts to break down jobs into easily repeated components and to devise more efficient tools and machines for performing them.[6]

CLASSICAL THEORY OF MOTIVATION theory holding that workers are motivated solely by money

EARLY BEHAVIORAL THEORY

In 1925, a group of Harvard researchers began a study at the Hawthorne Works of Western Electric outside Chicago. With an eye to increasing productivity, they wanted to examine the relationship between changes in the physical environment and worker output.

Signaling Sensitivity

These days, there's a lot of pressure placed on global companies to be "good corporate citizens"—to treat employees with respect and dignity, to be sensitive to local cultures, and to ensure that the laws of the host country are followed.

It's a rule of thumb that the happier the employee, the more productive and dedicated he or she will be. But communicating the fact that a firm has a stake in the satisfaction of its employees and the prosperity of its community is more easily said than done. For one thing, global companies employ people all over the world; there's no one unified group of people who share all the same values and all the same attitudes. In addition, because people take jobs for many different reasons, they may have very different expectations when it comes to pay and benefits and to the degree of commitment they're prepared to make to a corporate entity.

One way companies are trying to communicate more effectively with employees is through Web sites and in-house publications. The aim is to give employees around the world a sense of belonging to a community whose members have shared interests. At the same time, however, companies want to send the message that they're sensitive to employee differences—to the cultural and other forms of diversity that characterize their workforces and the communities in which they operate. Many global firms, for example, sponsor extensive local outreach programs in which they provide assistance to various groups in the communities where they conduct business.

There are still a lot of questions about the role of the corporation in an increasingly globalized world, and there have always been questions about the degree to which companies should exercise social responsibility in host communities. One thing, however, seems certain: Global companies are going to become a good deal more sophisticated in the way they communicate to both groups of stakeholders.

The results of the experiment were unexpected, even confusing. For example, increased lighting levels improved productivity. For some reason, however, so did lower lighting levels. Moreover, against all expectations, increased pay failed to increase productivity. Gradually, the researchers pieced together the puzzle. The explanation lay in the workers' response to the attention they were receiving. The researchers concluded that productivity rose in response to almost any management action that workers interpreted as special attention. This finding—known today as the **Hawthorne effect**—had a major influence on human relations theory, although in many cases it amounted simply to convincing managers that they should pay more attention to employees.

HAWTHORNE EFFECT tendency for productivity to increase when workers believe they are receiving special attention from management

Following the Hawthorne studies, managers and researchers alike focused more attention on the importance of good human relations in motivating employee performance. Stressing the factors that cause, focus, and sustain workers' behavior, most motivation theorists became concerned with the ways in which management thinks about and treats employees. The major motivation theories include the *human resources model*, the *hierarchy of needs model*, and *two-factor theory*.[7]

Human Resources Model: Theories X and Y In one important book, behavioral scientist Douglas McGregor concluded that managers had radically different beliefs about how best to use the human resources employed by a firm. He classified these beliefs into sets of assumptions that he labeled "Theory X" and "Theory Y." The basic differences between these two theories are shown in Table 8.1.

THEORY X theory of motivation holding that people are naturally lazy and uncooperative

Managers who subscribe to **Theory X** tend to believe that people are naturally lazy and uncooperative and must be either punished or rewarded to be made productive. Managers who are inclined to accept **Theory Y** tend to believe that people are naturally energetic, growth-oriented, self-motivated, and interested in being productive.

THEORY Y theory of motivation holding that people are naturally energetic, growth-oriented, self-motivated, and interested in being productive

TABLE 8.1 THEORY X AND THEORY Y

THEORY X	THEORY Y
People are lazy.	People are energetic.
People lack ambition and dislike responsibility.	People are ambitious and seek responsibility.
People are self-centered.	People can be selfless.
People resist change.	People want to contribute to business growth and change.
People are gullible and not very bright.	People are intelligent.

McGregor argued that Theory Y managers are more likely to have satisfied and motivated employees. Theory X and Y distinctions are somewhat simplistic and offer little concrete basis for action. Their value lies primarily in their ability to highlight and classify the behavior of managers in light of their attitudes toward employees.

Maslow's Hierarchy of Needs Model Psychologist Abraham Maslow's **hierarchy of human needs model** proposed that people have several different needs that they attempt to satisfy in their work. Maslow classified these needs into five basic types and suggested that they be arranged in the hierarchy of importance, as shown in Figure 8.3. According to Maslow, needs are hierarchical because lower-level needs must be met before a person will try to satisfy higher-level needs.

Once a set of needs has been satisfied, it ceases to motivate behavior. For example, if you feel secure in your job (that is, your security needs have been met), additional opportunities to achieve even more security, such as being assigned to a long-term project, will probably be less important to you than the chance to fulfill social or esteem needs, such as working with a mentor or becoming the member of an advisory board.

HIERARCHY OF HUMAN NEEDS MODEL theory of motivation describing five levels of human needs and arguing that basic needs must be fulfilled before people work to satisfy higher-level needs

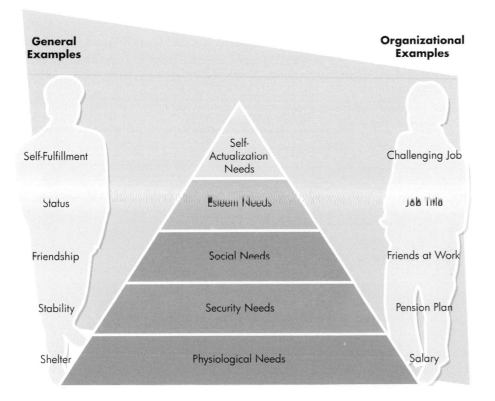

Figure 8.3
Maslow's Hierarchy of Human Needs

If, however, a lower-level need suddenly becomes unfulfilled, most people immediately refocus on that lower level. Suppose, for example, you are seeking to meet your self-esteem needs by working as a divisional manager at a major company. If you learn that your division and, consequently, your job may be eliminated, you might very well find the promise of job security at a new firm as motivating as a promotion once would have been at your old company.

Two-Factor Theory After studying a group of accountants and engineers, psychologist Frederick Herzberg concluded that job satisfaction and dissatisfaction depend on two factors: *hygiene factors*, such as working conditions, and *motivation factors*, such as recognition for a job well done.

According to Herzberg's **two-factor theory**, hygiene factors affect motivation and satisfaction only if they are absent or fail to meet expectations. For example, workers will be dissatisfied if they believe they have poor working conditions. If working conditions are improved, however, they will not necessarily become satisfied; they will simply not be dissatisfied. If workers receive no recognition for successful work, they may be neither dissatisfied nor satisfied. If recognition is provided, they will likely become more satisfied.

Figure 8.4 illustrates the two-factor theory. Note that motivation factors lie along a continuum from satisfaction to no satisfaction. Hygiene factors, in contrast, are likely to produce feelings that lie on a continuum from dissatisfaction to no dissatisfaction. Whereas motivation factors are directly related to the work that employees actually perform, hygiene factors refer to the environment in which they work.

This theory suggests that managers should follow a two-step approach to enhancing motivation. First, they must ensure that hygiene factors—working conditions, for example, or clearly stated policies—are acceptable. This practice will result in an absence of dissatisfaction. Then they must offer motivation factors—recognition or added responsibility—as a way to improve satisfaction and motivation.

> **TWO-FACTOR THEORY** theory of motivation holding that job satisfaction depends on two factors, hygiene and motivation

■■■ CONTEMPORARY MOTIVATION THEORY

Recently, other more complex models of employee behavior and motivation have been developed.[8] Two of the more interesting and useful ones are *expectancy theory* and *equity theory*.

Figure 8.4
Two-Factor Theory
of Motivation

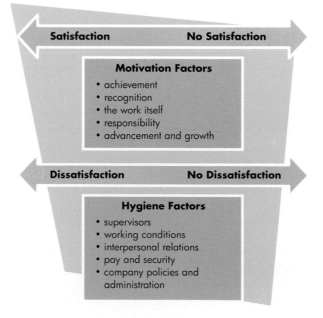

Figure 8.5   Expectancy Theory Model

Effort–Performance
Issue

Performance–Reward
Issue

Rewards–Personal
Goals
Issue

Expectancy Theory **Expectancy theory** suggests that people are motivated to work toward rewards that they want and that they believe they have a reasonable chance—or expectancy—of obtaining. A reward that seems out of reach is likely to be undesirable even if it is intrinsically positive. Figure 8.5 illustrates expectancy theory in terms of issues that are likely to be considered by an individual employee.

Consider the case of an assistant department manager who learns that her firm needs to replace a retiring division manager three levels above her in the organization. Even though she wants the job, she does not apply because she doubts she will be selected. In this case, she considers the performance-reward issue: She believes that her performance will not get her the position. She also learns that the firm is looking for a production manager on the night shift. She thinks she could get this job but does not apply because she does not want to work nights (the rewards–personal goals issue). Finally, she learns of an opening one level higher—department manager—in her own division. She may well apply for this job because she both wants it and thinks that she has a good chance of getting it. In this case, her consideration of all the issues has led to an expectancy that she can reach a goal.

Expectancy theory helps explain why some people do not work as hard as they can when their salaries are based purely on seniority. Paying employees the same whether they work very hard or just hard enough to get by removes the financial incentive for them to work harder. In other words, they ask themselves, "If I work harder, will I get a pay raise?" (the performance–reward issue) and conclude that the answer is no. Similarly, if hard work will result in one or more undesirable outcomes—for example, a transfer to another location or a promotion to a job that requires unpleasant travel (the rewards–personal goal issue)—employees will not be motivated to work hard.

Equity Theory **Equity theory** focuses on social comparisons—people evaluating their treatment by the organization relative to the treatment of others. This approach holds that people begin by analyzing inputs (what they contribute to their jobs in terms of time, effort, education, experience) relative to outputs (what they receive in return—salary, benefits, recognition, security). This comparison is very similar to the psychological contract. As viewed by equity theory, the result is a ratio of contribution to return. When they compare their own ratios with those of other employees, they ask whether their ratios are equal to, greater than, or less than those of the people with whom they are comparing themselves. Depending on their assessments, they experience feelings of equity or inequity. Figure 8.6 illustrates the three possible results of such an assessment.

For example, suppose a new college graduate gets a starting job at a large manufacturing firm. His starting salary is $45,000 a year, he gets an inexpensive company car, and he shares an assistant with another new employee. If he later learns that another new employee has received the same salary, car, and staff arrangement, he will feel equitably

EXPECTANCY THEORY theory of motivation holding that people are motivated to work toward rewards that they want and that they believe they have a reasonable chance of obtaining

EQUITY THEORY theory of motivation holding that people evaluate their treatment by the organization relative to the treatment of others

Figure 8.6
Equity Theory: Possible Assessments

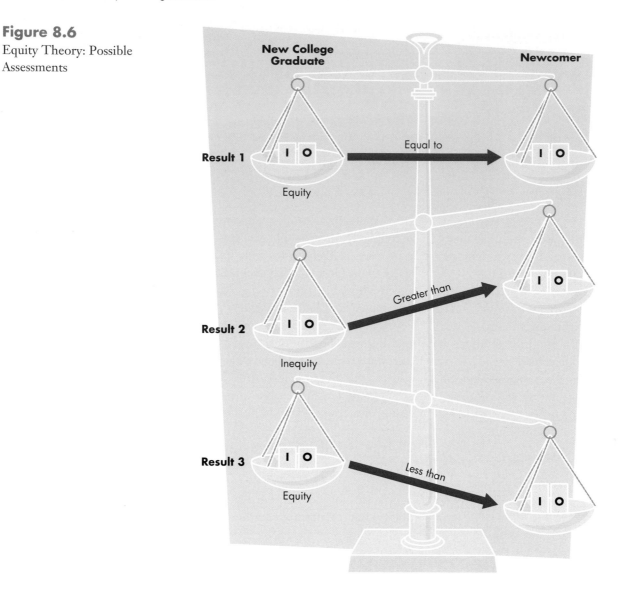

treated (result 1 in Figure 8.6). If the other newcomer, however, has received $70,000, a more expensive company car, and a personal assistant, he may feel inequitably treated (result 2 in Figure 8.6).

Note, however, that for an individual to feel equitably treated, the two ratios do not have to be identical, only equitable. Assume, for instance, that our new employee has a bachelor's degree and two years of work experience. Perhaps he learns subsequently that the other new employee has an advanced degree and 10 years of experience. After first feeling inequity, the new employee may conclude that the person with whom he compared himself is actually contributing more to the organization. That employee is equitably entitled, therefore, to receive more in return (result 3 in Figure 8.6).

When people feel they are being inequitably treated, they may do various constructive and some not so constructive things to restore fairness. For example, they may speak to their boss about the perceived inequity. Or (less constructively) they may demand a raise, reduce their efforts, work shorter hours, or just complain to their coworkers. They may also rationalize ("Management succumbed to pressure to promote a woman/Asian American"), find different people with whom to compare themselves, or leave their jobs.

SELF-CHECK QUESTIONS 4–6

You should now be able to answer Self-Check Questions 4–6.*

4 Multiple Choice Which of the following is **not** a major motivational theory?
(a) equity theory
(b) expectancy theory
(c) two-factor theory
(d) all are major motivational theories

5 True/False According to Maslow's hierarchy of needs, people will always be motivated more by self-esteem needs than by security needs.

6 Multiple Choice In Maslow's hierarchy of needs model, a prestigious job title can generally help satisfy which of the following set of needs?
(a) self-actualization needs
(b) esteem needs
(c) social needs
(d) security needs

***Answers to Self-Check Questions 4–6 can be found on p. 565.**

STRATEGIES AND TECHNIQUES FOR ENHANCING MOTIVATION

Understanding what motivates workers is only one part of the manager's job. The other part is applying that knowledge. Experts have suggested—and many companies have implemented—a range of programs designed to make jobs more interesting and rewarding, to make the work environment more pleasant, and to motivate employees to work harder.

■■■ REINFORCEMENT/BEHAVIOR MODIFICATION

Some companies try to control—and even alter or modify—workers' behavior through systematic rewards and punishments for specific behaviors. Such companies first try to define the specific behaviors that they want their employees to exhibit (working hard, being courteous to customers, stressing quality) and the specific behaviors they want to eliminate (wasting time, being rude to customers, ignoring quality). Then they try to shape employee behavior by linking positive reinforcement with desired behaviors and punishment with undesired behaviors.

Positive reinforcement is used when a company or manager provides a reward when employees exhibit desired behaviors—working hard, helping others, and so forth. When rewards are tied directly to performance, they serve as positive reinforcement. For example, paying large cash bonuses to salespeople who exceed quotas prompts them to work even harder during the next selling period. John Deere has adopted a reward system based on positive reinforcement. The firm gives pay increases when its workers complete college courses and demonstrate mastery of new job skills.

Punishment is designed to change behavior by presenting people with unpleasant consequences if they exhibit undesired behaviors. Employees who are repeatedly late for work, for example, may be suspended or have their pay docked. Similarly,

POSITIVE REINFORCEMENT reward that follows desired behaviors

PUNISHMENT unpleasant consequences of an undesirable behavior

entrepreneurship and new ventures

American Girl

Pleasant Rowland was looking for a Christmas gift for her two nieces in 1985 and Cabbage Patch dolls were all the rage. But Rowland felt that her nieces, ages 8 and 10, were too grown-up for baby dolls, and she thought Barbie was still a bit mature for them. She wanted something to spark the kids' imaginations, and when she couldn't find anything suitable, Rowland got the idea of a doll for "tweens"—preteen girls who are neither little children nor teenagers. The result was the American Girl collection of dolls, which grew to become a $700-million toy empire.

Rowland's extraordinary success was motivated by a number of factors. Her deep-seated convictions played a big part. She was looking for an image that was wholesome and empowering. "Here I was," she recalls, "in a generation of women at the forefront of redefining women's roles, and yet our daughters were playing with dolls that celebrated being a teen queen or a mommy. I knew I couldn't be the only woman in America who was unhappy with those choices. . . . Mothers," she adds, "yearned for a product that would both capture children's interest and allow little girls to be little girls for a little longer."

Then Rowland took a trip to Williamsburg, Virginia, where she was excited by the celebration of colonial America. "I remember . . . reflecting on what a poor job schools do of teaching history," she explains, "and how sad it was that more kids couldn't visit this fabulous classroom of living history." The two ideas—teaching history and designing better toys for preteens—collided, and as Rowland recalls, "The concept literally exploded in my brain. Once the idea had formed, I could think of nothing else. In one weekend, I wrote out the concept in great detail." Her concept was a series of books about girls growing up in different places and times in American history. The books would be accompanied by dolls, accessories, and toys.

When she presented the idea of the American Girl to investors, many of them told her that there was no profit in selling educational toys or dolls. Rowland, however, was confident that her line of unique educational products would sell, and she did eventually find the financing she needed to get started. And she was right: In the first four months, the Pleasant Company sold $1.7 million of dolls and books.

Office workers had to help with the sewing, and because the startup's cramped old warehouse was barely heated, they had to do it in mittens. Rowland thrived on the chaos. "For all the money the company made subsequently," she reports, "none of it was as fun or rewarding as that first million dollars." Money, however, was never the most important motivator for Rowland. She was already a millionaire from her book royalties and worked more for love than for money, and when she was diagnosed with cancer in 1989, work became her source of strength. "I never missed a day of work, and work is probably what saved me. I loved what I was doing."

Rowland eventually sold Pleasant Company to Mattel for $700 million. "Finally," she explains, "my vision was complete, my original business plan had been executed, and I was tired. It was time to sell the company." Has Rowland ever regretted the sale? Not at all. "As I walked out the door, I stopped and looked around at all I had built, expecting to be overwhelmed by sadness or loss. But no emotion came. . . . It was then that I realized that I had never felt I 'owned' American Girl. I had been its steward, and I had given it my best during the prime of my career. It was time for someone else to take care of it."

when the National Football League or Major League Baseball fines or suspends players found guilty of substance abuse, the organization is seeking to change players' behavior.

■■■ USING GOALS TO MOTIVATE BEHAVIOR

MANAGEMENT BY OBJECTIVES (MBO) set of procedures involving both managers and subordinates in setting goals and evaluating progress

Performance goals are also commonly used to direct and motivate behavior. The most frequent method for setting performance goals is called **management by objectives (MBO)**, which is a system of collaborative goal setting that extends from the top of an organization to the bottom. MBO involves managers and subordinates in setting goals and evaluating progress. After the program is started, the organization specifies its overall goals and plans. Managers then collaborate with each of their subordinates to set individual goals that will best contribute to the organization's goals. Managers meet periodically to review

"O.K., I messed up. He didn't have to rub my nose in it."

progress toward individual goals, and then, usually on an annual basis, goal achievement is evaluated and used as a basis for starting the cycle over again.

According to many experts, motivational impact is the biggest advantage of MBO. When employees sit down with managers to set upcoming goals, they learn more about companywide objectives, feel that they are an important part of a team, and see how they can improve companywide performance by reaching their own goals. If an MBO system is used properly, employees should leave meetings not only with an understanding of the value of their contributions but also with fair rewards for their performances. They should also accept and be committed to the moderately difficult and specific goals they have helped set for themselves.[9]

■■■ PARTICIPATIVE MANAGEMENT AND EMPOWERMENT

In **participative management and empowerment**, employees are given a voice in how they do their jobs and in how the company is managed—they become empowered to take greater responsibility for their own performance. Not surprisingly, participation and empowerment often makes employees feel more committed to organizational goals they have helped to shape.

Participation and empowerment can be used in large firms or small firms, both with managers and operating employees. For example, managers at General Electric who once needed higher-level approval for any expenditure over $5,000 now have the autonomy to make their own expense decisions up to as much as $50,000. At Adam Hat Company, a small firm that makes men's dress, military, and cowboy hats, workers who previously had to report all product defects to supervisors now have the freedom to correct problems themselves or even return products to the workers who are responsible for them. Sports gear company And1 also practices empowerment by allowing its designers considerable latitude in testing new ideas. For instance, a designer can make a few prototypes of a new product, distribute them to kids on a neighborhood basketball court, and then get their feedback.

Although some employees thrive in participative programs, such programs are not for everyone. People may be frustrated by responsibilities they are not equipped to handle. Moreover, participative programs may actually result in dissatisfied employees if workers see the invitation to participate as more symbolic than substantive. One key, say most experts, is to invite participation only to the extent that employees want to have input and only if participation will have real value for an organization.

PARTICIPATIVE MANAGEMENT AND EMPOWERMENT method of increasing job satisfaction by giving employees a voice in the management of their jobs and the company

This team of workers at Germany's Apollo car production plant work together to design and manufacture the Apollo sports car. Such teams often help firms make decisions more effectively, enhance communication, and lead to increased employee motivation and satisfaction.

■ ■ ■ TEAM MANAGEMENT

We have already noted the increased use of teams in organizations. Yet another benefit that some companies get from using teams is increased motivation and enhanced job satisfaction among those employees working in teams. Although teams are often less effective in traditional and rigidly structured bureaucratic organizations, they often help smaller, more flexible organizations make decisions more quickly and effectively, enhance companywide communication, and encourage organizational members to feel more like a part of an organization. In turn, these attitudes usually lead to higher levels of both employee motivation and job satisfaction.[10]

But managers should remember that teams are not for everyone. Levi Strauss, for example, encountered major problems when it tried to use teams. Individual workers previously performed repetitive, highly specialized tasks, such as sewing zippers into jeans, and were paid according to the number of jobs they completed each day. In an attempt to boost productivity, company management reorganized everyone into teams of 10 to 35 workers and assigned tasks to the entire group. Each team member's pay was determined by the team's level of productivity. In practice, however, faster workers became resentful of slower workers because they reduced the group's total output. Slower workers, meanwhile, resented the pressure put on them by faster-working coworkers. As a result, motivation, satisfaction, and morale all dropped, and Levi Strauss eventually abandoned the teamwork plan altogether.

■ ■ ■ JOB ENRICHMENT AND JOB REDESIGN

Whereas goal setting and MBO programs and empowerment can work in a variety of settings, *job enrichment* and *job redesign* programs are generally used to increase satisfaction in jobs significantly lacking in motivating factors.[11]

Job Enrichment Programs **Job enrichment** is designed to add one or more motivating factors to job activities. For example, *job rotation* programs expand growth opportunities by rotating employees through various positions in the same firm. Workers gain not only new skills but also broader overviews of their work and their organization. Other programs focus on increasing responsibility or recognition. At Continental Airlines, for example, flight attendants now have more control over their own scheduling. The jobs of flight service managers were enriched when they were given more responsibility and authority for assigning tasks to flight crew members.

JOB ENRICHMENT method of increasing job satisfaction by adding one or more motivating factors to job activities

Job Redesign Programs **Job redesign** acknowledges that different people want different things from their jobs. By restructuring work to achieve a more satisfactory fit between workers and their jobs, job redesign can motivate individuals with strong needs for career growth or achievement. Job redesign is usually implemented in one of three ways: through *combining tasks*, *forming natural work groups*, or *establishing client relationships*.

JOB REDESIGN method of increasing job satisfaction by designing a more satisfactory fit between workers and their jobs

Combining Tasks The job of combining tasks involves enlarging jobs and increasing their variety to make employees feel that their work is more meaningful. In turn, employees become more motivated. For example, the job done by a programmer who maintains computer systems might be redesigned to include some system design and system development work. While developing additional skills, the programmer also gets involved in the overall system development.

Forming Natural Work Groups People who do different jobs on the same projects are candidates for natural work groups. These groups are formed to help employees see the place and importance of their jobs in the total structure of the firm. They are valuable to management because the people working on a project are usually the most knowledgeable about it and the most capable problem solvers.

Establishing Client Relationships Establishing client relationships means letting employees interact with customers. This approach increases job variety. It gives workers both a greater sense of control and more feedback about performance than they get when their jobs are not highly interactive. For example, software writers at Microsoft watch test users work with programs and discuss problems with them directly rather than receive feedback from third-party researchers.

▪▪▪ MODIFIED WORK SCHEDULES

As another way of increasing job satisfaction, many companies are experimenting with *modified work schedules*—different approaches to working hours and the workweek. The two most common forms of modified scheduling are *work-share programs* and *flextime programs*, including alternative workplace strategies.[12]

Work-Share Programs At Steelcase, the country's largest maker of office furnishings, two very talented women in the marketing division both wanted to work only part-time. The solution: They now share a single full-time job. With each working 2.5 days a week, both got their wish and the job gets done—and done well. The practice, known as **work sharing** (or **job sharing**), has "brought sanity back to our lives," according to at least one Steelcase employee.

WORK SHARING (JOB SHARING) method of increasing job satisfaction by allowing two or more people to share a single full-time job

Job sharing usually benefits both employees and employers. Employees, for instance, tend to appreciate the organization's attention to their personal needs. At the same time, the company can reduce turnover and save on the cost of benefits. On the negative side, job-share employees generally receive fewer benefits than their full-time counterparts and may be the first to be laid off when cutbacks are necessary.

Flextime Programs and Alternative Workplace Strategies **Flextime programs** allow people to choose their working hours by adjusting a standard work schedule on a daily or weekly basis. There are limits to flextime. The Steelcase program, for instance, requires all employees to work certain core hours. This practice allows everyone to reach coworkers at a specified time of day. Employees can then decide whether to make up the rest of the standard eight-hour day by coming in and leaving early (by working 6:00 A.M. to 2:00 P.M. or 7:00 A.M. to 3:00 P.M.) or late (9:00 A.M. to 5:00 P.M. or 10:00 A.M. to 6:00 P.M.).

In one variation, companies may also allow employees to choose four, five, or six days on which to work each week. Some, for instance, may choose Monday through Thursday, others Tuesday through Friday. Still others may work Monday and Tuesday and Thursday and Friday and take Wednesday off. By working 10 hours over four work-days, employees still complete 40-hour weeks.

Telecommuting Kelly Ramsey-Dolson is an accountant employed by Ernst & Young. Because she has a young son, she does not want to be away from home more than she absolutely must. Ramsey-Dolson and the company have worked out an arrangement whereby she works at home two or three days a week and comes into the office the other days. Her home office is outfitted with a PC, high-speed Internet connection, and connects to the company's network, and she uses this technology to keep abreast of everything going on at the office.

Ramsey-Dolson is one of a rapidly growing number of U.S. workers who do a significant portion of their work via **telecommuting**—performing some or all of a job away from standard office settings. Among salaried employees, the telecommuter workforce grew by 21.5 percent in 1994—to 7.6 million—and then to 11 million in 1997; the number of telecommuters in 2001 exceeded 25.4 million employees. By 2004, experts suggested that as many as 35.5 million employees were using some form of telecommuting.

Advantages and Disadvantages of Modified Schedules and Alternative Workplaces Flextime gives employees more freedom in their professional and personal lives. It allows

FLEXTIME PROGRAMS method of increasing job satisfaction by allowing workers to adjust work schedules on a daily or weekly basis

TELECOMMUTING form of flextime that allows people to perform some or all of a job away from standard office settings

Cindy Mingo (standing) used to work on the assembly line at Rockwell Collins, a maker of avionics devices headquartered in Coralville, IA. Now she leads an RPI, or radical process improvement, team. Rockwell Collins depends on experienced employees and teams to cut production costs. This group is using Post-its to trace an assembly process and identify some bottlenecks in the process.

workers to plan around the work schedules of spouses and the school schedules of young children. Studies show that the increased sense of freedom and control reduces stress and improves individual productivity.

Companies also benefit in other ways. In urban areas, for example, such programs can reduce traffic congestion and similar problems that contribute to stress and lost work time. Furthermore, employers benefit from higher levels of commitment and job satisfaction. John Hancock Insurance, Atlantic Richfield, and Metropolitan Life are among the major U.S. corporations that have successfully adopted some form of flextime.

Conversely, flextime sometimes complicates coordination because people are working different schedules. In addition, if workers are paid by the hour, flextime may make it difficult for employers to keep accurate records of when employees are actually working.

As for telecommuting, it may not be for everyone. For example, consultant Gil Gordon points out that telecommuters are attracted to the ideas of "not having to shave and put on makeup or go through traffic, and sitting in their blue jeans all day." However, he suggests that would-be telecommuters ask themselves several other questions: "Can I manage deadlines? What will it be like to be away from the social context of the office five days a week?" One study has shown that even though telecommuters may be producing results, those with strong advancement ambitions may miss networking and rubbing elbows with management on a day-to-day basis.

Another obstacle to establishing a telecommuting program is convincing management that it can be beneficial for all involved. Telecommuters may have to fight the perception from both bosses and coworkers that if they are not being supervised, they are not working. Managers, admits one experienced consultant, "usually have to be dragged kicking and screaming into this. They always ask 'How can I tell if someone is working when I can't see them?'" By the same token, he adds, "that's based on the erroneous assumption that if you can see them, they are working." Most experts agree that reeducation and constant communication are requirements of a successful telecommuting arrangement. Both managers and employees must determine expectations in advance.

As we have illustrated in this chapter, employee behavior and motivation are important concepts for managers to understand. They are also complex processes that require careful consideration by managers. For example, a clumsy attempt to motivate employees to work harder without fully considering all factors can actually have just the opposite effect. But managers who do take the time to understand the people with whom they work can better appreciate their efforts. Another important factor that affects employee behavior is *leadership*, the subject of our next chapter.

Managers always ask "How can I tell if someone is working when I can't see them?" That's based on the erroneous assumption that if you can see them, they are working.

—HR consultant on managerial qualms about telecommuting

SELF-CHECK QUESTIONS 7–9

You should now be able to answer Self-Check Questions 7–9.*

7 **True/False** Positive reinforcement and punishment are techniques used to shape employee behavior.

8 **True/False** Management by objectives is a system of collaborative goal setting that extends from the top of an organization to the bottom.

9 **Multiple Choice** Which of the following is an example of a modified work schedule?

(a) work-share program
(b) flextime program
(c) telecommuting
(d) these are all examples of modified work schedules

*Answers to Self-Check Questions 7–9 can be found on p. 565.

CONTINUED FROM PAGE 238

THINKING ABOUT WORK AND PAY

Many white-collar workers have options to enhance their motivation and job satisfaction. But what about low-skill workers? *New York Times* journalist Daniel Akst points out that workplace unhappiness "is not a new phenomenon. Work is not a picnic. It's always tough for people." Akst admonishes his readers, "If you find the modern, air-conditioned workplace stressful—all that e-mail!—just think back to the work most Americans used to do." For instance, just contrast today's modern office work with farming, the most common occupation a century ago. Farmers at that time performed hard outdoor labor seven days per week, for uncertain pay, in social isolation, and with no benefits or retirement plans.

Just as a focus on the past shows us how really fortunate most middle-class workers truly are, so too does a comparison of middle- and working-class employees. The Bureau of Labor Statistics reports that in 2004, 6.4 million U.S. managers earned an average salary of $83,400, while 10.3 million food service workers earned only $17,400. The disparity is even greater when benefits and other rewards are considered.

Organizations face a stiff challenge in designing and creating jobs for low-skill workers that are richer and more rewarding. Even if pay were greater, motivation theory would predict that repetitive, routine jobs with little autonomy will not create worker happiness or motivation. Innovative job design for barbers, grounds workers, fishing crews, and nursing aides seems very difficult, yet could affect tens of millions of individuals nationwide.

The U.S. Census reports that 6.6 million individuals in households headed by full-time year-round workers were below the federal poverty threshold. If money and an appealing job create happiness, low-skill workers must be pretty unhappy. So, what's a manager to do? Perhaps the most basic suggestion is just this: remember that workers want to be treated with respect and dignity. Even if you can't pay them a lot of money or make their jobs exciting, you can nevertheless treat them as you would want to be treated if you were in their shoes. And, come to think of it, the same could be said of any worker performing any job.

QUESTIONS FOR DISCUSSION

1 Some experts warn that we are creating more and more disparity between higher-paid workers and lower-paid workers. If this is true, what are the implications?

2 Recall a low-skill, low-wage job you have held. What could your boss have done to motivate you?

3 Have you ever had a chance to change or modify a job so as to make it more interesting? If so, how? If not, select a job you can observe (such as a Starbucks barista) and then discuss how it could be made more interesting.

4 Are there some jobs that simply cannot be improved? If so, provide examples. If not, then why aren't all jobs made more interesting and motivating?

5 Describe the "perfect" job that you can envision for yourself. What would be the parts of the job that would really motivate you?

1 Identify and discuss the basic forms of behaviors that employees exhibit in organizations.

Employee behavior is the pattern of actions by the members of an organization that directly or indirectly influences the organization's effectiveness. *Performance behaviors* are the total set of work-related behaviors that the organization expects employees to display. *Organizational citizenship* refers to the behavior of individuals who make a positive overall contribution to the organization. *Counterproductive behaviors* are those that detract from, rather than contribute to, organizational performance.

2 Describe the nature and importance of individual differences among employees.

Individual differences are personal attributes that vary from one person to another. *Personality* is the relatively stable set of psychological attributes that distinguish one person from another. The *"big five" personality traits* are *agreeableness, conscientiousness, emotionality, extraversion,* and *openness. Emotional intelligence,* or *emotional quotient (EQ),* refers to the extent to which people are self-aware, can manage their emotions, can motivate themselves, express empathy for others, and possess social skills. *Attitudes* reflect our beliefs and feelings about specific ideas, situations, or other people. Especially important attitudes are *job satisfaction* and *organizational commitment.*

3 Explain the meaning and importance of psychological contracts and the person-job fit in the workplace.

A *psychological contract* is the overall set of expectations held by employees and the organization regarding what employees will contribute to the organization and what the organization will provide in return. A good *person-job fit* is achieved when the employee's contributions match the inducements the organization offers. Having a good match between people and their jobs can help enhance performance, job satisfaction, and motivation.

4 Identify and summarize the most important models and concepts of employee motivation.

Motivation is the set of forces that cause people to behave in certain ways. Early approaches to motivation were based first on the assumption that people work only for money and then on the assumption that social needs are the primary way to motivate people. The *hierarchy of human needs* model holds that people at work try to satisfy one or more of five different needs. The *two-factor theory* argues that satisfaction and dissatisfaction depend on *hygiene factors,* such as working conditions, and *motivation factors,* such as recognition for a job well done. *Expectancy theory* suggests that people are motivated to work toward rewards that they have a reasonable expectancy of obtaining. *Equity theory* focuses on social comparisons—people evaluating their treatment by the organization relative to the treatment of others.

5 Describe some of the strategies and techniques used by organizations to improve employee motivation.

There are several major strategies and techniques often used to make jobs more interesting and rewarding. *Positive reinforcement* is used when a company or manager provides a reward when employees exhibit desired behaviors. *Punishment* is designed to change behavior by presenting employees with unpleasant consequences if they exhibit undesired behaviors. *Management by objectives (MBO)* is a system of collaborative goal setting that extends from the top of an organization to the bottom. In *participative management and empowerment,* employees are given a voice in how they do their jobs and in how the company is managed. Using *teams* can also enhance motivation. *Job enrichment* adds motivating factors to job activities. *Job redesign* is a method of increasing job satisfaction by designing a more satisfactory fit between workers and their jobs. Some companies also use *modified work schedules*—different approaches to working hours. Common options include *work sharing (job sharing), flextime programs,* and *telecommuting.*

absenteeism (p. 240)

attitudes (p. 242)

"big five" personality traits (p. 241)

classical theory of motivation (p. 245)

counterproductive behavior (p. 240)

emotional intelligence (emotional
   quotient, EQ) (p. 242)

employee behavior (p. 238)

equity theory (p. 249)

expectancy theory (p. 249)

flextime programs (p. 256)

Hawthorne effect (p. 246)

hierarchy of human needs model (p. 247)

individual differences (p. 240)

job enrichment (p. 255)

job redesign (p. 255)

job satisfaction (p. 243)

management by
   objectives (MBO) (p. 252)

motivation (p. 245)

organizational citizenship (p. 239)

organizational commitment (p. 243)

participative management and
   empowerment (p. 253)

performance behaviors (p. 239)

personality (p. 240)

person-job fit (p. 244)

positive reinforcement (p. 251)

psychological contract (p. 243)

punishment (p. 251)

telecommuting (p. 256)

Theory X (p. 246)

Theory Y (p. 246)

turnover (p. 240)

two-factor theory (p. 248)

work sharing (or job sharing) (p. 255)

Questions for Review

1 Describe the psychological contract you currently have or have had in the past with an employer. If you have never worked, describe the psychological contract that you have with the instructor in this class.

2 Do you think that most people are relatively satisfied or dissatisfied with their work? What factors do you think most contribute to satisfaction or dissatisfaction?

3 Compare and contrast the hierarchy of human needs with the two-factor theory of motivation.

4 How can participative management programs enhance employee satisfaction and motivation?

Questions for Analysis

5 Some evidence suggests that recent college graduates show high levels of job satisfaction. Levels then drop dramatically as they reach their late twenties, only to increase gradually once they get older. What might account for this pattern?

6 As a manager, under what sort of circumstances might you apply each of the theories of motivation discussed in this chapter? Which would be easiest to use? Which would be hardest? Why?

7 Suppose you realize one day that you are dissatisfied with your job. Short of quitting, what might you do to improve your situation?

8 Describe what you would tell a low-skill worker performing a simple and routine job who wants more challenge and enjoyment from work.

Application Exercises

9 Assume you are about to start your own business. What might you do from the very beginning to ensure that your employees will be satisfied and motivated?

10 Interview the manager of a local manufacturing company. Identify as many different strategies for enhancing job satisfaction at that company as you can.

TOO MUCH OF A GOOD THING

Goal

To encourage you to apply different motivational theories to a workplace problem involving poor productivity.

Background Information

For years, working for George Uhe, a small chemicals broker in Paramus, New Jersey, made employees feel as if they were members of a big family. Unfortunately, this family was going broke because too few "members" were working hard enough to make money for it. Employees were happy, comfortable, complacent—and lazy.

With sales dropping in the pharmaceutical and specialty-chemicals division, Uhe brought in management consultants to analyze the situation and to make recommendations. The outsiders quickly identified a motivational problem affecting the sales force: Sales representatives were paid a handsome salary and received automatic, year-end bonuses regardless of performance. They were also treated to bagels every Friday and regular group birthday lunches that cost as much as $200. Employees felt satisfied but had little incentive to work very hard. Eager to return to profitability, Uhe's owners waited to hear the consultants' recommendations.

Method

Step 1

In groups of four, step into the role of Uhe's management consultants. Start by analyzing your client's workforce-motivation problems from the following perspectives (our questions focus on key motivational issues):

- *Job satisfaction and morale.* As part of a 77-year-old, family-owned business, Uhe employees were happy and loyal, in part because they were treated so well. Can high morale

have a downside? How can it breed stagnation, and what can managers do to prevent stagnation from taking hold?

- *Theory X versus Theory Y.* Although the behavior of these workers seems to make a case for Theory X, why is it difficult to draw this conclusion about a company that focuses more on satisfaction than on sales and profits?

- *Two-factor theory.* Analyze the various ways in which improving such motivational factors as recognition, added responsibility, advancement, and growth might reduce the importance of hygiene factors, including pay and security.

- *Expectancy theory.* Analyze the effect on productivity of redesigning the company's sales force compensation structure—namely, by paying lower base salaries while offering greater earnings potential through a sales-based incentive system. Why would linking performance with increased pay that is achievable through hard work motivate employees? Why would the threat of a job loss also motivate greater effort?

Step 2

Write a short report based on your analysis making recommendations to Uhe's owners. The goal of your report is to change the working environment in ways that will motivate greater effort and generate greater productivity.

FOLLOW-UP QUESTIONS

1 What is your group's most important recommendation? Why do you think it is likely to succeed?

2 Changing the corporate culture to make it less paternalistic may reduce employees' sense of belonging to a family. If you were an employee, would you consider a greater focus on profits to be an improvement or a problem? How would it affect your motivation and productivity?

3 What steps would you take to improve the attitude and productivity of longtime employees who resist change?

PRACTICING CONTROLLED BEHAVIOR

The Situation

Some companies try to control—or alter—workers' behavior through systematic rewards and punishments for specific behaviors. In other words, they first try to define the specific behaviors they want their employees to exhibit (such as working hard, being courteous to customers, stressing quality) and the specific behaviors they want them to eliminate (wasting time, being rude to customers, ignoring quality). They then try to shape employee behavior by linking positive reinforcement to desired behaviors and punishment to undesired behaviors.

Some critics, though, argue that these techniques rely too much on subconscious processes. That is, they equate these methods to laboratory experiments where you "give the rat some cheese when it pulls on the bar," and then it will pull on the bar again. Some people even question the ethics of this practice, since the target of the reward is not explicitly informed of how their behavior is being shaped.

The Dilemma

Assume that you are the new human resources manager in a medium-sized organization. Your boss has just ordered you to implement a behavior-modification program by creating a network of rewards and punishments to be linked to specific desired and undesired behaviors. Specifically, you have been instructed to specify a set of rewards that will be provided when people engage in "positive" behaviors (such as an encouraging e-mail from the boss when an employee exceeds production quotas) and punishments to be provided following "negative" behaviors (such as a critical e-mail from the boss).

However, you are uncomfortable with this approach because of how it manipulates people's behaviors without their consent. Instead, you would prefer to use rewards in a way that is consistent with expectancy theory—that is, by letting employees know in advance how they can most effectively reach the rewards they most want. You have tried to change your boss's mind but to no avail. She says to proceed with behavior modification with no further discussion.

QUESTIONS TO ADDRESS

1 What are the ethical issues in this case?
2 What do you think most managers would do in this situation?
3 What would you do?

TAKING ONE FOR THE TEAM

The Situation

You are a skilled technician who has worked for a major electronics firm for the past 10 years. You love your job—it is interesting, stimulating, and enjoyable, and you are well paid for what you do. The plant where you work is one of five manufacturing centers your firm operates in a major metropolitan area. The firm is currently developing a new prototype for one of its next-generation products. To ensure that all perspectives are reflected, the company has identified a set of technicians from each plant who will work together as a team for the next two months.

The Dilemma

You have just met with your new teammates and are quite confused about what you might do next. As it turns out, the technicians from two of the manufacturing centers have heard rumors that your company is planning to close at least three of the centers and move production to a lower-cost factory in another country. These individuals are very upset. Moreover, they have made it clear that they (1) do not intend to put forth much extra effort on this project and (2) they are all looking for new jobs. You and the other technicians, though, have heard none of these rumors. Moreover, these individuals seem as excited as you about their jobs.

Team Activity

First, working alone, write a brief summary of how you would handle this situation. For instance, would you seek more information or just go about your work? Would you start looking for another job, would you try to form a sub-group just with those technicians who share your views, or would you try to work with everyone?

Second, form a small group with some of your classmates. Share with each other the various ideas you each identified. Then, formulate a group description of what you think most people in your situation would do. Then, share your description with the rest of the class.

COMPUTING FAMILY VALUES: KINGSTON TECHNOLOGY

Learning Objectives

The purpose of this video is to help you:

1 Understand the importance of motivating employees.
2 Consider ways in which financial and nonfinancial rewards can motivate employees.
3 Explain how high morale can positively affect organizational performance.

Synopsis

California-based Kingston Technology is the world's largest independent manufacturer of computer memory products. Founded by John Tu and David Sun, Kingston employs more than 1,500 people but tries to make each employee feel like part of a family. Besides returning 10 percent of its profits to employees every year through a profit-sharing program, the company fosters mutual trust and respect between employees and management. Senior managers stay in touch with employees at all levels and conduct surveys to obtain employee feedback. For their part, employees report high job satisfaction and develop both personal and professional connections with their colleagues—boosting morale and motivation.

DISCUSSION QUESTIONS

1 **For analysis**: After Kingston's sale to Softbank, employees learned from news reports that Kingston's $100 million profit-sharing distribution was one of the largest in U.S. history. What was the likely effect of this publicity on employee morale?
2 **For analysis**: Are Kingston's managers applying Theory X or Theory Y in their relations with employees? How do you know?
3 **For application**: What kinds of survey questions should Kingston ask to gauge satisfaction and morale?
4 **For application**: What might Kingston management do to help employees satisfy higher-level needs such as self-actualization?
5 **For debate**: Do you agree with Kingston's policy of giving new employees profit-sharing bonuses even when they join the company just one week before profits are distributed? Support your position.

Online Exploration

Visit Kingston Technology's Web site (www.kingston.com) and follow the links to company information about its awards. From the company information page, follow the links to learn about the organization's values. How do these values support the founders' intention to create a family feeling within the company? How do they support employee satisfaction of higher-level needs? Why would Kingston post a list of corporate milestones (including the company's founding and the honors bestowed on it) on its Web site?

After reading this chapter, you should be able to:

1 Define *leadership* and distinguish it from management.

2 Summarize early approaches to the study of leadership.

3 Discuss the concept of situational approaches to leadership.

4 Describe transformational and charismatic perspectives on leadership.

5 Identify and discuss leadership substitutes and neutralizers.

6 Discuss leaders as coaches and examine gender and cross-cultural issues in leadership.

7 Describe strategic leadership, ethical leadership, and virtual leadership.

8 Relate leadership to decision making and discuss both rational and behavioral perspectives on decision making.

BRINGING THE BOUNTY BACK TO P&G

As the 1990s drew to a close, consumer products powerhouse Procter & Gamble (P&G) found itself in an unfamiliar rut. Fueled by such megabrands as Tide, Crest, Charmin, Downy, Pampers, Folgers, Bounty, and Pringles, the 1980s had been a decade of phenomenal growth, but in the 1990s—for the first time ever—P&G failed to meet its goal

LEADERSHIP AND DECISION MAKING

of doubling sales growth for each decade. Part of the problem was clear—turnover at the top. P&G had gone through three different CEOs during the 1990s, each with his own unique personality and individual view of how the firm should be run.

The last of the three, Durk Jager, was appointed in 1998. Jager was an avid reorganizer who moved no fewer than 110,000 workers into new jobs. His strategy also called for focusing attention on new products rather than bestsellers. Unfortunately, the innovations that he championed, such as Olay cosmetics, often bombed. He also liked the idea of putting American brand names on P&G's global products, but shoppers in Germany and Hong Kong didn't recognize such brands as "Pantene" and "Dawn," and overseas sales plummeted. Jager tried to acquire drug-makers Warner Lambert and American Home Products but dropped the idea under pressure from investors who thought the prices were too high.

Under Jager's leadership, P&G missed earnings targets and lost $70 billion in market value. To make matters worse, his aggressive personality didn't endear Jager to P&G employees. Insiders reported that morale was falling daily, and many senior managers felt as if they no longer knew what they were supposed to be doing. "I was lost," said one vice president. "It was like no one knew how to get anything done anymore." Jager was fired in mid-2000, after only 17 months on the job.

If there were 15 people sitting around the conference table, it wouldn't be obvious that he was the CEO.

—Industry analyst on P&G CEO Alan Lafley

The announcement of his replacement, 25-year P&G veteran Alan Lafley, was met with yawns and a $4 per share drop in share price. According to conventional wisdom, Jager had saddled the company with so many problems that only a dynamic, strong-willed successor stood a chance of turning things around. And by most accounts, that wasn't Lafley, whose low-key style and bespectacled appearance caused one industry analyst to comment that "If there were 15 people sitting around the conference table, it wouldn't be obvious that he was the CEO." *Fortune* magazine dubbed him "the un-CEO."

But to the surprise of many—and the shock of some—the quiet and unassuming Lafley has succeeded in turning around the stumbling manufacturer when other, more flamboyant leaders might well have failed. In some ways, he's even made it seem easy, demonstrating the virtues of back-to-basics strategy and honest, straightforward leadership. Lafley has also succeeded in restoring a sense of pride in the company and its products and has lifted employee morale in dramatic style.

Our opening story continues on page 285.

WHAT'S IN IT FOR ME?

In Chapter 8 we described the primary determinants of employee behavior and noted that managers can influence the behavior and enhance the motivation of employees. We now examine in more detail how leaders actually go about affecting employee behavior and motivating their performance. P&G CEO Alan Lafley, for instance, is clearly a leader. He understands what needs to be done and knows how to influence and motivate others. Why does understanding leadership matter to you? By mastering the material in this chapter, you'll benefit in two ways: (1) You'll better understand how you can more effectively function as a leader and (2) You'll have more insight into how your manager or boss strives to motivate you through his or her own leadership.

We start this chapter by taking a look at the nature of leadership. We then describe early approaches to leadership, as well as the situational perspective accepted today. Next, we examine leadership through the eyes of followers as well as alternatives to leadership. The changing nature of leadership and emerging issues in leadership are discussed next. Finally, we describe the very important related concept of decision making.

THE NATURE OF LEADERSHIP

LEADERSHIP the processes and behaviors used by someone, such as a manager, to motivate, inspire, and influence the behaviors of others

Because *leadership* is a term that is often used in everyday conversation, you might assume that it has a common and accepted meaning. It is a word that is often misused. We define **leadership** as the processes and behaviors used by someone, such as a manager, to motivate, inspire, and influence the behaviors of others. One of the biggest errors people make is assuming that leadership and management mean the same thing when they are really different concepts. A person can be a manager, a leader, both, or neither.[1] Some of the basic distinctions between the two are summarized in Table 9.1. On the left side of the table are four dimensions that differentiate leadership from management. The second and third columns show how each dimension differs when considered from the perspectives of managers versus leaders. For example, when they are

TABLE 9.1 KOTTER'S DISTINCTIONS BETWEEN MANAGEMENT AND LEADERSHIP

ACTIVITY	MANAGEMENT	LEADERSHIP
Creating an Agenda	**Planning and budgeting.** Establishing detailed steps and timetables for achieving needed results; allocating the resources necessary to make those needed results happen.	**Establishing direction.** Developing a vision of the future, often the distant future, and strategies for producing the changes needed to achieve that vision.
Developing a Human Network for Achieving the Agenda	**Organizing and Staffing.** Establishing some structure for accomplishing plan requirements, staffing that structure with individuals, delegating responsibility and authority for carrying out the plan, providing policies and procedures to help guide people, and creating methods or systems to monitor implementation.	**Aligning people.** Communicating the direction by words and deeds to all those whose cooperation may be needed to influence the creation of teams and coalitions that understand the vision and strategies and accept their validity.
Executing Plans	**Controlling and problem solving.** Monitoring results vs. plan in some detail, identifying deviations, and then planning and organizing to solve these problems.	**Motivating and Inspiring.** Energizing people to overcome major political, bureaucratic, and resource barriers to change by satisfying very basic, but often unfulfilled, human needs.
Outcomes	Produces a degree of predictability and order and has the potential to consistently produce major results expected by various shareholders (e.g., for customers, always being on time; for stockholders, being on budget).	Produces change, often to a dramatic degree, and has the potential to produce extremely useful change (e.g., new products that customers want, new approaches to labor relations that help make a firm more competitive)

executing plans, managers focus on monitoring results, and identifying deviations. In contrast, leaders focus on energizing people to overcome bureaucratic hurdles to help reach goals.

To further highlight the differences, consider the various roles of managers and leaders in a hospital setting. The chief of staff (chief physician) of a large hospital is clearly a manager by virtue of the position itself. At the same time, this individual may not be respected or trusted by others and may have to rely solely on the authority vested in the position to get people to do things. Thus, being a manager does not ensure that a person is also a leader—any given manager may or may not be a leader.

On the other hand, an emergency-room nurse with no formal authority may be quite effective at taking charge of a chaotic situation and directing others in how to deal with specific patient problems. Others in the emergency room may respond because they trust the nurse's judgment and have confidence in the nurse's decision-making skills. In this case, the emergency-room nurse is a leader but not a manager.

And finally, the head of pediatrics, supervising a staff of 20 other doctors, nurses, and attendants, may also enjoy the staff's complete respect, confidence, and trust. They readily take her advice and follow directives without question, and often go far beyond what is necessary to help carry out the unit's mission. Thus, the head of pediatrics is both a manager and a leader.

Organizations need both management and leadership if they are to be effective. For example, leadership is necessary to create and direct change and to help the organization get through tough times.[2] Management is necessary to achieve coordination and systematic results and to handle administrative activities during times of stability and predictability. Management in conjunction with leadership can help achieve planned orderly change, and leadership in conjunction with management can keep the organization properly aligned with its environment. In addition, managers and leaders also play a major role in establishing the moral climate of the organization and in determining the role of ethics in its culture.[3]

Leaders have always played important roles in society. For instance, even though Abraham Lincoln, Gandhi, and Eleanor Roosevelt lived at different times and worked in different areas, each is recognized as an exemplary leader. Early approaches to leadership attempted to identify the key traits or behaviors that characterized these and other leaders.

EARLY APPROACHES TO LEADERSHIP

Although leaders and leadership have profoundly influenced the course of human events, careful scientific study of them began only about a century ago. Early study focused on the *traits*, or personal characteristics, of leaders. Later research shifted to examine actual leader *behaviors*.

▪▪▪ TRAIT APPROACHES TO LEADERSHIP

Lincoln, Napoleon, Joan of Arc, Hitler, and Gandhi are names that most of us know quite well. Early researchers believed that notable leaders, such as these, had some unique set of qualities or traits that distinguished them from their peers. These traits were also thought to be relatively stable and enduring. Following this **trait approach to leadership**, researchers focused on identifying the essential leadership traits. The earliest researchers believed that important leadership traits included intelligence,

TRAIT APPROACH TO LEADERSHIP focused on identifying the essential traits that distinguished leaders

dominance, self-confidence, energy, activity (versus passivity), and knowledge about the job. These early studies resulted in a long list of additional traits. Unfortunately, the list quickly became so long that it lost any practical value. In addition, the results of many studies were inconsistent.

For example, one early argument was that effective leaders, such as Lincoln, tended to be taller than less effective leaders. But critics were quick to point out that Hitler and Napoleon, both effective leaders in their own way, were not tall. Some researchers have even tried to relate leadership to such traits as body shape, astrological sign, or handwriting patterns.

Although the trait approach was all but abandoned several decades ago, in recent years, it has resurfaced. For example, some researchers have again started to focus on a limited set of traits. These traits include emotional intelligence, mental intelligence, drive, motivation, honesty and integrity, self-confidence, knowledge of the business, and charisma. Some people even believe that biological factors, such as appearance or height, may play a role in leadership. However, it is too early to know whether these traits really do relate to leadership.

▪▪▪ BEHAVIORAL APPROACHES TO LEADERSHIP

In the late 1940s, most researchers began to shift away from the trait approach and to look at leadership as a set of actual behaviors. The goal of the **behavioral approach to leadership** was to determine what *behaviors* were employed by effective leaders. These researchers assumed that the behaviors of effective leaders differed somehow from the behaviors of less effective leaders, and that the behaviors of effective leaders would be the same across all situations.

This research led to the identification of two basic forms of leader behavior. While different researchers applied different names, the basic leader behaviors identified during this period were:

> **BEHAVIORAL APPROACH TO LEADERSHIP** focused on determining what behaviors are employed by leaders

- **Task-focused leader behavior**: Task-focused leader behavior occurs when a leader focuses on how tasks should be performed in order to meet certain goals and to achieve certain performance standards.
- **Employee-focused leader behavior**: Employee-focused leader behavior occurs when a leader focuses on the satisfaction, motivation, and well-being of his or her employees.

> **TASK-FOCUSED LEADER BEHAVIOR** leader behavior focusing on how tasks should be performed in order to meet certain goals and to achieve certain performance standards

During this period, people believed that leaders should always try to engage in a healthy dose of both behaviors, one to increase performance and the other to increase job satisfaction and motivation. Experts also began to realize that they could train managers to engage in these behaviors in a systematic manner. But they also discovered that there were other leader behaviors that needed to be considered, and that there were circumstances in which different combinations of leader behavior might be more effective than other combinations.

> **EMPLOYEE-FOCUSED LEADER BEHAVIOR** leader behavior focusing on satisfaction, motivation, and well-being of employees

For instance, suppose a new manager takes over a work site that is plagued by low productivity and whose workers, while perhaps satisfied, are not motivated to work hard. The leader should most likely focus on task-focused behaviors in order to improve lagging productivity. But now suppose the situation is different—productivity is very high but workers are stressed out about their jobs and have low levels of job satisfaction. In this instance, the manager should most likely concentrate on employee-focused behaviors so as to help improve job satisfaction. This line of thinking led to the creation of *situational theories*.

Figure 9.1   The Leadership Continuum

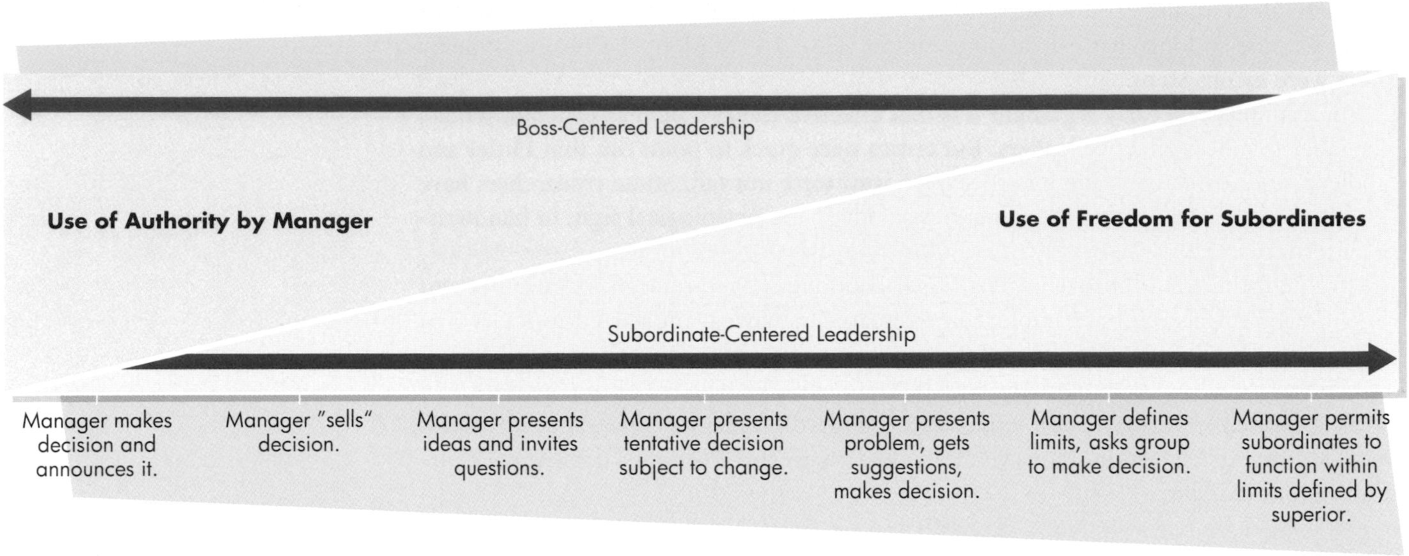

Boss-Centered Leadership

Use of Authority by Manager

Use of Freedom for Subordinates

Subordinate-Centered Leadership

| Manager makes decision and announces it. | Manager "sells" decision. | Manager presents ideas and invites questions. | Manager presents tentative decision subject to change. | Manager presents problem, gets suggestions, makes decision. | Manager defines limits, asks group to make decision. | Manager permits subordinates to function within limits defined by superior. |

THE SITUATIONAL APPROACH TO LEADERSHIP

SITUATIONAL APPROACH TO LEADERSHIP assumes that appropriate leader behavior varies from one situation to another

The **situational approach to leadership** assumes that appropriate leader behavior varies from one situation to another. This approach was first proposed as a continuum of leadership behavior, which is shown in Figure 9.1. This continuum ranges from the one extreme of having the leader make decisions alone (i.e., task-focused) to the other extreme of having employees make decisions with only minimal guidance from the leader. Each point on the continuum is influenced by *characteristics of the leader*, *his or her subordinates*, and the *situation*.

Leadership characteristics include the manager's value system, confidence in subordinates, personal inclinations, and feelings of security. Subordinate characteristics include the subordinates' need for independence, readiness to assume responsibility, tolerance for ambiguity, interest in the problem, understanding of goals, knowledge, experience, and expectations. Situational characteristics that affect decision making include the type of organization, group effectiveness, the problem itself, and time pressures.

Hence, the leadership continuum focused attention on leader behaviors as a continuum instead of being two simple alternatives, and that various elements of any given situation affect the success of any given leadership style. Although this framework pointed out the importance of situational factors, it was, however, only speculative. Later models have developed more detailed predictions of how different forms of leader behavior influence various goals.

SELF-CHECK QUESTIONS 1–3

You should now be able to answer Self-Check Questions 1–3.*

1 **True/False** All leaders are managers, and all managers are leaders.

2 **Multiple Choice** Which of the following is a trait that may play a role in leadership?

   (a) emotional intelligence
   (b) mental intelligence
   (c) charisma
   (d) all of the above

3 Multiple Choice The situational approach to leadership suggests that
(a) task-focused behavior is always effective for a leader

(b) employee-focused behavior is always effective for a leader
(c) effective leadership depends on the situation
(d) there are five forms of leader behavior

*Answers to Self-Check Questions 1–3 can be found on p. 565.

LEADERSHIP THROUGH THE EYES OF FOLLOWERS

Another recent perspective that has been adopted by some leadership experts focuses on how leaders are seen through the eyes of their followers. The two primary approaches to leadership through the eyes of followers are *transformational leadership* and *charismatic leadership*.

▪▪▪ TRANSFORMATIONAL LEADERSHIP

Transformational leadership focuses on the importance of leading for change (as opposed to leading during a period of stability). According to this view, much of what a leader does is relatively routine and simply involves carrying out what might be thought of as basic management "transactions"—assigning work, evaluating performance, making decisions, and so forth. Occasionally, however, the leader has to engage in transformational leadership to initiate and manage major change, such as managing a merger, creating a new work team, or redefining the organization's culture.

Thus, **transformational leadership** is the set of abilities that allows a leader to recognize the need for change, to create a vision to guide that change, and to execute the change effectively. On the other hand, **transactional leadership** is essentially the same as management in that it involves routine, regimented activities. Only a leader with tremendous influence can hope to perform both functions successfully. Some experts believe that change is such a vital organizational function that even successful firms need to change regularly to avoid becoming complacent and stagnant; accordingly, leadership for change is extremely important.

TRANSFORMATIONAL LEADERSHIP the set of abilities that allows a leader to recognize the need for change, to create a vision to guide that change, and to execute the change effectively

TRANSACTIONAL LEADERSHIP comparable to management, it involves routine, regimented activities

Gordon Bethune of Continental Airlines used transformational leadership to completely overhaul the firm. He was then able to become an effective transactional leader and led the firm through several more years of success.

Some leaders are able to adopt either transformational or transactional perspectives, depending on their circumstances. Others are able to do one or the other, but not both. For instance, when Gordon Bethune assumed the leadership role at Continental Airlines in the early 1990s, the firm was in desperate straits and heading for its third bankruptcy in a decade. The airline's equipment was old, the firm was heavily in debt, and its employee morale at an all-time low. Using dramatic transformational leadership, Bethune managed to completely overhaul the firm, revitalizing and transforming the airline to become one of the most successful and admired in the world. And after the transformation was complete, Bethune was then able to transition to become a highly effective transactional leader and led the firm through several more years of success before he retired in 2005.

At Walt Disney, however, the story was different. Michael Eisner took over the firm in the early 1990s as it had become stagnant and was heading into decline. Relying on transformational skills, he turned things around in dramatic fashion. Among many other things, he quickly expanded the company's theme parks, built new hotels, improved Disney's movie business, created a successful Disney cruise line, launched several other major initiatives, and changed the company into a global media powerhouse. But when the firm began to plateau and needed some time to let the changes all settle in, Eisner was unsuccessful at changing his own approach from transformational leadership to transactional leadership and was pressured into retiring.

■■■ CHARISMATIC LEADERSHIP

Charisma is a form of interpersonal attraction that inspires support and acceptance. **Charismatic leadership** is a type of influence based on the leader's personal charisma. All else being equal, someone with charisma is more likely to be able to influence others than someone without charisma. For example, a highly charismatic supervisor will be more successful in influencing a subordinate's behavior than a supervisor who lacks charisma. Thus, influence is a fundamental element of the charismatic leadership perspective.

The basic concept of charisma suggests that charismatic leaders are likely to have a lot of self-confidence, confidence in their beliefs and ideals, and a strong need to influence people. They also tend to communicate high expectations about follower performance and to express confidence in their followers. Continental Airlines CEO Gordon Bethune,

CHARISMATIC LEADERSHIP
type of influence based on the leader's personal charisma

Figure 9.2
Charismatic Leadership

described earlier, is an excellent example of a charismatic leader. Bethune skillfully blended a unique combination of executive skills, honesty, and playfulness. These qualities attracted a group of employees at Continental who were willing to follow his lead without question and to dedicate themselves to carrying out his decisions and policies with unceasing passion.[1] Other individuals who are or were seen as charismatic leaders include Herb Kelleher, Mary Kay Ash, Steve Jobs, Ted Turner, Martin Luther King, Jr., and Pope John Paul II. Unfortunately, however, charisma can also empower leaders in other directions. Adolf Hitler, for instance, had strong charismatic qualities.

Figure 9.2 portrays the three elements of charismatic leadership in organizations that most experts acknowledge today:

1 Charismatic leaders are able to envision likely future trends and patterns, to set high expectations for themselves and for others, and to behave in ways that meet or exceed those expectations.

2 Charismatic leaders are able to energize others by demonstrating personal excitement, personal confidence, and consistent patterns of success.

3 Charismatic leaders enable others by supporting them, empathizing with them, and expressing confidence in them.[5]

Charismatic leadership ideas are quite popular among managers today and are the subject of numerous books and articles.[6] Unfortunately, few studies have specifically attempted to test the meaning and impact of charismatic leadership. Lingering ethical concerns about charismatic leadership also trouble some people. They stem from the fact that some charismatic leaders inspire such blind faith in their followers that they may engage in inappropriate, unethical, or even illegal behaviors just because the leader instructed them to do so. This tendency likely played a role in the unwinding of both Enron and Arthur Andersen, as people followed orders from their charismatic bosses to hide information, shred documents, and mislead investigators.

Taking over a leadership role from someone with substantial personal charisma is also a challenge. For instance, the immediate successors to very successful charismatic football coaches like Vince Lombardi (Green Bay Packers), Steve Spurrier (University of Florida), and Tom Osborne (University of Nebraska) each failed to measure up to his predecessor's legacy and was subsequently fired.

SPECIAL ISSUES IN LEADERSHIP

Another interesting perspective on leadership focuses on *alternatives* to leadership. In some cases, certain factors may actually *substitute* for leadership, making actual leadership unnecessary or irrelevant. In other cases, factors may exist that *neutralize* or negate the influence of a leader even when that individual is attempting to exercise leadership.

TABLE 9.2 LEADERSHIP SUBSTITUTES AND NEUTRALIZERS

Individual Factors	• Individual professionalism • Individual ability, knowledge, and motivation • Individual experience and training • Indifference to rewards
Job Factors	• Structured/automated • Highly controlled • Intrinsically satisfying • Embedded feedback
Organization Factors	• Explicit plans and goals • Rigid rules and procedures • Rigid reward system not tied to performance • Physical distance between supervisor and subordinate
Group Factors	• Group performance norms • High level of group cohesiveness • Group interdependence

■■■ LEADERSHIP SUBSTITUTES

LEADERSHIP SUBSTITUTES
individual, task, and
organizational characteristics that
tend to outweigh the need for
a leader to initiate or direct
employee performance

Leadership substitutes are individual, task, and organizational characteristics that tend to outweigh the need for a leader to initiate or direct employee performance. In other words, if certain factors are present, the employee will perform his or her job capably, without the direction of a leader. Unlike other approaches, which assume that leadership in one form or another is always important, the premise of the leadership substitutes perspective is that leader behaviors may be irrelevant in some situations. Table 9.2 identifies several basic leadership substitutes.

Consider, for example, what happens when an ambulance with a critically injured victim screeches to the door of a hospital emergency room. Do the ER employees stand around waiting for someone to take control and instruct them on what to do? The answer is no—they are highly trained and well-prepared professionals who know how to respond, whom to depend on, whom to communicate with, how to work together as a team, and so forth. In short, they are fully capable of carrying out their jobs without someone playing the role of leader.

Individual ability, experience, training, knowledge, motivation, and professional orientation are among the characteristics that may substitute for leadership. Similarly, a task characterized by routine, a high degree of structure, and frequent feedback may also render leader behavior unnecessary. Or, if the task gives the subordinate enough intrinsic satisfaction, she or he may not need support from a leader. For instance, if a person truly loves his or her job and knows exactly how to perform it, no leadership is required to motivate the person to perform well.

Explicit plans and goals, rules and procedures, cohesive work groups, a rigid reward structure, and physical distance between supervisor and subordinate are organizational characteristics that may substitute for leadership. For example, if job goals are explicit and there are many rules and procedures for task performance, a leader providing directions may not be necessary.

■■■ LEADERSHIP NEUTRALIZERS

LEADERSHIP NEUTRALIZERS
factors that may render leader
behaviors ineffective

In other situations, even if a leader is present and attempts to engage in various leadership behaviors, those behaviors may be rendered ineffective—or neutralized—by various factors that can be called **leadership neutralizers**. Suppose, for example, that a relatively new and inexperienced leader is assigned to a work group composed of very experienced employees with long-standing performance norms and a high level of group cohesiveness. The norms and cohesiveness of the group may be so strong that there is nothing the new leader can do to change things. This pattern may also work in several different ways. The norms may dictate acceptable but not high performance, and the leader may be powerless to improve things because the group is so cohesive. Or, the norms may call for very high performance, and even a bungling and ineffective leader cannot cause any damage. In both cases, however, the process is the same—the leader's ability to alter the situation is neutralized by elements in that situation.

In addition to group factors, elements of the job itself may also limit a leader's ability to "make a difference." Consider, for example, employees working on a moving assembly line. Employees may only be able to work at the pace of the moving line, so performance quantity is constrained by the speed of the line. And if performance quality is also constrained (for example, by simple tasks and/or tight quality control procedures), the leader may again be powerless to influence individual work behaviors.

Finally, organizational factors can also neutralize at least some forms of leader behavior. Suppose a new leader is accustomed to using merit pay increases as a way to motivate people. But in his or her new job, pay increases are dictated by union contracts and are based primarily on employee seniority and cost-of-living. Or suppose that an employee is already at the top of the pay grade for his or her job. In either case, the leader's previous approach to motivating people has been neutralized and so new approaches will have to be identified.

SELF-CHECK QUESTIONS 4–6

You should now be able to answer Self-Check Questions 4–6.*

4 Multiple Choice A transformational leader functions best
(a) during a period of stability
(b) during a period of change
(c) when the leader lacks charisma
(d) none of the above

5 True/False Charisma in a leader may or may not be a good thing.

6 Multiple Choice A leadership substitute
(a) can never serve to replace a real leader
(b) is often used by charismatic leaders
(c) can replace a real leader in certain situations
(d) works best during periods of transformation

*Answers to Self-Check Questions 4–6 can be found on p. 565.

THE CHANGING NATURE OF LEADERSHIP

Various alternatives to leadership aside, many settings still call for at least some degree of leadership, although the nature of that leadership continues to evolve. Among the recent changes in leadership that managers should recognize are the increasing role of *leaders as coaches* as well as *gender and cross-cultural patterns* of leader behavior.

▪▪▪ LEADERS AS COACHES

We noted in Chapter 6 that many organizations today are using teams. Many other organizations are attempting to become less hierarchical—that is, to eliminate the old-fashioned command-and-control mentality often inherent in bureaucratic organizations and to motivate and empower individuals to work independently. In each case, the role of leaders is also changing. Whereas leaders were once expected to control situations, direct work, supervise people, closely monitor performance, make decisions, and structure activities, many leaders today are being asked to change how they manage people. Perhaps the best description of this new role is for the leader to become a *coach* instead of an *overseer*.[7]

Consider the metaphor from the standpoint of an actual coach of an athletic team. The coach plays a role in selecting the players for the team and deciding on the general direction to take (such as emphasizing offense versus defense). The coach also helps develop player talent and teaches them how to execute specific plays. But at game time, the coach stays on the sideline; it's up to the players themselves to execute plays and get the job done. And while the coach may get some of the credit for the victory, he or she didn't actually score any of the points.

From the standpoint of a business leader, a coaching perspective would call for the leader to help select team members and other new employees, to provide some general direction, to help train and develop the team and the skills of its members, and to help the team get the information and other resources it needs. The leader may also have to help resolve conflict among team members and mediate other disputes that arise. And coaches from different teams may need to play important roles in linking the activities and functions of their respective teams. But beyond these activities, the leader keeps a low profile and lets the group get its work done with little or no direct oversight from the leader.

Some leaders long accustomed to the traditional more directive approach may have trouble changing to a coaching role. But others seem to make the transition with little or no difficulty. Companies such as Texas Instruments, Halliburton, and YUM! Brands have developed very successful training programs to help their leaders learn how to become better coaches. Within the coaching role, some leaders have also excelled at taking on more responsibilities as a *mentor*—the role of helping a less-experienced person learn the ropes and to better prepare him or her to advance within the organization. Texas Instruments, again, has maintained a very successful mentoring program for years.

▪▪▪ GENDER AND LEADERSHIP

Another factor that is clearly altering the face of leadership is the growing number of women advancing to higher levels in organizations. Given that most leadership theories and research studies have focused on male leaders, developing a better understanding of how women lead is clearly an important next step. For example, do women and men tend to lead differently? Some early observers, for instance, predicted that (consistent with prevailing stereotypes) female leaders would be relatively warm, supportive, and nurturing as compared to their male counterparts. But in reality, research suggests that female leaders are not necessarily more nurturing or supportive than male leaders. Likewise, male leaders are not systematically more harsh, controlling, or task focused than female leaders. The one difference that does seem to arise in some cases is that women have a tendency to be slightly more democratic in making decisions, whereas men have a tendency to be somewhat more autocratic.[8]

There are two possible explanations for this pattern. One possibility is that women may tend to have stronger interpersonal skills than men and are able to better understand how to effectively involve others in making decisions. Men, on the other hand, may have weaker interpersonal skills and have a tendency to rely on their own judgment. The other possible explanation is that women may encounter more stereotypic resistance to their occupying senior roles. If this is the case, they may actively work to involve others in making decisions so as to help minimize any hostility or conflict.

Andrea Jung (left), CEO of Avon Products, and Condoleeza Rice (right), Secretary of State, are demonstrating the effectiveness with which women can be exceptional leaders. For instance, Jung has transformed Avon and made it a real powerhouse in its industry, and Rice is often the "face" of U.S. diplomacy as she travels the globe working with foreign leaders.

However, much more work needs to be done in order to better understand the dynamics of gender and leadership. Moreover, as the number of female leaders continues to grow, understanding what differences, if any, are likely to exist will become increasingly important. High-profile and successful female leaders, such as Andrea Jung (CEO of Avon Products) and Condoleezza Rice (Secretary of State), are demonstrating the effectiveness with which women can be exceptional leaders.

CROSS-CULTURAL LEADERSHIP

Another changing perspective on leadership relates to cross-cultural issues. In this context, *culture* is used as a broad concept to encompass both international differences and diversity-based differences within one culture. For instance, when a Japanese firm sends an executive to head up the firm's operation in the United States, that person will need to become acclimated to the cultural differences that exist between the two countries and consider changing his or her leadership style accordingly. Japan is generally characterized by *collectivism* (group before individual), whereas the U.S. is based more on *individualism* (individual before group). The Japanese executive, then, will find it necessary to recognize the importance of individual contributions and rewards and the differences in individual and group roles that exist in Japanese and U.S. businesses.

Similarly, cross-cultural factors also play a growing role in organizations as their workforces become more diverse. Most leadership research, for instance, has been conducted on samples or case studies involving white male leaders (since until several years ago most business leaders were white males). But as African Americans, Asian Americans, Hispanics, and members of other ethnic groups achieve leadership positions, it may be necessary to reassess how applicable current theories and models of leadership are when applied to an increasingly diverse pool of leaders.

EMERGING ISSUES IN LEADERSHIP

Finally, there are also three emerging issues in leadership that warrant discussion. These issues are *strategic leadership*, *ethical leadership*, and *virtual leadership*.

STRATEGIC LEADERSHIP

Strategic leadership is a new concept that explicitly relates leadership to the role of top management. **Strategic leadership** is a leader's ability to understand the

STRATEGIC LEADERSHIP leader's ability to understand the complexities of both the organization and its environment and to lead change in the organization so as to enhance its competitiveness

complexities of both the organization and its environment and to lead change in the organization so as to enhance its competitiveness.

To be effective as a strategic leader, a manager needs to have a thorough and complete understanding of the organization—its history, its culture, its strengths, and its weaknesses. In addition, the leader needs a firm grasp of the organization's external environment. This needs to include current business and economic conditions and circumstances as well as significant trends and issues on the horizon. The strategic leader also needs to recognize the firm's current strategic advantages and shortcomings. Steve Jobs, CEO of Apple Computer, is an effective strategic leader. A few years ago, Jobs recognized the potential growth of MP3 players and the fact that those devices used technology that is similar to that found in computers. He therefore directed the development of the Apple iPod, which has quickly become an enormously successful—and profitable—product.

In addition to Steven Jobs, Andrea Jung (CEO of Avon Products), Michael Dell (founder and CEO of Dell Computer), and Alan Lafley (CEO of P&G) have all been recognized as strong strategic leaders. On the other hand, Jurgen Schrempp (CEO of DaimlerChrysler), Raymond Gilmartin (CEO of Merck), and Scott Livengood (CEO of Krispy Kreme) were recently singled out for their poor strategic leadership.[3]

■■■ ETHICAL LEADERSHIP

ETHICAL LEADERSHIP leader behaviors that reflect high ethical standards

Most people have long assumed that business leaders are ethical people. But in the wake of recent corporate scandals at firms like Enron, Boeing, and WorldCom, faith in business leaders has been shaken. Perhaps now more than ever, high standards of ethical conduct are being held up as a prerequisite for effective leadership. More specifically, business leaders are being called on to maintain high ethical standards for their own conduct, to unfailingly exhibit ethical behavior, and to hold others in their organizations to the same standards—in short, to practice **ethical leadership**.

The behaviors of top leaders are being scrutinized more than ever, and those responsible for hiring new leaders for a business are looking more closely at the backgrounds of those being considered. And the emerging pressures for stronger corporate governance models are likely to further increase commitment to select only those individuals with high ethical standards for leadership positions in business and to hold them more accountable than in the past for both their actions and the consequences of those actions.

VIRTUAL LEADERSHIP leadership in settings where leaders and followers interact electronically rather than in face-to-face settings

■■■ VIRTUAL LEADERSHIP

Finally, **virtual leadership** is also emerging as an important issue for organizations. In earlier times, leaders and their employees worked together in the same physical location and engaged in personal (i.e., face-to-face) interactions on a regular basis. But in today's world, both leaders and their employees may work in locations that are far from one another. Such arrangements might include people telecommuting from a home office one or two days a week to people actually living and working far from company headquarters and seeing one another in person only very infrequently.

How then do managers carry out leadership when they do not have regular personal contact with their followers? And how do they help mentor and develop others? Communication between leaders and their subordinates will still occur, but it may be largely by telephone and e-mail. One implication may be that leaders in these situations may simply need to work harder at creating and maintaining relationships with their employees that go beyond words on a computer screen. While nonverbal communication, such as smiles and handshakes, may not be possible online, managers can instead

Great leaders find a balance between getting results and how they get them. A lot of people make the mistake of thinking that getting results is all there is to a job.

—Andrall Pearson, Director of YUM! Brands

entrepreneurship and new ventures

An Apple a Day

Steve Jobs, a cofounder of Apple Computer, was the visionary behind the first mass-market personal computer, while his cofounder, Steve Wozniak, was the technical wizard. The quirky, creative, and unique culture of Apple was greatly influenced by Jobs, the nonconformist CEO. Apple's unprecedented success helped paved the way for the PC boom of the 1980s. However, under pressure of competition from mainstream computer makers, such as IBM and Compaq, Apple's performance declined.

As the computer maker lost its strategic direction, Jobs was seen by some investors as having failed, and he reluctantly left Apple in 1985. One biography of Jobs sums up the turnover, saying, "While Jobs was a persuasive and charismatic evangelist for Apple, critics also claimed he was an erratic and tempestuous manager." In 1986, Jobs purchased Pixar from George Lucas and became CEO. The computer animation studio produced its first film, *Toy Story*, in 1995. And after a decade of mediocre results at Apple, Jobs was then coaxed into again taking the helm in 1997.

As Apple CEO, Jobs developed a reputation for brilliance, originality, and charm. At the same time, he could be arrogant and hypercritical. He expected others to meet his very high standards and was insulting when disappointed. One industry observer portrayed Jobs as intimidating and power hungry, while others said he commanded "a cult-like following from employees and consumers."

Yet, despite occasional criticism, Jobs is clearly a leader who can deliver success in businesses that are evolving, highly technical, and demanding. Writer Steven Berglas says, "Jobs, the enfant terrible widely reputed to be one of the most aggressive egotists in Silicon Valley, has an unrivaled track record when it comes to pulling development teams through start-ups." Referring to the bitter battles waged in the PC industry during the period of rapid growth, Berglas believes that Jobs is an empire builder who "held up IBM as the enemy he needed to destroy."

> *Steve never tells us what to do.*
>
> **—Pixar employee**

But would Jobs' charisma, confidence, and vision allow him to be a successful leader during times of prosperity and success? Berglas and some other industry observers predicted that Jobs would not be able to switch his leadership behavior to effectively manage the company during good times. However, as Apple's shares reached an all-time high of $80 and the company had the highest revenues and profits in its history in January 2006, Jobs has proved them wrong.

Indeed, he seems more unbeatable than ever. In a recent interview, Jobs discussed how his passion and focus enable the company to succeed in any type of situation or environment. "Lots of companies have tons of great engineers and smart people," said Jobs. "But ultimately, there needs to be some gravitational force that pulls it all together. . . . That's what was missing at Apple for a while. There were bits and pieces of interesting things floating around, but not that gravitational pull."

Today, Apple and Job are riding high. Pixar has released a series of wildly successful movies, such as *Monsters, Inc.*, *Finding Nemo*, and *The Incredibles*. Each film has grossed more than the previous one. *The Incredibles* had sales of $143 million in its opening weekend; the DVD sold five million copies on the first day of release, setting a daily record of $100 million. In early 2006, Disney bought Pixar, making Jobs the largest shareholder of that company.

As for Apple, it's also riding high. For instance, it has released several versions of the hugely popular iPod, supported by the company's online music store, iTunes. The recent iMac and Mac mini have also been bestsellers. And Apple has started making computers using Intel technology, making them much more compatible with PCs. Jobs' confidence is justified by the company's tremendous success and his confidence is growing. "Apple is doing the best work in its history," he says, "and there's a lot more coming." Jobs' uncanny blend of leadership and entrepreneurship has contributed in myriad ways to the successes of both Apple and Pixar, and will likely give Disney a boost as well.

make a point of adding a few personal words in an e-mail (whenever appropriate) to convey appreciation, reinforcement, or constructive feedback. Building on this, managers should then also take advantage of every opportunity whenever they are in face-to-face situations to go further than they might have done under different circumstances to develop a strong relationship.

But beyond these simple prescriptions, there is no theory or research to guide managers functioning in a virtual world. Hence, as electronic communications continues to pervade the workplace, researchers and managers alike need to work together to first help frame the appropriate issues and questions regarding virtual leadership and then to help address those issues and answer those questions.

LEADERSHIP, MANAGEMENT, AND DECISION MAKING

DECISION MAKING choosing one alternative from among several options

We noted earlier the differences and similarities between managing and leading. Decision making is another important related concept, and both managers and leaders must frequently make decisions. As we saw back in Chapter 5, **decision making**—choosing one alternative from among several options—is a critical management skill. Since we now have a better understanding of both management and leadership, we can explore in a bit more detail some of the essential elements of decision making.

▪▪▪ RATIONAL DECISION MAKING

Managers and leaders should strive to be rational in making decisions. Figure 9.3 shows the steps in the rational decision-making process.

Figure 9.3   Steps in the Rational Decision-Making Process

Step	Detail	Example
1. Recognizing and defining the decision situation	Some stimulus indicates that a decision must be made. The stimulus may be positive or negative.	The plant manager sees that employee turnover has increased by 5 percent.
2. Identifying alternatives	Both obvious and creative alternatives are desired. In general, the more important the decision, the more alternatives should be generated.	The plant manager can increase wages, increase benefits, or change hiring standards.
3. Evaluating alternatives	Each alternative is evaluated to determine its feasibility, its satisfactoriness, and its consequences.	Increasing benefits may not be feasible. Increasing wages and changing hiring standards may satisfy all conditions.
4. Selecting the best alternative	Consider all situational factors and choose the alternative that best fits the manager's situation.	Changing hiring standards will take an extended period of time to cut turnover, so increase wages.
5. Implementing the chosen alternative	The chosen alternative is implemented into the organizational system.	The plant manager may need permission from corporate headquarters. The human resource department establishes a new wage structure.
6. Following up and evaluating the results	At some time in the future, the manager should ascertain the extent to which the alternative chosen in step 4 and implemented in step 5 has worked.	The plant manager notes that six months later, turnover dropped to its previous level.

Recognizing and Defining the Decision Situation The first step in rational decision making is recognizing that a decision is necessary—that is, there must be some stimulus or spark to initiate the process. For example, when equipment malfunctions, managers must decide whether to repair it or to replace it. Similarly, a person taking the leadership role during an emergency must decide how best to protect everyone's safety. And the stimulus for a decision may be either positive or negative. Managers who must decide how to invest surplus funds, for example, face a positive decision situation. A negative financial stimulus could involve having to trim budgets because of cost overruns.

Inherent in making such a decision is the need to define precisely what the problem is. Managers must develop a complete understanding of the problem, its causes, and its relationship to other factors. This understanding comes from careful analysis and thoughtful consideration of the situation. Consider the situation currently being faced in the international air travel industry. Because of the growth of international travel related to business, education, and tourism, global carriers, such as Singapore Airlines, KLM, JAL, British Airways, and American Airlines, need to increase their capacity for international travel. Because most major international airports are already operating at or near capacity, adding a significant number of new flights to existing schedules is not feasible. As a result, the most logical alternative is to increase capacity on existing flights. Thus, Boeing and Airbus, the world's only manufacturers of large commercial aircraft, have recognized an important opportunity and have defined their decision situation as how best to respond to the need for increased global travel capacity.[10]

Identifying Alternatives Once the decision situation has been recognized and defined, the second step is to identify alternative courses of effective action. Developing both obvious, standard alternatives and creative, innovative alternatives is useful. In general, the more important the decision, the more attention is directed to developing alternatives. If the decision involves a multimillion-dollar relocation, a great deal of time and expertise will be devoted to identifying the best locations. For example, J. C. Penney spent two years searching before selecting the Dallas–Fort Worth area for its corporate headquarters when the firm decided to move from New York. However, if the problem is to choose a name for the company softball team, a leader can obviously devote much less time and energy on reaching a resolution.

Although managers should seek creative solutions, they must also recognize that various constraints often limit their alternatives. Common constraints include legal restrictions, moral and ethical norms, and constraints imposed by the power and authority of the manager, available technology, economic considerations, and unofficial social norms. After assessing the question of how to increase international airline capacity, Boeing and Airbus identified three different alternatives: They could independently develop new large planes, they could collaborate in a joint venture to create a single new large plane, or they could modify their largest existing planes to increase their capacity.

Evaluating Alternatives The third step in the decision-making process is evaluating each of the alternatives. For a small, struggling firm, an alternative requiring a huge financial outlay is probably out of the question. Other alternatives may not be feasible because of legal barriers. And limited human, material, and information resources may make other alternatives impractical. Managers must thoroughly evaluate all the alternatives in order to increase the chances that the alternative finally chosen will be successful. Airbus felt it would be at a disadvantage if it tried simply to enlarge its existing planes, because the Boeing 747 is already the largest aircraft being made and could readily be expanded to remain the largest. Boeing, meanwhile, was seriously concerned about the risk inherent in building a new and even larger plane, even if it shared the risk with Airbus as a joint venture.

Selecting the Best Alternative Choosing the best available alternative is the real crux of decision making. Even though many situations do not lend themselves to objective, mathematical analysis, managers and leaders can often develop subjective estimates and weights for choosing an alternative. Decision makers should also remember that finding multiple acceptable alternatives may be possible; selecting just one alternative and rejecting all the others might not be necessary. For example, Airbus proposed a joint venture with Boeing. Boeing, meanwhile, decided that its best course of action was to modify its existing 747 to increase its capacity. As a result, Airbus then decided to proceed on its own to develop and manufacture a new jumbo jet. Meanwhile, Boeing also decided that in addition to modifying its 747, it would also develop a new plane to offer as an alternative, albeit one not as large as the 747 or the proposed Airbus plane.

Implementing the Chosen Alternative After an alternative has been selected, managers and leaders must put it into effect. In some decision situations, implementation is fairly easy; in others, it is more difficult. In the case of an acquisition, for example, managers must decide how to integrate all the activities of the new business, including purchasing, human resource practices, and distribution, into an ongoing organizational framework. For example, when Hewlett-Packard first announced its acquisition of Compaq, managers also acknowledged that it would take at least a year to integrate the two firms into a single one.

Managers must also consider people's resistance to change when implementing decisions. The reasons for such resistance include insecurity, inconvenience, and fear of the unknown. When J. C. Penney decided to move its headquarters from New York to Texas, many employees resigned rather than relocate. Managers should anticipate potential resistance at various stages of the implementation process.

Managers should also recognize that even when all alternatives have been evaluated as precisely as possible and the consequences of each alternative have been weighed, unanticipated consequences are still likely. Any number of factors—unexpected cost increases, a less-than-perfect fit with existing organizational subsystems, or unpredicted effects on cash flow or operating expenses, for example—could develop after implementation has begun. For example, Boeing has set its engineers to work expanding the capacity of its 747 from today's 416 passengers to as many as 520 passengers by adding 30 feet to the plane's body. Boeing has also been developing another plane intended for international travel, the 787. Airbus engineers, meanwhile, are developing design concepts for a new jumbo jet equipped with escalators and elevators and capable of carrying 655 passengers. Airbus's development costs alone are estimated to be more than $12 billion.

Following Up and Evaluating the Results The final step in the decision-making process requires that managers and leaders evaluate the effectiveness of their decision—that is, they should make sure that the chosen alternative has served its original purpose. If an implemented alternative appears not to be working, they can respond in several ways. Another previously identified alternative (the original second or third choice, for instance) could be adopted. Or they might recognize that the situation was not correctly defined to begin with and start the process all over again. Finally, managers and leaders might decide that the original alternative is in fact appropriate but either has not yet had time to work or should be implemented in a different way.

At this point, both Boeing and Airbus are nearing the crucial period when they will learn whether they made good decisions. Airbus's A380 is expected to make its first commercial flight in 2007. Its final design allows seating for up to 850 people, and major airports around the world have been building new runways and terminal areas to accommodate the behemoth. Boeing's expanded 747 should be in service around the same time. Meanwhile, though, it appears that Boeing's secondary initiative for designing the new 787 may prove to be the best decision of all. A key element of the new plane is that

After a long decision-making process, Airbus decided to design its own jumbo jet. The Airbus A380's design allows seating for up to 850 people, and major airports around the world have been building new runways and terminal areas to accommodate the behemoth. Boeing, meanwhile, went through a similar decision-making process but concluded that the risks were too great to gamble on such an enormous project. Instead, the firm decided to modify its existing 747 design and develop a new fuel-efficient aircraft, the 787.

it is much more fuel-efficient than other international airplanes. Given the dramatic surge in fuel costs in recent years, a fuel-efficient option like the 787 is likely to be an enormous success. However, the 787 will not be available for passenger service until 2009, so its real impact will not be known for a few more years.[11]

■■■ BEHAVIORAL ASPECTS OF DECISION MAKING

If all decision situations were approached as logically as described in the previous section, more decisions would prove successful. Yet decisions are often made with little consideration for logic and rationality. Some experts have estimated that U.S. companies use rational decision-making techniques less than 20 percent of the time.[12] And even when organizations try to be logical, they sometimes fail. For example, when Starbucks opened its first coffee shops in New York, it relied on scientific marketing research, taste tests, and rational deliberation in making a decision to emphasize drip over espresso coffee. However, that decision proved wrong, as it became clear that New Yorkers strongly preferred the same espresso-style coffees that were Starbucks mainstays in the West. Hence, the firm had to reconfigure its stores hastily to meet customer preferences.

On the other hand, sometimes a decision made with little regard for logic can still turn out to be correct.[13] Important ingredients in how these forces work are behavioral aspects of decision making. These include *political forces*, *intuition*, *escalation of commitment*, and *risk propensity*.

Political Forces in Decision Making Political forces contribute to the behavioral nature of decision making. One major element of politics, *coalitions*, is especially relevant to decision making. A **coalition** is an informal alliance of individuals or groups formed to achieve a common goal. This common goal is often a preferred decision alternative. For example, coalitions of stockholders frequently band together to force a board of directors to make a certain decision.

Intuition **Intuition** is an innate belief about something, often without conscious consideration. Managers sometimes decide to do something because it "feels right" or they have a "hunch." This feeling is usually not arbitrary, however. Rather, it is based on years

COALITION an informal alliance of individuals or groups formed to achieve a common goal

INTUITION an innate belief about something, often without conscious consideration of experience and practice in making decisions in similar situations. Such an inner sense may help managers make an occasional decision without going through a full-blown rational sequence of steps. For example, the New York Yankees once contacted three major sneaker manufacturers—Nike, Reebok, and Adidas—and informed them that they were looking to make a sponsorship deal. While Nike and Reebok were carefully and rationally assessing the possibilities, managers at Adidas quickly realized that a partnership with the Yankees made a lot of sense for them. They responded very quickly to the idea and ended up hammering out a contract while the competitors were still analyzing details.[14] All managers, but most especially inexperienced ones, should be careful not to rely too heavily on intuition. If rationality and logic are continually flouted for "what feels right," the odds are that disaster will strike one day.

Escalation of Commitment Another important behavioral process that influences decision making is **escalation of commitment** to a chosen course of action. In particular, decision makers sometimes make decisions and then become so committed to the course of action suggested by that decision that they stay with it, even when it appears to have been wrong.[15] For example, when people buy stock in a company, they sometimes refuse to sell it even after repeated drops in price. They choose a course of action—buying the stock in anticipation of making a profit—and then stay with it even in the face of increasing losses. Moreover, after the value drops, they rationalize that they can't sell now because if they do, they will lose money.

ESCALATION OF COMMITMENT condition in which a decision maker becomes so committed to a course of action that she or he stays with it even when it appears to have been wrong

Risk Propensity and Decision Making The behavioral element of **risk propensity** is the extent to which a decision maker is willing to gamble when making a decision. Some managers are cautious about every decision they make. They try to adhere to the rational model and are extremely conservative in what they do. Such managers are more likely to avoid mistakes, and they infrequently make decisions that lead to big losses. Other managers are extremely aggressive in making decisions and are willing to take risks.[16] They rely heavily on intuition, reach decisions quickly, and often risk big investments on their decisions. As in gambling, these managers are more likely than their conservative counterparts to achieve big successes with their decisions; they are also more likely to incur greater losses.[17] The organization's culture is a prime ingredient in fostering different levels of risk propensity.

RISK PROPENSITY extent to which a decision maker is willing to gamble when making a decision

SELF-CHECK QUESTIONS 7–9

You should now be able to answer Self-Check Questions 7–9.*

7 Multiple Choice Which of these is an important emerging issue in leadership?
(a) strategic leadership
(b) ethical leadership
(c) virtual leadership
(d) all of the above

8 Multiple Choice Which of these is a central part of rational decision making?

(a) political forces
(b) intuition
(c) risk propensity
(d) none of the above

9 True/False Political forces contribute to the *behavioral* nature of decision making.

***Answers to Self-Check Questions 7–9 can be found on p. 565.**

CONTINUED FROM PAGE 266

TURNING THE TIDE

From day one as CEO, Alan Lafley knew that P&G could do a better job of selling its proven winners. One of his first acts as a leader was to allocate more resources to the managers of the company's top 10 brands. "The trick," he recalls, "was to find the few things that were really going to sell, and sell as many of them as you could . . . The essence of our strategy," he adds, "is incredibly simple, but I believe the simplicity is its power . . . It's Sesame Street–simple, but it works." For example, hair-care managers reinvented the way they marketed Pantene, the company's top-selling hair-care brand. Rather than position products by hair type (for oily hair or fine hair), new campaigns focused on the looks that customers wanted—for example, more curls or more volume. Sales went up by 8 percent.

Instead of insisting that new products be developed internally, Lafley also started acquiring small, idea-driven firms. He announced that 50 percent of the company's product innovations should come through such acquisitions. If the strategy proves successful, Lafley explains, "We would double the productivity of our current investment in R&D." Lafley also demands more marketability in new products, reminding researchers, "Innovation is in the consumer's eyes . . . It isn't a great innovation until [the customer] loves it and purchases it."

Lafley is shaking up P&G's staid culture in other ways, too. At the company's Cincinnati headquarters, product managers have moved out of executive suites to work more closely with employees. Wood paneling and oil paintings are coming down so that top managers can work as teams in modern, open spaces. The penthouse floor is now a learning center, where top executives conduct lessons and share knowledge with the workforce. "I really believe knowledge is power," says Lafley, "and translating knowledge into action in the marketplace is one of the things that distinguishes leadership."

Communication between managers, workers, board members, and even competitors has opened up. With a series of small changes, Lafley has had a powerful impact on P&G's performance. Since he took over, earnings regularly beat expectations, and the stock price has risen 70 percent. As for Lafley himself, he continues to emphasize the basics. "Nearly 2 billion times a day," he reminds his employees, "P&G products are put to the test when consumers use [them]. . . . When we get this right. . . . then we begin to earn the trust on which great brands are built."

I really believe knowledge is power, and translating knowledge into action in the marketplace is one of the things that distinguishes leadership.

—**Alan Lafley, CEO of P&G**

QUESTIONS FOR DISCUSSION

1 What does this case illustrate about the nature of leadership?

2 Compare and contrast the leadership approaches used by Jager and Lafley.

3 What does this case illustrate about the situational nature of leadership?

4 How would you characterize Lafley in terms of charismatic leadership?

5 How would you rate his performance in terms of transformational leadership, strategic leadership, and ethical leadership?

SUMMARY OF LEARNING OBJECTIVES

1 Define *leadership* and distinguish it from management.

Leadership refers to the processes and behaviors used by someone to motivate, inspire, and influence the behaviors of others. While leadership and management are often related, they are not the same thing. Leadership involves such things as developing a vision, communicating that vision, and directing change. Management, meanwhile, focuses more on outlining procedures, monitoring results, and working toward outcomes.

2 Summarize early approaches to the study of leadership.

The *trait approach to leadership* focused on identifying the traits of successful leaders. The earliest researchers believed that important leadership traits included intelligence, dominance, self-confidence, energy, activity (versus passivity), and knowledge about the job. More recent researchers have started to focus on traits such as emotional intelligence, drive, honesty and integrity, self-confidence, and charisma. The *behavioral approach* identified two basic and common leader behaviors: *task-focused* and *employee-focused* behaviors.

3 Discuss the concept of situational approaches to leadership.

The *situational approach to leadership* proposes that there is no single best approach to leadership. Instead, situational factors influence the approach to leadership that is most effective. This approach was proposed as a continuum of leadership behavior, ranging from having the leader make decisions alone to having employees make decisions with minimal guidance from the leader. Each point on the continuum is influenced by *characteristics of the leader*, *his or her subordinates*, and the *situation*.

4 Describe transformational and charismatic perspectives on leadership.

Transformational leadership (as distinguished from *transactional leadership*) focuses on the set of abilities that allows a leader to recognize the need for change, to create a vision to guide that change, and to execute the change effectively. *Charismatic leadership* is influence based on the leader's personal charisma. The basic concept of charisma suggests that charismatic leaders are likely to have self-confidence, confidence in their beliefs and ideals, and a need to influence people. They also tend to communicate high expectations about follower performance and to express confidence in their followers.

5 Identify and discuss leadership substitutes and neutralizers.

Leadership substitutes are individual, task, and organizational factors that tend to outweigh the need for a leader to initiate or direct employee performance. In other words, if certain factors are present, the employee will perform his or her job without the direction of a leader. Even if a leader attempts to engage in leadership behaviors, there exist *leadership neutralizers* that may render the leader's efforts ineffective. Such neutralizers include group cohesiveness as well as elements of the job itself.

6 Discuss leaders as coaches and examine gender and cross-cultural issues in leadership.

Many organizations expect their leaders to play the role of *coach*—to select team members, provide direction, train and develop, but otherwise allow the group to function autonomously. Another factor that is altering the face of leadership is the number of women advancing to higher levels. While there appear to be few differences between men and women leaders, the growing number of women leaders suggests a need for more study. Another changing perspective on leadership relates to cross-cultural issues. In this context, *culture* encompasses international differences and diversity-based differences within one culture.

7 Describe strategic leadership, ethical leadership, and virtual leadership.

Strategic leadership is the leader's ability to lead change in the organization so as to enhance its competitiveness. Business leaders are also being called on to practice *ethical leadership*—that is, to maintain high ethical standards for their own conduct, and to hold others in their organizations to the same standards. As more leaders and employees work in different settings, a better understanding of *virtual leadership* is also becoming more important.

8 Relate leadership to decision making and discuss both rational and behavioral perspectives on decision making.

Decision making—choosing one alternative from among several options—is a critical management and leadership skill. The *rational perspective* prescribes a logical process for making decisions. It involves six steps (1) recognizing and defining the decision situation, (2) identifying alternatives, (3) evaluating alternatives, (4) selecting the best alternative, (5) implementing the chosen alternative, and (6) following up and evaluating the results. The *behavioral perspective* acknowledges that things like *political forces*, *intuition*, *escalation of commitment*, and *risk propensity* are also important aspects of decision making.

☐☐☐☐☐☐☐☐☐☐   **KEY TERMS**

behavioral approach to
   leadership (p. 269)
charismatic leadership (p. 272)
coalition (p. 283)
decision making (p. 280)
employee-focused leader
   behavior (p. 269)

escalation of commitment (p. 284)
ethical leadership (p. 278)
intuition (p. 283)
leadership (p. 266)
leadership neutralizers (p. 274)
leadership substitutes (p. 274)
risk propensity (p. 284)

situational approach to leadership (p. 270)
strategic leadership (p. 277)
task-focused leader behavior (p. 269)
trait approach to leadership (p. 268)
transactional leadership (p. 271)
transformational leadership (p. 271)
virtual leadership (p. 278)

☐☐☐☐☐☐☐☐☐☐   **QUESTIONS AND EXERCISES**

Questions for Review

1   What are the basic differences between management and leadership?
2   Summarize the basic premises underlying the trait, behavioral, and situational approaches to leadership.
3   What are leadership substitutes and neutralizers?
4   List and briefly explain the steps in rational decision making.

Questions for Analysis

5   Identify five people you would consider to be excellent leaders. Explain why you feel that way about each.
6   What factors are present in your job that motivate you to perform without the direction of a leader? Are there factors that neutralize the efforts of your leader?
7   The impact of virtual leadership is likely to grow in the future. As a potential "follower" in a virtual leadership situation, what issues would be of most concern to you? What would the issues be from the perspective of the "leader" role in such a situation?
8   Identify and discuss examples of how your decision making has been affected by at least two of the behavioral processes noted in the chapter.

Application Exercises

9   Interview a senior manager at a local company. Ask that manager if he or she believes that leadership can be taught. What are the key implications of his or her position?
10   Review the running example in the textbook regarding the decisions made by Airbus and Boeing regarding new long-haul aircraft. Research the most current information available about the status of both planes. Based on the information you have available, which firm seems to have made the best decision?

LEARNING TO LEAD

Goal

To encourage you to appreciate your own strengths and weaknesses as they relate to critical leadership skills.

Background Information

While not all experts agree, most believe that businesses can teach their managers to become more effective leaders. Indeed, most large businesses devote considerable resources to identifying those managers with the most leadership potential and providing training and development opportunities for those managers to enhance and refine their leadership skills. One major U.S. energy company, for instance, has identified the following traits, characteristics, and skills as reflecting how it sees leadership:

- Personal integrity
- Decision-making skills
- Interpersonal skills
- Communication skills
- Strategic thinking skills
- Global awareness skills
- Financial management skills

Method

Step 1

Working alone or with classmates (as directed by your instructor), develop or describe indicators and measures a business could use to assess each of these traits, characteristics, and skills

in managers so as to most effecrtively select those with the strongest potential for leadership. That is, describe how you would go about selecting managers for special leadership training and development.

Step 2

Working alone or with classmates (again, as directed by your instructor), develop or describe the techniques and methods that might potentially serve to best enhance the traits, characteristics, and skills noted above. That is, having chosen those managers with the strongest potential for growth as leaders, describe how you would go about teaching and developing those individuals so as to enhance their leadership potential and capability.

FOLLOW-UP QUESTIONS

1 Comment on the traits, characteristics, and skills used by the energy company. Do you agree or disagree that these would differentiate between those who might be described as both managers and leaders versus those best described simply as managers? Are there others you might include?

2 How simple or easy would you expect it to be to select managers for leadership and development at this company?

3 Do you believe that leadership can be taught? What are the assumptions underlying your answer?

4 If you personally were selected for a program such as this, what would you expect to encounter during the training and development? What would you expect to be different after the training and development were complete?

EXERCISING CHARISMA

The Situation

Assume that you are the owner and CEO of a small but growing business. You see yourself as a mild and laid-back kind of person—one that is honest and effective as a manager, but not necessarily someone who strongly inspires and motivates others. This has never been a barrier to your success. You have made excellent decisions since founding your company and are respected by both your employees and the firm's external stakeholders.

Because your business is growing, about a year ago you found it necessary to hire some additional managers. One of these has been increasingly causing you concern. The manager in question, Bill Jackson, is a dynamic and charismatic person—all of the things you are not. Indeed, these qualities have already made him enormously liked by most people in the business. So far, though, Jackson has not really distinguished himself as a manager. He basically makes reasonable decisions and understands how to run his unit, but does not seem to be a real strategic thinker.

The Dilemma

A new competitor has just entered your market area. While you do not see this a major long-term threat, you have decided that you need for your business to "tighten its belt" a bit. You anticipate, for example, that your business revenues will shrink a bit this year (due to the new company) but will likely start to grow again within a year or so. Your senior financial manager has convinced you that the best course of action would be to terminate one of the newer managers you hired last year.

Your inclination is to terminate Jackson. The basis for this is your concern for how others in the business see him. For example, if you were to decide to retire (which you may want to do in a few years), you suspect there would be a strong and immediate groundswell of support for appointing Jackson as the CEO to take your place. You truly believe that this support would be based on his charisma and dynamic personality, but you also think that while he would be an adequate replacement, there are others in the business who would do a better job actually managing the firm. But given Jackson's enormous popularity, anyone else picked to replace you would at least initially have to work hard to overcome skepticism and disappointment. You are leaning toward terminating Jackson.

QUESTIONS TO ADDRESS

1 What are the ethical issues in this situation?
2 What do you think most managers would do in this situation?
3 What would you do?

FORCING THE HAND

The Situation

The Edda Corporation is a large manufacturing company that is assessing the market potential of four new products it has acquired the rights to produce.

The Dilemma

After some preliminary discussions, it seems apparent that two of the new products have market potential, but the others do not. However, the company's CEO, Lucy Shaw, wants to produce all the new products. After all, she is the one who approved the costly acquisition of rights, and it is she who will have to explain to the board of directors why some of the products she approved do not, after all, have market potential. But it is also she who will be accountable if the products are all manufacturered but end up performing poorly.

Edda Corporation's top managers have identified several options:

1 Approve all four products for production
2 Be completely frank and recommend approval of only two of the products.
3 Form a coalition with a team of engineers and work toward a proposal to modify the two less attractive products. The management team thinks this is viable, but it will also add some costs for product development and delay product introduction for about six months.

Team Activity

Assemble a group of four students and assign each group member to one of the following roles:

■ Lucy Shaw (CEO)
■ A member of the top management team
■ An Edda Corporation stockholder
■ A member of the Edda Corporation board of directors

ACTION STEPS

1 Before hearing any of your group's comments on this situation, and from the perspective of your assigned role, which option do you think is best for the company? Write down the reasons for your position.
2 Before hearing any of your group's comments on this situation, and from the perspective of your assigned role, what are the underlying ethical issues, if any, in this situation? Write down the issues.
3 Gather your group together and reveal, in turn, each member's comments on the three options. Next, reveal the ethical issues listed by each member.
4 Appoint someone to record main points of agreement and disagreement within the group. How do you explain the results? What accounts for any disagreement?
5 From an ethical standpoint, what does your group conclude is the most appropriate action that should have been taken by the Edda Corporation in this situation?
6 Develop a group response to the following question: Regardless of your current opinion of Lucy Shaw as a leader, what actions on her part now would cause you to think less of her as a leader? What actions would cause you to think more of her as a leader?

WHAT IS BUSINESS LEADERSHIP?

Learning Objectives
The purpose of this video is to help you:
1 Discuss different concepts of what it means to be a successful leader.
2 Understand how different leaders and their ideas of leadership affect organizations.

Synopsis
In this video, you'll see a brief introductory *ABC News* segment featuring business best sellers, including *Principle Centered Leadership* by Stephen R. Covey and *The Corporate Mystic* by Gay Hendricks and Kate Luderman, proponents of people-friendly leadership styles. You'll then listen to executives, managers, and frontline employees from Ernst & Young, Second City, the WNBA, and American Apparel share their own leadership insights. You'll hear their views on such things as the use of status by administrators, the qualities needed to coach a professional sports team of diverse players while staying focused on what is best for the organization as a whole, the centrality of entrepreneurial vision to corporate success, and the need for leaders to be open to new ideas.

DISCUSSION QUESTIONS
1 **For analysis**: What are some of the traits listed as good leadership traits by those interviewed in the video? Do you agree that these are real leadership traits? Why or why not?
2 **For analysis**: What traits of WNBA coaches can apply to leaders in general?
3 **For application**: How would you suggest that a new CEO use concepts of leadership in his or her day-to-day business activities?
4 **For debate**: Do you agree with Stephen Covey's notion that leaders should admit their mistakes, apologize, and ask for forgiveness? Why or why not?
5 **For debate**: Gay Hendricks and Kate Luderman, authors of *The Corporate Mystic*, say that leaders should always tell the truth and take responsibility for mistakes of the whole group. Do you agree with their philosophy? Why or why not?

Online Exploration
Using the Internet, research current business best-sellers that focus on leadership. What are the most current best sellers on leadership, and what do they claim makes a good leader? Then visit the Center for Creative Leadership at www.ccl.org. What sorts of coaching services does the Center offer?

After reading this chapter, you should be able to:

1 Define *human resource management* and explain how managers plan for their organization's human resource needs.

2 Identify the tasks in staffing a company and discuss ways in which organizations select, develop, and appraise employee performance.

3 Describe the main components of a compensation system and describe some of the key legal issues involved in hiring, compensating, and managing workers in today's workplace.

4 Discuss workforce diversity, the management of knowledge workers, and the use of a contingent workforce as important changes in the contemporary workplace.

5 Explain why workers organize into labor unions and describe the collective bargaining process.

LAS VEGAS GAMBLES ONLINE

Talk about daunting challenges! Imagine this assignment: Your boss tells you that you are responsible for hiring almost 10,000 new workers. But that's the easy part. You have to have them all prepared to start working on the same day, their job skills have to be impeccable, and there can be no mistakes. Oh, and just to make it interesting, you are not allowed to use

HUMAN RESOURCE MANAGEMENT AND LABOR RELATIONS

a single sheet of paper! Sound impossible? Well, that's just what a team of Las Vegas executives was asked to do.

In the few years since it opened, the Bellagio hotel and casino in Las Vegas has become one of the gambling mecca's most popular destinations. But before it opened, and behind the scenes, the Bellagio also gave human resource (HR) managers new insights into how to staff a new organization. The task facing the resort's HR executives was daunting: They had to hire 9,600 workers in 24 weeks and have everyone trained and on the payroll when the first customer walked through the door. The firm's HR team not only pulled this feat off without a hitch—it did it without using a single sheet of paper! Arte Nathan, vice president of human resources for the Bellagio, observed that "for us, hiring 9,600 people was like Desert Storm."

With the precision of a full-scale military operation, the Bellagio team designed and implemented one of the

For us, hiring 9,600 people was like Desert Storm.

—Arte Nathan, vice president of human resources at the Bellagio

most sophisticated HR selection systems ever devised. To apply for a position, applicants called and requested an appointment. They were then scheduled in batches to arrive at the resort's hiring center, where they filled out an application at a computer terminal. One hundred terminals were kept busy 12 hours a day, 6 days a week. As applications were submitted, employees at the checkout desk conducted unobtrusive assessments of the applicants' communication skills and overall demeanor, eliminating about 20 percent of the applicants.

Next came 27,000 interviews. For example, a hiring manager could sit at a PC and call up the highest-rated desk clerk candidates. The database system would rank order the candidates according to predetermined criteria. The manager could then call in, for example, three applicants for each open position for face-to-face interviews. An interview consisted of a set of structured questions. During an interview, the manager would discretely evaluate the responses to each question on a hidden keypad. These data were then fed back into the database.

If a manager wanted to hire a particular applicant, he or she could pull up a screen and check "Conduct background check." A team of investigators would then verify employment, military, and education history; for some jobs, a drug test was mandatory. About 8 percent of the applicants were rejected at this stage because of falsified information on their applications.

If a manager was ready to offer a job to a particular individual, another screen was used to check "Yes." When this happened, the applicant was invited to a job-offer meeting, which is when people were actually offered jobs. If they accepted, they then completed various required documents—again, in electronic form—for benefits and income tax purposes. They were also scheduled for relevant training sessions. And when the big day came and the Bellagio officially threw open its doors, 9,600 new employees were in place and ready to work. ■

Our opening story continues on page 317.

WHAT'S IN IT FOR ME?

Effectively managing human resources is the lifeblood of organizations. A firm that handles this activity has a much better chance for success than does a firm that simply goes through the motions. By understanding the material in this chapter, you'll be better able to understand (1) the importance of properly managing human resources in a unit or business you own or supervise and (2) why and how your employer provides the working arrangements that most directly affect you.

We start this chapter by explaining how managers plan for their organization's human resource needs. We'll also discuss ways in which organizations select, develop, and appraise employee performance and examine the main components of a compensation system. Along the way, we'll look at some key legal issues involved in hiring, compensating, and managing workers in today's workplace and discuss workforce diversity. Finally, we'll explain why workers organize into labor unions and describe the collective bargaining process. Let's get started with some basic concepts of human resource management.

THE FOUNDATIONS OF HUMAN RESOURCE MANAGEMENT

HUMAN RESOURCE MANAGEMENT (HRM) set of organizational activities directed at attracting, developing, and maintaining an effective workforce

Human resource management (HRM) is the set of organizational activities directed at attracting, developing, and maintaining an effective workforce. Human resource management takes place within a complex and ever-changing environmental context and is increasingly being recognized for its strategic importance.[1]

■■■ THE STRATEGIC IMPORTANCE OF HRM

Human resources are critical for effective organizational functioning. HRM (or *personnel*, as it is sometimes called) was once relegated to second-class status in many organizations, but its importance has grown dramatically in the last several years. This new importance stems from increased legal complexities, the recognition that human resources are a valuable means for improving productivity, and the awareness today of the costs associated with poor HRM.

Indeed, managers now realize that the effectiveness of their HR function has a substantial impact on a firm's bottom-line performance. Poor HR planning can result in spurts of hiring followed by layoffs—costly in terms of unemployment compensation payments, training expenses, and morale. Haphazard compensation systems do not attract, keep, and motivate good employees, and outmoded recruitment practices can expose a firm to expensive and embarrassing legal action. Consequently, the chief HR executive of most large businesses is a vice president directly accountable to the CEO, and many firms are developing strategic HR plans that are integrated with other strategic planning activities.

■■■ HR PLANNING

As you can see in Figure 10.1, the starting point in attracting qualified human resources is planning. In turn, HR planning involves job analysis and forecasting the demand for, and supply of, labor.

Job Analysis **Job analysis** is a systematic analysis of jobs within an organization. A job analysis results in two things:

■ The **job description** lists the duties and responsibilities of a job; its working conditions; and the tools, materials, equipment, and information used to perform it.
■ The **job specification** lists the skills, abilities, and other credentials and qualifications needed to perform the job effectively.

Job analysis information is used in many HR activities. For instance, knowing about job content and job requirements is necessary to develop appropriate selection methods, to create job-relevant performance appraisal systems, and to set equitable compensation rates.

JOB ANALYSIS systematic analysis of jobs within an organization

JOB DESCRIPTION description of the duties and responsibilities of a job, its working conditions, and the tools, materials, equipment, and information used to perform it

JOB SPECIFICATION description of the skills, abilities, and other credentials and qualifications required by a job

Figure 10.1
The HR Planning Process

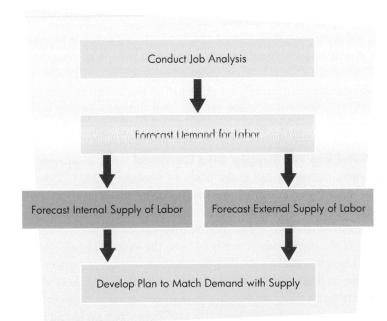

Forecasting HR Demand and Supply After managers fully understand the jobs to be performed within an organization, they can start planning for the organization's future HR needs. The manager starts by assessing trends in past HR usage, future organizational plans, and general economic trends. A good sales forecast is often the foundation, especially for smaller organizations. Historical ratios can then be used to predict demand for types of employees, such as manufacturing plant employees and sales representatives. Large organizations use much more complicated models to predict HR needs.

Forecasting the supply of labor is really two tasks:

1 Forecasting *internal supply*—the number and type of employees who will be in the firm at some future date.
2 Forecasting *external supply*—the number and type of people who will be available for hiring from the labor market at large.

The simplest approach merely adjusts present staffing levels for anticipated turnover and promotions. Again, however, large organizations use extremely sophisticated models to make these forecasts.

REPLACEMENT CHART list of each management position, who occupies it, how long that person will likely stay in the job, and who is qualified as a replacement

Replacement Charts At higher levels of an organization, managers plan for specific people and positions. The technique most commonly used is the **replacement chart**, which lists each important managerial position, who occupies it, how long that person will probably stay in it before moving on, and who (by name) is now qualified or soon will be qualified to move into it. This technique allows ample time to plan developmental experiences for people identified as potential successors to critical managerial jobs. Replacement charts were once actual paper documents—posters, charts, or files. Now, however, they are much more likely to be electronic.

EMPLOYEE INFORMATION SYSTEM (SKILLS INVENTORY) computerized system containing information on each employee's education, skills, work experiences, and career aspirations

Skills Inventories To facilitate both planning and identifying people for transfer or promotion, some organizations also have **employee information systems (skills inventories)**. These systems are also likely to be computerized; they contain information on each employee's education, skills, work experience, and career aspirations. Such a system can quickly locate every employee who is qualified to fill a position requiring, for example, a degree in chemical engineering, three years of experience in an oil refinery, and fluency in Spanish.

Forecasting the external supply of labor is a different problem altogether. How does a manager, for example, predict how many electrical engineers will be seeking work in California or Florida three years from now? To get an idea of the future availability of labor, planners must rely on information from outside sources, such as state employment commissions, government reports, and figures supplied by colleges on the number of students in major fields.

Matching HR Supply and Demand After comparing future demand and internal supply, managers can make plans to manage predicted shortfalls or overstaffing. If a shortfall is predicted, new employees can be hired, present employees can be retrained and transferred into understaffed areas, individuals approaching retirement can be convinced to stay on, or labor-saving or productivity-enhancing systems can be installed.

If the organization needs to hire, the external labor-supply forecast helps managers plan how to recruit according to whether the type of person needed is readily available or scarce in the labor market. The use of temporary workers also helps managers in staffing by giving them extra flexibility. If overstaffing is expected to be a problem, the main options are transferring the extra employees, not replacing individuals who quit, encouraging early retirement, and laying off people.

entrepreneurship and new ventures

The Guru for Fun Takes a Meeting with the V. P. of Buzz

Rather than dictating standard job titles, some new ventures and entrepreneurial firms now allow new hires to name their own jobs. Others even let employees *create* their own jobs. Some interesting twists have emerged.

It started with the Internet bubble in the mid-1990s. For example, Amy Berkus, a marketing coordinator at a small dot-com, changed her job title to "marketing mechanic." "Everyone was creating new titles in Internet-speak," recalls Berkus. "We wanted titles that conveyed team spirit and a fun atmosphere. . . . It just fit the time." Other catchy designations included "V.P. of Buzz," "Chief People Officer," "Guru of Fun," "Gladiator," and "Chief Evangelist." Under the right circumstances, such titles encouraged creativity and got employees to think differently about their jobs. They also let everyone know that the company was hip. "It was a matter of doing away with everything that seemed to reek of the old," explains business professor Donna Hoffman. "The feeling was, 'We're going to make new rules. We need new titles.'"

But the times have changed. Executive recruiter Marc Lewis observes that "as the market has cooled, the interest in creative and unusual job titles has diminished." Smaller companies (as well as some larger ones) are now trying to create images of legitimacy, respectability, and honesty. Berkus admits that "the traditional titles [like 'customer care manager' and 'production supervisor'] lend themselves more to the image of a stable company that is driving toward profitability."

> *The feeling was, "We're going to make new rules. We need new titles."*
>
> **—Donna Hoffman, business professor, on the tendency of dot-coms to embrace creative job titles**

Does a return to confidence-inspiring, snooze-inducing job titles mean that companies have abandoned the effort to encourage employee creativity? By no means. Innovation is just as important during tough times as during boom times. The method, however, has changed. Today, entrepreneurial firms that want to encourage and reward creativity aren't willing to settle for window dressing. They're changing the jobs themselves.

Employers are finding, for example, that basing positions on employee interests can be more effective than trying to fit unique individuals into predetermined job slots. Often, a customized job is a reward for high performance. Steve Gluckman, a bicycle designer for REI, a supplier of outdoor gear, worked his way up from service manager to designer over 13 years. An avid cyclist, he says, "Some people sing. Some people paint. I ride my bike. Like a ballet dancer, like a gymnast, like a skateboarder, I express myself in my job." Starbucks's coffee education manager, Aileen Carrell, travels around the world educating employees about coffee. "I was hired as temporary Christmas help in 1990," explains Carrell, "and I fell madly in love with the fact that coffees came from the most amazing places, like Sulawesi." After working as a store manager for several years, Carrell herself proposed the creation of her new position. Organizations will always have to define most of the jobs that have to be performed, but many are discovering that a little flexibility can lead to a lot of productivity.

STAFFING THE ORGANIZATION

When managers have determined that new employees are needed, they must then turn their attention to recruiting and hiring the right mix of people. Staffing the organization is one of the most complex and important tasks of good HRM. The task involves two processes: the process of acquiring staff from outside the company (*external staffing*) and the process of promoting staff from within (*internal staffing*). Both external and internal staffing, however, start with effective *recruiting*.

■■■ RECRUITING HUMAN RESOURCES

Once an organization has an idea of its future HR needs, the next phase is usually recruiting new employees. **Recruiting** is the process of attracting qualified persons to apply for the jobs that are open. Some recruits are found internally, whereas others come from outside of the organization.

RECRUITING process of attracting qualified persons to apply for jobs an organization is seeking to fill

Internal Recruiting **Internal recruiting** means considering present employees as candidates for openings. Promotion from within can help build morale and keep high-quality employees from leaving. In unionized firms, the procedures for notifying employees of internal job-change opportunities are usually spelled out in the union contract. For higher-level positions, a skills inventory system may be used to identify internal candidates, or managers may be asked to recommend individuals who should be considered.

External Recruiting **External recruiting** involves attracting people outside of the organization to apply for jobs. External recruiting methods include posting jobs on the company Web site or other job sites, such as Monster.com, holding campus interviews for potential college recruits, using employment agencies or executive search firms to scout out potential talent, seeking referrals by present employees, advertising in newspapers, magazines, or trade publications, and hiring "walk-ins" or "gate-hires" (people who show up without being solicited). A manager must select the most appropriate method for each job. The manager might, for example, use the state employment service to find a maintenance worker but not a nuclear physicist. Private employment agencies can be a good source of clerical and technical employees, and executive search firms specialize in locating top-management talent. Newspaper ads are often used because they reach a wide audience and allow applicants equal opportunity to find out about and apply for job openings.

When unemployment rates are low, employers must be relatively active and aggressive when seeking new employees. For instance, during one recent period of low unemployment, some companies (including Sprint, PeopleSoft, and Cognex) worked to stress how much "fun" it was to work for them, reinforcing this message with ice cream socials, karaoke contests, softball leagues, and free-movie nights. But when unemployment is relatively high, employers can be more passive, advertising their positions but waiting for potential employees to come to them.

▪▪▪ SELECTING HUMAN RESOURCES

Once the recruiting process has attracted a pool of applicants, the next step is to select someone to hire. The intent of the selection process is to gather from applicants information that will predict their job success and then to hire the candidates likely to be most successful. The organization can only gather information about factors that can be used to predict future performance. The process of determining the predictive value of information is called *validation*. For instance, measuring how far an athlete can throw a football tells little about his or her prowess as a golfer; but observing the person playing a round of golf will be insightful. If an employment criterion accurately predicts job performance, it is said to be valid. If a criterion does not predict performance, it lacks validity.

Application Forms The first step in selection is usually asking the candidate to fill out an application. An application form is an efficient method of gathering information about the applicant's previous work history, educational background, and other job-related demographic data. It should not contain questions about areas unrelated to the job, such as gender, religion, or national origin. Application forms are generally used informally to decide whether a candidate merits further evaluation, and interviewers use application forms to familiarize themselves with candidates before interviewing them. Application forms are seldom used for upper-level jobs; candidates for such positions usually provide the same information on their résumé. But applications are still widely used for most mid- to lower-level jobs.

Interviews are a very popular selection device. In a structured interview, questions are written in advance, and all interviewers follow the same question list with each candidate. For interviewing managerial or professional candidates, a somewhat less structured approach can be used.

Tests Employers sometimes ask candidates to take tests during the selection process. Tests of ability, skill, aptitude, or knowledge relevant to a particular job are usually the best predictors of job success, although tests of general intelligence or personality are occasionally useful as well. For example, if a manager is hiring an assistant who needs to be able to type at a rate of 80 words per minute, an excellent way to assess this ability would be to have prospective employees complete an objective typing exercise and then measure their speed. Some companies use the "big five" personality dimensions discussed in Chapter 8 to predict success; potential employees complete a test designed to measure the "big five" dimensions, and the scores are used to help make hiring decisions. In addition to being validated, tests should be administered and scored consistently. All candidates should be given the same directions, allowed the same amount of time, and offered the same testing environment, including temperature, lighting, and distractions.

Interviews *Interviews* are a very popular selection device, although they are sometimes a poor predictor of job success. For example, biases inherent in the way people perceive and judge others on first meeting affect subsequent evaluations. Interview validity can be improved by training interviewers to be aware of potential biases and by tightening the structure of the interview. In a structured interview, questions are written in advance, and all interviewers follow the same question list with each candidate. Such structure introduces consistency into the interview procedure and allows the organization to validate the content of the questions. For interviewing managerial or professional candidates, a somewhat less structured approach can be used. Although question areas and information-gathering objectives are still planned in advance, specific questions vary with the candidates' backgrounds.

In general, interviewers tend to ask about such things as a major project the employee has been involved with, why the person wants to leave their current employer, and so forth. As we will discuss more fully later, interviewers must steer clear of any questions that could appear to be related to gender (i.e., do you plan to start a family soon?), religion, ethnic origin, and so forth. The safest bet is to describe job-related issues and then ask the prospective employee if he or she can meet that condition. For example, it would be okay to ask something like "This job requires you to be away from home traveling on company business about 10 nights a month. Are you able to meet this requirement?"

Sometimes companies are looking for especially creative employees and may try to learn more about the individual's creativity during an interview. For instance, Microsoft

Top-Down Sensitivity

By definition, global companies must communicate with employees in many different countries and cultures, and a firm's success in communicating with local workers can mean success or failure in an overseas operation. The most successful global companies know how to talk to the people who work for them.

In some countries, the gap between managers and workers is quite wide, and managers are used to bridging it with orders that are simply to be followed. In many Asian cultures, for example, you simply don't question the boss's decisions or the policies of the company. In the United States, on the other hand, people are often encouraged to provide feedback and to say what they think. The gap is relatively narrow, and communication channels tend to be informal and wide open.

The same arrangements usually apply when it comes to dealing with workplace disputes. In some countries, such as Germany and Sweden, there's a formal system for ensuring that everyone involved gets a say in resolving workplace disputes. In these countries, although communication channels are always open, they're also highly structured.

But being culturally sensitive to local employees means much more than just knowing how to settle workplace disputes. As a rule, companies also need to convey a sense of good "citizenship" in the host country. This means respecting the social and cultural values of employees and communicating to them the fact that it cares about these things.

NEW CHALLENGES IN THE CHANGING WORKPLACE

As we have seen throughout this chapter, HR managers face several ongoing challenges in their efforts to keep their organizations staffed with effective workforces. To complicate matters, new challenges arise as the economic and social environments of business change. In the following sections, we look at several of the most important HRM issues facing business today.

■■■ MANAGING WORKFORCE DIVERSITY

WORKFORCE DIVERSITY the range of workers' attitudes, values, beliefs, and behaviors that differ by gender, race, age, ethnicity, physical ability, and other relevant characteristics

One extremely important set of HR challenges centers on **workforce diversity**—the range of workers' attitudes, values, beliefs, and behaviors that differ by gender, race, age, ethnicity, physical ability, and other relevant characteristics. In the past, organizations tended to work toward homogenizing their workforces, getting everyone to think and behave in similar ways. Partly as a result of affirmative action efforts, however, many U.S. organizations are now creating more diverse workforces, embracing more women, ethnic minorities, and foreign-born employees than ever before.

Figure 10.3 helps put the changing U.S. workforce into perspective by illustrating changes in the percentages of different groups of workers—males and females, whites, African Americans, Hispanics, Asians, and others—in the total workforce in the years 1986, 1996, and 2006. The picture is clearly one of increasing diversity. As of 2006, say experts, almost half of all workers in the labor force will be women and almost one-third will be African Americans, Hispanics, and Asians.

Today, organizations are recognizing not only that they should treat everyone equitably but also that they should acknowledge the individuality of each person they employ.

Figure 10.3   Changing Composition of the U.S. Workforce

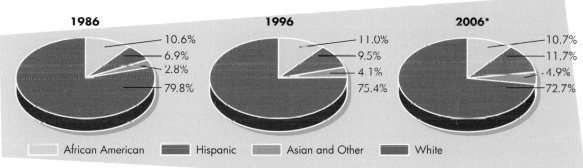

Numbers (in thousands)	1986	1996	2006	Percentage	1986	1996	2006
Total	117,834	133,944	148,847	Total	100.0	100.0	100.0
Men	65,422	72,087	78,226	Men	55.5	53.8	52.6
Women	52,412	61,857	70,620	Women	44.5	46.2	47.4
White, Non-Hispanic	94,026	100,915	108,166	White, Non-Hispanic	79.8	75.4	72.7
Men	52,442	54,451	56,856	Men	44.5	40.7	38.2
Women	41,583	46,464	51,310	Women	35.3	34.7	34.5
African American, Non-Hispanic	12,483	14,795	15,983	African American, Non-Hispanic	10.6	11.0	10.7
Men	6,279	7,091	7,347	Men	5.3	5.3	4.9
Women	6,204	7,704	8,636	Women	5.3	5.8	5.8
Hispanic Origin	8,076	12,774	17,401	Hispanic Origin	6.9	9.5	11.7
Men	4,948	7,646	10,235	Men	4.2	5.7	6.9
Women	3,128	5,128	7,166	Women	2.7	3.8	4.8
Asian and Other, Non-Hispanic	3,249	5,459	7,296	Asian and Other, Non-Hispanic	2.8	4.1	4.9
Men	1,753	2,899	3,788	Men	1.5	2.2	2.5
Women	1,496	2,561	3,508	Women	1.3	1.9	2.4

*Projection

They are also recognizing that diversity can be a competitive advantage. For example, by hiring the best people available from every single group rather than hiring from just one or a few groups, a firm can develop a higher-quality labor force. Similarly, a diverse workforce can bring a wider array of information to bear on problems and can provide insights on marketing products to a wider range of consumers.

We think it is important for our customers to look inside and see people like them. If they can't, the prospect of them becoming or staying our customers declines.

—Head of workforce diversity at IBM

▪▪▪ MANAGING KNOWLEDGE WORKERS

Traditionally, employees added value to organizations because of what they did or because of their experience. In the information age, however, many employees add value because of what they *know.*

The Nature of Knowledge Work Employees who add value because of what they know are usually called **knowledge workers**, and the skill with which they are managed is a major factor in determining which firms will be successful. Knowledge

KNOWLEDGE WORKERS employees who are of value because of the knowledge they possess

workers—including computer scientists, engineers, physical scientists, and game developers—provide special challenges for the HR manager. They tend to work in high-technology firms and are usually experts in some abstract knowledge base. They often like to work independently and tend to identify more strongly with their professions than with any organization—even to the extent of defining performance in terms recognized by other members of their professions.

As the importance of information-driven jobs grows, the need for knowledge workers continues to grow as well. But these employees require extensive and highly specialized training; they also tend to be highly paid. As a result, not every organization is willing to invest the money necessary to take advantage of these jobs. Even after knowledge workers are on the job, retraining and training updates are critical to prevent their skills from becoming obsolete. It has been suggested, for example, that the half-life of a technical education in engineering is about three years. The failure to update such skills will not only result in the loss of competitive advantage for the firm, but will also increase the likelihood that the knowledge worker will go to another firm that is more committed to updating his or her skills. Hence, HR managers must ensure that the proper training is prepared to enable knowledge workers to stay current while also making sure they are compensated at market rates.

Knowledge Worker Management and Labor Markets The demand for knowledge workers continues to grow at a steady pace. As a result, organizations that need these workers must introduce regular salary upgrades to pay their current knowledge workers enough to keep them. This is especially critical in areas in which demand is still growing, since even entry-level salaries for these employees are continuing to escalate.

The continuing demand for knowledge workers has inspired some fairly extreme measures for attracting them in the first place. High starting salaries and sign-on bonuses are common. British Petroleum Exploration was recently paying starting petroleum engineers with undersea platform-drilling knowledge—not experience, just knowledge—salaries in the six figures, plus sign-on bonuses of over $50,000 and immediate profit sharing. Even with these incentives, HR managers complain that in the Gulf Coast region, they cannot retain specialists because young engineers soon leave to accept even more attractive jobs with competitors.

Knowledge workers often prefer to work independently. Indeed, they frequently choose to work as consultants or independent contractors. However, this arrangement may cause complications for them in terms of securing adequate health care coverage. Self-employed marketing consultant Ann Quinn pays $740 a month for health insurance to cover herself, her daughter, and her husband. The carrier is a nonprofit organization called Working Today, which furnishes portable, affordable health insurance to freelance workers in New York City.

▪▪▪ CONTINGENT AND TEMPORARY WORKERS

A final contemporary HR issue of note involves the use of contingent and temporary workers. In recent years there has been an explosion in the use of such workers by organizations.

Trends in Contingent and Temporary Employment A **contingent worker** is a person who works for an organization on something other than a permanent or full-time basis. Categories of contingent workers include independent contractors, on-call workers, temporary employees (usually hired through outside agencies), and contract and leased employees. Another category is part-time workers. The financial services giant Citigroup, for example, makes extensive use of part-time sales agents to pursue new clients. About 10 percent of the employed U.S. workforce is subject to one of these alternative forms of employment relationships. Experts suggest, however, that this percentage is increasing.

CONTINGENT WORKER employee hired on something other than a full-time basis to supplement an organization's permanent workforce

Managing Contingent and Temporary Workers Given the widespread use of contingent and temporary workers, HR professionals must understand how to manage such employees most effectively. One key is careful planning. Even though one of the presumed benefits of using contingent workers is flexibility, it is still important to integrate such workers in a coordinated fashion. Rather than having to call in workers sporadically, and with no prior notice, organizations try to bring in specified numbers of workers for well-defined periods of time.

A second key is understanding contingent workers and acknowledging their advantages and disadvantages. That is, the organization must recognize what it can and can't achieve from the use of contingent and temporary workers. For instance, these workers may lack the firm-specific knowledge to perform as effectively as a permanent employee would perform. They are also less committed to the organization and less likely to engage in organizational citizenship behaviors.

Third, managers must carefully assess the real cost of using contingent workers. Many firms use contingent and temporary workers to save labor costs. Thus, the organization should be able to document its labor-cost savings. How much would it be paying people in wages and benefits if they were on permanent staff? How does this compare with the amount spent on contingent workers?

Finally, managers must fully understand the business strategy and decide in advance how they intend to integrate them into the organization. On a very simplistic level, for example, an organization with a large contingent workforce must decide how it will treat contingent workers relative to the permanent full-time workers. Should contingent workers have the same access to such employee benefits as counseling services and child-care? Should they be invited to the company holiday party? There are no right or wrong answers to such questions, but managers need to develop a strategy for integrating contingent workers according to some sound logic and then follow that strategy consistently.

DEALING WITH ORGANIZED LABOR

A **labor union** is a group of individuals working together to achieve shared job-related goals, such as higher pay, shorter working hours, more job security, greater benefits, or better working conditions. **Labor relations** refers to the process of dealing with employees who are represented by a union.

Labor unions grew in popularity in the United States in the nineteenth and early twentieth centuries. The labor movement was born with the Industrial Revolution,

LABOR UNION group of individuals working together to achieve shared job-related goals, such as higher pay, shorter working hours, more job security, greater benefits, or better working conditions

LABOR RELATIONS process of dealing with employees who are represented by a union

which also gave birth to a factory-based production system that carried with it enormous economic benefits. Job specialization and mass production allowed businesses to create ever-greater quantities of goods at ever-lower costs.

But there was a dark side to this era. Workers became more dependent on their factory jobs. Eager for greater profits, some owners treated their workers like other raw materials: resources to be deployed with little or no regard for any individual worker's well-being. Many businesses forced employees to work long hours—60-hour weeks were common, and some workers were routinely forced to work 12 to 16 hours a day. With no minimum-wage laws or other controls, pay was also minimal and safety standards virtually nonexistent. Workers enjoyed no job security and received few benefits. Many companies, especially textile mills, employed large numbers of children at poverty wages. If people complained, nothing prevented employers from firing and replacing them at will.

Unions appeared and ultimately prospered because they forced management to listen to the complaints of all workers rather than to just the few who were brave (or foolish) enough to speak out. The power of unions, then, comes from collective action. **Collective bargaining** (which we discuss more fully later in this chapter) is the process by which union leaders and managers negotiate common terms and conditions of employment for the workers represented by unions. Although collective bargaining does not often occur in small businesses, many midsize and larger businesses must engage in the process.

COLLECTIVE BARGAINING process by which labor and management negotiate conditions of employment for union-represented workers

▪▪▪ UNIONISM TODAY

Although understanding the historical context of labor unions is important, so too is appreciating the role of unionism today, especially trends in union membership, union-management relations, and bargaining perspectives.

Trends in Union Membership Since the mid-1950s, U.S. labor unions have experienced increasing difficulties in attracting new members. As a result, although millions of workers still belong to labor unions, union membership as a percentage of the total workforce has continued to decline at a very steady rate. In 1995, for instance, 14.9 percent of the U.S. workforce belonged to a labor union. Since that time, union membership as a percentage of the workforce has gradually but consistently declined to its present level of 12.5 percent (see Figure 10.4).

Just as union membership has continued to decline, so has the percentage of successful union-organizing campaigns. In the years immediately following World War II and continuing through the mid-1960s, most unions routinely won certification elections. In recent years, however, labor unions have been winning certification less than 50 percent of the times that workers are called upon to vote.

By the same token, unions still do win. Meat cutters at a Florida Wal-Mart store recently voted to unionize—the first-ever successful organizing campaign against the retailing giant. "You'll see a lot more attention to Wal-Mart now," exulted one AFL-CIO official. "It's not like Wal-Mart stands out as some unattainable goal."

From most indications, however, the power and significance of U.S. labor unions, while still quite formidable, are also measurably lower than they were just a few decades ago.

Trends in Union-Management Relations The gradual decline in unionization in the United States has been accompanied by some significant trends in union-management relations. In some sectors of the economy, perhaps most notably the automobile and steel industries, labor unions still remain quite strong. In these areas, unions have large memberships and considerable power in negotiating with

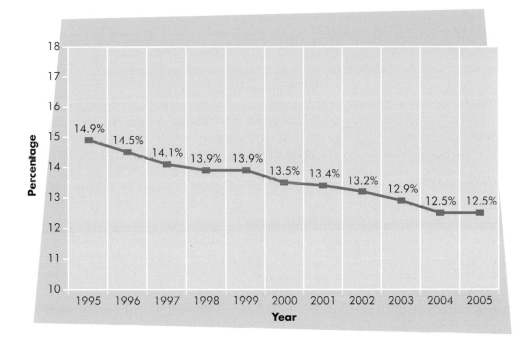

Figure 10.4
Percentage of Workers Who Belong to Unions, 1995–2005: Membership as a Percentage of Payrolls

management. The United Auto Workers (UAW), for example, is still one of the strongest unions in the United States.

In most sectors, however, unions are clearly in a weakened position, and as a result, many have taken more conciliatory stances in their relations with management. Increasingly, for instance, unions recognize that it is in their own best interests, as well as in those of the workers they represent, to work with management instead of working against it. Ironically, then, union-management relations are in many ways better today than they have been in many years.

The Future of Unions Despite declining membership and some loss of power, labor unions remain a major factor for U.S. businesses. Even though several of its members withdrew from the parent organization in 2005, the AFL-CIO, as well as independent major unions such as the Teamsters and the National Education Association (NEA), still play a major role in U.S. business. Some unions still wield considerable power, especially in the traditional strongholds of goods-producing industries.

COLLECTIVE BARGAINING

When a union has been legally certified, it assumes the role of official bargaining agent for the workers it represents. Collective bargaining is an ongoing process involving both the drafting and the administering of the terms of a labor contract.

■■■ REACHING AGREEMENT ON CONTRACT TERMS

The collective bargaining process begins when the union is recognized as the exclusive negotiator for its members. The bargaining cycle itself begins when union leaders meet with management representatives to agree on a contract. By law, both parties must sit down at the bargaining table and negotiate in good faith.

Figure 10.5
The Bargaining Zone

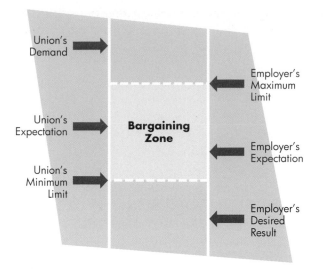

When each side has presented its demands, sessions focus on identifying the bargaining zone. The process is shown in Figure 10.5. For example, although an employer may initially offer no pay raise, it may expect to grant a raise of up to 6 percent. Likewise, the union may initially demand a 10-percent pay raise while expecting to accept a raise as low as 4 percent. The bargaining zone, then, is a raise between 4 and 6 percent. Ideally, some compromise is reached between these levels, and then the new agreement is submitted for a ratification vote by union membership.

Sometimes this process goes quite smoothly. At other times, the two sides cannot—or will not—agree. The speed and ease with which such an impasse is resolved depend in part on the nature of the contract issues, the willingness of each side to use certain tactics, such as strikes, and the prospects for mediation or arbitration.

■■■ CONTRACT ISSUES

In the past, most union-management bargaining situations were characterized by union demands for increases in wages, salaries, and benefits. Now, however, unions often find themselves fighting against wage cuts rather than striving for wage increases. Similarly, as organizations are more likely to seek lower health care and other benefits, a common goal of union strategy is to preserve what's already been won.

The labor contract itself can address an array of different issues. Most of these concern demands that unions make on behalf of their members. Issues that are typically most important to union negotiators include *compensation*, *benefits*, and *job security*. Certain *management rights* are also negotiated in most bargaining agreements.

Compensation The most common issue is compensation. One aspect of compensation is current wages. Unions want their employees to earn higher wages and try to convince management to raise wages for all or some employees. Of equal concern to unions is future compensation: wage rates to be paid during subsequent years of the contract. One common tool for securing wage increases is a **cost-of-living adjustment (COLA)**. Most COLA clauses tie future raises to the *Consumer Price Index (CPI)*, a government statistic that reflects changes in consumer purchasing power. The premise is that as the CPI increases by a specified amount during a given period of time, wages will automatically be increased. Almost half of all labor contracts today include COLA clauses.

Wage reopener clauses are now included in almost 10 percent of all labor contracts. Such a clause allows wage rates to be renegotiated at preset times during the

COST-OF-LIVING ADJUSTMENT (COLA) labor contract clause tying future raises to changes in consumer purchasing power

WAGE REOPENER CLAUSE clause allowing wage rates to be renegotiated during the life of a labor contract

life of the contract. For example, a union might be uncomfortable with a long-term contract based solely on COLA wage increases. A long-term agreement might be more acceptable, however, if management agrees to renegotiate wages every two years.

Benefits Employee benefits are also an important component in most labor contracts. Unions typically want employers to pay all or most of the costs of insurance for employees. Other benefits commonly addressed during negotiations include retirement benefits, paid holidays, and working conditions. Due to surging health-care costs, employee health insurance premiums have become a major point of contention in recent years.

Job Security Job security also remains an important agenda item in many bargaining sessions today. In some cases, a contract may dictate that if the workforce is reduced, seniority will be used to determine which employees keep their jobs. Unions are also increasingly setting their sights on preserving jobs for workers in the United States in the face of business efforts to outsource production in some sectors to countries where labor costs are cheaper. For example, the AFL-CIO has been an outspoken opponent of efforts to normalize trade relations with China, fearing that more businesses might be tempted to move jobs there.

Other Union Issues Other possible issues might include such specific details as working hours, overtime policies, rest period arrangements, differential pay plans for shift employees, the use of temporary workers, grievance procedures, and allowable union activities (dues collection, union bulletin boards, and so forth). In addition, labor and management in some industries, notably airlines and steel, are beginning to favor contracts that establish formal mechanisms for greater worker input into management decisions. Inland Steel, for example, recently granted its major union the right to name a member to the board of directors. Union officers can also attend executive meetings.

Management Rights Management wants as much control as possible over hiring policies, work assignments, and so forth. Unions, meanwhile, often try to limit management rights by specifying hiring, assignment, and other policies. At a DaimlerChrysler plant in Detroit, for example, the contract stipulates that three workers are needed to change fuses in robots: a machinist to open the robot, an electrician to change the fuse, and a supervisor to oversee the process. As in this case, contracts often bar workers in one job category from performing work that falls in the domain of another. Unions try to secure jobs by defining as many different categories as possible (the DaimlerChrysler plant has over 100). Management resists this practice, which limits flexibility and makes it difficult to reassign workers.

■■■ WHEN BARGAINING FAILS

An impasse occurs when, after a series of bargaining sessions, management and labor have failed to agree on a new contract or a contract to replace an agreement that is about to expire. Although it is generally agreed that both parties suffer when an impasse is reached and some action by one part against the other is taken, each side can use several tactics to support its cause until the impasse is resolved.

Union Tactics When their demands are not met, unions may bring a variety of tactics to the bargaining table. Chief among these are the strike, which may be supported by pickets and boycotts, and the work slowdown.

STRIKE labor action in which employees temporarily walk off the job and refuse to work

ECONOMIC STRIKE strike usually triggered by stalemate over one or more mandatory bargaining items

SYMPATHY STRIKE (SECONDARY STRIKE) strike in which one union strikes to support action initiated by another

WILDCAT STRIKE strike that is unauthorized by the strikers' union

PICKETING labor action in which workers publicize their grievances at the entrance to an employer's facility

BOYCOTT labor action in which workers refuse to buy the products of a targeted employer

WORK SLOWDOWN labor action in which workers perform jobs at a slower than normal pace

LOCKOUT management tactic whereby workers are denied access to the employer's workplace

STRIKEBREAKER worker hired as a permanent or temporary replacement for a striking employee

MEDIATION method of resolving a labor dispute in which a third party suggests, but does not impose, a settlement

Strikes A **strike** occurs when employees temporarily walk off the job and refuse to work. Most strikes in the United States are **economic strikes**, triggered by stalemates over mandatory bargaining items, including such noneconomic issues as working hours. For example, the New York City transit workers went on strike in December 2005. The union was seeking higher wages and a stronger pension plan for its members. However, a judge ordered an end to the strike, and transit workers went back to their jobs before the issues were settled.

Far fewer strikes occur today than in previous years. For example, 222 strikes were held in the United States in 1960, involving a total of 896,000 workers. In 1970, 2,468,000 workers took part in 381 strikes. In 1990, only 44 strikes involved only 185,000 workers. Since 1990, the annual number of strikes has ranged from a high of 43 (in 2004) to a low of 29 (in 1997).

Not all strikes are legal. **Sympathy strikes (secondary strikes)**, which occur when one union strikes in sympathy with action initiated by another, may violate the sympathetic union's contract. **Wildcat strikes**—strikes unauthorized by a union that occur during the life of a contract—deprive strikers of their status as employees and, thus, of the protection of national labor law.

Other Labor Actions To support a strike, a union faced with an impasse has recourse to additional legal activities:

- In **picketing**, workers march at the entrance to the employer's facility with signs explaining their reasons for striking.
- A **boycott** occurs when union members agree not to buy the products of a targeted employer. Workers may also urge consumers to boycott the firm's products.
- Another alternative to striking is a **work slowdown**. Instead of striking, workers perform their jobs at a much slower pace than normal. A variation is the *sickout*, during which large numbers of workers call in sick. Pilots at American Airlines engaged in a massive sickout a few years ago, causing the airline to cancel thousands of flights before a judge ordered them back into the cockpit.

Management Tactics Like workers, management can respond forcefully to an impasse with the following:

- **Lockouts** occur when employers deny employees access to the workplace. Lockouts are illegal if they are used as offensive weapons to give management a bargaining advantage. However, they are legal if management has a legitimate business need (for instance, avoiding a buildup of perishable inventory). Lockouts are actually quite rare today. Among the more visible lockouts in recent years, the ABC television network locked out its off-camera employees because they staged an unannounced one-day strike during a critical broadcasting period.
- A firm can also hire temporary or permanent replacements called **strikebreakers**. However, the law forbids the permanent replacement of workers who strike because of unfair practices. In some cases, an employer can obtain legal injunctions that either prohibit workers from striking or prohibit a union from interfering with its efforts to use replacement workers.

Mediation and Arbitration Rather than wield these often unpleasant weapons against one another, labor and management can agree to call in a third party to help resolve the dispute:

- In **mediation**, the neutral third party (the mediator) can suggest but cannot impose a settlement on the other parties.

- In **voluntary arbitration**, the neutral third party (the arbitrator) dictates a settlement between the two sides, which have agreed to submit to outside judgment.
- In some cases, arbitration is legally required to settle bargaining disputes. **Compulsory arbitration** is used to settle disputes between the government and public employees, such as firefighters and police officers.

Managing an organization's human resources is both a complex and an important undertaking. Most businesses can buy the same equipment and use the same technology as their competitors. But differences in employee talent and motivation are not easily copied. Consequently, most well-managed companies today recognize the value provided by their employees and strive to insure that the HR function is managed as efficiently and effectively as possible.

VOLUNTARY ARBITRATION
method of resolving a labor dispute in which both parties agree to submit to the judgment of a neutral party

COMPULSORY ARBITRATION
method of resolving a labor dispute in which both parties are legally required to accept the judgment of a neutral party

SELF-CHECK QUESTIONS 7–9

You should now be able to answer Self-Check Questions 7–9.*

7 Multiple Choice In general, which of the following is true about workforce diversity?
(a) it is decreasing
(b) it is increasing
(c) it remains constant
(d) it is becoming less important to business

8 True/False In recent years, the number of contingent workers has increased.

9 Multiple Choice Which of the following is true about union membership in recent years?
(a) it has generally remained constant
(b) it has generally changed in unknown ways because of new privacy laws
(c) generally, it has steadily increased
(d) generally, it has steadily declined

*Answers to Self-Check Questions 7–9 can be found on p. 565.

CONTINUED FROM PAGE 294

THE LOGISTICS OF HIRING EN MASSE

The massive hiring plan at the Bellagio almost staggers the imagination. But in reality, many firms must routinely plan to hire large numbers of people in a coordinated fashion. Las Vegas itself reflects a microcosm of this task with each massive new casino that is opened. The Mandalay Bay, the Venetian, and similar mega-resorts have had to do the same thing as the Bellagio. In other outposts, Disney must hire thousands of new employees to staff each new theme park it opens, Toyota must hire thousands for each new factory it builds, and Royal Caribbean must hire thousands for each new cruise ship it launches.

Wal-Mart, however, is in the midst of a hiring explosion that may eventually make these examples truly passé. Wal-Mart has announced a goal of hiring 1 million new people over the next five years. About 800,000 of these will be to fill newly created jobs, while the other 200,000 will be replacements for retirees and other employees forecasted to leave the firm. That's akin to hiring the state of Rhode Island or the city of Dallas.

So what does the giant retailer plan to do? For one thing, it may need to up its pay grades a bit and offer more benefits. For another, it plans to step up its college recruiting for potential new store managers. And it hopes to entice the spouses, children, and other relatives of its current employees to join its ranks. If Wal-Mart is successful, it may end up revolutionizing not only the retailing industry but the HRM function as well.

QUESTIONS FOR DISCUSSION

1 What are the unique challenges faced when firms must hire massive numbers of people?

2 Identify at least five factors that might disrupt a firm's massive hiring plans.

3 Compare and contrast the challenges faced by the Bellagio and Wal-Mart.

4 What other employment situations might be able to use the Bellagio's model?

5 Suppose a firm had to reduce its staff by several thousand workers in a short period of time. What might it learn from the Bellagio?

1 Define *human resource management* and explain how managers plan for their organization's human resource needs.

Human resource management (HRM) is the set of organizational activities directed at attracting, developing, and maintaining an effective workforce. *Job analysis* is a systematic analysis of jobs within an organization resulting in two things: a *job description* and a *job specification*. Managers must plan for future HR needs by assessing past trends, future plans, and general economic trends. Forecasting labor supply is really two tasks: (a) *forecasting internal supply* and (b) *forecasting external supply*. The next step in HR planning is matching HR supply and demand. If a shortfall is predicted, new employees can be hired.

2 Identify the tasks in staffing a company and discuss ways in which organizations select, develop, and appraise employee performance.

Staffing an organization means recruiting and hiring the right mix of people. *Recruiting* is the process of attracting qualified persons to apply for open jobs, either from within the organization or from outside the organization. The next step is the *selection process*—gathering information that will predict applicants' job success and then hiring candidates. Common selection techniques include application forms; tests of ability, aptitude, or knowledge; and interviews. New employees must be trained and allowed to develop job skills. *On-the-job training* occurs while the employee is at work. *Off-the-job training* takes place off-site where controlled environments allow focused study. Some firms use *vestibule training*—off-the-job training in simulated work environments. In larger firms, *performance appraisals* show how well workers are doing their jobs.

3 Describe the main components of a compensation system and describe some of the key legal issues involved in hiring, compensating, and managing workers in today's workplace.

A *compensation system* is the total package of rewards that a firm offers employees in return for their labor. Although *wages* and *salaries* are key parts of all compensation systems, most also include incentives and employee benefits programs. Beyond a certain point, money motivates employees only when tied directly to performance. One way to establish this link is the use of *incentive programs*—special pay programs designed to motivate performance. *Benefits*—compensation other than wages and salaries—account for a large percentage of compensation budgets. The law requires most companies to provide social security benefits and *workers' compensation insurance*. Most companies provide health, life, and disability insurance; retirement plans pay pensions to workers when they retire.

HR management is influenced by the law. One area of HR regulation is *equal employment opportunity*—regulation to protect people from discrimination in the workplace. Because illegal discrimination is based on a prejudice about classes of individuals, laws protect various classes. A *protected class* consists of individuals who share one or more common characteristics as indicated by a given law (such as race, color, religion, gender, age, national origin, and so forth).

4 Discuss workforce diversity, the management of knowledge workers, and the use of a contingent workforce as important changes in the contemporary workplace.

Workforce diversity refers to the range of workers' attitudes, values, beliefs, and behaviors that differ by gender, race, age, ethnicity, physical ability, and other relevant characteristics. Many U.S. organizations regard diversity as a competitive advantage. Employees who add value because of what they know are usually called *knowledge workers*, and managing them skillfully helps to determine which firms will be successful in the future. *Contingent workers*, including independent contractors, on-call workers, temporary employees, contract and leased employees, and part-time employees, work for organizations on something other than a permanent or full-time basis.

5 Explain why workers organize into labor unions and describe the collective bargaining process.

A *labor union* is a group of individuals working together to achieve shared job-related goals. *Labor relations* refers to the process of dealing with employees represented by a union. The *collective bargaining* cycle begins when union leaders and management meet to agree on a contract. Each presents its demands, and then the two sides identify a *bargaining zone*. When a compromise is reached, the agreement is voted on by union members.

An *impasse* occurs when management and labor fail to agree on a contract. Each side can use several tactics to support its cause until the impasse is resolved. The most important union tactic is the *strike*. Unions may also use *picketing*. Under a *boycott*, union members agree not to buy the products of a targeted employer. During a *work slowdown*, workers perform their jobs at a much slower pace than normal. During a *sickout*, large numbers of workers call in sick. Management may resort to *lockouts*—denying employees access to the workplace. A firm can also hire strikebreakers, but the law forbids the permanent replacement of workers who strike because of unfair practices.

Rather than use these tactics, labor and management can call in a third party to help resolve the dispute. Common options include *mediation, voluntary arbitration*, and *compulsory arbitration*.

KEY TERMS

affirmative action plan (p. 305)

benefits (p. 304)

bonus (p. 303)

boycott (p. 316)

cafeteria benefits plan (p. 304)

collective bargaining (p. 312)

compensation system (p. 301)

compulsory arbitration (p. 317)

contingent worker (p. 311)

cost-of-living adjustment
(COLA) (p. 314)

economic strike (p. 316)

employee information system (skills
inventory) (p. 296)

employment at will (p. 307)

equal employment opportunity (p. 305)

Equal Employment Opportunity
Commission (EEOC) (p. 305)

external recruiting (p. 298)

gainsharing plan (p. 304)

hostile work environment (p. 307)

human resource management
(HRM) (p. 294)

incentive program (p. 303)

internal recruiting (p. 298)

job analysis (p. 295)

job description (p. 295)

job specification (p. 295)

knowledge workers (p. 309)

labor relations (p. 312)

labor union (p. 311)

lockout (p. 316)

mediation (p. 316)

merit salary system (p. 303)

Occupational Safety and Health Act
of 1970 (OSHA) (p. 306)

off-the-job training (p. 300)

on-the-job training (p. 300)

pay for performance
(or variable pay) (p. 303)

pay-for-knowledge plan (p. 304)

performance appraisal (p. 301)

picketing (p. 316)

profit-sharing plan (p. 303)

protected class (p. 305)

quid pro quo harassment (p. 307)

recruiting (p. 297)

replacement chart (p. 296)

salary (p. 301)

sexual harassment (p. 306)

strike (p. 316)

strikebreaker (p. 316)

sympathy strike (secondary
strike) (p. 316)

vestibule training (p. 301)

voluntary arbitration (p. 317)

wage reopener clause (p. 314)

wages (p. 301)

wildcat strike (p. 316)

work slowdown (p. 316)

workers' compensation
insurance (p. 304)

workforce diversity (p. 308)

QUESTIONS AND EXERCISES

Questions for Review

1 What are the advantages and disadvantages of internal and external recruiting? Under what circumstances is each more appropriate?

2 Why is the formal training of workers so important to most employers? Why don't employers simply let people learn about their jobs as they perform them?

3 What different forms of compensation do firms typically use to attract and keep productive workers?

4 Why do workers in some companies unionize whereas workers in others do not?

Questions for Analysis

5 What are your views on drug testing in the workplace? What would you do if your employer asked you to submit to a drug test?

6 Workers at Ford, GM, and DaimlerChrysler are represented by the UAW. However, the UAW has been unsuccessful in its attempts to unionize U.S. workers employed at Toyota, Nissan, and Honda plants in the United States. Why do you think this is so?

7 What training do you think you are most likely to need when you finish school and start your career?

8 How much will benefit considerations affect your choice of an employer after graduation?

Application Exercises

9 Interview an HR manager at a local company. Focus on a position for which the firm is currently recruiting applicants and identify the steps in the selection process.

10 Interview the managers of two local companies, one unionized and one nonunionized. Compare the wage and salary levels, benefits, and working conditions of employees at the two firms.

A LITTLE COLLECTIVE BRAINSTORMING

Goal
To help you understand why some companies unionize and others do not.

Background Information
You've been working for the same nonunion company for five years. Although there are problems in the company, you like your job and have confidence in your ability to get ahead. Recently, you've heard rumblings that a large group of workers wants to call for a union election. You're not sure how you feel about this because none of your friends or family are union members.

Method

Step 1
Come together with three other "coworkers" who have the same questions as you. Each person should target two companies to learn about their union status. Avoid small businesses. Choose large corporations such as General Motors, Intel, and Sears. As you investigate, answer the following questions:

■ Is the company unionized?
■ Is every worker in the company unionized, or just selected groups of workers? Describe the groups.
■ If a company is unionized, what is the union's history in that company?
■ If a company is unionized, what are the main labor-management issues?

■ If a company is unionized, how would you describe the current status of labor-management relations? For example, is it cordial or strained?
■ If a company is not unionized, what factors are responsible for its nonunion status?

To learn the answers to these questions, contact the company, read corporate annual reports, search the company's Web site, contact union representatives, or do research on a computerized database.

Step 2
Go to the Web site of the AFL-CIO (www.aflcio.org) to learn more about the current status of the union movement. Then with your coworkers, write a short report about the advantages of union membership.

Step 3
Research the disadvantages of unionization. A key issue to address is whether unions make it harder for companies to compete in the global marketplace.

FOLLOW-UP QUESTIONS

1 Based on everything you learned, are you sympathetic to the union movement? Would you want to be a union member?
2 Are the union members you spoke with or read about satisfied or dissatisfied with their union's efforts to achieve better working conditions, higher wages, and improved benefits?
3 What is the union's role when layoffs occur?
4 Based on what you learned, do you think the union movement will stumble or thrive in the years ahead?

OPERATING TACTICALLY

The Situation

Assume that you work as a manager for a medium-sized, nonunion company that is facing its most serious union organizing campaign in years. Your boss, who is determined to keep the union out, has just given you a list of things to do in order to thwart the efforts of the organizers. For example, he has suggested each of the following tactics:

- Whenever you learn about a scheduled union meeting, you should schedule a "worker appreciation" event at the same time. He wants you to offer free pizza and to give cash prizes, which winners have to be present to receive.
- He wants you to look at the most recent performance evaluations of the key union organizers and to terminate the one with the lowest overall evaluation.
- He wants you to make an announcement that the firm is seriously considering such new benefits as on-site child care, flexible work schedules, telecommuting options, and exercise facilities. Although you know that the firm is indeed looking into these benefits, you also know that, ultimately, your boss will provide far less lavish benefits than he wants you to intimate.

The Dilemma

When you questioned the ethics—and even the legality—of these tactics, your boss responded by saying, "Look, all's fair in love and war, and this is war." He went on to explain that he was seriously concerned that a union victory might actually shut down the company's domestic operations altogether, forcing it to move all of its production capacities to lower-cost foreign plants. He concluded by saying that he was really looking out for the employees, even if he had to play hardball to help them. You easily see through his hypocrisy, but you also recognize some potential truth in his warning: If the union wins, jobs may actually be lost.

QUESTIONS TO ADDRESS

1 What are the ethical issues in this situation?
2 What are the basic arguments for and against extreme measures to fight unionization efforts?
3 What do you think most managers would do in this situation? What would you do?

HANDLING THE LAYOFFS

The Situation
The CEO of a moderate-sized company is developing a plan for laying off some members of the company workforce. He wants each manager to rank his or her employees according to the order in which they should be laid off, from first to last.

The Dilemma
One manager has just asked for help. He is new to his position and has little experience to draw from. The members of the manager's team are as follows:

- Tony Jones: white male, 10 years with the company, average performer, reportedly drinks a lot after work
- Amanda Wiggens: white female, very ambitious, 3 years with company, above-average performer, puts in extra time at work; is known to be abrasive when dealing with others
- Jorge Gonzalez: Latino, 20 years with the company, average performer, was laid off before but then called back when business picked up
- Dorothy Henderson: white female, 25 years with company, below-average performer, has filed five sexual harassment complaints in last 10 years
- Wanda Jackson: African American female, 8 years with company, outstanding performer, is rumored to be looking for another job

- Jerry Loudder: white male, single parent, 5 years with company, average performer
- Martha Strawser: white female, 6 years with company, excellent performer but spotty attendance, is putting husband through college

Team Activity
Assemble a group of four students. Your group has agreed to provide the manager with a suggested rank ordering of the manager's employees.

ACTION STEPS
1 Working together, prepare this list, ranking the manager's employees according to the order in which they should be laid off, from first to last.
2 As a group, discuss the underlying ethical issues in this situation and write them down.
3 As a group, brainstorm any legal issues involved in this situation and write them down.
4 Do the ethical and legal implications of your choices always align?
5 Do the ethical and performance implications of your choices always align?

PART 3: PEOPLE IN ORGANIZATIONS

Goal of the Exercise

At this point, your business has an identity and you've described the factors that will affect your business and how you will operate it. Part 3 of the business plan project asks you to think about your employees, the jobs they will be performing, and the ways in which you can lead and motivate them.

Exercise Background: Part 3 of the Business Plan

To complete this part of the plan, you need to refer back to the organizational chart that you created in Part 2. In this part of the business plan exercise, you'll take the different job titles you created in the organizational chart and give thought to the *skills* that employees will need to bring to the job *before* they begin. You'll also consider *training* you'll need to provide *after* they are hired, as well as how you'll compensate your employees. Part 3 of the business plan also asks you to consider how you'll lead your employees and keep them happy and motivated.

Your Assignment

Step 1

Open the *Business Plan* file you began working on in Parts 1 and 2.

Step 1

For the purposes of this assignment, you will answer the questions in "Part 3: People in Organizations:"

1 What do you see as the "corporate culture" of your business? What types of employee behaviors, such as organizational citizenship, will you expect?
   Hint: Will your business demand a casual environment or a more professional environment? Refer to the discussion on employee behavior in Chapter 8 for information on organizational citizenship and other employee behaviors.

2 What is your philosophy on leadership? How will you manage your employees day-to-day?
   Hint: Refer to the discussion on leadership in Chapter 9, to help you formulate your thoughts.

3 Looking back at your organizational chart in Part 2, briefly create a job description for each team member.

Hint: As you learned in Chapter 10, a job description lists the duties and responsibilities of a job; its working conditions; and the tools, materials, equipment, and information used to perform it. Imagine your business on a typical day. Who is working and what is each person's responsibilities?

4 Next, create a job specification for each job, listing the skills and other credentials and qualifications needed to perform the job effectively.
   Hint: As you write your job specifications, consider what you would write if you were making an ad for the position. What would the new employee need to bring to the job in order to qualify for the position?

5 What sort of training, if any, will your employees need once they are hired? How will you provide this training?
   Hint: Refer to the discussion of training in Chapter 10. Will you offer your employees on-the-job training? Off-the-job training? Vestibule training?

6 A major factor in retaining skilled workers is a company's compensation system—the total package of rewards that it offers employees in return for their labor. Part of this compensation system includes wages/salaries. What wages or salaries will you offer for each job? Why did you decide on that pay rate?
   Hint: Refer to Chapter 10 for more information on forms of compensation. You may also want to check out sites like www.salary.com, which includes a salary wizard you can use to determine how much people with different job titles are making in your area and across the United States.

7 As you learned in Chapter 10, incentive programs are special programs designed to motivate high performance. What incentives will you use to motivate your workforce?
   Hint: Be creative and look beyond a simple answer, such as giving pay increases. Ask yourself, who are my employees and what is important to them? Refer to Chapter 10 for more information on the types of incentives you may want to consider.

Note: Once you have answered the questions, save your Word document. You'll be answering additional questions in later chapters.

MANAGING THE HUMAN SIDE OF BUSINESS: PARK PLACE ENTERTAINMENT

Learning Objectives

The purpose of this video is to help you:

1 Recognize the ways in which human resource management contributes to organizational performance.

2 Understand how and why HR managers make plans and decisions about staffing.

3 Identify some of the ways in which HR managers handle evaluation and development.

Synopsis

Park Place Entertainment owns and operates resorts and casinos around the world. Its HR department is responsible for hiring, training, and managing a diverse group of more than 52,000 employees. Because its customers come from many countries and speak many languages, the company seeks employees from diverse backgrounds and varies the recruitment process for different properties in different areas. HR managers have created specific job descriptions for each position, instituted programs for employee and management development, and established incentive programs to reward good performance. Park Place's 360-degree evaluation method allows supervisors to get performance feedback from the employees they supervise.

DISCUSSION QUESTIONS

1 **For analysis:** What are the advantages and disadvantages of centralizing the recruiting process at a company such as Park Place Entertainment?

2 **For analysis:** Why did Park Place begin the restructuring of its HR department by standardizing training for supervisors?

3 **For application:** What steps might Park Place HR managers take to reduce employee turnover at particular resorts?

4 **For application:** How might Park Place encourage employees to refer friends as candidates for open positions?

5 **For debate:** Rather than hiring employees when business booms and then laying them off when it slumps, should Park Place temporarily rehire retired employees during peak periods? Support your chosen position.

Online Exploration

Visit the Park Place Entertainment Web site at (www.ballys.com) and browse the home page to find the names and locations of the company's resorts and casinos. Then, follow the company information link to find information on career opportunities and company benefits. What kinds of jobs are featured on the Web site? How does Park Place arrange jobs? How does the firm make it convenient for applicants to submit résumés online? Why would Park Place put so much emphasis on Internet recruiting?

PART IV:
PRINCIPLES
OF MARKETING

DELL-IVERING ON CONSUMER ELECTRONICS

There's good reason why competitors don't match Dell's success in selling computers. From the outset, Michael Dell's vision recognized a market with different kinds of potential users—the business sector, nonbusiness organizations, such as schools and other

MARKETING PROCESSES AND CONSUMER BEHAVIOR

institutions, as well as the growing segment of PC users in homes—each with different needs and resources. Choosing to focus more on the business and institutional segments, Dell envisioned an unheard-of combination of service features for PC customers: high-quality products, lowest cost, ease in ordering and receiving products, live interaction with expert technical assistance for building a PC "the way you like it," efficient manufacturing with super-fast deliveries, and after-sales communications to ensure product performance and keep users informed about upgrades for their PCs.

The market response has been overwhelming, resulting in Dell's dominant position as industry leader with $49 billion sales in 2005. Competitors are struggling to copy Dell's low-price-high-value way of doing business.

As if that's not enough to cause headaches in the PC industry, Dell has launched itself into the broader consumer electronics market. Today's giant electronics retailers, such as Circuit City and Best Buy, may soon be looking over their shoulders if Dell's customer-friendly business model is successfully carried over into flat-panel TVs, DVD recorders, MP3 players, and digital cameras. By partnering with Yahoo! Music, MusicMatch, and Napster To Go, Dell offers online music downloading for over 1 million songs on the same popular Web site where PC users buy other Dell products. Commenting on the company's new thrust, Chairman Michael Dell states, "The whole new ballgame is these worlds [computing and consumer electronics] converging, and that's a world we're comfortable in."

Dell's brand is strong among consumers. It gives us confidence we can proceed with a forked strategy.

—Dell CEO Kevin Rollins

But will they necessarily succeed? Some experts think the crossover into consumer products could be a problem because Dell's primary PC focus has been on business and institutional markets. Not to worry, asserts Dell CEO Kevin Rollins: "Dell's brand is strong among consumers. It gives us confidence we can proceed with a forked strategy." ■

Our opening story continues on page 352.

WHAT'S IN IT FOR ME?

The core of Michael Dell's vision is to provide exceptional value to customers so they will come back again and again. Marketing is a business tool that embraces the notion of providing value to customers to ensure commercial success. By grasping this chapter's presentation of marketing methods and ideas, you'll benefit in two ways: (1) You'll be better prepared to use marketing in your career as both employee and manager and (2) You'll be a more informed consumer with greater awareness of how businesses use marketing to gain your purchases.

We'll start this chapter by looking at some marketing basics and forces that constitute the external marketing environment. We'll then look at the marketing plan and the components of the marketing mix, and we'll discuss market segmentation and how it is used in target marketing. Next, we'll look at key factors that influence the buying processes of consumers and organizational buyers. Finally, we'll explore how new products are developed and see how branding and packaging help establish their identity in the marketplace.

WHAT IS MARKETING?

MARKETING "a set of processes for creating, communicating, and delivering value to customers and for managing customer relationships in ways that benefit the organization and its stakeholders"

What comes to mind when you think of marketing? Most of us think of marketing as advertisements for detergents and soft drinks. Marketing, however, encompasses a much wider range of activities. The American Marketing Association defines **marketing** as "a set of processes for creating, communicating, and delivering value to customers and for managing customer relationships in ways that benefit the organization and its stakeholders."[1] In this section, we begin by looking at how marketing focuses on providing value and utility for consumers. We then explore the marketing environment and the development of marketing strategy. Finally, we focus on the four activities that compose the *marketing mix*: developing, pricing, placing, and promoting products.

▪▪▪ PROVIDING VALUE AND SATISFACTION

What attracts buyers to one product instead of another? Although our desires for the many goods and services available to us may be unbounded, limited financial resources force most of us to be selective. Accordingly, consumers buy products that offer the best value when it comes to meeting their needs and wants.

VALUE relative comparison of a product's benefits versus its costs

Value and Benefits **Value** compares a product's benefits with its costs. *Benefits* include not only the functions of the product but also the emotional satisfaction associated with owning, experiencing, or possessing it. But every product has costs, including sales price, the expenditure of the buyer's time, and even the emotional costs of making a purchase decision. A satisfied buyer perceives the benefits derived from the purchase to be greater than its costs. Thus, the simple but important ratio for value is derived as follows:

$$Value = \frac{Benefits}{Costs}$$

The marketing strategies of leading firms focus on increasing value for customers. Marketing resources are deployed to add benefits and decrease costs of products to provide greater value. Satisfying customers may mean developing an entirely new product that performs better (provides greater benefits) than existing products. Or, it may entail keeping a store open extra hours during a busy season (adding the benefit of greater shopping convenience). Some firms simply offer price reductions (the benefit of lower cost). Customers may also gain benefits from an informational promotion that explains how a product can be used in new ways.

Value and Utility To understand how marketing creates value for customers, we need to know the kind of benefits that buyers get from a firm's goods or services. As we discussed in Chapter 7, products provide consumers with **utility**—the ability of a product to satisfy a human want or need. Marketing strives to provide four kinds of utility—*form utility*, *time utility*, *place utility*, and *ownership utility*—in the following ways:

UTILITY ability of a product to satisfy a human want or need

- **Form utility.** Marketing has a voice in *designing products* with features customers want.
- **Time utility.** Marketing creates sales agreements that stipulate *when* products will be delivered to customers.
- **Place utility.** Marketing creates sales agreements that stipulate *where* products will be delivered to customers.
- **Ownership utility.** Marketing arranges for transferring *product ownership* to customers by setting *selling prices*, setting *terms for customer credit payments*, and providing *ownership documents*.

Because they determine product features, and the timing, place, and terms of sale that provide utility and add value for customers, marketers must understand customers' wants and needs. Their methods for creating utility are described in this and the following chapter.

■■■ GOODS, SERVICES, AND IDEAS

The marketing of tangible goods is obvious in everyday life. You walk into a department store where an employee asks if you'd like to try a new cologne. A pharmaceutical company proclaims the virtues of its new cold medicine. Your local auto dealer offers an economy car at an economy price. These products—the cologne, the cold medicine, and the car—are all **consumer goods**: tangible goods that you, the consumer, may buy for personal use. Firms that sell goods to consumers for personal consumption are engaged in *consumer marketing*.

CONSUMER GOODS physical products purchased by consumers for personal use

Marketing also applies to **industrial goods**: physical items used by companies to produce other products. Surgical instruments and bulldozers are industrial goods, as are such components and raw materials as integrated circuits, steel, and unformed plastic. Firms that sell goods to other companies are engaged in *industrial marketing*.

INDUSTRIAL GOODS physical products purchased by companies to produce other products

But marketing techniques are also applied to **services**—products with intangible (nonphysical) features, such as professional advice, improved safety procedures, timely

SERVICES products having nonphysical features, such as time, expertise, or an activity that can be purchased

information for decisions, or a resort vacation. *Service marketing*—the application of marketing for services—continues to be a major growth area in the United States. Insurance companies, airlines, investment counselors, health clinics, and public accountants all engage in service marketing, both to individuals (consumer markets) and to other companies (industrial markets). Thus, the terms *consumer marketing* and *industrial marketing* include services as well as goods.

Finally, marketers also promote *ideas*. Big-screen ads in theaters, for example, remind us to respect copyrighted property by refraining from pirating movies or CDs. Other ads stress the advantages of avoiding fast foods, wearing our seat belts, or quitting smoking.

RELATIONSHIP MARKETING
marketing strategy that
emphasizes lasting relationships
with customers and suppliers

Relationship Marketing Although marketing often focuses on single transactions for products, services, or ideas, marketers also take a longer-term perspective. Thus, **relationship marketing** emphasizes building lasting relationships with customers and suppliers. Stronger relationships—including stronger economic and social ties—can result in greater long-term satisfaction and customer loyalty.[2] Commercial banks, for example, offer economic incentives to encourage longer-lasting relationships. Long-time customers who purchase a certain number of the bank's products (for example, checking accounts, savings accounts, and loans) accumulate credits toward free or reduced-price products or services, such as free investment advice.

Data Warehousing and Data Mining for Building Customer Relationships Like many other marketing areas, the ways that marketers go about building relationships with customers have changed dramatically. The power of computers coupled with the availability of information on consumer preferences has allowed marketers to better predict what customers will want and buy. The compiling and storage of consumer data, known as *data warehousing*, provides the raw materials from which marketers can extract information that enables them to better know their customers and supply more of what they need. *Data mining* automates the massive analysis of data by using computers to sift, sort, and search for previously undiscovered clues about what customers look at, react to, and how they might be influenced. The hoped-for result is a clearer picture of how marketing can more effectively use resources to build closer relationships with customers.

Toronto-based Fairmont Resort Hotels, for example, used data mining to rebuild its customer-relations package by finding out what kinds of vacations their customers prefer, and then placed ads where they were more likely to reach those customers. When data mining revealed the worldwide destinations of Fairmont customers, it helped determine Fairmont's decision to buy their customers' number-one preference—the Savoy in London.[3] We'll discuss data warehousing and data mining in more detail in Chapter 13.

▪▪▪ THE MARKETING ENVIRONMENT

Marketing strategies are not determined unilaterally by any business, not even by marketers as experienced as those at Coca-Cola and P&G. Rather, they are strongly influenced by powerful outside forces. As you see in Figure 11.1, every marketing program must recognize the factors in a company's *external environment*, which we defined in Chapter 1 as everything outside an organization's boundaries that might affect it, including the *political-legal*, *sociocultural*, *technological*, *economic*, and *competitive* environments. In this section, we'll discuss how these environments affect the marketing environment in particular.

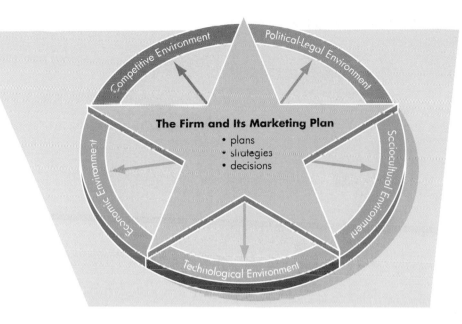

Figure 11.1
The External Marketing
Environment

Political-Legal Environment Political activities, both foreign and domestic, have profound effects on marketing. For example, legislation on the use of cell phones in cars and the Clean Air Act have determined the destinies of entire industries. Marketing managers try to maintain favorable political-legal environments in several ways. To gain public support for products and activities, marketers use ad campaigns to raise public awareness of local, regional, or national issues. Companies contribute to political candidates and frequently support the activities of political action committees (PACs) maintained by their respective industries.

Sociocultural Environment More people are working in home offices, the number of Hispanic-speaking families is increasing, and low-carb food preferences reflect a continuing concern for healthy lifestyles. These and other trends reflect the values, beliefs, and ideas that shape U.S. society.

Changing social values force companies to develop and promote new products for both individual consumers and industrial customers. For example, although most of us value privacy, Web surfers have discovered that a loss of privacy is often a price for the convenience of Internet shopping. Web sites regularly collect information about your surfing habits to use for marketing purposes and to sell to other firms. Responding to the growing demand for better privacy protection, firms like iNetPrivacy offer new products, such as Anonymity 4 Proxy software, which allows you to surf the Internet anonymously.

Technological Environment New technologies create new goods (such as global positioning systems) and services (such as online courses). New products make existing products obsolete (digital chips are fast replacing film for cameras), and many products change our values and lifestyles. In turn, lifestyle changes often stimulate new products not directly related to the new technologies themselves. Cell phones, for example, not only facilitate business communication but free up time for recreation and leisure. The Internet has become a medium for selling, buying, and distributing products from your own home to customers around the world.

Economic Environment Because they determine spending patterns by consumers, businesses, and governments, economic conditions influence marketing plans for product offerings, pricing, and promotional strategies. Marketers are concerned with such

Marketing strategies are strongly influenced by powerful outside forces. For example, new technologies create new products, such as the Chinese cell phone "gas station" kiosk shown here. Called shouji jiayouzhan in Chinese, these kiosks enable customers to recharge their cell phones just as they would refuel their cars. The screens on the kiosks also provide marketers with a new way to display ads to waiting customers.

economic variables as inflation, interest rates, and recession. Thus, they monitor the general business cycle to anticipate trends in consumer and business spending.

Traditionally, economic analysis focused on the national economy. Increasingly, however, as nations form more complex economic connections, the global economy is more prominent in the thinking of marketers everywhere. U.S. auto drivers felt the bite of global influence in 2006 when the price of crude oil reached an all-time high—more than $70 a barrel. This jump in price reflected a variety of circumstances in the global economic environment: Prices rose because traders were afraid of terrorism in the Middle East, and gas prices went up because demand had surged, especially in the United States and China. The possible repercussions include reduced consumer spending on other products, lower corporate profits, and inflation.

Competitive Environment   In a competitive environment, marketers must convince buyers that they should purchase one company's products rather than those of some other seller. Because both consumers and commercial buyers have limited resources, every dollar spent on one product is no longer available for other purchases. Each marketing program, therefore, seeks to make its product the most attractive. Expressed in business terms, a failed program loses the buyer's dollar forever (or at least until it is time for the next purchase decision).

To promote products effectively, marketers must first understand which of three types of competition they face:

SUBSTITUTE PRODUCT product that is dissimilar from those of competitors but that can fulfill the same need

- **Substitute products** may not look alike or they may seem very different from one another, but they can fulfill the same need. For example, your cholesterol level may be controlled with either of two competing products: a physical fitness program or a drug regimen. The fitness program and the drugs compete as substitute products.

BRAND COMPETITION competitive marketing that appeals to consumer perceptions of benefits of products offered by particular companies

- **Brand competition** occurs between similar products, such as the auditing services provided by the large accounting firms of Ernst & Young and KPMG. Brand competition is based on buyers' perceptions of the benefits of products offered by particular companies.

■ **International competition** matches the products of domestic marketers against those of foreign competitors—such as a flight on Swissair versus Delta Airlines. The intensity of international competition has been heightened by the formation of alliances, such as the European Union and NAFTA.

INTERNATIONAL COMPETITION competitive marketing of domestic products against foreign products

Having identified the kind of competition, marketers can then develop a strategy for attracting more customers.

■■■ STRATEGY: THE MARKETING MIX

A company's **marketing managers** are responsible for planning and implementing all the activities that result in the transfer of goods or services to its customers. These activities culminate in the **marketing plan**—a detailed strategy for focusing marketing efforts on consumer needs and wants. Therefore, marketing strategy begins when a company identifies a consumer need and develops a product to meet it.

In planning and implementing strategies, marketing managers develop the four basic components (often called the "Four Ps") of the **marketing mix**: *product, pricing, place,* and *promotion.*

MARKETING MANAGER manager who plans and implements the marketing activities that result in the transfer of products from producer to consumer

MARKETING PLAN detailed strategy for focusing marketing efforts on consumer needs and wants

MARKETING MIX the combination of product, pricing, promotion, and distribution strategies used to market products

Product Marketing begins with a **product**—a good, a service, or an idea designed to fill a consumer need or want. Conceiving and developing new products is a constant challenge for marketers, who must always consider the factor of change—changing technology, changing consumer wants and needs, and changing economic conditions. Meeting consumer needs often means changing existing products to keep pace with emerging markets and competitors.

PRODUCT good, service, or idea that is marketed to fill consumer needs and wants

Product Differentiation Producers often promote particular features of products in order to distinguish them in the marketplace. **Product differentiation** is the creation of a feature or image that makes a product differ enough from existing products to attract consumers. For example, Jann Wenner started *Rolling Stone* magazine in 1967, and it's been the cash cow of Wenner Media ever since. In 1985, Wenner bought *Us* magazine and set out to

PRODUCT DIFFERENTIATION creation of a product feature or product image that differs enough from existing products to attract consumers

Wenner Media Chair and CEO Jann Wenner is hoping that greater product differentiation between his *Us Weekly* magazine and rival *People* will attract more customers.

compete with *People*, one of the industry giants. Wenner's latest strategy calls for greater differentiation between the two products. *People* is news driven, reporting on ordinary people as well as celebrities, and Wenner plans to punch up *Us Weekly* with more coverage of celebrity sex and glitter. So far, he hasn't been successful: *People* reaches 3.7 million readers, *Us Weekly* about 900,000.[4]

Pricing   *Pricing* a product—selecting the best price at which to sell it—is often a balancing act. On the one hand, prices must support a variety of costs—operating, administrative, and research costs as well as marketing costs. On the other hand, prices can't be so high that consumers turn to competitors. Successful pricing means finding a profitable middle ground between these two requirements.

Both low- and high-price strategies can be effective in different situations. Low prices, for example, generally lead to larger sales volumes. High prices usually limit market size but increase profits per unit. High prices may also attract customers by implying that a product is of high quality. We discuss pricing in more detail in Chapter 12.

DISTRIBUTION part of the marketing mix concerned with getting products from producers to consumers

Place (Distribution)   In the marketing mix, *place* refers to **distribution**. Placing a product in the proper outlet—for example, a retail store—requires decisions about several activities, all of which are concerned with getting the product from the producer to the consumer. Decisions about warehousing and inventory control are distribution decisions, as are decisions about transportation options.

Firms must also make decisions about the *channels* through which they distribute products. Many manufacturers, for example, sell goods to other companies that, in turn, distribute them to retailers. Others sell directly to major retailers, such as Target and Wal-Mart. Still others sell directly to final consumers. We explain distribution decisions further in Chapter 12.

Promotion   The most visible component of the marketing mix is no doubt *promotion*, which refers to techniques for communicating information about products. The most important promotional tools include *advertising*, *personal selling*, *sales promotions*, *publicity* and *public relations*. We describe promotional activities more fully in Chapter 12.

SELF-CHECK QUESTIONS 1–3

You should now be able to answer Self-Check Questions 1–3.*

1 **Multiple Choice** Marketers know that consumers buy products that offer the best value. Which of the following is **not** true regarding value for the buyer?
   (a) it is related to the buyer's wants and needs
   (b) it is the comparison of a product's benefits versus its costs
   (c) it cannot be measured
   (d) market strategies focus on increasing it

2 **Multiple Choice** All of the following are elements in the marketing mix (the Four *P*s of marketing) except:

   (a) pricing
   (b) place (or distribution)
   (c) promotion
   (d) potential

3 **True/False** A program in which a bank offers free services to long-standing customers is an example of relationship marketing.

*****Answers to Self-Check Questions 1–3 can be found on p. 565.**

TARGET MARKETING AND MARKET SEGMENTATION

Marketers have long known that products cannot be all things to all people. Buyers have different tastes, goals, lifestyles, and so on. The emergence of the marketing concept and the recognition of consumer needs and wants led marketers to think in terms of **target markets**—groups of people with similar wants and needs, who can be expected to show interest in the same products. Selecting target markets is usually the first step in the marketing strategy.

Target marketing requires **market segmentation**—dividing a market into categories of customer types or "segments." Once they have identified segments, companies may adopt a variety of strategies. Some firms market products to more than one segment. General Motors, for example, offers compact cars, vans, trucks, luxury cars, and sports cars with various features and at various price levels. GM's strategy is to provide an automobile for nearly every segment of the market.

In contrast, some businesses offer a narrower range of products, such as the specialty retailer Sunglass Hut International, aiming toward fewer segments. Note that segmentation is a strategy for analyzing *consumers*, not products. Once a target segment is identified, the marketing of products for that segment begins. The process of fixing, adapting, and communicating the nature of the product itself is called *product positioning*.

TARGET MARKET group of people that has similar wants and needs and that can be expected to show interest in the same products

MARKET SEGMENTATION process of dividing a market into categories of customer types

▪▪▪ IDENTIFYING MARKET SEGMENTS

By definition, members of a market segment must share some common traits that affect their purchasing decisions. In identifying segments, researchers look at several different influences on consumer behavior. Three of the most important are *geographic*, *demographic*, and *psychographic variables*.

Geographic Variables Many buying decisions are affected by the places people call home. The heavy rainfall in Washington State, for instance, means that people there buy more umbrellas than people in the Sunbelt. Urban residents don't need agricultural equipment, and sailboats sell better along the coasts than on the Great Plains. **Geographic variables** are the geographical units, from countries to neighborhoods, that may be considered in a segmentation strategy.

These patterns affect decisions about marketing mixes for a huge range of products. For example, consider a plan to market down-filled parkas in rural Minnesota. Demand will be high and price competition intense. Local newspaper ads may be effective, and the best retail location may be one that is easily reached from several small towns.

Although the marketability of some products is geographically sensitive, others enjoy nearly universal acceptance. Coke, for example, gets more than 70 percent of its sales from international markets. It is the market leader in Great Britain, China, Germany, Japan, Brazil, and Spain. Pepsi's international sales are about 15 percent of Coke's. In fact, Coke's chief competitor in most countries is some local soft drink, not Pepsi, which earns 78 percent of its income at home.

GEOGRAPHIC VARIABLES geographical units that may be considered in developing a segmentation strategy

Demographic Variables **Demographic variables** describe populations by identifying traits, such as age, income, gender, ethnic background, marital status, race, religion, and social class. For example, several general consumption characteristics can be attributed to certain age groups (18–25, 26–35, 36–45, and so on). Table 11.1 lists some

DEMOGRAPHIC VARIABLES characteristics of populations that may be considered in developing a segmentation strategy

possible demographic breakdowns. Depending on the marketer's purpose, a segment can be a single classification (*aged 20–34*) or a combination of categories (*aged 20–34, married without children, earning* $25,000–$34,999).

For example, Hot Topic is a California-based chain that specializes in clothes, accessories, and toys designed to appeal to the Generation Y and Millennials—a demographic consisting of American consumers between 13 and 17. The theme is music—anything from rock and rockabilly to rave and acid rap—because it's the biggest influence on the demographic's fashion tastes.

Psychographic Variables Markets can also be segmented according to such **psychographic variables** as lifestyles, interests, and attitudes. For example, Burberry, whose raincoats have been a symbol of British tradition since 1856, has repositioned itself as a global luxury brand, like Gucci and Louis Vuitton. The strategy, which resulted in a 31-percent sales increase, calls for attracting a different type of customer—the top-of-the-line, fashion-conscious individual—who shops at stores like Neiman Marcus and Bergdorf Goodman.[5]

Psychographics are particularly important to marketers because, unlike demographics and geographics, they can be changed by marketing efforts. For example, Polish companies have overcome consumer resistance by promoting the safety and desirability of using credit cards rather than depending solely on cash. One product of changing attitudes is a booming economy and the emergence of a robust middle class. The increasing number

PSYCHOGRAPHIC VARIABLES consumer characteristics, such as lifestyles, opinions, interests, and attitudes, that may be considered in developing a segmentation strategy

TABLE 11.1 DEMOGRAPHIC VARIABLES

Age	Under 5, 5–11, 12–19, 20–34, 35–49, 50–64, 65+
Education	Grade school or less, some high school, graduated high school, some college, college degree, advanced degree
Family Life Cycle	Young single, young married without children, young married with children, older married with children under 18, older married without children under 18, older single, other
Family Size	1, 2–3, 4–5, 6+
Income	Under $9,000, $9,000–$14,999, $15,000–$24,999, $25,000–$34,999, $35,000–$45,000, over $45,000
Nationality	African, American, Asian, British, Eastern European, French, German, Irish, Italian, Latin American, Middle Eastern, Scandinavian
Race	Native American, Asian, African American, Caucasian
Religion	Buddhist, Catholic, Hindu, Jewish, Muslim, Protestant
Sex	Male, female

"I'd get out of children and into older people."

of Polish households with TVs, appliances, automobiles, and houses is defining the status of Poland's middle class as the most stable in the former Soviet bloc.[6]

UNDERSTANDING CONSUMER BEHAVIOR

Although marketing managers can tell us what features people want in a new refrigerator, they cannot tell us why they buy particular refrigerators. What desire are consumers fulfilling? Is there a psychological or sociological explanation for why they purchase one product and not another? These questions and many others are addressed in the study of **consumer behavior**—the study of the decision process by which people buy and consume products.

CONSUMER BEHAVIOR study of the decision process by which people buy and consume products

■■■ INFLUENCES ON CONSUMER BEHAVIOR

To understand consumer behavior, marketers draw heavily on such fields as psychology and sociology. The result is a focus on four major influences on consumer behavior: *psychological, personal, social,* and *cultural*. By identifying which influences are most active in certain circumstances, marketers try to explain consumer choices and predict future buying behavior.

1 *Psychological influences* include an individual's motivations, perceptions, ability to learn, and attitudes.
2 *Personal influences* include lifestyle, personality, and economic status.
3 *Social influences* include family, opinion leaders (people whose opinions are sought by others), and such reference groups as friends, coworkers, and professional associates.
4 *Cultural influences* include culture (the way of living that distinguishes one large group from another), subculture (smaller groups, such as ethnic groups, with shared values), and social class (the cultural ranking of groups according to such criteria as background, occupation, and income).

Although these factors can have a strong impact on a consumer's choices, their effect on actual purchases is sometimes weak or negligible. Some consumers, for example, exhibit high **brand loyalty**—they regularly purchase products because they are satisfied with their performance. Such people (for example, users of Maytag appliances) are less subject to influence and stick with preferred brands. On the other hand, the clothes you wear and the food you eat often reflect social and psychological influences on your consumer behavior.

BRAND LOYALTY pattern of regular consumer purchasing based on satisfaction with a product

■■■ THE CONSUMER BUYING PROCESS

Students of consumer behavior have constructed various models to help show how consumers decide to buy products. Figure 11.2 presents one such model. At the core of this and similar models is an awareness of the many influences that lead to consumption. Ultimately, marketers use this information to develop marketing plans.

Problem/Need Recognition This process begins when the consumer recognizes a problem or need. After strenuous exercise, for example, you may realize that you're thirsty. Need recognition also occurs when you have a chance to change your buying habits. When you obtain your first job after graduation, your new income may let you buy things that were once too expensive for you. You may find that you need professional clothing, apartment furnishings, and a car. American Express and Citibank cater to such shifts in needs when they market credit cards to college seniors.

Information Seeking Having recognized a need, consumers often seek information. The search is not always extensive, but before making major purchases, most people seek information from personal sources, public sources, and experience. Before buying an exercise bike, for example, you may read about bikes in *Consumer Reports* or you may test-ride several bikes.

Evaluation of Alternatives If you're in the market for skis, you probably have some idea of who makes skis and how they differ. Perhaps accumulated knowledge during the information-seeking stage is combined with what you knew beforehand. By analyzing product attributes (color, price, prestige, quality, service record), you'll compare products before deciding which one best meets your needs.

RATIONAL MOTIVES reasons for purchasing a product that are based on a logical evaluation of product attributes

Purchase Decision Ultimately, consumers make purchase decisions. "Buy" decisions are based on rational motives, emotional motives, or both. **Rational motives**

Figure 11.2   The Consumer Buying Process

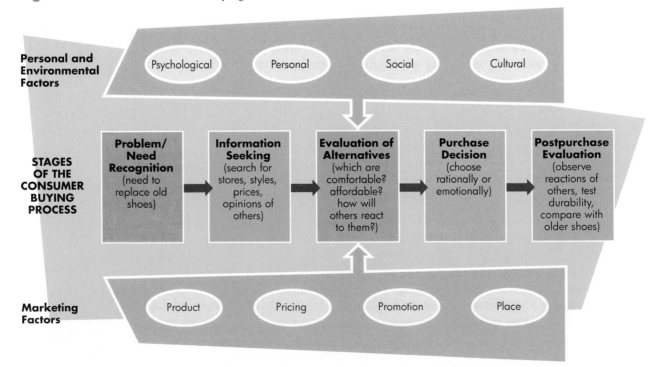

involve the logical evaluation of product attributes: cost, quality, and usefulness. **Emotional motives** involve nonobjective factors and include sociability, imitation of others, and aesthetics. For example, you might buy the same brand of jeans as your friends to feel comfortable in a certain group, not because your friends happen to have the good sense to prefer durable, comfortably priced jeans.

EMOTIONAL MOTIVES reasons for purchasing a product that are based on nonobjective factors

Postpurchase Evaluation Marketing does not stop with the sale of a product. What happens *after* the sale is important. Marketers want consumers to be happy after buying products so that they are more likely to buy them again. Because consumers do not want to go through a complex decision process for every purchase, they often repurchase products they have used and liked. Not all consumers are satisfied with their purchases. These buyers are not likely to purchase the same product(s) again and are much more apt to broadcast their experiences than are satisfied customers.

ORGANIZATIONAL MARKETING AND BUYING BEHAVIOR

In the consumer market, buying and selling transactions are visible to the public. Equally important, though far less visible, are *organizational* (or *commercial*) *markets*. Some 23 million U.S. organizations buy goods and services to be used in creating and delivering consumer products. Marketing to these buyers involves various kinds of markets and buying behaviors different from those in consumer markets.

ORGANIZATIONAL MARKETS

Organizational or commercial markets fall into three categories: *industrial, reseller*, and *government/institutional markets*. Taken together, these markets do about $27 trillion in business annually—more than two times the amount done in the U.S. consumer market.[7]

Industrial Market The **industrial market** includes businesses that buy goods to be converted into other products or that are used up during production. It includes farmers, manufacturers, and some retailers. For example, clockmaking company Seth Thomas buys electronics, metal components, and glass to make clocks for the consumer market. The company also buys office supplies, tools, and factory equipment—items never seen by clock buyers—that are used during production.

INDUSTRIAL MARKET organizational market consisting of firms that buy goods that are either converted into products or used during production

Reseller Market Before products reach consumers, they pass through a **reseller market** consisting of intermediaries, including wholesalers and retailers, that buy and resell finished goods. For example, as a leading distributor of parts and accessories for the  pleasure boat market, Coast Distribution System buys lights, steering wheels, and propellers and resells them to marinas and boat-repair shops. On resold products, 700,000 U.S. wholesalers have annual sales of $2.7 trillion. Some 3 million U.S. retailers purchase merchandise that, when resold, is valued at $3.2 trillion per year.[8]

RESELLER MARKET organizational market consisting of intermediaries that buy and resell finished goods

Government and Institutional Market In addition to federal and state governments, there are some 87,000 local governments (municipalities, counties, and school districts) in the United States. State and local governments annually spend nearly $3 trillion for durable goods, nondurables, services, and construction.[9] The **institutional market** consists of nongovernmental organizations, such as hospitals, churches, museums, and charities, that also use supplies and equipment as well as legal, accounting, and transportation services.

INSTITUTIONAL MARKET organizational market consisting of such nongovernmental buyers of goods and services as hospitals, churches, museums, and charitable organizations

▪▪▪ ORGANIZATIONAL BUYING BEHAVIOR

In some respects, organizational buying behavior bears little resemblance to consumer buying practices. Differences include the buyers' purchasing skills and an emphasis on buyer-seller relationships.

Differences in Buyers Unlike most consumers, organizational buyers are professional, specialized, and expert (or at least well-informed):

- As *professionals*, organizational buyers are trained in methods for negotiating purchase terms. Once buyer-seller agreements have been reached, they also arrange for formal contracts.
- As a rule, industrial buyers are company *specialists* in a line of items. As one of several buyers for a large bakery, for example, you may specialize in food ingredients. Another buyer may specialize in baking equipment (industrial ovens and mixers), whereas a third may buy office equipment and supplies.
- Industrial buyers are often *experts* about the products they buy. On a regular basis, organizational buyers study competing products and alternative suppliers by attending trade shows, by reading trade magazines, and by conducting technical discussions with sellers' representatives.

Differences in the Buyer-Seller Relationship Consumer-seller relationships are often impersonal, short-lived, one-time interactions. In contrast, industrial situations often involve frequent and enduring buyer-seller relationships. The development of a long-term relationship provides each party with access to the technical strengths of the other as well as the security of knowing what future business to expect. Thus, a buyer and a supplier may form a design team to create products of benefit to both. Accordingly, industrial sellers emphasize personal selling by trained representatives who understand the needs of each customer.

SELF-CHECK QUESTIONS 4–6

You should now be able to answer Self-Check Questions 4–6.*

4 **True/False** Target marketing requires market segmentation.

5 **Multiple Choice** The following is **not** a stage in the consumer buying process:
(a) substitution purchase
(b) evaluation of alternatives
(c) information seeking
(d) problem/need recognition

6 **True/False** In terms of market size, organizational buying in the United States is economically much more significant than consumer buying.

*Answers to Self-Check Questions 4–6 can be found on p. 565.

WHAT IS A PRODUCT?

In developing the marketing mix for any product, whether goods or services, marketers must consider what consumers really buy when they purchase products. Only then can these marketers plan strategies effectively. We begin this section where product strategy begins: By understanding that every product is a *value package* that provides benefits to satisfy the needs and wants of customers. Next, we describe the major *classifications of products*, both consumer and industrial. Finally, we discuss the most important component in the offerings of any business: its *product mix*.

▦▪■ THE VALUE PACKAGE

Whether it is a physical good, a service, or some combination of the two, customers get value from the various benefits, features, and even intangible rewards associated with a product. **Product features** are the qualities, tangible and intangible, that a company builds into its products, such as a 12-horsepower motor on a lawn mower. However, as we discussed earlier, to attract buyers, features also must provide *benefits*: The lawn mower must produce an attractive lawn. The owner's pleasure in knowing that the mower is nearby when needed is an intangible reward.

Today's consumer regards a product as a bundle of attributes—benefits and features—that, taken together, marketers call the **value package**. Increasingly, buyers expect to receive products with greater value—with more benefits and features at reasonable costs. Consider, for example, the possible attributes in a personal computer value package:

PRODUCT FEATURE tangible and intangible qualities that a company builds into a product

VALUE PACKAGE product marketed as a bundle of value-adding attributes, including reasonable cost

- Easy access to understandable prepurchase information
- Choices in keyboards, monitors, and memory and processing capacities
- Features, such as built-in DVD/CD burners
- Choices of color and design
- Attractive software packages
- Attractive prices
- Fast, simple ordering via the Internet
- Secure credit card purchasing
- Assurance of speedy delivery
- Warranties
- Easy access to technical support
- Prestige of owning a state-of-the art system

Although the computer includes physical *features*—processing devices and other hardware—most items in the value package are services or intangibles that, collectively, add value by providing *benefits* that increase the customer's satisfaction. Reliable data processing is certainly a benefit, but so too are pride of ownership, access to technical support, and a feeling of security. Today, more firms compete on the basis of enhanced value packages. They find that the addition of a simple new service often pleases customers far beyond the cost of providing it. Just making the purchase transaction more convenient, for example, adds value by sparing customers long waits and cumbersome paperwork.

Look at the ad in Figure 11.3 for SAS Institute, a major designer of statistical software. SAS emphasizes not the technical features of its products and not even the criteria that companies use in selecting software—efficiency, compatibility, and support. Rather, the ad focuses on the customer-oriented benefits that a buyer of SAS software can expect from using the firm's products: "SAS gives 1-800-FLOWERS.COM the power to know how to cultivate brand loyalty through quality customer relationships." The product's benefits are being marketed as part of a complete value package.

Figure 11.3 The Product: Features and Benefits

CONVENIENCE GOOD/CONVENIENCE SERVICE inexpensive good or service purchased and consumed rapidly and regularly

SHOPPING GOOD/SHOPPING SERVICE moderately expensive, infrequently purchased good or service

SPECIALTY GOOD/SPECIALTY SERVICE expensive, rarely purchased good or service

EXPENSE ITEM industrial product purchased and consumed rapidly and regularly for daily operations

■■■ **CLASSIFYING GOODS AND SERVICES**

We can classify products according to expected buyers, who fall into two groups: buyers of *consumer products* and buyers of *industrial products*. As we saw earlier in this chapter, the consumer and industrial buying processes differ significantly. Marketing products to consumers is vastly different from marketing products to other companies.

Classifying Consumer Products

Consumer products are commonly divided into three categories that reflect buyer behavior:

1. **Convenience goods** (such as milk and newspapers) and **convenience services** (such as those offered by fast-food restaurants) are consumed rapidly and regularly. They are inexpensive and are purchased often and with little output of time and effort.

2. **Shopping goods** (such as stereos and tires) and **shopping services** (such as insurance) are more expensive and are purchased less often than convenience products. Consumers often compare brands, sometimes in different stores. They may also evaluate alternatives in terms of style, performance, color, price, and other criteria.

3. **Specialty goods** (such as wedding gowns) and **specialty services** (such as catering for wedding receptions) are extremely important and expensive purchases. Consumers usually decide on precisely what they want and will accept no substitutes. They often go from store to store, sometimes spending a great deal of money and time to get a specific product.

Classifying Industrial Products
Depending on how much they cost and how they will be used, industrial products can be divided into two categories:

1. **Expense items** are goods or services that are consumed within a year by firms producing other goods or supplying other services. The most obvious expense items are industrial goods used directly in the production process (for example, bulkloads of tea processed into tea bags).

2. **Capital items** are permanent (expensive and long-lasting) goods and services. They have expected lives of more than a year and, typically, of several years. Buildings (offices, factories), fixed equipment (water towers, baking ovens), and accessory equipment (computers, airplanes) are *capital goods. Capital services* are those for which long-term commitments are made, such as building and equipment maintenance or legal

services. Because capital items are expensive and purchased infrequently, they often involve decisions by high-level managers.

▪▪▪ THE PRODUCT MIX

The group of products that a company makes available for sale, whether consumer, industrial, or both, is its **product mix**. Black & Decker, for example, makes toasters, vacuum cleaners, electric drills, and a variety of other appliances and tools. 3M makes everything from Post-it Notes to laser optics.

Product Lines Many companies, such as a simple coffee shop for sit-down or takeout, begin with a single product. Over time, they find that the initial product fails to suit every consumer shopping for the product type. To meet market demand, they introduce similar products—such as flavored coffees and various roasts—designed to reach more coffee drinkers. For example, Starbucks stores expanded the line of coffees by adding various Italian-style espresso beverages that include mochas, cappucinos, and lattes—hot and iced—and flavored blended cremes. A group of products that are closely related because they function in a similar manner (e.g., flavored coffees) or are sold to the same customer group (e.g., stop-in coffee drinkers) who will use them in similar ways is a **product line**.

Companies may extend their horizons and identify opportunities outside existing product lines. The result—*multiple* (or *diversified*) *product lines*—is evident at Starbucks. Beyond just serving beverages to customers at coffee bars, Starbucks has a line of home-brewing equipment (grinders, presses, espresso machines, coffeemakers, and bar blenders), a line of Starbucks supermarket products (premium ice creams, coffee liqueur, bottled frappucino, canned espresso, and packaged coffees), music products (in-store CD sales and Starbucks Hear Music on XM Satellite Radio), and a line of industry services (office service including brewing equipment and bags of coffee). Multiple product lines allow a company to grow rapidly and can help to offset the consequences of slow sales in any one product line.

DEVELOPING NEW PRODUCTS

To expand or diversify product lines—in fact, just to survive—firms must develop and introduce streams of new products. Faced with competition and shifting consumer preferences, no firm can count on a single successful product to carry it forever. Even products that have been popular for decades need constant renewal. Consider one of America's most-used books: *Webster's New World College Dictionary*. Published for more than 50 years, this popular reference book requires periodic renewal. The latest edition, for example, was updated with 7,000 new entries plus new uses and meanings for existing words to reflect technological innovation, language changes, and new pronunciations.

In this section, we focus on the process by which companies develop new goods and services.

▪▪▪ THE NEW PRODUCT DEVELOPMENT PROCESS

Over the past five years, the demand for food and beverage ingredients has grown more than 4 percent per year, reaching more than $5 billion annually. Flavors and flavor enhancers are the biggest part of that growth, especially artificial sweeteners. However, companies that develop and sell these products face a big problem: It costs between $30 million and $50 million and can take as long as 8 to 10 years to get a new product through the approval process at the Food and Drug Administration (FDA).

Testing, both for FDA approval and for marketing, can be the most time-consuming stage of development. For example, Acesulfame K beverage sweetener, which is made by Hoechst Celanese, has been through more than 90 safety studies and a thousand technical studies to see how it performs in various kinds of beverages.[10] Thus, cashing in on the growth of the food- and beverage-ingredients market requires an immense amount of time, patience, and money.

Product development is a long and expensive process, and like Hoechst Celanese, many firms have research and development (R&D) departments for exploring new product possibilities. Why do they devote so many resources to exploring product possibilities, rejecting many seemingly good ideas along the way? First, high *mortality rates* for new ideas mean that only a few new products reach the market. Second, for many companies, *speed to market* with a product is as important as care in developing it.

Product Mortality Rates It is estimated that it takes 50 new product ideas to generate one product that finally reaches the market. Even then, only a few of these survivors become *successful* products. Many seemingly great ideas have failed as products. Creating a successful new product has become increasingly difficult—even for the most experienced marketers. Why? The number of new products hitting the market each year has increased dramatically: More than 25,000 new household, grocery, and drugstore items are introduced annually. In just one recent year, the beverage industry alone launched 1,500 new products with 3,200 packaging variations.[11] At any given time, however, the average supermarket carries a total of only 20,000 to 25,000 different items. Because of lack of space and customer demand, about 9 out of 10 new products will fail. Those with the best chances are innovative and deliver unique benefits.

Speed to Market The more rapidly a product moves from the laboratory to the marketplace, the more likely it is to survive. By introducing new products ahead of competitors, companies establish market leadership. They become entrenched in the market before being challenged by newer competitors. How important is **speed to market**—that is, a firm's success in responding to customer demand or market changes? One study reports that a product that is only three months late to market (three months behind the leader) loses 12 percent of its lifetime profit potential. At six months, it will lose 33 percent.

SPEED TO MARKET strategy of introducing new products to respond quickly to customer or market changes

At Equity Marketing, engineers like Mark Barbato and Frank Kautzman used to design toys by sculpting models out of clay. Now they use "rapid prototyping," a technology that allows several employees to work simultaneously on 3D "models" that can then be e-mailed to clients for instant review. It now takes five days instead of three weeks to make an initial sculpture.

▪▪▪ THE PRODUCT LIFE CYCLE

When a product reaches the market, it enters the **product life cycle (PLC)**: A series of stages through which it passes during its commercial life. Depending on the product's ability to attract and keep customers, its PLC may be a matter of months, years, or decades. Strong, mature products (such as Clorox bleach and H&R Block tax preparation) have had long productive lives.

PRODUCT LIFE CYCLE (PLC)
series of stages in a product's commercial life

Stages in the PLC The life cycle for both goods and services is a natural process in which products are born, grow in stature, mature, and finally decline and die. Look at the two graphics in Figure 11.4. In Figure 11.4(a), the four phases of the PLC are applied to several products with which you are familiar:

1 **Introduction.** This stage begins when the product reaches the marketplace. Marketers focus on making potential consumers aware of the product and its benefits. Extensive promotional and development costs erase all profits.

2 **Growth.** If the new product attracts enough consumers, sales start to climb rapidly. The product starts to show a profit, and other firms move rapidly to introduce their own versions.

Figure 11.4
Products in the Life Cycle: Stages, Sales, Cost, and Profit

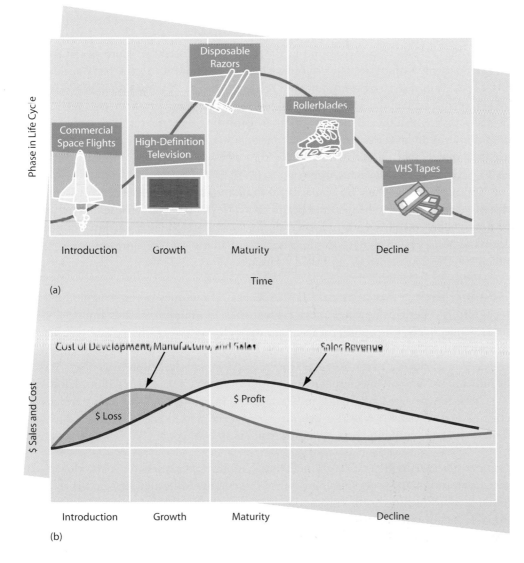

3 Maturity.   Sales growth starts to slow. Although the product earns its highest profit level early in this stage, increased competition eventually forces price cutting and lower profits. Toward the end of the stage, sales start to fall.

4 Decline.   Sales and profits continue to fall, as new products in the introduction stage take away sales. Firms end or reduce promotional support (ads and salespeople) but may let the product linger to provide some profits.

Figure 11.4(b) plots the relationship of the PLC to a product's typical sales, costs, and profits (losses). Although the early stages of the PLC often show financial losses, increased sales for successful products recover earlier losses and continue to generate profits until the decline stage. For most products, profitable life spans are short—thus, the importance placed by so many firms on the constant replenishment of product lines.

IDENTIFYING PRODUCTS

As we noted earlier, developing a product's features is only part of a marketer's job. Marketers must also identify products so that consumers recognize them. Two important tools for this task are *branding* and *packaging*.

▪▪▪ BRANDING PRODUCTS

BRANDING process of using symbols to communicate the qualities of a product made by a particular producer

Coca-Cola is the best-known brand in the world. Some Coke executives claim that if all the company's other assets were obliterated, they could go to the bank and borrow $100 billion on the strength of the brand name alone. Brand names, such as Coca-Cola, and emblems, such as the McDonald's golden arches, are symbols that characterize products and distinguish them from one another. **Branding** is a process of using symbols to communicate the qualities of a particular product made by a particular producer. Brands are designed to signal uniform quality: Customers who try and like a product can return to it by remembering its name or its logo.

BRAND AWARENESS extent to which a brand name comes to mind when the consumer considers a particular product category

Several benefits result from successful branding, including *brand loyalty* (which we discussed earlier in this chapter) and **brand awareness**—the brand name that first comes to mind when you consider a particular product category. What company, for example, comes to mind when you need to ship a document a long way on short notice? For many people, FedEx has the necessary brand awareness.

Gaining Brand Awareness   The expensive, sometimes fierce struggle for brand recognition is perhaps nowhere more evident than in branding battles among dot-com firms. Collectively, the top Internet brands—Google, America Online, Yahoo!, eBay, and Amazon.com—spend billions a year, even though only Google (ranked thirty-eighth) has cracked the ranks of the top 50 global brands.[12] Moreover, the mounting costs of establishing a brand identity mean that many more would-be e-businesses will probably fail.

With its growing importance in nearly every industry, marketers are finding more effective, less expensive ways for gaining brand awareness. Recent successes have been found with two methods: *product placements* and *viral marketing*.

PRODUCT PLACEMENTS a promotional tactic for brand exposure in which characters in television, film, music, magazines, or video games use a real product that is visible to viewers

Product Placements   Television commercials can be a real turnoff for many viewers, but when entertainment programming returns, it gets our full attention. And that's when marketers are turning up the promotional juice with **product placements**—a promotional tactic for brand exposure in which characters in television, film, music, magazines, or video games use a real product that is visible to viewers. Television placements are widespread: The Chevrolet Impala logo was inset in a *CSI* episode, and *The Office* character Michael Scott is heard to say, "I love my new Levi's." Films, too, are replete with placements for brand awareness: *I, Robot* and *The Transporter 2* used Audis, and the Nokia phone was used in *Cellular*. In print placements, Hewlett-Packard computers appear exclusively in the photo layouts in the IKEA catalog.[13]

Product placements are effective because the message is delivered in an attractive setting that holds the consumer's interest. When used in successful films and TV shows, the brand's association with famous performers is an implied celebrity endorsement. The idea is to legitimize the brand in the mind of the consumer. In all, nearly $5 billion is spent annually on product placements, especially in television, and major marketers such as P&G are putting more into product placements instead of television advertisements.

Viral Marketing Another method for increasing brand awareness is **viral marketing**, which relies on word-of-mouth and the Internet to spread information like a "virus" from person to person about products and ideas. Messages about new cars, sports events, and numerous other goods and services flow via the Internet among potential customers who pass the information on to others. Using various formats—games, contests, chat rooms, and bulletin boards—marketers encourage potential customers to try out products and tell other people about them.[14]

How effective can it be? Viral marketing can lead to consumer awareness faster and with wider reach than traditional media messages—and at a lower cost. It works for two reasons. First, people rely on the Internet for information that they used to get from newspapers, magazines, and television. Equally important, however, is the interactive element: The customer becomes a participant in the process of spreading the word by forwarding information to other Internet users. For instance, the Organic Trade Association probably got more than it bargained for in choosing viral marketing to raise awareness about organic foods. They hired Free Range Studios to make a parody movie based on *Star Wars: Episode III—Revenge of the Sith*, for release on the Internet just six hours before the real movie's debut in theaters. The result was *Grocery Store Wars*, starring the endearing puppet adventures of Tofu-D2, Chewbroccoli, Cuke Skywalker, and ObiWan Cannoli. It was a landslide hit for gaining exposure: More than 8 million viewers visited www.storewars.org to be entertained about organic foods and, as word spread about the film's clever characters and humor, millions more were attracted by additional coverage on CNN and in *USAToday*.[15]

Types of Brand Names Just about every product has a brand name. Generally, different types of brand names—national, licensed, or private—increase buyers' awareness of the nature and quality of competing products. When consumers are satisfied with a product, marketers try to build brand loyalty among the largest possible segment of repeat buyers.

National Brands **National brands** are produced by, widely distributed by, and carry the name of the manufacturer. These brands (for example, Scotch tape or Scope mouthwash) are often widely recognized by consumers because of national advertising campaigns, and they are, therefore, valuable assets. Because the costs of developing a national brand are high, some companies use a national brand on several related products. P&G now markets Ivory shampoo, capitalizing on the name of its bar soap and dishwashing liquid.

Licensed Brands We have become used to companies (and even personalities) selling the rights to put their names on products. These are called **licensed brands**. For example, the popularity of auto racing is generating millions in revenues for the NASCAR brand, which licenses its name on car accessories, ladies and men's apparel, headsets, and

VIRAL MARKETING a promotional method that relies on word of mouth and the Internet to spread information like a "virus" from person to person about products and ideas

NATIONAL BRAND brand-name product produced by, widely distributed by, and carrying the name of a manufacturer

LICENSED BRAND brand-name product for whose name the seller has purchased the right from an organization or individual

How many of these brand logos are you able to recognize?

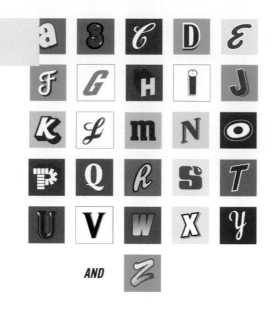

AND

countless other items with the names of drivers such as Martin, Johnson, Stewart, and Edwards. Harley-Davidson's famous logo—emblazoned on boots, eyewear, gloves, purses, lighters, and watches—brings the motorcycle maker more than $210 million annually. Along with brands such as Coors and Ferrari, licensing for character-based brands—Punisher, Spiderman Chicken Little—are equally lucrative. Marketers exploit brands because of their public appeal—the image and status that consumers hope to gain by associating with them.

Private Brands When a wholesaler or retailer develops a brand name and has a manufacturer put it on a product, the resulting name is a **private brand** (or **private label**). Sears, which carries such lines as Craftsman tools, Canyon River Blues denim clothing, and Kenmore appliances, is a well-known seller of private brands.

PRIVATE BRAND (PRIVATE LABEL) brand-name product that a wholesaler or retailer has commissioned from a manufacturer

■■■ PACKAGING PRODUCTS

PACKAGING physical container in which a product is sold, advertised, or protected

With a few exceptions (such as fresh fruits and vegetables and structural steel), products need some form of **packaging** to reduce the risk of damage, breakage, or spoilage, and to increase the difficulty of stealing small products. A package also serves as an in-store advertisement that makes the product attractive, displays the brand name, and identifies features and benefits. Advances in materials have created added uses, too, for packaging. A paper-based material that doubles as a cooking container has made Budget Gourmet dinners a low-cost entry in the dinner-entrée market. No-drip bottles have enhanced sales of Clorox bleach.

THE INTERNATIONAL MARKETING MIX

Marketing internationally means mounting a strategy to support global business operations. Foreign customers, for example, differ from domestic buyers in language, customs, business practices, and consumer behavior. If they go global, marketers must reconsider each element of the marketing mix—product, pricing, place, and promotion.

entrepreneurship and new ventures

DVDs as Easy as Netflix.com

What happens when you're a week late in returning a rented copy of a movie, and get hit with a $39 late fee? If you're Reed Hastings, you think, "There's got to be a better way." That's how Hastings came up with the idea for a new product: online DVD subscription services. When the online store was launched, back in 1999, VCRs were all the rage, but Hastings believed consumer tastes would change and DVDs would soon sweep the market. Those projections were prophetic: Today, more than 4 million Netflix subscribers get their choice of price and service level: They pay a monthly fee in any of eight subscription plans, granting members different "rental" services based on their monthly fee. With a library of 45,000 titles and revenues approaching $700 million for 2005, Hastings' ambitious near-term projections call for 100,000 films and 20 million subscribers by 2010. Can Netflix reach such lofty goals? Industry trends are favorable—in-store rentals are falling 6 percent annually, while Internet rentals are projected to increase by 50 percent for 2006 alone.

This former Peace Corps volunteer who once taught math in Swaziland is an admitted DVD evangelist with a spirit for doing business in a big way: "The only way to build a successful business is to make a bet that some macro trend will happen . . . I would like Netflix to transform the movie business." So great is his confidence that his personal stake in the company is $150 million, from proceeds of a software company he founded and later sold for $750 million in the mid-1990s.

> *The only way to build a successful business is to make a bet that some macro trend will happen . . . I would like Netflix to transform the movie business.*
>
> **—Reed Hastings, founder of Netflix, the online DVD rental store**

How well does Netflix stack up against the competition? Apparently, customers appreciate the value package they receive, including fast front-door delivery service and no late fees. Shipping 1 million DVDs a day from 35 shipping centers throughout the United States, 90 percent of subscribers receive one-day delivery. In a rare setback for Wal-Mart, the nation's largest retailer surrendered its DVD rental operation to Netflix in 2005. Rental giant Blockbuster, with 8,900 stores and more than 50 million in-store customers, has garnered just 25 percent of the online market while Netflix, with its larger selection of films, nationwide reach, and faster delivery speed, enjoys a whopping 70 percent. Little wonder, then, that Hastings is betting on a lofty future for his company.

▪▪▪ INTERNATIONAL PRODUCTS

Some products can be sold abroad with virtually no changes. Budweiser, Coca-Cola, and Marlboros are the same in Peoria, Illinois, and Paris, France. In other cases, U.S. firms have had to create products with built-in flexibility—for example, an electric shaver that is adaptable to either 115- or 230-volt outlets, so travelers can use it in both U.S. and European electrical outlets. Frequently, however, domestic products require a major redesign for buyers in foreign markets. To sell computers in Japan, for example, Apple had to develop a Japanese-language operating system.

▪▪▪ INTERNATIONAL PRICING

When pricing for international markets, marketers must consider the higher costs of transporting and selling products abroad. For example, because of the higher costs of buildings, rent, equipment, and imported meat, a McDonald's Big Mac that sells for $3.15 in the United States has a price tag of $4.93 in Switzerland.

▪▪▪ INTERNATIONAL DISTRIBUTION

In some industries, delays in starting new international distribution networks can be costly. Therefore, companies with existing distribution systems often enjoy an advantage. Many companies have avoided time delays by buying existing businesses with already-established networks. P&G, for example, bought Revlon's Max Factor and Betrix cosmetics, both of which have distribution and marketing networks in foreign markets.

▪▪▪ INTERNATIONAL PROMOTION

Occasionally, a good ad campaign is a good campaign just about anywhere. Quite often, however, U.S. promotional tactics do not succeed in other countries. Many Europeans believe that a product must be inherently shoddy if a company resorts to any advertising, particularly the American hard-sell variety.

International marketers are ever more aware of cultural differences that can cause negative reactions to improperly advertised products. Some Europeans, for example, are offended by TV commercials that show weapons or violence. Meanwhile, cigarette commercials that are banned from U.S. television thrive in many Asian and European markets. Product promotions must be carefully matched to local customs and cultural values.

Because of the need to adjust the marketing mix, success in international markets is hard won. But whether a firm markets in domestic or international markets, the basic principles of marketing still apply; only their implementation changes.

SMALL BUSINESS AND THE MARKETING MIX

Many of today's largest firms were yesterday's small businesses. Behind the success of many small firms lies a skillful application of the marketing concept and an understanding of each element in the marketing mix.

Small-Business Products Some new products and firms are doomed at the start because few consumers want or need what they have to offer. Many fail to estimate realistic market potential, and some offer new products before they have clear pictures of their target segments.

In contrast, a thorough understanding of what customers want has paid off for many small firms. Take, for example, the case of Little Earth Productions, a company that makes fashion accessories, such as handbags. Originally, the company merely considered how consumers would use its handbags. But after examining shopping habits, Little Earth Productions redesigned for better in-store display. Because stores can give handbags better visibility by hanging them instead of placing them on floors or low countertops, Little Earth Productions added small handles specifically for that purpose.

Small-Business Pricing Haphazard pricing can even sink a firm with a good product. Small-business pricing errors usually result from a failure to estimate operating expenses accurately. Owners of failing businesses have often been heard to say, "I didn't realize how much it costs to run the business!" But when small businesses set prices by carefully assessing costs, many earn satisfactory profits.

Small-Business Distribution Perhaps the most critical aspect of distribution for small businesses is facility location, especially for new service businesses. The ability of many small businesses to attract and retain customers depends partly on the choice of location.

In distribution as in other aspects of the marketing mix, however, smaller companies may have advantages over larger competitors, even in highly complex industries. Everex Systems of Fremont, California, sells personal computers to wholesalers and dealers through a system that the company calls *zero response time*. Because Everex Systems is small and flexible, phone orders can be reviewed every two hours and factory assembly adjusted to match demand.

Small-Business Promotion Successful small businesses plan for promotional expenses as part of start-up costs. Some hold down costs by using less expensive

say what you mean

Never Give a German a Yellow Rose

Good things come in small packages—right? Not in cultures in which the size of the package says a lot about its value. More is better in some places, while big is wasteful in others. Color is important, too. White signifies death and mourning in China, while red means good luck and prosperity. Never give a German an even number of roses—it's bad luck. And don't give a German any number of yellow roses because yellow is associated with jealousy. In Japan, avoid putting any four things in any single package—the number four is bad luck.

What does all of this superstition have to do with business? Packaging, color, quantity, and the way a product is presented can determine whether something's going to sell or sit on the shelf.

Almost all cultures have an unwritten set of rules when it comes to using words, colors, numbers, and images. Displaying images of animate objects—humans or otherwise—is frowned on in some Islamic cultures, while in Italy and Brazil, nakedness (or even near nakedness) always sells. Americans like to

see their flag on packages; it's a good way of displaying one's patriotism. In some cultures, however, commercializing the national emblem is in bad taste.

If you're giving someone a package in Japan, don't expect the recipient to open it in front of you—it's not polite. But if someone gives you something in the United States, it's rude not to show your delight immediately. Be careful of what you call things, too. Even in English-speaking countries, you can get into a lot of trouble by using culturally inaccurate names. If you want to market flip-flops in New Zealand, you'd better call them *jandals*. How about cookies in England? Put *biscuits* on the label.

And finally, speaking of food, beef in a hamburger in India is taboo, but you can't go wrong with a lamb burger in Saudi Arabia. Americans use chopsticks in Thai restaurants, but you won't find too many Thais using them. If you want to keep something cool in Australia, put it in an *eskie*—which is what Americans call a cooler. Sometimes the name says it all, and sometimes it doesn't.

Know the culture and you'll know something about its market. Nothing beats a little research and a lot of cultural sensitivity.

promotional methods. Local newspapers, for example, are sources of publicity when they publish articles about new or unique businesses. Other small businesses identify themselves and their products with associated groups, organizations, and events. Thus, a crafts gallery might join with a local art league to organize public showings of their combined products.

SELF-CHECK QUESTIONS 7–9

You should now be able to answer Self-Check Questions 7–9.*

7 **Multiple Choice** When viewed as a value package for the buyer, a product is a bundle of attributes consisting of the following:
   (a) benefits
   (b) features
   (c) intangible rewards
   (d) all of the above

8 **True/False** The *product mix* is the group of products that a company makes available for sale and within which it may have several *product lines*.

9 **Multiple Choice** Which of the following is **not** true of the international marketing mix?

   (a) products that sell for a given price in the United States may sell at a different price in another country
   (b) an ad campaign that is good in domestic markets will also be good in international markets
   (c) a company can speed up its international distribution activities by buying an existing business in another country
   (d) cultural differences can cause negative reactions to products because of the way they are advertised

***Answers to Self-Check Questions 7–9 can be found on p. 565.**

CONTINUED FROM PAGE 328

CAN DELL SHOCK THE ELECTRONICS WORLD?

For masses of electronics lovers, Dell's entry into the broader consumer electronics market comes as welcome news. Consumers will see prices fall, whereas retailers will experience what might be called "reverse sticker shock": Sellers currently enjoying net profit margins of 25 to 40 percent on consumer electronics may have to survive on the modest 10 percent margin to which PC sellers are accustomed.

Dell's promotional efforts, at first, are aimed at building brand familiarity. Electronics lovers who are accustomed to brands such as Sony and Samsung may be surprised to see the Dell name on TVs, pocket PCs, MP3 players, and the Digital Jukebox, among its upcoming line of products. Winning a massive customer base is essential for high-volume sales, but because consumer buying habits don't change overnight, no one at Dell expects to dominate the electronics market the way it does in PCs. Before buying an expensive flat-screen TV, for example, consumers want to *see* the quality of its picture firsthand rather than looking through catalogs or a Web site. As Forrester Research analyst Jed Kolko notes, "With video products it's harder to demonstrate value online." Consumers hold similar reservations about the sound quality of audio products as well. So, only with the passage of time can Dell establish relationships with consumers by informing them and convincing them to switch over from an already-crowded list of competing sellers.

QUESTIONS FOR DISCUSSION

1 What sociocultural and technological factors have influenced the growth of the consumer electronics market?

2 What demographics would you use to define the flat-screen TV target market? How about the target market for home PCs?

3 Identify the main factors favoring success for Dell's crossover into consumer electronics, such as MP3 players and flat-screen TVs. What prominent factors suggest major problems or even failure for this crossover attempt?

4 Applying this chapter's definition of product value to Dell's plans, what are the benefits in Dell's consumer electronics offerings? What are the costs?

5 Applying this chapter's definition of product value to electronics retailers, such as Best Buy or Circuit City, what are their benefits and costs? How well or poorly does Dell's product value ratio stack up against its competitors' ratios?

1 Explain the concept of marketing and identify the five forces that constitute the external marketing environment.

Marketing is responsible for delivering value and satisfaction to customers at a profit. After identifying customers' needs and wants, it develops plans to satisfy them by creating products, establishing their prices, methods for distributing them, and ways for promoting them to potential customers. Marketing is successful if satisfied buyers perceive that the benefits derived from each purchase outweigh its costs, and if the firm, in exchange for providing the products, meets its organizational goals. Five outside factors comprise a company's external environment and influence its marketing programs: (1) *political and legal actions*, (2) *sociocultural factors*, (3) *technological changes*, (4) *economics*, and (5) *competition*.

2 Explain the purpose of a marketing plan and identify the four components of the marketing mix.

The *marketing plan* is a detailed strategy for focusing marketing efforts on meeting consumer needs and wants. In planning and implementing strategies, marketing managers focus on the four elements (Four *P*s) of the *marketing mix*: (1) *products* for consumers, (2) *pricing* of products, (3) *distribution* of products to consumers (*place*), and (4) *promotion* of products.

3 Explain market segmentation and how it is used in target marketing.

Marketers think in terms of *target markets*—groups of people who have similar wants and needs and who can be expected to show interest in the same products. Target marketing requires *market segmentation*—dividing a market into customer types or "segments." Members of a market segment must share some common traits that influence purchasing decisions. The following are three influences: (1) *Geographic variables* are the geographical units that may be considered in developing a segmentation strategy. (2) *Demographic variables* describe populations by identifying such traits as age, income, gender, ethnic background, marital status, race, religion, and social class. (3) *Psychographic variables* include lifestyles, interests, and attitudes.

4 Describe the key factors that influence the consumer buying process.

One consumer behavior model considers five influences that lead to consumption: (1) *Problem/need recognition*: The buying process begins when the consumer recognizes a problem or need. (2) *Information seeking*: Having recognized a need, consumers seek information. (3) *Evaluation of alternatives*: Consumers compare products to decide which product best meets their needs. (4) *Purchase decision*: "Buy" decisions are based on rational motives, emotional motives, or both. *Rational motives* involve the logical evaluation of product attributes, such as cost, quality, and usefulness. *Emotional motives* involve nonobjective factors and include sociability, imitation of others, and aesthetics. (5) *Postpurchase evaluations*: Marketers want consumers to be happy after the consumption of products so that they are more likely to buy them again.

5 Discuss the three categories of organizational markets.

(1) The *industrial market* consists of businesses that buy goods to be converted into other products or that are used during production. (2) Before products reach consumers, they pass through a *reseller market* consisting of intermediaries that buy finished goods and resell them. (3) The *government and institutional market* includes federal, state, and local governments, and nongovernmental buyers—hospitals, churches, and charities—that purchase goods and services needed for serving their clients.

6 Explain the definition of a product as a value package and classify goods and services.

Customers buy products to receive value that satisfies a want or a need. Thus, a successful product is a *value package*—a bundle of attributes that, taken together, provides the right features and offers the right benefits. *Features* are the qualities, tangible and intangible, that are included with the product. To be satisfying, features must provide *benefits*. The value package has services and features that add value by providing benefits that increase the customer's satisfaction.

Products (both goods and services) can be classified according to expected buyers as either *consumer products* or *industrial products*. *Convenience products* are inexpensive goods and services that are consumed rapidly and regularly. *Shopping products* are more expensive and are purchased less often than convenience products. *Specialty products* are extremely important and expensive goods and services. Industrial products are classified as either *expense items* or *capital items*. *Expense items* are consumed within a year. *Capital items* are expensive and long-lasting goods and services that have expected lives of several years.

7 Describe the key considerations in the new product development process.

To expand or diversify product lines, new products must be developed and introduced. Many firms have research and development (R&D) departments for continuously exploring new product possibilities because high mortality rates for new ideas result in only a few new products reaching the market. Even then, only a few of these survivors become successful products. *Speed to market*—how fast a firm responds with new products or market changes—determines a product's profitability and success. A continuous product development process is necessary because every product has a *product life cycle*—a series of stages through which it passes during its commercial life. The development of new products, then, is the source for renewal of the firm's product offerings in the marketplace.

8 Explain the importance of branding and packaging.

Branding and *packaging* identify products so that consumers recognize them. The goal in developing a brand is to distinguish a product from others and to signal its uniform quality so that consumers develop a preference for that particular brand name. Most products need some form of *packaging*—a physical container in which it is sold, advertised, or protected. A package makes the product attractive, displays the brand name, and identifies features and benefits. It also reduces the risk of damage, breakage, or spoilage, and it lessens the likelihood of theft.

9 Discuss the challenges that arise in adopting an international marketing mix.

If they go global, marketers must reconsider each element of the marketing mix—product, pricing, place, and promotion—because foreign customers differ from domestic buyers in language, customs, business practices, and consumer behavior. While some products can be sold abroad with virtually no changes, others require major redesign. When pricing for international markets, marketers must consider differences in the costs of transporting and selling products abroad. In some industries, delays in starting new international distribution networks can be costly, so companies with existing distribution systems enjoy an advantage. Often, U.S. promotional tactics do not succeed in other countries, so different promotional methods must be developed. Product promotions, therefore, must be carefully matched to local customs and cultural values.

10 Identify the ways that small businesses can benefit from an understanding of the marketing mix.

Each element in the marketing mix—product, price, place, and promotion—can determine success or failure for any small business. Many *products* are failures because consumers don't need or want what they have to offer. A more realistic market potential can be gained by getting a clearer picture of what target segments want in a new product. Small-business *pricing* errors usually result from a failure to estimate operating expenses accurately. By carefully assessing costs, small businesses can set prices that earn satisfactory profits. Perhaps the most crucial aspect of *place*, or distribution, for small businesses is location because it determines the ability to attract customers. Although *promotion* can be expensive and is essential for small businesses, especially at startup, costs can be reduced by using less expensive promotional methods. Local newspaper articles and television cover business events, thus providing free public exposure.

QUESTIONS AND EXERCISES

Questions for Review

1 What are the key similarities and differences between consumer buying behavior and organizational buying behavior?

2 Why and how is market segmentation used in target marketing?

3 How is the concept of the value package useful in marketing to consumers and industrial customers?

4 What are the various classifications of consumer and industrial products? Give an example of a good and a service for each category other than those discussed in the text.

Questions for Analysis

5 Select an everyday product (personal fitness training, CDs, dog food, cell phones, or shoes, for example). Show how different versions of your product are aimed toward different market segments. Explain how the marketing mix differs for each segment.

6 Select a second everyday product and describe the consumer buying process that typically goes into its purchase.

7 Consider a service product, such as transportation, entertainment, or health care. What are some ways that more customer value might be added to this product? Why would your improvements add value for the buyer?

8 How would you expect the branding and packaging of convenience, shopping, and specialty goods to differ? Why? Give examples to illustrate your answers.

Application Exercises

9 Interview the marketing manager of a local business. Identify the degree to which this person's job is focused on each element in the marketing mix.

10 Select a product made by a foreign company and sold in the United States. What is the product's target market? What is the basis on which the target market is segmented? Do you think that this basis is appropriate? How might another approach, if any, be beneficial? Why?

DEALING WITH VARIABLES

Goal

To encourage you to analyze the ways in which various market segmentation variables affect business success.

Background Information

You and four partners are thinking of purchasing a heating and air conditioning (H/AC) dealership that specializes in residential applications priced between $2,000 and $40,000. You are now in the process of deciding where that dealership should be located. You are considering four locations: Miami, Florida; Westport, Connecticut; Dallas, Texas; and Spokane, Washington.

Method

Step 1

Working with your partnership group, do library research to learn how H/AC makers market residential products. Check for articles in the *Wall Street Journal*, *Business Week*, *Fortune*, and other business publications.

Step 2

Continue your research by focusing on the specific marketing variables that define each prospective location. Check Census Bureau and Department of Labor data at your library and on the Internet and contact local chambers of commerce (by phone and via the Internet) to learn about the following factors for each location:

1 Geography
2 Demography (especially age, income, gender, family status, and social class)
3 Psychographic factors (lifestyles, interests, and attitudes)

Step 3

As a group, determine which location holds the greatest promise as a dealership site. Base your decision on your analysis of market segment variables and their effects on H/AC sales.

FOLLOW-UP QUESTIONS

1 Which location did you choose? Describe the segmentation factors that influenced your decision.
2 Identify the two most important variables that you believe will affect the dealership's success. Why are these factors so important?
3 Which factors were least important? Why?
4 When equipment manufacturers advertise residential H/AC products, they often show them in different climate situations (winter, summer, or high-humidity conditions). Which market segments are these ads targeting? Describe these segments in terms of demographic and psychographic characteristics.

DRIVING A LEGITIMATE BARGAIN

The Situation

A firm's marketing methods are sometimes at odds with the consumer's buying process. This exercise illustrates how ethical issues can become entwined with personal selling activities, product pricing, and customer relations.

The Dilemma

In buying his first new car, Matt visited showrooms and Web sites for every make of SUV. After weeks of reading and test-driving, he settled on a well-known Japanese-made vehicle with a manufacturer's suggested retail price of $34,500 for the 2007 model. The price included accessories and options that Matt considered essential. Because he planned to own the car for at least five years, he was willing to wait for just the right package rather than accept a lesser-equipped car already on the lot. Negotiations with Gary, the sales representative, continued for two weeks. Finally, a sales contract was signed for $30,600, with delivery due no more than two or three months later if the vehicle had to be special-ordered from the factory and earlier if Gary found the exact car when he searched other dealers around the country. On April 30, to close the deal, Matt had to write a check for $1,000.

Matt received a call on June 14 from Angela, Gary's sales manager: "We cannot get your car before October," she reported, "so it will have to be a 2008 model. You will have to pay the 2008 price." Matt replied that the agreement called for a stated price and delivery deadline for 2007, pointing out that money had exchanged hands for the contract. When asked what the 2008 price would be, Angela responded that it had not yet been announced. Angrily, Matt replied that he would be foolish to agree now on some unknown future price. Moreover, he didn't like the way the dealership was treating him. He told Angela to send him back everything he had signed; the deal was off.

QUESTIONS TO ADDRESS

1 Given the factors involved in the consumer buying process, how would you characterize the particular ethical issues in this situation?

2 From an ethical standpoint, what are the obligations of the sales representative and the sales manager regarding the pricing of the product in this situation?

3 If you were responsible for maintaining good customer relations at the dealership, how would you handle this matter?

CLEANING UP IN SALES

The Situation

Selling a product—whether a good or a service—requires the salesperson to believe in it, to be confident of his or her sales skills, and to keep commitments made to clients. Because so many people and resources are involved in delivering a product, numerous uncertainties and problems can give rise to ethical issues. This exercise encourages you to examine some of the ethical issues that can surface in the selling process for industrial products.

The Dilemma

Along with 16 other newly hired graduates, Denise Skilsel has just completed the sales training program for a new line of high-tech machinery that Cleaning Technologies Corporation (CTC) manufactures for industrial cleaners. As a new salesperson, Denise is eager to meet potential clients, all of whom are professional buyers for companies—such as laundries and dry cleaners, carpet cleaners, and military cleaners—that use CTC products or those of competitors. Denise is especially enthusiastic about several facts that she learned during training: CTC's equipment is the most technically advanced in the industry, carries a 10-year performance guarantee, and is safe—both functionally and environmentally.

The first month was difficult but successful: In visits to seven firms, Denise successfully closed three sales, earning large commissions (pay is based on sales results) as well as praise from the sales manager. Moreover, after listening to her presentations, two more potential buyers had given verbal commitments and were about to sign for much bigger orders than any Denise had closed to date. As she was catching her flight to close those sales, Denise received two calls—one from a client and one from a competitor. The client, just getting started with CTC equipment, was having some trouble: Employees stationed nearby were getting sick when the equipment was running. The competitor told Denise that the U.S. Environmental Protection Agency (EPA) had received complaints that CTC's new technology was environmentally unsafe because of noxious emissions.

Team Activity

Assemble a group of four students and assign each group member to one of the following roles:

- Denise: CTC salesperson (employee)
- CTC sales manager (employer)
- CTC customer
- CTC investor

ACTION STEPS

1. Before hearing any of your group's comments on this situation, and from the perspective of your assigned role, what do you recommend Denise should say to the two client firms she is scheduled to visit? Write down your recommendation.
2. Gather your group together and reveal, in turn, each member's recommendation.
3. Appoint someone to record main points of agreement and disagreement within the group. How do you explain the results? What accounts for any disagreement?
4. Identify any ethical issues involved in group members' recommendations. Which issues, if any, are more critical than others?
5. From an ethical standpoint, what does your group finally recommend Denise should say to the two client firms she is scheduled to visit? Explain your result.
6. Identify the advantages and drawbacks resulting from your recommendations.

VIDEO EXERCISE

PUTTING YOURSELF IN THE CONSUMER'S SHOES: SKECHERS USA

Learning Objectives

The purpose of this video is to help you:

1 Describe the role of the Four *P*s in a company's marketing mix.
2 Explain how a company shapes its market research to fit its marketing goals.
3 Discuss the effectiveness of target marketing and segmentation in analyzing consumers.

Synopsis

Skechers USA enjoys a reputation for producing footwear that combines comfort with innovative design. It has built its product line into a globally recognized brand distributed in more than 110 countries. From its corporate headquarters in Manhattan Beach, California, Skechers has engineered steady growth in market share while competing against some powerful players in the high-ticket athletic shoe industry.

Since its start in 1992, Skechers has burnished its image as a maker of hip footwear through a savvy marketing strategy that calls for catering to a closely targeted consumer base. Maintaining brand integrity and its reputation for innovation is a crucial goal in all of Skechers' product development and marketing activities.

In this video, Director of Public Relations Kelly O'Connor discusses her work and the marketing activities that are critical to maintaining Skechers' edge in the highly competitive footwear marketplace. She describes the company's goal of creating a megabrand with an image, personality, and "feel" that can be translated and marketed globally. Skechers has been successful in brand building by means of an "Ask, Don't Tell" approach to product development and marketing: It aims to find out what the market wants and then appeal to customers' wants rather than trying to influence the market with the products that it makes available.

DISCUSSION QUESTIONS

1 **For analysis**: Which of the Four *P*s of the marketing mix seems to govern Skechers' marketing strategy? Why? How do you suppose Skechers alters elements of its American marketing mix to attract consumers in international markets?
2 **For application**: Skechers collects a lot of primary data in its market research. What kinds of primary data does the company prefer to gather? Why do these kinds of data suit its marketing goals? How do the data suit the firm's consumer base? Given Skechers' fairly limited consumer base, are there other types of research data that you would recommend?
3 **For analysis**: Describe Skechers' target market and explain how company marketers segment it. How effective is this strategy in analyzing customers? How successful are Skechers' marketing efforts among 12- to 24-year-olds (and consumers wishing they were in that demographic segment)?
4 **For application**: Discuss the impact of brand loyalty on the sale of Skechers products. Building brand loyalty is a major effort that presents both opportunities and challenges to marketers and product developers. What are some of the opportunities and challenges encountered by Skechers' marketing managers?
5 **For application**: How do you think Skechers might expand its current product lines? What other new products might Skechers research, such as clothing or accessories? How could the company go about investigating the market potential for such products?

Online Exploration

Go online to find out about the product lines and target markets of such companies as Nike (www.nike.com), Reebok (www.reebok.com), Lady Foot Locker (www.ladyfootlocker.com), and FUBU (www.fubu.com). How does the approach to segmentation at these companies compare with Skechers' approach?

After reading this chapter, you should be able to:

1 Identify the various pricing objectives that govern pricing decisions and describe the price-setting tools used in making these decisions.

2 Discuss pricing strategies that can be used for different competitive situations and identify the pricing tactics that can be used for setting prices.

3 Explain the meaning of *distribution mix* and identify the different channels of distribution.

4 Describe the role of wholesalers and explain the different types of retailing.

5 Describe the role of e-intermediaries and explain how they add value for advertisers and consumers on the Internet.

6 Define *physical distribution* and describe the major activities in the physical distribution process.

7 Identify the important objectives of promotion, discuss the considerations in selecting a promotional mix, and discuss advertising promotions.

8 Outline the tasks involved in personal selling, describe the various types of sales promotions, and distinguish between publicity and public relations.

THE NOSTALGIA MERCHANTS

Why did Reuben Harley think that throwbacks—replicas of old sports jerseys—would catch on? Call it instinct, street smarts, or whatever you will, he trusted his personal tastes. While making a living doing odd jobs in his West Philly neighborhood, he saved money to buy classic jerseys of legendary players such as Julius Irving, Nolan Ryan, and

PRICING, DISTRIBUTING, AND PROMOTING PRODUCTS

Jackie Robinson from century-old Mitchell & Ness's retail store. When people would ask where he got the oversize Hank Aaron jersey he was wearing, the 300-pound-plus Harley wouldn't tell them because he wanted them all as his own. "But just seeing the cat's reaction, I knew this could really catch on," he says. And so it began for this high school graduate who, eventually, teamed up with Peter Capolino, the then 58-year-old owner of Mitchell & Ness Nostalgia Company (M&N). Together, in just two years' time, they changed M&N into the nation's best-known marketer of clothing for urban teen African Americans.

But just seeing the cat's reaction, I knew this could really catch on.

—Entrepreneur Reuben Harley, on the inspiration for marketing throwback sports clothing

Harley's self-styled promotional efforts started by focusing on celebrities—rappers and pro athletes—who could afford the $250 to $470 price tag for these intricately-stitched designs with authentic team colors. He began meeting them by going uninvited to their parties in New York and Philadelphia nightclubs, soon becoming a trusted acquaintance with his charming and unassuming personality. When shown samples of M&N's jerseys, hip-hop great Sean (Diddy) Combs immediately bought them, as did rapper Fabulous. Basketball star Jermaine O'Neal, who owns over 150 throwbacks, says, "Acquiring the hottest model is a competitive sport among teammates." Soon, entertainment stars were seen wearing throwbacks on MTV and Black Entertainment Television.

With so much brand visibility, it's little wonder that M&N has been turned into the industry's most imitated seller of authentic old sports jerseys. Sales jumped from

$2.8 million in 2000 to $25 million in 2002, then to more than $40 million in 2003. By 2005, the throwbacks' popularity had created a problem: Unauthorized sales of counterfeit versions by street vendors and Internet sites amounted to $11 million. In becoming the industry's brand leader, there's no doubting who the prime mover is for M&N's success: "I consider it a miracle that Reuben fell into my lap. He deserves all the credit," says Capolino. ∎

Our opening story continues on page 386.

WHAT'S IN IT FOR ME?

Peter Capolino didn't grasp the market potential for M&N's products before Reuben Harley launched his self-developed promotional strategy for throwback jerseys. Personal selling, combined with promotion through entertainment personalities, catapulted M&N's throwbacks into national prominence. By understanding this chapter's methods for pricing, distributing, and promoting products, you, too, can benefit in three ways: (1) You'll be better prepared to use the concepts of pricing, distributing, and promoting products in your career as both employee and manager; (2) as a consumer, you'll have a clearer picture of how a product's promotion and distribution affect its selling price, causing it to rise or fall; and (3) as a future investor, you'll be better prepared to evaluate a company's marketing program and its competitive potential before buying the company's stock.

In this chapter, we'll look at three of the Four *P*s of the marketing mix. We'll start this chapter by looking at the concept of *pricing* and the price-setting tools used in making pricing decisions. We'll then look at *place*—the distribution mix and the different channels and methods of distribution. We'll then look at *promotion* and discuss the considerations in selecting a promotional mix. Finally, we'll discuss the tasks involved in personal selling and various types of sales promotions.

DETERMINING PRICES

PRICING process of determining what a company will receive in exchange for its products

As we saw in Chapter 11, product development managers decide what *products* a company will offer to customers. In **pricing**, the second major component of the marketing mix, managers decide what the company will get in exchange for its products. In this section, we first discuss the objectives that influence a firm's pricing decisions. Then, we describe the major tools that companies use to meet those objectives.

■■■ PRICING TO MEET BUSINESS OBJECTIVES

PRICING OBJECTIVES goals that sellers hope to attain in pricing products for sale

eBay, the popular Internet auction site, has a straightforward pricing structure that's a consumer favorite: Let buyers make offers until a price is finally settled. While eBay sellers hope for a high price, they sometimes are willing to give up some profit in return for a quick sale. Unfortunately, the eBay pricing model, one-on-one price setting, isn't feasible for all companies with lots of customers and products. **Pricing objectives** are the goals that sellers hope to achieve in pricing products for sale. Some companies set prices to maximize profits and, therefore, have *profit-maximizing pricing objectives*. Some firms want to dominate the market or secure high market share and, therefore, have *market share pricing objectives*. Pricing decisions are also influenced by the need to compete in the marketplace, by social and ethical concerns, and even by corporate image.

Profit-Maximizing Objectives Pricing to maximize profits is tricky. If prices are set too low, the company will probably sell many units of a product but may miss the chance to make additional profits on each unit (and may even lose money on each exchange). If prices are set too high, the company will make a large profit on each item but will sell fewer units. Again, the firm loses money. It may also be left with excess inventory and may have to reduce or even close production operations. To avoid these problems, companies try to set prices to sell the number of units that will generate the highest possible total profits.

In calculating profits, managers weigh sales revenues against costs for materials and labor. They also consider the capital resources (plant and equipment) that the company ties up to generate a given level of profit. The costs of marketing (such as maintaining a large sales staff) can also be substantial. To use these resources efficiently, many firms set prices to cover costs and achieve a targeted level of return for owners.

Market Share Objectives In the long run, a business must make a profit to survive. Even so, companies often set initially low prices for new products. Because they are willing to accept minimal profits, even losses, to get buyers to try products, these companies use pricing to establish **market share**—a company's percentage of the total industry's sales for a specific product type. Even with established products, market share may outweigh profit as a pricing objective. Consider Arturo ("Arte") Moreno, who made a fortune in billboards and then bought baseball's Anaheim Angels in 2003, when the team's attendance ranked a mundane seventh out of 14 American league teams. In a business characterized by soaring costs and red ink, Moreno (the sport's first minority owner) decided on an unexpected strategy: He cut prices on tickets and concessions. Why? His team plays in the huge Los Angeles market, but unfortunately, the L.A. Dodgers are in the same market, and the Angels have never been able to garner a proportionate share. Moreno is counting on attracting enough fans to offset his lower margins. For the 2005 season, Angels attendance had risen by 30 percent above 2003, into the second-place ranking in the league.

MARKET SHARE a company's percentage of the total industry's sales for a specific product

Arturo Moreno, owner of baseball's Anaheim Angels, is betting that more fans will come to the team's games when prices are cut on tickets and concessions.

▪▪▪ PRICE-SETTING TOOLS

Whatever a company's objectives, managers like to measure the potential impact before deciding on final prices. Two tools used for this purpose are *cost-oriented pricing* and *breakeven analysis*. Although each can be used alone, both are often used because they provide different kinds of information for determining prices that will allow the company to reach its objectives.

COST-ORIENTED PRICING pricing that considers the firm's desire to make a profit and its need to cover production costs

Cost-Oriented Pricing **Cost-oriented pricing** considers the firm's desire to make a profit and its need to cover production costs. A music store manager would price CDs by calculating the cost of making them available to shoppers. He or she would include the costs of store rent, employee wages, utilities, product displays, insurance, and the manufacturer's price.

MARKUP amount added to an item's cost to sell it at a profit

Let's assume that the manufacturer's price is $8 per CD. If the store sells CDs for $8, it won't make any profit. Nor will it make a profit if it sells CDs for $8.50 each—or even $10 or $11. To be profitable, the company must charge enough to cover product and other costs. Together, these factors determine the **markup**—the amount added to an item's cost to sell it at a profit. In this case, a reasonable markup of $7 over costs means a $15 selling price. Markup, when stated as a percentage of selling price, is calculated as follows:

$$\text{Markup percentage} = \frac{\text{Markup}}{\text{Sales price}} \times 100\%$$

For our CD retailer, the markup percentage is 46.7:

$$\text{Markup percentage} = \frac{\$7}{\$15} \times 100\% = 46.7\%$$

Out of every $1.00 taken in, $0.467 will be gross profit. Out of this profit, the store must still pay rent, utilities, insurance, and all other costs.

For experienced price-setters, an even simpler method uses a standard percentage of cost-of-goods to determine the markup amount. Many retailers, for example, use 100 percent of cost-of-goods as the standard markup. If the manufacturer's price is $8 per CD, markup (100 percent) is also $8, so selling price is $16. It's a quick-and-easy method, but should only be used in established businesses with a proven track record.

VARIABLE COST cost that changes with the quantity of a product produced and sold

FIXED COST cost that is incurred regardless of the quantity of a product produced and sold

BREAKEVEN ANALYSIS for a particular selling price, assessment of the seller's costs versus revenues at various sales volumes

Breakeven Analysis: Cost-Volume-Profit Relationships Using cost-oriented pricing, a firm will cover **variable costs**—costs that change with the number of units of a product produced and sold. Variable costs include materials bought to make the product, sales commissions, and mailing or delivering the product to customers. It will also make some money to pay **fixed costs**—costs, such as annual rent, insurance, and utilities, that must be paid *regardless of the number of units produced and sold*.

But how many units must the company sell before all costs, both variable and fixed, are covered, and it begins to make a profit? What if too few units are sold? And what happens if sales are greater than expected? The answers depend on costs, selling price, and number of units sold. **Breakeven analysis** assesses costs versus revenues for various sales volumes. It shows, at any particular selling price, the financial result—the amount of loss or profit—for each possible volume of sales.

Figure 12.1
Breakeven Analysis

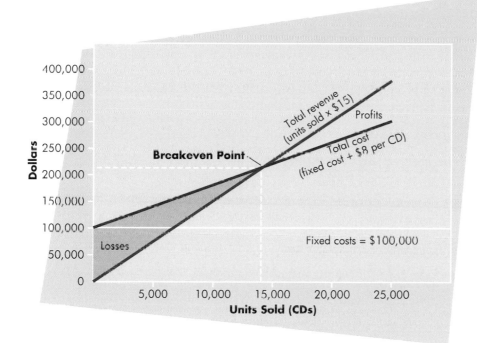

To continue our music store example, suppose that the *variable cost* for each CD (in this case, the cost of buying the CD from the producer) is $8. This means that the store's annual variable costs depend on how many CDs are sold—the number of CDs sold times the $8 cost for each CD. Say that *fixed costs* for keeping the store open for one year are $100,000. The number of CDs sold does not affect these costs. Costs for lighting, rent, insurance, and salaries are steady no matter how many CDs are sold. Therefore, what we want to know is this: How many CDs must be sold *so that total revenues exactly cover both* fixed and variable costs? The answer is the **breakeven point**, which is 14,286 CDs. We arrive at this number through the following equation:

BREAKEVEN POINT sales volume at which the seller's total revenue from sales equals total costs (variable and fixed) with neither profit nor loss

$$\text{Breakeven point (in units)} = \frac{\text{Total Fixed Cost}}{\text{Price} - \text{Variable Cost}} = \frac{\$100,000}{\$15 - \$8} = 14,286 \text{ CDs}$$

Look at Figure 12.1. If the store sells fewer than 14,286 CDs, it loses money for the year. If sales go over 14,286, profits grow by $7 for each additional CD. If the store sells exactly 14,286 CDs, it will cover all its costs but earn zero profit.

Zero profitability at the breakeven point can also be seen by using the profit equation:

Profit = Total Revenue − (Total Fixed Cost + Total Variable Cost)
   = (14,286 CDs × $15) − ($100,000 Fixed Cost + [14,286 CDs × $8 Variable Cost])
$0 = ($214,290) − ($100,000 + $114,288) (rounded to the nearest whole CD)

PRICING STRATEGIES AND TACTICS

The pricing tools discussed in the previous section help managers set prices on specific goods. They do not, however, help them decide on pricing philosophies for diverse competitive situations. In this section, we discuss pricing *strategy*—pricing as a planning activity. We then describe some basic pricing *tactics*: ways in which managers implement a firm's pricing strategies.

▪▪▪ PRICING STRATEGIES

How important is pricing as an element in the marketing mix and in the marketing plan? Because pricing has a direct impact on revenues, it is extremely important. Moreover, it is a very flexible tool. It is certainly easier to change prices than to change products or distribution channels. In this section, we focus on the ways in which pricing strategies can result in widely differing prices for very similar products.

Pricing Existing Products A firm has three options for pricing existing products:

1 Pricing above prevailing market prices for similar products
2 Pricing below market prices
3 Pricing at or near market prices

Pricing above the market takes advantage of the common assumption that higher price means higher quality. Godiva chocolates and Patek Phillipe watches price high by promoting prestige and quality images. In contrast, both Budget and Dollar car-rental companies promote themselves as low-priced alternatives to Hertz and Avis. Pricing below prevailing market price works if a firm offers a product of acceptable quality while keeping costs below those of higher-priced competitors.

PRICE SKIMMING setting an initially high price to cover new product costs and generate a profit

PENETRATION PRICING setting an initially low price to establish a new product in the market

Pricing New Products When introducing new products, companies must often choose between two pricing policies: very high prices or very low prices. **Price skimming**—setting an initially high price to cover costs and generate a profit—may generate a large profit on each item sold. The revenue is often needed to cover development and introduction costs. Skimming works only if marketers can convince consumers that a new product is truly different from existing products. In contrast, **penetration pricing**—setting an initially low price to establish a new product in the market—seeks to create consumer interest and stimulate trial purchases.

Fixed Versus Dynamic Pricing for E-Business The electronic marketplace has introduced a highly variable pricing system as an alternative to more conventional—and more stable—pricing structures for both consumer and business-to-business (B2B) products. Dynamic pricing works because information flow on the Web notifies millions of buyers of instantaneous changes in product availability. To attract sales that might be lost under traditional fixed-price structures, sellers can alter prices privately, on a one-to-one, customer-to-customer basis.[1] Roy Cooper, for example, scours the markets of Quito, Ecuador, for tapestries, baskets, and religious relics. He pays $10 to $15 for selected items and then posts them on eBay, where they usually sell at substantial markups. His online enterprise nets Cooper about $1,300 a month ($2,500 in November and December). His Ecuadorean suppliers, whose average income is $1,460 a year, seem happy with their share; in a country where only 2.7 percent of the population has ever been online, very few people have ever heard of dynamic pricing.

At present, fixed pricing is still the most common option for cybershoppers. E-tail giant Amazon.com has maintained this practice as its pricing strategy for its 16 million retail items. That situation, however, is beginning to change as dynamic-price challengers, such as eBay and Priceline.com, grow in popularity.

Roy Cooper uses the Internet to negotiate prices privately with buyers and sellers, one-on-one, to buy and sell native folk art objects.

■■■ PRICING TACTICS

Regardless of its pricing strategy, a company may adopt one or more *pricing tactics*. Companies selling multiple items in a product category often use **price lining**—offering all items in certain categories at a limited number of prices. With price lining, a department store, for example, predetermines three or four *price points* at which a particular product will be sold. If price points for men's suits are $175, $250, and $400, all men's suits will be priced at one of these three prices.

Psychological pricing takes advantage of the fact that customers are not completely rational when making buying decisions. One type of psychological pricing, **odd-even pricing**, is based on the theory that customers prefer prices that are not stated in even dollar amounts. Thus, customers regard prices of $1,000, $100, $50, and $10 as significantly higher than $999.95, $99.95, $49.95, and $9.95, respectively. Finally, sellers must often resort to price reductions—**discounts**—to stimulate sales.

PRICE LINING setting a limited number of prices for certain categories of products

PSYCHOLOGICAL PRICING pricing tactic that takes advantage of the fact that consumers do not always respond rationally to stated prices

ODD-EVEN PRICING psychological pricing tactic based on the premise that customers prefer prices not stated in even dollar amounts

DISCOUNT price reduction offered as an incentive to purchase

SELF-CHECK QUESTIONS 1–3

You should now be able to answer Self-Check Questions 1–3.*

1 **Multiple Choice** Suppose your main pricing objective is to establish a new product in the marketplace. The appropriate pricing strategy for this objective Is:
(a) market-share pricing
(b) dynamic pricing
(c) psychological pricing
(d) penetration pricing

2 **True/False** With price skimming, sellers set an initially low price to create consumer interest and stimulate trial purchases for a new product.

3 **True/False** Consider the pricing tactics in the clothing department of a department store. If the department uses price lining, then it cannot also use odd-even pricing.

*Answers to Self-Check Questions 1–3 can be found on p. 565.

THE DISTRIBUTION MIX

DISTRIBUTION MIX the combination of distribution channels by which a firm gets its products to end users

We have already seen that a company needs a good product mix and effective pricing. But the success of any product also depends on its **distribution mix**: the combination of distribution channels by which a firm gets products to end users. In addition to consumers, industrial users are important because every company is a customer that buys other companies' products. In this section, we consider some of the many factors in the distribution mix for all users. First, we look at the role of the target audience and explain the need for intermediaries. Then, we discuss basic distribution strategies.

■■■ INTERMEDIARIES AND DISTRIBUTION CHANNELS

INTERMEDIARY individual or firm that helps to distribute a product

WHOLESALER intermediary who sells products to other businesses for resale to final consumers

RETAILER intermediary who sells products directly to consumers

Once called *middlemen*, **intermediaries** help to distribute a producer's goods, either by moving them or by providing information that stimulates their movement from sellers to customers. **Wholesalers** are intermediaries who sell products to other businesses for resale to final consumers. **Retailers** sell products directly to consumers. Whereas some firms rely on independent intermediaries, others employ their own distribution networks and sales forces.

DISTRIBUTION CHANNEL network of interdependent companies through which a product passes from producer to end user

Distribution of Goods and Services A **distribution channel** is the path that a product follows from producer to end user. Figure 12.2 shows how four popular distribution channels can be identified according to the kinds of channel members involved in getting products to buyers. Note first that all channels begin with a producer and end either with a consumer or an industrial (business) user.

DIRECT CHANNEL distribution channel in which a product travels from producer to consumer without intermediaries

Channel 1: Direct Distribution In a **direct channel**, the product travels from the producer to the consumer or to the industrial buyer, without intermediaries. Using their own sales forces, companies such as Avon, Dell, Geico, and Tupperware use this channel. Direct distribution is prominent on the Internet for thousands of products ranging from books and automobiles to insurance and vacation packages sold directly by producers to users. Most business goods, especially those bought in large quantities, are sold directly by the manufacturer to the industrial buyer.

Figure 12.2
Channels of Distribution

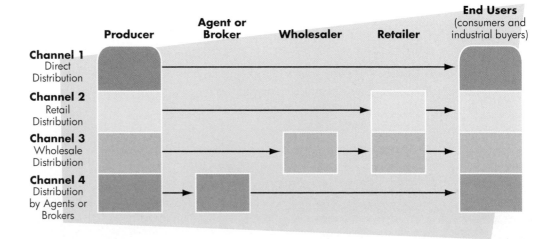

At the plant of the world's largest auto parts supplier, Delphi Automotive Systems, Jessica V. Prince assembles fuel pumps according to a process that she helped engineers and consultants design. The auto parts are shipped from the plant to an auto manufacturer, illustrating a direct (producer to customer) channel of distribution.

Channel 2: Retail Distribution In Channel 2, producers distribute consumer products through retailers. Goodyear, for example, maintains its own system of retail outlets. Levi's has its own outlets but also produces jeans for other retailers. Large outlets, such as Wal-Mart, buy merchandise directly from producers. Many industrial buyers rely on this channel: Businesses shop at office supply retailers, such as Staples, Office Depot, and Office Max, that are designed for industrial users.

Channel 3: Wholesale Distribution Once the most widely used method of nondirect distribution, Channel 2 requires a large amount of floor space, both for storing merchandise and for displaying it in stores. Faced with the rising cost of store space, many retailers found that they could not afford both retail and storage space. Thus, wholesalers entered the distribution network to take over more of the storage function. The combination convenience store/gas station is an example of Channel 3. With approximately 90 percent of the space used to display merchandise, only 10 percent is left for storage and office facilities. Wholesalers relieve the space problem by storing merchandise for retailers and restocking store displays frequently.

Channel 4: Distribution by Agents or Brokers Channel 4 uses *sales agents* or *brokers* who represent producers and sell to consumers, industrial users, or wholesalers. They receive commissions based on the prices of the goods they sell. **Sales agents** generally deal in the related product lines of a few producers, and form long-term relationships to represent those producers and meet the needs of steady customers. Consider Vancouver-based Uniglobe Travel International, a travel agency representing airlines, car-rental companies, hotels, and tour companies. Uniglobe Travel International books flight reservations and arranges complete recreational travel services for consumers. The firm also services companies whose employees need lodging and transportation for business travel. In contrast to agents, **brokers** match numerous sellers and buyers as needed, often without knowing in advance who they will be. Both the real estate industry and stock exchanges rely on brokers to match buyers and sellers of property.

SALES AGENT independent intermediary who generally deals in the related product lines of a few producers and forms long-term relationships to represent those producers and meet the needs of steady customers

BROKER independent intermediary who matches numerous sellers and buyers as needed, often without knowing in advance who they will be

The Pros and Cons of Nondirect Distribution Each link in the distribution chain makes a profit by charging a markup or commission. Thus, nondirect distribution means higher prices: The more members in the channel—the more intermediaries—the higher the final price.

Figure 12.3   The Value-Adding Intermediary

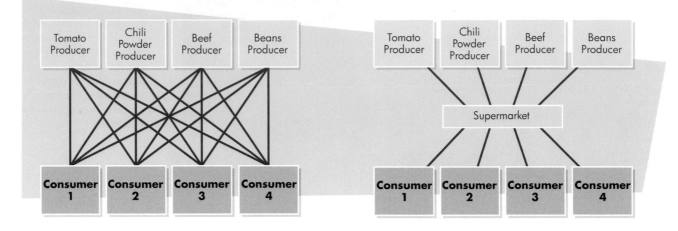

Intermediaries, however, can provide *added value* by saving consumers both time and money. Moreover, the value accumulates with each link in the supply chain. Intermediaries provide time-saving information and make the right quantities of products available where and when consumers need them. Consider Figure 12.3, which illustrates the problem of making chili without the benefit of a common intermediary—the supermarket. As a consumer, you would obviously spend a lot more time, money, and energy if you tried to gather all the ingredients from one producer at a time. In any case, even if we did away with intermediaries, you would not eliminate either their tasks or the costs entailed by performing those tasks. They exist because they do necessary jobs in cost-efficient ways.

WHOLESALING

Now that you know something about distribution channels, we can consider more closely the role of intermediaries. Wholesalers, for example, provide a variety of services to buyers of products for resale or business use. In addition to storing and providing an assortment of products, some wholesalers offer delivery, credit, and product information.

Most wholesalers are independent operations that sell various consumer or business goods produced by a variety of manufacturers. They buy products from manufacturers and sell them to other businesses. They own the goods that they resell and usually provide storage and delivery. They provide additional value-adding services for customers, including credit, marketing advice, and merchandising services, such as marking prices and setting up displays.

Unlike wholesalers, agents and brokers do not own their merchandise. Rather, they serve as sales and merchandising arms for producers or sellers who do not have their own sales forces. The value of agents and brokers lies in their knowledge of markets and their merchandising expertise. They show sale items to potential buyers and, for retail stores, they provide such services as shelf and display merchandising and advertising layout. They remove open, torn, or dirty packages, arrange products neatly, and generally keep goods attractively displayed. Many supermarket products are handled through brokers.

RETAILING

There are more than three million retail establishments in the United States. Most of them are small, often consisting of owners and part-time help. Indeed, over one-half of the nation's retailers account for less than 10 percent of all retail sales. Retailers also include huge operations, such as Wal-Mart, the largest employer in the United States, and Sears. Although there are large retailers in many other countries—Kaufhof in Germany, Carrefour in France, and Daiei in Japan—most of the world's largest retailers are U.S. businesses.

■■■ TYPES OF RETAIL OUTLETS

U.S. retail operations vary widely by type as well as size. We can classify them in various ways: by their pricing strategies, location, range of services, or range of product lines. Choosing the right types of retail outlets is a crucial aspect of every seller's distribution strategy. In this section, we describe U.S. retail stores by using three classifications: *product line retailers*, *bargain retailers*, and *convenience stores*.

Product Line Retailers Retailers featuring broad product lines include **department stores**, which are organized into specialized departments: shoes, furniture, women's petite sizes, and so on. Stores are usually large, handle a wide range of goods, and offer a variety of services, such as credit plans and delivery. Similarly, **supermarkets** are divided into departments of related products: food products, household products, and so forth. They stress low prices, self-service, and wide selection.

In contrast, **specialty stores** are small stores that carry one line of related products. They serve specific market segments with full product lines in narrow product fields and often feature knowledgeable sales personnel. Sunglass Hut International, for example, has 1,500 outlets with a deep selection of competitively priced sunglasses.

Bargain Retailers **Bargain retailers** carry wide ranges of products and come in many forms. The first **discount houses** sold large numbers of items (such as TVs and other appliances) at substantial price reductions to cash-only customers. As name-brand items became more common, they offered better product assortments while still transacting cash-only sales in low-rent facilities. As they became firmly entrenched, they began moving to better locations, improving decor, and selling better-quality merchandise at higher prices. They also began offering a few department store services, such as credit plans and noncash sales.

Catalog showrooms mail catalogs to attract customers into showrooms to view display samples, place orders, and wait briefly while clerks retrieve orders from attached warehouses. **Factory outlets** are manufacturer-owned stores that avoid wholesalers and retailers by selling merchandise directly from factory to consumer. The **wholesale club** offers large discounts on a wide range of brand-name merchandise to customers who pay annual membership fees. Costco Wholesale Corporation has a $45 annual membership fee and two million members that shop in its 400 warehouse stores.

Convenience Stores Neighborhood food retailers, such as 7-Eleven and Circle K stores, are **convenience store** chains, which offer ease of purchase: They stress easily accessible locations, extended store hours, and speedy service. They differ from most bargain retailers in that they do not feature low prices. Like bargain retailers, they control prices by keeping in-store service to a minimum.

DEPARTMENT STORE large product-line retailer characterized by organization into specialized departments

SUPERMARKET large product-line retailer offering a variety of food and food-related items in specialized departments

SPECIALTY STORE retail store carrying one product line or category of related products

BARGAIN RETAILER retailer carrying a wide range of products at bargain prices

DISCOUNT HOUSE bargain retailer that generates large sales volume by offering goods at substantial price reductions

CATALOG SHOWROOM bargain retailer in which customers place orders for catalog items to be picked up at on-premises warehouses

FACTORY OUTLET bargain retailer owned by the manufacturer whose products it sells

WHOLESALE CLUB bargain retailer offering large discounts on brand-name merchandise to customers who have paid annual membership fees

CONVENIENCE STORE retail store offering easy accessibility, extended hours, and fast service

DIRECT-RESPONSE RETAILING
form of nonstore retailing by
direct interaction with customers
to inform them of products and to
receive sales orders

**MAIL ORDER (CATALOG
MARKETING)** form of nonstore
retailing in which customers place
orders for catalog merchandise
received through the mail

TELEMARKETING form of
nonstore retailing in which the
telephone is used to sell directly
to consumers

DIRECT SELLING form of
nonstore retailing typified
by door-to-door sales

■■■ NONSTORE RETAILING

Some of the largest retailers sell all or most of their products without brick-and-mortar stores. Certain types of consumer goods and services—food products, pinball, jukeboxes, pool and cigarettes—sell well from vending machines located outdoors, in schools, hospitals and restaurants. But even at $110 billion per year, vending machine sales still make up less than 3 percent of all U.S. retail sales.[2]

Nonstore retailing also includes **direct-response retailing**, in which firms contact customers directly to inform them about products and to receive sales orders. **Mail order** (or **catalog marketing**), such as that practiced by Crate & Barrel and Sharper Image, is a popular form of direct-response retailing. Less popular in recent years is **telemarketing**—the use of the telephone to sell directly. While it is growing rapidly in Canada and Great Britain, it suffered a downturn in the United States with recent state and national do-not-call registries, and some are predicting a near-collapse as more households object to intrusive phone calls. Finally, more than 600 U.S. companies use **direct selling** to sell door-to-door or through home-selling parties. Avon Products, alone, has some four million door-to-door sales representatives in 100 countries.[3]

say what you mean

Keeping Channels Clear

Merely securing a major distributor is not a guarantee of success in any market. Distributors often carry a huge range of products and usually have different incentives for getting different products to market. Using intermediaries to distribute products around the world requires an understanding of cultural differences, especially when it comes to communicating with channel partners whose cultural values—such as what's an incentive and what's not—are not the same as your own.

Most communication with distributors is written— e-mails, faxes, letters, and so forth. Your distributor must be able to understand what you need, so here are a few tips for communicating with foreign members of your distribution channel. Don't be too casual or informal when you're e-mailing businesspeople in Germany—you may give them the wrong idea about your commitment to the partnership and even turn them off to you and your firm. German businesspeople expect to be addressed by Mr., Mrs., and other appropriate titles, and they will expect you to observe a certain level of formality in all communications. Latin Americans, on the other hand, tend to appreciate a personal touch—for example, a reference to family or health early in the communication. If you're an American, you probably expect succinct, matter-of-fact messages; you don't even mind bulleted lists of things to be discussed.

If distributors don't understand the value or benefits of your new product features, they're less likely to market them successfully. In many cases, explaining things in culturally specific slang or jargon just confuses foreign distributors. Do not, however, expect Singaporeans or Filipinos to tell you voluntarily that they don't understand your technical terms. They'd lose face. You're better off anticipating communication challenges and focusing on such questions as how they would recommend improving your sales in their markets. You're bound to get a list of polite suggestions that may not only be useful but that also should help you determine whether your communications are effective.

Finally, remember that your distributor is probably the best person to ask about the local market. You may want to consider translating your marketing and product materials to ensure that foreign distributors understand the features and benefits of your products. Typically, they're representing numerous products, and communicating clearly with them will make it easier for them to represent your products.

THE ASCENT OF THE E-INTERMEDIARY

The ability of e-commerce to bring together millions of widely dispersed consumers and businesses has changed the types and roles of intermediaries. **E-intermediaries** are Internet-based channel members who perform one or both of two functions: (1) They collect information about sellers and present it to consumers, or (2) they help deliver Internet products to buyers. We will examine three types of e-intermediaries: *syndicated sellers, shopping agents,* and *e-retailers.*

E-INTERMEDIARY Internet distribution channel member that assists in delivering products to customers or that collects information about various sellers to be presented to consumers

■■■ SYNDICATED SELLERS

Syndicated selling occurs when one Web site offers another a commission for referring customers. Here's how it works. With nearly 20 million users each month, Expedia.com is the world's leading online travel service. Expedia's Web page shows a list of car rental companies, such as Dollar Rent A Car. When Expedia customers click on the Dollar banner for a car rental, they are transferred from the Expedia site to the Dollar site. Dollar pays Expedia a fee for each booking that comes through this channel. Although the new intermediary increases the cost of Dollar's supply chain, it adds value for customers. Travelers avoid unnecessary cyberspace searches and are efficiently guided to a car-rental agency.[4]

SYNDICATED SELLING e-commerce practice whereby a Web site offers other Web sites commissions for referring customers

■■■ SHOPPING AGENTS

Shopping agents (e-agents) help Internet consumers by gathering and sorting information. Although they don't take possession of products, they know which Web sites and stores to visit, give accurate comparison prices, identify product features, and help consumers complete transactions by presenting information in a usable format—all in a matter of seconds. PriceScan.com is among the better known cyber-shopping agents, but there are many others as well. Since e-agents have become so plentiful, unsure shoppers are turning to rating sites, such as eSmarts.com, that evaluate and compare e-agents. In essence, we're witnessing the emergence of new e-intermediaries that specialize in providing information about e-agents!

SHOPPING AGENT (E-AGENT) e-intermediary (middleman) in the Internet distribution channel that assists users in finding products and prices but that does not take possession of products

■■■ ELECTRONIC RETAILING

E-retailing sales reached $71 billion in 2004, as some 80 million households with PCs went online to shop.[5] **Electronic retailing** is made possible by communications networks that let sellers post product information on consumers' PCs. Use of the Internet to interact with customers—to inform, sell to, and distribute to them—is booming. In addition to large companies, more than four million U.S. small businesses have their own Web sites, and more are on the way. Figure 12.4 tells the story of this growth by showing the percentages of small businesses with Web sites (Figure 12.4a), of those planning to post Web sites (Figure 12.4b), and of the marketing functions that owners expect sites to perform (Figure 12.4c).[6]

ELECTRONIC RETAILING nonstore retailing in which information about the seller's products and services is connected to consumers' computers, allowing consumers to receive the information and purchase the products in the home

Electronic Catalogs **E-catalogs** use the Internet to display products for both retail and business customers. Using electronic displays (instead of traditional mail catalogs), firms give millions of users instant access to pages of product information. The seller avoids mail-distribution and printing costs, and once an online catalog is in place, there is little cost in maintaining and accessing it. Recognizing these advantages, about 85 percent of all catalogers are now on the Internet, with sales via Web sites accounting for 10 percent of all catalog sales. The top-rated consumer e-catalogs include JCPenney (number 1), Fingerhut

E-CATALOG nonstore retailing in which the Internet is used to display products

Figure 12.4 Small Business and the Web

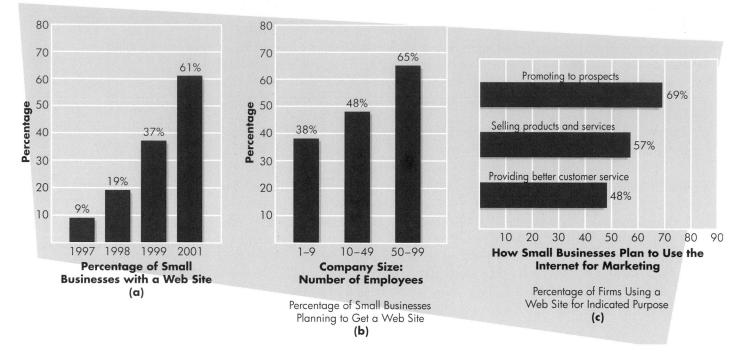

Percentage of Small Businesses with a Web Site
(a)

Percentage of Small Businesses Planning to Get a Web Site
(b)

How Small Businesses Plan to Use the Internet for Marketing

Percentage of Firms Using a Web Site for Indicated Purpose
(c)

(number 3), L. L.Bean (number 7), and Victoria's Secret (number 8). Top B2B e-catalogs include Dell Computer (number 1) and Office Depot (number 5).[7]

Electronic Storefronts and Cybermalls

Today, a seller's Web site is an **electronic storefront** (or *virtual storefront*) from which consumers collect information about products and buying opportunities, place orders, and pay for purchases. Producers of large product lines, such as Dell, dedicate storefronts to their own product lines. Other sites, such as Songsearch.com, which offers music CDs and DVD movies, are category sellers whose storefronts feature products from many manufacturers.

Search engines like Yahoo! serve as **cybermalls**: collections of virtual storefronts representing diverse products. After entering a cybermall, shoppers can navigate by choosing from a list of stores (L.L. Bean or Macy's), product listings (computers or MP3 players), or departments (apparel or bath/beauty). When your virtual shopping cart is full, you check out and pay your bill. The value-added properties of cybermalls are obvious: speed, convenience, 24-hour access, and efficient searching.

Interactive and Video Marketing

Today, both retail and B2B customers interact with multimedia sites using voice, graphics, animation, film clips, and access to live human advice. One good example of **interactive marketing** is LivePerson.com, a leading provider of real-time sales and customer service for over 3,000 Web sites. When customers log on to the sites of Toyota, Earthlink, Hewlett Packard, Verizon, Microsoft—all of which are LivePerson clients—they can enter a live chat room where a service operator initiates a secure one-on-one text chat. Questions and answers go back and forth to help customers get answers to specific questions before deciding on a product. Another form of interaction is the so-called banner ad that changes as the user's mouse moves about the page, revealing new drop-down, check, and search boxes.

Video marketing, a long-established form of interactive marketing, lets viewers shop at home from TV screens by phoning in or e-mailing orders. Most cable systems offer video marketing through home-shopping channels that display and demonstrate products and allow viewers to phone in or e-mail orders. One U.S. network, QVC, also operates in the United Kingdom, Germany, Mexico, and South America.

ELECTRONIC STOREFRONT commercial Web site in which customers gather information about products and buying opportunities, place orders, and pay for purchases

CYBERMALL collection of virtual storefronts (business Web sites) representing a variety of products and product lines on the Internet

INTERACTIVE MARKETING nonstore retailing that uses a Web site to provide real-time sales and customer service

VIDEO MARKETING nonstore retailing to consumers via home television

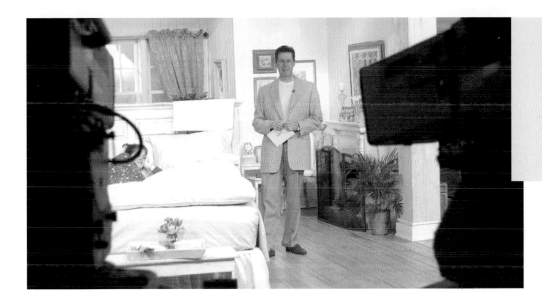

QVC host Bob Bowersox is getting ready to offer bedding made by Northern Lights, which distributes regularly through the TV home-shopping channel. Northern Lights markets through such electronic-retailing outlets as eBay and Shopping.com as well as QVC, which also sells online through its Web site and through six outlet stores.

PHYSICAL DISTRIBUTION

Physical distribution refers to the activities needed to move products from manufacturer to consumer. Its purpose is to make goods available when and where consumers want them, keep costs low, and provide services to satisfy customers. Thus, physical distribution includes *warehousing* and *transportation operations*. Because of its importance for customer satisfaction, some firms have adopted distribution as their marketing strategy of choice.

PHYSICAL DISTRIBUTION activities needed to move a product efficiently from manufacturer to consumer

▪▪▪ WAREHOUSING OPERATIONS

Storing, or **warehousing**, is a major part of distribution management. In selecting a strategy, managers must keep in mind both the different characteristics and costs of warehousing operations. **Private warehouses** are owned by a single manufacturer, wholesaler, or retailer. Most are run by large firms that deal in mass quantities and need regular storage. J. C. Penney, for example, maintains its own warehouses to facilitate the movement of products to its retail stores.

WAREHOUSING physical distribution operation concerned with the storage of goods

PRIVATE WAREHOUSE warehouse owned by and providing storage for a single company

Public warehouses are independently owned and operated. Because companies rent only the space they need, these facilities are popular with firms needing storage only during peak periods. They are also used by manufacturers who need multiple storage locations to get products to multiple markets.

PUBLIC WAREHOUSE independently owned and operated warehouse that stores goods for many firms

▪▪▪ TRANSPORTATION OPERATIONS

Because the highest cost faced by many companies is that of physically moving a product, cost is a major consideration in choosing transportation methods. But firms must also consider other factors: the nature of the product, the distance it must travel, the speed with which it must be received, and customer wants and needs.

Transportation Modes The major transportation modes are trucks, railroads, planes, water carriers, and pipelines. Differences in cost are most directly related to delivery speed.

Specializing in long-haul shipping, U.S. Express Enterprises employs nearly 6,000 drivers to operate 5,300 trucks and 12,000 trailers. Trucks have satellite capabilities, anticollision radar, vehicle-detection sensors, and computers for shifting through 10 speeds, and roomy cabs have sleepers, refrigerators, and microwaves.

Trucks With more than three million drivers, trucks haul more than two-thirds of all tonnage carried by all modes of U.S. freight transportation. The advantages of trucks include flexibility for any-distance distribution, fast service and dependability. Increasing truck traffic, however, is raising safety and courtesy concerns on the highways.

Planes Air is the fastest mode of transportation for physical goods. Air freight customers benefit from lower inventory carrying by eliminating the need to store items that might deteriorate. Shipments of fresh fish, for example, can be picked up by restaurants each day, avoiding the risk of spoilage from packaging and storing. Air freight, however, is the most expensive form of transportation.

Water Carriers Water, by contrast, is the least expensive mode but, unfortunately, also the slowest. Networks of waterways—oceans, rivers, and lakes—let water carriers reach many areas throughout the world. Boats and barges are used mostly for moving bulky products (such as oil, grain, and gravel). Long-distance ships are specially constructed to hold large standardized containers.

Railroads Railroads can economically transport high volume, heavy, bulky items, such as cars, steel, and coal. However, their delivery routes are limited by fixed, immovable rail tracks.

Pipelines Like water transport, pipelines are slow. Used to transport liquids and gases, they are also inflexible, but for specialized products they provide economical and reliable delivery. Lack of adaptability to other products makes pipelines an unimportant transportation method for most industries.

▪▪▪ PHYSICAL DISTRIBUTION AND E-CUSTOMER SATISFACTION

ORDER FULFILLMENT all activities involved in completing a sales transaction, beginning with making the sale and ending with on-time delivery to the customer

New e-commerce companies often focus on sales, only to discover that delays in after-sale distribution cause customer dissatisfaction. Any delay in physical distribution is a breakdown in fulfillment. **Order fulfillment** begins when the sale is made: It involves getting the product to each customer in good condition and on time. But the volume of a firm's transactions can be huge, and fulfillment performance—in terms of timing, content, and terms of payment—has been a source of irritation to many e-business customers.

To improve on-time deliveries, many businesses maintain distribution centers and ship from their own warehouses. Other e-tailers, however, outsource order filling to distribution specialists, such as the giant UPS e-logistics and the much smaller Atomic Box, to gain reliable performance. Both Atomic Box and UPS process orders, ship goods, provide information about product availability and order status, and handle returns. To perform these tasks, the client's computer system must be networked with that of the distribution specialist.

■■■ DISTRIBUTION AS A MARKETING STRATEGY

Distribution is an increasingly important way of competing for sales. Instead of just offering advantages in product features and quality, price, and promotion, many firms have turned to distribution as a cornerstone of business strategy. This approach means assessing and improving the entire stream of activities—wholesaling, warehousing, and transportation—involved in getting products to customers.

Consider, for example, the distribution system of National Semiconductor, one of the world's largest computer-chip makers. Finished microchips are produced in plants around the world and shipped to customers, such as IBM, Toshiba, and Compaq, which also run factories around the globe. Chips originally sat waiting at one location after another—on factory floors, at customs, in distributors' facilities, and in customers' warehouses. Typically, they traveled 20,000 different routes on as many as 12 airlines and spent time in 10 warehouses before reaching customers. National has streamlined the system by shutting down six warehouses and now airfreights chips worldwide from a single center in Singapore. Every activity—storage, sorting, and shipping—is run by FedEx. By outsourcing the activities, National's distribution costs have fallen, delivery times have been reduced by half, and sales have increased.

SELF-CHECK QUESTIONS 4–6

You should now be able to answer Self-Check Questions 4–6.*

4 True/False The distribution mix is the combination of products that a firm offers for distribution to end users.

5 Multiple Choice Which of the following is **not true** regarding intermediaries and distribution channels?
  (a) wholesalers sell products to other businesses, which resell them to final customers
  (b) intermediaries are retailers that move goods or information to customers
  (c) intermediaries provide added value for customers

  (d) marketers of consumer products and industrial products use distribution channels for getting products to customers

6 Multiple Choice Which of the following is **not true** regarding retailing and retail outlets?
  (a) factory outlets and warehouse clubs are examples of bargain retailers
  (b) department stores offer a wide range of goods and customer services
  (c) mail-order retailers offer deep price discounts
  (d) electronic retailing relies on communication networks connecting sellers to buyers' computers

*Answers to Self-Check Questions 4–6 can be found on p. 565.

PROMOTION aspect of the marketing mix concerned with the most effective techniques for communicating information about and selling a product

In this chapter's opening case, Reuben Harley developed the promotional methods that launched sky-rocketing sales of throwback jerseys. As we noted in Chapter 11, **promotion** refers to techniques for communicating information about products. It is part of the *communication mix*: the total message any company sends to consumers about its product. Promotional techniques, especially advertising, must communicate the uses, features, and benefits of products. Sales promotions also include various programs that add value beyond the benefits inherent in the product. It's nice to get a quality product at a good price but even better when you get a rebate or a bonus pack with "20 percent more free." In promoting products, then, marketers have an array of tools at their disposal.

PROMOTIONAL OBJECTIVES

The ultimate objective of any promotion is to increase sales. In addition, marketers may use promotion to *communicate information*, *position products*, *add value*, and *control sales volume*. Promotion, first and foremost, communicates information about the product. Users cannot buy products unless they know about them. Information may advise customers that a product exists, educate them about the product's features, and tell what the product will do for them.

POSITIONING process of establishing an identifiable product image in the minds of consumers

As we saw in Chapter 11, **positioning** is the process of establishing an easily identi-fiable product image in the minds of consumers by fixing, adapting, and communicating the nature of the product itself. First, the firm must identify which market segments are likely to purchase its product and how its product measures up against competitors. Only then can it focus on promotional choices for differentiating its product and positioning it in the minds of the target audience.

Promotional mixes are often designed to communicate a product's *value-added benefits*. Burger King shifted its promotional mix by cutting back on advertising dollars and using the money for customer discounts: Getting the same food at a lower price is a value-added benefit. Finally, by increasing promotions during slow periods, firms that experience seasonal sales patterns (for example, greeting-card companies) can keep pro-duction and distribution systems *running evenly* and stabilize sales volume throughout the year.

THE PROMOTIONAL MIX

PROMOTIONAL MIX combination of tools used to promote a product

Four of marketing's most powerful promotional tools are *advertising*, *personal selling*, *sales promotions*, and *publicity and public relations*. The best combination of these tools—the best **promotional mix**—depends on many factors. The most important is the target audience, with its unique characteristics. As an example, two generations from now, 25 percent of the U.S. workforce will be Hispanic. The rise in Latinos' dis-posable income—29 percent, to $652 billion—since 2001 has made them a potent economic force, and marketers are scrambling not only to redesign products that will appeal to them, but to find more effective ways of promoting products to Hispanic consumers. Spanish-language media is one obvious outlet: The audience for programming from Univision, the biggest Spanish-language media company in the United States—with television, radio, music, and Internet—has ballooned by 44 percent since 2001.

The Target Audience: Promotion and the Buyer Decision Process In establishing a promotional mix, marketers match promotional tools with the five stages in the buyer decision process:

1 The process begins when buyers first recognize the need to make a purchase. At this stage, marketers should make sure that buyers are aware of their products. Advertising and publicity, which can reach many people quickly, are important at this stage.

2 Buyers want to learn about available products, so they search for information to "see what's out there." At this stage, advertising and personal selling are important because both can be used to educate consumers.

3 Buyers like to compare competing products to better understand what features and benefits are available. At this stage, personal selling can be vital. Sales representatives can demonstrate product quality and performance in comparison with competitors' products.

4 Buyers choose products that are a good value and purchase them. At this stage, sales promotion is effective because it can give consumers an incentive to buy. Personal selling can help by bringing products to convenient purchase locations.

5 Buyers evaluate products after the purchase by using them, noting (and remembering) their strengths and deficiencies. At this stage, advertising, or even personal selling, is sometimes used to remind consumers that they made wise purchases.

Figure 12.5 summarizes the effective promotional tools for each stage of the consumer buying process.

▪▪▪ ADVERTISING PROMOTIONS

Advertising is paid, nonpersonal communication, by which an identified sponsor informs an audience about a product. In 2004, U.S. firms spent $264 billion on advertising— $98 billion of it by just 100 companies.[8] Let's take a look at the different types of advertising media, noting some of the advantages and limitations of each.

ADVERTISING promotional tool consisting of paid, nonpersonal communication used by an identified sponsor to inform an audience about a product

Advertising Media Consumers tend to ignore the bulk of advertising messages that bombard them; they pay attention to what interests them. Marketers must find out who their customers are, which media they pay attention to, what messages appeal to them,

Figure 12.5 The Consumer Buying Process and the Promotional Mix

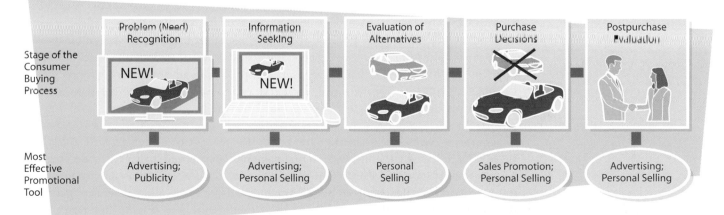

| Stage of the Consumer Buying Process | Problem (Need) Recognition | Information Seeking | Evaluation of Alternatives | Purchase Decisions | Postpurchase Evaluation |
| Most Effective Promotional Tool | Advertising; Publicity | Advertising; Personal Selling | Personal Selling | Sales Promotion; Personal Selling | Advertising; Personal Selling |

Figure 12.6
Top 10 Network TV Advertisers

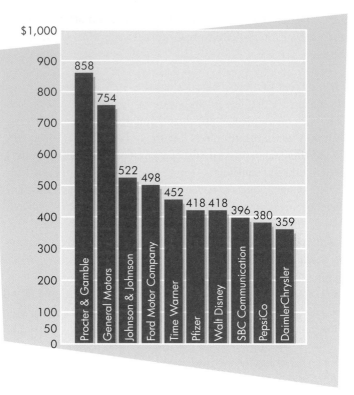

and how to get their attention. Thus, marketers use several different **advertising media**—specific communication devices for carrying a seller's message to potential customers—each having its advantages and drawbacks. The combination of media through which a company advertises is called its **media mix**.

Television With 26 percent of all advertising outlays, television is the most widely used medium. Figure 12.6 shows U.S. network-TV advertising expenditures for top-spending firms.[9] Information on viewer demographics for particular programs allows advertisers to use sight, sound, and motion for aiming their commercials at target audiences. Although television reaches more people than any other medium, the brevity of TV ads makes it a poor medium for educating viewers, and TV is also the most expensive medium. For example, companies such as Pepsi, Anheuser-Busch, FedEx, and Mastercard paid an average of $2.5 million for 30-second spots during Super Bowl XL.[10]

Direct Mail Direct-mail advertisements, which account for 20 percent of all advertising outlays, involve printed ads mailed directly to consumers' homes or places of business.[11] Direct mail allows a seller to select its audience and personalize its message. Although many people discard junk mail, advertisers can predict in advance how many recipients will take a mailing seriously. Moreover, these recipients display stronger-than-average interest in an advertised product and are more likely than most to buy it.

Newspapers Newspapers account for about 18 percent of all advertising outlays.[12] Because each local market has at least one daily newspaper, newspapers provide excellent coverage, reaching more than 200 million U.S. adults daily. Newspaper ads are flexible—they can easily be changed from day to day. By the same token, newspapers are generally thrown out after one day, and because their readership is so broad, they don't allow advertisers to target audiences very well.

Magazines Magazine ads account for roughly 12 percent of all advertising.[13] The huge variety of magazines provides a high level of ready market segmentation. With plenty of space for detailed information, magazines allow attractive photographs and artwork. Because magazines have long lives and tend to be passed around, magazine ads over time get increased exposure. They must, however, be submitted well in advance, and there is rarely a guarantee of where an ad will appear in a magazine.

Radio About 7 percent of all advertising outlays go to radio.[14] Over 227 million people—or 96 percent of all persons aged 12 and older in the United States—listen to the radio each day, and radio ads are inexpensive. For example, a small business in a Midwestern town of 100,000 people pays about $20 for a 30-second local radio spot. (A television spot costs over $250.) Because stations are usually segmented into categories, such as rap, country, jazz, talk, or news, audiences are largely segmented. Unfortunately, radio ads, like TV ads, go by quickly, and people tend to use the radio as background noise while doing other things.

Internet Although Internet advertising has great potential, many marketers recognize its limitations. In particular, consumers don't want to wade through Web pages cluttered with distracting graphics and pop-ups. Some experts contend that most commercial ads on the Internet are never read by anyone, but Internet advertising accounts for about 3 percent of U.S. ad expenditures.[15] The Internet's capability for targeted advertising is especially appealing because, unlike other media, advertisers can measure the success of messages: Electronic tracking counts how many people respond to each ad and identifies which ads generate more purchases, what sales margins result from each sale, and which ads attract the most attention from target audiences.

Outdoor Outdoor advertising—billboards, signs, and ads on buses, street furniture, taxis, stadiums, and subways—makes up about 2 percent of all advertising, but it's growing faster—at 8 percent per year—than newspapers, magazines, and television.[16] These ads are inexpensive, face little competition for consumers' attention, and provide high repeat exposure. Once regarded as visually inferior to other media, advances in graphics—with animation, dynamic images, and vibrant colors—have fueled the revival in spending. On the downside, outdoor ads can present only limited information, and advertisers have little control over audiences.

Other A combination of other media, including catalogs, sidewalk handouts, skywriting, telephone calls, special events, movies, and door-to-door communication, make up the remaining 12 percent of all U.S. advertising.[17]

■■■ PERSONAL SELLING

In the oldest form of sales, **personal selling**, a salesperson communicates one-on-one with potential customers to identify their needs and align them with the seller's products. In our opening case, Reuben Harley invested a lot of time getting acquainted with potential customers—entertainment personalities—by going uninvited to parties and forming social relationships. Thereafter, he made sure they noticed the eye-catching throwback jerseys. As with all personal selling, Reuben Harley's presence lent credibility to the product because it allowed buyers to interact with and ask questions of the seller. Because presentations are generally made to only one or two individuals at a time, personal selling is the most expensive form of promotion per contact.

PERSONAL SELLING
promotional tool in which a salesperson communicates one-on-one with potential customers

ORDER PROCESSING personal selling task in which salespeople receive orders and see to their handling and delivery

CREATIVE SELLING personal selling task in which salespeople try to persuade buyers to purchase products by providing information about their benefits

MISSIONARY SELLING personal selling task in which salespeople promote their firms and products rather than try to close sales

Personal Selling Tasks An important aspect of sales force management is developing salespeople for performing three basic tasks of personal selling. In **order processing**, a salesperson receives an order and sees to its handling and delivery. Route salespeople, who call on regular customers to check inventories, are often order processors. With the customer's consent, they may decide on the sizes of re-orders, fill them directly from their trucks, and even stock shelves. In other situations, however, when potential customers are not aware that they need or want a product, **creative selling** can help to persuade buyers to purchase by providing information and demonstrating the product's benefits. Creative selling is crucial for industrial products and high-priced consumer products, such as cafeteria-management services and cars, for which buyers comparison shop.

Finally, a salesperson may use **missionary selling** to promote a company and its products rather than simply to close a sale. For example, when drug company representatives promote drugs to doctors, the salesperson is not trying to sell pharmaceuticals to the physician but is making the doctor aware of the company and its products. If missionary selling is successful, the doctor will remember and recommend the company's products to others.

Depending on the product and company, sales jobs usually require individuals to perform all three tasks—order processing, creative selling, and missionary selling—to some degree.

■■■ ■ SALES PROMOTIONS

SALES PROMOTION short-term promotional activity designed to encourage consumer buying, industrial sales, or cooperation from distributors

Sales promotions are short-term promotional activities designed to encourage consumer buying, industrial sales, or cooperation from distributors. They are important because they increase the likelihood that buyers will try products. They also enhance product recognition and can increase purchase size and sales revenues.

COUPON sales promotion technique in which a certificate is issued entitling the buyer to a reduced price

PREMIUM sales promotion technique in which offers of free or reduced-price items are used to stimulate purchases

POINT-OF-SALE (POS) DISPLAY sales promotion technique in which product displays are located in certain areas to stimulate purchase or to provide information on a product

TRADE SHOW sales promotion technique in which various members of an industry gather to display, demonstrate, and sell products

Types of Sales Promotions Most consumers have taken part in a variety of sales promotions such as free *samples* (giveaways) that let customers try products without risk. When you use a certificate entitling you to savings off regular prices, you are participating in a **coupon** promotion. It may be used to encourage customers to try new products, to lure customers away from competitors, or to induce customers to buy more of a product. **Premiums** are free or reduced-price items, such as pencils, coffee mugs, and six-month low-interest credit cards, given to consumers in return for buying a specified product. *Contests* can boost sales by rewarding high-producing distributors and sales representatives with vacation trips to Hawaii or Paris. Consumers, too, may win prizes by entering their cats in the Purina Cat Chow calendar contest, for example, by submitting entry blanks from the backs of cat food packages.

To grab customers' attention as they move through stores, companies use **point-of-sale (POS) displays**. Located at the ends of aisles or near checkout counters, POS displays make it easier for customers to find products and easier for sellers to eliminate competitors from consideration. In addition to physical goods, POS pedestals also provide services, namely information for consumers. Bank lobbies and physicians waiting rooms, for example, have computer-interactive kiosks inviting clients to learn more about bank products and educational information about available treatments on consumer-friendly touch-screen displays. For B2B promotions, industries sponsor **trade shows** where companies rent booths to display and demonstrate products to customers who have a special interest or who are ready to buy.

entrepreneurship and new ventures

Capitalizing on the VirTus of Experience

Marian Marchese didn't start off planning to be in business for herself. As vice president of account services at an ad agency, she discovered that her boss had a peculiar way of holding down costs: When people rose to certain salary levels, he fired them and replaced them with younger employees. That was why one day Marchese, who had just scraped together the down payment on a house, found herself jobless on the streets of Philadelphia.

"I resolved at that moment," she recalls, "that I would never allow anyone to do this to me again." So she took a chance and started her own ad agency, which later became part of a successful partnership. In 1995, Marchese and Joe Barone, convinced that the Internet was transforming the advertising and marketing industries, founded a new partnership—an Internet company called VirTu—that was more profitable within eight months than the ad agency had been in 11 years.

Today, VirTu—a strategic marketing company—shows clients how to combine traditional or offline services (such as direct-response retailing) and interactive or online services (such as Web site development and digital technologies) for conducting both B2B and B2C marketing activities. Starting with strategic planning, VirTu helps clients in developing multi-channel marketing systems and methods for online and offline branding. Then, it gives them help in designing and programming processes for reaching their business goals. VirTu's three competencies—marketing, creative communications design, and technology—provide each client company with a unified approach to reaching its customers.

In applying past experiences to new ideas, Marchese and Barone not only recognized the possibilities for a new venture but also went on to implement those ideas. Right now, VirTu's possibilities include going public and joining forces with other companies that are interested in the secrets to VirTu's success.

■ ■ ■ PUBLICITY AND PUBLIC RELATIONS

Publicity is information about a company, a product, or an event transmitted by the general mass media to attract public attention. To the delight of marketers with tight budgets, publicity is free. On the downside, however, media reporters and writers, not marketers, usually have control over publicity, and because it is presented in a news format, consumers often regard it as objective and credible. In 2005, for example, U.S. fast-food patrons were horrified when a customer said she found a human fingertip in a bowl of Wendy's chili. The spreading news—a publicity nightmare—had an immediate, bruising effect on the food-chain's reputation. The financial damage? About $15 million in lost sales in six weeks forced layoffs and reduced hours.[18]

In contrast to publicity, **public relations** is company-influenced information that seeks either to build good relations with the public or to deal with unfavorable events. A firm will try to establish goodwill with customers (and potential customers) by performing and publicizing its public-service activities. In the Wendy's case, CEO Jack Schuessler's public relations response was decisive and focused: First-and-foremost, protect the brand and tell the truth. That meant there would be no payoff or settlement to keep it out of the news. Instead, Wendy's enlisted cooperation with the health department and police, did visual inspections, polygraphed employees, publicly announced a hotline for tips, and offered a reward for information, all leading to the conclusion that the reported episode was a hoax. Energetic public relations was an effective promotional tool for clearing the Wendy's name and preserving the company's reputation.[19]

PUBLICITY promotional tool in which information about a company, a product, or an event is transmitted by the general mass media to attract public attention

PUBLIC RELATIONS company-influenced information directed at building goodwill with the public or dealing with unfavorable events

My first response was "I cannot believe it. This is a hoax. And we have to get to the bottom of it. We have to protect the brand; tell the truth."

—Jack Schuessler, CEO of Wendy's International, commenting on the notorious fingertip incident, which turned out to be a hoax

SELF-CHECK QUESTIONS 7–9

You should now be able to answer Self-Check Questions 7–9.*

7 Multiple Choice In regard to marketing promotions, all of the following are correct **except**:

(a) the ultimate objective of any promotion is to establish an easily identifiable product image

(b) the promotional mix can provide value-added benefits

(c) the choice of a promotional mix should consider the target audience

(d) personal selling can be effective when potential buyers have questions about the seller's products

8 Multiple Choice Which of the following is **true** about advertising media?

(a) TV is the most-used medium and reaches the most people

(b) one benefit of newspaper ads is that they have long lives

(c) advertisers who want fast, immediate impact prefer magazines

(d) the success of an Internet ad cannot be measured as easily as the success of ads in other media

9 Multiple Choice Suppose your chief personal selling strategy is to persuade buyers that there are benefits to your company's product, especially buyers who are unfamiliar with its features and uses. The appropriate name for this type of selling is:

(a) order extraction

(b) missionary selling

(c) prospecting

(d) creative selling

*Answers to Self-Check Questions 7–9 can be found on p. 566.

CONTINUED FROM PAGE 364

IS NOSTALGIA JUST A FAD?

Reuben Harley was 17 years old in 1991 when he bought his first throwback—a 1983 Andre Thornton Cleveland Indians jersey—at Mitchell & Ness (M&N), a tiny retail shop in city-center Philadelphia. In 2001, while watching an Outcast music video, Harley realized he owned (bought over the years on layaway) the same throwback jerseys the performers were wearing. Soon thereafter, an Oprah Winfrey TV show about "following your dreams" inspired him to pursue selling, not just buying, vintage jerseys. Today, after joining Peter Capolino, M&N's jerseys are wholesaled to some 220 retailers around the country.

The potential market as seen by Harley was worlds apart from Capolino's pre-2001 vision for M&N: Harley envisioned an urban, largely African American youth segment that idolizes basketball players with baggy shorts and bigger, brightly colored jerseys with striking patterns in double-knits and mesh. Capolino, in contrast, was aiming for middle-aged collectors of sports items, mostly from its retro-baseball line with body-hugging gray flannels. At an age in life when established businesspeople might take a safer path, Capolino made a gutsy call in deciding to go along with Harley. "It's an all-sport thing, but guys identify with basketball players more than anybody," says Harley. Now basketball, instead of baseball, accounts for the largest share of M&N's business.

Because it holds exclusive licenses from the National Football League, Major League Baseball, the National Basketball Association, and the National Hockey League, M&N can reproduce authentic jerseys that have been out of circulation for at least five years. Therein, according to Harley, lies the staying power of M&N's throwbacks: "This isn't a fad. These uniforms are the history of sports. Styles come and go, but you can't change the '79 Magic Johnson jersey." That's why they captured an enthusiastic audience, even at such hefty prices as $325 for a 1979 Willie Stargell Pirates, $450 for the 1963 Lance Alworth Chargers, $300 for the 1983–1984 Sidney Moncrief Bucks, and $250 for the 1966–1967 Dave Bing Pistons.

QUESTIONS FOR DISCUSSION

1 Which promotional tools are most prominent in Reuben Harley's marketing strategy for M&N's products?
2 In what ways do you believe M&N's pre-2001 promotional strategy differs from its current promotional strategy?
3 What kinds of advertising promotions, if any, are being used for the M&N marketing strategy? Would you advise using a different mix of advertising?
4 What kind of promotional mix(es) would you recommend as most effective for reaching M&N's target market(s)?
5 Why is personal selling so effective for M&N? What factors have led to its effectiveness?

1 Identify the various pricing objectives that govern pricing decisions and describe the price-setting tools used in making these decisions.

Two major pricing objectives are (1) *Pricing to maximize profits*: With prices set too low, the seller misses the chance to make additional profits on each of the many units sold. With prices set too high, a larger profit will be made on each unit, but fewer units will be sold. (2) *Market share objectives*: Pricing is used for establishing market share. The seller is willing to accept minimal profits, even losses, to get buyers to try products. Two basic tools are (1) *Cost-oriented pricing* begins by determining total costs for making products available to shoppers, then a figure for profit is added in to arrive at a selling price. (2) *Breakeven analysis* assesses total costs versus revenues for various sales volumes. It shows, at each possible sales volume, the amount of loss or profit for any chosen sales price. It also shows the *breakeven point*: the number of sales units for total revenue to equal total costs.

2 Discuss pricing strategies that can be used for different competitive situations and identify the pricing tactics that can be used for setting prices.

Pricing for existing products can be set above, at, or below market prices for similar products. High pricing is often interpreted as meaning higher quality and prestige, while low pricing may attract greater sales volume. Strategies for new products include *price skimming*—setting an initially high price to cover costs and generate a profit—and *penetration pricing*—setting a low price to establish a new product in the market. Strategies for e-businesses include dynamic versus fixed pricing. *Dynamic pricing* establishes individual prices by real-time interaction between the seller and each customer on the Internet. *Fixed pricing* is the traditional one-price-for-all arrangement.

Three tactics are often used for setting prices: (1) With *price lining*, any product category (such as lady's shoes) will be set at three or four price levels, and all shoes will be priced at one of those levels. (2) *Psychological pricing* acknowledges that customers are not completely rational when making buying decisions, as with *odd-even pricing* where customers regard prices such as $10 as being significantly higher than $9.95. (3) *Discount pricing* uses price reductions to stimulate sales.

3 Explain the meaning of *distribution mix* and identify the different channels of distribution.

The combination of distribution channels for getting products to end users—consumers and industrial buyers—is the *distribution mix*. *Intermediaries* help to distribute a producer's goods by moving them from sellers to customers: *Wholesalers* sell products to other businesses, which resell them to final users. *Retailers*, *sales agents*, and *brokers* sell products directly to end users. In the simplest of four distribution channels, the producer sells directly to users. Channel 2 includes a retailer, Channel 3 involves both a retailer and a wholesaler, and Channel 4 includes an agent or broker. *p 370*

4 Describe the role of wholesalers and explain the different types of retailing.

Wholesalers provide a variety of services—delivery, credit arrangements, and product information—to buyers of products for resale or business use. In buying and reselling an assortment of products, wholesalers provide storage, marketing advice, and assist customers by marking prices and setting up displays. *Retail stores* range from broad product-line department stores and supermarkets, to small specialty stores for specific market segments seeking narrow product lines. With retail stores, there is always an intermediary that moves products from producers to users. Various kinds of nonstore retailing include *direct-response retailing*, *mail order* (or *catalog marketing*), *telemarketing*, and *direct selling*. Many nonstore retailers do not use intermediaries but, instead, use direct-to-consumer contact by the producer.

5 Describe the role of e-intermediaries and explain how they add value for advertisers and consumers on the Internet.

E-intermediaries are Internet-based channel members who perform one or both of two functions: (1) They collect information about sellers and present it to consumers and (2) they help deliver Internet products to buyers. There are three types of e-intermediaries: (1) *Syndicated selling* occurs when a Web site offers other Web sites a commission for referring customers. (2) *Shopping agents* (*e-agents*) help Internet consumers by gathering and sorting information (such as comparison prices and product features) for making purchases. They add value for sellers by listing sellers' Web addresses for consumers. (3) *Electronic retailers* use the Internet to interact with customers to inform, sell to, and distribute products to them. *E-catalogs* are electronic displays that give instant worldwide access to pages of product information. *Electronic storefronts* and *cybermalls* provide collections of virtual storefronts at which Internet shoppers collect information about products, place orders, and pay for purchases.

6 **Define *physical distribution* and describe the major activities in the physical distribution process.**

Physical distribution is all activities needed to move products from producers to consumers, making them available when and where customers want, at reasonable cost. Physical distribution activities include providing customer services, warehousing, and transportation of products. *Warehouses* provide storage for products, whereas *transportation operations* physically move products from suppliers to customers. Trucks, railroads, planes, water carriers (boats and barges), and pipelines are the major transportation modes used in the distribution process.

7 **Identify the important objectives of promotion, discuss the considerations in selecting a promotional mix, and discuss advertising promotions.**

Although the ultimate goal of *promotion* is to increase sales, other goals include communicating information, positioning a product, adding value, and controlling sales volume. In deciding on the appropriate *promotional mix*—the best combination of promotional tools (e.g., advertising, personal selling, public relations)—marketers must consider the good or service being offered, characteristics of the target audience, the buyer's decision process, and the promotional mix budget. *Advertising* is paid, nonpersonal communication, by which an identified sponsor informs an audience about a product. Marketers use several different *advertising media*—specific communication devices for carrying a seller's message to potential customers—each having its advantages and drawbacks. The combination of media through which a company advertises is called its *media mix*.

8 **Outline the tasks involved in personal selling, describe the various types of sales promotions, and distinguish between publicity and public relations.**

Personal selling tasks include *order processing*, *creative selling*, and *missionary selling*. Sales promotions include *point-of-sale* (*POS*) displays to attract consumer attention, help them find products in stores, and provide product information. Other sales promotions give purchasing incentives, such as *samples* (customers can try products without having to buy them), *coupons* (a certificate for price reduction), and *premiums* (free or reduced-price rewards for buying products). At *trade shows*, B2B sellers rent booths to display products to industrial customers. *Contests* intend to stimulate sales, with prizes to high-producing intermediaries and consumers who use the seller's products.

Publicity is information about a company, a product, or an event transmitted by the general mass media to attract public attention. Control of the message's content is determined by outside writers and reporters. In contrast to publicity, *public relations* is company-influenced information that seeks to either build good relations with the public or to deal with unfavorable events.

KEY TERMS

advertising (p. 381)

advertising media (p. 382)

bargain retailer (p. 373)

breakeven analysis (p. 366)

breakeven point (p. 367)

broker (p. 371)

catalog showroom (p. 373)

convenience store (p. 373)

cost-oriented pricing (p. 366)

coupon (p. 384)

creative selling (p. 384)

cybermall (p. 376)

department store (p. 373)

direct channel (p. 370)

direct selling (p. 374)

direct-response retailing (p. 374)

discount (p. 369)

discount house (p. 373)

distribution channel (p. 370)

distribution mix (p. 370)

e-catalog (p. 375)

e-intermediary (p. 375)

electronic retailing (p. 375)

electronic storefront (p. 376)

factory outlet (p. 373)

fixed cost (p. 366)

interactive marketing (p. 376)

intermediary (p. 370)

mail order (catalog
    marketing) (p. 374)

market share (p. 365)

markup (p. 366)

media mix (p. 382)

missionary selling (p. 384)

odd-even pricing (p. 369)

order fulfillment (p. 378)

order processing (p. 384)

penetration pricing (p. 368)

personal selling (p. 383)

physical distribution (p. 377)

point-of-sale (POS)
    display (p. 384)

positioning (p. 380)

premium (p. 384)

price lining (p.369)

price skimming (p. 368)

pricing (p. 364)

pricing objectives (p. 364)

private warehouse (p. 377)

promotion (p. 380)

promotional mix (p. 380)

psychological pricing (p. 369)

public relations (p. 385)

public warehouse (p. 377)

publicity (p. 385)

retailer (p. 370)

sales agent (p. 371)

sales promotion (p. 384)

shopping agent (e-agent) (p. 375)

specialty store (p. 373)

supermarket (p. 373)

syndicated selling (p. 375)

telemarketing (p. 374)

trade show (p. 384)

variable cost (p. 366)

video marketing (p. 376)

warehousing (p. 377)

wholesale club (p. 373)

wholesaler (p. 370)

QUESTIONS AND EXERCISES

Questions for Review

1 How does breakeven analysis help managers measure the potential impact of prices?

2 Discuss the goal of price skimming and penetration pricing.

3 Identify the channels of distribution. In what key ways do they differ from one another?

4 Explain how e-agents or brokers differ from traditional agents and brokers.

5 Select four advertising media and compare the advantages and disadvantages of each.

Questions for Analysis

6 Suppose that a small publisher selling to book distributors has fixed operating costs of $600,000 each year and variable costs of $3.00 per book. How many books must the firm sell to break even if the selling price is $6.00?

7 Choose two advertising campaigns: one that you think is effective and one that you think is ineffective. What makes one campaign better than the other?

8 Give examples of two products that typify the products sold to shoppers through each form of nonstore retailing. Explain why different products are best suited to each form of nonstore retailing.

Application Exercises

9 Select a product and analyze pricing objectives for it. What information would you want if you were to adopt a profit-maximizing objective? A market-share objective?

10 Select a product and identify the media used in its promotion. On the whole, do you think the campaign is effective? Why or why not?

GREETING START-UP DECISIONS

Goal

To encourage you to analyze the potential usefulness of two promotional methods—personal selling and direct mail—for a start-up greeting card company.

Background Information

You are the marketing adviser for a local start-up company that makes and sells specialty greeting cards in a city of 400,000. Last year's sales totaled 14,000 cards, including personalized holiday cards, birthday cards, and special-events cards for individuals. Although revenues increased last year, you see a way of further boosting sales by expanding into card shops, grocery stores, and gift shops. You see two alternatives for entering these outlets:

1 Use direct mail to reach more individual customers for specialty cards.

2 Use personal selling to gain display space in retail stores.

Your challenge is to convince the owner of the start-up company which alternative is the more financially sound decision.

Method

Step 1

Get together with four or five classmates to research the two kinds of product segments: personalized cards and retail store cards. Find out which of the two kinds of marketing promotions will be more effective for each of the two segments. What will be the reaction to each method of customers, retailers, and card-company owners?

Step 2

Draft a proposal to the company owner. Leaving budget and production details to other staffers, list as many reasons as possible for adopting direct mail. Then, list as many reasons as possible for adopting personal selling. Defend each reason. Consider the following reasons in your argument:

■ **Competitive environment.** Analyze the impact of other card suppliers that offer personalized cards and cards for sale in retail stores.

■ **Expectations of target markets.** Who buys personalized cards and who buys ready-made cards from retail stores?

■ **Overall cost of the promotional effort.** Which method, direct mail or personal selling, will be more costly?

■ **Marketing effectiveness.** Which promotional method will result in greater consumer response?

FOLLOW-UP QUESTIONS

1 Why do you think some buyers want personalized cards? Why do some consumers want ready-made cards from retail stores?

2 Today's computer operating systems provide easy access to software for designing and making cards on home PCs. How does the availability of this product affect your recommendation?

3 What was your most convincing argument for using direct mail? For using personal selling?

4 Can a start-up company compete in retail stores against industry giants, such as Hallmark and American Greetings?

THE CHAIN OF RESPONSIBILITY

The Situation

Because several stages are involved when distribution chains move products from supply sources to end consumers, the process offers ample opportunity for ethical issues to arise. This exercise encourages you to examine some of the ethical issues that can emerge during transactions among suppliers and customers.

The Dilemma

A customer bought an expensive wedding gift at a local store and asked that it be shipped to the bride in another state. Several weeks after the wedding, the customer contacted the bride, who had not confirmed the arrival of the gift. It hadn't arrived. Charging that the merchandise had not been delivered, the customer requested a refund from the retailer. The store manager uncovered the following facts:

- All shipments from the store are handled by a well-known national delivery firm.
- The delivery firm verified that the package had been delivered to the designated address two days after the sale.

- Normally, the delivery firm does not obtain recipient signatures; deliveries are made to the address of record, regardless of the name on the package.

The gift giver argued that even though the package had been delivered to the right address, it had not been delivered to the named recipient. It turns out that, unbeknownst to the gift giver, the bride had moved. It stood to reason, then, that the gift was in the hands of the new occupant at the bride's former address. The manager informed the gift giver that the store had fulfilled its obligation. The cause of the problem, she explained, was the incorrect address given by the customer. She refused to refund the customer's money and suggested that the customer might want to recover the gift by contacting the stranger who received it at the bride's old address.

QUESTIONS TO ADDRESS

1 What are the responsibilities of each party—the customer, the store, the delivery firm—in this situation?

2 From an ethical standpoint, in what ways is the store manager's action right? In what ways is it wrong?

3 If you were appointed to settle this matter, what actions would you take?

A BIG PUSH FOR PUBLICITY

The Situation

J Company is known as a "good citizen" and prides itself on publicity it receives from sponsoring civic programs and other community projects. J Company's executive vice president, Ms. Q, has just been named chairperson of annual fundraising for MAS, a large coalition of community services that depend on voluntary donations. In the highly visible chairperson's role, Ms. Q has organized the support of officials at other firms to ensure that the fundraising target is met or surpassed.

The Dilemma

Ms. Q began a J Company meeting of 30 department managers to appeal for 100 percent employee participation in MAS giving in the fundraising drive: "We will have 100 percent participation here." As follow-up the week before the drive officially started, Ms. Q met with each manager, saying: "I expect you to give your fair share and for you to ensure that all your employees do likewise. I don't care what it takes, just do it. Make it clear that employees will at least donate cash. Even better, get them to sign up for weekly payroll deductions to the MAS fund because it nets more money than one-time cash donations."

An hour after meeting with Ms. Q, Nathan Smith was both surprised and confused. As a newly appointed department manager, he was unsure how to go about soliciting donations from his 25 employees. Remembering Ms. Q's comment, "I don't care what it takes, just do it," Nathan wondered what to do if someone did not give. Personally, too, he was feeling uneasy. How much should he give? With his family's pressing financial needs, he would rather not give money to MAS. He began to wonder if his donation to MAS would affect his career at J Company.

Team Activity

Assemble a group of four to five students and assign each group member to one of the following roles:

- Nathan Smith (employee)
- Ms. Q (employer)
- Director of MAS (customer)
- J Company stockholder (investor)
- J Company CEO (use this role only if your group has at least five members)

ACTION STEPS

1 Before hearing any of your group's comments, and from the perspective of your assigned role, do you think there are any *ethical issues* with J Company's fundraising program? If so, write them down.

2 Before hearing any of your group's comments, and from the perspective of your assigned role, are any *problems* likely to arise from J Company's fundraising program? If so, write them down.

3 Together with your group, share the ethical issues you identified. Then, share the potential problems you listed. Did the different roles you were assigned result in different ethical issues and problems?

4 For the various ethical issues that were identified, decide as a group which one is the most important for J Company to resolve. Likewise, for potential problems that were identified, which is the most important one for J Company?

5 From an ethical standpoint, what does your group recommend be done to resolve the most important ethical issue? How should the most important problem be resolved? Identify the advantages and drawbacks of your recommendations.

PART 4: PRINCIPLES OF MARKETING

Goal of the Exercise

So far, your business has an identity, you've described the factors that will affect your business, and you've examined your employees, the jobs they'll be performing, and the ways in which you can motivate them. Part 4 of the business plan project asks you to think about marketing's Four *Ps*—*product*, *price*, *place (distribution)*, and *promotion*—and how they apply to your business. You'll also examine how you might target your marketing toward a certain group of consumers.

Exercise Background: Part 4 of the Business Plan

In Part 1, you briefly described what your business will do. The first step in Part 4 of the plan is to more fully describe the product (good or service) you are planning to sell. Once you have a clear picture of the product, you'll need to describe how this product will "stand out" in the marketplace—that is, how will it differentiate itself from other products?

In Part 1, you also briefly described who your customers would be. The first step in Part 4 of the plan is to describe your ideal buyer, or target market, in more detail, listing their income level, educational level, lifestyle, age, and so forth. This part of the business plan project also asks you to discuss the price of your products, as well as where the buyer can find your product.

Finally, you'll examine how your business will get the attention and interest of the buyer through its *promotional mix*—advertising, personal selling, sales promotions, and publicity and public relations.

This part of the business plan encourages you to be creative. Have fun! Provide as many details as you possibly can, as this reflects an understanding of your product and your buyer. Marketing is all about finding a need and filling it. Does your product fill a need in the marketplace?

Your Assignment

Step 1

Open the saved *Business Plan* file you began working on in Parts 1 to 3.

Step 2

For the purposes of this assignment, you will answer the following questions in "Part 4: Principles of Marketing:"

1. Describe your target market in terms of age, education level, income, and other demographic variables.
   Hint: Refer to Chapter 11 for more information on the aspects of target marketing and market segmentation that you may want to consider. Be as detailed as possible about who you think your customers will be.

2. Describe the features and benefits of your product or service.
   Hint: As you learned in Chapter 11 a product is a bundle of attributes—features and benefits. What features does your product have—what does it look like and what does it do? How will the product benefit the buyer?

3. How will you make your product stand out in the crowd?
   Hint: There are many ways to stand out in the crowd, such as a unique product, outstanding service, or a great location. What makes your great idea special? Does it fill an unmet need in the marketplace? How will you differentiate your product to make sure that it succeeds?

4. What pricing strategy will you choose for your product, and what are the reasons for this strategy?
   Hint: Refer to this chapter for more information on pricing strategies and tactics. Since your business is new, so is the product. Therefore, you probably want to choose between price skimming and penetration pricing. Which will you choose, and why?

5. Where will customers find your product or service? (That is, what issues of the distribution mix should you consider?)
   Hint: If your business does not sell its product directly to consumers, what types of retail stores will sell your product? If your product will be sold to another business, which channel of distribution will you use? Refer to this chapter for more information on aspects of distribution you may want to consider.

6. How will you advertise to your target market? Why have you chosen these forms of advertisement?
   Hint: Marketers use several different advertising media—specific communication devices for carrying a seller's message to potential customers—each having its advantages and drawbacks. Refer to this chapter, for a discussion of the types of advertising media you may wish to consider here.

7. What other methods of promotion will you use, and why?
   Hint: There's more to promotion than simple advertising. Other methods include personal selling, sales promotions, and publicity and public relations. Refer to the discussion of promotion in this chapter for ideas on how to promote your product that go beyond just advertising.

Note: Once you have answered the questions, save your Word document. You'll be answering additional questions in later chapters.

THROUGH THE GRAPEVINE: CLOS DU BOIS WINERY

Learning Objectives

The purpose of this video is to help you:

1 Understand how a company works with wholesalers and retailers to make its products available to consumers.
2 Discuss the factors that affect a company's distribution strategy.
3 Consider physical distribution goals and challenges.

Synopsis

Riding a tidal wave of U.S. consumer interest in California wines, Clos du Bois Winery sells its wines from coast to coast. The company now produces and ships more than one million cases of wine every year, although less than 20 percent is sold in California. The winery works through a network of statewide and regional distributors that sell to retailers and restaurants which, in turn, serve the wine to consumers. For efficient order fulfillment and inventory management, Clos du Bois ships from a central warehouse to more than 300 wholesaler warehouses around the United States. To ensure that quality is not compromised by temperature extremes, the company also pays close attention to the details of physical distribution. Now, the company is tapping the infrastructure of parent company Allied Domecq to arrange for wider distribution in Europe.

DISCUSSION QUESTIONS

1 **For analysis**: Why does Clos du Bois sell through wholesalers rather than sell to retailers and restaurants?
2 **For analysis**: How does the U.S. pattern of table wine consumption affect the winery's domestic distribution strategy?
3 **For application**: What might Clos du Bois do when its supply of a certain vintage is quite limited?
4 **For application**: What effect does the cost of storing and shipping Clos du Bois wine have on the prices paid by retailers and, ultimately, consumers?
5 **For debate**: Given its long-term relationships with established wholesalers, should Clos du Bois lobby against direct sales of wine to U.S. consumers through Internet channels? Support your position.

Online Exploration

Visit the Web site of the Clos du Bois Winery at (www.closdubois.com) and (if you are of legal drinking age in your state) enter and read what the company says about its wines, winery, and wine club. Also, follow the link to explore the trade site and find out where Clos du Bois wines are sold. Considering the winery's dependence on distributors, why would it invest so heavily in a consumer-oriented Web site? What channel conflict might be caused by this site? If you cannot legally enter the winery's Web site, use your favorite search engine (such as Google) to see whether other online retailers are selling this wine. If so, why would Clos du Bois make its wine available through these intermediaries?

PART V: MANAGING INFORMATION

After reading this chapter, you should be able to:

1. Discuss the impacts information technology has had on the business world.

2. Identify the IT resources businesses have at their disposal and how these resources are used.

3. Describe the role of information systems, the different types of information systems, and how businesses use such systems.

4. Identify the threats and risks information technology poses on businesses.

5. Describe the ways in which businesses protect themselves from the threats and risks information technology poses.

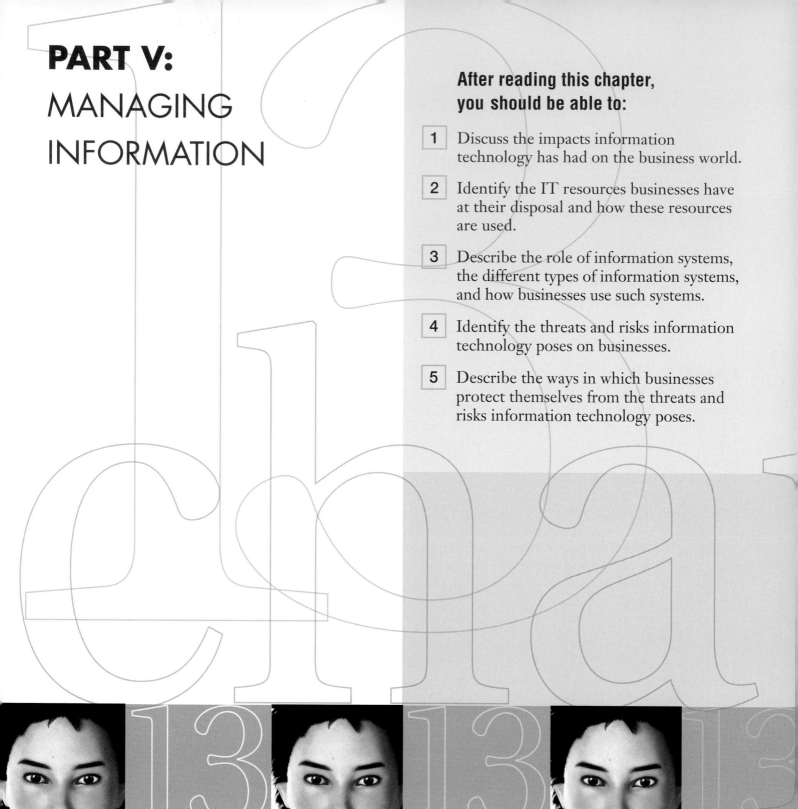

LETTING TECHNOLOGY BE YOUR GUIDE

Have you ever seen an ATM—an automated teller machine—that talked to you when you made a deposit, answering any questions you might have? Or what about an ATM that lets you deposit cash and checks without an envelope? NCR Corporation, the world's largest maker of ATMs, is hoping that some day you will.

INFORMATION TECHNOLOGY FOR BUSINESS

Headed by Mark Hurd, NCR is a leading supplier of information technology products—data warehousing and data mining systems, e-business networks, and electronic payment systems—that it sells to other businesses. Hurd has aspirations especially of becoming the leading developer of hi-tech ATMs and point-of-sale (POS) machines for the soon-to-be self-service economy. "There will be a continual drive to get consumers to do more of the work and enjoy it—at places where we shop," says Hurd, whose futuristic ambitions are unfolding in Dundee, Scotland, the site of NCR's research center for ATMs of the future. At the center, visitors get a smiling welcome from Maddy—NCR's cheery electronic greeter—followed by demonstrations of the latest ATM technology. Speaking in any language, Maddy shows visitors the newest in solar-power POS and ATM machines, anti-theft protection devices that stain money with ink if a machine is violated, radio-frequency identification devices that enable you to load money electronically into your cell phone, and machines that can even accept stacks of checks and cash without envelopes.

The most imaginative NCR innovation, perhaps, is Maddy herself. She's what is called an "avatar"—a computer-generated character driven by NCR's text-to-speech software—that you'll be seeing soon on the screen of your ATM. This virtual human greets customers by name, offers special promotions based on the customer's profile

Getting the right character is vital. Customers have to be comfortable with the image and voice of the character. You have to get the look, the sound, and the feel right.

—Mark Grossi, NCR's chief technology officer, commenting on the development of a human-like, computer-generated character coming soon to your ATM screen

from NCR's data-mining software, then explains how to use the machine. When customers select a self-service transaction, for example, Maddy talks them through the necessary steps. When users want more information, they can call on Maddy for help, right at the ATM. For NCR's technology designers, getting the human touch—without the human—is a challenge. "Getting the right character is vital," says NCR's chief technology officer Mark Grossi. "Customers have to be comfortable with the image and voice of the character. You have to get the look, the sound, and the feel right."

NCR hopes characters like Maddy will be a digital jack-of-all-trades, providing you with everything you need in a self-service mode, where you need it, when you need it—and at the same time reducing expensive human labor costs. ■

Our opening story continues on page 419.

WHAT'S IN IT FOR ME?

NCR's ATMs and POS machines have come a long way from their humble beginnings as cash registers. Facilitating information exchanges, in digital form, between customers and service providers, the machines are prime examples of how firms have to keep up with the pace of technology, or risk perishing. By understanding this chapter's discussion on the impact of technology on business, you'll have a clearer picture of how technology is used by and affects business, and how, as an employee, manager, or consumer, you can use technology to your best advantage.

We'll start this chapter by looking at ways in which technology has changed the business landscape. We'll then turn our attention to the building blocks of technology—the technological resources companies have at their disposal today. Next, we'll look at how companies make use of these resources in information systems, helping them make sense of all the data they collect. Finally, we'll talk about the threats technology poses to businesses as well as the ways in which businesses are protecting themselves from these threats.

IT IMPACTS

INFORMATION TECHNOLOGY (IT) the various appliances and devices for creating, storing, exchanging, and using information in diverse modes, including visual images, voice, multimedia, and business data

No matter where we go, we can't escape the impacts of **information technology (IT)**—the various appliances and devices for creating, storing, exchanging, and using information in diverse modes, including visual images, voice, multimedia, and business data. We see ads all the time for the latest cell phones, iPods, laptops, and Microsoft products, and most of us connect daily to the Internet. E-mail has become a staple in business, and even such traditionally "low-tech" businesses as nail salons and garbage collection companies are becoming dependent on the Internet, computers, and networks. As consumers, we interact with databases every time we withdraw money from an ATM, order food at McDonalds, or check on the status of a package at UPS.com. Technology and its effects are evident everywhere.

The effect IT has had on businesses is immeasurable—in fact, the growth of IT has changed the very structure of business organizations. Its adoption has altered the workforces in many companies, contributed to greater flexibility in dealing with customers, and changed the way that employees interact with each other. **E-commerce** (short for *electronic commerce*)—the use of the Internet and other electronic means for retailing and business-to-business transactions—has created new market relationships around the

E-COMMERCE the use of the Internet and other electronic means for retailing and business-to-business transactions

globe. In this section, we'll look at how businesses are using IT to bolster productivity, improve operations and processes, create new opportunities, and communicate and work in ways not possible before.

■■■ CREATING PORTABLE OFFICES: PROVIDING REMOTE ACCESS TO INSTANT INFORMATION

The packing list for Jodi Randolf's upcoming fishing trip reflects her new outlook on where, when, and how work gets done. It reads, in part, as follows: (1) fly rod, (2) dry-pack food, (3) BlackBerry, (4) tent. Five years earlier, a much longer list included a cell phone, road and area maps, phone directory, appointments calendar, office files, and client project folders, all of which are replaced now by just one item—her BlackBerry—a wireless handheld messaging device that allows her to take the office with her, wherever she goes.

For a project manager like Randolf, the BlackBerry is more than just a cell phone. With its continuous connection, there's no dialing in; incoming e-mail is displayed instantly, at the same moment it arrives on her PC back at the office. Even in the wilderness, Randolf can place phone calls and read new e-mail messages. Along with Internet browsing, there's access to desktop tools—such as an organizer and an address book—for managing work and staying in touch with customers, suppliers, and employees from any location.

Technology such as the mobile messaging capabilities built into devices such as the BlackBerry offer businesses powerful tools that save time and travel expenses. They also mean that a geographic separation between the workplace and headquarters is more common. Employees no longer work only at the office or the factory, nor are all of a company's operations performed at one place. When using such devices, offsite employees have continuous access to information, instead of being forced to be at a desk to access their files and the Internet. Such benefits have attracted more than three million enthusiastic subscribers, making BlackBerry the leader in the handheld wireless industry.[1]

The BlackBerry wireless handheld messaging device allows employees to take the office with them.

ENABLING BETTER SERVICE BY COORDINATING REMOTE DELIVERIES

Meanwhile, with access to the Internet, company activities may be geographically scattered but remain coordinated through a networked system that provides better service for customers. Many businesses, for example, coordinate activities from one centralized location, but their deliveries flow from several remote locations, often at lower cost. When you order furniture—for example, a chair, a sofa, a table, and two lamps—from an Internet storefront, the chair may come from a warehouse in Philadelphia and the lamps from a manufacturer in California; the sofa and table may be shipped direct from different suppliers in North Carolina. Beginning with the customer's order, activities are coordinated through the company's network, as if the whole order were being processed at one place. It avoids the expensive in-between step of first shipping all the items to a central location.

CREATING LEANER, MORE EFFICIENT ORGANIZATIONS

Networks and technology are also leading to leaner companies with fewer employees and simpler structures. Because networks enable firms to maintain information linkages among both employees and customers, more work and customer satisfaction can be accomplished with fewer people. Bank customers can dial into a 24-hour information system and monitor their accounts without employee assistance. Instructions that once were given to assembly workers by supervisors are now delivered to workstations electronically. For example, truck drivers delivering freight used to return to the trucking terminal to receive instructions from supervisors on reloading for the next delivery. Today, one dispatcher using IT has replaced several supervisors. Instructions to the fleet arrive on electronic screens in trucks on the road so drivers know in advance what will be happening next.

ENABLING INCREASED COLLABORATION

Collaboration among internal units and with outside firms is greater when firms use collaboration software and other IT communications devices, which we'll discuss later in this chapter. Companies are learning that complex problems can be solved better through IT-supported collaboration, either with formal teams or spontaneous interaction among people and departments. The design of new products, for example, was once an engineering responsibility. Now it is a shared activity using information from people in marketing, finance, production, engineering, and purchasing who, collectively, determine the best design. For example, when designing its 777 aircraft, Boeing gained collaboration from not just engineers but also from passengers (who wanted electronic outlets to recharge personal electronic devices), cabin crews (who wanted more bathrooms and wider aisles), and air-traffic controllers (who wanted larger, safer airbrakes).

ENABLING GLOBAL EXCHANGE

The global reach of IT is enabling business collaboration on a scale that was unheard of before. Consider Lockheed Martin's gigantic contract for designing the Joint Strike Fighter and supplying thousands of the planes in different versions for the United

States, Britain, Italy, Denmark, Canada, and Norway over the next 20 years. Lockheed can't do the job alone; in just the startup phase, it is collaborating with Britain's BAE Systems along with more than 70 U.S. and 18 international subcontractors at some 190 locations. An Australian manufacturer of aviation communications and a Turkish electronics supplier entered the project in 2005, joining seven other Australian and two other Turkish firms already on board. Over the project's 20-year life, more than 1,500 firms will supply everything from radar systems, to engines, to bolts. Currently, 40,000 remote computers are collaborating on the project using Lockheed's Internet-based system. Web collaboration on a massive scale is essential for coordinating design, testing, and construction while avoiding delays, holding down costs, and maintaining quality.[2]

IMPROVING MANAGEMENT PROCESSES

IT has also changed the nature of the management process. The activities and methods of today's manager differ significantly from those that were common just a few years ago. At one time, upper-level managers didn't concern themselves with all of the detailed information filtering upward from the workplace because it was expensive to gather, slow in coming, and quickly became out of date. Workplace management was delegated to middle and first-line managers.

With databases, specialized software, and networks, however, instantaneous information is accessible and useful to all levels of management. For example, consider *enterprise resource planning (ERP)*: an information system for organizing and managing a firm's activities across product lines, departments, and geographic locations. The ERP stores real-time information on work status and upcoming transactions and notifies employees when action is required if certain schedules are to be met. It coordinates internal operations with activities of outside suppliers and notifies customers of upcoming deliveries and billings. Consequently, more managers use it routinely for planning and controlling operations. Today, a manager at Hershey Foods, for example, uses ERP to check on the current status of any customer order for Kisses or Jolly Ranchers, inspect productivity statistics for each workstation, and analyze the delivery performance on any shipment. Managers can better coordinate company-wide performance. They can identify departments that are working well together and those that are lagging behind schedule and creating bottlenecks.

PROVIDING FLEXIBILITY FOR CUSTOMIZATION

IT networks and other IT advances also create new manufacturing capabilities that enable businesses to offer customers greater variety and faster delivery cycles. Whether it's a personal computer from Dell, one of Motorola's cordless phones, or a Rawlings baseball glove, today's design-it-yourself world has become possible through fast, flexible manufacturing using IT networks. At San Francisco-based Timbuk2's Web site, for example, you can "build your own" custom messenger bag at different price levels with choices of size, fabric, color combinations, accessories, liner material, strap, and even left- or right-hand access.[3] The principle is called **mass-customization**: Although companies produce in large volumes, each unit features the unique options the customer prefers. With IT, the old standardized assembly line has become quickly adaptable because workers have instantaneous access to assembly instructions for all the product options, and equipment can be changed quickly for each customer's order.

MASS-CUSTOMIZATION
Although companies produce in large volumes, each unit features the unique options the customer prefers

Figure 13.1
Networking for Mass
Customization

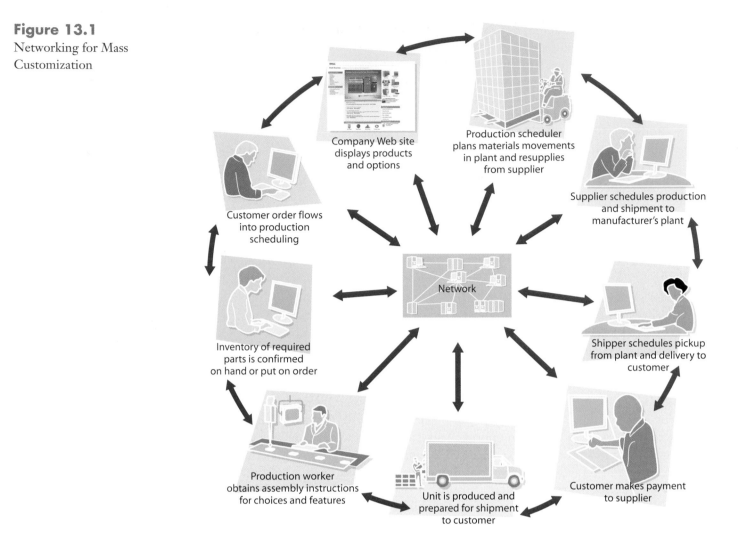

As shown in Figure 13.1, flexible production and speedy delivery depend on an integrated network of information to coordinate all the activities among customers, manufacturers, suppliers, and shippers.

■■■ PROVIDING NEW BUSINESS OPPORTUNITIES

Not only is IT improving existing businesses, it is creating entirely new businesses where none existed before. For big businesses, this means developing new products, offering new services, and reaching new clients. Only a few years ago, the multibillion-dollar behemoth known as Google was a fledgling search engine. Today, that company boasts not just a search engine but instant messaging, e-mail, and auction features as well.

The IT landscape has also presented small business owners with new e-business opportunities. Consider Richard Smith. His love for stamp collecting began at age seven. Now, some 40 years after saving that first stamp, he's turned his hobby into a profitable eBay business. Each day begins at the PC in his home office, scanning eBay's listings for items available and items wanted by sellers and buyers around the world. With more than 3,000 sales transactions to date, Richard maintains a perfect customer rating and recently earned more than $4,000 on a single eBay transaction.

Just how does Richard, like others, make eBay work for him? To assist start-up businesses, eBay's services network is a ready-made online business model, not just an auction market. Services range from credit financing to protection from fraud and misrepresentation, information security, international currency exchanges, and post-sales management. These activities enable users like Richard to complete sales transactions, deliver merchandise, and get new merchandise for future resale, all from the comfort of their own homes.

Meanwhile, eBay's PayPal system—an online financial institution processes $20 billion in transactions annually. As a seller, Richard receives payments into his PayPal account from buyers using credit cards, debit cards, bank accounts, or from their PayPal accounts. When buying merchandise, he can pay in any of six currencies, including the Euro and Japanese Yen, with PayPal making the conversion between U.S. dollars and the seller's currency.

Using eBay's integrated online services, Richard, like many others who have an eBay business, has found a profitable new career.

▪▪▪ IMPROVING THE WORLD AND OUR LIVES

Can advancements in IT really make the world a better place? Hospitals and medical equipment companies certainly think so. For example, when treating combat injuries, surgeons at Walter Reed National Military Medical Center now rely on high-tech graphics displays that are converted into three-dimensional physical models for presurgical planning. These 3-D mockups of shoulders, femurs, and facial bones give doctors the opportunity to see and feel the anatomy as it will be seen in the operating room, before they even use their scalpels.[4] Meanwhile, vitamin-sized cameras that patients swallow are providing doctors with computer images of the insides of the human body, helping them to make better diagnoses for such ailments as ulcers and cancer.[5]

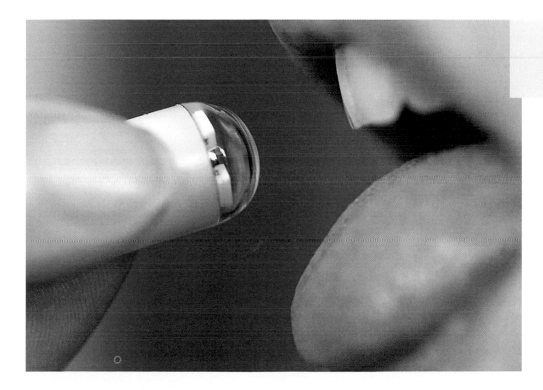

After this capsule is swallowed, the camera inside it can transmit 50,000 images during its eight-hour journey through the digestive tract.

SELF-CHECK QUESTIONS 1–3

You should now be able to answer Self-Check Questions 1–3.*

1 **Multiple Choice** Which of the following is **not** true about information technology (IT):
   (a) the term *information technology* includes the various appliances and devices for creating, storing, exchanging, and using information
   (b) e-commerce is the use of the Internet and other electronic means for retailing and business-to-business transactions
   (c) BlackBerry's mobile messaging capabilities save time and travel expenses but they prevent a geographic separation between the workplace and headquarters
   (d) with IT networks, more work and customer satisfaction can be accomplished with fewer people

2 **True/False** Companies with mass customization produce in large volumes, yet each unit features the unique options the customer prefers.

3 **Multiple Choice** Which of the following is **not** true about information technology (IT):
   (a) due to time limitations for completing Lockheed Martin's airplane project, global Web collaboration cannot be used for designing and testing the aircraft
   (b) IT networks enable instantaneous access to information on the status of current operations to all levels of management
   (c) customers have gained greater product variety and faster product deliveries because of IT
   (d) Richard Smith's stamp-selling business on eBay is an example of new business opportunities that are created by information technology

***Answers to Self-Check Questions 1–3 can be found on p. 566.**

IT BUILDING BLOCKS: BUSINESS RESOURCES

We've discussed how IT is affecting the global business landscape, but what are the tools that make it work? The Internet and e-mail are vital factors. So, too, are other communications technologies, networks, hardware devices, and software. In this section, we'll take a brief look at various IT resources that businesses have at their disposal.

THE INTERNET AND OTHER COMMUNICATION RESOURCES

INTERNET a gigantic system of interconnected computers—more than 100 million computers in over 100 countries

WORLD WIDE WEB a standardized code for accessing information and transmitting data over the Internet; the common language that allows information sharing on the Internet

The Internet—and its companion system, the World Wide Web—are today among the world's most powerful communication technologies. Over 68 percent of Americans use the Internet,[6] with the number growing daily. The **Internet** is a gigantic system of interconnected computers—more than 100 million computers in over 100 countries make up the Internet we know today. The **World Wide Web**, however, is a standardized code for accessing information and transmitting data over the Internet. It provides the common language that allows information sharing on the Internet. The Internet and the Web both serve individual computers with information and provide communication flows among separate networks around the world. For thousands of businesses, the Internet is replacing the telephone, fax machine, and standard mail as the primary communications tool.

The Internet has spawned a number of other business communications technologies, including *intranets*, *extranets*, *electronic conferencing*, and *VSAT satellite communications*.

Intranets Many companies have extended Internet technology internally by maintaining internal Web sites linked throughout the firm. These private networks, or **intranets**, are accessible only to employees. "The internal web is the backbone of Ford's business today," says Ford Motor Company Chief Information Officer Bud Mathaisel. Its intranet connects 175,000 workstations in Asia, Europe, and the United States to thousands of Ford Web sites containing private information on Ford's employee benefits, production management tools, and product design resources. Sharing information on engineering, distribution, and marketing has reduced the lead time for getting new models into production and has shortened customer delivery times.[7]

INTRANET an organization's private network of internally linked Web sites accessible only to employees

Extranets **Extranets** allow outsiders limited access to a firm's internal information network. The most common application allows buyers to enter a system to see which products are available for sale and delivery, thus providing convenient product availability information. Industrial suppliers are often linked into customers' information networks so that they can see planned production schedules and prepare supplies for customers' upcoming operations. The extranet at Chaparral Steel, for example, lets customers shop electronically through its storage yards and gives them electronic access to Chaparral's planned inventory of industrial steel products.

EXTRANET a system that allows outsiders limited access to a firm's internal information network

Electronic Conferencing **Electronic conferencing** allows groups of people to communicate simultaneously from various locations via e-mail, phone, or video. One form, called *dataconferencing*, allows people in remote locations to work simultaneously on one document: Working as a team, they can revise a marketing plan or draft a press release. *Videoconferencing* allows participants to see one another on video screens while the conference is in progress. For example, Lockheed Martin's Joint Strike Fighter project, discussed earlier, uses Internet collaboration systems with both voice and video capabilities. Although separated by oceans, partners can communicate as if they were in the same room for redesigning components and production schedules. Electronic conferencing is attractive to many businesses because it eliminates travel and saves money.

ELECTRONIC CONFERENCING IT that allows groups of people to communicate simultaneously from various locations via e-mail, phone, or video

VSAT Satellite Communications Another Internet technology businesses use to communicate is **VSAT satellite communications**. VSAT (short for *Very Small Aperture Terminal*) systems have a transmitter-receiver (*transceiver*) that sits outdoors with a direct line-of-sight to a satellite. The hub—a ground station computer at the company's headquarters—sends signals to and receives signals from the satellite, exchanging voice, video, and data transmissions. An advantage of VSAT is privacy. A company that operates its own VSAT system has total control over its communications without dependence on other companies. A firm might use VSAT to exchange sales and inventory information, advertising messages, and visual presentations between headquarters and store managers at remote sites. For example, stores in Minneapolis, London, and Boston might communicate with headquarters in New York, sending and receiving digital data via a satellite, as shown in Figure 13.2.

VSAT SATELLITE COMMUNICATIONS a network of geographically dispersed transmitter-receivers (transceivers) that send signals to and receive signals from a satellite, exchanging voice, video, and data transmissions

■■■ NETWORKS: SYSTEM ARCHITECTURE

A **computer network** is a group of two or more computers linked together by some form of cabling (fiber-optic, coaxial, or twisted wire) or by wireless technology to share data or resources, such as a printer. The most common type of network used in

COMPUTER NETWORK a group of two or more computers linked together by some form of cabling or by wireless technology to share data or resources, such as a printer

Figure 13.2
A VSAT Satellite
Communication Network

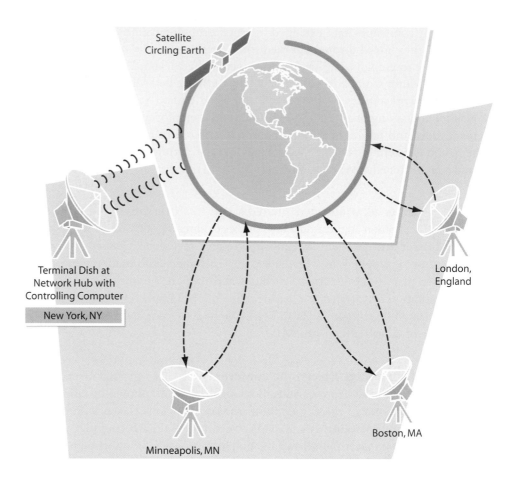

Satellite
Circling Earth

Terminal Dish at
Network Hub with
Controlling Computer

New York, NY

London,
England

Boston, MA

Minneapolis, MN

CLIENT-SERVER NETWORK a
common business network in
which *clients* make requests for
information or resources and
servers provide the services

businesses is a **client-server network**. In client-server networks, *clients* are usually the laptop or desktop computers through which users make requests for information or resources. *Servers* are the computers that provide the services shared by users. In big organizations, servers are usually assigned a specific task. For example, in a local university or college network, an *application server* stores the word-processing, spreadsheet, and other programs used by all computers connected to the network. A *print server* controls the printer, stores printing requests from client computers, and routes jobs as the printer becomes available. An *e-mail server* handles all incoming and outgoing e-mail. With a client-server system, users can share resources and Internet connections—and avoid costly duplication.

Networks can be classified according to geographic scope and means of connection (either wired or wireless).

WIDE AREA NETWORK (WAN)
computers that are linked over
long distances through telephone
lines, microwave signals, or
satellite communications

Wide Area Networks (WANs) Computers that are linked over long distances—statewide or even nationwide—through telephone lines, microwave signals, or satellite communications make up what are called **wide area networks (WANs)**. Firms can lease lines from communications vendors or maintain private WANs. Wal-Mart, for example, depends heavily on a private satellite network that links 5,000 retail stores to its Bentonville, Arkansas, headquarters.

LOCAL AREA NETWORK (LAN)
computers that are linked in a
small area, such as all of a firm's
computers within a single
building

Local Area Networks (LANs) In **local area networks (LANs)**, computers are linked in a smaller area, such as all of a firm's computers within a single building. On cable TV's Home Shopping Network, for example, hundreds of operators at the HSN facility are united by a LAN for entering call-in orders. The arrangement requires only one computer system with one database and one software system.

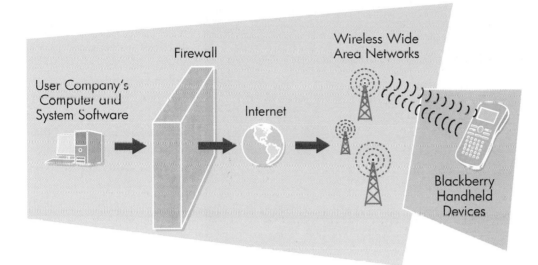

Figure 13.3
BlackBerry Wireless Internet
Architecture

Wireless Networks Wireless networks use airborne electronic signals to link network computers and devices. Like wired networks, wireless networks can reach across long distances or exist within a single building or small area. For example, the BlackBerry system shown in Figure 13.3 consists of devices that send and receive transmissions on **wireless wide area networks (WWANS)** of more than 100 service providers—such as Cellular One (United States), T-Mobile (United Kingdom and United States), and Vodafone (Italy)—in over 40 countries. The wireless format that the system relies on to control wireless messaging is supplied by Research in Motion (RIM), the company that makes the BlackBerry, and is installed on the user-company's computer. The *firewall* provides privacy protection. We'll discuss firewalls in more detail later in the chapter.

> **WIRELESS WIDE AREA NETWORK (WWAN)** a network that uses airborne electronic signals instead of wires to link computers and electronic devices over long distances

Wi-Fi You've no doubt heard of "hotspots"—specific locations such as coffee shops, hotels, and airport terminals that provide wireless Internet connections for people on the go. Each hotspot, or **Wi-Fi** (short for *wireless fidelity*) access point, is actually its own small network, called a **wireless local area network (Wireless LAN or WLAN).** Although wireless service is free at some hotspots, others charge a fee—a daily or hourly rate—for the convenience of Wi-Fi service.

> **WI-FI** short for *wireless fidelity*; a wireless local area network

The benefit of Wi-Fi is that you're not tethered to a wire for accessing the Internet. Employees can wait for a delayed plane in the airport and still be connected to the Internet through their wireless-enabled laptop. However, as with every technology, Wi-Fi has limitations, including a short range of distance. This means that your laptop's Internet connection can be severed if you move further than about 300 feet from the hotspot. In addition, thick walls, construction beams, and other obstacles can interfere with the signals sent out by the network. So, while a city may have hundreds of hotspots, your laptop must remain near one to stay connected. This distance limitation is expected to be improved soon by *WiMax* (*Worldwide Interoperability for Microwave Access*), the next step in wireless advancements, with its wireless range of 30 miles.

> **WIRELESS LOCAL AREA NETWORK** a local area network with wireless access points for PC users

▪▪▪ HARDWARE AND SOFTWARE

Any computer network or system needs **hardware**—the physical components, such as keyboards, monitors, system units, and printers. In addition to the laptops, desktop computers, and BlackBerrys mentioned earlier, *handheld computers* are also used often in businesses. For example, Wal-Mart employees roam the store aisles using handhelds to identify, count, and

> **HARDWARE** the physical components of a computer network, such as keyboards, monitors, system units, and printers

Figure 13.4

3-D computer modeling software gives engineers a better idea of where oil might be located.

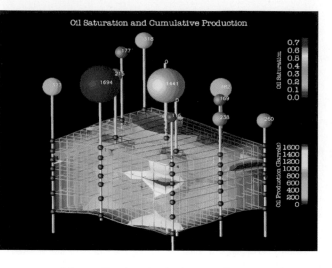

SOFTWARE programs that tell the computer's hardware what resources to use and how

order items, track deliveries, and update backup stock at distribution centers to keep store shelves replenished with merchandise.

The other essential in any computer system is **software**: programs that tell the computer how to function. Software includes *system software*, such as Microsoft Windows, which tells the computer's hardware how to interact with the software, what resources to use, and how. It also includes *application software*, such as Microsoft Excel and Adobe PhotoShop, which are programs that meet the needs of specific users. Some application programs are used to address such common, long-standing needs as database management and accounting and inventory control, whereas others have been developed for a variety of specialized tasks. For example, IBM's Visualization Data Explorer software uses data from field samples to model the underground structure of an oil field. The imagery in Figure 13.4, for example, provides engineers with better information on oil location and reduces the risk of their hitting less productive holes.

We noted earlier the advantages of collaboration among any firm's internal units and with outside firms. Remote collaboration is made possible with *groupware*—software that connects group members for e-mail distribution, electronic meetings, message storing, appointments and schedules, and group writing. Linked by groupware, people can collaborate from their own desktop PCs, even if they're remotely located. It is especially useful when people work together regularly and rely heavily on information sharing. Groupware systems include IBM Lotus Domino 6.5, Microsoft Exchange Server 2003, and Novell GroupWise 6.5.

INFORMATION SYSTEMS: HARNESSING THE COMPETITIVE POWER OF IT

INFORMATION SYSTEM (IS) a system that uses IT resources to convert data into information and to collect, process, and transmit that information for use in decision making

Business today relies on information management in ways that no one could foresee a decade ago. Managers now treat IT as a basic organizational resource for conducting daily business. At major firms, every activity—designing services, ensuring product delivery and cash flow, evaluating personnel—is linked to *information systems*. An **information system (IS)** is a system that uses IT resources and enables managers to take **data**—raw facts and figures that, by themselves, may not have much meaning—and turn that data into **information**—the meaningful, useful interpretation of data. Information systems also enable managers to collect, process, and transmit that information for use in decision making.

DATA raw facts and figures that, by themselves, may not have much meaning

One company well-known for its strategic use of information systems is Wal-Mart. The nerve center for company operations is a centralized IS in Bentonville, Arkansas. The IS drives costs down and raises efficiency because the same methods and systems are applied for all 5,000-plus stores in Europe, Asia, and the Americas. Data on the billions of sales transactions—time, date, place—flows to Bentonville. Keeping track of nearly 700 million stock keeping units (SKUs) weekly, the information system enforces uniform

INFORMATION the meaningful, useful interpretation of data

say what you mean

Are You E-mailing Me?

Just because we have international communication tools, such as the Internet, we can't simply ignore local culture when we're communicating with someone in another country. It's always a good idea to remember who's on the other end of the T-3 line.

Americans are notoriously informal when talking to one another. The same goes for our e-mail communications, and the Internet enables us to spread the message of informality all over the world. Unfortunately, however, being too informal in your e-mail can send the wrong message. In some places, you'll come across as too familiar (or even too aggressive). In some cultures, including the United Kingdom, Germany, and Japan, people like a little formality, even in their e-mail.

For example, be careful about using first names or a casual tone in electronic communications. Pay attention to your grammar: Sloppy language is often a turnoff, and many people automatically regard it as a sign of poor education. Try to organize your message in a logical way. In some cultures, an e-mail message is perceived as a letter with a formal structure.

Don't always expect people to reply to e-mails immediately. Different cultures have different concepts of time, and a person's concept of time plays a big part in his or her sense of when to respond to messages. Demanding an immediate response in Brazil or Mexico is a good way to send your message to the bottom of the electronic pile. Finally, remember that a lot of people are bombarded with e-mail, and many of them regard dealing with a constant barrage of communications as a strain on their time. Communicate with them electronically only when you have something that needs to be said sooner rather than later or when you need a question answered.

As usual, the bottom line in communications is knowing the culture in which your message is going to be received. Find out something about the culture of the person with whom you're dealing before you engage him or her in electronic conversation.

---

reordering and delivery procedures—on packaging, timing, and quantities—for more than 30,000 suppliers. It regulates the flow of the more than five billion cases through its distribution centers, and deliveries by nearly 8,000 Wal-Mart truck drivers, to its stores.

Beyond the firm's daily operations, information systems are also crucial in planning. Managers routinely use the IS to decide on products and markets for the next 5 to 10 years. The company's vast database enables marketing managers to analyze demographics and is also used for financial planning, materials handling, and electronic funds transfers with suppliers and customers.

Wal-Mart, like most businesses, regards its information as a private resource—an asset that's planned, developed, and protected. It's not surprising, therefore, that they have **information systems managers** who operate the systems used for gathering, organizing, and distributing information, just as they have production, marketing, and finance managers.

Incoming information to Wal-Mart managers arrives in various forms—reports, memos, databases, and e-mails. They use many of the IT resources we discussed earlier— the Internet, communication technologies, networks, hardware, and software—to sift through information and apply it to their jobs. The question facing many businesses today, however, is how to use that information most effectively. In this section, we'll explore the process of *data mining* as well the types of information systems that are available to businesses.

INFORMATION SYSTEMS MANAGERS managers who operate the systems used for gathering, organizing, and distributing information

■■■ LEVERAGING INFORMATION RESOURCES: DATA WAREHOUSING AND DATA MINING

Almost everything you do leaves a trail of information about you. Your preferences in movie rentals, television viewing, Internet sites, and groceries; the destinations of your phone calls, your credit card charges, your financial status; personal information about age, gender, marital status, and even health—these are just a few of the items about each of us that are stored in scattered databases. The behavior patterns of millions of users can be traced by analyzing files of information gathered over time from their Internet usage and in-store purchases.

DATA WAREHOUSING the collection, storage, and retrieval of data in electronic files

The collection, storage, and retrieval of such data in electronic files is called **data warehousing**. For managers, the data warehouse is a goldmine of information about their business.[8] The Wal-Mart data warehouse, for example, has a storage capacity of over 570 terabytes (a thousand billion bytes) of data. That's larger than all the Web pages on the Internet. Or, if each byte was a car, that would be nearly 88,000 cars for every person on earth.

DATA MINING the application of electronic technologies for searching, sifting, and reorganizing pools of data to uncover useful information

Data Mining After collecting information, managers use **data mining**—the application of electronic technologies for searching, sifting, and reorganizing pools of data to uncover useful information. By mining the data in the data warehouse, managers can better plan for new products, set prices, and identify trends and shopping patterns. When Hurricane Ivan was approaching Pensacola, Florida, for example, Wal-Mart's planning system indicated a rise in demand for Kellogg's Strawberry Pop-Tarts so additional shipments were sent.[9] Wal-Mart data about demographics, markdowns, returns, and inventory levels, for example, can be used by managers to forecast sales, conduct merchandise planning so store shelves will be stocked, and determine the effects of marketing promotions.[10]

Companies also use data collected on the Internet to gather information on user behavior—who has bought which products and how many, over what Web sites individuals bought the products, how they paid, and so on. By analyzing what consumers actually do, businesses can determine what subsequent purchases they are likely to make and then send them tailor-made ads.

Information Linkages with Suppliers The top priority for Wal-Mart's IS—improving in-stock reliability—requires integration of Wal-Mart's and suppliers' activities with store sales. That's why P&G, Johnson & Johnson, and other suppliers

Wal-Mart's IT people gathered outside to be photographed as *InformationWeek's* business technology "Team of the Year."

connect into Wal-Mart's information system to observe up-to-the-minute sales data on individual items, by store. They can use the system's computer-based tools—spreadsheets, sales forecasting, weather information—to forecast sales demand and plan delivery schedules. Coordinated planning avoids excessive inventories, speeds up deliveries, and holds down costs throughout the supply chain while keeping shelves stocked for retail customers.

■■■ TYPES OF INFORMATION SYSTEMS

In a sense, the term *information system* may be a misnomer. It suggests that there is one system when, in fact, employees have many different responsibilities and decision-making needs, and one IS can't handle such a range of requirements. In reality, the IS may be a set of several information systems that share information while serving different levels of the organization, different departments, or different operations. Because they work on different kinds of problems, managers and their employees have access to the specialized information systems that satisfy their different information needs.

In addition to different types of users, each business *function*—marketing, human resources, accounting, production, finance—has its own information needs, as do groups working on major projects. Each user group and department, therefore, may need a special IS.

Information Systems for Knowledge Workers As we discussed in Chapter 10, *knowledge workers* are employees for whom information and knowledge are the raw materials of their work, such as engineers, scientists, and IT specialists who rely on IT to design new products or create new processes. For example, to develop new materials at a flooring company, knowledge workers may need information on the chemical properties of adhesives. Therefore, they use *knowledge information systems*. The purpose of such systems is to supply a flow of new knowledge that can be integrated into the company to strengthen it. A **knowledge information system** supports knowledge workers by providing resources to create, store, use, and transmit new knowledge for useful applications. It provides databases to organize and retrieve information, and computational power for data analysis. Word processing programs, spreadsheets, graphics capabilities, and desktop publishing are available for fast, effective communications.

KNOWLEDGE INFORMATION SYSTEM information system that supports knowledge workers by providing resources to create, store, use, and transmit new knowledge for useful applications

Specialized support systems, such as computer-aided design and simulation modeling, have also increased the productivity of knowledge workers. **Computer-aided design (CAD)** helps knowledge workers design products by simulating them and displaying them in 3-D graphics. Products ranging from cell phones to auto parts are created with CAD because it creates faster designs at lower cost than manual modeling methods. The older method—making handcrafted prototypes from wood, plastic, or clay—is replaced with rapid prototyping: The CAD system electronically transfers instructions to a computer-controlled machine that builds the prototype.

COMPUTER-AIDED DESIGN (CAD) IS with software that helps knowledge workers design products by simulating them and displaying them in three-dimensional graphics

In archaeology, CAD is helping scientists uncover secrets hidden in fossils using 3-D computer models of skeletons, organs, and tissues constructed with digital data from CT (computed tomography) scans of dinosaur fossils. From these models, scientists have learned, for example, that the giant Apatosaurus' neck curved downward, instead of high in the air as once thought. By seeing how the animals' bones fit together, and the structure of cartilage, ligaments, and vertebrae, scientists are discovering more about how these prehistoric creatures interacted with their environment.[11]

The 3-D computer model of this dinosaur is constructed from digital scans of fossilized tissue.

Information Systems for Managers Each manager's information activities and IS needs vary according to his or her functional area (accounting or marketing and so forth) and management level. The following are some popular information systems used by managers for different purposes.

MANAGEMENT INFORMATION SYSTEM (MIS) computer system that supports managers by providing information—reports, schedules, plans, and budgets—that can be used for making decisions

Management Information Systems Management information systems (MIS) support managers by providing reports, schedules, plans, and budgets that can then be used for making decisions. For day-to-day activities, managers use information to oversee the details of departments or projects. For example, at Walsworth Publishing Company, managers rely on detailed information—current customer orders, staffing schedules, employee attendance, production schedules, equipment status, materials availability—for moment-to-moment decisions during the day. For mid-range action—looking weeks or months ahead—they rely on information to plan such activities as personnel training, materials movements, and cash flows. They also need to anticipate the status of the jobs and projects assigned to their departments. What stage is a job at now? When will it be finished? When will there be openings so other jobs can start? Many MIS—cash flow, sales, production scheduling, shipping—are indispensable for helping managers find answers to such questions.

For longer-range decisions on business strategy, Walsworth managers need information to analyze trends in the publishing industry and overall company performance in order to make long-range plans. They need both external and internal information, current and futuristic, to compare current performance data to data from previous years and to analyze consumer trends and economic forecasts.

DECISION SUPPORT SYSTEM (DSS) interactive system that creates virtual business models for a particular kind of decision and tests them with different data to see how they respond

Decision Support Systems Managers that face a particular kind of decision repeatedly can get assistance from **decision support systems (DSS)**—interactive systems that create virtual business models and test them with different data to see how they respond. When faced with decisions on plant capacity, for example, Walsworth managers can use a capacity DSS. The manager inputs data on anticipated sales, working capital, and customer-delivery requirements. The data flows into the DSS processor, which then simulates the plant's performance under the proposed data conditions. After experimenting with various data conditions, the DSS makes recommendations on the best levels of plant capacity for each future time period.

entrepreneurship and new ventures

Upgrading to a Radio Frequency Future

Radio Frequency Identification (RFID) is a powerful new technology with potential applications for nearly every civilian industry—manufacturing, logistics, mining, transportation—and in military activities as well. Wal-Mart is the leader in piloting its application to retailing, for tracking inventory. It's a better way to make sure that products are on the store shelf when customers want them. After a successful test program in 140 stores, Wal-Mart Chief Information Officer Linda Dillman declared: "This technology has a bigger potential to make a difference in retailing than anything we've ever done."

An RFID code number is assigned to each item when it is manufactured. The code has unique information about the item—the product name, date of manufacture, current location, expiration date, and so on. The code is stored on an RFID label, or smart tag, containing a microchip and a tiny ribbon-like antenna overlaid on a piece of tape or label. It looks like a thin strip of tape attached to a container (e.g., a can of soda), or embedded in a carton (e.g., in a cardboard case of soda). The tag can communicate by radio signals with RFID scanners, either handheld or located in a fixed position. The scanner then retrieves the product's information, such as its current location and the selling price at the store's checkout. A computer updates the information as the product moves from stage to stage so it can be used for shipping, shelf restocking, pricing, and so on.

As an example, consider a can of soda bought from a vending machine. Its RFID code information—tracing its path through the supply chain to the consumer and, even later, to disposal—tells the product name, where it was canned, when,

container size, when it left the factory, the distributor that received it, location of the vending machine, date you bought it, where the can was deposited after you finished, when and where the can reached the recycling station, and date of destruction of the can and its RFID code label. The stage-to-stage data updating is done remotely via radio-wave communications between code label and scanners.

As compared with today's barcode scanning, RFID is much faster and more flexible. Radio waves from RFID scanners can communicate with many tags simultaneously, instead of barcode's one-tag-at-a-time scanning with laser beams. Imagine pushing a loaded grocery cart past an overhead scanner that reads all items simultaneously before you reach the grocery checkout stand, where an itemized total awaits you. The RFID data instantaneously launches replenishment orders for all the grocery items through the supply chain to refill the store shelves.

It will take years before Wal-Mart can fully implement RFID because it depends on participation throughout the supply chain, from factory to warehouse to storeroom. The buildup of the technology will require billions of tags, thousands of scanners, and huge-capacity data banks with remote access all along the supply chain. By the end of 2006, some 20,000 Wal-Mart suppliers will be participating so that incoming merchandise is accurately identified and matched up against on-the-shelf requirements. Thereafter, the remaining 10,000 suppliers will be added in along with those of other retailers that will follow Wal-Mart's IT leadership.

SELF-CHECK QUESTIONS 4–6

You should now be able to answer Self-Check Questions 4–6.*

4 **True/False** The Internet and the World Wide Web are interchangeable terms meaning the same thing.

5 **Multiple Choice** Which of the following is true about information technology business resources:
  (a) intranets are networks for public access to information about company activities
  (b) extranets are backup systems for access when the firm's normal network breaks down
  (c) the BlackBerry system has devices that send and receive transmissions on WWANs

  (d) Wal-Mart's data mining and data warehousing capabilities are about the same as those for most other firms

6 **True/False** The purpose of knowledge information systems is to support knowledge workers by providing resources to create, store, use, and transmit new knowledge for useful applications.

***Answers to Self-Check Questions 4–6 can be found on p. 566.**

IT RISKS AND THREATS

As with other technologies throughout history, IT has attracted abusers that are set on doing mischief, with severity ranging from mere nuisance to outright destruction. Hackers break into computers, stealing personal information and company secrets, and launching attacks on other computers. Meanwhile, the ease of information sharing on the Internet has proven costly for companies who are having an increasingly difficult time protecting their intellectual property, and viruses have crashed millions of computers and have cost companies millions. In this section, we'll look at these and other IT risks. In the next section, we'll discuss ways in which businesses are protecting themselves from them.

■■■ HACKERS

HACKER cybercriminal who gains unauthorized access to a computer or network, either to steal information, money, or property or to tamper with data

"Breaking and entering" no longer refers merely to physical intrusion. Today, it applies to IT intrusions as well. **Hackers** are cybercriminals who gain unauthorized access to a computer or network, either to steal information, money, or property or to tamper with data. For example, one 16-year-old British hacker recently got into the U.S. Air Force's top command-and-control facility 150 times. From there, he got into the computers of several defense contractors and the South Korean Atomic Research Institute.

Wireless mooching is a growing industry for cybercriminals. In just five minutes, a *St. Petersburg Times*, Florida, reporter using a laptop found six unprotected wireless networks that were wide open to outside users. Once inside an unsecured wireless network, hackers use it to commit identity theft and to steal credit card numbers, among other activities. When police officers try to track down these criminals, they're long gone, leaving you, the network host, exposed to criminal prosecution.

I'll guarantee there are tons of people out there who have their wireless network being exploited but have no idea . . . As we see more people using wireless, we'll see more people being victimized.

—Special Agent Bob Breeden, head of Florida's computer crime division[12]

One common reason hackers break into a computer network is to launch *denial of service (DOS) attacks*. DOS attacks flood networks or Web sites with bogus requests for information and resources, thereby shutting the networks or Web sites down and making it so that legitimate users can no longer access them. Such attacks cost companies across the world millions in lost productive time and revenue.

■■■ IDENTITY THEFT

IDENTITY THEFT unauthorized stealing of personal information (such as social security number and address) to get loans, credit cards, or other monetary benefits by impersonating the victim

Once inside a computer network, hackers are able to commit **identity theft**, the unauthorized stealing of personal information (such as social security number and address) to get loans, credit cards, or other monetary benefits by impersonating the victim.

Not all identity theft is committed by hackers, though. Clever crooks get information on unsuspecting victims by digging in trash, luring Internet users to bogus Web sites, and stealing mail. Take the case of an e-mail from America Online notifying a customer of a billing problem with her AOL accounts. The e-mail, displaying AOL logos and legitimate-looking links, requests personal information—credit card numbers, social security numbers, and banking accounts with passwords and PIN numbers. When the customer clicks on the AOL Billing Center link, she is transferred to a spoofed (falsified) AOL-looking Web page, where she submits the requested information—into the hands of the thief. Her accounts soon are empty. The thief in this case used *phishing* or *pharming*—e-mailing a deceptive, real-looking imitation of a popular Web site (e.g., AOL, PayPal, or your local bank) as bait, to masses of recipients, tricking them into giving up personal information.

With more than 30 million victims, identity theft it is the fastest growing crime in the United States. Although such theft often goes undetected, lawbreakers increasingly are receiving stiff penalties. For example, a Michigan hacker was recently sentenced to nine years in prison for breaking into a computer system and stealing credit card account numbers of customers in a Lowe's home improvement store.[13]

∎∎∎ INTELLECTUAL PROPERTY THEFT

Information is so valuable as an asset that most companies enforce security precautions to protect it. Nearly every company faces the dilemma of protecting product plans, new inventions, industrial processes, and other **intellectual property**: a product of the mind—something produced by the intellect, with great expenditure of human effort—that has commercial value. Its ownership and right to its use may be protected by patent, copyright, trademark, and other means.

Hackers often break into company networks to steal company or trade secrets. But it's not just hackers who are doing the stealing. Because the chances of getting caught seem slim, home users continue, illegally, to download unpaid-for movies, music, and other resources from file-swapping networks. Recent estimates conservatively indicate industry losses in the United States at $5 billion in music, $13 billion for software, and $4 billion in movies each year. The Commerce Department estimates that illegal product usage in the global market is costing U.S. companies $200 billion annually.[14]

INTELLECTUAL PROPERTY a product of the mind—something produced by the intellect, with great expenditure of human effort—that has commercial value

∎∎∎ COMPUTER VIRUSES, WORMS, AND TROJAN HORSES

Another IT risk facing businesses is rogue programmers who disrupt IT operations by contaminating and destroying software, hardware, or data files. Viruses, worms, and Trojan horses are three kinds of malicious programs that, once installed, can shut down any computer system. A *computer virus* exists in a file that attaches itself to a program and migrates from computer to computer as a shared program or as an e-mail attachment. It does not infect the system unless the user opens the contaminated file, and users typically are unaware they are spreading the virus by file-sharing. It can, for example, quickly copy itself over and over again, using up all available memory and effectively shutting down the computer.

Worms are a particular kind of virus that travel from computer to computer within networked computer systems, without your needing to open any software to spread the contaminated file. In a matter of days, the notorious Blaster Worm infected some 400,000 computer networks, destroying files and even allowing outsiders to take over computers remotely. The worm replicates itself rapidly, sending out thousands of copies to other computers in the network. Traveling through Internet connections and e-mail address books in the network's computers, it absorbs system memory and shuts down network servers, Web servers, and individual computers.

Unlike viruses, a *Trojan horse* does not replicate itself. Instead, it most often comes into the computer, at your request, masquerading as a harmless, legitimate software product or data file. Once installed, the damage begins. For instance, it may simply redesign desktop icons or, more maliciously, delete files and destroy information.

▪▪■ SPYWARE

As if forced intrusion isn't bad enough, Internet users unwittingly invite spies—masquerading as a friendly file available as a "giveaway" or shared among individual users on their PCs. This so-called **spyware** is downloaded by users that are lured by "free" software. Once installed, it crawls around to monitor the host's computer activities, gathering e-mail addresses, credit card numbers, passwords, and other inside information that it transmits back to someone outside the host system. Spyware authors assemble incoming stolen information to create their own "intellectual property" that they then sell to other parties to use for marketing/advertising purposes or for identity theft.[15]

▪▪■ SPAM

We've all received **spam**—junk e-mail sent to a mailing list or a newsgroup (an online discussion group).[16] Spam is a greater nuisance than postal junk mail because the Internet is open to the public, e-mail costs are negligible, and massive mailing lists are accessible through file-sharing or by theft. Spam operators send unwanted messages ranging from explicit pornography to hate mail to advertisements, and even destructive computer viruses. In addition to wasting users' time, it also consumes a network's bandwidth, thereby reducing the amount of data that can be transmitted in a fixed amount of time for useful purposes. U.S. industry experts estimate spam's damage in lost time and productivity at more than $9 billion annually.[17]

IT PROTECTION MEASURES

Security measures against intrusion and viruses are a constant challenge. In this section, we'll discuss the main ways in which businesses guard themselves against intrusion, identity theft, and viruses by using firewalls, special software, and encryption.

▪▪■ PREVENTING UNAUTHORIZED ACCESS: FIREWALLS

Many systems guard against unauthorized access by requiring users to have protected passwords. This helps ensure that intruders are unable to access your computer or the data on it. However, many firms rely on additional safeguards, such as firewalls. **Firewalls** are security systems with special software or hardware devices designed to keep computers safe from hackers. Figure 13.5 shows how a firewall works. The firewall is located where the two networks—the Internet and the company's internal network—meet. It contains two components for filtering each incoming message:

- The company's *security policy*—Access rules that identify every type of message that the company doesn't want to pass through the firewall.
- A *router*—A table of available routes or paths, a "traffic switch" that determines which routes or paths on the network to send each message after it is tested against the security policy.

Only those messages that meet the conditions of the user's security policy are routed through the firewall and permitted to flow between the two networks. Messages that fail the access test are blocked and cannot flow between the two networks. As we saw earlier, a firewall is used for protecting the BlackBerry wireless system from intrusion.

Figure 13.5
How a Firewall Works

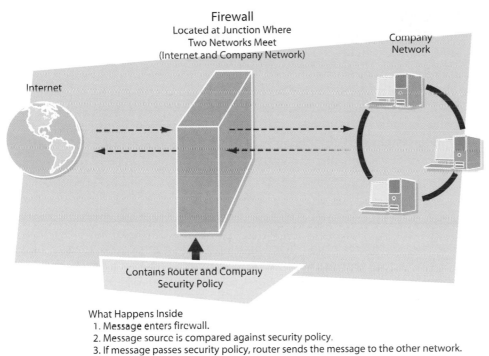

Firewall
Located at Junction Where
Two Networks Meet
(Internet and Company Network)

Company
Network

Internet

Contains Router and Company
Security Policy

What Happens Inside
1. Message enters firewall.
2. Message source is compared against security policy.
3. If message passes security policy, router sends the message to the other network.
   Otherwise, router closes the gate to prevent entry.

▪▪▪ PREVENTING IDENTITY THEFT

While foolproof prevention is impossible, steps can be taken to avoid being victimized. A visit to the Identity Theft Resource Center (www.idtheftcenter.org) is a valuable first step to get information on everything from scam alerts to victim issues—including assistance on lost and stolen wallets—to media resources, current laws, and prevention of identity theft in the workplace.

The Fair and Accurate Credit Transactions Act (FACTA), which took effect in 2005, strengthens identity-theft protections by specifying how organizations must destroy information instead of dropping it in a dumpster. It applies to records containing credit or social security information, including check stubs and tax forms. When a company disposes of such documents, they must be shredded, pulverized, or burned, and all electronic records (in computers and databases) must be permanently removed to keep them out of the hands of intruders.[18]

▪▪▪ PREVENTING VIRUSES: ANTI-VIRUS SOFTWARE

Combating viruses, worms, and Trojan horses has become a major industry for systems designers and software developers. Installation of any of hundreds of **anti-virus software** products protects systems by searching incoming e-mail and data files for "signatures" of known viruses and virus-like characteristics. Contaminated files are discarded or placed in quarantine for safekeeping.

Many viruses take advantage of weaknesses in operating systems, such as Microsoft Windows, in order to spread and propagate. Network administrators must make sure that the computers on their systems are using the most up-to-date operating system that includes the latest security protection.

ANTI-VIRUS SOFTWARE
product that protects systems by searching incoming e-mails and data files for "signatures" of known viruses and virus-like characteristics

▪▪▪ PROTECTING ELECTRONIC COMMUNICATIONS: ENCRYPTION SOFTWARE

Security for electronic communications is another concern for businesses. Unprotected e-mail can be intercepted, diverted to unintended computers, and opened, revealing contents to intruders. Protective software is available to guard against those intrusions, adding a layer of security by encoding e-mails so that only intended recipients can open them. The **encryption system** works by locking an e-mail message to a unique code number (digital fingerprint) for each computer so only that computer can open and read the message.[19]

ENCRYPTION SYSTEM software that assigns an e-mail message to a unique code number (digital fingerprint) for each computer so only that computer, not others, can open and read the message

▪▪▪ AVOIDING SPAM AND SPYWARE

To help their employees avoid privacy invasion and to improve productivity, businesses often install anti-spyware and spam filtering software on their systems. While dozens of anti-spyware products provide protection—software such as Webroot's Spy Sweeper and the Microsoft AntiSpyware Beta—they must be continually updated to keep pace with new spyware techniques.

The federal CAN-SPAM Act of 2003 requires the Federal Trade Commission to shield the public from falsified header information, sexually explicit e-mails that are not so labeled, Internet spoofing (using trickery to make a message appear as if it came from a trusted source), and hijacking of computers through worms or Trojan horses. While it cannot be prevented entirely, spam is abated by many Internet service providers (ISPs) that ban the spamming of ISP subscribers. An ISP in Iowa was recently awarded $1 billion in a lawsuit against 300 spammers that jammed the ISP system with an astounding 10 million e-mails a day. Anti-spam groups, too, promote the public's awareness of known spammers. The Spamhaus Project (www.spamhaus.org), for example, maintains a list—Register of Known Spam Operators (ROKSO)—of over 200 professional spammers that are responsible for over 80 percent of spam traffic in North America and Europe.

SELF-CHECK QUESTIONS 7–9

You should now be able to answer Self-Check Questions 7–9.*

7 Multiple Choice Which of the following is true about IT risks and threats:

(a) phishing or pharming uses a deceptive imitation of a real Web site as bait to trick Web users into giving up personal information

(b) unauthorized downloading of music or movies from file-swapping networks is a form of intellectual property theft

(c) spyware sometimes masquerades as a friendly file available as a "giveaway" for downloading to PC users

(d) all of the above are true

8 Multiple Choice Which of the following is true about protection measures against IT risks and threats:

(a) firewalls cannot protect against intrusions by hackers

(b) identity theft can be reduced by carefully disposing of documents and electronic records containing personal information

(c) anti-virus software is designed to prevent system intrusions by hackers

(d) encryption systems are useful for preventing massive spam intrusions

9 True/False Anti-spyware and spam filtering software can help businesses protect employees against privacy invasion and improve productivity.

*Answers to Self-Check Questions 7–9 can be found on p. 566.

CONTINUED FROM PAGE 398

THE POINT OF CASHING IN

Mark Hurd is positioning NCR's future on the fact that labor-intensive service companies haven't yet taken advantage of POS devices but will do so soon. Moreover, the customer data in those service companies contain a wealth of information and, with assistance from NCR's data-mining systems, can make self-service enjoyable for customers, and profitable too. By using new IT devices, transactions that rely on employees for interfacing with customers—hotel check-ins, patient check-ins at the doctor's office, airport check-ins, and retail shopping to name a few—are ripe for changeover to self-service. Hurd believes his company is uniquely prepared for endless new POS applications beyond ATMs because there's more to NCR's equipment than just the POS server that meets the customer's eye. Behind the scenes, software is prowling through gigantic data warehouses, combing for clues about consumer buying patterns. By linking those technologies to digital salesclerks—such as "Maddy"—POS applications can revolutionize retailing and other applications involving interactions with customers.

Consider Hurd's futuristic vision for shopping. The supermarket shopper enters a loyalty card number into an electronic recorder that accompanies the cart and tracks the shopper's location, aisle-by-aisle, using infrared beacons from the ceiling. Data-mining software reviews the shopper's history to create special offers, customized to the individual's preferences, gives directions for finding specific items, and reminds them of items they might have forgotten. The shopping trip ends with self-service checkouts without having to empty their cart. Consumers, aided with easy-to-use technology, do more of the work while creating mounds of new information for retailers.

QUESTIONS FOR DISCUSSION

1 Do you think people would like and use more self-service technologies in the near future? Why or why not?
2 What industries, in addition to those mentioned in the case, are good prospects for adopting NCR's POS technologies? For at least three such industries, identify reasons why you believe they are good prospects.
3 From your experiences as a shopper, what weaknesses, if any, can you think of in NCR's POS technologies? What is your assessment of the seriousness of those weaknesses?
4 Suppose you were designing a "digital salesclerk." What are the operational features that you consider most important for customer satisfaction? Explain.
5 Do you see any potential ethical issues in the use NCR's POS technologies? Explain.

1 Discuss the impacts information technology has had on the business world.

The growth of IT has changed the very structure of business organizations. Its adoption provides new modes of communication, including portable offices, resulting in the geographic separation of the workplace from headquarters for many employees. By providing instantaneous access to company information, IT has altered the workforces in many companies, enabling them to streamline with fewer employees and simpler structures. It also contributes to greater flexibility in serving customers and enables closer coordination with suppliers. IT's global reach facilitates project collaboration with remote business partners and the formation of new market relationships around the globe. Just as electronic collaboration has changed the way employees interact with each other, IT networks have created new manufacturing flexibility for mass customization, and Internet access has brought new opportunities for small businesses.

2 Identify the IT resources businesses have at their disposal and how these resources are used.

The Internet and the Web serve computers with information and provide communication flows among networks around the world. For many businesses, the Internet is replacing the telephone, fax machine, and standard mail as the primary communications tool. To support internal communications, many companies maintain internal Web sites—*intranets*—accessible only to employees. Some firms give limited network access to outsiders via *extranets* for coordination with suppliers and customers. *VSAT satellite networks* provide private long-distance communications for voice, video, and data transmissions. *Computer networks* (wide area networks, local area networks) enable the sharing of information, hardware, software, and other resources over wired or wireless connections. *Hardware* refers to the computer's physical components. *Software* includes programs to meet specific user needs, such as groupware with voice and video connections for remote collaboration.

3 Describe the role of information systems, the different types of information systems, and how businesses use such systems.

An *information system (IS)* enables users to collect, process, and transmit information for use in decision making. *Knowledge information systems* support knowledge workers by providing resources to create, store, use, and transmit new knowledge for useful applications. *Management information*

systems (MIS) support managers by providing reports, schedules, plans, and budgets that can then be used for making decisions at all levels ranging from detailed daily activities to long-range business strategies. The many uses of information systems include experimenting to test the effectiveness of potential decisions, data mining to identify shopping trends and to plan for new products, and planning delivery schedules from suppliers and to customers.

4 Identify the threats and risks information technology poses on businesses.

IT has attracted abusers that do mischief, with severity ranging from mere nuisance to outright destruction, costing companies millions. *Hackers* break into computers, stealing personal information and company secrets, tampering with data, and launching attacks on other computers. Once inside a computer network, hackers are able to commit *identity theft*, the unauthorized stealing of personal information to get loans, credit cards, or other monetary benefits by impersonating the victim. Even the ease of information sharing on the Internet poses a threat: It has proven costly for companies who are having a difficult time protecting their *intellectual property*, such as software products, movies, and music. Another IT risk facing businesses is system shutdown and destruction of software, hardware, or data files by *viruses*, *worms*, and *Trojan horses*. Spam's damage, too, is costly in terms of lost time and productivity.

5 Describe the ways in which businesses protect themselves from the threats and risks information technology poses.

Most systems guard against unauthorized access by requiring users to have protected passwords. In addition, many firms rely on safeguards, such as *firewalls*, so that only messages that meet the conditions of the company's security policy are permitted to flow through the network. Firms can protect against identity theft by using assistance from advisory sources, such as the Identity Theft Resource Center, and by implementing the identity-theft protection provisions of the federal FACTA rule for maintaining and destroying personal information records. To combat viruses, worms, and Trojan horses, *anti-virus software* products search incoming e-mail and data files for "signatures" of known viruses and virus-like characteristics. Contaminated files are discarded or placed in quarantine for safe-keeping. Additional intrusion protection is available by installing *anti-spyware* and *spam filtering software*.

KEY TERMS

anti-virus software (p. 417)

client-server network (p. 406)

computer network (p. 405)

computer-aided design
   (CAD) (p. 411)

data (p. 408)

data mining (p. 410)

data warehousing (p. 410)

decision support system (DSS) (p. 412)

e-commerce (p. 398)

electronic conferencing (p. 405)

encryption system (p. 418)

extranet (p. 405)

firewall (p. 416)

hacker (p. 414)

hardware (p. 407)

identity theft (p. 414)

information (p. 408)

information system (IS) (p. 408)

information systems managers (p. 409)

information technology
   (IT) (p. 398)

intellectual property (p. 415)

Internet (p. 404)

intranet (p. 405)

knowledge information
   system (p. 411)

local area network (LAN) (p. 406)

management information
   system (MIS) (p. 412)

mass-customization (p. 401)

software (p. 408)

spam (p. 416)

spyware (p. 416)

VSAT satellite communications (p. 405)

wide area network (WAN) (p. 406)

Wi-Fi (p. 407)

wireless local area network (wireless
   LAN or WLAN) (p. 407)

wireless wide area network
   (WWAN) (p. 407)

World Wide Web (p. 404)

QUESTIONS AND EXERCISES

Questions for Review

1 Why must a business manage information as a resource?

2 How can electronic conferencing increase a company's productivity and efficiency?

3 Why do different users in an organization need different kinds of information from the information system?

4 Why has the BlackBerry become a popular tool among business people?

5 What is the definition of *intellectual property*? List three examples of intellectual property.

Questions for Analysis

6 Describe how a company might use data warehousing and data mining in its information system to better plan for new products.

7 Aside from the eBay example in this chapter, describe one or more ways that IT presents new business opportunities for small businesses.

8 Give three examples (other than those in this chapter) of how a company can become leaner and more efficient by adopting IT.

Application Exercises

9 Consider your daily activities—as a consumer, student, parent, friend, homeowner or renter, car driver, employee, etc.—and think about the ways that you are involved in transactions with IT systems. Make a list of your recent IT encounters and then recall instances in those encounters that you revealed personal information that could be used to steal your identity. Are some encounters in your list riskier than others? Why or why not?

10 Describe the computer network at your school. Identify its components and system architecture. What features either promote or inhibit intrusions from hackers? What features either promote or inhibit intellectual property theft? What features either promote or inhibit computer viruses and spam?

THE ART AND SCIENCE OF POINT-AND-CLICK RESEARCH

Goal

To learn how to use the Web to conduct research more effectively.

Background Information

In a survey of nearly 2,000 Web users, two-thirds said they used the Web to obtain work-related information. With an estimated one billion pages of information on the Web, the challenge for business users is: How best to find what they're seeking.

Method

You'll need a computer and access to the Web to complete this exercise.

Step 1

Get together with three classmates and decide on a business-related research topic. Choose a topic that interests you—for example, "Business Implications of the War in Iraq," "Labor Disputes in Professional Sports," or "Marketing Music Lessons to Parents of Young Children."

Step 2

Search the following sites for information on your topic (dividing sites among group members to speed the process):

- Dogpile (www.dogpile.com)
- Excite (www.excite.com)
- Google (www.google.com)
- Yahoo! (www.yahoo.com)

Take notes as you search so that you can explain your findings to other group members.

Step 3

Working as a group, answer the following questions about your collective search:

1 Which sites were the easiest to use?
2 Which sites offered the most helpful results? What specific factors made these sites better than the others?
3 Which sites offered the least helpful results? What were the problems?
4 Why is it important to learn the special code words or symbols, called *operators*, that target a search? (Operators are words such as *AND*, *OR*, and *NOT* that narrow search queries. For example, using *AND* in a search tells most search engines to look only for sites in which all words appear in the results—American *AND* Management *AND* Association.)

FOLLOW-UP QUESTIONS

Research the differences between *search engines* and *subject directories*. Given your topic, would a search engine or a subject directory be more helpful for your research?

1 Why is it important to learn how to use a search site's Help function?
2 Look into some of the sites' Advanced Search pages. How do these pages affect your searches?
3 How has the Web changed the nature of business research?

CAUGHT IN A CYBER BIND

The Situation

Time pressures to complete project assignments, coupled with easy access to the Internet, can present interesting temptations. This exercise illustrates how ethical issues may arise in using information from the Internet.

The Dilemma

Suppose you are assigned to write a report that requires research into a business problem. In searching the Internet, you find mounds of published articles that discuss the problem, but most of them are complicated write-ups using technical terms that you don't completely understand. As the deadline approaches, you realize that you can't figure out a logical, sensible format for writing the report. You then recall, from conversations with colleagues, two possible solutions for your problem: (1) From the many articles found on the Internet, you can select the best-sounding phrases, sentences, and paragraphs, arrange them into a logical sequence, and piece them together as your final report or (2) You can hire an Internet report-writing service at $15 per page to write your report. Chances of being detected are slim.

QUESTIONS TO ADDRESS

1 Given the factors in this situation, what, if any, ethical issues exist?

2 Would you adopt either of the two "possible solutions" listed above? Why or Why not?

3 If a friend was confronted with this same situation and asked your opinion, what advice would you offer?

THIS GAME IS GETTING SERIOUS

The Situation

Interactive games have become big-time entertainment for millions of enthusiasts playing side by side or among contestants anywhere on the Internet. Amidst the fun, questions can arise about the use of intellectual property and the ownership obligations of gamers. This exercise encourages you to examine some of the ethical issues that can surface in gaming.

The Dilemma

Tracy was enamored with a new adventure-and-strategy game from the moment she bought it. Her favorite character—Goddess Diaphanese—had accumulated overwhelming powers, thanks to Tracy's gaming skills and lots of trial and error, during two months of intense competition. Opponents were consistently overwhelmed by Diaphanese's mystical powers, and her ability to foresee the future, ward off attacks with invincible armor, and elevate her intellect to outsmart opponents in this virtual universe. Tracy's Diaphanese was, in effect, an invincible game character.

Another gamer wanted to buy Tracy's personal version of the game, but she decided instead to list it for sale on a popular Internet auction site. The bid price rose to over 10 times the original game price when Tracy got an e-mail from the manufacturer objecting to her sale of the game, stating that both the game name and the character itself are intellectual properties of the firm. The message insisted that she withdraw the product from auction.

Tracy's response to the company stated that her game cartridge—including the unique version of the powerful Goddess Diaphanes—was not the same product she purchased months earlier but, instead, was entirely different due to months of thoughtful game playing. Accordingly, she was selling her creation—a one-of-a-kind, new product.

Team Activity

Assemble a group of four students and assign each group member to one of the following roles:
- Tracy
- auction winner buying Tracy's version of the game
- manufacturer of the game
- investor/owner of the company that manufactures the game

ACTION STEPS

1 Before hearing any of your group's comments, and from the perspective of your assigned role, write down the ethical issues, if any, that you see in this situation.

2 Before hearing any of your group's comments, what actions do you think your assigned role should have taken in this situation? Write down your recommended actions.

3 Gather your group together and reveal, in turn, each member's comments and recommendations.

4 Appoint someone to record main points of agreement and disagreement within the group. How do you explain the results? What accounts for any disagreement?

5 From an ethical standpoint, what does your group recommend Tracy do?

SPACE-AGE INFORMATION SYSTEMS: BOEING SATELLITE SYSTEMS

Learning Objectives

The purpose of this video is to help you:

1 Understand why a business must manage information.
2 Consider the role of information systems in an organization.
3 Understand how information systems and communications technology contribute to efficiency and performance.

Synopsis

Boeing Satellite Systems, the world's leading manufacturer of commercial communications satellites, is a wholly owned subsidiary of Boeing and serves customers in 14 countries. Boeing's IS collects and analyzes data from all departments and then disseminates the results to help management make decisions for boosting performance, productivity, and competitiveness. The chief information officer also oversees security precautions, disaster recovery plans, and procedures for safeguarding valuable data. In addition, each of the company's more than 8,000 employees is equipped with a personal computer or laptop that can also serve as a television to receive broadcasts about company activities.

DISCUSSION QUESTIONS

1 **For analysis**: What role do information systems play at Boeing Satellite Systems?

2 **For analysis**: What are some of the ways in which IT can improve productivity and performance at Boeing Satellite Systems?

3 **For application**: What potential problems might Boeing Satellite Systems have encountered when introducing computer kiosks into factory operations?

4 **For application**: In addition to scenes of Boeing-made satellite launches, what else should the company broadcast over employee computers? Why?

5 **For debate**: Should Boeing Satellite Systems try to prevent potential abuses by using software for monitoring employee use of PCs and laptops? Support your position.

Online Exploration

Visit the Boeing Satellite Systems Web site at www.boeing.com/satellite and search for more information about the firm's state-of-the-art integration and test facility. Also browse the site to see what the company says about its use of information systems and communication technology. Why would the company discuss technology in detail on a public Web site? What specific benefits of information systems does Boeing Satellite Systems highlight? Why are these benefits important to customers who buy satellites?

1 Explain the role of accountants and distinguish between the kinds of work done by public accountants, private accountants, management accountants, and forensic accountants.

2 Explain how the accounting equation is used.

3 Describe the three basic financial statements and show how they reflect the activity and financial condition of a business.

4 Explain the key standards and principles for reporting financial statements.

5 Describe how computing financial ratios can help users get more information from financial statements to determine the financial strengths of a business.

6 Discuss the role of ethics in accounting.

WHAT NUMBERS CAN BE CRUNCHED OFFSHORE?

Planning on an accounting career for job security? If so, you might want to take a second look at what's happening with business process outsourcing (BPO). BPO is the use of third parties to perform services (not manufacturing) that a company would otherwise do internally.

THE ROLE OF ACCOUNTANTS AND ACCOUNTING INFORMATION

Universities and hospitals, for example, outsource cafeteria operations to food service firms, retailers outsource human resources (HR) activities to HR firms, and manufacturing companies outsource shipping and delivery activities to UPS, FedEx, and other delivery specialists that do the job better, at lower cost. Worldwide finance and accounting outsourcing topped $38 billion in 2004, up from $12 billion just five years earlier.

The outsourcer's basic philosophy is that businesses do best when they focus on their core activities rather than getting sidetracked into noncore activities that, for many firms, include accounting. "Finance and accounting take up a lot of time and energy," says Accenture partner John Gillespie. "There are generally a lot of people involved, lots of staff development, staff planning, accounting controls, processing issues, and a lot of routine stuff that frankly you don't need your high flyers in finance to be worried about. Outsourcing allows client companies to focus on their core business."

[There is] a lot of routine stuff that frankly you don't need your high flyers in finance to be worried about.

—*Accenture partner John Gillespie, on why companies outsource accounting*

Offshore outsourcing (*offshoring*)—using third parties in other countries—is expected to surpass $24 billion for U.S. business processes in 2007. The biggest area of growth is in back-office—behind-the-scenes—professional services that have low customer contact and require little customization, such as radiology analysis (for example, x-rays, CT scans, MRIs), computer software development, engineering (for example, product design, testing, and analysis), and basic accounting services. Standardized processes are easily exported for service abroad, thanks to the Internet's global reach. Accounting's basic number-crunching activities—payroll, accounts receivable, accounts payable, cash accounting, and inventory valuation—are easily outsourced because once the U.S. accounting rules are learned, they apply equally to all U.S. customers. Data for these activities are transmitted for offshore processing, then results are transmitted back to the outsourcer. With fast-developing technologies, especially in multimedia communications systems and collaborative groupware, digital proximity can provide enough depth in the accountant-client relationship to allow even further outsourcing in accounting. ■

Our opening story continues on page 449.

WHAT'S IN IT FOR ME?

Whether it's done locally or, as our opening case illustrates, outsourced to a foreign firm, every business uses a myriad of accounting services. By understanding this chapter's discussion of accountants, their methods, and their responsibilities, you'll benefit in three ways: (1) if you're thinking about starting your own business, you'll discover your obligations for reporting your firm's financial status, (2) as an employee or union member, you'll see how to evaluate your company's financial condition and its prospects for the future, and (3) as an interested citizen, you'll learn about accounting ethics and regulatory requirements for maintaining the public's trust in the U.S. business system.

In this chapter, we look at the role of accountants—public accountants, private accountants, management accountants, and forensic accountants. We also examine how the accounting equation is used in accounting and describe the three basic financial statements. Finally, we explain the key standards and principles for reporting financial statements and discuss accounting ethics. But first, let's look at some accounting basics.

WHAT IS ACCOUNTING AND WHO USES ACCOUNTING INFORMATION?

ACCOUNTING comprehensive system for collecting, analyzing, and communicating financial information

BOOKKEEPING recording of accounting transactions

ACCOUNTING INFORMATION SYSTEM (AIS) organized procedure for identifying, measuring, recording, and retaining financial information for use in accounting statements and management reports

Accounting is a comprehensive system for collecting, analyzing, and communicating financial information. It measures business performance and translates the findings into information for management decisions. Accountants also prepare performance reports for owners, the public, and regulatory agencies. To perform these functions, accountants keep records of taxes paid, income received, and expenses incurred, and they assess the effects of these transactions on business activities. By sorting and analyzing thousands of such transactions, accountants can determine how well a business is being managed and how financially strong it is.[1] **Bookkeeping** is just one phase of accounting—the recording of transactions. Accounting itself is much more comprehensive than bookkeeping because accounting involves more than merely recording information.

Because businesses engage in thousands of transactions, ensuring consistent, dependable financial information is mandatory. This is the job of the **accounting information system (AIS)**—an organized procedure for identifying, measuring, recording, and retaining financial information so that it can be used in accounting statements and management reports. The system includes all of the people, reports, computers, procedures, and resources that are needed to compile financial transactions.[2]

Users of accounting information are numerous:

■ *Business managers* use it to develop goals and plans, set budgets, and evaluate future prospects.

■ *Employees and unions* use it to plan for and receive compensation and such benefits as health care, vacation time, and retirement pay.

- *Investors and creditors* use it to estimate returns to stockholders, determine growth prospects, and decide whether a firm is a good credit risk.
- *Tax authorities* use it to plan for tax inflows, determine the tax liabilities of individuals and businesses, and ensure that correct amounts are paid on time.
- *Government regulatory agencies* rely on it to fulfill their duties toward the public. The Securities and Exchange Commission (SEC), for example, requires firms to file financial disclosures so that potential investors have valid information about their financial status.

WHO ARE ACCOUNTANTS AND WHAT DO THEY DO?

At the head of the AIS is the **controller**, who manages a firm's accounting activities. As chief accounting officer, the controller ensures that the AIS provides the reports and statements needed for planning, controlling, decision making, and other management activities. This range of activities requires different types of accounting specialists. In this section, we begin by distinguishing between the two main fields of accounting: *financial* and *managerial*. Then, we discuss the different functions and activities of *certified public accountants*, *private accountants*, *management accountants*, and *forensic accountants*.

CONTROLLER person who manages all of a firm's accounting activities (chief accounting officer)

FINANCIAL VERSUS MANAGERIAL ACCOUNTING

In any company, two fields of accounting—financial and managerial—can be distinguished by the users they serve. It is both convenient and accurate to classify users as those outside the company and those inside the company. We can use this same distinction to classify accounting systems as *financial* or *managerial*.[3]

Financial Accounting A firm's **financial accounting** system is concerned with external information users—the firm's external stakeholders: consumer groups, unions, stockholders, suppliers, creditors, and government agencies. It regularly prepares income statements and balance sheets, as well as other financial reports published for shareholders and the public. All these documents focus on the activities of the company as a whole rather than on individual departments or divisions.[4]

FINANCIAL ACCOUNTING field of accounting concerned with external users of a company's financial information

Managerial Accounting **Managerial (management) accounting** serves internal users. Managers at all levels need information to make departmental decisions, monitor projects, and plan future activities. Other employees also need accounting information. To make product or operations improvements, engineers must know certain costs. To set performance goals, salespeople need past sales data organized by geographic region. Purchasing agents use information on materials costs to negotiate terms with suppliers.

MANAGERIAL (MANAGEMENT) ACCOUNTING field of accounting that serves internal users of a company's financial information

CERTIFIED PUBLIC ACCOUNTANTS

Certified public accountants (CPAs) offer accounting services to the public. They are licensed by a state after passing an exam prepared by the American Institute of Certified Public Accountants (AICPA), which also provides technical support and discipline in matters of ethics. Whereas some CPAs work as individual practitioners, many form or join existing partnerships or professional corporations. More than

CERTIFIED PUBLIC ACCOUNTANT (CPA) accountant licensed by the state and offering services to the public

40,000 CPA firms are active in the United States, but one-half of their total revenues go to the four biggest firms: Deloitte Touche Tohmatsu, Ernst & Young, KPMG LLP, and PriceWaterhouseCoopers. In addition to prominence in the United States, international operations are important for all four of these companies.

CPA Services Virtually all CPA firms, whether large or small, provide auditing, tax, and management services. Larger firms earn up to 60 percent of their revenue from auditing services, and consulting services constitute another growth area. Smaller firms earn most of their income from tax and management services.

Auditing An **audit** examines a company's AIS to determine whether financial reports reliably represent its operations.[5] Organizations must provide audit reports when applying for loans, selling stock, or when going through a major restructuring. Independent auditors who do not work for the company must ensure that clients' accounting systems follow **generally accepted accounting principles (GAAP)**—the accounting guidelines governing the content and form of financial reports. GAAP is formulated by the Financial Accounting Standards Board (FASB) of the AICPA and should be used to determine whether a firm has controls to prevent errors and fraud.[6] The Securities and Exchange Commission (SEC) is the U.S. government agency that legally enforces accounting and auditing rules and procedures. Ultimately, the auditor will certify whether the client's reports comply with GAAP.

Tax Services **Tax services** include assistance not only with tax-return preparation but also with tax planning. A CPA's advice can help a business structure (or restructure) operations and investments and perhaps save millions of dollars in taxes. Staying abreast of tax-law changes is no simple matter. Some critics charge that tax changes have become a full-time vocation among some state and federal legislators who add increasingly complicated laws and technical corrections on taxation each year.

Management Advisory Services As consultants, accounting firms provide **management advisory services** ranging from personal financial planning to planning corporate mergers. Other services include production scheduling, computer-feasibility studies, and AIS

AUDIT systematic examination of a company's accounting system to determine whether its financial reports reliably represent its operations

GENERALLY ACCEPTED ACCOUNTING PRINCIPLES (GAAP) accounting guidelines that govern the content and form of financial reports

TAX SERVICES assistance provided by CPAs for tax preparation and tax planning

MANAGEMENT ADVISORY SERVICES assistance provided by CPA firms in areas such as financial planning, information systems design, and other areas of concern for client firms

Sometimes, companies ignore GAAP and accountants fail to disclose violations. Jamie Olis was a mid-level executive at Texas-based energy producer Dynegy. To cover up the company's financial difficulties, Olis helped devise an accounting scheme to disguise a $300 million loan as cash flow. Higher-level financial officers were sentenced to 5 years in jail; Olis got 24 years. Loss to Dynegy investors was estimated at $100 million.

TABLE 14.1 CORE COMPETENCIES FOR ACCOUNTING

Strategic and Critical Thinking Skills	The accountant can provide competent advice for strategic action by combining data, knowledge, and insight.
Communications and Leadership Skills	The accountant can exchange information meaningfully in a variety of business situations with effective delivery and interpersonal skills.
Focus on the Customer, Client, and Market	The accountant can meet the changing needs of clients, customers, and employers better than the competition and can anticipate those needs better than competitors.
Skills in Interpreting Converging Information	The accountant can interpret new meaning by combining financial and nonfinancial information into a broader understanding that adds more business value.
Technology Skills	The accountant can use technology to add value to activities performed for employers, customers, and clients.

design. Some firms even assist in executive recruitment. On the staffs of the largest CPA firms are engineers, architects, mathematicians, and psychologists, who are available for consulting.

Noncertified Public Accountants Many accountants don't take the CPA exam; others work in the field while getting ready for it or while meeting requirements for state certification. Many small businesses, individuals, and even larger firms rely on these noncertified public accountants for income tax preparation, payroll accounting, and financial-planning services.

The CPA Vision Project The recent talent shortage in accounting has led the profession to rethink its culture and lifestyle.[7] With grassroots participation from CPAs, educators, and industry leaders, the AICPA, through its *CPA Vision Project*, is redefining the role of the accountant for today's world economy. The Vision Project identifies a unique combination of skills, technology, and knowledge—called **core competencies for accounting**—that will be necessary for the future CPA. As Table 14.1 shows, those skills go far beyond the ability to "crunch numbers." They include certain communications skills, along with skills in critical thinking and leadership. Indeed, the CPA Vision Project foresees CPAs who combine specialty skills with a broad-based orientation in order to communicate more effectively with people in a wide range of business activities.

CORE COMPETENCIES FOR ACCOUNTING the combination of skills, technology, and knowledge that will be necessary for the future CPA

■■■■ **PRIVATE ACCOUNTANTS AND MANAGEMENT ACCOUNTANTS**

To ensure integrity in reporting, CPAs are always independent of the firms they audit. As employees of accounting firms, they provide services for many clients. However, many businesses also hire their own salaried employees—**private accountants**—to perform day-to-day activities.

PRIVATE ACCOUNTANT salaried accountant hired by a business to carry out its day-to-day financial activities

Private accountants perform numerous jobs. An internal auditor at ConocoPhillips might fly to the North Sea to confirm the accuracy of oil-flow meters on offshore petroleum drilling platforms. A supervisor responsible for $2 billion in monthly payouts to vendors and employees may never leave the executive suite, with duties such as hiring and training, assigning projects, and evaluating performance of accounting personnel. Large businesses employ specialized accountants in such areas as budgets, financial planning, internal auditing, payroll, and taxation. In small businesses, a single person may handle all accounting tasks.

MANAGEMENT ACCOUNTANT
private accountant who provides
financial services to support
managers in various business
activities within a firm

**CERTIFIED MANAGEMENT
ACCOUNTANT (CMA)**
professional designation awarded
by the Institute of Management
Accountants in recognition of
management accounting
qualifications

Most private accountants are **management accountants** who provide services to support managers in various activities (marketing, production, engineering, and so forth). Many hold the **certified management accountant (CMA)** designation, awarded by the Institute of Management Accountants (IMA), recognizing qualifications of professionals who have passed IMA's experience and examination requirements. With some 70,000 worldwide members, IMA is dedicated to supporting accounting professionals to create quality internal controls and financial practices in their companies.

∎∎∎ FORENSIC ACCOUNTANTS

FORENSIC ACCOUNTING the
practice of accounting for legal
purposes

Forensic accounting is the fastest growing area in accounting. Sometimes known as "the private eyes of the corporate culture," forensic accountants must be good detectives. They look behind the corporate façade instead of accepting financial records at face value. In combining investigative skills with accounting, auditing, and the instincts of a bloodhound, they assist in the investigation of business and financial issues that may have application to a court of law. **Forensic accounting** is the use of accounting for legal purposes.[8]

Forensic accountants may be called upon—by law enforcement agencies, insurance companies, law firms, and business firms—for both investigative accounting and litigation support in crimes against companies, crimes by companies, and civil disagreements. They may be found conducting criminal investigations of Internet scams and misuse of government funds. Civil cases often require investigating and quantifying claims of personal injury loss due to negligence, and analyzing financial issues in matrimonial disputes. Forensic accountants also assist business firms in tracing and recovering lost assets from employee business fraud or theft.

Investigative Accounting A forensic accountant, at times, may be asked to investigate a trail of financial transactions behind a suspected crime, as in a money laundering scheme or an investment swindle. Try your hand, for example, at "Catch Me If You Can," the popular interactive forensic accounting game sponsored by the AICPA (at www.startheregoplaces.com). The forensic accountant, being familiar with the legal concepts and procedures of the case, identifies financial evidence—documents, bank accounts, phone calls, computer records, people—that may be pertinent, analyzes financial evidence, and presents accounting conclusions and their legal implications. They develop reports, exhibits, and documents to communicate their findings.

Litigation Support Forensic accountants assist in the application of accounting evidence for judicial proceedings by preparing and preserving evidence for judicial proceedings. They also assist by presenting visual aids to support trial evidence, by testifying as expert witnesses, and, especially, in determining economic damages in any case before the court. A divorce attorney, for example, may suspect that assets are being understated and request financial analysis by a forensic accountant. A movie producer may need a forensic accountant's help in determining damages for breach of contract by an actress that quits before the film is completed.

**CERTIFIED FRAUD EXAMINER
(CFE)** professional designation
administered by the Association
of Certified Fraud Examiners in
recognition of qualifications for
a specialty area within forensic
accounting

Certified Fraud Examiners A specific specialty area within forensic accounting—the **Certified Fraud Examiner (CFE)** designation—is administered by the Association of

Certified Fraud Examiners. The CFE's activities focus specifically on fraud-related issues: fraud detection, evaluating accounting systems for weaknesses and fraud risks, investigating white collar crime on behalf of law enforcement agencies, evaluating internal organizational controls for fraud prevention, and expert witnessing. The CFE examination covers four areas:

1 *Criminology and ethics.* Includes theories of fraud prevention and ethical situations.
2 *Financial transactions.* Examines types of fraudulent financial transactions incurred in accounting records.
3 *Fraud investigation.* Pertains to tracing illicit transactions, evaluating deception, and interviewing and taking statements.
4 *Legal elements of fraud.* Includes rules of evidence, criminal and civil law, and rights of the accused and accuser.

Eligibility to take the exam includes both educational and experience requirements. While a minimum of a Bachelor's degree is required, it does not have to be in accounting or any other specific field of study. Candidates without a Bachelor's degree, but with fraud-related professional experience, may substitute two years of experience for each year of academic study. Experience requirements for certification include at least two years in any of several of fraud-related areas, such as auditing, criminology, fraud investigation, or law.[9]

▪▪▪ FEDERAL RESTRICTIONS ON CPA SERVICES AND FINANCIAL REPORTING: SARBOX

While expanding into new services for clients, and amidst the torrent of financial scandals, CPA firms have encountered some obstacles. The financial wrongdoings associated with companies such as ImClone Systems, Tyco, WorldCom, Enron, Arthur Andersen, and others have not gone unnoticed in legislative circles. Federal regulations, in particular the **Sarbanes-Oxley Act of 2002 (Sarbox)**, have been enacted to restore public trust in corporate accounting practices. Sarbox's numerous provisions are a direct response to corporate America's widely publicized financial abuses.

Sarbox restricts the kinds of nonaudit services that CPAs can provide. Under the new law, for example, a CPA firm can help design a client's financial information system, but not if it also does the client's auditing. Hypothetically, an unscrupulous accounting firm's audit might intentionally overlook a client's false financial statements if, in return, the client rewards the accounting firm with a contract for lucrative nonaccounting services, such as management consulting. This was a core allegation in the Enron–Arthur Andersen scandal. By prohibiting auditing and nonauditing services to the same client, Sarbox encourages audits that are independent and unbiased.

Sarbox Compliance Requirements Sarbox imposes new requirements on virtually every financial activity, from top to bottom, in publicly traded corporations. CFOs and CEOs, for example, have to pledge that the company's finances are correct and must vouch for the methods and internal controls used to get those numbers. Companies have to provide a system that is safe for employees throughout the company—potential whistleblowers—to anonymously report unethical accounting practices and illegal activities without fear of retaliation. Sarbox imposes severe

SARBANES-OXLEY ACT OF 2002 (SARBOX) enactment of federal regulations to restore public trust in accounting practices by imposing new requirements on financial activities in publicly traded corporations

TABLE 14.2 SELECTED PROVISIONS OF THE SARBANES-OXLEY ACT

Creates a national Accounting Oversight Board that, among other activities, must establish the ethics standards used by CPA firms in preparing audits.

Requires that auditors retain audit working papers for specified periods of time (they cannot destroy audit records).

Requires auditor rotation by prohibiting the same person from being the lead auditor for more than five consecutive years.

Requires that the CEO and CFO certify that the company's financial statements are true, fair, and accurate.

Prohibits corporations from extending personal loans to executives and directors.

Requires that the audited company disclose whether it has adopted a code of ethics for its senior financial officers.

Requires that the SEC regularly review each corporation's financial statements.

Prevents employers from retaliating against research analysts that write negative reports.

Imposes criminal penalties on auditors and clients for falsifying, destroying, altering, or concealing records (10 years in prison).

Imposes fine or imprisonment (up to 25 years) on any person that defrauds shareholders.

Increases penalties for mail and wire fraud from 5 to 20 years in prison.

Establishes criminal liability for failure of corporate officers to certify financial reports.

criminal penalties for persons committing fraud, failing to report fraudulent acts, or destroying financial records.[10]

The full gamut for Sarbox compliance covers such wide-ranging issues as ethics requirements for corporations, establishment of a federal oversight board, new rules applied to auditing firms, obligations of employees, protections for employees, and penalties for noncompliance. Table 14.2 provides brief descriptions for several of Sarbox's many provisions.

SELF-CHECK QUESTIONS 1–3

You should now be able to answer Self-Check Questions 1–3.*

1 Multiple Choice Which of the following statements is **not true**?
(a) users of accounting information include business managers, investors, unions, and government agencies
(b) many, but not all, private accountants hold the CMA designation
(c) the Sarbanes-Oxley Act prohibits a CPA firm from providing management advisory services to a client company if it also does auditing for that company
(d) a Bachelor's degree in accounting is a minimum requirement for the CFE designation

2 True/False Auditing services, as provided by CPA firms for client companies, are primarily concerned with managerial accounting.

3 Multiple Choice Which of the following statements is **not true** regarding the Sarbanes-Oxley Act?
(a) upon completion of an audit, auditors are required to destroy audit working papers to preserve the privacy of the client company's information
(b) CEOs and CFOs must certify that the company's financial statements are true, fair, and accurate
(c) companies have to provide a system that is safe for employees to anonymously report unethical and illegal accounting practices without fear of retaliation
(d) Sarbox regulations were enacted to restore public trust in corporate accounting practices

*Answers to Self-Check Questions 1–3 can be found on p. 566.

THE ACCOUNTING EQUATION

All accountants rely on record keeping to enter and track transactions. Underlying all record-keeping procedures is the most basic tool of accounting: the **accounting equation**. At various points in the year, accountants use the equation to balance the data pertaining to the firm's financial transactions:

$$\text{Assets} = \text{Liabilities} + \text{Owners' Equity}$$

After each financial transaction (e.g., payments to suppliers, sales to customers, wages to employees), the accounting equation must be in balance. If it isn't, then an accounting error has occurred. To better understand the importance of this equation, we must understand the terms *assets*, *liabilities*, and *owners' equity*.

Assets and Liabilities An **asset** is any economic resource that is expected to benefit a firm or an individual who owns it. Assets include land, buildings, equipment, inventories, and payments due the company (accounts receivable). Google, the Internet search and information provider, for example, held assets amounting to $3.31 billion at year-end 2004.[11]

A **liability** is a debt that the firm owes to an outside party. The total of Google's liabilities—all the debt owed to others—was $0.38 billion at the end of 2004.

Owners' Equity You may have heard of the *equity* that a homeowner has in a house—that is, the amount of money that could be made by selling the house and paying off the mortgage. Similarly, **owners' equity** is the amount of money that owners would receive if they sold all of a company's assets and paid all of its liabilities. Google's financial reports for 2004 declared shareholders' equity of $2.93 billion. For the Google example, we see that the accounting equation is in balance, as it should be:

$$\text{Assets} = \text{Liabilities} + \text{Owners' Equity}$$
$$\$3.31 = \$0.38 + \$2.93 \text{ billion}$$

We can rewrite the equation to highlight how owners' equity relates to its assets and liabilities:

$$\text{Assets} - \text{Liabilities} = \text{Owners' Equity}$$

It means the same thing as *net worth*: The difference between what the firm owns (assets) minus what it owes (liabilities) is its net worth or owners' equity. If a company's assets exceed its liabilities, owners' equity is *positive*. At Google, owners' equity is $2.93 billion (= $3.31 – $0.38). If the company goes out of business, the owners will receive some cash (a gain) after selling assets and paying off liabilities. If liabilities outweigh assets, owners' equity is *negative*; assets are insufficient to pay off all debts and the firm is bankrupt. If the company goes out of business, the owners will get no cash and some creditors won't be paid. Owners' equity is meaningful for both investors and lenders. Before lending money to owners, for example, lenders want to know the amount of owners' equity in a business. A larger owners' equity indicates greater security for lenders. Owners' equity consists of two sources of capital:

1 The amount that the owners originally invested
2 Profits (also owned by the owners) earned by and reinvested in the company

When a company operates profitably, its assets increase faster than its liabilities. Owners' equity, therefore, will increase if profits are retained in the business instead of paid out as dividends to stockholders. Owners' equity also increases if owners invest more of their own money to increase assets. However, owners' equity can shrink if the company operates at a loss or if owners withdraw assets.

ACCOUNTING EQUATION
Assets = Liabilities + Owners' Equity; used by accountants to balance data for the firm's financial transactions at various points in the year

ASSET any economic resource expected to benefit a firm or an individual who owns it

LIABILITY debt owed by a firm to an outside organization or individual

OWNERS' EQUITY amount of money that owners would receive if they sold all of a firm's assets and paid all of its liabilities

The inventory at this Ford dealership is among the company's assets: The cars constitute an economic resource because the firm will benefit financially as it sells them.

FINANCIAL STATEMENTS

FINANCIAL STATEMENT any of several types of reports summarizing a company's financial status to stakeholders and to aid in managerial decision making

As noted previously, accountants summarize the results of a firm's transactions and issue reports to help managers make informed decisions. Among the most important reports are **financial statements**, which fall into three broad categories—*balance sheets*, *income statements*, and *statements of cash flows*. Together, these reports indicate the firm's financial health and what affected it. In this section, we discuss these three types of financial statements as well as the function of the budget as an internal financial statement. We conclude by explaining the most important reporting practices and the standards that guide accountants in drawing up financial statements.

■■■ BALANCE SHEETS

BALANCE SHEET financial statement that supplies detailed information about a firm's assets, liabilities, and owners' equity

Balance sheets supply detailed information about the accounting equation factors: *assets*, *liabilities*, and *owners' equity*. Because they also show a firm's financial condition at one point in time, they are sometimes called *statements of financial position*. Figure 14.1 is a simplified presentation of the balance sheet for Google, Inc.

Assets Again, an *asset* is any economic resource that a company owns and from which it expects to get some future benefit. From an accounting standpoint, most companies have three types of assets: *current*, *fixed*, and *intangible*.

CURRENT ASSET asset that can or will be converted into cash within a year

LIQUIDITY ease with which an asset can be converted into cash

Current Assets **Current assets** include cash and assets that can be converted into cash within a year. The act of converting something into cash is called *liquidating*. Assets are normally listed in order of **liquidity**—the ease of converting them into cash. Debts, for example, are usually paid in cash. A company that needs but cannot generate cash—a company that's not "liquid"—may be forced to sell assets at reduced prices or even to go out of business.

By definition, cash is completely liquid. *Marketable securities* purchased as short-term investments are slightly less liquid but can be sold quickly. These include stocks or bonds of other companies, government securities, and money market certificates. Many companies

Figure 14.1   Google's Balance Sheet

Google, Inc.
Summary of Balance Sheet (condensed)
as of December 31, 2004
(in thousands)

Assets		Liabilities and Owner's Equity	
Current assets:		**Current liabilities:**	
Cash	$426,873	Accounts payable	$32,672
Marketable securities	1,705,424	Other	307,696
Other	561,168	**Total current liabilities**	**$340,368**
Total current assets	**$2,693,465**		
		Long-term liabilities:	
Fixed assets:		All long-term debts	43,927
Property and equipment, net	$378,916	**Total long-term liabilities**	**$43,927**
Other	47,083		
Total fixed assets	**$425,999**	**Total liabilities**	**$384,295**
		Owners equity:	
Intangible assets:		Paid-in capital	$2,338,585
Intangible assets	71,069	Retained earnings	590,471
Goodwill	122,818	**Total owners equity**	**$2,929,056**
Total Intangible assets	**$193,887**		
Total assets	**$3,313,351**	**Total liabilities and owners equity**	**$3,313,351**

Google's balance sheet for year ended December 31, 2004. The balance sheet shows clearly that the firm's total assets are equal to its total liabilities and owners' equity.

hold other nonliquid assets such as *merchandise inventory*—the cost of merchandise that's been acquired for sale to customers and is still on hand. Google has no merchandise inventory because it sells services rather than physical goods.

Fixed Assets **Fixed assets** (such as land, buildings, and equipment) have long-term use or value, but as buildings and equipment wear out or become obsolete, their value decreases. Accountants use **depreciation** to spread the cost of an asset over the years of its useful life. To reflect decreasing value, accountants calculate an asset's useful life in years, divide its worth by that many years, and subtract the resulting amount each year. Every year, therefore, the remaining value (or "net" value) decreases on the books. In Figure 14.1, Google shows fixed assets of $0.426 (rounded) billion after depreciation.

Intangible Assets Although their worth is hard to set, **intangible assets** have monetary value in the form of expected benefits. These usually include the cost of obtaining rights or privileges, such as patents, trademarks, copyrights, and franchise fees. **Goodwill** is the amount paid for an existing business beyond the value of its other assets. A purchased firm, for example, may have a particularly good reputation or location. Google declares both intangibles and goodwill as intangible assets in its balance sheet.

Liabilities Like assets, liabilities are often separated into different categories. **Current liabilities** are debts that must be paid within one year. These include **accounts payable (payables)**—unpaid bills to suppliers for materials as well as wages and taxes that must be paid in the coming year. Google has current liabilities of $0.34 (rounded) billion.

FIXED ASSET asset with long-term use or value, such as land, buildings, and equipment

DEPRECIATION accounting method for distributing the cost of an asset over its useful life

INTANGIBLE ASSET nonphysical asset, such as a patent or trademark, that has economic value in the form of expected benefit

GOODWILL amount paid for an existing business above the value of its other assets

CURRENT LIABILITY debt that must be paid within one year

ACCOUNTS PAYABLE (PAYABLES) current liability consisting of bills owed to suppliers, plus wages and taxes due within the coming year

LONG-TERM LIABILITY debt that is not due for at least one year

PAID-IN CAPITAL money that is invested in a company by its owners

RETAINED EARNINGS earnings retained by a firm for its use rather than paid out as dividends

Long-term liabilities are debts that are not due for at least a year. These normally represent borrowed funds on which the company must pay interest. The long-term liabilities of Google are $.044 (rounded) billion.

Owners' Equity The final section of the balance sheet in Figure 14.1 shows owners' equity broken down into *paid-in capital* and *retained earnings*. When Google was first formed, it sold a small amount of common stock that provided its first paid-in capital. With an initial public offering (IPO) in 2004, Google began selling its stock to the public, thus creating additional funds that were needed for expansion. **Paid-in capital** is additional money invested by owners. Google's paid-in capital had grown to $2.34 (rounded) billion by year-end 2004.

Retained earnings are net profits kept by a firm rather than paid out as dividend payments to stockholders. They accumulate when profits, which can be distributed to stockholders, are kept instead for the company's use. At the close of 2004, Google had retained earnings of $0.59 billion. The total of stockholders' equity—paid-in capital plus retained earnings—had grown to $2.93 billion.

The balance sheet for any company, then, is a barometer for its financial condition at one point in time. By comparing the current balance sheet with those of previous years, creditors and owners can better interpret the firm's financial progress and future prospects in terms of changes in its assets, liabilities, and owners' equity.

■■■ INCOME STATEMENTS

INCOME STATEMENT (PROFIT-AND-LOSS STATEMENT) financial statement listing a firm's annual revenues and expenses so that a bottom line shows annual profit or loss

REVENUES funds that flow into a business from the sale of goods or services

COST OF REVENUES costs that a company incurs to obtain revenues from other companies

The **income statement** is sometimes called a **profit-and-loss statement** because its description of revenues and expenses results in a figure showing the firm's annual profit or loss. In other words,

$$\text{Revenues} - \text{Expenses} = \text{Profit (or Loss)}$$

Popularly known as the *bottom line*, profit or loss is probably the most important figure in any business enterprise. Figure 14.2 shows the 2004 income statement for Google, whose bottom line was $0.40 (rounded) billion. The income statement is divided into four major categories: *revenues*, *cost of revenues*, *operating expenses*, and *net income*. Unlike a balance sheet, which shows the financial condition at a specific *point in time*, an income statement shows the financial results that occurred during a *period of time*, such as a month, quarter, or year.

Revenues When a law firm receives $250 for preparing a will or a supermarket collects $65 from a grocery shopper, both are receiving **revenues**—the funds that flow into a business from the sale of goods or services. In 2004, Google reported revenues of $3.2 (rounded) billion from the sale of advertising and Web search services to Google Network members, such as America Online.

Cost of Revenues (Cost of Goods Sold) In the Google income statement, the **cost of revenues** section shows the costs of obtaining the revenues from other companies during the year. These are fees Google must pay its network members—revenue sharing from advertising income—and also include expenses arising from the operation of Google's data centers, including labor, energy, and costs of processing customer transactions. The cost of revenues for Google in 2004 was $1.46 (rounded) billion.

While cost of revenues is a relevant income statement category for service providers like Google, it is not used by goods producers. Instead, income statements for firms, such

Figure 14.2   Google's Income Statement

Google, Inc.
Summary of Income Statement (condensed)
as of December 31, 2004
(in thousands)

Revenues (gross sales)		**$3,189,223**
Cost of revenues	1,457,653	
Gross profit		1,731,570
Operating expenses:		
Sales and marketing	246,300	
Administrative and general	845,078	
Total operating expenses		**$1,091,378**
Operating income (before taxes)		640,192
Income taxes*		241,073
Net income		**$399,119**

*approximated

Google's income statement for year ended December 31, 2004. The final entry on the income statement, the bottom line, reports the firm's profit or loss.

as P&G, use the corresponding category, **cost of goods sold**: costs of obtaining materials to make products sold during the year.

Gross Profit Managers are often interested in **gross profit**, a preliminary, quick-to-calculate profit figure, that considers just two pieces of data—revenues and cost of revenues (the direct costs of getting those revenues)—from the income statement. To calculate gross profit, subtract cost of revenues from revenues obtained by selling the firm's products. The gross profit for Google in 2004 was $1.73 (rounded) billion.

Operating Expenses
In addition to costs directly related to generating revenues, every company has general expenses ranging from erasers to the CEO's salary. Like cost of revenues and cost of goods sold, **operating expenses** are resources that must flow out of a company if it is to earn revenues. As shown in Figure 14.2, Google had operating expenses of $1.09 billion (rounded).

Sales and marketing expenses result from activities related to selling goods or services, such as sales force salaries and advertising expenses. *Administrative and general expenses*, such as management salaries and maintenance costs, are related to the general management of the company.

Operating and Net Income
Operating income compares the gross profit from operations against operating expenses. This calculation for Google ($1.73 billion – $1.09 billion) reveals an operating income, or income before taxes, of $0.64 billion. Subtracting income taxes from operating income ($0.64 billion – $0.24 billion) reveals **net income (net profit or net earnings)**. Google's net income for the year was $0.40 billion (rounded).

The step-by-step information in the income statement shows how a company obtained its net income for the period, making it easier for shareholders and other stakeholders to evaluate the firm's financial health.

COST OF GOODS SOLD costs of obtaining materials for making the products sold by a firm during the year

GROSS PROFIT a preliminary, quick-to-calculate profit figure calculated from the firm's revenues minus its cost of revenues (the direct costs of getting the revenues)

OPERATING EXPENSES costs, other than the cost of revenues, incurred in producing a good or service

OPERATING INCOME gross profit minus operating expenses

NET INCOME (NET PROFIT, NET EARNINGS) gross profit minus operating expenses and income taxes

Figure 14.3

Google's Statement of Cash Flows

> **Google, Inc.**
> **Summary of Statement of Cash Flows (condensed)**
> **as of December 31, 2004**
> **Increase (Decrease) in Cash**
> **(in thousands)**
>
> | | | |
> |---|---|---|
> | **Net cash provided by operating activities** | | **$977,044** |
> | | | |
> | Cash flows from investment activities: | | |
> | Payment for purchase of property, equipment, and securities | (1,901,356) | |
> | **Net cash used in investing activities** | | **(1,901,356)** |
> | | | |
> | Cash flows from financing activities: | | |
> | Proceeds from sale of stock (IPO) | 1,161,080 | |
> | Other | 41,110 | |
> | **Net cash provided by financing activities** | | **1,202,190** |
> | | | |
> | Net increase in cash | | 277,878 |
> | Cash at beginning of year | | 148,995 |
> | **Cash at end of year** | | **$426,873** |

Google's statement of cash flows for year ended December 31, 2004. The final entry shows year-end cash position resulting from operating activities, investing activities, and financing activities.

▪▪▪ STATEMENTS OF CASH FLOWS

STATEMENT OF CASH FLOWS
financial statement describing a firm's yearly cash receipts and cash payments

Some companies prepare only balance sheets and income statements. However, the SEC requires all firms whose stock is publicly traded to issue a third report: The **statement of cash flows**, which describes yearly cash receipts and cash payments. Since it provides the most detail about how the company generates and uses cash, some investors and creditors consider it one of the most important statements of all. A statement of cash flows, like that in Figure 14.3 for Google, shows the effects on cash of three aspects of the business: *operating activities*, *investing activities*, and *financing activities*.

- **Cash Flows from Operations.** This first section of the statement concerns main operating activities: cash transactions involved in buying and selling goods and services. For the Google example, it reveals how much of the year's cash balance results from the firm's main line of business—sales of advertising and web search services. Operating activities at Google contributed net cash inflows amounting to $0.98 (rounded) billion for 2004.
- **Cash Flows from Investing.** The second section reports net cash used in or provided by investing. It includes cash receipts and payments from buying and selling stocks, bonds, property, equipment, and other productive assets. These sources of cash are not the company's main line of business. Purchases of property, equipment, and securities made by Google consumed $1.9 (rounded) billion of net cash. A cash outflow is shown in parentheses.
- **Cash Flows from Financing.** The third section reports net cash from all financing activities. It includes cash inflows from borrowing or issuing stock, as well as outflows for payment of dividends and repayment of borrowed money. Google received $1.16 (rounded) billion from the public offering of Google stock and another $0.04 (rounded) billion from other sources. Financing activities provided a net cash inflow of $1.2 (rounded) billion.

The overall change in cash from these three sources is an increase of $0.28 (rounded) billion for the year. The amount is added to the beginning cash (from the 2003 balance sheet), to arrive at 2004's ending cash position of $0.43 (rounded) billion. When creditors and stockholders know how a firm obtained and used funds during the course of a year, it's easier for them to interpret year-to-year changes in the balance sheet and income statement.

THE BUDGET: AN INTERNAL FINANCIAL STATEMENT

For planning, controlling, and decision making, the most important internal financial statement is the **budget**—a detailed report on estimated receipts and expenditures for a future period of time. Although that period is usually one year, some companies also prepare three- or five-year budgets, especially when considering major capital expenditures.

BUDGET detailed statement of estimated receipts and expenditures for a future period of time

Budgets are also useful for keeping track of weekly or monthly performance. For example, P&G evaluates business units monthly by comparing actual financial results with monthly budgets. Discrepancies signal potential problems and spur action to improve financial performance.

Although the accounting staff coordinates the budget process, it needs input from many areas regarding proposed activities and required resources. Figure 14.4 is a sales budget for a hypothetical wholesaler—Perfect Posters. In preparing the budget, accounting must obtain from the sales group projections for units to be sold and expected expenses for the coming year. Then, accounting draws up the final budget and, throughout the year, compares the budget to actual expenditures and revenues. The budget differs from the other statements we have discussed in that budgets are not shared outside the company; hence the "internal financial statement" title.

Figure 14.4   Perfect Posters' Sales Budget

Perfect Posters, Inc.
555 RIVERVIEW, CHICAGO, IL 60606

Perfect Posters, Inc.
Sales Budget
First Quarter, 2007

	January	February	March	Quarter
Budgeted sales (units)	7,500	6,000	6,500	20,000
Budgeted selling price per unit	$3.50	$3.50	$3.50	$3.50
Budgeted sales revenue	**$26,250**	**$21,000**	**$22,750**	**$70,000**
Expected cash receipts:				
From December sales	$26,210			$26,210
From January sales	17,500	$8,750		26,250
From February sales		14,000	$7,000	21,000
From March sales			15,200	15,200
Total cash receipts:	**$43,710**	**$22,750**	**$22,200**	**$88,660**

REPORTING STANDARDS AND PRACTICES

Accountants follow standard reporting practices and principles when they prepare external reports. The common language dictated by standard practices is designed to give external users confidence in the accuracy and meaning of financial information. Spelled out in GAAP, these principles cover a range of issues, such as when to recognize revenues from operations and how to make full public disclosure of financial information. Without such standards, users of financial statements wouldn't be able to compare information from different companies, and they would misunderstand—or be led to misconstrue—a company's true financial status.

Revenue Recognition and Activity Timing The reporting of revenue inflows, and the timing of other transactions, must abide by accounting principles that govern financial statements. As noted previously, revenues are funds that flow into a business as a result of operating activities during an accounting period. **Revenue recognition**, for example, is the formal recording and reporting of revenues at the appropriate time. Although a firm earns revenues continuously as it makes sales, earnings are not reported until the *earnings cycle* is completed. This cycle is complete under two conditions:

REVENUE RECOGNITION
formal recording and reporting of
revenues at the appropriate time

1 The sale is complete and the product delivered.
2 The sale price has been collected or is collectible (accounts receivable).

The end of the earnings cycle determines the timing for revenue recognition in a firm's financial statements. Suppose a toy company in January signs a sales contract to supply $1,000 of toys to a retail store, with delivery scheduled in February. Although the sale is completed in January, the $1,000 revenue should not then be recognized because the toys have not been delivered and the sale price is not yet collectible, so the earnings cycle is incomplete. Revenues are recorded in the accounting period—February—in which the product is delivered and collectible (or collected). This practice ensures that the statement gives a fair comparison of what was gained (revenues) in return for the resources that were given up (costs of materials, labor, and other production and delivery expenses) for the transaction.

The timing of other activities, too, not just revenue recognition, is guided by GAAP reporting requirements. The SEC, for example, brought charges against America Online for fraudulently inflating the numbers of AOL subscribers it reported to the investment community, both before and after its merger with Time Warner in 2001. AOL violated the recognition principle by reporting memberships that the company knew had not been, and mostly would not be, activated by prospective customers. The unlikely activations stem from "bulk subscription sales" to other companies that, in turn, distributed them to employees that most often would not subscribe, but were all counted as subscribers in AOL's reports to the financial community. Since subscriptions were not activated, the number of subscribers in AOL's quarterly financial reports was bloated. The investment community, believing AOL's overstated new-subscriber growth rate, was misled into overvaluing AOL's financial prospects and its stock value.[12]

Full Disclosure Garden.com, the Internet startup we introduced in the Prologue to this text, issued "Management's Discussion and Analysis of Financial Condition and Results of Operations" containing the following comments:

Since inception we have incurred significant losses. . . . We expect to experience operating losses and negative cash flow for the foreseeable future. . . . As a result, we will need to generate significant revenues to achieve and maintain profitability. . . . We cannot assure you that we will be successful in addressing these risks, and our failure to do so could have a negative impact on our business, operating results and financial condition.

Within one year of this now-prophetic report, Garden.com closed its doors having accumulated losses amounting to more than $75 million.[13]

The Garden.com incident is an example of GAAP's **full disclosure** guideline. It means that financial statements should not include just numbers but should also furnish management's interpretations and explanations of those numbers so that users can better understand information in the statements. Because they know about events inside the company, the people in management prepare additional information to explain certain events or transactions or to disclose the circumstances behind certain results.

FULL DISCLOSURE guideline that financial statements should not include just numbers but should also furnish management's interpretations and explanations of those numbers

SELF-CHECK QUESTIONS 4–6

You should now be able to answer Self-Check Questions 4–6.*

4 Multiple Choice The end-of-year balance sheet for Millie's fruit stand includes the following data: assets = $22,000; owners' equity = $2,500; liabilities = $21,500. Given this information, which of the following is **true**?
   (a) assets are increasing faster than liabilities
   (b) profits are being reinvested in the firm
   (c) retained earnings for the year have increased
   (d) an accounting error has occurred

5 True/False Three financial statements—balance sheets, income statements, and statements of cash flows—provide useful information for indicating a firm's financial health and what affected it.

6 Multiple Choice Which of the following is **not true** regarding a company's financial statements?
   (a) the balance sheet shows the financial condition at a point in time, whereas the income statement shows financial results that occurred during a period of time
   (b) the accounting practice called full disclosure means that the company's financial statements must be released for distribution to the public, including all of the firm's stakeholders
   (c) a company's budget is an internal financial statement that usually is not released to the public
   (d) the SEC requires all firms whose stock is publicly traded to issue a statement of cash flows

***Answers to Self-Check Questions 4–6 can be found on p. 566.**

ANALYZING FINANCIAL STATEMENTS

Financial statements present a lot of information, but what does it all *mean*? How, for example, can statements help investors decide what stock to buy or help lenders decide whether to extend credit? Answers to such questions for various stakeholders—employees, managers, unions, suppliers, the government, customers—can be answered as follows: Statements provide data, which can, in turn, reveal trends and be applied to various *ratios* (comparative numbers). We can then use these trends and ratios to evaluate a firm's financial health, its progress, and its prospects for the future.

Ratios are normally grouped into three major classifications:

1 **Solvency ratios** for estimating short-term and long-term risk
2 **Profitability ratios** for measuring potential earnings
3 **Activity ratios** for evaluating management's use of assets

SOLVENCY RATIO financial ratio, either short- or long-term, for estimating the borrower's ability to repay debt

PROFITABILITY RATIO financial ratio for measuring a firm's potential earnings

ACTIVITY RATIO financial ratio for evaluating management's efficiency in using a firm's assets

entrepreneurship and new ventures

How Can You Account for a Good Beer?

At Toronto, Ontario's Black Oak Brewing Company, founders Ken Woods and John Gagliardi may be the perfect pair to survive in Canada's highly competitive beer market. Although each brings different skills to the joint venture, they share a vision: to make—and sell—the highest-quality beer possible. Gagliardi, certified as a brewmaster by the world-renowned Siebel Institute in 1993, is the quality-control expert whose responsibilities include ensuring the consistency and character of every batch of Black Oak. He admits that as a businessman, he is "first and foremost" a beer lover. "It's got to have the right taste and the perfect clarity and quality. We won't settle for anything less than the best, because we know our customers are going to be expecting a high-quality beer," says Gagliardi.

Woods is a CMA and a member of the Society of Management Accountants of Canada, who shares his partner's enthusiastic interest in beer and brewing. For 10 years, he devoted his evenings to developing both his bartending skills and his concepts of beers and brewery operations. Since opening Black Oak in 1999, they've managed to develop award-winning beers, such as Black Oak Nut Brown Ale. But they also know that even a great-tasting beer will go sour if you can't produce and sell it profitably.

Woods's accounting background enables him to set up and monitor management and financial procedures, such as the cost controls for buying equipment and raw materials at the right price. Accounting expertise is especially important because the company's cash flows are affected by the terms of payment negotiated with suppliers and by its procedures for collecting sales revenues. Working in finance and purchasing departments while earning his CMA credentials, Woods learned a lot about payables and receivables. He also produced staff expense reports and tax documents and set up standards for keeping operating costs under control. Being a CMA, says Woods, "is really helpful because it firms up everything you need to know in the marketplace."

Depending on the decisions to be made, a user may apply none, some, or all of these ratios. Data for calculating the ratios come from the firm's balance sheet and income statement.

■■■ SOLVENCY RATIOS: BORROWER'S ABILITY TO REPAY DEBT

What are the chances that a borrower will be able to repay a loan and the interest due? This question is first and foremost in the minds of bank lending officers, managers of pension funds and other investors, suppliers, and the borrowing company's own financial managers. Solvency ratios provide measures of the firm's ability to meet its debt obligations.

The Current Ratio and Short-Term Solvency Short-run survival depends on the ability to pay the company's immediate debts. Such payments require cash. **Short-term solvency ratios** measure a company's liquidity and its ability to pay immediate debts. The most commonly used of these is the **current ratio**, or "banker's ratio," that measures a company's ability to meet current obligations out of current assets. It reflects a firm's ability to generate cash to meet obligations through the normal, orderly process of selling inventories and collecting revenues from customers. It is calculated by dividing current assets by current liabilities. The higher a firm's current ratio, the lower the risk to investors.

As a rule, a current ratio is satisfactory at 2:1 or higher—that is, if current assets more than double current liabilities. A smaller ratio may indicate that a firm will have trouble paying its bills.

SHORT-TERM SOLVENCY RATIO financial ratio for measuring a company's ability to pay immediate debts

CURRENT RATIO financial ratio for measuring a company's ability to pay current debts out of current assets

How does Google measure up? Look again at the balance sheet in Figure 14.1. Judging from current assets and current liabilities at the end of 2004, we see that

$$\frac{\text{Current assets}}{\text{Current liabilities}} = \frac{\$2.69 \text{ billion}}{\$0.34 \text{ billion}} = 7.9$$

How does this ratio compare with those of other companies? Not bad: It's higher than the industry average of 1.4 for companies that provide business services. The 7.9 current ratio indicates Google is a good short-run credit risk.

Long-Term Solvency Stakeholders are also concerned about long-term solvency. Has a company been overextended by borrowing so much that it will be unable to repay debts in future years? A firm that can't meet its long-term debt obligations is in danger of collapse or takeover—a risk that makes creditors and investors quite cautious. To evaluate a company's risk of running into this problem, creditors turn to the balance sheet to see the extent to which a firm is financed through borrowed money. Long-term solvency is calculated by dividing **debt**—total liabilities—by owners' equity. The lower a firm's debt, the lower the risk to investors and creditors. Companies with more debt may find themselves owing so much that they lack the income needed to meet interest payments or to repay borrowed money.

Leverage Sometimes, high debt can be not only acceptable but also desirable. Borrowing funds gives a firm **leverage**—the ability to make otherwise unaffordable investments. In *leveraged buyouts*, firms have willingly taken on sometimes huge debt to buy out other companies. If owning the purchased company generates profits above the cost of borrowing the purchase price, leveraging often makes sense. Unfortunately, many buyouts have caused problems because profits fell short of expected levels or because rising interest rates increased payments on the buyer's debt.

DEBT a company's total liabilities

LEVERAGE ability to finance an investment through borrowed funds

■■■ PROFITABILITY RATIOS: EARNINGS POWER FOR OWNERS

It's important to know whether a company is solvent in both the long and the short term, but risk alone is not an adequate basis for investment decisions. Investors also want some indication of the returns they can expect. Potential shareholders ask, "As an owner of this company, how much financial return would I get?" Evidence of earnings power is available from profitability ratios, such as *earnings per share*.

Earnings per Share Defined as net income divided by the number of shares of common stock outstanding, **earnings per share** determines the size of the dividend that a firm can pay shareholders. As an indicator of a company's wealth potential, investors use this ratio to decide whether to buy or sell the firm's stock. As the ratio goes up, stock value increases because investors know that the firm can better afford to pay dividends. Naturally, stock loses market value if financial statements report a decline in earnings per share. For Google, we can use the net income total from the income statement in Figure 14.2, together with the number of outstanding shares of stock, to calculate earnings per share as follows:

EARNINGS PER SHARE profitability ratio measuring the net profit that the company earns for each share of outstanding stock

$$\frac{\text{Net income}}{\text{Number of common shares outstanding}} = \frac{\$399,119,000}{272,781,000 \text{ shares of stock}} = \$1.46 \text{ per share}$$

"It's up to you now, Miller. The only thing that can save us is an accounting breakthrough."

This means that Google had net earnings of $1.46 (rounded) for each share of stock during 2004. As a baseline for comparison, note that Time Warner's recent earnings were $0.58 per share, while Microsoft earned $1.18.

■■■ ACTIVITY RATIOS: HOW EFFICIENTLY IS THE FIRM USING ITS RESOURCES?

The efficiency with which a firm uses resources is linked to profitability. As a potential investor, you want to know which company gets more mileage from its resources. Information obtained from the income statement can be used for *activity ratios* to measure this efficiency. For example, two firms use the same amount of resources or assets to perform a particular activity. If Firm A generates greater profits or sales, it has used its resources more efficiently and so enjoys a better activity ratio. It may apply to various activities, such as the use of advertising, sales, or inventory management. Consider the activity of using the firm's resources to increase its sales. As an example, suppose from its income statements we find that Google increases its annual sales revenues and does it without increasing its own operating costs. Its operating activity has become more efficient. Investors like to see these year-to-year increases in efficiencies because it means the company is getting "more bang for the buck"—revenues are increasing faster than costs.

BRINGING ETHICS INTO THE ACCOUNTING EQUATION

"I'm becoming the Mother Teresa of corporate integrity," says Lynn Brewer, one of the internal whistleblowers that first shed light on Enron's corporate scandal, also implicating Arthur Andersen, its auditor. She quickly became aware of unethical accounting practices soon after arriving at Enron and, she says, there were strong incentives to keep it quiet. That was just the beginning. When Enron declared bankruptcy in 2001, there

say what you mean

Technically Speaking

The meeting for department heads began when the general manager asked, "Well, how did we do last month compared to the budget?" "On a static-budget basis," replied the head of accounting, "unfavorable variances were realized for variable expenses and total expenses. Favorable budget variances were realized for units sold, sales revenues, and operating income." She paused and then continued: "On a flexible-budget basis, unfavorable variances were realized on variable expenses, fixed expenses, total expenses, and operating income." After a moment of silence, the general manager said, "What does all that mean?"

An interesting situation. The key element—and the problem—is specialization. Specialists tend to develop their own languages so that they can communicate with one another efficiently and clearly. Communicating with outsiders, however, presents problems. In our sample meeting, the general manager asked for information from a specialist (an accountant) in front of nonaccountants. The presentation, though technically accurate, didn't inform anyone who didn't understand the special language of accounting. The technical detail just sidetracked everyone; the purpose of the meeting was lost in a flurry of jargon.

How could this situation have been avoided from the outset? The first step is recognizing the existence of specialized languages and working to foster communications across specialty areas. Good accountants develop skills for communicating with nonaccountants. The second step is the awareness that any one question can be answered in a variety of ways and various levels of technical detail, depending on the audience. The general manager, beforehand, should have clarified the purpose of the budget discussion so that accounting would be better prepared to deliver understandable and useful information for this audience.

---

were about 6,000 whistle-blowing reports to the SEC against all U.S. companies for the entire year. By 2005, the number of such reports had grown to over 450,000 per month—meaning there were more whistle-blowing reports than U.S. companies.[14]

■■■ WHY ACCOUNTING ETHICS?

The purpose of ethics in accounting is to maintain public confidence in business institutions, financial markets, and the products and services of the accounting profession. Without ethics, all of accounting's tools and methods would be meaningless because their usefulness depends, ultimately, on veracity in their application.

AICPA's Code of Professional Conduct The **code of professional conduct** for public accountants in the United States is maintained and enforced by the AICPA. The Institute identifies six ethics-related areas—listed in Table 14.3—with which accountants must comply to maintain certification. Comprehensive details for compliance in each area are spelled out in the AICPA Code of Professional Conduct. The IMA maintains a similar code to provide ethical guidelines for the management accounting profession.

In reading the AICPA's Code, you can see that it forbids misrepresentation and fraud in financial statements. Deception certainly violates the call for exercising moral judgments (in "Responsibilities"), is contrary to the public interest (by deceiving investors) and does not honor the public trust (in "The Public Interest"). Misleading statements destroy the public's confidence in the accounting profession and in business in general. While the Code prohibits such abuses, its success depends, ultimately, on its acceptance and use by the professionals it governs.

CODE OF PROFESSIONAL CONDUCT the code of ethics for CPAs as maintained and enforced by the AICPA

TABLE 14.3 OVERVIEW OF THE CODE OF ETHICS FOR CPAs

Membership in the American Institute of Certified Public Accountants is voluntary. By accepting membership, a certified public accountant assumes an obligation of self-discipline above and beyond the requirements of laws and regulations.

Responsibilities	In carrying out their responsibilities as professionals, members should exercise sensitive professional and moral judgments in all their activities.
The Public Interest	Members should accept the obligation to act in a way that will serve the public interest, honor the public trust, and demonstrate commitment to professionalism.
Integrity	To maintain and broaden public confidence, members should perform all professional responsibilities with the highest sense of integrity.
Objectivity and Independence	A member should maintain objectivity and be free of conflicts of interest in discharging professional responsibilities. A member in public practice should be independent in fact and appearance when providing auditing and other attestation services.
Due Care	A member should observe the profession's technical and ethical standards, strive continually to improve competence and the quality of services, and discharge professional responsibility to the best of the member's ability.
Scope and Nature of Services	A member in public practice should observe the Principles of the Code of Professional Conduct in determining the scope and nature of services to be provided.

Violations of Accounting Ethics and GAAP Unethical and illegal accounting violations have dominated the popular press in recent years. Some of the more notorious cases, listed in Table 14.4, violated the public's trust, ruined retirement plans for thousands of employees, and caused shutdowns and lost jobs. As you read each case, you should be able to see how its violation relates to the presentation of balance sheets and income statements in this chapter. In each case, adversity would have been prevented if employees had followed the code of professional conduct. In each case, nearly all of the code's six ethics-related areas were violated. And in every case, "professionals" willingly participated in unethical behavior. Such was the impetus for Sarbox.

Ethics Means Doing the Right Thing Amidst a flurry of unscrupulous activity, ethics remains an area where one person who is willing to "do the right thing" can make a difference. And they do, every day. Refusing to turn a blind eye to unethical accounting around her at Enron, Lynn Brewer tried to alert people inside about misstatements of the company's assets. When that failed, she, along with colleagues Sherron Watkins and Margaret Ceccioni, talked with the U.S. Committee on Energy and Commerce to voice concerns about Enron's condition. Maintaining personal and professional integrity, to Brewer, was an overriding concern, and she acted accordingly.

TABLE 14.4 EXAMPLES OF UNETHICAL AND ILLEGAL ACCOUNTING ACTIONS

CORPORATION	ACCOUNTING VIOLATION
AOL Time Warner	America Online (AOL) inflated ad revenues to keep stock prices high before and after merging with Time Warner.
Cendant	Inflated income in financial statements by $500 million through fraud and errors.
HCA, Columbia/HCA	Defrauded Medicare, Medicaid, and TRICARE through false cost claims and unlawful billings (must pay $1.7 billion in civil penalties, damages, criminal fines, and penalties).
Tyco	Dennis Kozlowski illegally used company funds to buy expensive art for personal possession (he received an 8- to 25-year prison sentence).
Waste Management	Overstated income in financial statements (false and misleading reports) by improperly calculating depreciation and salvage value for equipment.
WorldCom	Hid $3.8 billion in expenses to show an inflated (false) profit instead of loss in annual income statement.

SELF-CHECK QUESTIONS 7–9

You should now be able to answer Self-Check Questions 7–9.*

7 Multiple Choice Which of the following items is **not true** regarding financial ratios?

(a) solvency ratios, such as the current ratio, are useful to lending officers and others who are interested in the firm's ability to repay debt

(b) investors watch earnings per share as an indicator of the firm's earnings power and ability to pay dividends

(c) activity ratios are used as an indicator of the company's efficiency in performing a particular activity, such as sales, advertising, or inventory management

(d) the SEC requires that three kinds of ratios—solvency, profitability, and activity—be published in the financial statements of firms whose stock is publicly traded

8 True/False Ratios based on data from financial statements provide useful information for evaluating a firm's financial health, its progress, and its prospects for the future.

9 Multiple Choice Which of the following statements is **not true** regarding accounting ethics:

(a) the code of professional conduct for public accountants in the United States is maintained and enforced by the SEC

(b) the purpose of ethics in accounting is to maintain public confidence in business institutions, financial markets, and the accounting profession

(c) inflating revenues to keep stock prices high and hiding expenses to show inflated (false) profits are examples of unethical income-statement manipulation that have been publicly disclosed in recent years.

(d) by accepting membership in the AICPA, a CPA has an obligation of self-discipline above and beyond the requirements of laws and regulations

***Answers to Self-Check Questions 7–9 can be found on p. 566.**

CONTINUED FROM PAGE 428

ACCOUNTING TAKES A TRIP ABROAD

India, with its abundance of well-educated and highly skilled employees, has become the back office of the world. In medical services, for example, x-ray images are digitally transmitted to India, where skilled radiologists evaluate them, then transmit the results back to U.S. client hospitals. Accounting skills, too, are plentiful, with average salaries just one-fifth of those in Western countries and, as a former British colony, India has a widespread English-speaking culture. With over one-third of its college graduates speaking more than two languages fluently, and many speaking as many as six, India is well-positioned as an international outsourcing provider. Its Chartered Accountant designation for ensuring professionalism is similar in rigor and esteem to the U.S. CPA certification. It comes as no surprise, then, that Deloitte Touche forecasts India's financial and accounting services will be boosted by some one million new back-office jobs and technology-related positions, moved there by the world's top 100 financial companies by 2008.

In addition to cost savings, clients also expect better quality—more accurate and faster reporting—from outsourcing. As Peter Smith, a partner in the PricewaterhouseCoopers Business Process Outsourcing division, notes, "There's a different feeling when you're providing the service externally, as opposed to internally. There's a greater expectation from the client. They really do expect a much better service." On the downside, however, outsourcing increases the risk to data security. Placing private information in faraway hands, especially in the absence of clear-cut legislation on data privacy and security (as in India), increases chances of violating the client's trust in accounting integrity.

While India holds the premier position today in offshore work, others—Australia, Ireland, Malaysia, the Philippines, and South Africa—are gearing up with low-cost, high-technology expertise in the battle of accounting outsourcing destinations. Among the brightest contenders, if it can overcome a non-English-speaking tradition, is China, with its population of one billion, rapid economic growth, low-cost labor, and serious investment in technical education. Its stated goal is to become the world's top outsourcing destination for accounting.

QUESTIONS FOR DISCUSSION

1 What factors do you think are most important to consider in deciding which parts of your firm's accounting system, if any, are appropriate for outsourcing?

2 Suppose the accounting firm that prepares your income tax return outsources the work to a third-party tax-service provider. Do you think the accounting firm should get your permission before outsourcing the work? Explain why or why not.

3 Suppose you are hoping for an accounting career. How does the trend toward offshore outsourcing threaten your career prospects? In what ways does it provide new opportunities?

4 What steps might a firm take to ensure that its private information is safeguarded by its offshore accounting provider?

5 What ethical issues, if any, are involved in a decision about outsourcing a firm's accounting activities? Explain.

SUMMARY OF LEARNING OBJECTIVES

1 Explain the role of accountants and distinguish between the kinds of work done by public accountants, private accountants, management accountants, and forensic accountants.

The role of accountants is to maintain a comprehensive system for collecting, analyzing, and communicating financial information for use by external constituents and within firms for planning controlling, and decision making. It measures business performance and translates the results into information for management decisions. *Certified public accountants (CPAs)* are licensed professionals who provide auditing, tax, and management advisory services for other firms and individuals. CPAs are always independent of the firms they audit. Many businesses hire their own salaried employees—*private accountants*—to perform internal accounting activities, such as auditing, taxation, cost analysis, and budgeting. Most private accountants are *management accountants* who provide services to support managers in various activities (marketing, production, engineering, and so forth). *Forensic accountants* use accounting for legal purposes by providing investigative and litigation support in crimes against companies, crimes by companies, and civil cases.

2 Explain how the accounting equation is used.

Accountants use the following equation to balance the data pertaining to financial transactions:

$$\text{Assets} - \text{Liabilities} = \text{Owners' Equity}$$

After each financial transaction (e.g., payments to suppliers, sales to customers, wages to employees), the accounting equation must be in balance. If it isn't, then an accounting error has occurred. The equation also provides an indication of the firm's financial health. If assets exceed liabilities, owners' equity is positive; if the firm goes out of business, owners will receive some cash (a gain) after selling assets and paying off liabilities. If liabilities outweigh assets, owners' equity is negative; assets aren't enough to pay off debts. If the company goes under, owners will get no cash and some creditors won't be paid, thus losing their remaining investments in the company.

3 Describe the three basic financial statements and show how they reflect the activity and financial condition of a business.

Accounting summarizes the results of a firm's transactions and issues reports to help managers and other stakeholders make informed decisions. The class of reports known as *financial statements* is divided into three categories. (1) The *balance sheet* (sometimes called the *statement of financial position*) supplies detailed information about the accounting equation factors—assets, liabilities, and owners' equity—that together are a barometer of the firm's financial condition at a given point in time. By comparing the current balance sheet with those of previous years, creditors and owners can better interpret the firm's financial progress and future prospects. (2) The *income statement* (sometimes called a *profit-and-loss statement*) describes revenues and expenses to show a firm's annual profit or loss during a period of time, such as a year. (3) A publicly traded firm must issue a *statement of cash flows*, which describes its yearly cash receipts (inflows) and payments (outflows). It shows the effects on cash during the year from three kinds of business activities: (a) cash flows from operations, (b) cash flows from investing, and (c) cash flows from financing. The statement of cash flows then reports the overall change in the company's cash position at the end of the accounting period.

4 Explain the key standards and principles for reporting financial statements.

Accountants follow standard reporting practices and principles when they prepare financial statements. Otherwise, users wouldn't be able to compare information from different companies, and they might misunderstand—or be led to misconstrue—a company's true financial status. The following are two of the most important standard reporting practices and principles: (1) *Revenue recognition* is the formal recording and reporting of revenues in financial statements. All firms earn revenues continuously as they make sales, but earnings are not reported until the earnings cycle is completed. This cycle is complete under two conditions: (a) The sale is complete and the product delivered; (b) The sale price has been collected or is collectible. This practice assures interested parties that the statement gives a fair comparison of what was gained for the resources that were given up. (2) *Full disclosure* recognizes that a firm's managers have inside knowledge—beyond just the numbers reported in its financial statements—that can explain certain events, transactions, or otherwise disclose the circumstances behind certain results. Full disclosure means that financial statements include management interpretations and explanations to help external users understand the financial information contained in statements.

5 Describe how computing financial ratios can help users get more information from financial statements to determine the financial strengths of a business.

Financial statements provide data that can be applied to *ratios* (comparative numbers). Ratios can then be used to analyze the financial health of a company in terms of solvency, profitability, and efficiency in performing activities. Ratios can help creditors, investors, and managers assess a firm's current status and check a firm's progress by comparing current with past statements. *Solvency ratios* use balance sheet data to measure the firm's ability to meet (repay) its debts. The *current ratio* measures the ability to meet current (short-term) liabilities out of current assets. *Long-term solvency ratios* compare the firm's total liabilities (including long-term debt) against the owners' equity. High indebtedness (a high ratio) can be risky because it requires payment of interest and repayment of borrowed funds that may not be available. *Profitability ratios*, such as earnings per share, measure current and potential earnings. *Activity ratios* reflect management's use of assets by measuring the efficiency with which a firm uses its resources for a particular activity, such as sales, advertising, or inventory management. Sales efficiency, for example, can be measured from income statement data for annual sales revenues as compared with sales expenses. Sales efficiency has increased if the year-to-year growth in sales revenues is larger than the growth in sales expenses.

6 Discuss the role of ethics in accounting

The purpose of ethics in accounting is to maintain public confidence in business institutions, financial markets, and the products and services of the accounting profession. Without ethics, all of accounting's tools and methods would be meaningless because their usefulness depends, ultimately, on truthfulness in their application. Accordingly, professional accounting associations enforce codes of professional conduct that include ethics-related areas, such as the accountant's responsibilities, the public interest, integrity, and due care. The associations include ethics as an area of study to meet requirements for certification. The codes prohibit, among other areas, misrepresentation and fraud in financial statements. While the accounting profession relies generally on self-compliance to professional codes, accounting associations maintain ethical conduct committees to receive allegations, hold hearings, reach settlements, and impose penalties for misconduct. The flare-up of unethical and illegal corporate accounting violations was the impetus for the Sarbanes-Oxley Act of 2002, thus placing even greater emphasis and public awareness on the importance of ethics in accounting.

KEY TERMS

accounting (p. 428)

accounting equation (p. 435)

accounting information
system (AIS) (p. 428)

accounts payable (payables) (p. 437)

activity ratio (p. 443)

asset (p. 435)

audit (p. 430)

balance sheet (p. 436)

bookkeeping (p. 428)

budget (p. 441)

Certified Fraud Examiner (CFE) (p. 432)

certified management accountant
(CMA) (p. 432)

certified public accountant (CPA) (p. 429)

code of professional conduct (p. 447)

controller (p. 429)

core competencies for accounting (p. 431)

cost of goods sold (p. 439)

cost of revenues (p. 438)

current asset (p. 436)

current liability (p. 437)

current ratio (p. 444)

debt (p. 445)

depreciation (p. 437)

earnings per share (p. 445)

financial accounting (p. 429)

financial statement (p. 436)

fixed asset (p. 437)

forensic accounting (p. 432)

full disclosure (p. 443)

generally accepted accounting
principles (GAAP) (p. 430)

goodwill (p. 437)

gross profit (p. 439)

income statement (profit-and-loss
statement) (p. 438)

intangible asset (p. 437)

leverage (p. 445)

liability (p. 435)

liquidity (p. 436)

long-term liability (p. 438)

management accountant (p. 432)

management advisory services (p. 430)

managerial (management)
accounting (p. 429)

net income (net profit, net
earnings) (p. 439)

operating expenses (p. 439)

operating income (p. 439)

owners' equity (p. 435)

paid-in capital (p. 438)

private accountant (p. 431)

profitability ratio (p. 443)

retained earnings (p. 438)

revenue recognition (p. 442)

revenues (p. 438)

Sarbanes-Oxley Act of 2002
(Sarbox) (p. 433)

short-term solvency ratio (p. 444)

solvency ratio (p. 443)

statement of cash flows (p. 440)

tax services (p. 430)

QUESTIONS AND EXERCISES

Questions for Review

1 Who are the users of accounting information and for what purposes do they use it?

2 Identify the three types of services performed by CPAs.

3 Explain the ways in which financial accounting differs from managerial (management) accounting.

4 Discuss the activities and services performed by forensic accountants.

5 What are the three basic financial statements, and what major information does each contain?

6 Explain how financial ratios allow managers to gain additional information from financial statements.

Questions for Analysis

7 If you were planning to invest in a company, which of the three types of financial statements would you most want to see? Why?

8 Suppose that you, as the manager of a company, are making changes to fully comply with provisions of the Sarbanes-Oxley Act. Your company traditionally has relied on CPA firms for auditing, tax services, and management services. What are the major changes that will be needed in your company?

Application Exercises

9 Interview an accountant at a local firm. How does the firm use budgets? How does budgeting help managers plan business activities? How does budgeting help them control activities? Give examples.

10 Interview the manager of a local retailer, wholesale business, or manufacturing firm about the role of ethics in that company's accounting practices. Is ethics in accounting an important issue to the manager? If the firm has its own private accountants, what measures are taken for ensuring ethical practices internally? What steps, if any, does the company take to maintain ethical relationships in its dealings with CPA firms?

☐☐☐☐☐☐☐☐☐☐ **BUILDING YOUR BUSINESS SKILLS**

PUTTING THE BUZZ IN BILLING

Goal

To encourage you to think about the advantages and disadvantages of using an electronic system for handling accounts receivable and accounts payable.

Method
Step 1

As the CFO of a Midwestern utility company, you are analyzing the feasibility of switching from a paper to an electronic system. You decide to discuss the ramifications of the choice with three associates (choose three classmates to take on these roles). Your discussion requires that you research electronic payment systems now being developed. Specifically, using online and library research, you must find out as much as you can about the electronic bill-paying systems being developed by Visa International, Intuit, IBM, and the Checkfree Corporation.

Step 2

After you have researched this information, brainstorm the advantages and disadvantages of switching to an electronic system.

FOLLOW-UP QUESTIONS

1 What cost savings are inherent in the electronic system for both your company and its customers? In your answer, consider such costs as handling, postage, and paper.

2 What consequences would your decision to adopt an electronic system have on others with whom you do business, including manufacturers of check-sorting equipment, the U.S. Postal Service, and banks?

3 Switching to an electronic system would mean a large capital expense for new computers and software. How could analyzing the company's income statement help you justify this expense?

4 How are consumers likely to respond to paying bills electronically? Are you likely to get a different response from individuals than you get from business customers?

GIVE AND TAKE WITH ACCOUNTING CLIENTS

The Situation

CPAs rely on access to private information from clients for preparing financial documents. As professionals, accountants also charge fees for their services. Occasionally, however, the obligations of both parties become blurred when disputes arise, causing strained client-CPA relationships.

The Dilemma

Aaron Ault delivered original expense and income records so that his CPA, Katrina Belinski, could prepare financial statements for Ault's small business firm. Three months later, Katrina delivered the completed financial statements together with a fee for services to Ault. Aaron was surprised at what he regarded as excessive fees in the accountant's invoice and refused to make payment. Katrina, in turn, refused Ault's request for return of his original documents until such time as Ault paid for services rendered.

Unable to retrieve his documents, Ault filed a complaint with the Professional Ethics Executive Committee of the AICPA. The charge was violation of Rule 501—Acts Discreditable. Upon hearing the case, a settlement agreement was reached between the AICPA and the accountant. Its stipulations included the flowing: (1) A two year suspension from membership in the AICPA and (2) the accused must complete the AICPA course entitled Professional Ethics, with a passing grade of 90 or above.

QUESTIONS TO ADDRESS

1 What are the ethical issues in this situation?
2 What are the basic arguments for and against Aaron Ault's position in this situation? For and against Katrina Belinski's position?
3 What do you think of the AICPA's ruling in this situation? What would you do if you were placed in the role of ethics representative for the AICPA?

CONFIDENTIALLY YOURS

The Situation

Accountants are often entrusted with private, sensitive information that should be used confidentially. In this exercise, you're encouraged to think about ethical considerations that might arise when an accountant's career choices come up against a professional obligation to maintain confidentiality.

The Dilemma

Assume that you're the head accountant in Turbatron, a large electronics firm that makes components for other manufacturing firms. Your responsibilities include preparing Turbatron's financial statements that are then audited for financial reporting to shareholders. In addition, you regularly prepare confidential budgets for internal use by managers responsible for planning departmental activities, including future investments in new assets. You've also worked with auditors and CPA consultants that assess financial problems and suggest solutions.

Now let's suppose that you're approached by another company, Electroblast, one of the electronics industry's most successful firms, and offered a higher-level position. If you accept, your new job will include developing Electroblast's financial plans and serving on the strategic planning committee. Thus, you'd be involved not only in developing strategy but also in evaluating the competition, perhaps even using your knowledge of Turbatron's competitive strengths and weaknesses.

Your contractual commitments with Turbatron do not bar you from employment with other electronics firms.

Team Activity

Assemble a group of four to five students and assign each group member to one of the following roles:
- Head accountant (leaving Turbatron)
- General manager of Turbatron
- Shareholder of Turbatron
- Customer of Turbatron
- General manager of Electroblast (if your team has five members)

ACTION STEPS

1 Before hearing any of your group's comments on this situation, and from the perspective of your assigned role, are any ethical issues confronting the head accountant in this situation? If so, write them down.

2 Return to your group and reveal ethical issues identified by each member. Were the issues the same among all roles or did differences in roles result in different issues?

3 Among the ethical issues that were identified, decide as a group which one is most important for the head accountant. Which is most important for Turbatron?

4 What does your group finally recommend be done to resolve the most important ethical issue(s)?

5 What steps do you think Turbatron might take in advance of such a situation to avoid any difficulties it now faces?

PART 5: MANAGING INFORMATION

Goal of the Exercise

This part of the business plan project asks you to think about your business in terms of *information technology needs* and *costs*.

Exercise Background: Part 5 of the Business Plan

In Chapter 13 we discussed the major impact that IT—computers, the Internet, software, and so on—has had on businesses today. This part of the business plan asks you to assess how you will use technology to improve your business. Will you, for example, use a database to keep track of your customers? How will you protect your business from hackers and other IT security risks?

This part of the business plan also asks you to consider the costs of doing business, such as salaries, rent, and utilities. You'll also be asked to complete the following financial statements:

■ *Balance Sheet.* The balance sheet is a foundation for financial reporting. This report identifies the valued items of the business (its *assets*) as well as the debts that it owes (its *liabilities*). This information gives the owner and potential investors a "snapshot" into the health of the business.

■ *Income Statement (or Profit-and-Loss Statement).* This is the focus of the financial plan. This document will show you what it takes to be profitable and successful as a business owner for your first year.

Your Assignment

Step 1

Open the saved *Business Plan* file you began working on in Parts 1 to 4.

Step 2

For the purposes of this assignment, you will answer the following questions in "Part 5: Managing Information":

1 What kinds of IT resources will your business require?

Hint: Think about the employees in your business and what they will need in order to do their jobs. What computer hardware and software will they need? Will your business need a network and an Internet connection? What type of network? Refer to Chapter 13 for a discussion on IT resources you may want to consider.

2 How will you use IT to keep track of your customers and potential customers?

Hint: Many businesses—even small businesses—use databases to keep track of their customers. Will your business require a database? What about other information systems? Refer to Chapter 13 for more information on these topics.

3 What are the *costs* of doing business? Equipment, supplies, salaries, rent, utilities, and insurance are just some of these expenses. Estimate what it will cost to do business for one year.

Hint: The *Business Plan Student Template* provides a table for you to insert the costs associated with doing business. Note that these are just estimates—just try your best to include accurate costs for the expenses you think will be a part of doing business.

4 How much will you charge for your product? How many products do you believe that you can sell in one year (or how many customers do you think your business can attract)? Multiply the price that you will charge by the number of products that you hope to sell or the amount you hope each customer will spend. This will give you an estimate of your *revenues* for one year.

Hint: You will use the amounts you calculate in the costs and revenues questions in this part of the plan in the accounting statements in the next part, so be as realistic as you can.

5 Create a balance sheet and an income statement (profit-and-loss statement) for your business.

Hint: You will have two options for creating these reports. The first option is to use the Microsoft Word versions that are found within the *Business Plan Student Template* itself. The second option is to use the specific Microsoft Excel templates created for each statement, which are found on the book's Companion Website at www.prenhall.com/ebert. These Excel files are handy to use because they already have the worksheet calculations preset—all you have to do is "plug in" the numbers and the calculations will be performed automatically for you. If you make adjustments to the different values in the Excel worksheets, you'll automatically see how changes to expenses, for example, can improve the "bottom line."

Note: Once you have answered the questions, save your Word document. You'll be answering additional questions in later chapters.

ACCOUNTING FOR BILLIONS OF BURGERS: MCDONALD'S

Learning Objectives

The purpose of this video is to help you:

1 Understand the challenges that a company may face in managing financial information from operations in multiple countries.

2 Consider ways in which managers and investors use financial information reported by a public company.

3 Understand how different laws and monetary systems can affect the accounting activities of a global corporation.

Synopsis

Collecting, analyzing, and reporting financial data from 27,000 restaurants in 119 countries are not easy tasks, as the accounting experts at McDonald's are well aware. Every month, individual restaurants send their sales figures to be consolidated with data from other restaurants at the local or country level. From there, the figures are sent to country-group offices and then to one of three major regional offices before going to their final destination at McDonald's headquarters in Oak Brook, Illinois. In the past, financial information arrived in Illinois in bits and pieces, sent by courier, mail, and fax. Today, local and regional offices enter month-end figures into a special secure Web site, enabling the corporate controller to produce financial statements and projections for internal and external use.

DISCUSSION QUESTIONS

1 **For analysis:** Why does McDonald's use "constant currency" comparisons when reporting its financial results?

2 **For analysis:** What types of assets might McDonald's list under depreciation in its financial statements?

3 **For application:** What effect do corporate income tax rates in the countries where McDonald's operates have on the income statements prepared at McDonald's local offices?

4 **For application:** What problems might arise if individual restaurants were required to enter sales data directly on the company's centralized accounting Web site instead of following the current procedure of sending it through country and regional channels?

5 **For debate:** To help investors and analysts better assess the company's worldwide financial health, should McDonald's be required to disclose detailed financial results for every country and region? Support your position.

Online Exploration

Visit the McDonald's corporate Web site at www.mcdonalds.com/corporate. Locate the most recent financial report (quarterly or annual) and examine both overall and regional results. What aspects of its results does McDonald's highlight in this report? Which regions are doing particularly well? Which are lagging? How does management explain any differences in performance? What does McDonald's say about its use of constant currency reporting?

After reading this chapter, you should be able to:

1   Define *money* and identify the different forms that it takes in the nation's money supply.

2   Describe the different kinds of financial institutions that compose the U.S. financial system and explain the services they offer.

3   Explain how financial institutions create money and describe the means by which they are regulated.

4   Discuss the functions of the Federal Reserve System and describe the tools that it uses to control the money supply.

5   Identify three important ways in which the money and banking system is changing.

6   Discuss some of the institutions and activities in international banking and finance.

1 USD	36
1 GBP	52
1 AUD	18
1 CHF	24
1 CAD	22

GOING WITH THE CURRENCY

Euros, pesos, dollars, and yen—money comes in all sizes and stripes, and most everyone seems to want more of it. With today's global activities, travelers, shoppers, investors, and businesses often convert their dollars into other currencies, and when it comes to choosing one currency over others, the best choice changes from day to day. Why?

MONEY AND BANKING

Because every currency's value changes, reflecting global supply and demand—what traders are willing to pay—for one currency relative to others. At any one time, then, some currencies are "strong"—selling at a higher price and worth more—while others are "weak." Most people would prefer a "strong" currency, right? Well, not so fast. Using money for international activities, for example, taking a vacation, is one of those "good news–bad news" situations.

Consider the euro, up as much as 36 percent against the U.S. dollar since 2000. As a citizen in one of the 12 euro-area countries—for example, France—you chose wisely in delaying that U.S. vacation until 2005. Each euro in 2005 paid for about $1.20 of the trip, but it would have covered only $0.92 in 2000. That's the good news: The stronger euro means more purchasing power against the weaker dollar. It's bad news, though, for French innkeepers because Americans go elsewhere to avoid expensive European travel—it takes $1.20 for €1 of vacation cost, up from $0.92 five years earlier. Simply put, that $0.92 cup of coffee at a French sidewalk café in 2000 now costs you $1.20. In this example of U.S. dollar to euro, your purchasing power has declined as the dollar has weakened against the euro.

The stronger euro is proving to be a stumbling block for Europe's economy, especially for industries that export to non-euro countries with weaker currencies. Prices had

We are seriously worried about the negative consequences of the super-strong euro on . . . Europe.

—a member of Morgan Stanley's European economic team, on the competitive standing of European companies

to be increased, for example, on German-made Mercedes and BMW auto exports to the United States to cover euro-based manufacturing costs, causing weaker demand and sales. For 2005, one industry expert estimates that Europe's exports fell 6 percent, and in recent years, European firms lost 8 to 10 percent in revenue growth due to weakness of the dollar.

While the weaker dollar has hurt many European firms, others have gained by increasing their U.S. investments. When DaimlerChrysler, for example, produces Mercedes M-class autos in Alabama, it pays in weaker dollars for manufacturing them, exports cars to Europe, and sells in euros for windfall profits. On balance, however, euro-based firms are facing sagging sales, with slower revenue growth due to a strong euro.

"We are seriously worried about the negative consequences of the super-strong euro on . . . Europe," says a member of Morgan Stanley's European economic team. Euro-zone companies are less competitive against global counterparts, and Europe's economic recovery is slower than expected. Even so, the European Central Bank (ECB) refuses to weaken the euro by cutting interest rates. With lower rates, the supply of euros would increase, and the price of euros would fall—stimulating Europe's economy. But, the ECB fears, it would also stimulate too much inflation. In contrast, the U.S. Federal Reserve's rapid rate slashing in years up to 2004 is credited with weakening the dollar and stimulating the U.S. economy for the steady growth that continued into 2006. As pressures mount, some observers expect the ECB, too, will concede by cutting interest rates to weaken the euro. ∎

Our opening story continues on page 482.

WHAT'S IN IT FOR ME?

As our opening story illustrates, buyers and sellers both are concerned with the supply of money and its purchasing power at home and abroad. If you want to understand where money comes from, and how to get the most benefits from it, then this chapter will be useful. The chapter explains what money is, where it comes from, how the supply of money grows, and the kinds of services available to money users from the financial services industry. These topics are essential for knowing what's available in the money supply, and using it effectively.

In this chapter, we talk about the forms money takes and the different kinds of financial institutions that compose the U.S. financial system and the services they offer. We also examine how financial institutions create money and the means by which these institutions are regulated. Finally, we discuss the Federal Reserve System, ways in which the money and banking system is changing, and key concepts and activities in international banking and finance. Let's first look at a basic question: What exactly is money?

WHAT IS MONEY?

When someone asks you how much money you have, do you count the dollar bills and coins in your pockets? Do you include your checking and savings accounts? What about stocks and bonds? Do you count your car? Taken together, the value of all these combined is your personal wealth. Not all of it, however, is "money." In this section, we consider more precisely what *money* is and does.

∎∎∎ THE CHARACTERISTICS OF MONEY

Under the Celts, some 2,500 years ago, ancient Ireland had a simple agrarian economy. Instead of using coins, the cow was the unit of exchange. Modern money, in contrast, often takes the form of stamped metal or printed paper—U.S. dollars, euros, Japanese yen—issued by governments. Theoretically, however, just about any object can serve as **money** if it is *portable*, *divisible*, *durable*, and *stable*. To appreciate these qualities, imagine using something that lacks them—for example, a 1,000-pound cow:

MONEY any object that is portable, divisible, durable, and stable and that serves as a medium of exchange, a store of value, and a measure of worth

- **Portability.** Try lugging 1,000 pounds of cow from shop to shop. In contrast, modern currency is light and easy to handle.
- **Divisibility.** Suppose you want to buy a hat, a book, and a radio from three different stores. How would you divide your "cow-money"? Is a pound of its head worth as much as a pound of leg? Modern currency is easily divisible into smaller parts, each with a fixed value. A dollar, for example, can be exchanged for 10 dimes. Units of money can be easily matched with the value of all goods.
- **Durability.** Regardless of whether you "spend" it, your cow will lose value every day (it will eventually die and become too smelly to be worth anything). Modern currency, however, neither dies nor spoils, and if it wears out, it can be replaced. It is also hard to counterfeit—certainly harder than cattle-breeding or rustling more cows.
- **Stability.** If cows were in short supply, you might be able to make quite a deal for yourself. In the middle of an abundant cow year, however, the market would be flooded with cows. Sellers of goods would soon have enough cows and would refuse to produce anything for which they could get only cows, so the value of cows would fall. The ups and downs of cow money would be unpredictable. The value of our paper money also fluctuates, but it is considerably more stable than cows. Its value is related to what we can buy with it.

∎∎∎ THE FUNCTIONS OF MONEY

Imagine a successful cow rancher who needs a new fence for his stockyard. In a *barter economy*—one in which goods are exchanged directly for one another—he would have to find someone who not only needs a cow (or parts of one) but who is also willing to exchange a fence for it. If no fence maker wants a cow, the rancher must find someone else—for example, a wagon maker—who does want a cow. Then, the rancher must hope that the fence maker will trade for his new wagon. Barter is inefficient in comparison with money. In a money economy, the rancher would sell his cow, receive money, and exchange the money for such goods as a new fence.

Money serves three functions:

1 **It is a medium of exchange.** Like the rancher "trading" money for a new fence, we use money as a way of buying and selling things. Without money, we would be bogged down in a system of barter.

2 **It is a store of value.** Pity the rancher whose cow gets sick on Monday and who wants to buy some clothes on the following Saturday, by which time the cow may have died and lost its value. In the form of currency, however, money can be used for future purchases and "stores" value.

3 **It is a measure of worth.** Money lets us measure the relative values of goods and services. It acts as a measure of worth because all products can be valued and accounted

Instead of using a modern monetary system, traders like Muhammad Essa, in Quetta, Pakistan, transfer funds through handshakes and code words. The ancient system is called *hawala*, which means *trust* in Arabic. The worldwide *hawala* system, though illegal in most countries, moves billions of dollars past regulators annually and is alleged to be the system of choice for terrorists because it leaves no paper trail.

for in terms of money. For example, the concepts of "$1,000 worth of clothes" or "$500 in labor costs" have universal meaning because everyone deals with money every day.

■■■ M-1: THE SPENDABLE MONEY SUPPLY

For money to serve its basic functions, both buyers and sellers must agree on its value. That value depends in part on its *supply*—how much money is in circulation. When the money supply is high, the value of money drops. When it is low, that value increases.

Unfortunately, it is not easy to measure the supply of money. One of the most commonly used measures, known widely as **M-1**, counts only the most liquid, or spendable, forms of money—cash, checks, and checking accounts:

M-1 measure of the money supply that includes only the most liquid (spendable) forms of money

- Paper money and metal coins are **currency (cash)** issued by the government. Currency is widely used for small exchanges, and the law requires creditors to accept it in payment of debts.

CURRENCY (CASH) government-issued paper money and metal coins

- A **check** is essentially an order instructing a bank to pay a given sum to a "payee." Although not all sellers accept them as payment, many do. Checks are usually acceptable in place of cash because they are valuable only to specified payees and can be exchanged for cash.

CHECK demand deposit order instructing a bank to pay a given sum to a specified payee

- **Checking accounts**, which are known as **demand deposits**, are counted as money because their funds may be withdrawn at any time—"on demand."

CHECKING ACCOUNT (DEMAND DEPOSIT) bank account funds, owned by the depositor, that may be withdrawn at any time by check or cash

These are all noninterest-bearing or low–interest-bearing forms of money. As of January 2006, M-1 in the United States totaled $1.37 trillion.[1]

■■■ M-2: M-1 PLUS THE CONVERTIBLE MONEY SUPPLY

M-2 measure of the money supply that includes all the components of M-1 plus the forms of money that can be easily converted into spendable forms

M-2, a second measure of the money supply, is often used for economic planning by businesses and government agencies. **M-2** includes everything in M-1 plus other forms of money that are not quite as liquid—items that are invested for the short term but are easily converted to spendable forms. The major components of M-2 are M-1, *time deposits, money market mutual funds,* and *savings accounts.* Totaling $6.6 trillion in January 2006, M-2 accounts for two-thirds of the nation's money supply.[2] It measures the store of monetary value available for financial transactions by individuals and small businesses. As this overall level of money increases, more is available for consumer purchases and business investment. When the supply is tightened, less money is available; financial transactions, spending, and business activity slow down.

Unlike demand deposits, **time deposits**, such as certificates of deposit (CDs), have a fixed term (e.g., 3 months, 6 months, or 2 years) and are intended to be held to maturity. They cannot be transferred by check, and they pay higher interest rates than checking accounts. Time deposits in M-2 include only accounts of less than $100,000 that can be redeemed on demand, with penalties for early withdrawal.

Operated by investment companies that bring together pools of assets from many investors, **money market mutual funds** buy a collection of short-term, low-risk financial securities. Ownership of and profits (or losses) from the sale of these securities are shared among the fund's investors.

Figure 15.1 shows how the two measures of money, M-1 and M-2, have grown since 1964. For many years, M-1 was the traditional measure of liquid money. Because it was closely related to gross domestic product, it served as a reliable predictor of the nation's economic health. As you can see, however, this situation changed in the early 1980s, with

TIME DEPOSIT bank funds that have a fixed term of time to maturity and cannot be withdrawn earlier or transferred by check

MONEY MARKET MUTUAL FUND fund of short-term, low-risk financial securities purchased with the pooled assets of investor-owners

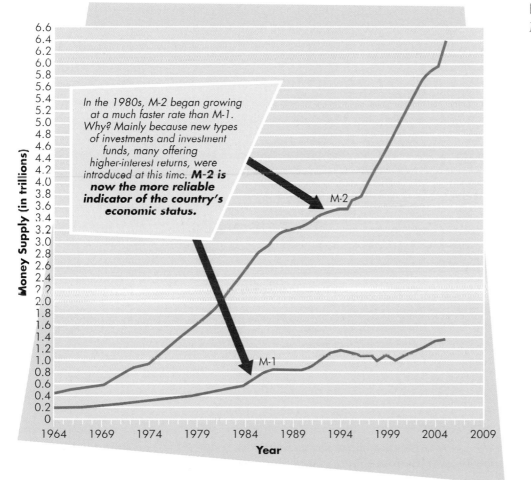

Figure 15.1
Money Supply Growth

In the 1980s, M-2 began growing at a much faster rate than M-1. Why? Mainly because new types of investments and investment funds, many offering higher-interest returns, were introduced at this time. **M-2 is now the more reliable indicator of the country's economic status.**

the introduction of new types of investments and the easier transfer of money among investment funds to gain higher interest returns. As a result, M-2 today is regarded as a more reliable measure than M-1.

▪▪▪ M-3: M-2 PLUS LESS LIQUID DEPOSITS

M-3 measure of the money supply that includes all the components of M-2 plus less liquid deposits of large institutional depositors

The third money measure—**M-3**—includes all of M-2 plus somewhat less liquid deposits in large time deposits and sizable money market funds by large institutions—investment companies, brokerages, and pension funds. In January 2006, M-3 was $9.5 trillion.[3]

▪▪▪ CREDIT CARDS: PLASTIC MONEY?

Citigroup is the world's largest credit-card issuer, with nearly 120 million accounts in North America alone and another 21 million in 42 other countries. It is estimated that more than 163 million U.S. cardholders carry 1.4 billion cards. Spending with general-purpose credit cards in the United States is estimated at $1.9 trillion—almost half of all transactions—for the year 2004.[4] The use of cards, such as Visa, MasterCard, and Discover, has become so widespread that many people refer to them as "plastic money." Credit cards, however, are not money and, accordingly, are not included in M-1, M-2, or M-3 when measuring the nation's money supply.

While consumers enjoy the convenience of credit cards, they also are finding that irresponsible use of the cards can be hazardous to your financial health. A discussion on managing the use of credit cards is presented in Appendix III: Personal Finance.

SELF-CHECK QUESTIONS 1–3

You should now be able to answer Self-Check Questions 1–3.*

1 **Multiple Choice** Suppose you possess paper money on which the printing will eventually be so faint that merchants won't accept it. In terms of its characteristics, your money does not possess:
   (a) stability
   (b) durability
   (c) divisibility
   (d) portability

2 **True/False** "I can spend my $2,000 now to buy a new TV, or I can save it until later to buy something else." In this example, money is serving its function as a store of value.

3 **Multiple Choice** The following is **not** true regarding the U.S. money supply:
   (a) credit cards ("plastic money") are included in M-2 but not in M-1
   (b) checking accounts are also known as demand deposits
   (c) as measured by M-2, the money supply is always greater than when measured by M-1
   (d) time deposits and money market mutual funds are included in M-2

***Answers to Self-Check Questions 1–3 can be found on p. 566.**

Money Talks

Money makes the world go round. Or so they say. But in different cultures, people put different spins on monetary transactions. In some countries—Japan is a good example—money is exchanged with a good deal of respect, even down to the way it's physically handled. You'll often find little trays and dishes next to cash registers where notes and coins are placed for people to pick up. Rarely is money passed from hand to hand. In Japan, too, it's not good form to talk too much about how much you make or have in the bank. These are private matters. The same goes in the United Kingdom, where it's often considered bad manners to talk about money.

In some places—and the United States is one of them—attitudes toward money and talking about it are far more relaxed. You'll find people freely discussing how much they make, how much they paid for their houses, and how much they're worth. Notes and coins themselves are exchanged with very little formality.

Typically, people pitch bills on a counter or slap them into someone's hand with little ceremony.

In many countries—the United States included—money is an important element of national identity: It helps to distinguish a country from its neighbors, and people often feel a touch of pride toward their national currencies. A lot of people don't like to see denominations of national currency removed from circulation or altered in design.

That's just what happened in Europe beginning in 2002, when the currencies of 12 nations were replaced by a new currency—the euro. Officials worried that many Europeans would be reluctant to give up their unique currencies in favor of common notes and coins. After all, the German deutschmark and the French franc were important symbols of national identity. But when the time came to make the switch, old currencies disappeared swiftly, and Europeans quickly became used to the cash and coinage. Ultimately, what's important is what you can buy with your money.

THE U.S. FINANCIAL SYSTEM

Many forms of money, such as checking accounts and savings accounts, depend on the existence of financial institutions that provide money-related services to both individuals and businesses. Just how important are these financial institutions, how do they work, and what are some of the services that they offer? In the sections that follow, we explain their role as creators of money and discuss the regulation of the U.S. banking system.

■■■ FINANCIAL INSTITUTIONS

The main function of financial institutions is to ease the flow of money from users with surpluses to those with deficits. They do this by attracting funds into checking and savings accounts. In turn, the incoming funds will be issued as loans to individuals and businesses, and perhaps invested in government securities. In this section, we discuss each of the major types of financial institutions: *commercial banks, savings and loan associations, mutual savings banks and credit unions*, and various organizations known as *nondeposit institutions*.

Commercial Banks The United States today boasts some 8,000 federally insured **commercial banks**—companies that accept deposits that they use to make loans, earn profits, pay interest to depositors, and pay dividends to owners. Commercial banks range from the very largest institutions in New York, such as Citigroup, Bank of America, and JPMorganChase, to tiny banks dotting the rural landscape. Bank liabilities—holdings

COMMERCIAL BANK company that accepts deposits that it uses to make loans, earn profits, pay interest to depositors, and pay dividends to owners

owed to others—include checking accounts and savings accounts. U.S. banks hold assets totaling more than $9 trillion, consisting of a wide variety of loans to individuals, businesses, and governments.[5]

Diversification and Mergers In recent years, financial industry competitors have grown faster than commercial banks in the United States. As consumers continue to look for better financial services, commercial banks find themselves with a dwindling share of the market. Business borrowers today can get loans from investment banks (which are not the same as commercial banks, as we will explain in Chapter 16), such as Merrill Lynch, which has provided billions of dollars in commercial loans, formerly the province of commercial banks. Savers, too, have switched their savings into money market funds, stocks, and bonds that are offered by companies such as Charles Schwab instead of into the traditional savings accounts offered by banks.

In efforts to regain competitiveness, banks were merging at a record-setting pace in the 1990s, a trend that continues today. The resulting companies hold larger shares of the financial market, diversify their offerings, and the lines become blurred between traditional banking and nonbank financial institutions. Citigroup, for example, was formed as the result of a 1998 merger between Citicorp (a commercial bank) and Travelers Group (which includes investment bank Salomon Smith Barney). Today, Citicorp is the third largest U.S. commercial bank, and its parent—Citigroup—is the largest U.S. financial services company, with over $1.5 trillion in assets.[6] The company offers one-stop shopping on a global scale for both consumers and businesses, including private banking, credit-card services, mortgages, mutual funds, stock brokerage services, insurance, and loans.

Commercial Interest Rates Every bank receives a major portion of its income from interest paid on loans by borrowers. As long as terms and conditions are clearly revealed to borrowers, banks are allowed to set their own interest rates, within rate limits set by each state. Traditionally, the lowest rates were made available to the bank's most creditworthy commercial customers. That rate is called the **prime rate**. Most commercial loans are set at markups over prime, like prime + 1, which means 1 percent over the prime rate. However, the prime rate is no longer a strong force in setting loan rates. Borrowers can now get funds less expensively from other sources, including foreign banks that set lower interest rates. To remain competitive, U.S. banks now offer some commercial loans at rates below prime. Figure 15.2 shows the changes in the prime rate since 1994.[7]

Savings and Loan Associations Like commercial banks, **savings and loan associations (S&Ls)** accept deposits, make loans, and are owned by investors. Most S&Ls were created to encourage savings habits and provide financing for homes; they

> *The only way banks can compete is to transform themselves into successful retailers of financial services, which involves dramatic, not incremental change.*
>
> —Thomas Brown, banking analyst

PRIME RATE interest rate available to a bank's most creditworthy customers

SAVINGS AND LOAN ASSOCIATION (S&L) financial institution accepting deposits and making loans primarily for home mortgages

Figure 15.2
The Prime Rate

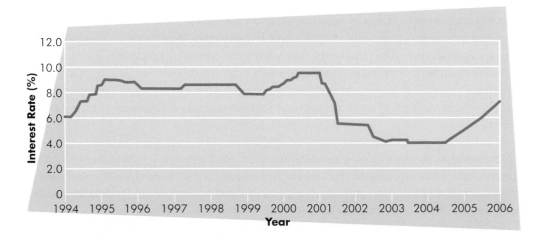

did not offer check services. Traditionally, they loaned money primarily for home mortgages. Many of them, however, have ventured into a variety of other investments. S&Ls in the United States now hold $1.5 trillion in assets and deposits of nearly $1 trillion.[8]

Mutual Savings Banks and Credit Unions In **mutual savings banks**, all depositors are considered owners of the bank. All profits, therefore, are divided proportionately among depositors, who receive dividends. Some 1,400 U.S. mutual savings banks attract most of their funds in the form of savings deposits, and funds are loaned out in the form of mortgages.

A **credit union** is a nonprofit, cooperative financial institution owned and run by its members. Its purpose is to promote *thrift*—careful management of one's money or resources—and to provide members with a safe place to save and borrow at reasonable rates. Members pool their funds to make loans to one another. Each credit union decides whom it will serve, such as a group of employees, people in a particular community, or members of an association. Most universities, for example, have credit unions, as does the U.S. Navy. Currently, 9,500 U.S. credit unions serve nearly 82 million members and hold more than $500 billion in assets.[9]

Nondeposit Institutions A variety of other organizations take in money, provide interest or other services, and make loans. They are called *nondeposit institutions* because, unlike commercial banks, inflowing funds are intended for purposes other than earning interest for depositors. Four of the most important are *pension funds*, *insurance companies*, *finance companies*, and *securities investment dealers*.

1 A **pension fund** is a pool of funds that is managed to provide retirement income for its members. *Public pension funds* include Social Security and $2 trillion in retirement programs for state and local government employees. *Private pension funds*, operated by employers, unions, and other private groups, cover about 90 million people and have total assets of $7 trillion.[10]

2 **Insurance companies** collect large pools of funds from the premiums charged for coverage. Funds are invested in stocks, real estate, and other assets. Earnings pay for insured losses, such as death benefits, automobile damage, and health-care expenses.

3 **Finance companies** are institutions that specialize in making loans to businesses and consumers. *Commercial finance companies* lend to businesses needing capital or long-term funds. They may, for example, lend to a manufacturer that needs new assembly-line equipment. *Consumer finance companies* devote most of their resources to small noncommercial loans to individuals.

4 **Securities investment dealers (brokers)**, such as Merrill Lynch and A. G. Edwards & Sons, buy and sell stocks and bonds on the New York and other stock exchanges for client investors. They also invest in securities—they buy stocks and bonds for their own accounts in hopes of reselling them later at a profit. These companies hold large sums of money for transfer between buyers and sellers. (We discuss the activities of brokers and investment bankers more fully in Chapter 16.)

MUTUAL SAVINGS BANK financial institution whose depositors are owners sharing in its profits

CREDIT UNION nonprofit, cooperative financial institution owned and run by its members, usually employees of a particular organization

PENSION FUND nondeposit pool of funds managed to provide retirement income for its members

INSURANCE COMPANY nondeposit institution that invests funds collected as premiums charged for insurance coverage

FINANCE COMPANY nondeposit institution that specializes in making loans to businesses and consumers

SECURITIES INVESTMENT DEALER (BROKER) financial institution that buys and sells stocks and bonds both for investors and for its own accounts

▪▪▪ SPECIAL FINANCIAL SERVICES

The finance business today is a highly competitive industry. No longer is it enough for commercial banks to accept deposits and make loans. Most, for example, also offer bank-issued credit cards and safe-deposit boxes. In addition, many offer pension, trust, international, and brokerage services and financial advice. Most offer ATMs and electronic money transfer.

INDIVIDUAL RETIREMENT ACCOUNT (IRA) tax-deferred pension fund that wage earners set up to supplement retirement funds

Pension and Trust Services Most banks help customers establish savings plans for retirement. **Individual retirement accounts (IRAs)** are tax-deferred pension funds that wage earners and their spouses can set up to supplement other retirement funds. The annual amount of contributions allowed in an IRA from the employee's wages, and other conditions for participation, depend on the type of account—*traditional IRA*, *Roth IRA*, or *"Educational" IRA*. Advantages and drawbacks to various kinds of IRAs are discussed in Appendix III. Banks provide IRA services by supplying information on investment vehicles available for IRAs (CDs, mutual funds, stocks, and so forth), and by receiving funds and investing them as directed by customers.

TRUST SERVICES management by a bank of an estate, investments, or other assets on behalf of an individual

Many commercial banks offer **trust services**—the management of funds left "in the bank's trust." In return for a fee, the trust department will perform such tasks as making your monthly bill payments and managing your investment portfolio. Trust departments also manage the estates of deceased persons.

International Services The three main international services offered by banks are *currency exchange*, *letters of credit*, and *banker's acceptances*. Suppose a U.S. company wants to buy a product from a Japanese supplier. For a fee, it can use one or more of three services offered by its bank:

1 It can exchange U.S. dollars for Japanese yen at a U.S. bank and then pay the supplier in yen.

2 It can pay its bank to issue a **letter of credit**—a promise by the bank to pay the Japanese firm a certain amount if specified conditions are met.

LETTER OF CREDIT bank promise, issued for a buyer, to pay a designated firm a certain amount of money if specified conditions are met

3 It can pay its bank to draw up a **banker's acceptance**, which promises that the bank will pay some specified amount at a future date.

A banker's acceptance requires payment by a particular date. Letters of credit are payable only after certain conditions are met. The Japanese supplier, for example, may not be paid until shipping documents prove that the merchandise has been shipped from Japan.

BANKER'S ACCEPTANCE bank promise, issued for a buyer, to pay a designated firm a specified amount at a future date

Financial Advice and Brokerage Services Many banks, both large and small, help their customers manage their money. Depending on the customer's situation, the bank, in its role as financial advisor, may recommend different investment opportunities.

"And, hey, don't kill yourself trying to pay it back. You know our motto—'What the hell, it's only money.'"

The recommended mix might include CDs, mutual funds, stocks, and bonds. Many banks also serve as securities intermediaries, using their own stockbrokers to buy and sell securities and their own facilities to hold them.

Electronic Funds Transfer Electronic funds transfer (EFT) provides for payments and collections by transferring financial information via electrical impulses over wire, cable, or microwave. Consumers enjoy EFT's convenience and speed at the checkout stand using debit cards instead of writing checks. In addition, EFT systems provide automatic payroll deposit, ATM transactions, bill payment, and automatic funds transfer. Such systems can help a businessperson close an important business deal by transferring money from San Francisco to Miami within a few minutes at less expense than paper check payments. The U.S. Treasury reports that it costs $0.83 to issue a check payment, but only $0.08 to issue an EFT payment.[11]

Automated Teller Machines Automated teller machines (ATMs) are among the most popular EFT systems. They allow customers to withdraw money, make deposits, transfer funds between accounts, and access information on their accounts. About 352,000 machines are now located in U.S. bank buildings and other locations. Bank of America, with 12,000 units, is this country's leading owner of ATMs. U.S. bank customers conduct nearly 14 billion ATM transactions a year, with each machine being used an average of 3,300 times a month.[12]

Increasingly, ATMs have become global fixtures. Among the world's more than one million ATMs, most are located outside the United States. Asia, with 32 percent of the world's total, is the leading region for ATMs, followed by North America (31 percent), Western Europe (25 percent), and Latin America (8 percent). Many U.S. banks now offer international ATM services. Citicorp installed Shanghai's first 24-hour ATM and was the first foreign bank to receive approval from the People's Bank of China to issue local currency through ATMs.

> **ELECTRONIC FUNDS TRANSFER (EFT)** communication of fund-transfer information over wire, cable, or microwave

> **AUTOMATED TELLER MACHINE (ATM)** electronic machine that allows bank customers to conduct account-related activities 24 hours a day, 7 days a week

■■■ FINANCIAL INSTITUTIONS AS CREATORS OF MONEY

In the course of their activities, financial institutions provide a special service to the economy: They create money. This is not to say that they mint bills and coins. Rather, by taking in deposits and making loans, they expand the money supply.

Devout Muslims can't pay or receive interest—a fact that tends to complicate banking operations. Because money has to work in order to earn a return, institutions like the Shamil Bank in Bahrain invest deposits directly in such ventures as real estate and pay back profit shares rather than interest.

Figure 15.3
How Banks Create Money

Deposit	Money Held in Reserve by Bank	Money to Lend	Total Supply
$100.00	$10.00	$90.00	**$190.00**
90.00	9.00	81.00	**271.00**
81.00	8.10	72.90	**343.90**
72.90	7.29	65.61	**409.51**
65.61	6.56	59.05	**468.56**

As Figure 15.3 shows, the money supply expands because banks are allowed to loan out most (although not all) of the money they take in from deposits. Suppose you deposit $100 in your bank. If banks are allowed to loan out 90 percent of all their deposits, then your bank will hold $10 in reserve and loan $90 of your money to borrowers. (You still have $100 on deposit.) Meanwhile, a borrower—or the people paid—will deposit the $90 loan in a bank. The borrower's bank will then have $81 (90 percent of $90) available for new loans. The banks, therefore, have turned your original $100 into $271 ($100 + $90 + $81). The chain continues, with borrowings from one bank becoming deposits in the next.

■■■ REGULATION OF THE BANKING SYSTEM

Because commercial banks are essential to the creation of money, the government regulates them to ensure a sound and competitive financial system. Later in this chapter, we'll see how the Federal Reserve System regulates many aspects of U.S. banking. Other federal and state agencies also regulate banks to ensure that the failure of some will not cause the public to lose faith in the banking system itself.

FEDERAL DEPOSIT INSURANCE CORPORATION (FDIC) federal agency that guarantees the safety of deposits up to $100,000 in the financial institutions that it insures

Federal Deposit Insurance Corporation The **Federal Deposit Insurance Corporation (FDIC)** preserves confidence in the U.S. financial system by supervising banks and insuring deposits in banks and thrift institutions. The FDIC is a government agency, created by Franklin Delano Roosevelt to restore public confidence in banks during the Depression era. More than 99 percent of the nation's commercial banks pay fees for membership in the FDIC. In return, the FDIC guarantees the safety of all deposits of every account owner up to the current maximum of $100,000. If a bank collapses, the FDIC promises to pay each depositor for losses up to $100,000. A person with more money can establish accounts in more than one bank to protect sums in excess of $100,000. (A handful of the nation's 8,000 commercial banks are insured by states rather than by the FDIC.)

To insure against multiple bank failures, the FDIC maintains the right to examine the activities and accounts of all member banks. Such regulation was effective from 1941 through 1980, when fewer than 10 banks failed per year. At the beginning of the 1980s, however, banks were deregulated, and between 1981 and 1990, losses from nearly 1,100 bank failures depleted the FDIC's reserve fund. In recent years, the FDIC has raised the premiums charged to member banks to keep up with losses incurred by failed banks.

SELF-CHECK QUESTIONS 4–6

You should now be able to answer Self-Check Questions 4–6.*

4 Multiple Choice Suppose you have accumulated substantial wealth that you want to leave to your now-infant children when they reach age 40. Which of the following financial services is most appropriate for your purposes?
(a) individual retirement account
(b) pension fund
(c) banker's acceptance
(d) bank trust services

5 True/False All the following financial institutions offer loan services: credit unions, mutual savings banks, savings and loan associations, commercial banks, and finance companies.

6 Multiple Choice Suppose that you deposit $250 in your local bank, which is allowed to loan out 85 percent of its deposits. Also, suppose that your bank loans out the maximum allowable to borrowers who, in turn, deposit the borrowed money in their banks. These banks also loan out the maximum allowable funds. In total, banks have turned your original $250 into which of the following amounts?
(a) $643.12
(b) $319.75
(c) $750.00
(d) $487.37

Answers to Self-Check Questions 4–6 can be found on p. 566.

THE FEDERAL RESERVE SYSTEM

Perched atop the U.S. financial system and regulating many aspects of its operation is the Federal Reserve System. Established by Congress in 1913, the **Federal Reserve System (the Fed)** is the nation's central bank. In this section, we describe the structure of the Fed, its functions, and the tools that it uses to control the nation's money supply.

FEDERAL RESERVE SYSTEM (THE FED) central bank of the United States, which acts as the government's bank, serves member commercial banks, and controls the nation's money supply

▪▪▪ THE STRUCTURE OF THE FED

The Fed consists of a board of governors, a group of reserve banks, and member banks. As originally established by the Federal Reserve Act of 1913, the system consisted of 12 relatively autonomous banks and a seven-member committee whose powers were limited to coordinating the activities of those banks. By the 1930s, however, both the structure and function of the Fed had changed dramatically. Figure 15.4 shows the structure of the Federal Reserve System today.

The Board of Governors The Fed's board of governors consists of seven members appointed by the president for overlapping terms of 14 years. The chair of the board serves on major economic advisory committees and works actively with the administration to formulate economic policy. The board plays a large role in controlling the money supply. It alone determines the reserve requirements, within statutory limits, for depository institutions. It also works with other members of the Fed to set discount rates and handle the Fed's sale and purchase of government securities.

Figure 15.4
Structure of the Federal
Reserve System

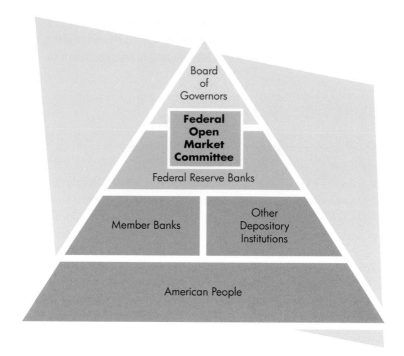

Reserve Banks The Fed consists of 12 administrative areas and 12 banks. Each Federal Reserve Bank holds reserve deposits from and sets the discount rate for commercial banks in its region. Reserve Banks also play a major role in the nation's check-clearing process.

Open Market Committee The Federal Open Market Committee is responsible for formulating the Fed's monetary policies to promote economic stability and growth by managing the nation's money supply. Its members include the Board of Governors, the president of the New York Federal Reserve Bank, and the presidents of four other Reserve Banks, who serve on a rotating basis.

Member Banks All nationally chartered commercial banks are members of the Fed, as are some state-chartered banks. The accounts of all member bank depositors are automatically covered by the FDIC.

Other Depository Institutions Although many state-chartered banks, credit unions, and S&Ls do not belong to the Fed, they are subject to its regulations, pay deposit insurance premiums, and are covered by the FDIC.

▪▪▪ THE FUNCTIONS OF THE FED

In addition to chartering national banks, the Fed serves as the federal government's bank and the "bankers' bank," regulating a number of banking activities. Most importantly, it controls the money supply. In this section, we describe these functions in some detail.

The Government's Bank Two of the Fed's activities are producing the nation's paper currency and lending money to the government. The Fed decides how many bills to produce and how many to destroy. To lend funds to the government, the Fed buys bonds issued by the Treasury Department. The borrowed money is then used to help finance the national deficit.

The Bankers' Bank Individual banks that need money can borrow from the Fed and pay interest on the loans. In addition, the Fed provides storage for commercial banks, which are required to keep funds on reserve at a Federal Reserve Bank.

Check Clearing The Fed also clears checks, some 56 million of them each day, for commercial banks. To understand the check-clearing process, imagine that you are a photographer living in New Orleans. To participate in a workshop in Detroit, you must send a check for $50 to the Detroit studio. Figure 15.5 traces your check through the clearing process:

1 You send your check to the Detroit studio, which deposits it in its Detroit bank.
2 The Detroit bank deposits the check in its own account at the Federal Reserve Bank of Chicago.
3 The check is sent from Chicago to the Atlanta Federal Reserve Bank for collection because you, the check writer, live in the Atlanta district.
4 Your New Orleans bank receives the check from Atlanta and deducts the $50 from your personal account.
5 Your bank then has $50 deducted from its deposit account at the Atlanta Federal Reserve Bank.
6 The $50 is shifted from Atlanta to the Chicago Federal Reserve Bank. The studio's Detroit bank gets credited, whereupon the studio's account is then credited $50. Your bank mails the canceled check back to you.

Depending on the number of banks and the distances between them, a check will clear in two to six days. Until the process is completed, the studio's Detroit bank cannot spend the $50 deposited there. Meanwhile, your bank's records will continue to show $50 in your account. Each day, approximately $1 billion in checks is processed by the system.

Figure 15.5
Clearing a Check

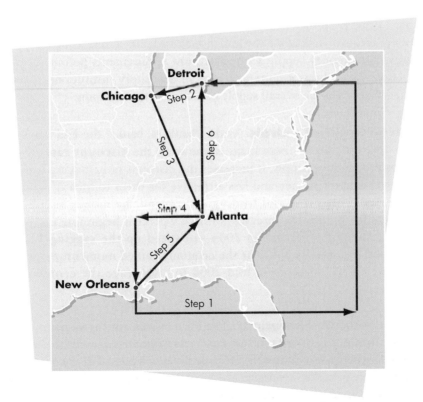

FLOAT total amount of checks written but not yet cleared through the Fed

The term **float** refers to all the checks in the process at any one time: Checks that have been written and are not yet cleared.

Controlling the Money Supply The Fed is responsible for the conduct of U.S. monetary policy—the management of the nation's economic growth by managing money supply and interest rates. By controlling these two factors, the Fed influences the ability and willingness of banks throughout the country to loan money.

MONETARY POLICY management of the nation's economic growth by managing the money supply and interest rates

Inflation Management As we defined in Chapter 1, *inflation* is a period of widespread price increases throughout an economic system. It occurs if the money supply grows too large. Demand for goods and services increases, and the prices of everything rise. (In contrast, too little money means that an economy will lack the funds to maintain high levels of employment.) Because commercial banks are the main creators of money, much of the Fed's management of the money supply takes the form of regulating the supply of money through commercial banks.

▪▪▪ THE TOOLS OF THE FED

According to the Fed's original charter, its primary duties were to supervise banking and to manage the nation's currency. The duties of the Fed evolved, however, along with a predominant philosophy of monetary policy. That policy includes an emphasis on the broad economic goals as discussed in Chapter 1, especially growth and stability. The Fed's role in controlling the nation's money supply stems from its role in setting policies to help reach these goals. To control the money supply, the Fed uses four primary tools: *reserve requirements*, *discount rate controls*, *open-market operations*, and *selective credit controls*.

RESERVE REQUIREMENT percentage of its deposits that a bank must hold in cash or on deposit with the Fed

Reserve Requirements The **reserve requirement** is the percentage of its deposits that a bank must hold, in cash or on deposit, with a Federal Reserve bank. High requirements mean that banks have less money to lend. Thus, a high reserve requirement reduces the money supply. Conversely, low requirements permit the supply to expand. Because the Fed sets requirements for all depository institutions, it can adjust them to make changes to the overall supply of money in the economy.

DISCOUNT RATE interest rate at which member banks can borrow money from the Fed

Discount Rate Controls As the "bankers' bank," the Fed loans money to banks. The interest rate on these loans is known as the **discount rate**. If the Fed wants to reduce the money supply, it increases the discount rate, making it more expensive for banks to borrow money and less attractive for them to loan it. Conversely, low rates encourage borrowing and lending and expand the money supply. The Fed used a series of discount rate decreases—from 6.0 percent beginning in May 2000 down to a historic low of 1 percent in 2004—to speed up the sagging U.S. economy. The Fed then reversed its policy as the economy gained momentum, gradually increasing the rate to 5.25 percent in mid-2006 to discourage the economy from becoming overheated.[13]

OPEN-MARKET OPERATIONS the Fed's sales and purchases of securities in the open market

Open-Market Operations The third instrument for monetary control is probably the Fed's most important tool. **Open-market operations** refer to the Fed's sale and purchase of securities (usually U.S. Treasury notes and bonds) in the open market, as directed by the open-market committee. Open-market operations are particularly effective because they act quickly and predictably on the money supply. How so? The Fed buys

entrepreneurship and new ventures

Your Check Is Not in the Mail

Pete Kight recognized the advantages of electronic funds transfer (EFT) when, at age 24, he started CheckFree in his grandmother's basement. Now, as CEO of the dominant firm in the world of electronic bill-payments systems, Kight's goal is to change a traditional way of life by replacing check writing with electronic payments. His biggest challenge is getting people accustomed to the idea of abandoning checkbooks and manual recordkeeping. "When consumers understand the benefits, they will want it," Kight insists. Until the masses sign on, however, Kight has to balance rising revenues (most recently, an annual increase of 10 percent, to $606 million) against first-ever profits ($10 million for the same year). CheckFree needs more revenue, and the only way that Kight can get it is by inducing more people to switch to electronic bill paying.

CheckFree offers Online Payment Service (OPS) for online billing and payments of any bill, to any company, from any person. OPS is available (for a fee of up to $15 per month) from any of 657 providers—including banks, credit unions, brokerages, and Internet portals—powered by CheckFree technology. If you sign up with a preferred provider, such as Yahoo!, Bank of America, or CheckFree

itself, you specify the companies and individuals whose bills you want to receive and view online. In turn, your billing—for example, for utilities, car payments, credit cards, cable TV, or the mortgage—comes with CheckFree. Your personalized account displays e-bills for online viewing, including amount owed and due date, and it even sends e-mail reminders for upcoming due dates. You choose dates of payment, dollar amounts, and which bills to pay, with no envelopes, no stamps, and no check writing. Billers benefit from the flow of electronic funds while avoiding slower, more costly paperwork transactions.

In growing from a one-person start-up to a six-state firm with more than 1,800 employees, Kight's expanded vision for the future is to "enable anyone to pay for anything, anywhere electronically over the Internet." As of 2004, however, consumers have been slow to adopt the concept: One consulting group estimates that just over 9 percent of the nation's 16 billion consumer bills were delivered online. Undaunted, however, and encouraged by steady growth, huge market potential, and its leadership position in the industry, CheckFree continues its quest to revolutionize the U.S. banking system by making the checkbook obsolete.

securities from dealers. Because the dealer's bank account is credited for the transaction, its bank has more money to lend, and so this transaction expands the money supply. The opposite happens when the Fed sells securities.

Selective Credit Controls The Fed can exert considerable influence over business activity by exercising **selective credit controls**. The Fed may set special requirements for consumer stock purchases, as well as credit rules for other consumer purchases.

As we will see in Chapter 16, investors can set up credit accounts with stockbrokers to buy stocks and bonds. A margin requirement set by the Fed stipulates the amount of credit that the broker can extend to the customer. For example, a 60 percent margin rate means that approved customers can purchase stocks having $100,000 market value with $60,000 in cash (60 percent of $100,000) and $40,000 in loans from the dealer. If the Fed wants to increase securities transactions, it can lower the margin requirement. Customers can then borrow greater percentages of their purchase costs from dealers, thus increasing their purchasing power and the amount of securities that they can buy.

Within stipulated limits, the Fed is also permitted to specify the conditions of certain credit purchases. This authority extends to such conditions as allowable down payment percentages for appliance purchases and repayment periods on automobile loans. The Fed has chosen to not use these powers in recent years.

SELECTIVE CREDIT CONTROLS
The Fed's authority to set both margin requirements for consumer stock purchases and credit rules for other consumer purchases

THE CHANGING MONEY AND BANKING SYSTEM

The U.S. money and banking systems continue to change today, just as they have in past decades. Enforcement of anti-terrorism regulations deters criminal misuse of the financial system. The expansion of interstate banking offers efficiencies by allowing banks to consolidate services and eliminate duplicated activities. And electronic technologies affect how you obtain money and how much interest you pay for it.

■■■ ANTI-TERRORISM REGULATIONS: THE BANK SECRECY ACT (BSA) AND USA PATRIOT ACT

Under provisions of the Bank Secrecy Act (BSA), the U.S. Department of the Treasury recently imposed a $24 million fine on the New York branch of Arab Bank. The Jordan-based bank, which operates in 30 countries worldwide, failed to implement anti-money–laundering controls—that would prevent concealing the origin of funds generated by illegal means—required of all financial institutions operating in the United States. The enforcement of BSA regulations—enacted in 1970 and re-awakened by the 9/11 tragedy—require financial institutions to formulate methods, such as monitoring and keeping records of customer transactions, to deter funding of crimes. It includes tracking and reporting on suspicious transactions, such as a sudden increase in wire transfers or cash transactions exceeding $10,000, to cut off funding of terrorist activities.

USA Patriot Act and the Customer Identification Program (CIP) The *USA Patriot Act*, passed in 2001, is designed to reduce terrorism risks by requiring banks to better know the customer's true identity. Financial institutions are required to obtain and verify four pieces of information for every customer: name, address, date of birth, and social security (or tax identification) number. They must also implement a *customer identification program (CIP)* to verify identities, keep records of customer activities, and, for new customers, compare identities with government lists of terrorists. Enforcement resides with examiners from the Department of the Treasury.[14]

■■■ INTERSTATE BANKING

The expanding geographic reach in banking is exemplified by Woodforest National Bank, a tiny Texas company that's teaming up with the world's biggest retailer by putting bank branches in more than 70 Wal-Mart stores in North Carolina by 2007.[15] Although interstate banking is commonplace, it is a relatively new development. The Interstate Banking Efficiency Act—passed into law in 1994—allows banks to enter (gradually) into interstate banking—the operation of banks or branches across state lines. It also mandates regulation by government agencies to ensure proper operation and competition. Three key provisions in this act are the following:

1 The ultimate *size* of any bank is limited. No one company can control more than 10 percent of nationwide insured deposits. No bank can control more than 30 percent of a state's deposits (each state is empowered to set its own limit).

2 Affiliated banks in other states can be converted into full-fledged interstate branches.

3 Banks cannot establish out-of-state branches primarily to gain deposits. They must also provide credit services (loans) to meet the needs of the host community. The branch must demonstrate a loan-to-deposit ratio that compares favorably to the average for all banks in the host state.

Interstate banking offers certain efficiencies. For example, it allows banks to consolidate services and eliminate duplicated activities. Opponents, however, remain concerned that some banks will gain undue influence, dominate other banks, and hinder competition. Looking beyond the interstate perspective, today's banks are expanding into global operations that present even greater opportunities and complexities for international financial services.

▪▪▪ THE IMPACT OF ELECTRONIC TECHNOLOGIES

Like so many other businesses, banks are increasingly adopting technology to improve efficiency and customer service levels. In addition to EFT systems, such as ATMs, banks offer telephone, TV, and Internet banking, which allow customers to make around-the-clock transactions. Each business day, more than $2 trillion exists in and among banks and other financial institutions in purely electronic form. Each year, the Fed's Fedwire funds transfer system—the world's largest electronic payments system—processes $400 trillion in transactions for some 9,300 financial institutions.

Check 21: Making the Paper Check Go Away While check writing remains the payment of choice in the United States, the paper check is expected to be stepping out of the check-clearing process. The *Check Clearing for the 21st Century Act (Check 21)* became federal law in 2004. It allows banks to present a substitute check for payment instead of the original check. The result, when fully implemented by U.S. banks, will be less paper handling, reduced reliance on physical transportation, faster collection times, and elimination of expensive float. Under Check 21, the receiving bank makes an electronic image of the paper check and sends the image to the paying bank, near or far, for instant payment instead of waiting days for the paper check to wind its way back to the sender. The days of writing a check, mailing it, and having several days to put money in the account to cover it are numbered, so check writers need to be prepared for faster check clearing.[16]

Blink Credit Card Help is on the way for customers who don't want to stand in line at checkout counters. A new "blink" technology is replacing the magnetic strips that were embedded in credit cards for the past 30 years. The result is a "contactless" payment system—consumers can wave the card in front of the merchant's terminal, at the gas pump, or in a department store and be on their way instead of waiting to swipe and sign. The blink card contains a computer chip that sends radio frequency signals, including customer information, and the transaction is authorized. Radio frequency identification, while new to credit cards, is familiar on toll roads with electronic passes that avoid waiting in line to pay.

Debit Cards One of the electronic offerings from the financial industry that has gained popularity is the debit card. Unlike credit cards, **debit cards** allow only the transfer of money between accounts. They do not increase the funds at an individual's disposal. They can, however, be used to make retail purchases. Debit cards are used as payment for nearly 20 percent of all U.S. consumer transactions, as compared with 23 percent by credit card payments.[17]

DEBIT CARD plastic card that allows an individual to transfer money between accounts

POINT-OF-SALE (POS) TERMINAL electronic device that allows customers to pay for retail purchases with debit cards

In stores with **point-of-sale (POS) terminals**, customers insert cards that transmit to terminals information relevant to their purchases. The terminal relays the information directly to the bank's computer system. The bank automatically transfers funds from the customer's account to the store's account.

SMART CARD credit-card-size plastic card with an embedded computer chip that can be programmed with electronic money

Smart Cards The so-called **smart card** is a credit-card-size plastic card with an embedded computer chip that can be programmed with "electronic money." Also known as *electronic purses* or *stored-value cards*, smart cards have existed for more than a decade. Phone callers, shoppers, and travelers in Europe and Asia are the most avid users, holding the majority of the more than four billion cards in circulation. Although small by European standards, card usage in North America continues to grow, reaching nearly 500 million cards in 2005. They are most popular in gas pump payments, followed by prepaid phone service, ATMs, self-operated checkouts, vending machines, and automated banking services.[18]

E-CASH electronic money that moves between consumers and businesses via digital electronic transmissions

E-Cash The revolutionary world of electronic money, known as **e-cash**, is money that moves via digital transmissions on the Internet, outside the established network of banks, checks, and paper currency overseen by the Fed. Companies as varied as e-cash specialist Mondex and giant Citicorp have developed their own forms of electronic money that allow consumers and businesses to spend money more conveniently, quickly, and cheaply than they can through the banking system.

How does e-cash work? Traditional currency is used to buy electronic funds, which are downloaded over phone lines into a PC or a portable "electronic wallet" that can store and transmit e-cash. E-cash is purchased from any company that issues (sells) it, including Mondex, Citicorp, and other financial institutions. When shopping online—for example, to purchase jewelry—a shopper sends digital money to the merchant instead of using checks, credit cards, or online banking to transfer cash. Businesses can purchase supplies and services electronically from any merchant that accepts e-cash. It flows from the buyer's into the seller's e-cash funds, which are instantaneously updated and stored on a microchip. Unlike smart cards, e-cash balances in the customer's account, at the end of the day, can be converted back into dollars in the customer's conventional banking account.

Although e-cash transactions are cheaper than handling checks and the paper records involved with conventional money, some potential problems can arise. Hackers, for example, may break into e-cash systems and drain them instantaneously. If the issuer's computer system crashes, it is conceivable that money "banked" in memory may be lost forever. Finally, regulation and control of e-cash systems remain largely nonexistent, with virtually none of the protection that covers government-controlled money systems.

INTERNATIONAL BANKING AND FINANCE

Electronic technologies now permit nearly instantaneous financial transactions around the globe. The subsequent country-to-country transactions result in an *international payments process* that moves money between buyers and sellers on different continents. Beyond the loosely structured agreements among countries, there is no worldwide system of policy making for international banking.

THE INTERNATIONAL PAYMENTS PROCESS

When transactions are made between buyers and sellers in different countries, exactly how are payments made? Financial settlements are simplified through the services provided by their banks. For example, payments from U.S. buyers start at a local bank that

Tellers at the Bank of Baghdad in the capital's Karrada neighborhood work with customers to convert Iraqi dinars into euros for sending payments from Iraq to a French seller.

converts them from dollars into the foreign currency of the sellers—for example, into euros to be sent to a seller in Greece. At the same time, payments from separate transactions also are flowing in the other direction: Greek businesses are buying products from U.S. sellers. The Greek buyers instruct their local bank to convert euros into dollars and send payment to the sellers' U.S. bank.

In this example, how much money actually flows between the two banks? If trade between the two countries is in balance—if money inflows and outflows are equal for both countries—then *money does not actually have to flow between the two countries.* Within each bank, the dollars spent by local importers offset the dollars received by local exporters. If inflows and outflows are not in balance at the U.S. bank (or at the Greek bank), then a flow of money—either to Greece or to the United States—is made to cover the difference.

■■■ INTERNATIONAL BANK STRUCTURE

There is no worldwide banking system that is comparable, in terms of policy making and regulatory power, to the system of any industrialized nation. Rather, worldwide banking stability relies on a loose structure of agreements among individual countries or groups of countries.

The World Bank and the IMF Two United Nations agencies, the World Bank and the International Monetary Fund, help to finance international trade. Unlike true banks, the **World Bank** (technically the International Bank for Reconstruction and Development), a U.N. agency, provides only a very limited scope of services. For instance, it funds national improvements by making loans to build roads, schools, power plants, and hospitals. The resulting improvements eventually enable borrowing countries to increase productive capacity and international trade.

Another U.N. agency, the **International Monetary Fund (IMF)**, is a group of some 150 nations that have combined resources for the following purposes:

- To promote the stability of exchange rates
- To provide temporary, short-term loans to member countries
- To encourage members to cooperate on international monetary issues
- To encourage development of a system for international payments

WORLD BANK U.N. agency that provides a limited scope of financial services, such as funding improvements in underdeveloped countries

INTERNATIONAL MONETARY FUND (IMF) U.N. agency consisting of about 150 nations that have combined resources to promote stable exchange rates, provide temporary short-term loans, and serve other purposes

The IMF makes loans to nations suffering from temporary negative trade balances. By making it possible for these countries to continue buying products from other countries, the IMF facilitates international trade. However, some nations have declined IMF funds rather than accept the economic changes that the IMF demands. For example, some developing countries reject the IMF's requirement that they cut back social programs and spending in order to bring inflation under control.

SELF-CHECK QUESTIONS 7–9

You should now be able to answer Self-Check Questions 7–9.*

7 Multiple Choice Suppose the Fed decides that the nation's money supply is too large and takes action to reduce it. Which of the following Fed actions is **not** appropriate for reducing the money supply?
(a) sell securities
(b) increase the reserve requirement
(c) decrease the discount rate
(d) increase the margin rate for stock purchases

8 Multiple Choice Which of the following electronic technologies allows money to move among consumers and businesses outside the established network of banks and money supplies overseen by the Fed?
(a) debit cards
(b) e-cash
(c) smart cards
(d) credit cards

9 True/False The World Bank is the global regulatory authority that supervises the international banking system and monitors the international payments process.

*Answers to Self-Check Questions 7–9 can be found on p. 566.

CONTINUED FROM PAGE 462

TAKING AN INTEREST IN MONEY

In managing the money supply and interest rates, the Fed strongly influences the dollar's strength against other currencies. The European Central Bank (ECB) has the same role in the 12-nation euro zone, the world's second-largest economic system. While both systems have struggled for economic recovery, their central banks adopted dissimilar monetary policies in the years since 2000, with contrasting results.

Consider the U.S. economy's recent growth, with a 45-year low federal funds rate—the interest rate governing overnight interbank loans—at 1 percent until mid-2004, high productivity, moderate unemployment, a weak dollar, low inflation, and strong economic recovery. Europe's monetary position, in contrast, clings to a policy of higher interest rates—standing at 2 percent—and a strengthening euro has risen by some 50 percent against the dollar since its low in mid-2001.

Europe's economic results are disappointing. In a growing global economy, exports, for example, remain less competitive—continue to fall—while imports to European markets are more competitive. Overall economic growth in the region was 1.4 percent for 2005 versus a robust 4.0 percent for the United States. The region's unemployment is nearly 9 percent, and productivity gains are modest. While U.S. corporate profits have recovered to their peaks in 2000, German profits are off 74 percent, French profits are down 67 percent, and Italian profits are off 25 percent. In short, the still-fragile economic recovery is sluggish.

Interest rate is a key policy variable in accounting for differences in U.S. and euro-zone results. The raising of interest rates tends to increase an economic system's currency value, whereas lowering the rate has the opposite effect. The Fed began raising U.S. rates in mid-2004, up to 5.25 percent by mid-2006, to dampen the bustling U.S. economy. It also strengthened the dollar so it could now buy €1 for about $1.20. Even so, the ECB recognizes the need for lower rates to stimulate the European recovery and further narrow the euro-dollar gap. As the two interest rates move in opposite directions, we can expect further strengthening of the dollar against the euro and a reversal of positions, somewhat, between the two economic systems.

QUESTIONS FOR DISCUSSION

1 In late 2000, €1 stood at US$0.92, whereas it reached a peak of nearly US$1.30 in early 2004. What does this change mean to you as a U.S. importer of euro-zone products? What does it mean if you are an exporter of U.S. goods to the euro zone?

2 Under what economic conditions might you expect the Fed to raise interest rates? To lower them? Explain.

3 Consider the policy position taken by the ECB. Why do you suppose it held to a 2 percent target inflation rate and a 2 percent interest rate for the European community's post-recession recovery?

4 Why do you think the Fed reversed trends by raising the interest rate governing overnight interbank loans from the recent 45-year low? How might a rate increase affect inflation, if at all?

5 Suppose you are a businessperson planning to build a new facility in either the United States or the euro zone. How might your choice of where and when to build be influenced by monetary policies of the ECB and the Fed?

SUMMARY OF LEARNING OBJECTIVES

1 Define *money* and identify the different forms that it takes in the nation's money supply.

Any item that's *portable*, *divisible*, *durable*, and *stable* satisfies the basic characteristics of money. Money also serves as a *medium of exchange*, a *store of value*, and a *measure of worth*. The nation's money supply is usually measured in three ways. *M-1* includes the most liquid (or spendable) forms of money: currency (cash), checks, and checking accounts (demand deposits). *M-2* includes M-1 plus other forms of money that are not quite as liquid but are converted easily to spendable forms: time deposits, money market funds, and savings accounts. *M-3* includes all of M-2 plus somewhat less liquid deposits, mainly by large institutions, in large time deposits and money market funds.

2 Describe the different kinds of financial institutions that compose the U.S. financial system and explain the services they offer.

Commercial banks offer checking accounts and accept deposits that they use to make loans and earn profits for shareholders. They also offer (1) pension and trust services, (2) international services, (3) financial advice and brokerage services, (4) ATMs, and (5) other forms of electronic banking. *Savings and loan associations* also accept deposits and make loans, primarily for home mortgages. In *mutual savings banks*, all depositors are owners of the bank, and all profits are divided among them. *Credit unions* are nonprofit cooperative financial institutions, owned and run by their members who pool their funds to make loans to one another at reasonable rates. Other organizations called *nondeposit institutions*—pension funds, insurance companies, finance companies, and securities investment dealers—take in money, provide interest or other services, and make loans.

3 Explain how financial institutions create money and describe the means by which they are regulated.

The money supply expands because banks can loan out most of the money they take in from deposits. The loans create additional deposits as follows: Out of a deposit of $100, the bank may hold $10 in reserve and loan 90 percent—$90—to borrowers. There will still be the original $100 on deposit, and borrowers will also deposit the $90 loans in their banks. Now, the borrowers' banks have $81 of new deposits available for new loans (90 percent of $90). Banks, therefore, have turned the original $100 deposit into $271 ($100 + $90 + $81) of deposits.

The government regulates commercial banks to ensure a sound financial system. The *Federal Deposit Insurance Corporation (FDIC)* insures deposits and guarantees the safety of all deposits up to $100,000. To ensure against failures, the FDIC examines the activities and accounts of all member banks.

4 Discuss the functions of the Federal Reserve System and describe the tools that it uses to control the money supply.

The *Federal Reserve System (the Fed)* is the nation's central bank. As the government's bank, the Fed produces currency and lends money to the government. As the bankers' bank, it lends money to member banks, stores reserve funds for banks, and clears checks for them. The Fed's Open Market Committee is responsible for formulating the monetary policies to promote economic stability and growth by managing the nation's money supply. Among its tools for controlling the money supply, the Fed specifies *reserve requirements*, it sets the *discount rate* at which it lends money to banks, and it conducts *open-market operations* to buy and sell securities. It also exerts influence through selective *credit controls*.

5 Identify three important ways in which the money and banking system is changing.

(1) The Bank Secrecy Act requires financial institutions to deter funding of crimes. The USA Patriot Act requires banks to implement a customer identification program to verify identities and compare them with government lists of terrorists. (2) The Interstate Banking Efficiency Act allows banks to operate across state lines. (3) In addition to EFT systems, banks offer telephone, TV, and Internet banking. *Electronic check clearing* speeds up the check-clearing process, and the "blink" credit card speeds up consumer checkout by replacing magnetic strip cards with contactless cards. *Debit cards* allow the transfer of money from the cardholder's account directly to others' accounts. The *smart card* can be programmed with "electronic money" at ATM machines or at home.

6 Discuss some of the institutions and activities in international banking and finance.

Country-to-country transactions rely on an international payments process that moves money between buyers and sellers in different nations. If trade between two countries is in balance—if money inflows and outflows are equal for both countries—money does not have to flow between the two countries. If inflows and outflows are not in balance, then a flow of money between them is made to cover the difference.

Because there is no worldwide banking system, global banking stability relies on agreements among countries. Two United Nations agencies help to finance international trade: (1) The *World Bank* funds loans for national improvements so borrowers can increase productive capacity and international trade. (2) The *International Monetary Fund* makes loans to nations suffering from temporary negative trade balances and to provide economic and monetary stability for the borrowing country.

KEY TERMS

automated teller machine (ATM) (p. 471)

banker's acceptance (p. 470)

check (p. 464)

checking account (demand
   deposit) (p. 464)

commercial bank (p. 467)

credit union (p. 469)

currency (cash) (p. 464)

debit card (p. 479)

discount rate (p. 476)

e-cash (p. 480)

electronic funds transfer (EFT) (p. 471)

Federal Deposit Insurance Corporation
   (FDIC) (p. 472)

Federal Reserve System (the Fed) (p. 473)

finance company (p. 469)

float (p. 476)

individual retirement account
   (IRA) (p. 470)

insurance company (p. 469)

International Monetary Fund
   (IMF) (p. 481)

letter of credit (p. 470)

M-1 (p. 464)

M-2 (p. 464)

M-3 (p. 466)

monetary policy (p. 476)

money (p. 463)

money market mutual fund (p. 465)

mutual savings bank (p. 469)

open-market operations (p. 476)

pension fund (p. 469)

point-of-sale (POS) terminal (p. 480)

prime rate (p. 468)

reserve requirement (p. 476)

savings and loan association
   (S&L) (p. 468)

securities investment dealer
   (broker) (p. 469)

selective credit controls (p. 477)

smart card (p. 480)

time deposit (p. 465)

trust services (p. 470)

World Bank (p. 481)

QUESTIONS AND EXERCISES

Questions for Review

1 Explain the four characteristics of money.
2 What are the components of M-1? Of M-2? Of M-3?
3 Explain the roles of commercial banks, savings and loan associations, credit unions, and nondeposit institutions in the U.S. financial system.
4 Describe the structure of the Federal Reserve System.
5 Show how the Fed uses the discount rate to manage inflation in the U.S. economy.

Questions for Analysis

6 Do you think credit cards should be counted in the money supply? Why or why not? Support your argument by using the definition of *money*.
7 Should commercial banks be regulated, or should market forces be allowed to determine the kinds of loans and the interest rates for loans and savings deposits? Why?

8 Identify a purchase made by you or a family member in which payment was made by check. Draw a diagram to trace the steps in the clearing process followed by that check.

Application Exercises

9 Start with a $1,000 deposit and assume a reserve requirement of 15 percent. Now trace the amount of money created by the banking system after five lending cycles.
10 Interview the manager of a local commercial bank. Identify the ways in which the bank has implemented requirements of the Bank Secrecy Act and the USA Patriot Act. What costs has the bank incurred to implement the federal requirements?

FOUR ECONOMISTS IN A ROOM

Goal

To encourage you to understand the economic factors considered by the Fed in determining current interest rates.

Background Information

One of the Fed's most important tools in setting monetary policy is the adjustment of the interest rates it charges member banks to borrow money. To determine interest rate policy, the Fed analyzes current economic conditions from its 12 districts. Its findings are published eight times a year in a report commonly known as the "Beige Book."

Method

Step 1

Working with three other students, access the Fed's Web site at www.federalreserve.gov. Look for the heading "Monetary Policy," and then click on the subheading "Beige Book." When you reach that page, read the summary of the current report.

Step 2

Working with group members, study each of the major summary sections:

- Consumer spending
- Manufacturing
- Construction and real estate
- Banking and finance
- Nonfinancial services
- Labor market, wages, and pricing
- Agriculture and natural resources

Working with team members, discuss ways in which you think key information contained in the summary might affect the Fed's decision to raise, lower, or maintain interest rates.

Step 3

At your library, find back issues of *Barron's*, the highly respected weekly financial publication. Look for the issue published immediately following the appearance of the most recent "Beige Book." Search for articles analyzing the report. Discuss with group members what the articles say about current economic conditions and interest rates.

Step 4

Based on your research and analysis, what factors do you think the Fed will take into account to control inflation? Working with group members, explain your answer in writing.

Step 5

Working with group members, research what the Fed chairperson says about interest rates. Do the chairperson's reasons for raising, lowering, or maintaining rates agree with your group's analysis?

FOLLOW-UP QUESTIONS

1 What are the most important factors in the Fed's interest rate decision?

2 Consider the old joke about economists that goes like this: When there are four economists in a room analyzing current economic conditions, there are at least eight different opinions. Based on your research and analysis, why do you think economists have such varying opinions?

TELLING THE ETHICAL FROM THE STRICTLY LEGAL

The Situation

When upgrading services for convenience to customers, commercial banks are concerned about setting prices that cover all costs so that, ultimately, they make a profit. This exercise challenges you to evaluate one banking service—ATM transactions—to determine if any ethical issues also should be considered in a bank's pricing decisions.

The Dilemma

A regional commercial bank in the western United States has more than 300 ATMs serving the nearly 400,000 checking and savings accounts of its customers. Customers are not charged a fee for their 30 million ATM transactions each year, as long as they use their bank's ATMs. For issuing cash to noncustomers, however, the bank charges a $2 ATM fee. The bank's officers are reexamining their policies on ATM surcharges because of public protests against other banks with similar surcharges in Santa Monica, New York City, and Chicago. Iowa has gone even further, becoming the first state to pass legislation that bans national banks from charging ATM fees for noncustomers. To date, the courts have ruled that the access fees are legal, but some organizations—such as the U.S. Public Interest Research Group (PIRG)—continue to fight publicly against them.

In considering its current policies, our western bank's vice president for community relations is concerned about more than mere legalities. She wants to ensure that her company is "being a good citizen and doing the right thing." Any decision on ATM fees will ultimately affect the bank's customers, its image in the community and industry, and its profitability for its owners.

QUESTIONS TO ADDRESS

1 From the standpoint of a commercial bank, can you find any economic justification for ATM access fees?

2 Based on the scenario described for our bank, do you find any ethical issues in this situation? Or do you find the main issues legal and economic rather than ethical?

3 As an officer for this bank, how would you handle this situation?

BANKER'S PREDICAMENT: NATIONAL SECURITY VERSUS CUSTOMER PRIVACY

The Situation

Since 9/11, many citizens are hearing about information activities by organizations that before 9/11 were considered intrusive. Under provisions of the Bank Secrecy Act and the USA Patriot Act, for example, financial institutions now scour transactions of customers more intensely than before. Does increased monitoring of transactions information raise any ethical problems for customers, owners, or employees?

The Dilemma

Bill Decker got irritated when his application to open a checking account at Forthright National Bank was delayed by lengthy identification-verifying procedures at the bank. Months later he was offended to learn that the bank was tracking deposit and checking activities in his account. As he vented his anger to Gloria Liu, the employee that reviews customers' transactions, she tried to explain the bank's obligations to do their part in detecting suspicious activities and preventing terrorism. Surprised by these comments, Bill insisted on finding out just how much Gloria knows about his personal financial situation. "Do you know who I have transactions with through your bank? Are you tracking them, too? With whom are you sharing this information? Does it affect my credit rating?" As the conversation heated up, Gloria decided that her boss, Carolyn Kleen, should be called, especially when Bill indicated that assistance from a civil liberties group might be appropriate for addressing his privacy concerns.

Team Activity

Assemble a group of four students and assign each group member to one of the following roles:

- Bill Decker (bank customer)
- Gloria Liu (bank employee)
- Carolyn Kleen (vice president, financial security)
- Karl Marcks (bank stockholder, investor)

ACTION STEPS

1 Before hearing any of your group's comments on this situation, and from the perspective of your assigned role, do you think there are any ethical issues with Forthright National Bank's security-screening program? If so, write them down.

2 Before hearing any of your group's comments, and from the perspective of your assigned role, what do you think are the main problems with the bank's security-screening program? Write them down.

3 Return to your group and share the ethical issues and problems identified by each member. Were the issues and problems the same among all roles, or did difference in roles result in different issues and problems?

4 Among the ethical issues identified, decide as a group which one is most important for the bank to resolve. Likewise, for potential problems, which is the most important one for the bank?

5 What does your group recommend be done to resolve the most important ethical issue? How should the most important problem be resolved?

☐☐☐☐☐☐☐☐☐☐ ▮ **VIDEO EXERCISE**

FUNDING THE BUSINESS WORLD: COAST BUSINESS CREDIT

Learning Objectives

The purpose of this video is to help you to:

1 Recognize how and why banks use customer deposits as the basis of loans.
2 Understand the role of banks and financial services firms in providing funding for business expansion, operations, and acquisitions.
3 Identify the risks that financial services firms take when loaning money to businesses.

Synopsis

Coast Business Credit, a division of Southern Pacific Bank, provides money for business. When evaluating the risk that a loan will not be repaid, Coast carefully considers the borrower's collateral, cash flow, and management. Business customers may apply for a short-term line of credit, a long-term loan, or other types of financing for a variety of purposes. One company may need operating capital; another may need money to make a major acquisition or to expand. Coast analyzes each lending opportunity in terms of potential risk, potential profit, and—in some cases—the ability to create or save jobs and, thus, benefit the community at large.

DISCUSSION QUESTIONS

1 **For analysis**: How might the amount of time deposits gathered by parent company Southern Pacific Bank affect the loans made by Coast Business Credit?
2 **For analysis**: If the Fed lowers the discount rate by a significant amount, what would be the likely effect on business loan rates?
3 **For application**: What type of collateral might Coast Business Credit prefer when considering a loan application?
4 **For application**: In addition to collateral, Coast Business Credit looks at cash flow and management when considering a loan application. Why is management such an important element?
5 **For debate**: Should Coast Business Credit establish a separate lending department specifically for financing Internet start-ups? Support your chosen position.

Online Exploration

Visit the Coast Business Credit Web site at www.coastbusiness-credit.com. After browsing the home page, follow the links to learn more about Coast Business Credit. What types of loans will Coast make? To what types of businesses? Why does Coast explain its financial offerings in such detail? Why would it mention the names of its parent company, its affiliates, and its FDIC coverage on its Web site? How does Coast make it easy for businesses to make contact?

**After reading this chapter,
you should be able to:**

1 Describe the role of securities markets
and explain the difference between
primary securities markets and secondary
securities markets.

2 Discuss the value to shareholders of
common stock and preferred stock and
identify the major stock exchanges and
stock markets.

3 Distinguish among various types of bonds
in terms of their issuers and safety.

4 Describe the investment opportunities
offered by mutual funds.

5 Describe the risk-return relationship, and
discuss the use of diversification and asset
allocation for investments.

6 Explain the process by which securities
are bought and sold.

7 Explain how securities markets are
regulated.

WANNA BET (ON A SURE THING)?

Sounds incredible, doesn't it, that someone can bet on events from the past? It turns out
that's what's been going on in the $7 trillion scandal-laden mutual funds industry. Some
funds managers have been making transactions after the market outcomes are known!

SECURITIES AND INVESTMENTS

16

It's what you might call a "sure thing" a great way to erase market risk and take profits that are inaccessible to honest investors.

It's called "late trading"—trading in fund shares after the market closes, at the close-of-trade price—and it's illegal. After the 4:00 P.M. (Eastern Standard Time) cutoff, when the day's closing price is known, preferred customers get to trade—buy or sell—at the pre-4:00 P.M. price. It's like betting after the game is over when you know the outcome. After-close trading is supposed to happen at the next day's closing price. However, the Securities and Exchange Commission's (SEC) enforcement director, Stephen Cutler, told a Senate hearing in late 2003 that about 10 percent of fund groups may have engaged in late trading, and as many as one-fourth of the nation's largest mutual funds firms helped favored clients by allowing illegal late trading. New York Attorney General Eliot Spitzer, after months of investigating abuses by investment firms, points out that preferential trading arrangements for big-money clients can be draining off billions of dollars from ordinary investors in mutual funds.

By late 2003, as word of the scandal rocked the once-trusted industry, several big state pension funds announced decisions to take money out of the offending mutual funds. At Putman Investments, Lawrence Lasser, CEO since 1987, was ousted, and four managers were fired. For Iowa Treasurer Michael Fitzgerald, Putnam's housecleaning wasn't enough: He fired Putnam by withdrawing $586 million of the state's pension fund.

> *It's a matter of trust. Lasser got paid an outrageous amount of money, and he should have known what was going on.*
>
> —Iowa Treasurer Michael Fitzgerald, on withdrawing Iowa pension funds from Putnam Investments

SELF-CHECK QUESTIONS 4–6

You should now be able to answer Self-Check Questions 4–6.*

4 Multiple Choice Which of the following is **not true** about bonds?

(a) a bond is a promise by the issuer to pay the buyer a certain amount of money at a future date

(b) corporate bonds issued by U.S. companies involve less money than U.S. government and municipal bonds

(c) secured bonds can reduce risk to holders because the issuing firms pledge assets in case of default

(d) government bonds are among the safest investments available

5 True/False Suppose a well-respected corporation has decided to issue bonds for raising capital but also does not want to pledge specific property as security. Is the following statement true or false? A debenture is well suited to this firm's objectives.

6 Multiple Choice Suppose you have $20,000 to invest. Your goal is to maximize capital appreciation over the next 20 years. Which of the following would be the most suitable kind of mutual fund for meeting your objectives?

(a) municipal bond fund

(b) balanced fund

(c) money market fund

(d) aggressive growth fund.

*Answers to Self-Check Questions 4–6 can be found on p. 566.

BUYING AND SELLING SECURITIES

The process of buying and selling securities—stocks, bonds, and mutual funds—involves several steps. First, you must find out about possible investments and match them to your investment objectives. Then, you must select a broker and open an account. Only then can you place orders and make different types of transactions.

■■■ FINANCIAL INFORMATION SERVICES

Have you ever looked at the financial section of your daily newspaper and wondered what all those tables and numbers mean? It is a good idea to know how to read stock, bond, and mutual fund quotations if you want to invest in them. Fortunately, this skill is easily mastered.

Stock Quotations Daily transactions for NYSE and NASDAQ common stocks are reported in most city newspapers. Figure 16.3 shows part of a past listing from the *Wall Street Journal*, with columns numbered 1 through 11. Let's analyze the listing for the company at the top, Gap Inc.:

■ The first column ("YTD % CHG") shows the stock price percentage change for the calendar year to date. Gap's common stock price has increased 4 percent since the beginning of that year.

■ The next two columns ("High" and "Low") show the highest and lowest prices paid for one share of Gap stock *during the past year*. Note that stock prices throughout are expressed in dollars per share. In the past 52 weeks, then, Gap's stock ranged in value from $24.13 to $16.71 per share. This range reveals a moderately volatile stock price.

■ The fourth column ("Stock") is the abbreviated company name (in this case, Gap Inc).

The Personality of a Risk Taker

Thanks to the risks entailed in setting up her own business, Lucy Marcus, founder of London-based Marcus Venture Consulting, has become an expert at assessing the risk involved in starting up a new business, investing in it, and managing it. In many ways, risk is the mainstay of Marcus's business. Her clients include individuals, companies, and pension funds—investors seeking a clear picture of the risks posed by potential investment opportunities. They want answers to such questions as "If I invest in XYZ Venture Capital Fund, how well will it be managed? What kind of financial return can I expect?"

As one of a handful of senior female executives in the private equity industry, Marcus has to gain the trust of all sorts of clients by demonstrating dependable judgment about risk. It's a business with few women in leadership roles. To encourage women in the equities industry, Marcus set up a network called HighTech Women—a 2,500-member discussion group for women to meet and mentor one another. "HighTech Women was something

I kept going to conferences and being one of four women in a roomful of 200 CEOs.

—Lucy Marcus, head of Marcus Venture Consulting

I had to do," she explains. "I kept going to conferences and being one of four women in a roomful of 200 CEOs. I found that I'd meet the most interesting people in the ladies' room."

As an entrepreneur advising other entrepreneurs, Marcus's outlook is influenced by a number of personal characteristics. For professional reasons, she won't tell anyone her age: "I'm too young for some people and too old for others." She regards herself as a maverick who's too outspoken for the average corporate environment, and she thinks people should be judged on what they achieve. She admires people who do different and interesting work, who buck trends, and who know what they're talking about. She claims to be a quick judge of character and admits that she has to work hard at networking because she doesn't make friends with everybody. She avoids focusing solely on the business she's in, but that doesn't mean that she's not passionate about what she does. "I couldn't do something I wasn't passionate about," she says, "because I couldn't put the energy into it."

■ The NYSE symbol for the stock—GPS—is listed in column 5 ("Sym").

■ The sixth column ("Div") indicates that Gap pays an annual cash dividend of $0.09 per share. This amount can be compared with payouts by other companies.

■ Column 7 ("Yld %") is the *dividend yield* expressed as a percentage of the stock's current price (shown in column 10). Gap's dividend yield is 0.4 percent (0.09/24.15, rounded).

Figure 16.3 Reading a Stock Quotation

❶	❷	❸	❹	❺	❻	❼	❽	❾	❿	⓫
YTD	52 Week					Yld		Vol		Net
% Chg	High	Low	Stock	Sym	Div	%	PE	100s	Close	Chg
4.0	24.13	16.71	Gap Inc	GPS	.09	.4	20	40017	24.15	0.05
9.7	30.30	18.85	GardnrDenvr	GDI			18	712	26.19	0.40
8.3	13.75	7.26	Gartner	IT			49	3657	12.25	−0.10
10.9	12.99	7.14	GartnerB	ITB			48	208	12.07	−0.08
−12.0	6.85	3.16	Gateway	GTW			dd	19218	4.05	0.07
−3.7	32.70	17.70	GaylEnt	GET			dd	2104	28.75	0.01
5.5	11.82	7.66	GenCorp	GY	.12	1.1	cc	1065	11.36	0.04
27.8	68.25	29.85	Genentech	DNA			cc	17664	59.81	−0.04
−1.7	10.23	4.31	GenlCbl	BGC			dd	2381	8.01	0.18
5.8	97	65.64	GenDynam	GD	1.44	1.5	18	8120	95.63	−0.09
0.5	34.57	26.90	GenElec	GE	.80	2.6	20	171098	31.12	−0.14

Potential buyers can compare this yield with returns they might get from alternative investments.

- Column 8 ("PE") shows the **price-earnings ratio**—the current price of the stock divided by the firm's current annual earnings per share (not shown in Figure 16.3). On this day, Gap's PE is 20, which means that investors are willing to pay $20 for each $1 of reported profits to own Gap stock. This figure can be compared with PE ratios of other stocks when deciding which is the better investment. The PE for some stocks is indicated as *cc*—a code meaning the stock's PE was greater than 100—or *dd* to indicate the stock had negative earnings for the past four quarters.

- The last three columns detail the *day's trading*. Column 9 ("Vol 100s") shows the *number of shares* (in hundreds) that were traded—in this case, 40,017. Some investors interpret increases in trading volume as an indicator of forthcoming price changes in a stock.

- Column 10 ("Close") shows that Gap's *last sale of the day* was for $24.15.

- The final column ("Net Chg") shows the *difference between the previous day's close and the close on the day being reported*. The closing price of Gap stock is $0.05 higher than it was on the previous business day. Day-to-day changes are indicators of recent price stability or volatility.

The listings also report unusual conditions of importance to investors. An *s* next to the stock symbol, for example, would indicate either a *stock split* (a division of stock that gives stockholders a greater number of shares but that does not change each individual's proportionate share of ownership) or an extra stock dividend paid by the company during the past 52 weeks. An *n* accompanying a stock symbol would indicate that this stock was newly issued during the past 52 weeks. The stock listings contain an index explaining the various codes for unusual conditions.

Bond Quotations Daily quotations on selected corporate bonds from the NYSE are also published in the financial news, although the listing is not extensive. Bond quotations contain essentially the same type of information as stock quotations. One difference is that the year in which it is going to mature is listed beside each bond.

Mutual Funds Quotations Selling prices for mutual funds are reported daily or weekly in most city newspapers. Additional investor information is also available in the financial press. Figure 16.4 shows a partial listing of T. Rowe Price funds from *Barron's: Mutual Funds*, a prominent weekly financial newspaper. The alphabetical listing includes the three funds—Balanced, Science and Technology, and Short-Term Bond—discussed previously, whereas the published list would include all of Price's more than 90 different funds.

Figure 16.4
Reading a Mutual Fund Quotation

❶	❷	❸	❹	❺	❻	❼	❽
52 Week		Fund	Close	Wk's	% Return		
High	Low	Name	NAV	Chg	1-Wk	YTD	3-Yrs
Price Funds:							
19.04	16.51	Balanced *n*	18.37	−0.01	−0.1	+0.4	+7.8
20.00	15.03	SciTec *n*	18.29	−0.21	−1.1	−2.7	−33.4
4.90	4.75	Sht-Bd *n*	4.75	−0.01	−0.2	−0.3	−13.5

The fund's **net asset value (NAV)**—the current market value of one share—is, perhaps, the key term for understanding the quotations. The fund managers calculate NAV at day's end by taking the fund's net assets—securities it owns, plus cash and any accumulated earnings, minus liabilities—and dividing the remainder by the number of shares owned by all shareholders. Again, let's focus on the first fund listed in the figure, the Balanced fund:

NET ASSET VALUE (NAV)
current market value of one share

- Column 1 shows the fund's highest (at that time) *net asset value (NAV)*—$19.04—during the past 52 weeks.
- Column 2 contains the 52-week low NAV, $16.51.
- Column 3 lists the company name (Price Funds) at the top and the individual fund names beneath the company name. The *n* code indicates no front-end or back-end sales charge (a *no-load fund*).
- Column 4 lists the NAV—$18.37—at the close of the most recent week.
- Column 5 shows the *net asset value change*—the dollar gain or loss based on the previous week's NAV. The Balanced fund closed $0.01 lower this week than in the previous week.
- The next three columns report *each fund's recent and longer-term performance*. These numbers reflect the percentage change in NAV. These three columns show the return of the fund (percentage return) for the most recent past week (column 6), current year-to-date (column 7), and the last 3 years (column 8).

Unlike stocks and bonds, shares of mutual funds are not traded on any organized market. Instead, they are sold directly to each investor by the company that creates the funds. You may buy mutual funds from any of the many companies that offer them, such as Vanguard or Fidelity Investments, by calling their 800 numbers or visiting their Web sites and setting up an account.

Market Indexes Although they do not indicate the status of individual securities, **market indexes** provide useful summaries of overall price trends, both in specific industries and in the stock market as a whole. Market indexes, for example, reveal bull and bear market trends. **Bull markets** are periods of rising stock prices. Periods of falling stock prices are called **bear markets**.

MARKET INDEX summary of price trends in a specific industry and/or the stock market as a whole

As Figure 16.5 shows, the years 1981 to the beginning of 2000 boasted a strong bull market, the longest in history. Inflation was under control as business flourished in a healthy economy. In contrast, the period 2000 to 2003 was characterized by a bear market. Financial failures closed many dot-com firms, sluggish sales abroad decreased U.S. exports, terrorism on September 11, 2001, brought a halt to business activity, and corporate misconduct led to a downcast mood among investors. Then, the bull market resumed after 2003 on into 2006. As you can see, the data that characterized such periods are drawn from three leading market indexes: the Dow Jones, Standard & Poor's, and NASDAQ Composite.

BULL MARKET period of rising stock prices

BEAR MARKET period of falling stock prices

The Dow The **Dow Jones Industrial Average (DJIA)** is the most widely cited U.S. market index. The Dow measures the performance of U.S. financial markets by focusing on 30 blue-chip companies as reflectors of economic health. The Dow is an average of the stock prices for these 30 large firms and, by tradition, traders and investors use it as a barometer of the market's overall movement. Because it includes only 30 of the thousands of companies on the market, the Dow is only an approximation of the overall market's price movements.

DOW JONES INDUSTRIAL AVERAGE (DJIA) market index based on the prices of 30 of the largest industrial firms listed on the NYSE

Over the decades, the Dow has been revised and updated to reflect the changing composition of U.S. companies and industries. The most recent modification occurred in 2004, when three companies were added—insurance giant American International Group, pharmaceuticals goliath Pfizer, telecom titan Verizon—replacing AT&T, Eastman

Figure 16.5
Bull and Bear Markets

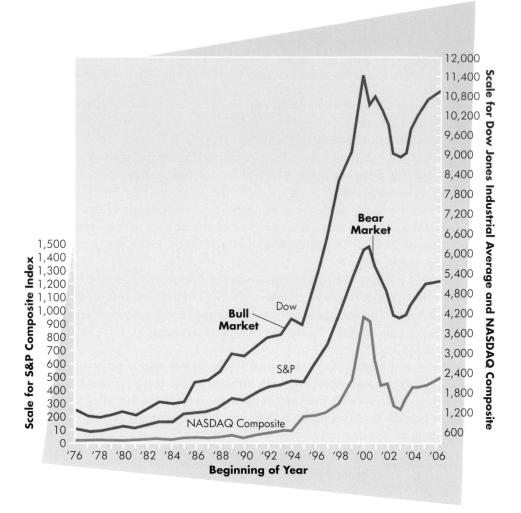

Kodak, and International Paper. These changes better reflect today's information-based economy and the increasing prominence of financial services and pharmaceuticals, versus the declining importance of some traditional companies.

The Dow average is computed as the sum of the current prices of the 30 stocks divided not by 30 (as might be expected) but rather by a number that compensates for stock splits and each stock's available number of shares. On January 19, 2006, for example, the value of that divisor was 0.12493117. Each day, the divisor's value is printed in the *Wall Street Journal*, as is the DJIA.

The S&P 500 Because it considers very few firms, the Dow is a limited gauge of the overall U.S. stock market. **Standard & Poor's Composite Index** is a broader report. It consists of 500 stocks, including 400 industrial firms, 40 utilities, 40 financial institutions, and 20 transportation companies. Because the index average is weighted according to the total market values of each stock, the more highly valued companies exercise a greater influence on the index.

The NASDAQ Composite Because it considers more stocks, some Wall Street observers regard the **NASDAQ Composite Index** as the most important of all market indexes. Unlike the Dow and the S&P 500, all NASDAQ-listed companies, not just a selected few, are included in the index, for a total of more than 3,300 firms (both domestic and foreign)—more than most other indexes.

STANDARD & POOR'S COMPOSITE INDEX market index based on the performance of 400 industrial firms, 40 utilities, 40 financial institutions, and 20 transportation companies

NASDAQ COMPOSITE INDEX value-weighted market index that includes all NASDAQ-listed companies, both domestic and foreign

Figure 16.6
The Stock Markets:
Comparative Dollar Volume
of Trades

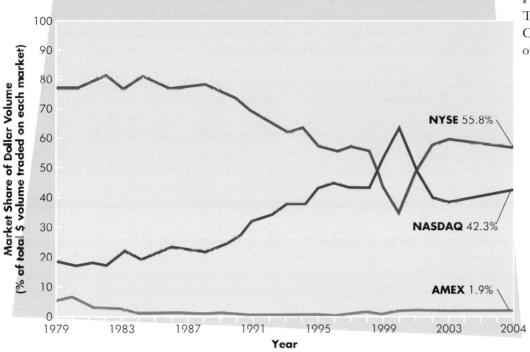

The popularity of the NASDAQ Index goes hand in hand with investors' growing interest in technology and small-company stocks. Compared with other markets, the NASDAQ market has enjoyed a remarkable level of activity. By 1998, so many shares were being traded on NASDAQ that its share of market surpassed that of the NYSE. Figure 16.6 shows the steady growth in the dollar volume of NASDAQ trades, which continued to capture market share through 1999. Thereafter, however, while the NASDAQ traded more shares than the NYSE, the dot-com downfall led to lower per-share prices, especially for technology and small-company stocks, such that the NASDAQ's annual dollar volume fell below the NYSE's. For 2004, the NYSE's $11.6 trillion trading volume once again engulfed the NASDAQ's nearly $8.8 trillion.

▦▦■ PLACING ORDERS

After doing your own research and getting recommendations from your broker, you can choose to place several different types of orders:

■ A **market order** requests that a broker buy or sell a certain security at the prevailing market price at the time of the order. For example, look again at Figure 16.3. On that day, your broker would have sold your Gap stock at a price near $24.15.
■ Note that when you gave your order to sell, you did not know exactly what the market price would be. This situation can be avoided with limit and stop orders, which allow for buying and selling only if certain price conditions are met. A **limit order** authorizes the purchase of a stock only if its price is less than or equal to a specified limit. For example, an order to buy at $25 a share means that the broker is to buy if and only if the stock becomes available for a price of $25 or less. A **stop order** instructs the broker to sell if a stock price falls to a certain level. For example, an order of $20 on a particular stock means that the broker is to sell that stock if and only if its price falls to $20 or below.

MARKET ORDER order to buy or sell a security at the market price prevailing at the time the order is placed

LIMIT ORDER order authorizing the purchase of a stock only if its price is equal to or less than a specified amount

STOP ORDER order authorizing the sale of a stock if its price falls to or below a specified level

ROUND LOT purchase or sale of stock in units of 100 shares

ODD LOT fraction of a round lot

■ Orders also differ by size. An order for a **round lot** requests 100 shares of a particular stock or some multiple thereof. Fractions of round lots are called **odd lots**. Because an intermediary—an *odd-lot broker*—is often involved, odd-lot trading is usually more expensive than round-lot trading.

■■■ FINANCING PURCHASES

When you place a buy order of any kind, you must tell your broker how you will pay for the purchase. For example, you might maintain a cash account with your broker. Then, as you buy and sell stocks, your broker adds proceeds to your account while deducting commissions and purchase costs. Like almost every product in today's economy, securities can also be purchased on credit.

MARGIN percentage of the total sales price that a buyer must put up to place an order for buying stock

Margin Trading Stocks can be bought on **margin**—that is, the buyer can put down a portion of the stock's price. The rest is borrowed from the buyer's broker, who then holds the purchased stock as collateral until the loan is repaid. Controlled by the Fed, the *margin requirement* has remained fixed at 50 percent in recent decades.

Margin trading offers a significant advantage: It provides additional buying power beyond the investor's limited funds, thus allowing larger purchases and the chance for greater profits through market appreciation. Although investors often recognize possible profits to be made in margin trading, they sometimes fail to consider that losses, too, can be amplified. Investors who focus on the upside benefits in bull markets think the market trend will continue upward, and they are less sensitive to the downside risks of margin trading. With more investors buying on debt, more of them can head for a serious accelerated crash when the market plunges. Bradley Skolnick, president of the North American Securities Administrators Association, voices the opinion held by many investment experts: "A lot of people are purchasing rather speculative, high-risk stocks with borrowed money, and that's a source of concern for me. In a volatile market, trading on margin can find you in a whole lot of hurt very quickly."[13]

In a volatile market, trading on margin can find you in a whole lot of hurt very quickly.

—Bradley Skolnick, president of the North American Securities Administrators Association

SHORT SALE stock sale in which an investor borrows securities from a broker to be sold and then replaced at a specified future date

Short Sales In addition to lending money, brokerages also lend securities. A **short sale** begins when you borrow a security from your broker and sell it (one of the few times that it is legal to sell something that you do not own). At a given point in the future, you must restore an equal number of shares of that issue to the brokerage, along with a fee for the use of the borrowed shares.

SECURITIES MARKET REGULATION

In addition to regulation by government agencies, both the *National Association of Securities Dealers (NASD)* and the NYSE exercise self-regulation to maintain the public trust and to ensure professionalism in the financial industry.

■■■ NASD AND SECURITIES REGULATION

NATIONAL ASSOCIATION OF SECURITIES DEALERS (NASD) the largest private-sector, securities-regulation organization in the world

The **National Association of Securities Dealers (NASD)** is the largest private-sector, securities-regulation organization in the world. Every broker/dealer in the United States who conducts securities business with the public is required by law to be a member of the NASD. The NASD includes dealers (not just brokers) who must pass qualification exams and meet certain standards for financial soundness. The privilege of trading in the market is granted by federal regulators and by the NASD.

■■■ NYSE SELF-REGULATION

A visible example of self-regulation is the NYSE's actions in establishing so-called *circuit breakers*—trading rules for reducing excessive market volatility, limiting mass or panic selling, and promoting investor confidence—that suspend trading for a preset length of time. Adopted first in 1988, with the approval of the SEC, the rules suspend trading on the NYSE whenever the market begins spiraling out of control during a single day. The 1988 rules stipulated that trading would halt for one hour on any day when the DJIA dropped 250 points and would close for two hours with any 400-point decline. The interruption provides a "cooling off" period that slows trading activity, gives investors time to reconsider their trading positions, and allows computer programs to be revised or shut down.

Because circuit-breaker thresholds are updated periodically to keep up with the Dow's growth, the following single-day declines are the current triggers that will halt trading in the securities and futures markets:

- A 10 percent drop in the DJIA before 2:00 P.M. halts trading for one hour.
- A 20 percent drop before 1:00 P.M. halts trading for two hours; if after 1:00 P.M., trading halts for the day.
- A 30 percent drop at any time halts trading for the day.

Although circuit-breaker rules were initiated in response to severe market plunges in October 1987 and October 1988, they were not triggered until October 27, 1997, when the DJIA fell 350 points at 2:35 P.M. and 550 points at 3:30 P.M., for an overall 7 percent plunge that shut down trading for the day (the trigger thresholds in 1997 were different from today's thresholds).

One oft-cited cause of sudden market fluctuations is **program trading**—the portfolio-trading strategy involving the sale or purchase of a group of stocks valued at $1 million or more, often triggered by computerized trading programs that can be launched without human supervision or control. It works in the following way: As market values change and economic events transpire during the course of a day, computer programs of large stock traders, such as insurance companies, are busy recalculating the future values of stocks. Once a calculated value reaches a critical point, the program automatically signals a buy or sell order. Because electronic trading could cause the market to spiral out of control, it has contributed to the establishment of circuit breakers.

PROGRAM TRADING large purchase or sale of a group of stocks, often triggered by computerized trading programs that can be launched without human supervision or control

■■■ THE SECURITIES AND EXCHANGE COMMISSION

To protect the investing public and to maintain smoothly functioning markets, the SEC oversees the ways securities are issued. The SEC regulates the public offering of new securities by requiring that all companies file prospectuses before proposed offerings

PROSPECTUS registration statement filed with the SEC before the issuance of a new security

commence. To protect investors from fraudulent issues, a **prospectus** contains pertinent information about both the offered security and the issuing company. False statements are subject to criminal penalties.

Insider Trading The SEC also enforces laws against **insider trading**—the use of special knowledge about a firm for profit or gain. In December 2005, for example, a U.S. Attorney announced that a federal grand jury in Denver returned an indictment charging Joseph P. Nacchio, the former CEO of Qwest Communications, with 42 counts of insider trading. The indictment states that during 2001, Nacchio, while in possession of nonpublic information about Qwest's financial health, accelerated his sale of Qwest stock—selling more than $100,000,000 worth of Qwest common stock—in violation of insider trading laws. The indictment states that Nacchio, because of his insider position, knew that the company was underperforming at levels far below Qwest's publicly stated financial targets. The indictment seeks forfeiture of the proceeds of the resulting illegal stock trades. As stated by the U.S. attorney: "Insider trading is a crime. Corporate executives are prohibited from enriching themselves while the public remains in the dark about the true financial condition of their companies." Each insider trader count carries a penalty of up to 10 years in prison and a $1,000,000 fine.[14]

INSIDER TRADING illegal practice of using special knowledge about a firm for profit or gain

The SEC also offers a reward to any person who provides information leading to a civil penalty for illegal insider trading. The courts can render such a penalty of up to three times the illegal profit that was gained, and the reward can, at most, be 10 percent of that penalty.

Along with the SEC's enforcement efforts, the stock exchanges and securities firms, as members of the NASD, cooperate in detecting and stopping insider action. In any given year, the NASD may refer more than a hundred cases to the SEC for charges of possible insider trading. In addition, the NASD's self-regulation results in actions ranging from fining member firms and officers to barring or suspending them.

Blue-Sky Laws State governments also regulate the sale of securities. For example, commenting that some promoters would sell stock "to the blue sky itself," one legislator's speech led to the phrase **blue-sky laws** and the passage of statutes requiring securities to be registered with state officials. In addition, securities dealers must be registered and licensed by the states in which they do business. Finally, states may prosecute for the sale of fraudulent securities.

BLUE-SKY LAWS laws requiring securities dealers to be licensed and registered with the states in which they do business

SELF-CHECK QUESTIONS 7–9

You should now be able to answer Self-Check Questions 7–9.*

7 Multiple Choice Which of the following is **not** true about printed stock quotations, like those published in the *Wall Street Journal*?
(a) the percentage change in the stock's price for the year is shown
(b) the company's annual cash dividend is reported
(c) a stock's high and low prices for any given day are reported

(d) the difference between closing prices on successive days is shown

8 True/False The DJIA is the most widely cited American index because it approximates the market's overall price movements more accurately than other indexes.

9 True/False The SEC oversees the ways securities are issued and regulates the public offering of new securities.

*Answers to Self-Check Questions 7–9 can be found on p. 566.

CONTINUED FROM PAGE 492

A STRONG CASE FOR REGULATION

Scandal has tarnished this industry that was once trusted and regarded as a safe, conservative investment by most of the 90 million people—and half of the nation's households—with money in U.S. stock mutual funds. Industry abuses will ultimately affect millions of investors in 401(k) retirement plans and the investments of big pension plans covering government and company employees. Late trading, especially, is nefarious because it gives an unfair information advantage over other investors. If big news breaks after the 4:00 P.M. closing—news that will almost certainly affect the next day's securities markets—late traders are nearly ensured of a next-day quick profit or avoidance of a loss.

In late 2003, three agencies announced they were investigating Richard Strong, board chairman of Strong Mutual Funds, for his personal trading of the company's funds. The SEC, the New York Attorney General's Office, and the Wisconsin Department of Financial Institutions looked into alleged improper trading that may have benefited him, his family, and friends. Former SEC attorney Mercer Bullard called Strong "a model of the kinds of conflicts of interest that shouldn't even be allowed in the mutual fund industry." In resigning as board chairman of the $42 billion fund, Strong said he would reimburse investors for any losses they suffered because of his trading.

While news of more abuses rolled in, an indignant U.S. Congress proposed possible remedies and pledged that new, stiffer SEC regulations will eventually emerge. Meanwhile, the SEC and the NASD brought actions seeking injunctions, penalties, and financial relief for investors against several more illicit brokerages and mutual funds. Under a 2004 settlement with the SEC, Richard Strong agreed to pay $60 million for improper gains and civil penalties, the company agreed to pay $80 million, and all $140 million is being used to compensate investors. Richard Strong agreed to be barred from the financial industry for life.

Richard Strong is a model of the kinds of conflicts of interest that shouldn't even be allowed in the mutual fund industry.

—Former SEC attorney, on market-timing violations at Strong Mutual Funds

QUESTIONS FOR DISCUSSION

1 Why do you suppose the SEC was slow in detecting the industry's late-trading abuses?

2 Do you believe the penalties imposed on Richard Strong and the company are appropriate? How much, if any, restitution should they have been required to make to Strong Mutual Funds investors?

3 Suppose you are the manager of one of the equity funds for a large mutual funds firm. What steps would you take to ensure compliance with SEC and state regulations by your employees?

4 As an employee working at a mutual funds firm, what would you do if you suspected other employees of doing late trading?

5 Think of an after-hours news event that is (or was) likely to result in a next-day decline in the stock market. Now, think of an event that would increase market prices. Why do you think the market would fall for the one example and would increase for the other?

1 Describe the role of securities markets and explain the difference between primary and secondary securities markets.

By facilitating the buying and selling of securities, the *securities markets* provide the capital that companies rely on for survival. They also provide investment opportunities for individuals and businesses. Three kinds of securities—*stocks*, *bonds*, and *mutual funds*—each represent different kinds of secured, or financially valuable claims on the part of investors. *Primary securities* markets involve the buying and selling of new stocks and bonds, either in public offerings or through private placements. *Secondary markets* involve the trading for the general public of existing stocks and bonds through such familiar bodies as the New York Stock Exchange, the American Stock Exchange, and the NASDAQ market.

2 Discuss the value to shareholders of common stock and preferred stock and identify the major stock exchanges and stock markets.

Common stock affords investors voting rights and the prospect of dividend income and capital gains in market value. *Preferred stock* income is less risky than dividend income from common shares because preferred shareholders must be paid dividends before common shareholders. Both common stock and preferred stock are traded on *stock exchanges* including *floor-based exchanges*, *electronic markets*, and in *over-the-counter markets*. Floor-based exchanges include the *New York Stock Exchange, American Stock Exchange*, and *regional and foreign exchanges*. *NASDAQ* is the world's largest electronic stock market. In OTC markets, dealers negotiate with one another to buy and sell.

3 Distinguish among various types of bonds in terms of their issuers and safety.

A *bond* is an IOU—a promise by the issuer to pay the buyer a certain amount of money by a specified future date, usually with interest paid at regular intervals. Bonds differ in terms of maturity dates, tax status, and level of repayment risk versus potential yield to bondholders. *U.S. government bonds* are backed by government institutions and agencies. *Municipal bonds*, which are offered by state and local governments to finance projects, are also usually safe, and the interest is ordinarily tax exempt. *Corporate bonds* are issued by companies to gain long-term funding. Corporate bonds may be *secured* (backed by pledges of the issuer's assets) or *unsecured* (*debentures*). The safety of bonds is rated by Moody's and Standard & Poor's.

4 Describe the investment opportunities offered by mutual funds.

Companies called *mutual funds* pool investments from individuals and organizations to purchase a portfolio of stocks, bonds, and other securities. Investors in *no-load funds* are not charged sales commissions when they buy in or sell out. Those in *load funds* pay commissions of 2 to 8 percent. Funds that stress conservative growth, current income, and preservation of capital are called *balanced mutual funds*. *Aggressive growth funds* emphasize maximum long-term capital growth. *Stability and safety funds* strive for stable current income and preserving capital against market fluctuations.

5 Describe the risk-return relationship, and discuss the use of diversification and asset allocation for investments.

The risk-return relationship is the principle that investors expect to receive higher returns for riskier investments and lower returns for safer investments. Diversification and asset allocation are tools for helping investors achieve the desired risk-return balance for an investment portfolio. *Diversification* means buying several different kinds of investments to reduce the risk of loss if the value of any one security should fall. *Asset allocation* is the proportion of overall money invested in each of various investment alternatives so that the overall risks for the portfolio are low, moderate, or high, depending on the investor's objectives and preferences.

6 Explain the process by which securities are bought and sold.

First, you need to match possible investments to your investment objectives. Then, a broker must be selected and an account opened so you can make transactions. Investors can then place different types of orders. *Market orders* are orders to buy or sell at current prevailing prices. Investors may also issue *limit orders* or *stop orders* that are to be executed only if prices rise to or fall below specified levels. *Round lots* are purchased in multiples of 100 shares. *Odd lots* are purchased in fractions of round lots. Securities can be bought on *margin*, by borrowing money from the broker, or as part of *short sales* in which investors sell securities that are borrowed from brokers and returned at a later date.

7 Explain how securities markets are regulated.

In addition to government regulation, both the NASD and the NYSE exercise self-regulation. The NYSE established so-called *circuit breakers*—trading rules for discouraging panic selling, reducing excessive volatility, and promoting investor confidence—to suspend trading when markets threaten to spin out of control. The SEC protects investors from fraudulent issues by requiring all companies to file prospectuses before proposed securities offerings can be sold to the public. The SEC also enforces laws against *insider trading*. State governments enforce so-called *blue-sky laws*, and securities dealers must be licensed by the states in which they do business.

KEY TERMS

asset allocation (p. 505)

bear market (p. 509)

bearer (coupon) bond (p. 502)

blue-chip stock (p. 494)

blue-sky laws (p. 514)

bond (p. 501)

book value (p. 494)

bull market (p. 509)

capital gain (p. 495)

common stock (p. 493)

corporate bond (p. 502)

debenture (p. 503)

diversification (p. 505)

dividend (p. 493)

Dow Jones Industrial Average
(DJIA) (p. 509)

government bond (p. 502)

Initial public offering (IPO) (p. 497)

insider trading (p. 514)

investment bank (p. 493)

limit order (p. 511)

load fund (p. 503)

margin (p. 512)

market appreciation (p. 496)

market index (p. 509)

market order (p. 511)

market value (p. 493)

municipal bond (p. 502)

mutual fund (p. 503)

NASDAQ Composite Index (p. 510)

National Association of Securities
Dealers (NASD) (p. 512)

National Association of Securities
Dealers Automated Quotation
(NASDAQ) system (p. 499)

net asset value (NAV) (p. 509)

no-load fund (p. 503)

odd lot (p. 512)

over-the-counter (OTC)
market (p. 499)

par value (p. 493)

portfolio (p. 503)

preferred stock (p. 495)

price-earnings ratio (p. 508)

primary securities market (p. 492)

program trading (p. 513)

prospectus (p. 514)

registered bond (p. 502)

risk-return relationship (p. 504)

round lot (p. 512)

secondary securities market (p. 493)

secured bond (p. 502)

securities (p. 492)

Securities and Exchange Commission
(SEC) (p. 493)

securities market (p. 492)

short sale (p. 512)

Standard & Poor's Composite
Index (p. 510)

stock (p. 493)

stock broker (p. 496)

stock exchange (p. 496)

stop order (p. 511)

QUESTIONS AND EXERCISES

Questions for Review

1 What is the role of securities markets?

2 Which one of the three measures of common stock value is most important? Why?

3 How do government, municipal, and corporate bonds differ from one another?

4 Based on the risk-return relationship, would you expect to receive higher or lower returns for a safe investment versus a risky investment?

5 In what ways is diversification useful for managing securities portfolios?

6 How does the SEC regulate securities markets?

Questions for Analysis

7 Which kind of broker—full service or discount—would you use for buying and selling common stocks? Why?

8 Which type of mutual fund would be most appropriate for your investment purposes at this time? Why?

9 Using a newspaper, select a recent day's transactions for a stock on the NYSE, a stock on the AMEX, a NASDAQ stock, and a mutual fund. Explain each element in the listing.

Application Exercises

10 Suppose you buy 100 shares of stock at a price of $73.64 per share. Exactly one year later you sell it at the market price of $87.13 per share. During the year of ownership, the company paid cash dividends of $1.60 per share. Calculate the amount of market appreciation for your investment.

11 Interview the financial manager of a local business or your school. What are the investment goals of this person's organization? What securities does it use?

12 Contact a securities dealer and request information about setting up an account for trading securities. What are the broker's policies regarding buy/sell orders, credit terms, cash account requirements, services, and commissions/fees?

MARKET UPS AND DOWNS

Goal

To encourage you to understand the forces that affect fluctuations in stock prices.

Background Information

Investing in stocks requires an understanding of the various factors that affect stock prices. These factors may be intrinsic to the company itself or part of the external environment.

- Internal factors relate to the company itself, such as an announcement of poor or favorable earnings, earnings that are more or less than expected, major layoffs, labor problems, new products, management issues, and mergers.
- External factors relate to world or national events, such as the war in Iraq, the Asian currency crisis, weather conditions that affect sales, the Fed's adjustment of interest rates, and employment figures that were higher or lower than expected.

By analyzing these factors, you will often learn a lot about why a stock did well or why it did poorly. Being aware of these influences will help you anticipate future stock movements.

Method

Step 1

Working alone, choose a common stock that has experienced considerable price fluctuations in the past few years. Here are several examples (but there are many others): IBM, J. P. Morgan Chase, AT&T, Amazon.com, Oxford Health Care, and Apple Computer. Find the symbol for the stock (for example, J. P. Morgan Chase is JPM) and the exchange on which it is traded (JPM is traded on the NYSE).

Step 2

At your library, find the Daily Stock Price Record, a publication that provides a historical picture of daily stock closings.

There are separate copies for the NYSE, the AMEX, and the NASDAQ markets. Find your stock, and study its trading pattern.

Step 3

Find four or five days over a period of several months or even a year when there have been major price fluctuations in the stock. (A two- or three-point price change from one day to the next is considered major.) Then research what happened on that day that might have contributed to the fluctuation. The best place to begin is with the *Wall Street Journal* or on the business pages of a national newspaper, such as the *New York Times* or the *Washington Post*.

Step 4

Write a short analysis that links changes in stock price to internal and external factors. As you analyze the data, be aware that it is sometimes difficult to know why a stock price fluctuates.

Step 5

Get together with three other students who studied different stocks. As a group, discuss your findings, looking for fluctuation patterns.

FOLLOW-UP QUESTIONS

1 Do you see any similarities in the movement of the various stocks during the same period? For example, did the stocks move up or down at about the same time? If so, do you think the stocks were affected by the same factors? Explain your thinking.

2 Based on your analysis, did internal or external factors have the greater impact on stock price? Which factors had the more long-lasting effect? Which factors had the shorter effect?

3 Why do you think it is so hard to predict changes in stock price on a day-to-day basis?

ARE YOU ENDOWED WITH GOOD JUDGMENT?

The Situation

Every organization faces decisions about whether to make conservative or risky investments. Let's assume that you have been asked to evaluate the advantages and drawbacks of conservative versus risky investments, including all relevant ethical considerations, by Youth Dreams Charities (YDC), a local organization that assists low-income families in gaining access to educational opportunities. YDC is a not-for-profit firm that employs a full-time professional manager to run daily operations. Overall, governance and policy making reside with a board of directors—10 part-time, community-minded volunteers who are entrusted with carrying out YDC's mission.

For the current year, 23 students receive tuition totaling $92,000 paid by YDC. Tuition comes from annual fund-raising activities (a white-tie dance and a seafood carnival) and from financial returns from YDC's $2.1 million endowment. The endowment has been amassed from charitable donations during the past 12 years, and this year it has yielded some $84,000 for tuitions. The board's goal is to increase the endowment to $4 million in five years to provide $200,000 in tuition annually.

The Dilemma

Based on the finance committee's suggestions, the board is considering a change in YDC's investment policies. The current, rather conservative, approach invests the endowment in low-risk instruments that have consistently yielded a 5-percent annual return. This practice has allowed the endowment to grow modestly (at about 1 percent per year). The remaining investment proceeds (4 percent) flow out for tuition. The proposed plan would invest one-half of the endowment in conservative instruments and the other half in blue-chip stocks. Finance committee members believe that—with market growth—the endowment has a good chance of reaching the $4 million goal within five years. While some board members like the prospects of faster growth, others think the proposal is too risky. What happens if, instead of increasing, the stock market collapses and the endowment shrinks? What will happen to YDC's programs then?

QUESTIONS TO ADDRESS

1 Why might a conservative versus risky choice be different at a not-for-profit organization than at a for-profit organization?
2 What are the main ethical issues in this situation?
3 What action should the board take?

SERVING TWO MASTERS: TORN BETWEEN COMPANY AND CLIENT

The Situation

Employees in financial services firms are sometimes confronted by conflicting allegiances between the company and its clients. In managing customers' stock portfolios, for example, the best timing for buy and sell decisions for clients' financial positions may not be the most profitable for the financial manager's firm. Investment managers, as a result, must choose a "right" course of action for reconciling possible conflicting interests.

The Dilemma

George Michaels is a customer portfolio manager employed by Premier Power Investments Company, one of the top 10 financial services firms on the West Coast. His 35 clients—individual investors—have portfolios with market values ranging from $200,000 to $2 million in stocks, bonds, and mutual funds. Clients generally rely on George's recommendations to buy, sell, or hold each security based on his knowledge of their investment goals and risk tolerance, along with his experience in keeping up with market trends and holding down transactions costs. Premier Power Investments Company earns sales commissions ranging from 2 percent to 4 percent of market value for each buy and sell transaction.

On Monday morning, George's boss, Vicky Greene, informs George that due to Premier Power Investments Company's sagging revenues, it is to everyone's benefit to increase the number of transactions in customers' portfolios. She suggests that he find some different and attractive securities to replace existing securities for his customers. As George thinks about possible ways for accelerating his buy and sell recommendations, he has qualms about the motivation behind Vicky's comments. He is unsure what to do.

Team Activity

Assemble a group of four to five students and assign each group member to one of the following roles:

- George Michaels (employee)
- Vicky Greene (employer)
- Portfolio owner (customer)
- Owner (one of many outside shareholders of Premier Power Investments Company)
- SEC representative (use this role only if your group has at least five members)

ACTION STEPS

1 Before hearing any of your group's comments on this situation, and from the perspective of your assigned role, do you think there are any ethical issues with this situation? If so, write them down.

2 Return to your group and reveal any ethical issues that were identified by each member. Be especially aware to see if the different roles resulted in different kinds of ethical issues. Why might role differences result in dissimilar priorities on ethical issues?

3 For the various ethical issues that were identified, decide as a group which one is the most important for Premier Power Investments to resolve. Which issue is second in importance?

4 From an ethical standpoint, what does your group finally recommend be done to resolve the most important ethical issue? To resolve the second most important ethical issue?

CRAFTING A BUSINESS PLAN

PART 6: FINANCIAL ISSUES

Goal of the Exercise

In this final part of the business plan project, you'll consider how you'll finance your business as well as create an executive summary for your plan.

Exercise Background: Part 6 of the Business Plan

In the previous part of the business plan, you discussed the costs of doing business, as well as how much revenue that you expect to earn in one year. It's now time to think about how to finance the business. To get a "great idea" off the ground requires money. But how will you get these funds?

You'll then conclude this project by creating an *executive summary*. The purpose of the executive summary is to give the reader a quick snapshot into your proposed business. Although this exercise comes at the end of the project, once you're done writing it, you'll end up placing the executive summary at the *beginning* of your completed business plan.

Your Assignment

Step 1

Open the saved *Business Plan* file you began working on in Parts 1 to 5.

Step 2

For the purposes of this assignment, you will answer the following questions, shown in "Part 6: Financial Issues:"

1 How much money will you need to get your business started?

Hint: Refer back to Part 5 of the plan, where you analyzed the costs involved in running your business. Approximately how much will you need to get your business started?

2 How will you finance your business? For example, will you seek out a bank loan? Borrow from friends? Sell stocks or bonds initially or as your business grows?

Hint: Refer to Chapter 16 for information on securities, such as stocks and bonds. Refer also to Appendix I: Financial Risk and Risk Management and Chapter 3 for more information on sources of short-term and long-term funds.

3 Now, create an executive summary for your business plan. The executive summary should be brief—no more than two pages long—and should cover the following points:

- The name of your business
- Where your business will be located
- The mission of your business
- The product or service you are selling
- Who your ideal customers are
- How your product or business will stand out in the crowd
- Who the owners of the business are and what experience they have
- An overview of the future prospects for your business and industry

Hint: At this point, you've already answered all of these questions, so what you need to do here is put the ideas together into a "snapshot" format. The executive summary is really a sales pitch—it's the investor's first impression of your idea. Therefore, as with all parts of the plan, write in a clear and professional way.

Congratulations on completing the business plan project!

□□□□□□□□□□ **VIDEO EXERCISE**

INFORMATION PAYS OFF: MOTLEY FOOL

Learning Objectives

The purpose of this video is to help you to:

1 Identify the wide variety of investments available to individuals.
2 Describe the process by which securities are bought and sold.
3 Recognize the risks involved in commodities and other investments.

Synopsis

Despite news reports about lottery winners and other overnight millionaires, individuals have a better chance of getting rich if they learn to select investments that are appropriate for their long-term financial goals. Experts advise looking for investments that will beat inflation and keep up with or—ideally—beat general market returns. You can invest in preferred or common stock, newly issued stock from IPOs, managed or index mutual funds, bonds, or commodities. These investments, however, are far from risk-free. Thus, if you're planning to invest, you might want to educate yourself about securities and investment strategies by surfing Web sites such as the Motley Fool (www.fool.com).

DISCUSSION QUESTIONS

1 **For analysis**: Why is the SEC concerned about stock rumors that circulate on the Internet?
2 **For application**: What should you consider when deciding whether to buy and sell stock through a broker, through a Web-based brokerage, or directly through the company issuing the stock?
3 **For application**: If you were about to retire, why might you invest in preferred stock rather than common stock?
4 **For debate**: Should stock rumors that circulate on the Internet be covered by the individual's constitutional right to freedom of speech rather than be regulated by the SEC? Support your chosen position.

Online Exploration

Mutual funds that seek out environmentally and socially conscious firms in which to invest are becoming more popular because they offer investors a way to earn returns that don't offend their principles. Investigate the following Web sites: www.efund.com, www.ethicalfunds.com, and www.domini.com. What types of firms does each fund avoid? What type does each prefer? Would you choose one of these funds if you wanted to invest in a mutual fund? Explain your answer.

FINANCIAL RISK AND RISK MANAGEMENT

THE ROLE OF THE FINANCIAL MANAGER

In small and large firms alike, the business activity known as **finance** (or **corporate finance**) typically entails four responsibilities:

1 Determining a firm's long-term investments
2 Obtaining the funds to pay for those investments
3 Conducting the firm's everyday financial activities
4 Helping to manage the risks that the firm takes

As we saw in Chapter 7, production managers plan and control the output of goods and services. In Chapter 11, we saw that marketing managers plan and control the development and marketing of products. Similarly, **financial managers** plan and control the acquisition and dispersal of a firm's financial resources. In this section, we discuss how those activities are channeled into specific plans for protecting—and enhancing—a firm's financial well-being.

FINANCE (CORPORATE FINANCE) activities concerned with determining a firm's long-term investments, obtaining the funds to pay for them, conducting the firm's everyday financial activities, and managing the firm's risks

FINANCIAL MANAGER manager responsible for planning and controlling the acquisition and dispersal of a firm's financial resources

RESPONSIBILITIES OF THE FINANCIAL MANAGER

Financial managers collect funds, pay debts, establish credit, obtain loans, control cash balances, and plan for future financial needs. But a financial manager's overall objective is to increase a firm's value—and stockholders' wealth. Whereas accountants create data to reflect a firm's financial status, financial managers make decisions for improving that status. Financial managers, then, must ensure that a company's earnings exceed its costs—that it earns a profit. In sole proprietorships and partnerships, profits translate directly into increases in owners' wealth. In corporations, profits translate into an increase in the value of common stock.

The various responsibilities of the financial manager in increasing a firm's wealth fall into two general categories: *cash-flow management* and *financial planning.*

Cash-Flow Management To increase a firm's value, financial managers must ensure that it always has enough funds on hand to purchase the materials and human resources it needs to produce goods and services. At the same time, some funds may be invested to earn more money for the firm. This activity—**cash-flow management**—requires careful planning. If excess cash balances are allowed to sit idle instead of being invested, a firm loses the returns that it could have earned.

How important to a business is the management of its idle cash? One study has revealed that companies averaging $2 million in annual sales typically hold $40,000 in noninterest-bearing accounts. Larger companies hold even larger sums. More companies, however, are learning that these idle funds can become working funds. For example, by locating idle cash and putting it to work, they can avoid borrowing from outside sources. The savings on interest payments can be substantial.

Financial Planning The cornerstone of effective financial management is the development of a financial plan. A **financial plan** describes a firm's strategies for reaching some future financial position. In constructing the plan, a financial manager must ask several questions:

- What amount of funds does the company need to meet immediate needs?
- When will it need more funds?
- Where can it get the funds to meet both its short- and long-term needs?

To answer these questions, a financial manager must develop a clear picture of why a firm needs funds. Managers must also assess the relative costs and benefits of potential funding sources.

> **CASH-FLOW MANAGEMENT** management of cash inflows and outflows to ensure adequate funds for purchases and the productive use of excess funds

> **FINANCIAL PLAN** a firm's strategies for reaching some future financial position

WHY DO BUSINESSES NEED FUNDS?

Every company must spend money to survive. According to the simplest formula, funds that are spent on materials, wages, and buildings eventually lead to the creation of products, revenues, and profits. In planning for funding requirements, financial managers must distinguish between two kinds of expenditures: *short-term (operating) expenditures* and *long-term (capital) expenditures.*

SHORT-TERM (OPERATING) EXPENDITURES

> **SHORT-TERM (OPERATING) EXPENDITURES** payments incurred regularly in a firm's everyday business activities

Short-term (operating) expenditures are payments incurred regularly in a firm's *everyday business activities.* To manage these outlays, managers must pay attention to *accounts payable, accounts receivable,* and *inventories.* The measures used by some firms in managing the funds are known as *working capital.*

Accounts Payable In Chapter 14, we defined *accounts payable* as unpaid bills owed to suppliers for materials, plus wages and taxes due within the upcoming year. For most companies, this is the largest single category of short-term debt. To plan for funding flows, financial managers want to know in advance the amounts of new accounts payable, as well as when they must be repaid. For information about such obligations and needs—for example, the quantity of supplies required by a certain department in an upcoming period—financial managers must rely on other managers.

Accounts Receivable A company's **accounts receivable** consist of funds due from customers who have bought on credit. A sound financial plan requires financial managers to project accurately both how much credit is advanced to buyers and when they will make payments on their accounts. For example, managers at Kraft Foods must know how many dollars' worth of cheddar cheese Kroger's supermarkets will order each month; they must also know Kroger's payment schedule. Because accounts receivable represent an investment in products for which a firm has not yet received payment, they temporarily tie up its funds. The seller wants to receive payment as quickly as possible.

ACCOUNTS RECEIVABLE funds due from customers who have bought on credit

Inventories Between the time a firm buys raw materials and the time it sells finished products, it ties up funds in **inventory**—materials and goods that it will sell within the year. Failure to manage inventory can have grave financial consequences. Too little inventory of any kind can cost a firm sales. Too much inventory means tied-up funds that cannot be used elsewhere. In extreme cases, a company may have to sell excess inventory at low profits simply to raise cash.

INVENTORY materials and goods that are held by a company that it will sell within the year

Working Capital **Working capital** consists of a firm's net current assets on hand—the difference between a firm's current assets and current liabilities. It is a liquid asset out of which current debts can be paid. A company calculates its working capital by adding up the following:

WORKING CAPITAL difference between a firm's current assets and current liabilities

- Inventories—raw materials, work-in-process, and finished goods on hand
- Accounts receivable (minus accounts payable)

How much money is tied up in working capital? *Fortune* 500 companies typically devote $0.20 of every $1.00 of sales—about $800 billion total—to working capital. What are the benefits of reducing these sums? The following are two very important pluses:

1 Every dollar that is not tied up in working capital becomes a dollar of more useful cash flow.
2 Reduction of working capital raises earnings permanently.

The second advantage results from the fact that money costs money (in interest payments and the like). Reducing working capital, therefore, saves interest payments.

■■■ LONG-TERM (CAPITAL) EXPENDITURES

In addition to needing funds for operating expenditures, companies need funds to cover **long-term expenditures**—purchases of fixed assets. As we saw in Chapter 14, *fixed assets* are items with long-term use or value, such as land, buildings, and machinery.

LONG-TERM EXPENDITURES purchases of fixed assets

Long-term expenditures are usually more carefully planned than short-term expenditures because they pose special problems. They differ from short-term expenditures in the following ways, all of which influence the ways that long-term outlays are funded:

- Unlike inventories and other short-term assets, they are not normally sold or converted into cash.

- Their acquisition requires a very large investment.
- They represent a binding commitment of company funds that continues long into the future.

SOURCES OF SHORT-TERM FUNDS

Firms can call on many sources for the funds they need to finance day-to-day operations and to implement short-term plans. These sources include *trade credit*, *secured loans*, and *unsecured loans*.

TRADE CREDIT

TRADE CREDIT granting of credit by one firm to another

Accounts payable are not merely expenditures. They also constitute a source of funds for the buying company. Until it pays its bill, the buyer has the use of *both* the purchased product and the price of the product. This situation results when the seller grants **trade credit**, which is effectively a short-term loan from one firm to another. The most common form, **open-book credit**, is essentially a good-faith agreement. Buyers receive merchandise along with invoices stating credit terms. Sellers ship products on faith that payment will be forthcoming.

OPEN-BOOK CREDIT form of trade credit in which sellers ship merchandise on faith that payment will be forthcoming

SECURED SHORT-TERM LOANS

SECURED LOAN loan for which the borrower must provide collateral

COLLATERAL borrower-pledged legal asset that may be seized by lenders in case of nonpayment

For most firms, bank loans are an important source of short-term funding. Such loans almost always involve promissory notes in which the borrower promises to repay the loan plus interest. In **secured loans**, banks also require **collateral**: a legal interest in certain assets that can be seized if payments are not made as promised. Collateral may be in the form of inventories or accounts receivable, and most businesses have other types of assets that can be pledged. Some, for example, own marketable securities, such as stocks or bonds of other companies. Many more own fixed assets, such as land, buildings, or equipment. Fixed assets, however, are generally used to secure long-term rather than short-term loans. Most short-term business borrowing is secured by inventories and accounts receivable.

When a loan is made with inventory as a collateral asset, the lender lends the borrower some portion of the stated value of the inventory. When accounts receivable are used as collateral, the process is called **pledging accounts receivable**. In the event of nonpayment, the lender may seize the receivables.

PLEDGING ACCOUNTS RECEIVABLE using accounts receivable as loan collateral

UNSECURED SHORT-TERM LOANS

UNSECURED LOAN loan for which collateral is not required

With an **unsecured loan**, the borrower does not have to put up collateral. In many cases, however, the bank requires the borrower to maintain a *compensating balance*—the borrower must keep a portion of the loan amount on deposit with the bank in a noninterest-bearing account.

The terms of the loan—amount, duration, interest rate, and payment schedule—are negotiated between the bank and the borrower. To receive an unsecured loan, then, a firm must ordinarily have a good banking relationship with the lender. Once an agreement is made, a **promissory note**—a formal, written promise to pay—will be executed

PROMISSORY NOTE a formal, written promise to pay

and the funds will be transferred to the borrower. Although some unsecured loans are one-time-only arrangements, many take the form of *lines of credit, revolving credit agreements*, or *commercial paper*.

Line of Credit and Credit Agreements A **line of credit** is a standing agreement between a bank and a business in which the bank promises to lend the firm a maximum amount of funds on request. In a **revolving credit agreement**, a lender agrees to make some amount of funds available on a continuing basis. The lending institution guarantees that these funds will be available when sought by the borrower. In return for this guarantee, the bank charges the borrower a *commitment fee* for holding the line of credit open. This fee is payable even if the customer does not borrow any funds. It is often expressed as a percentage of the loan amount (usually .5 percent to 1 percent of the committed amount).

LINE OF CREDIT standing arrangement in which a lender agrees to make available a specified amount of funds upon the borrower's request

REVOLVING CREDIT AGREEMENT arrangement in which a lender agrees to make funds available on demand and on a continuing basis

COMMERCIAL PAPER short-term securities, or notes, containing a borrower's promise to pay

Commercial Paper Some firms can raise short-term funds by issuing **commercial paper**: short-term securities, or notes, containing the borrower's promise to pay. Because it is backed solely by the issuing firm's promise to pay, commercial paper is an option for only the largest and most creditworthy firms.

How does commercial paper work? Corporations issue commercial paper with a certain face value. Buying companies pay less than that value. At the end of a specified period (usually 30 days to 90 days), the issuing company buys back the paper *at face value*. The difference between the price paid and the face value is the buyer's profit. For the issuing company, the cost is usually lower than prevailing interest rates on short-term loans.

SOURCES OF LONG-TERM FUNDS

Firms need long-term funding to finance expenditures on fixed assets: the buildings and equipment needed to conduct their businesses. They may seek long-term funds through *debt financing* (from outside the firm) or through *equity financing* (by drawing on internal sources). In addition to these options, there is a middle-ground option called *hybrid financing*.

■■■ DEBT FINANCING

Long-term borrowing from sources outside the company—**debt financing**—is a major component of most firms' long-term financial planning. Long-term debts are obligations that are payable more than one year after they are originally issued. The two primary sources of such funding are *long-term loans* and the sale of *corporate bonds*.

DEBT FINANCING long-term borrowing from sources outside a company

Long-Term Loans Most corporations get long-term loans from commercial banks, usually those with which they have developed long-standing relationships. Credit companies (such as Household Finance Corporation), insurance companies, and pension funds also grant long-term business loans.

Long-term loans are attractive to borrowers for several reasons:

■ Because the number of parties involved is limited, loans can often be arranged very quickly.

■ The firm need not make public disclosure of its business plans or the purpose for which it is acquiring the loan. (In contrast, the issuance of corporate bonds, discussed next, requires such disclosure.)

- The duration of the loan can easily be matched to the borrower's needs.
- If the firm's needs change, loans usually contain clauses making it possible to change terms.

Long-term loans also have some disadvantages. Borrowers, for example, may have trouble finding lenders to supply large sums. Long-term borrowers may also face restrictions as conditions of the loan. For example, they may have to pledge long-term assets as collateral or agree to take on no more debt until the loan is paid.

Corporate Bonds As we saw in Chapter 16, a *corporate bond*, like commercial paper, is a contract—a promise by the issuer to pay the holder a certain amount of money on a specified date. Unlike issuers of commercial paper, however, bond issuers do not pay off quickly. In many cases, bonds may not be redeemable for 30 years. Also, unlike commercial paper, most bonds pay bondholders a stipulated sum of annual or semiannual interest. If the company fails to make a bond payment, it is said to be *in default*.

Bonds are the major source of long-term debt financing for most corporations. They are attractive when firms need large amounts for long periods of time. The issuing company also gains access to large numbers of lenders through nationwide bond markets and stock exchanges. On the other hand, bonds entail high administrative and selling costs. They may also require stiff interest payments, especially if the issuing company has a poor credit rating.

◼◼◼◼ EQUITY FINANCING

EQUITY FINANCING use of common stock and/or retained earnings to raise long-term funding

Although debt financing often has strong appeal, looking inside the company for long-term funding is sometimes preferable. In small companies, for example, founders may increase personal investments in their own firms. In most cases, **equity financing** means issuing common stock or retaining the firm's earnings. Both options involve putting the owners' capital to work.

Common Stock By issuing shares of stock, the company gets the funds it needs for buying land, buildings, and equipment. Suppose that the founders of a hypothetical company, called Sunshine Tanning, invested $10,000 by buying the original 500 shares of common stock (at $20 per share) in 1996. The company used these funds to buy equipment, and it succeeded financially. By 2006, it needed funds for expansion. A pattern of profitable operations and regularly paid dividends now allows Sunshine Tanning to raise $50,000 by selling 500 new shares of stock at $100 per share. This $50,000 would constitute *paid-in capital*—additional money, above the par value of its original stock sale, paid directly to a firm by its owners. As Figure AI.1 shows, this additional paid-in capital would increase total stockholders' equity to $60,000.

Note that the use of equity financing by means of common stock can be expensive because paying dividends is more expensive than paying bond interest. Why? Because interest paid to bond holders is a business expense and, therefore, a tax deduction for the firm. Payments of cash dividends to shareholders are not tax deductible.

Retained Earnings As presented in Chapter 14, *retained earnings* are net profits retained for the firm's use rather than paid out in dividends to stockholders. If a company uses retained earnings as capital, it will not have to borrow money and pay interest. If a firm has a history of reaping profits by reinvesting retained earnings, it may be very attractive to some investors. Retained earnings, however, mean smaller dividends for shareholders. This practice may decrease the demand for—and the price of—the company's stock.

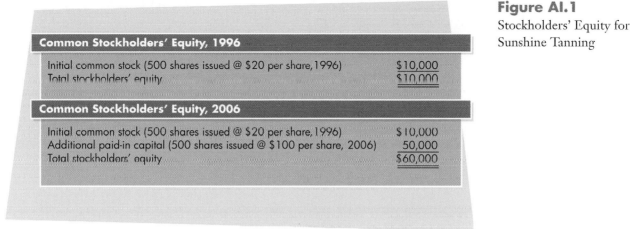

Figure AI.1
Stockholders' Equity for Sunshine Tanning

For example, if Sunshine Tanning had net earnings of $50,000 in 2006, it could pay a $50-per-share dividend on its 1,000 shares of common stock. However, Sunshine plans to remodel at a cost of $30,000, intending to retain $30,000 in earnings to finance the project. Then, only $20,000—$20 per share—will be available for shareholders.

■■■ HYBRID FINANCING: PREFERRED STOCK

A middle ground between debt financing and equity financing is the use of *preferred stock* (see Chapter 16). Preferred stock is a hybrid because it has some of the features of both corporate bonds and common stocks. As with bonds, payments on preferred stock are fixed amounts, such as $6 per share per year. Unlike bonds, however, preferred stock never matures; like common stock, it can be held indefinitely. In addition, preferred stockholders have first rights (over common stockholders) to dividends.

A major advantage to the issuer is the flexibility of preferred stock. Because preferred stockholders have no voting rights, the stock secures funds for the firm without jeopardizing corporate control of its management. Furthermore, corporations are not obligated to repay the principal and can withhold payment of dividends in lean times.

■■■ CHOOSING BETWEEN DEBT AND EQUITY FINANCING

An aspect of financial planning is striking a balance between debt and equity financing. Because a firm relies on a mix of debt and equity to raise the cash needed for capital outlays, that mix is called its **capital structure**. Financial plans contain targets for capital structure; an example would be 40 percent debt and 60 percent equity—but choosing a target is not easy. A wide range of mixes is possible, and strategies range from conservative to risky.

CAPITAL STRUCTURE relative mix of a firm's debt and equity financing

The most conservative strategy is all-equity financing and no debt: A company has no formal obligations to make financial payouts. As we have seen, however, equity is an expensive source of capital. The riskiest strategy is all-debt financing. Although less expensive than equity funding, indebtedness increases the risk that a firm will be unable to meet its obligations (and even go bankrupt). Somewhere between the two extremes, financial planners try to find mixes that will increase stockholders' wealth with a reasonable exposure to risk.

FINANCIAL MANAGEMENT FOR SMALL BUSINESS

New business success and failure are often closely related to adequate or inadequate funding. For example, one study of nearly 3,000 new companies revealed a survival rate of 84 percent for new businesses with initial investments of at least $50,000. Those with less funding have a much lower survival rate. Why are so many start-ups underfunded? For one thing, entrepreneurs often underestimate the value of establishing *bank credit* as a source of funds and use trade credit ineffectively. In addition, they are notorious for not planning cash flow needs properly.

■■■ ESTABLISHING BANK AND TRADE CREDIT

Some banks have liberal credit policies and offer financial analysis, cash-flow planning, and suggestions based on experiences with other local firms. Some provide loans to small businesses in bad times and work to keep them going. Some do not. Obtaining credit, therefore, begins with finding a bank that can—and will—support a small firm's financial needs. Once a line of bank credit is obtained, the small business can seek more liberal credit policies from other businesses. Sometimes, for example, suppliers give customers longer credit periods—45 days or 60 days rather than 30 days. Liberal trade credit terms with their suppliers let firms increase short-term funds and avoid additional borrowing from banks.

Obtaining long-term loans is more difficult for new businesses than for established companies. With unproven repayment ability, start-up firms usually pay higher interest rates than older firms. If a new enterprise displays evidence of sound financial planning, however, the SBA may support a guaranteed loan.

Start-up firms without proven financial success usually must present a business plan to demonstrate that the firm is a good credit risk. The business plan is a document that tells potential lenders why the money is needed, the amount, how the money will be used to improve the company, and when it will be paid back.

■■■ PLANNING FOR CASH-FLOW REQUIREMENTS

Although all businesses should plan for their cash flows, this planning is especially important for small businesses. Success or failure may hinge on anticipating those times when either cash will be short or excess cash can be expected.

Figure AI.2 shows possible cash inflows, cash outflows, and net cash position (inflows minus outflows) month by month for Slippery Fish Bait Supply Company, a highly seasonal business. Bait stores buy heavily from Slippery Fish Bait Supply Company during the spring and summer months. Revenues outpace expenses, leaving surplus funds that can be invested. During fall and winter, however, expenses exceed revenues. Slippery Fish Bait Supply Company must borrow funds to keep going until revenues pick up again in spring. Comparing predicted cash inflows from sales with outflows for expenses shows the firm's expected monthly cash-flow position.

Such information can be invaluable for the small-business manager. By anticipating shortfalls, for example, financial managers can seek funds in advance and minimize their costs. By anticipating excess cash, a manager can plan to put the funds to work in short-term, interest-earning investments.

Figure AI.2
Projected Cash Flow for Slippery Fish Bait Supply Company

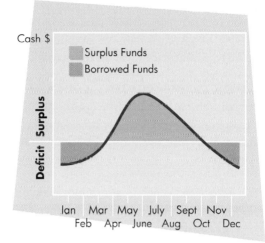

RISK MANAGEMENT

Financial risks are not the only risks faced every day by companies (and individuals). In this section, we describe other types of risks that businesses face and analyze some of the ways in which they typically manage them.

▪▪▪ COPING WITH RISK

Businesses constantly face two basic types of **risk**—uncertainty about future events. **Speculative risks**, such as financial investments, involve the possibility of gain or loss. **Pure risks** involve only the possibility of loss or no loss. Designing and distributing a new product, for example, is a speculative risk. The product may fail, or it may succeed and earn high profits. In contrast, the chance of a warehouse fire is a pure risk.

> **RISK** uncertainty about future events

> **SPECULATIVE RISK** risk involving the possibility of gain or loss

> **PURE RISK** risk involving only the possibility of loss or no loss

For a company to survive and prosper, it must manage both types of risk in a cost-effective manner. We can define the process of **risk management** as conserving the firm's earning power and assets by reducing the threat of losses due to uncontrollable events. In every company, each manager must be alert for risks to the firm and their impact on profits. The risk-management process usually entails five steps:

> **RISK MANAGEMENT** process of conserving the firm's earning power and assets by reducing the threat of losses due to uncontrollable events

Step 1: Identify Risks and Potential Losses Managers analyze a firm's risks to identify potential losses. For example, a firm with a fleet of delivery trucks can expect that one of them will eventually be involved in an accident. The accident may cause bodily injury to the driver or others, may cause physical damage to the truck or other vehicles, or both.

Step 2: Measure the Frequency and Severity of Losses and Their Impact To measure the frequency and severity of losses, managers must consider both history and current activities. How often can the firm expect the loss to occur? What is the likely size of the loss in dollars? For example, our firm with the fleet of delivery trucks may have had two accidents per year in the past. If it adds trucks, however, it may reasonably expect the frequency of accidents to increase.

Step 3: Evaluate Alternatives and Choose the Techniques That Will Best Handle the Losses Having identified and measured potential losses, managers are in a better position to decide how to handle them. With this third step, they generally have four choices: *risk avoidance, control, retention,* or *transfer.*

RISK AVOIDANCE practice of avoiding risk by declining or ceasing to participate in an activity

Risk Avoidance A firm opts for **risk avoidance** by declining to enter or by ceasing to participate in a risky activity. For example, the firm with the delivery trucks could avoid any risk of physical damage or bodily injury by closing down its delivery service. Similarly, a pharmaceutical maker may withdraw a new drug for fear of liability suits.

RISK CONTROL practice of minimizing the frequency or severity of losses from risky activities

Risk Control When avoidance is not practical or desirable, firms can practice **risk control**—the use of loss-prevention techniques to minimize the frequency or severity of losses. A delivery service, for example, can prevent losses by training its drivers in defensive-driving techniques, mapping out safe routes, and conscientiously maintaining its trucks.

RISK RETENTION practice of covering a firm's losses with its own funds

Risk Retention When losses cannot be avoided or controlled, firms must cope with the consequences. When such losses are manageable and predictable, the firm may decide to cover them out of company funds. The firm is said to assume or retain the financial consequences of the loss; hence, the practice is known as **risk retention**. For example, the firm with the fleet of trucks may find that vehicles suffer vandalism averaging $500 per year. Depending on its coverage, the company may find it cheaper to pay for repairs out of pocket rather than to submit claims to its insurance company.

RISK TRANSFER practice of transferring a firm's risk to another firm

Risk Transfer When the potential for large risks cannot be avoided or controlled, managers often opt for **risk transfer**. They transfer the risk to another firm—namely, an insurance company. In transferring risk to an insurance company, a firm buys insurance to protect itself against theft, physical damage to trucks, and bodily injury to drivers and others involved in an accident.

Step 4: Implement the Risk-Management Program The means of implementing risk-management decisions depend on both the technique chosen and the activity being managed. For example, risk avoidance for certain activities can be implemented by purchasing those activities from outside providers—for example, hiring delivery services instead of operating delivery vehicles. Risk control might be implemented by training employees and designing new work methods and equipment for on-the-job safety. For situations in which risk retention is preferred, reserve funds can be set aside out of revenues. When risk transfer is needed, implementation means selecting an insurance company and buying the right policies.

Step 5: Monitor Results Because risk management is an ongoing activity, follow-up is always essential. New types of risks, for example, emerge with changes in customers, facilities, employees, and products. Insurance regulations change, and new types of insurance become available. Consequently, managers must continuously monitor a company's risks, reevaluate the methods used for handling them, and revise them as necessary.

INSURANCE PREMIUM fee paid to an insurance company by a policyholder for insurance coverage

■■■ INSURANCE AS RISK MANAGEMENT

INSURANCE POLICY a formal agreement to pay the policyholder a specified amount in the event of certain losses

To deal with some risks, both businesses and individuals may choose to purchase one or more of the products offered by insurance companies. Insurance is purchased by paying **insurance premiums**—payments to an insurance company to buy a policy and keep it active. In return, the insurance company issues an **insurance policy**—a formal agreement to pay the policyholder a specified amount in the event of certain losses. In some cases, the insured party must also pay a **deductible**: an agreed-upon amount of the loss that the insured must absorb prior to reimbursement. Buyers find insurance appealing

DEDUCTIBLE an amount of the loss that the insured must absorb prior to reimbursement

for a very basic reason: In return for a relatively small sum of money, they are protected against larger losses, some of them potentially devastating. Accordingly, buying insurance is a risk-management activity for dealing with chance losses.

With insurance, then, individuals and businesses share risks by contributing to a fund out of which those who suffer losses are paid. But why are insurance companies willing to accept these risks for other companies? Insurance companies make profits by taking in more premiums than they pay out to cover policyholders' losses. Although many policyholders are paying for protection against the same type of loss, by no means will all of them suffer such a loss.

Insurable Versus Uninsurable Risks Like every business, insurance companies must avoid certain risks. Insurers divide potential sources of loss into *insurable risks* and *uninsurable risks*. They issue policies only for insurable risks. Although there are some exceptions, an insurable risk must meet the following four criteria:

1 *Predictability*: The insurer must be able to use statistical tools to forecast the likelihood of a loss. For example, an auto insurer needs information about the number of vehicle accidents in the past year to estimate the expected number of accidents for the following year. With this information, the insurer can translate expected numbers and types of accidents into expected dollar losses. The same forecast also helps insurers determine premiums charged to policyholders.

2 *Casualty*: A loss must result from an *accident*, not from an intentional act by the policyholder. Insurers do not have to cover damages if a policyholder deliberately sets fire to corporate headquarters. To avoid paying in cases of fraud, insurers may refuse to cover losses when they cannot determine whether policyholders' actions contributed to them.

3 *Unconnectedness*: Potential losses must be random and must occur independently of other losses. No insurer can afford to write insurance when a large percentage of those who are exposed to a particular kind of loss are likely to suffer such a loss. One insurance company would not want all the hurricane coverage in Louisiana or all the earthquake coverage in California. By carefully choosing the risks that it will insure, an insurance company can reduce its chances of a large loss or insolvency.

4 *Verifiability*: Insured losses must be verifiable as to cause, time, place, and amount. Did an employee develop emphysema because of a chemical to which she was exposed or because she smoked 40 cigarettes a day for 30 years? Did the policyholder pay the renewal premium before the fire destroyed his factory? Were the goods stolen from company offices or from the president's home? What was the insurable value of the destroyed inventory? When all these points have been verified, payment by the insurer goes more smoothly.

Special Forms of Insurance for Business Many forms of insurance are attractive to both businesses and individuals. For example, homeowners are as concerned about insuring property from fire and theft as are businesses. Life insurance, too, including group policies, is important both to individuals and for protecting a company's human assets. Businesses, however, have some additional special insurable concerns. In this section, we discuss forms of insurance that cover four kinds of business risks: *liability, property, business interruption, key person insurance*, and *business continuation agreements*.

Liability Insurance Liability means responsibility for damages in case of accidental or deliberate harm to individuals or property. **Liability insurance** covers losses resulting from damage to people or property when the insured party is judged liable.

A business is liable for any injury to an employee when the injury arises from activities related to the occupation. When workers are permanently or temporarily disabled by

LIABILITY INSURANCE
insurance covering losses resulting from damage to people or property when the insured party is judged liable

WORKERS' COMPENSATION COVERAGE coverage provided by a firm to employees for medical expenses, loss of wages, and rehabilitation costs resulting from job-related injuries or disease

PROPERTY INSURANCE insurance covering losses resulting from physical damage to or loss of the insured's real estate or personal property

BUSINESS INTERRUPTION INSURANCE insurance covering income lost during times when a company is unable to conduct business

KEY PERSON INSURANCE special form of business insurance designed to offset expenses entailed by the loss of key employees

BUSINESS CONTINUATION AGREEMENT special form of business insurance whereby owners arrange to buy the interests of deceased associates from their heirs

job-related accidents or disease, employers are required by law to provide **workers' compensation coverage** for medical expenses, loss of wages, and rehabilitation services. U.S. employers now pay out approximately $63 billion in workers' compensation premiums each year, much of it to public insurers.

Property Insurance   Firms purchase **property insurance** to cover injuries to themselves resulting from physical damage to or loss of real estate or personal property. Property losses may result from fire, lightning, wind, hail, explosion, theft, vandalism, or other destructive forces.

Business Interruption Insurance   In some cases, loss to property is minimal in comparison to loss of income. A manufacturer, for example, may have to close down for an extended time while repairs to fire damage are being completed. During that time, the company is not generating income. Even so, however, certain expenses—such as taxes, insurance premiums, and salaries for key personnel—may continue. To cover such losses, a firm may buy **business interruption insurance**.

Key Person Insurance   Many businesses choose to protect themselves against loss of the talents and skills of key employees, either from death or other departure. For example, if a salesperson who annually rings up $2.5 million dies or takes a new job, the firm will suffer loss. It will also incur recruitment costs to find a replacement and training expenses once a replacement is hired. **Key person insurance** is designed to offset both lost income and additional expenses.

Business Continuation Agreements   Who takes control of a business when a partner or associate dies? Surviving partners are often faced with the possibility of having to accept an inexperienced heir as a management partner. This contingency can be handled in **business continuation agreements**, whereby owners make plans to buy the ownership interest of a deceased associate from his or her heirs. The value of the ownership interest is determined when the agreement is made. Special policies can also provide survivors with the funds needed to make the purchase.

THE LEGAL CONTEXT OF BUSINESS

In this appendix, we describe the basic tenets of U.S. law and show how these principles work through the court system. We'll also survey a few major areas of business-related law.

THE U.S. LEGAL AND JUDICIAL SYSTEMS

Laws are the codified rules of behavior enforced by a society. In the United States, laws fall into three broad categories according to their origins: *common*, *statutory*, and *regulatory*. After discussing each of these types of laws, we'll briefly describe the three-tier system of courts through which the judicial system administers the law in the United States.

LAWS codified rules of behavior enforced by a society

■■■ TYPES OF LAW

Law in the United States originates primarily with English common law. Its sources include the U.S. Constitution, state constitutions, federal and state statutes, municipal ordinances, administrative agency rules and regulations, executive orders, and court decisions.

Common Law Court decisions follow *precedents*, or the decisions of earlier cases. Following precedent lends stability to the law by basing judicial decisions on cases anchored in similar facts. This principle is the keystone of **common law**: the body of decisions handed down by courts ruling on individual cases. Although some facets of common law predate the American Revolution (and even hearken back to medieval Europe), common law continues to evolve in the courts today.

COMMON LAW body of decisions handed down by courts ruling on individual cases

535

STATUTORY LAW law created by constitutions or by federal, state, or local legislative acts

Statutory Law Laws created by constitutions or by federal, state, or local legislative acts constitute **statutory law**. For example, Article I of the U.S. Constitution is a statutory law that empowers Congress to pass laws on corporate taxation, the zoning authority of municipalities, and the rights and privileges of businesses operating in the United States.

State legislatures and city councils also pass statutory laws. Some state laws, for example, prohibit the production or sale of detergents containing phosphates, which are believed to be pollutants. Nearly every town has ordinances specifying sites for certain types of industries or designating areas where cars cannot be parked during certain hours.

REGULATORY (ADMINISTRATIVE) LAW law made by the authority of administrative agencies

Regulatory Law Statutory law and common law have long histories. Relatively new is **regulatory** (or **administrative) law**: law made by the authority of administrative agencies. By and large, the expansion of U.S. regulatory law has paralleled the nation's economic and technological development. Lacking the technical expertise to develop specialized legislation for specialized business activities, Congress established the first administrative agencies to create and administer the needed laws in the late 1800s. Before the early 1960s, most agencies concerned themselves with the *economic* regulation of specific areas of business—for example, transportation or securities. Since then, many agencies have been established to pursue narrower *social* objectives. They focus on issues that cut across different sectors of the economy—clean air, for example, or product testing.

Today a host of agencies, including the Equal Employment Opportunity Commission (EEOC), the Environmental Protection Agency (EPA), the Food and Drug Administration (FDA), the Federal Trade Commission (FTC), and the Occupational Safety and Health Administration (OSHA), regulate U.S. business practices.

Agencies and Legislation Although Congress retains control over the scope of agency action, once passed, regulations have the force of statutory law. Government regulatory agencies act as a secondary judicial system, determining whether regulations have been violated and imposing penalties. A firm that violates OSHA rules, for example, may receive a citation, a hearing, and perhaps a heavy fine. Much agency activity consists of setting standards for safety or quality and monitoring the compliance of businesses. The FDA, for example, is responsible for ensuring that food, medicines, and even cosmetics are safe and effective.

Congress has created many new agencies in response to pressure to address social issues. In some cases, agencies were established in response to public concern about corporate behavior. The activities of these agencies have sometimes forced U.S. firms to consider the public interest almost as routinely as they consider their own financial performance.

The Move Toward Deregulation Although government regulation has benefited U.S. business in many ways, it is not without its drawbacks. Businesspeople complain—with some justification—that government regulations require too much paperwork. For example, to comply with just one OSHA regulation for a year, Goodyear once generated 345,000 pages of computer reports weighing 3,200 pounds. It now costs Goodyear $35.5 million each year to comply with the regulations of six government agencies, and it takes 36 employee-years annually (the equivalent of one employee working full time for 36 years) to fill out the required reports.

DEREGULATION elimination of rules that restrict business activity

Many people in both business and government support broader **deregulation**: the elimination of rules that restrict business activity. Advocates of both regulation and deregulation claim that each acts to control business expansion and prices, increase government efficiency, and right wrongs that the marketplace cannot or does not handle itself. Regulations, such as those enforced by the EEOC, for example, are supposed to control undesirable business practices in the interest of social equity. In contrast, the court-ordered breakup of AT&T was prompted by a perceived need for greater market efficiency. For these and other reasons, the federal government began deregulating certain industries in the 1970s.

It is important to note that the United States has been at the forefront of all industrialized nations with regard to the deregulation of key industries—financial services, transportation, telecommunications, and a host of others. A 1996 law, for instance, allowed the seven "Baby Bells"—regional phone companies created when AT&T was broken up—to compete for long-distance business. It also allowed cable television and telephone companies to enter each other's markets by offering any combination of video, telephone, and high-speed data communications services. Many analysts contend that such deregulation is now and will become an even greater advantage in an era of global competition. Deregulation, they argue, is a primary incentive to innovation.

According to this view, deregulated industries are forced to innovate in order to survive in fiercely competitive industries. Those firms that are already conditioned to compete by being more creative will outperform firms that have been protected by regulatory climates in their home countries. "What's important," says one economist, "is that competition energizes new ways of doing things." The U.S. telecommunications industry, proponents of this view say, is twice as productive as its European counterparts because it is the only such industry forced to come out from under a protective regulatory umbrella.

■■■ THE U.S. JUDICIAL SYSTEM

Laws are of little use unless they are enforced. Much of the responsibility for law enforcement falls to the courts. Although few people would claim that the courts are capable of resolving every dispute, there often seem to be more than enough lawyers to handle them all: There are 140 lawyers for every 100,000 people in the United States. Litigation is a significant part of contemporary life, and we have given our courts a voice in a wide range of issues, some touching personal concerns, some ruling on matters of public policy that affect all our lives.

The Court System   There are three levels in the U.S. judicial system—*federal*, *state*, and *local*. These levels reflect the federalist structure of a system in which a central government shares power with state or local governments. Federal courts were created by the U.S. Constitution. They hear cases on questions of constitutional law, disputes relating to maritime laws, and violations of federal statutes. They also rule on regulatory actions and on such issues as bankruptcy, postal law, and copyright or patent violation. Both the federal and most state systems embody a three-tiered system of *trial*, *appellate*, and *supreme courts*.

Trial Courts   At the lowest level of the federal court system are the **trial courts**, general courts that hear cases not specifically assigned to another court. A case involving contract violation would go before a trial court. Every state has at least one federal trial court, called a *district court*.

TRIAL COURT general court that hears cases not specifically assigned to another court

Trial courts also include special courts and administrative agencies. Special courts hear specific types of cases, such as cases involving tax evasion, fraud, international disputes, or claims against the U.S. government. Within their areas of jurisdiction, administrative agencies also make judgments much like those of courts.

Courts in each state system deal with the same issues as their federal counterparts. However, they may rule only in areas governed by state law. For example, a case involving state income tax laws would be heard by a state special court. Local courts in each state system also hear cases on municipal ordinances, local traffic violations, and similar issues.

Appellate Courts A losing party may disagree with a trial court ruling. If that party can show grounds for review, the case may go before a federal or state **appellate court**. These courts consider questions of law, such as possible errors of legal interpretation made by lower courts. They do not examine questions of fact. There are now 13 federal courts of appeal, each with 3 to 15 judges. Cases are normally heard by three-judge panels.

Supreme Courts Cases still not resolved at the appellate level can be appealed to the appropriate state supreme courts or to the U.S. Supreme Court. If it believes that an appeal is warranted or that the outcome will set an important precedent, the U.S. Supreme Court also hears cases appealed from state supreme courts. Each year, the U.S. Supreme Court receives about 5,000 appeals but typically agrees to hear fewer than 200.

BUSINESS LAW

Most legal issues confronted by businesses fall into one of six basic areas: *contract, tort, property, agency, commercial,* or *bankruptcy law.* These areas cover a wide range of business activity.

▪▪▪ CONTRACT LAW

A **contract** is any agreement between two or more parties that is enforceable in court. As such, it must meet six conditions. If all these conditions are met, one party can seek legal recourse from another if the other party breaches (violates) the terms of the agreement.

1 *Agreement.* Agreement is the serious, definite, and communicated offer and acceptance of the same terms. For example, an auto parts supplier offers in writing to sell rebuilt engines to a repair shop for $500 each. If the repair shop accepts the offer, the two parties have reached an agreement.

2 *Consent.* A contract is not enforceable if any of the parties has been affected by an honest mistake, fraud, or pressure. For example, a restaurant manager orders a painted sign, but the sign company delivers a neon sign instead.

3 *Capacity.* To give real consent, both parties must demonstrate legal **capacity** (competence). A person under legal age (usually 18 or 21) cannot enter into a binding contract.

4 *Consideration.* An agreement is binding only if it exchanges **considerations**— items of value. If your brother offers to paint your room for free, you cannot sue him if he changes his mind. Note that items of value do not necessarily entail money. For example, a tax accountant might agree to prepare a homebuilder's tax return in exchange for a new patio. Both services are items of value. Contracts need not be rational, nor must they provide the best possible bargain for both sides. They need only include legally sufficient consideration. The terms are met if both parties receive what the contract details.

5 *Legality.* A contract must be for a lawful purpose and must comply with federal, state, and local laws and regulations. For example, an agreement between two competitors to engage in *price fixing*—to set a mutually acceptable price—is not legal.

6 *Proper form.* A contract may be written, oral, or implied from conduct. It must be written, however, if it involves the sale of land or goods worth more than $500. It must be written if the agreement requires more than a year to fulfill—for example, a contract for employment as an engineer on a 14-month construction project. All changes to written contracts must also be in writing.

Breach of Contract What can one party do if the other fails to live up to the terms of a valid contract? Contract law offers a variety of remedies designed to protect the reasonable expectations of the parties and, in some cases, to compensate them for actions taken to enforce the agreement. As the injured party to a breached contract, any of the following actions might occur:

- You might cancel the contract and refuse to live up to your part of the bargain. For example, you might simply cancel a contract for carpet shampooing if the company fails to show up.
- You might sue for damages up to the amount that you lost as a result of the breach. You might sue the original caterer if you must hire a more expensive caterer for your wedding reception because the original company canceled at the last minute.
- If money cannot repay the damage you suffered, you might demand specific performance—require the other party to fulfill the original contract. For example, you might demand that a dealer in classic cars sell you the antique Stutz Bearcat he agreed to sell you and not a classic Jaguar instead.

▪▪▪ TORT LAW

Tort law applies to most business relationships *not governed by contracts*. A **tort** is a *civil*—that is, noncriminal—injury to people, property, or reputation for which compensation must be paid. For example, if a person violates zoning laws by opening a convenience store in a residential area, he or she cannot be sent to jail as if the act were a criminal violation. But a variety of other legal measures can be pursued, such as fines or seizure of property. Trespass, fraud, defamation, invasion of privacy, and even assault can be torts, as can interference with contractual relations and wrongful use of trade secrets. There are three classifications of torts: *intentional, negligence,* and *product liability.*

Intentional Torts **Intentional torts** result from the deliberate actions of another person or organization—for instance, a manufacturer knowingly fails to install a relatively inexpensive safety device on a product. Similarly, refusing to rectify a product design flaw, as in the case of the space shuttle *Challenger* disaster, can render a firm liable for an intentional tort. The actions of employees on the job may also constitute intentional torts—for example, an overzealous security guard who wrongly accuses a customer of shoplifting. To remedy torts, courts will usually impose **compensatory damages**: payments intended to redress an injury actually suffered. They may also impose **punitive damages**: fines that exceed actual losses suffered by plaintiffs and that are intended to punish defendants.

Negligence Torts Ninety percent of tort suits involve charges of **negligence**—conduct falling below legal standards for protecting others against unreasonable risk. If a company installs a pollution-control system that fails to protect a community's water supply, it may later be sued by an individual who gets sick from drinking the water.

Negligence torts may also result from employee actions. For example, the captain of an Exxon oil supertanker, the *Valdez*, ran aground in Alaska and spilled 11 million gallons of crude oil into coastal fishing waters. A jury subsequently ordered Exxon to pay $5 billion in punitive damages to 34,000 fishermen and other plaintiffs. The firm responsible for pipeline operations at the Valdez, Alaska, terminal (which is partially owned by Exxon) also agreed to pay plaintiffs in the same case $98 million in damages. In a separate case, Exxon

TORT civil injury to people, property, or reputation for which compensation must be paid

INTENTIONAL TORT tort resulting from the deliberate actions of a party

COMPENSATORY DAMAGES monetary payments intended to redress injury actually suffered because of a tort

PUNITIVE DAMAGES fines imposed over and above any actual losses suffered by a plaintiff

NEGLIGENCE conduct falling below legal standards for protecting others against unreasonable risk

paid $20 million in damages to villages whose food supply had been destroyed. And even before any of these awards were handed down, Exxon had already spent $2.1 billion on the cleanup effort and paid $1.3 billion in civil and criminal penalties.

PRODUCT LIABILITY tort in which a company is responsible for injuries caused by its products

Product Liability Torts In cases of **product liability**, a company may be held responsible for injuries caused by its products. According to a special government panel on product liability, about 33 million people are injured and 28,000 killed by consumer products each year.

STRICT PRODUCT LIABILITY principle that liability can result not from a producer's negligence but from a defect in the product itself

Strict Product Liability Since the early 1960s, businesses have faced a number of legal actions based on the relatively new principle of **strict product liability**: the principle that liability can result not from a producer's negligence but from a defect in the product itself. An injured party need show only that

1 The product was defective.
2 The defect was the cause of injury.
3 The defect caused the product to be unreasonably dangerous.

Many recent cases in strict product liability have focused on injuries or illnesses attributable to toxic wastes or other hazardous substances that were legally disposed of. Because plaintiffs need not demonstrate negligence or fault, these suits frequently succeed. The number of such suits promises to increase.

∎∎∎ PROPERTY LAW

PROPERTY anything of value to which a person or business has sole right of ownership

As the name implies, *property law* concerns property rights. But what exactly is "property"? Is it the land under a house? The house itself? A car in the driveway? A dress in the closet? The answer in each case is yes: In the legal sense, **property** is anything of value to which a person or business has sole right of ownership. Property is technically those rights.

Within this broad general definition, we can divide property into four categories:

TANGIBLE REAL PROPERTY land and anything attached to it

1 **Tangible real property** is land and anything attached to it. A house and a factory are both tangible real property, as are built-in appliances or the machines inside the buildings.

TANGIBLE PERSONAL PROPERTY any movable item that can be owned, bought, sold, or leased

2 **Tangible personal property** is any movable item that can be owned, bought, sold, or leased. Examples are automobiles, clothing, stereos, and cameras.

3 **Intangible personal property** cannot be seen but exists by virtue of written documentation. Examples are insurance policies, bank accounts, stocks and bonds, and trade secrets.

INTANGIBLE PERSONAL PROPERTY property that cannot be seen but that exists by virtue of written documentation

4 **Intellectual property** is created through a person's creative activities. Books, articles, songs, paintings, screenplays, and computer software are all intellectual property.

INTELLECTUAL PROPERTY property created through a person's creative activities

Protection of Intellectual Rights The U.S. Constitution grants protection to intellectual property by means of copyrights, trademarks, and patents. Copyrights and patents apply to the tangible expressions of an idea—not to the ideas themselves. You could not copyright the idea of cloning dinosaurs from fossil DNA. Michael Crichton could copyright his novel, *Jurassic Park*, which is a tangible result of that idea, and sell the film rights to producer-director Steven Spielberg. Both creators are entitled to the profits, if any, that may be generated by their tangible creative expressions.

Copyrights **Copyrights** give exclusive ownership rights to the creators of books, articles, designs, illustrations, photos, films, and music. Computer programs and even semiconductor chips are also protected. Copyrights extend to creators for their entire lives and to their estates for 70 years thereafter.

COPYRIGHT exclusive ownership right belonging to the creator of a book, article, design, illustration, photo, film, or musical work

Trademarks Because the development of products is expensive, companies must prevent other firms from using their brand names. Often, they must act to keep competitors from seducing consumers with similar or substitute products. A producer can apply to the U.S. government for a **trademark**—the exclusive legal right to use a brand name.

Trademarks are granted for 20 years and may be renewed indefinitely if a firm continues to protect its brand name. If a firm allows the brand name to lapse into common usage, it may lose protection. Common usage takes effect when a company fails to use the ® symbol to indicate that its brand name is a registered trademark. It also takes effect if a company seeks no action against those who fail to acknowledge its trademark. Recently, for example, the popular brand-name sailboard Windsurfer lost its trademark. Like *trampoline*, *yo-yo*, and *thermos*, *windsurfer* has become the common term for the product and can now be used by any sailboard company.

TRADEMARK exclusive legal right to use a brand name or symbol

Patents **Patents** provide legal monopolies for the use and licensing of manufactured items, manufacturing processes, substances, and designs for objects. A patentable invention must be *novel*, *useful*, and *nonobvious*. Patents are valid for 20 years, with the term running from the date on which the application was *filed*, not the date on which the patent itself was *issued*.

PATENT exclusive legal right to use and license a manufactured item or substance, manufacturing process, or object design

Restrictions on Property Rights Property rights are not always absolute. For example, rights may be compromised under any of the following circumstances:

- Owners of shorefront property may be required to permit anglers, clam diggers, and other interested parties to walk near the water.
- Utility companies typically have rights called *easements*, such as the right to run wire over private property or to lay cable or pipe under it.
- Under the principle of **eminent domain**, the government may, upon paying owners fair prices, claim private land to expand roads or erect public buildings.

EMINENT DOMAIN principle that the government may claim private land for public use by buying it at a fair price

■■■ ■ AGENCY LAW

The transfer of property—whether the deeding of real estate or the transfer of automobile title—often involves agents. An **agent** is a person who acts for, and in the name of, another party, called the **principal.** The most visible agents are those in real estate, sports, and entertainment. Many businesses, however, use agents to secure insurance coverage and handle investments. Every partner in a partnership and every officer and director in a corporation are agents of that business. Courts have also ruled that both a firm's employees and its outside contractors may be regarded as its agents.

AGENT individual or organization acting for and in the name of, another party

PRINCIPAL individual or organization authorizing an agent to act on its behalf

Authority of Agents Agents have the authority to bind principals to agreements. They receive that authority, however, from the principals themselves; they cannot create their own authority. An agent's authority to bind a principal can be express, implied, or apparent.

For example, Ellen is a salesperson in Honest Sam's Used Car Lot. Her written employment contract gives her **express authority** to sell cars, to provide information to prospective buyers, and to approve trade-ins up to $2,000. Derived from the custom of

EXPRESS AUTHORITY agent's authority, derived from written agreement, to bind a principal to a certain course of action

IMPLIED AUTHORITY agent's authority, derived from business custom, to bind a principal to a certain course of action

APPARENT AUTHORITY agent's authority, based on the principal's compliance, to bind a principal to a certain course of action

used-car dealers, she also has **implied authority** to give reasonable discounts on prices and to make reasonable adjustments to written warranties. Furthermore, Ellen may—in the presence of Honest Sam—promise a customer that she will match the price offered by another local dealer. If Honest Sam assents—perhaps merely nods and smiles—Ellen may be construed to have the **apparent authority** to make this deal.

Responsibilities of Principals Principals have several responsibilities to their agents. They owe agents reasonable compensation, must reimburse them for related business expenses, and should inform them of risks associated with their business activities. Principals are liable for actions performed by agents *within the scope of their employment*. If agents make untrue claims about products or services, the principal is liable for making amends. Employers are similarly responsible for the actions of employees. Firms are often liable in tort suits because the courts treat employees as agents.

Businesses are increasingly being held accountable for *criminal* acts by employees. Court findings, for example, have argued that firms are expected to be aware of workers' propensities for violence, to check on their employees' pasts, and to train and supervise employees properly. Suppose that a delivery service hires a driver with a history of driving while intoxicated. If the driver has an accident with a company vehicle while under the influence of alcohol, the company may be liable for criminal actions.

■■■ COMMERCIAL LAW

Managers must be well acquainted with the most general laws affecting commerce. Specifically, they need to be familiar with the provisions of the *Uniform Commercial Code*, which sets down rules regarding *warranties*.

The Uniform Commercial Code For many years, companies doing business in more than one state faced a special problem: Laws governing commerce varied, sometimes widely, from state to state. In 1952, however, the National Conference of Commissioners on Uniform State Laws and the American Law Institute drew up the **Uniform Commercial Code (UCC)**. Accepted by every state except Louisiana, the UCC describes the rights of buyers and sellers in transactions. One key area of coverage by the UCC, contracts, was discussed earlier. Another key area is warranties.

A **warranty** is a seller's promise to stand by its products or services if a problem occurs after the sale. Warranties may be express or implied. The terms of an **express warranty** are specifically stated by the seller. For example, many stereo systems are expressly warranted for 90 days. If they malfunction within that period, they can be returned for full refunds.

An **implied warranty** is dictated by law. Implied warranties embody the principle that a product should (1) fulfill the promises made by advertisements and (2) serve the purpose for which it was manufactured and sold. If you buy an advertised frost-free refrigerator, the seller implies that the refrigerator will keep your food cold and that you will not have to defrost it. It is important to note, however, that warranties, unlike most contracts, are easily limited, waived, or disclaimed. Consequently, they are the source of more tort action, as dissatisfied customers seek redress from producers.

UNIFORM COMMERCIAL CODE (UCC) body of standardized laws governing the rights of buyers and sellers in transactions

WARRANTY seller's promise to stand by its products or services if a problem occurs after the sale

EXPRESS WARRANTY warranty whose terms are specifically stated by the seller

IMPLIED WARRANTY warranty, dictated by law, based on the principle that products should fulfill advertised promises and serve the purposes for which they are manufactured and sold

■■■ BANKRUPTCY LAW

At one time, individuals who could not pay their debts were jailed. Today, however, both organizations and individuals can seek relief by filing for **bankruptcy**—the court-granted permission not to pay some or all debts.

BANKRUPTCY permission granted by the courts to individuals and organizations not to pay some or all of their debts

Many individuals and businesses file for bankruptcy each year, and their numbers continue to increase. Why do individuals and businesses file for bankruptcy? Cash-flow problems and drops in farm prices caused many farmers, banks, and small businesses to go bankrupt. In recent years, large enterprises such as Continental Airlines have sought the protection of bankruptcy laws as part of strategies to streamline operations, cut costs, and regain profitability.

Three main factors account for the increase in bankruptcy filings:

1 The increased availability of credit
2 The "fresh-start" provisions in current bankruptcy laws
3 The growing acceptance of bankruptcy as a financial tactic

In some cases, creditors force an individual or firm into **involuntary bankruptcy** and press the courts to award them payment of at least part of what they are owed. Far more often, however, a person or business chooses to file for court protection against creditors. In general, individuals and firms whose debts exceed total assets by at least $1,000 may file for **voluntary bankruptcy**.

INVOLUNTARY BANKRUPTCY bankruptcy proceedings initiated by the creditors of an indebted individual or organization

VOLUNTARY BANKRUPTCY bankruptcy proceedings initiated by an indebted individual or organization

Business Bankruptcy   A business bankruptcy may be resolved by one of three plans:

1 Under a *liquidation plan*, the business ceases to exist. Its assets are sold and the proceeds are used to pay creditors.
2 Under a *repayment plan*, the bankrupt company simply works out a new payment schedule to meet its obligations. The time frame is usually extended, and payments are collected and distributed by a court-appointed trustee.
3 *Reorganization* is the most complex form of business bankruptcy. The company must explain the sources of its financial difficulties and propose a new plan for remaining in business. Reorganization may include a new slate of managers and a new financial strategy. A judge may also reduce the firm's debts to ensure its survival. Although creditors naturally dislike debt reduction, they may agree to the proposal, since 50 percent of one's due is better than nothing at all.

Legislation passed since 1994 has made some major revisions in bankruptcy laws. For example, it is now easier for individuals with up to $1 million in debt to make payments under installment plans instead of liquidating assets immediately. In contrast, the new law restricts how long a company can protect itself in bankruptcy while continuing to do business. Critics have charged that many firms have succeeded in operating for many months under bankruptcy protection. During that time, they were able to cut costs and prices, not only competing with an unfair advantage but dragging down overall industry profits. The new laws place time limits on various steps in the filing process. The intended effect is to speed the process and prevent assets from being lost to legal fees.

THE INTERNATIONAL FRAMEWORK OF BUSINESS LAW

Laws can vary dramatically from country to country, and many businesses today have international markets, suppliers, and competitors. It follows that managers need a basic understanding of the international framework of business law that affects the ways in which they can do business.

National laws are created and enforced by countries. The creation and enforcement of international law are more complicated. For example, if a company shipping merchandise between the United States and Mexico breaks an environmental protection law, to whom is that company accountable? The answer depends on several factors. Which country enacted the law in question? Where did the violation occur? In which country is the alleged violator incorporated?

Issues, such as pollution across borders, are matters of **international law**: the very general set of cooperative agreements and guidelines established by countries to govern the actions of individuals, businesses, and nations themselves.

International law has several sources. One source is custom and tradition. Among countries that have been trading with each other for centuries, many customs and traditions governing exchanges have gradually evolved into practice. Although some trading practices still follow ancient unwritten agreements, there has been a clear trend in more recent times to approach international trade within a more formal legal framework. Key features of that framework include a variety of formal trade agreements.

Another important source of international law is the formal trade treaties nations negotiate with one another. As we discussed in Chapter 4, agreements governing such entities as the WTO and the EU, for instance, also provide legal frameworks within which participating nations agree to abide.

MANAGING YOUR PERSONAL FINANCES

For many people, the goal of financial success isn't being wealthy: It's the things that they can do with wealth. That's why chapter one in so many financial success stories deals with a hard reality: Like it or not, dealing with personal finances is a life-long job. As a rule, it involves a life-altering choice between two options:

1 Committing to the rational management of your personal finances—controlling them as a way of life and helping them grow.
2 Letting the financial chips fall where they may and hoping for the best (which seldom happens).

Option 1 results in greater personal satisfaction and financial stability. Ignoring your finances, on the other hand, invites frustration, disappointment, and, quite often, financial distress.

In Chapter 16 and Appendix I, we discussed the activities of financial managers—clarifying financial goals, determining short-term and long-term funding needs, and managing risk. Many of those same activities and principles of organizational finance pertain to personal finance as well. In managing your own finances and pursuing your own personal financial goals, you must consider similar issues of cash management, financial planning and control, investment alternatives, and risk management. Let's start by looking at one key factor in success: the personal financial plan. We'll then discuss the steps in the planning process and show how you can make better decisions to manage your personal finances.

BUILDING YOUR FINANCIAL PLAN

FINANCIAL PLANNING process of looking at one's current financial condition, identifying one's goals, and anticipating requirements for meeting those goals

Financial planning is the process of looking at your current financial condition, identifying your goals, and anticipating what you'll need to do to meet those goals. Once you've determined the assets you need to meet your goals, you'll then identify the best sources and uses of those assets for eventually reaching your goals. But remember: Because your goals and financial position will change as you enter different life stages, your plan should always make room for revision. Figure AIII.1 summarizes a step-by-step approach to personal financial planning.

ASSESSING YOUR CURRENT FINANCIAL CONDITION

PERSONAL NET WORTH value of one's total assets minus one's total liabilities (debts)

The first step in developing a personal financial plan is assessing your current financial position. Your **personal net worth** is the value of all your assets, including cash or a car, minus all your liabilities (debts), such as car loans and student loans. Bear in mind that personal net worth is a measure of *your wealth at the present time*. The worksheet in Figure AIII.2 provides some sample calculations for developing your own personal "balance sheet." Because assets and liabilities change over time, updating your balance sheet not only allows you to monitor changes but also provides more accurate information for realistic budgeting and planning.

DEVELOP YOUR FINANCIAL GOALS

Your personal balance sheet lets you review your current overall financial condition. Once you know where you presently stand, you can move on to step 2 in financial planning: setting specific financial goals for the future. This includes setting three different

Figure AIII.1

Developing a Personal Financial Plan

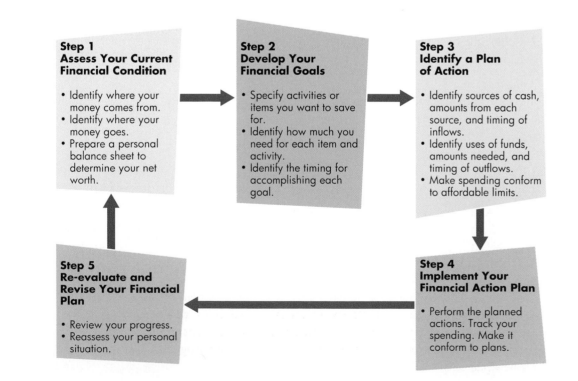

Step 1
Assess Your Current Financial Condition

- Identify where your money comes from.
- Identify where your money goes.
- Prepare a personal balance sheet to determine your net worth.

Step 2
Develop Your Financial Goals

- Specify activities or items you want to save for.
- Identify how much you need for each item and activity.
- Identify the timing for accomplishing each goal.

Step 3
Identify a Plan of Action

- Identify sources of cash, amounts from each source, and timing of inflows.
- Identify uses of funds, amounts needed, and timing of outflows.
- Make spending conform to affordable limits.

Step 5
Re-evaluate and Revise Your Financial Plan

- Review your progress.
- Reassess your personal situation.

Step 4
Implement Your Financial Action Plan

- Perform the planned actions. Track your spending. Make it conform to plans.

Assets: What You Own	Example Numbers	Your Numbers
LIQUID ASSETS:		
1. Cash	$ 300	
2. Savings	+ 3,700	
3. Checking	+ 1,200	
INVESTMENTS:		
4. IRAs	+ 12,400	
5. Securities	+ 500	
6. Retirement Plan	+ —	
7. Real Estate (other than primary residence)	+ —	
HOUSEHOLD:		
8. Cars (market value)	+ 18,000	
9. House (market value)	+ —	
10. Furniture	+ 3,400	
11. Personal Property	+ 6,600	
12. Other assets	—	
13. Total Assets (add lines 1-12)	**= $46,100**	
Liabilities (Dept): What You Owe		
CURRENT LIABILITIES:		
14. Credit card balance	$ 1,300	
15. Unpaid bills due	+ 1,800	
16. Alimony and child support	+ —	
LONG-TERM LIABILITIES:		
17. Home mortgage	+ —	
18. Home equity loan	+ —	
19. Car loan	+ 4,100	
20. Student loan	+ 3,600	
21. Other liabilities	+ 2,400	
22. Total Liabilities (add lines 14-21)	**= $13,200**	
Net Worth		
23. Total Assets (line 13)	$46,100	
24. Less: Total Debt (line 22)	– 13,200	
25. Results: Net Worth	**= $32,900**	

types of goals: *immediate goals* (within one year), *intermediate goals* (within five years), and *long-term goals* (more than five years). The worksheet in Figure AIII.3 will help you establish these goals. By thinking about your finances in three different time frames, you'll be better able to set measurable goals and completion times when calculating your future financial needs. It also lets you set priorities for rationing your resources if, at some point, you're not able to pursue all of your goals.

Because subsequent planning steps—step 3 (identifying a plan of action) and step 4 (implementing your plan)—will affect your assets and liabilities, your balance sheet will change over time. That's why step 5 (reevaluating and revising your plan) needs periodic updating to reflect your current net worth, to monitor your progress, and to help you start a new planning cycle.

Figure AIII.3   Worksheet for Setting Financial Goals

Name the Goal	Financial Requirement (amount) for This Goal	Time Frame for Accomplishing Goal	Importance (1= highest, 5 = lowest)
Immediate Goals:			
Live in a better apartment	_____	_____	_____
Establish an emergency cash fund	_____	_____	_____
Pay off credit card debt	_____	_____	_____
Other	_____	_____	_____
Intermediate Goals:			
Obtain adequate life, disability, liability, property insurance	_____	_____	_____
Save for wedding	_____	_____	_____
Save to buy new car	_____	_____	_____
Establish regular savings program (5% of gross income)	_____	_____	_____
Save for college for self	_____	_____	_____
Pay off major outstanding debt	_____	_____	_____
Make major purchase	_____	_____	_____
Save for home remodeling	_____	_____	_____
Save for down payment on a home	_____	_____	_____
Other	_____	_____	_____
Long-Term Goals:			
Pay off home mortgage	_____	_____	_____
Save for college for children	_____	_____	_____
Save for vacation home	_____	_____	_____
Increase personal net worth to $___ in ___ years.	_____	_____	_____
Achieve retirement nest egg of $___ in ___ years.	_____	_____	_____
Accumulate fund for travel in retirement	_____	_____	_____
Save for long-term care needs	_____	_____	_____
Other	_____	_____	_____

THE TIME VALUE OF MONEY

TIME VALUE OF MONEY principle that invested money grows by earning interest or yielding some other form of return

The **time value of money** is perhaps the single most important concept in personal finance. The concept of *time value* recognizes the basic fact that, while it's invested, money grows by earning interest or yielding some other form of return. Whenever you make everyday purchases, you're giving up interest that you could have earned with the same money if you'd invested it instead. From a financial standpoint, "idle" or uninvested money—money that could be put to work earning more money—is a wasted resource.

▪▪▪ WHY MONEY GROWS

The value of time stems from the principle of **compound growth**—the compounding of interest paid over given time periods: With each additional time period, interest payments accumulate and earn even more interest, thus, multiplying the earning capacity of the investment.

> **COMPOUND GROWTH** how a sum of money grows by paying interest on the principal of an investment, as well as paying interest on previously earned interest, over several time periods

For example, you invest $1.00 today at 10 percent annual interest. As you can see from Figure AIII.4, you'll have $1.10 at the end of one year (your $1.00 original investment plus $0.10 in interest). If you reinvest your whole $1.10, you'll earn interest on both your first year's interest and your original investment. During year 2, therefore, your savings will grow to $1.21 (your $1.10 reinvestment plus $0.11 in interest). Each year's interest will be greater than the previous year's. The interest accumulated over a single time period may seem rather modest, but when you add it up over many periods, the growth can be impressive. After about 7 1/2 years at 10 percent, your original $1.00 will have doubled. If you had invested $10,000, you'd have $20,000.

The Rule of 72 How long does it take to double an investment? A handy rule of thumb is called the "Rule of 72." You can find the number of years needed to double your money by dividing the annual interest rate (in percent) into 72. If, for example, you reinvest annually at 8 percent, you'll double your money in about 9 years:

$$\frac{72}{8} = 9 \text{ years to double the money}$$

The Rule of 72 can also calculate how much interest you must get if you want to double your money in a given number of years: Simply divide 72 by the desired number of years. If you want to double your money in 10 years, you need to get 7.2 percent:

$$\frac{72}{10} = 7.2 \text{ percent interest needed to double the money}$$

Finally, the Rule of 72 highlights the downside as well as the upside of compound growth: Compound growth provides greater wealth for savers who receive interest. It also means increased indebtedness for borrowers who don't repay borrowed money and let the debt grow at a given interest rate. As we have seen, for example, an 8-percent rate doubles the principal every 9 years:

$$\frac{72}{8} = 9 \text{ years to double the money}$$

Figure AIII.4
Calculating Compound Growth

Year	Beginning Amount	+	Annual Interest Earned	=	Ending Amount
1	$1.000	+	$0.100[0.10 X $1.000 = $0.10]	=	$1.100
2	1.100	+	0.110[0.10 X $1.100 = $0.11]	=	1.210
3	1.210	+	0.121[0.10 X $1.210 = $0.121]	=	1.331
4	1.331	+	0.133[0.10 X $1.331 = $0.133]	=	1.464
5	1.464	+	0.146[0.10 X $1.464 = $0.146]	=	1.610
6	1.610	+	0.161[0.10 X $1.610 = $0.161]	=	1.771
7	1.771	+	0.177[0.10 X $1.771 = $0.177]	=	1.948
8	1.948	+	0.195[0.10 X $1.948 = $0.195]	=	2.143

When money is borrowed for a period of 36 years, the amount owed doubles every 9 years, so the doubling occurs 4 times during the 36 years:

$$\frac{36}{9} = 4 \text{ cycles of doubling during 36 years}$$

At 4 percent interest rate, by contrast, money doubles every 18 years, according to the Rule of 72. Therefore, during the 36 years the money doubles only twice—accumulating to $4,000. We see the accumulated difference between the growth of debt for 8 percent versus 4 percent interest rates. The lesson for the personal-finance manager is clear: When *investing* (or saving), seek *higher* interest rates because money will double more frequently; when *borrowing*, seek *lower* interest rates because indebtedness will grow more slowly.

▪▪▪ MAKING BETTER USE OF YOUR TIME VALUE

Most people want to save for the future, either for things they need—down payments on a house, college tuition, and so on—or for nonessentials (luxury items and recreation). The sooner you get started, the greater your financial power will be: You will have taken advantage of the time value of money for a longer period of time.

Consider the following example. Coworkers Ellen and Barbara are both planning to retire in 25 years. Over that period, each can expect a 10-percent annual return on investment (the U.S. stock market has averaged more than 10 percent for the past 75 years). Their savings strategies, however, are different: Whereas Barbara begins saving immediately, Ellen plans to start later but invest larger sums. Barbara will invest $2,000 annually for each of the next five years (years 1 through 5), for a total investment of $10,000. She'll let interest accumulate through year 25. Ellen, meanwhile, wants to live a little larger by spending rather than saving for the next 10 years. Then, for years 11 through 20, she'll start saving $2,000 annually, for a total investment of $20,000. She, too, will allow annual returns to accumulate until year 25, when both she and Barbara retire. Will Ellen have a larger retirement fund in year 25 because she's ultimately contributing twice as much as Barbara?

Not by a long shot: Barbara's retirement wealth will be much larger—$90,364 versus Ellen's $56,468—even though she invested only half as much ($10,000 versus $20,000). We explain the disparity by crunching all the numbers in Figure AIII.5. Barbara's advantage lies in timing—namely, the length of her savings program. Her money is invested longer—over a period of 21 to 25 years—with interest compounding over that range of time. Ellen's earnings are compounded over a shorter period—6 to 15 years. Granted, Ellen may have had more fun in years 1 to 5, but Barbara's retirement prospects look brighter.

▪▪▪ TIME VALUE AS A FINANCIAL-PLANNING TOOL

How much must you set aside today in order to accumulate enough money for something you want tomorrow? By its very nature, financial planning takes into account not only future needs (vacations, a wedding, major purchases, retirement) but also sources of funds for meeting those needs. Timing, however, is important: The timing of financial transactions will determine whether your plan works or doesn't work the way you intend. Start by considering the time value of money at the outset of your planning cycle. In this respect, various time-based tables for financial calculations are quite useful.[1]

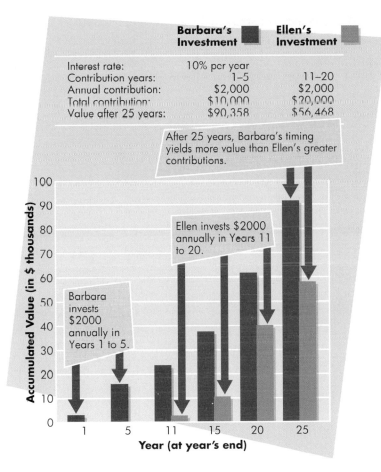

Figure AIII.6, for example, shows how much a $1.00 investment will grow over different lengths of time and at different interest rates. Let's see how we can use this tool for financial planning.

Having recently inherited $50,000, Jason wants to invest for his old age. Specifically, he wants to accumulate a $200,000 nest egg by the time he reaches 55 (30 years from now). He also wants to spend some of the money while he's young enough to enjoy it, but he doesn't know how much he'll have left to spend after he's determined the amount needed to meet his retirement goal.

To help Jason with his planning, we first need to focus on our 30-year investment; thus, $n = 30$ in Figure AIII.6. As you can see, the accumulated value of that investment depends on the annual interest rate. At 4 percent, for instance, the growth factor is 3.243. Over 30 years, therefore, $1.00 invested now will grow to $3.243. Our question is this: If $1.00 invested now yields $3.243, how many dollars must we invest now to accumulate $200,000 in 30 years? The answer is fairly simple. If $1.00 provides $3.243 in 30 years, and if we want to accumulate $200,000, we divide $200,000 by $3.243 to determine Jason needs to invest $61,671 to reach his retirement goal.

Jason's worksheet, which is shown in Figure AIII.7, reveals trial calculations made with three different interest rates—conservative, moderate, optimistic—available from alternative investments. As you can see, a 4-percent return on investment won't provide the desired $200,000. If he gets only 4 percent, Jason would have to invest $61,671; but he has only $50,000. If he invested the entire $50,000 at 4 percent, he'd end up with just $162,150—

$$\$50,000 \times \$3.243 = \$162,150$$

—which is well below his $200,000 goal.

Figure AIII.6
Timetable for Growing $1.00

n	1%	2%	4%	6%	8%	10%
1	1.010	1.020	1.040	1.060	1.080	1.100
2	1.020	1.040	1.082	1.124	1.166	1.210
3	1.030	1.061	1.125	1.191	1.260	1.331
4	1.041	1.082	1.170	1.262	1.360	1.464
5	1.051	1.104	1.217	1.338	1.469	1.611
6	1.062	1.126	1.265	1.419	1.587	1.772
7	1.072	1.149	1.316	1.504	1.714	1.949
8	1.083	1.172	1.369	1.594	1.851	2.144
9	1.094	1.195	1.423	1.689	1.999	2.358
10	1.105	1.219	1.480	1.791	2.159	2.594
15	1.161	1.346	1.801	2.397	3.172	4.177
20	1.220	1.486	2.191	3.207	4.661	6.727
25	1.282	1.641	2.666	4.292	6.848	10.834
30	1.348	1.811	3.243	5.743	10.062	17.449

Note:
n = Number of time periods
% = Various interest rates

Jason has two choices: Find a higher-paying investment or, if he's willing to settle for 4 percent, reduce the amount of his desired nest egg. To make his decision, Jason can use the trial data contained in Figure AIII.7. Projecting an investment at 8 percent, he needs to allocate only about $20,000 to start his nest egg and still have more than $30,000 for other uses. If he considers the 8-percent investment too risky, he may opt for the safer 6-percent return; in that case, he'd still have $15,175 left ($50,000 –$34,825) to spend now.

Figure AIII.7   Nest Egg Worksheet: Three Investment Possibilities

	Investment Returns (annual rate)			Your numbers %
	Conservative 4%	**Moderate 6%**	**Optimistic 8%**	
Ending amount after 30 years:	$200,000	$200,000	$200,000	_____
Growth factor (from table):	3.243	5.743	10.062	_____
Amount* to invest now (end amount/ growth factor):	$61,671** ($200,000/3.243)	$34,825 ($200,000/5.743)	$19,877 ($200,000/10.062)	_____

*Rounded to nearest whole dollar.
**This amount is greater than the available $50,000.

CONSERVING MONEY BY CONTROLLING IT

Several steps in the financial-planning process call for conserving money by paying attention to where it goes—by keeping spending within affordable limits and understanding what you're spending your money on. As too many people have found out the hard way, a major pitfall in any financial plan is the temptation to spend too much, especially when credit is so easy to get. Consumers often lose track of how much they spend, and, to make matters worse, some don't consider the costly finance charges associated with easy credit. Because many credit-card issuers target college students and recent graduates with tempting offers appealing to the desire for financial independence, we'll use the following section to explain the financial costs entailed by credit cards. Keep in mind, however, that the same lessons apply equally to other loans—home mortgages, cars, and student financial aid.

▪▪▪ CREDIT CARDS: KEYS TO SATISFACTION OR FINANCIAL HANDCUFFS?

Although some credit cards don't charge annual fees, all of them charge interest on unpaid (outstanding) balances. Because credit-card debt is one of the most expensive sources of funds, you need to understand the costs before you start charging instead of being surprised when you open your bill. For one thing, many card users don't realize how much interest they're paying or how long it will take them to pay off their bills.

Some states post Web sites to help consumers understand credit-card costs. Figure AIII.8 reprints part of a page from California's "Minimum Payment Credit Card Calculation," which can be accessed at www.dfi.ca.gov/ab865/ChartAB865.pdf. Using the table as a guide, let's consider the following situation. Suppose you owe $5,000 for credit-card purchases, and your card company requires a minimum monthly payment (minimum payment due—or MPD) of 5 percent of the unpaid balance. The interest rate is 18 percent APR (annual percentage rate) on the outstanding balance. (By the way, this rate isn't unusually high: Some rates are well above 20 percent.)

Figure AIII.8 reflects an account with $5,000 outstanding balance at the end of last month. *This is the amount on which your interest of 18 percent APR is charged.* Remember,

Figure AIII.8   Paying Off Credit-Card Debt

Balance = $5,000 APR	MPD 3% Months	MPD 3% Costs	MPD 5% Months	MPD 5% Costs	MPD 10% Months	MPD 10% Costs
6%	144	$5,965.56	92	$5,544.58	50	$5,260.74
9%	158	$6,607.74	96	$5,864.56	51	$5,401.63
12%	175	$7,407.50	102	$6,224.26	53	$5,550.32
18%	226	$9,798.89	115	$7,096.70	55	$5,873.86
21%	266	$11,704.63	123	$7,632.92	57	$6,050.28

Note:
MPD = Minimum Payment Due.
APR = Annual Percentage Rate.

too, that your card company requires a *minimum monthly payment due (MPD) of 5 percent* of the current balance. Let's assume that you pay only the monthly minimum and ask ourselves two questions:

1 How many months will it take to pay off the $5,000?
2 How much interest will you have paid when you do pay it off?

To answer these questions, let's look at Figure AIII.8. Remember that your card has an MPD of 5 percent, so we start by finding the MPD 5 percent column. Next, we remember that the APR is 18 percent, so we find the row on the left that corresponds to an 18 percent APR. Where this row intersects with the MPD 5 percent column is the number of months it will take you to pay off $5,000: 115 months. That's approximately 9 1/2 years! And remember: This number assumes that your balance gradually diminishes to zero because you add *no other purchases to the card.* Your total payment of $7,096.70 covers your $5,000 debt plus $2,096.70 in interest charges. An immediate cash payoff, therefore, would save you $2,096.70 in interest payments.

Why does repayment take so long? In Figure AIII.9, we run through some sample calculations for the first two months in your 115-month repayment process. Your minimum monthly payment decreases because your ending balance gets smaller with each monthly payment. Your $250 payment in February includes $75 in interest owed on the $5,000 balance in the previous month. At 18 percent APR, interest on $5,000 would be $900 for a year (0.18 × $5,000), but for one month (January), it's only 1/12 of that amount—$75. You're paying the rest of your February installment of $175 ($250 – $75) on the principal amount, thereby reducing the month-end balance to $4,825. If we carry out these calculations over 115 months, we find that, when your account is paid in full, you've made "payments on principal" of $5,000 and interest payments of $2,096.70.

Practice Paying Off Your Debt Using the method illustrated in Figure AIII.9, you should be able to answer the following questions about credit-card repayment (the answers appear at the end of this appendix):

1 According to the data in Figure AIII.9, your minimum monthly payment for April would be which of the following? (a) $232.81; (b) $253.47; (c) $230.56; (d) $226.18.
2 According to the data in Figure AIII.9, for April, the interest owed on your previous balance would be which of the following? (a) $70.43; (b) $71.94; (c) $69.84; (d) $68.32.
3 According to the data in Figure AIII.9, for April, your ending balance owed on principal would be which of the following? (a) $4,182.16; (b) $4,493.16; (c) $4,517.22; (d) $4,334.97.

Figure AIII.9 Calculating Minimum Monthly Payments

Month	Minimum Monthly Payment (5% of Previous Ending Balance)	=	Interest Owed on Previous Balance* (1/12 X .18 X Previous Balance)	+	Payment on Principal	Ending Balance Owed on Principle
January	—		—		—	$5,000.
February	$250. [0.05 X $5,000]	=	$75. [1/12 X 0.18 X $5,000]	+	$175.	$4,825. [5,000 – 175]
March	$241.25 [0.05 X 4,825]	=	$72.38 [1/12 X 0.18 X 4,825]	+	$168.87	$4,656.13 [4,825 – 168.87]

*Monthly interest is calculated using 1/12 of annual interest rate.

▪▪■ SAVE YOUR MONEY: LOWER INTEREST RATES AND FASTER PAYMENTS

A closer look at Figure AIII.8 confirms two principles for saving money that you can apply when borrowing from any source, not just credit cards: Look for lower interest rates and make faster repayments.

Seeking Lower Interest Rates Because higher interest rates mean more expensive money, you save money with lower interest rates. With a little research, you'll find that potential creditors charge different rates (ranging from below 10 percent to over 20 percent APR among credit-card issuers). How much can you save? Look again at Figure AIII.8 and compare the cost of borrowing $5,000 at 18 percent with the cost of borrowing it at 9 percent. If you assume the same 5-percent minimum monthly payment, how much interest does 9 percent save you over the life of the repayment? The answer is $1,232.14 ($864.56 instead of $2,096.70). That's a nearly 59-percent savings.

Making Faster Payments Because money has a time value, lenders charge borrowers according to the length of time for which they borrow it. In general, longer lending periods increase the cost, while shorter periods are cheaper. Accordingly, borrowers often speed up payments to cut interest costs. Using Figure AIII.8, for example, compare the costs of the 5 percent MPD (required monthly payment of 5 percent on the remaining balance) with the faster 10 percent MPD. The faster schedule cuts the repayment period from 115 to 55 months and, at 18 percent APR, reduces interest costs by $1,222.84.

What if you combined both faster repayment and the lower interest rate (9 percent versus 18 percent)? You'd cut your total interest cost to just $450.30—a savings of $1,695.07 over the amount you'd pay if you made slower repayments at the higher rate.

We'll say it one more time: When borrowing money, look for lower interest rates and make faster repayments.

▪▪■ DECLINING ASSET VALUE: A BORROWER'S REGRET

Financially speaking, nothing's more disappointing than buying an expensive item only to discover that it's not worth what you paid. Some of this loss in asset value can be avoided through realistic planning and spending—by knowing and staying within your financial means. Excessive spending gets costly fast. Spending on cars is a good example. New cars can be a temptation, especially with long-term loans—up to 72 months—that reduce monthly payments to seemingly affordable levels. The real problem comes when borrowers realize that the asset is depreciating faster than the loan balance: The car's market value in year five is less than that year's loan payments, and there's still another year left to pay. In the event that an accident totals the car, the borrower owes more money than is received from the insurance company. A better strategy for those with limited resources is to buy a less expensive car and, if borrowing is necessary, get a low-interest, short-term loan.

FINANCIAL COMMITMENTS OF HOME OWNERSHIP

Should you rent or buy the roof you need over your head? The answer to that question involves a variety of considerations, including life stage, family needs, career, financial situation, and preferred lifestyle. If you decide to buy, for example, you have to ask yourself how much house you can afford. To answer that question, you need to ask yourself a number of questions about your personal financial condition and your capacity for borrowing.

■■■ TO BUY OR NOT TO BUY: THAT IS THE QUESTION

Renting is attractive because you can move in without making an initial investment (or at least making a hefty down payment). That's why it's a popular choice among young adults, especially singles with limited budgets and people whose lifestyles aren't congenial to settling down in a fixed location. Flexibility, mobility, and freedom from obligations of maintenance and upkeep are important advantages. Financially speaking, however, rent payments are cash outflows that provide future financial benefits to owners instead of renters.

By the same token, first-time homebuyers cite the prospect of future financial gain as an attractive reason for buying. The financial inducements are powerful, including home equity, increasing property values, and tax advantages. You can see if buying is a good idea for you by consulting a "rent-versus-buy calculator" on the Web, such as the one at www.mortgage-calc.com. By letting you try various interest rates, down payments, loan lengths, and rental costs, calculators specify the financial advantages of renting or buying under a wide range of financial circumstances.

Many younger adults with children report that they choose to buy because they want privacy, space, and the freedom to choose a neighborhood. Finally, most home buyers say that they get satisfaction from a sense of ownership—from having their own property. Figure AIII.10 summarizes the key considerations in deciding whether to rent or buy a place to live.

■■■ HOW MUCH HOUSE CAN YOU AFFORD?

For most people, buying a home is the biggest investment they'll ever make. Unfortunately, many people make a mistake once they've made the decision to buy: They buy a house that they can't afford. In addition, new homebuyers quickly discover that the

Figure AIII.10   To Buy or Not to Buy

Renting	Buying
• No down payment to get started	• Must make payments for mortgage, property taxes, and insurance
• Flexibility to leave	• Equity builds up over time
• No obligation for upkeep or improvements	• More privacy
• No groundskeeping	• Value of property may increase
• Easy cash-flow planning (a single monthly payment)	• Lower income taxes: mortgage-interest and property tax payments reduce taxable income
• May provide access to recreation and social facilities	• Financial gains from selling house can be exempt from taxes
• Rental conditions may be changed by owner	• Greater control over use of property and improvements
• Timing for repairs controlled by owner	• The home can become a source of cash by refinancing with another mortgage loan or a home-equity loan

typical demands of ownership—especially the demand on their time and other resources for maintaining and improving a home—tend to cut into the money left over for recreation, eating out, taking vacations, and so on. You can reduce the financial pressure by calculating in advance a realistic price range—one that not only lets you buy a house but also lets you live a reasonably pleasant life once you're in it.

Most people need a loan to buy a house or a condominium. A **mortgage loan** is a loan that's secured by the property—the home—being purchased. Because the size of a loan depends on the cost of the property, both borrowers and lenders want to know whether the buyer can afford the house they want. How can you determine how much you can afford? One time-tested (though somewhat conservative) rule of thumb cautions the buyer to keep the price below 2 1/2 times his or her annual income. If your income is $48,000, look for a house priced below $120,000.

MORTGAGE LOAN loan secured by property being purchased

Any such calculation, however, will give you just a rough estimate of what you can afford. There are other considerations. What you can afford also depends on how much money you have for a down payment and how much you can borrow. Lending institutions want to determine a buyer's borrowing capacity—the borrower's ability to meet the *recurring costs* of buying and owning.

PITI What are those recurring costs? Every month, the homeowner must pay principal (pay back some of the borrowed money), along with interest, taxes, and homeowner's insurance—PITI, for short. Because all four costs are greater for more expensive homes, the buyer's monthly obligation depends on how much house he or she has bought. The size of principal and interest payments depends on (1) the mortgage amount, (2) the length of the mortgage loan, and (3) the interest rate. For any borrowed amount, the larger your monthly payment, the faster you'll pay off your loan. As Figure AIII.11 shows, monthly payments on loans are lower for longer-term loans and higher for larger interest rates.

In evaluating loan applications, lenders use PITI calculations to estimate the buyer's financial capacity—his or her ability to meet monthly payments. To determine how much someone is likely to lend you, calculate 28 percent of your gross monthly income (that is, before taxes and other deductions). If your PITI costs don't exceed that figure, your loan application probably will receive favorable consideration. With a monthly gross income of $4,000, for example, your PITI costs shouldn't exceed $1,120 (28 percent of $4,000). Additional calculations show a house price of $162,382 is the most this borrower can afford. Figure AIII.12 gives a sample calculation, and you should be able to make step-by-step computations by plugging your own numbers into the worksheet.

Figure AIII.11
Monthly Payments on a $10,000 Loan

Interest Rate (%)	Length of Loan				
	3 Years	5 Years	10 Years	20 Years	30 Years
5.0	$299.71	$188.71	$106.07	$66.00	$53.68
6.0	304.22	193.33	111.02	71.64	59.96
6.5	306.49	195.66	113.55	74.56	63.21
7.0	308.77	198.01	116.11	77.53	66.53
8.0	313.36	202.76	121.33	83.65	73.38
9.0	318.00	207.58	126.68	89.98	80.47
10.0	322.67	212.47	132.16	96.51	87.76
11.0	327.39	217.42	137.76	103.22	95.24
12.0	332.14	222.44	143.48	110.11	102.86

Other Debt In evaluating financial capacity, lenders also look at any additional outstanding debt, such as car loans, student loans, and credit-card bills. As a general guideline, they will accept indebtedness (including PITI) that amounts to 36 percent of gross income. Remember: Because PITI itself can be up to 28 percent, you might be allowed as little as 8 percent in other long-term debt. With your $4,000 monthly gross income, your total debt should be less than $1,440 (which allows $1,120 for PITI and $320 for other debt). If your total debt exceeds $1,440, you may have to settle for a smaller loan than the one you calculated with the PITI method.

If you want to go into more detail about your own payment capabilities, Web sites, such as www.mortgages.interest.com provide mortgage calculators for testing interest rates, lengths of loans, and other personal financial information.

Figure AIII.12
Worksheet for PITI Calculations

ASSUMPTIONS:

30-year mortgage
Closing costs (fees for property, survey, credit report, title search,
   title insurance, attorney, interest advance, loan origination) = $5,000
Funds available for closing costs and down payment = $25,000
Interest rate on mortgage = $6\frac{1}{2}\%$ per year
Estimated real estate taxes = $200 per month
Estimated homeowner's insurance = $20 month

Example Numbers	Your Numbers
1. Monthly income, gross (before taxes or deductions)........$4,000	_____
2. Apply PITI ratio (0.28 X amount on line 1) to determine borrower's payment capacity: 0.28 X $4,000 = ...$1,120	_____
3. Determine mortgage payment (principal and interest) by subtracting taxes and insurance from PITI (line 2)...–$ 220	_____
4. Result: Maximum mortgage payment (principal and interest)................................. $900	_____
5. Using Table Figure AIII.11, find the monthly mortgage payment on a $10,000 loan at $6\frac{1}{2}\%$ interest for 30 years... $63.21	_____
6. Since each $10,000 loan requires a $63.21 monthly payment, how many $10,000 loans can the borrower afford with the $900 payment capacity? The answer is determined as follows: $900.00/$63.21 = 14.2382 loans of $10,000 each.	_____
7. Result: Maximum allowable mortgage loan [calculated as follows: 14.2382 loans (from line 6 above) X $10,000 per loan] = ...**$142,382**	_____
8. Result: Maximum house price borrower can afford using PITI (amount of house that can be bought with available funds):	
From loan...........................$142,382	_____
From down payment...........$ 25,000	_____
Less clothing cost..............–$ 5,000	_____
...............**$162,382**	_____

CASHING OUT FROM TAX AVOIDANCE (LEGALLY)

Although personal expenditures always require cash outflows, some also have the reverse effect—namely, reducing your tax bill and saving you some cash. Individual retirement accounts (IRAs) and some education savings accounts have this effect. (Before you commit any money to these instruments or activities, check with an expert on tax regulations; they change from time to time.)

▪▪▪ THE IRA TAX BREAK

With a **traditional Individual Retirement Account (IRA)** you can make a tax-deductible savings deposit of up to $4,000 in years 2005 through 2007, and $5,000 in 2008 (the amount ultimately depends on your income level). IRAs are long-term investments, intended to provide income after age 59 1/2. If you're intending to save for the distant future anyway, an IRA boasts immediate cash advantages over a typical savings account. Why? Because your current taxable income is reduced by the amount of your contribution.

> **TRADITIONAL INDIVIDUAL RETIREMENT ACCOUNT (IRA)** provision allowing individual tax-deferred retirement savings

Here's how it works: You're a qualified employee with a federal income tax rate of 20 percent in year 2006. If you contribute $4,000 to an IRA, you avoid $800 in income taxes (0.20 × $4,000 = $800) that you would have owed if you had treated the $4,000 as normal income or put it into a standard savings account. Your untaxed contributions and their accumulated earnings will be taxed later, when you withdraw money from your IRA. Why is this a tax break? The idea of the IRA is based on the assumption that, after you retire, you're likely to have less total income and will have to pay less tax on the money withdrawn as income from your IRA.

IRA Risks If you take money out of an IRA prematurely, you'll probably get hit with a 10-percent penalty. This provision poses a financial risk, especially to people who haven't determined whether they can afford an IRA investment in the first place. If, for example, you underestimate your future cash requirements, you may have to withdraw money before you reach 59 1/2. You can, however, make penalty-free withdrawals under certain circumstances: buying a first home, paying college expenses, and paying large medical bills.

The unpredictability of future income-tax rates also poses a financial risk. If tax rates increase substantially, future IRA withdrawals may be taxed at higher rates—perhaps high enough to offset the amount of your original tax savings.

Roth IRA Versus Traditional IRA The **Roth IRA** is the reverse of the traditional IRA in three respects:

> **ROTH IRA** provision allowing individual retirement savings with tax-free accumulated earnings

1 Your initial Roth contribution is not tax deductible.

2 You can withdraw any amount of your initial contribution at any time without penalty.

3 When you withdraw them after the age of 59 1/2 you don't have to pay taxes on accumulated earnings.

This last feature gives long-term participants a significant advantage because accumulated earnings typically far outweigh the initial contribution. Look, for example, at Figure AIII.13. Although you pay an extra $1,285 in front-end taxes, you get $40,732 additional cash at retirement—and even more if income-tax rates have increased.

Figure AIII.13 Cash Flows: Roth IRA Versus Traditional IRA

Assumptions:
Initial contribution and earnings average 10-percent growth annually.
Initial contribution and earnings remain invested for 40 years.
Income tax rate is 30 percent.

	Traditional IRA	Roth IRA
Initial cash contribution to IRA	$3,000	$3,000
Income tax paid initially: $4,285 income X 30% tax rate = $1,285 tax	0	1,285
Total initial cash outlay	**$3,000**	**$4,285**
Accumulated earnings (40 years)	$132,774	$132,774
Initial contribution	+ 3,000	+ 3,000
Total available for distribution after 40 years	= $135,774	= $135,774
Income tax at time of distribution	− $40,732	0
After-tax distribution (cash)	**= $95,042**	**= $135,774**

IRAs and Education Depending on your income level, you can contribute up to $2,000 per year to a Coverdell Education Savings Account (also known as an *Education IRA*) for each child under age 18. As with the Roth IRA, your initial contribution is not tax deductible, your earnings are tax-free, and you pay no tax on withdrawals to pay for qualified education expenses. Unlike the Roth IRA, the Education IRA requires that you use the money by the time your child reaches age 30. Funds that you withdraw but don't use for stipulated education expense are subject to taxation plus a 10-percent penalty.

PROTECTING YOUR NET WORTH

With careful attention, thoughtful saving and spending, and skillful financial planning (and a little luck), you can build up your net worth over time. In addition to steps for accumulating net worth, every financial plan should consider steps for preserving it. One approach involves the risk-return relationship that we discussed in Chapter 16. Do you prefer to protect your current assets, or are you willing to risk them in return for greater growth? At various life stages, and whenever you reach a designated level of wealth, you should adjust your asset portfolio to conform to your risk and return preferences—conservative, moderate, or aggressive.

Why Buy Life Insurance? You can also think of life insurance as a tool for financial preservation. As explained in Appendix I, a life insurance policy is a promise to pay beneficiaries after the death of an insured party. In return, insurance companies collect *premiums*—payments from the insurance purchaser—during his or her lifetime.

What Does Life Insurance Do? From a personal-finance perspective, the purpose of life insurance is to replace income on which someone else is dependent, upon the death of the policyholder. Accordingly, the amount of insurance you need depends on how many other people rely on your income. Insurance, for example, makes sense for the married parent who is a family's sole source of income. On the other hand, a single person with no financial dependents, including unmarried college students, needs little or no insurance and will probably prefer to put their money to other uses until the need for insurance coverage arises.

How Much Should I Buy? The more insurance you buy, the more it's going to cost you. To estimate the amount of coverage you need, begin by adding up all of your annual expenses—rent, food, clothing, transportation, schooling, debts to be paid—that you pay for the dependents who'd survive you. Then multiply the total by the number of years that you want the insurance to cover your dependents. Typically, this sum will amount to several times your current annual income. Many policyholders, especially during the life stages of highest need—are insured for 10 to 20 times their annual salaries.

Why Consider Term Insurance? *Term insurance* pays a predetermined benefit when death occurs during the stipulated term—for example, 10, 20, or 30 years—covered by the policy. If the insured outlives the term, the policy loses its value and simply ceases. When it is in force, however, the insured knows that it will provide funds to beneficiaries if he or she dies. Term-life premiums are significantly lower than premiums for whole life insurance.

Unlike term life, *whole-life insurance*—also known as *cash-value insurance*—remains in force as long as premiums are paid. In addition to paying a death benefit, whole life accumulates cash value over time—a form of savings. Once the insured reaches a point at which he or she no longer needs the coverage, paid-in money can be withdrawn. Whole-life savings, however, earn less interest than most alternative forms of investment.

How Much Does It Cost? The cost of insurance depends on how much you buy. But it also depends on your life expectancy and other risk factors that insurers determine statistically. Premiums are higher for people whose life expectancies are shorter, whether because of gender, age, weight, occupation, or preexisting health conditions.

The lower cost of term insurance is an important consideration, not just for people on limited incomes, but also for those seeking higher returns from other types of investment. A healthy 30-year-old, nonsmoking female, for example, can expect to pay about $360 a year for a $300,000 term policy and about $600 to $700 a year for a $1 million term policy. Depending on the insurer and the conditions of coverage, whole life may cost the same person up to 10 times as much as term. To get the best match between your policy and your personal situation, therefore, you should evaluate the terms and conditions of a variety of policies. You can get convenient comparisons on Web sites such as IntelliQuote.com.

Answers to "Practice Paying Off Your Debt"

1 Item (a) is the correct answer, obtained as follows:
   Minimum monthly payment
   (5 percent of previous ending balance)
   April $232.81 = (0.05 × $4,656.13)

2 Item (c) is the correct answer, obtained as follows:
   Interest owed on previous balance
   (1/12 × 0.18 × previous balance):
   April 69.84 = (1/12 × 0.18 × $4,656.13)

3 Item (b) is the correct answer, obtained as follows:

Payment on principal (monthly payment − monthly interest)	Ending balance owed on principal (previous balance − payment on principal)
April $162.97 = ($232.81 − $69.84)	$4,493.16 = ($4,656.13 − $162.97)

ANSWERS TO SELF-CHECK QUESTIONS

CHAPTER 1

1 **(c)** Technological environment (See the section on "The External Environments of Business" on pages 6–8)
2 **(b)** Government regulations and controls (See the section on "Factors of Production" on pages 8–11)
3 **False** (See the section on "Types of Economic Systems" on pages 11–13)
4 **(d)** The law of demand (See the section on "Demand and Supply in a Market Economy" on pages 13–15)
5 **(c)** Shoppers will buy fewer eggs (See the section on "Demand and Supply in a Market Economy" on pages 13–15)
6 **False** (See the section on "Private Enterprise and Competition in a Mixed Economy" on pages 15–18)
7 **(b)** Inflation (See the section on "Economic Indicators" on pages 18–27)
8 **(c)** They mean different things but are usually close in value (See the section on "Economic Growth, Aggregate Output, and Standard of Living" on pages 18–23)
9 **False** (See the section on "Managing the U.S. Economy" on pages 26–27)

CHAPTER 2

1 **(b)** Employee behavior toward the organization (See the section on "Business and Managerial Ethics" on pages 40–41)
2 **(d)** Regulation (See the section on "Assessing Ethical Behavior" on pages 41–43)
3 **False** (See the section on "Company Practices and Business Ethics" on pages 43–46)
4 **True** (See the section on "Social Responsibility" on pages 46–59)
5 **(d)** All of these (See the section on "The Stakeholder Model of Responsibility" on pages 46–49)
6 **(c)** Growing skepticism and concern regarding responsible corporate governance (See the section on "Contemporary Social Consciousness" on pages 50–51)

7 **(a)** Responsibility toward the board of directors (See the section on "Areas of Social Responsibility" on pages 51–59)
8 **(d)** All of these (See the section on "Approaches to Social Responsibility" on pages 60–61)
9 **False** (See the section on "Social Responsibility and the Small Business" on pages 62–63)

CHAPTER 3

1 **(d)** One that is independently owned and managed and does not dominate its market (See the section on "What Is a "Small" Business?" on pages 74–78)
2 **(b)** Manufacturing (See the section on "Popular Areas of Small Business Enterprise" on pages 76–78)
3 **False** (See the section on "Entrepreneurial Characteristics" on pages 79–80)
4 **False** (See the section on "Crafting a Business Plan" on pages 80–81)
5 **(d)** Personal resources (See the section on "Financing the Small Business" on pages 83–84)
6 **(c)** Employee theft or sabotage (See the section on "Reasons for Failure" on page 87)
7 **(d)** All of the above (See the section on "Sole Proprietorships" on pages 90)
8 **True** (See the section on "Partnerships" on pages 90–91)
9 **(a)** All of the above are corporations (See the section on "Types of Corporations" on pages 93–94)

CHAPTER 4

1 **False** (See the section on "Import–Export Balances" on pages 115–119)
2 **True** (See the section on "Import–Export Balances" on pages 115–119)
3 **(b)** A country can produce something that is cheaper and/or of higher quality than any other country (See the section on "Forms of Competitive Advantage" on pages 120–121)

4 False (See the section on "Levels of International Involvement" on pages 124–125)

5 True (See the section on "Levels of International Involvement" on pages 124–125)

6 (a) Foreign direct investment (See the section on "International Organizational Structures" on pages 125–126)

7 (d) Transportation differences (See the section on "Barriers to International Trade" on pages 127–130)

8 (b) Exchange rate parameters (See the section on "Legal and Political Differences" on pages 128–130)

9 False (See the section on "The Protectionism Debate" on pages 129–130)

CHAPTER 5

1 False (See the section on "The Management Process" on pages 144–147)

2 True (See the section on "Levels of Management" on pages 147–148)

3 (b) Operations (See the section on "Areas of Management" on pages 148–149)

4 (c) Conceptual skills (See the section on "Basic Management Skills" on pages 150–153)

5 (b) Global and technology (See the section on "Management Skills for the Twenty-First Century" on pages 152–153)

6 False (See the section on "Basic Management Skills" on pages 150–153)

7 (a) Goals show the government what the firm hopes to achieve (See the section on "Setting Business Goals" on pages 155–156)

8 (d) Deciding which division to sell if a firm runs short of cash (See the section on "Contingency Planning and Crisis Management" on pages 159–161)

9 True (See the section on "Kinds of Goals" on pages 155–156)

CHAPTER 6

1 False (See the section on "What is Organizational Structure?" on pages 174–175)

2 (c) Assembly line worker (See the section on "The Building Blocks of Organizational Structure" on pages 176–177)

3 (a) Sequence (See the section on "Departmentalization" on pages 177–179)

4 (c) Narrow (See the section on "Distributing Authority: Centralization and Decentralization" on pages 180–183)

5 (d) All of these are part of the delegation process (See the section on "The Delegation Process" on page 183)

6 True (See the section on "Three Forms of Authority" on pages 183–185)

7 (b) Process structure (See the section on "Basic Forms of Organizational Structure" on pages 185–192)

8 True (See the section on "Organizational Design for the Twenty-First Century" on pages 191–192)

9 False (See the section on "Informal Organization" on pages 192–193)

CHAPTER 7

1 False (See the section on "What Does *Operations* Mean Today?" on pages 204–205)

2 (d) Foot surgery is a good example of a low-contact operation. (See the section on "Operations Processes" on pages 207–208)

3 (a) Many services cannot be produced ahead of time and then stored. (See the section on "Creating Value Through Operations" on pages 205–208)

4 True (See the section on "Business Strategy as the Driver of Operations" on pages 209–211)

5 (a) An assembly line is a good example of a product layout. (See the section on "Layout Planning" on pages 213–214)

6 (b) Methods improvements are possible in goods-producing operations but are usually impossible in service operations. (See the section on "Operations Planning" on pages 211–216)

7 (c) JIT creates smooth materials movements by adding more storage space for inventories. (See the section on "Materials Management" on pages 219–220)

8 (b) In controlling for quality, managers should establish specific standards and measurements. (See the section on "Quality Improvement and Total Quality Management" on pages 221–224)

9 (b) A company using a supply chain strategy always focuses on the next stage (either incoming or outgoing) in the chain. (See the section on "Adding Value Through Supply Chains" on pages 224–225)

CHAPTER 8

1 (c) Agreeableness (See the section on "Personality at Work" on pages 240–242)

2 True (See the section on "Psychological Contracts" on pages 243–244)

3 **True** (See the section on "The Person-Job Fit" on page 244)

4 **(d)** All are popular motivational theories (See the section on "Basic Motivation Concepts and Theories" on pages 245–248)

5 **False** (See the section on "Maslow's Hierarchy of Needs Model" on pages 247–248)

6 **(b)** Esteem needs (See the section on "Maslow's Hierarchy of Needs Model" on pages 247)

7 **True** (See the section on "Reinforcement/Behavior Modification" on pages 251–252)

8 **True** (See the section on "Using Goals to Motivate Behavior" on pages 252–253)

9 **(d)** These are all examples of modified work schedules (See the section on "Modified Work Schedules" on pages 255–257)

CHAPTER 9

1 **False** (See the section on "The Nature of Leadership" on pages 266–267)

2 **(d)** All of the above (See the section on "Trait Approaches to Leadership" on pages 268–269)

3 **(c)** Effective leadership depends on the situation (See the section on "The Situational Approach to Leadership" on pages 270–271)

4 **(b)** During a period of change (See the section on "Transformational Leadership" on pages 271–272)

5 **True** (See the section on "Charismatic Leadership" on pages 272–273)

6 **(c)** Can replace a real leader in certain situations (See the section on "Leadership Substitutes" on page 274)

7 **(d)** All of the above (See the section on "Emerging Issues in Leadership" on pages 277–280)

8 **(d)** None of the above (See the section on "Rational Decision Making" on pages 280–284)

9 **True** (See the section on "Behavioral Aspects of Decision Making" on pages 283–284)

CHAPTER 10

1 **False** (See the section on "Job Analysis" on page 295)

2 **False** (See the section on "Forecasting HR Demand and Supply" on page 296)

3 **(c)** Polygraph exam (See the section on "Selecting Human Resources" on pages 298–300)

4 **(d)** All of these (See the section on "Training" on pages 300–301)

5 **(a)** Individual incentive (See the section on "Incentive Programs" on pages 302–304)

6 **True** (See the section on "Equal Employment Opportunity" on page 305)

7 **(b)** It is increasing (See the section on "Managing Workforce Diversity" on pages 308–309)

8 **True** (See the section on "Trends in Contingent and Temporary Employment" on pages 311)

9 **(d)** Generally, it has steadily declined (See the section on "Unionism Today" on pages 312–313)

CHAPTER 11

1 **(c)** It cannot be measured (See the section on "Providing Value and Satisfaction" on pages 328–329)

2 **(d)** Potential (See the section on "Strategy: The Marketing Mix" on pages 333–334)

3 **True** (See the section on "Goods, Services, and Ideas" on pages 329–334)

4 **True** (See the section on "Target Marketing and Market Segmentation" on pages 335–336)

5 **(a)** Substitution purchase (See the section on "The Consumer Buying Process" on pages 338–339)

6 **True** (See the section on "Organizational Markets" on page 339)

7 **(d)** All of the above (See the section on "The Value Package" on page 341)

8 **True** (See the section on "The Product Mix" on page 343)

9 **(b)** An ad campaign that is good in domestic markets will also be good in international markets. (See the section on "The International Marketing Mix" on pages 348–349)

CHAPTER 12

1 **(d)** Penetration pricing (See the section on "Pricing Strategies" on page 368)

2 **False** (See the section on "Pricing Strategies" on page 368)

3 **False** (See the section on "Pricing Tactics" on page 369)

4 **False** (See the section on "The Distribution Mix" on pages 370–372)

5 **(b)** Intermediaries are retailers who move goods or information to customers (See the section on "Intermediaries and Distribution Channels" on pages 370–372)

6 **(c)** Mail-order retailers offer deep price discounts (See the section on "Retailing" on pages 372–374)

7 (a) The ultimate objective of any promotion is to establish an easily identifiable product image (See the section on "Promotional Objectives" on page 380)

8 (a) TV is the most-used media and reaches the most people (See the section on "Advertising Promotions" on pages 381–383)

9 (d) Creative selling (See the section on "Personal Selling" on pages 383–384)

CHAPTER 13

1 (c) BlackBerry's mobile messaging capabilities save time and travel expenses but they prevent a geographic separation between the workplace and headquarters (See the section on "IT Impacts" on pages 398–403)

2 True (See the section on "IT Impacts" on pages 398–403)

3 (a) Due to time limitations for completing Lockheed Martin's airplane project, global Web collaboration cannot be used for designing and testing the aircraft (See the section on "IT Impacts" on pages 398–403)

4 False (See the section on "The Internet and Other Communication Resources" on pages 404–408)

5 (c) The BlackBerry system has devices that send and receive transmissions on WWANs (See the section on "Networks: System Architecture" on pages 405–407)

6 True (See the section on "Types of Information Systems" on pages 411–413)

7 (d) All of the above are true (See the section on "IT Risks and Threats" on pages 414–416)

8 (b) Identity theft can be reduced by carefully disposing of documents and electronic records containing personal information (See the section on "IT Protection Measures" on pages 416–418)

9 True (See the section on "IT Protection Measures" on pages 416–418)

CHAPTER 14

1 (d) A Bachelor's degree in accounting is a minimum requirement for the CFE designation. (See the sections on "What Is Accounting and Who Uses Accounting Information?" and "Who Are Accountants and What Do They Do?" on pages 429–434)

2 False (See the section on "Certified Public Accountants" on pages 429–431)

3 (a) Upon completion of an audit, auditors are required to destroy audit working papers to preserve the privacy of the client company's information. (See the section on "Federal Restrictions on CPA Services and Financial Reporting: Sarbox" on pages 433–434)

4 (d) An accounting error has occurred (See the sections on "The Accounting Equation" on page 435)

5 True (See the section on "Financial Statements" on pages 436–438)

6 (b) The accounting practice called full disclosure means that the company's financial statements must be released for distribution to the public, including all of the firm's stakeholders. (See the sections on "Financial Statements" and "Reporting Standards and Practices" on pages 436–443)

7 (d) The SEC requires that three kinds of ratios—solvency, profitability, and activity ratios—be published in the financial statements of firms whose stock is publicly traded. (See the section on "Analyzing Financial Statements" on pages 443–446)

8 True (See the section on "Financial Statements" on pages 443–446)

9 (a) The code of professional conduct for public accountants in the U.S. is maintained and enforced by the SEC. (See the section on "Bringing Ethics into the Accounting Equation" on pages 446–448)

CHAPTER 15

1 (b) durability (See the section on "The Characteristics of Money" on page 463)

2 True (See the section on "The Functions of Money" on pages 463–464)

3 (a) Credit cards ("plastic money") are included in M-2 but not in M-1. (See the sections on M-1, M-2, and M-3 on pages 464–466)

4 (d) bank trust services (See the section on "Special Financial Services" on pages 469–471)

5 True (See the section on "Financial Institutions" on pages 467–469)

6 (a) $643.12 (See the section on "Financial Institutions as Creators of Money" on pages 471–472)

7 (c) decrease the discount rate (See the section on "The Tools of the Fed" on pages 476–477)

8 (b) e-cash (See the section on "The Impact of Electronic Technologies" on pages 479–480)

9 False (See the section on "International Banking and Finance" on pages 480–482)

CHAPTER 16

1 (d) Shares of preferred stock have priority over common shares for dividend distributions (See the section on "Stocks" on pages 493–500)

2 False (See the section on "Stocks" on pages 493–500)

3 (c) The number of shares traded on the floor of the Nasdaq Stock Market is greater than at the NYSE (See the section on "Stocks" on pages 493–500)

4 (b) Corporate bonds issued by U.S. companies involve less money than U.S. government and municipal bonds (See the section on "Bonds" on pages 501–503)

5 True (See the section on "Bonds" on pages 501–503)

6 (d) Aggressive growth fund (See the section on "Mutual Funds" on pages 503–504)

7 (c) A stock's high and low prices for any given day are reported (See the section on "Buying and Selling Securities" on pages 506–512)

8 False (See the section on "Buying and Selling Securities" on pages 506–512)

9 True (See the section on "The Securities and Exchange Commission" on pages 513–514)

NOTES, SOURCES, AND CREDITS

REFERENCE NOTES

CHAPTER 1

[1] See Paul Heyne, Peter J. Boetke, and David L. Prychitko, *The Economic Way of Thinking*, 10th ed. (Upper Saddle River, NJ: Prentice Hall, 2003), 171–176.

[2] See Karl E. Case and Ray C. Fair, *Principles of Economics*, 6th ed., updated (Upper Saddle River, NJ: Prentice Hall, 2003), 103–105.

[3] See Henry R. Cheeseman, *Business Law: Legal, E-Commerce, Ethical, and International Environments*, 5th ed. (Upper Saddle River, NJ: Prentice Hall, 2004), 920–923, 928–930.

[4] Case and Fair, *Principles of Economics*, 432–433.

[5] See Olivier Blanchard, *Macroeconomics*, 3rd ed. (Upper Saddle River, NJ: Prentice Hall, 2003), 24–26.

[6] See Jay Heizer and Barry Render, *Operations Management*, 7th ed. (Upper Saddle River, NJ: Prentice Hall, 2004), 14.

[7] This section is based on Paul Heyne, Peter J. Boettke, and David L. Prychitko, *The Economic Way of Thinking*, 10th ed. (Upper Saddle River, NJ: Prentice Hall, 2003), 491–493.

[8] See Warren J. Keegan, *Global Market Management*, 7th ed. (Upper Saddle River, NJ: Prentice Hall, 2002), 39–42.

[9] This section follows Ronald M. Ayers and Robert A. Collinge, *Economics: Explore and Apply*, (Upper Saddle River, NJ: Prentice Hall, 2004), 163–167.

[10] See Heyne, Boettke, and Prychitko, *The Economic Way of Thinking*, 403–409, 503–504.

[11] See "The New Fed," *Business Week*, November 7, 2005, pp. 30–34.

CHAPTER 2

[1] William G. Symonds with Geri Smith, "The Tax Games Tyco Played," *Business Week*, July 1, 2002, 40–41.

[2] "Tyco Votes to Stay Offshore," *Business Week*, March 6, 2003.

[3] This section follows the logic of Gerald F. Cavanaugh, *American Business Values with International Perspectives*, 4th ed. (Upper Saddle River, NJ: Prentice Hall, 1998), Chapter 3.

[4] See Manuel G. Velasquez, *Business Ethics: Concepts and Cases*, 5th ed. (Upper Saddle River, NJ: Prentice Hall, 2002), Chapter 2. See also John R. Boatright, *Ethics and the Conduct of Business*, 4th ed. (Upper Saddle River, NJ: Prentice Hall, 2003), 34–35, 57–59.

[5] "Camera Phones Don't Click at Work," *USA Today*, January 12, 2005, 1B.

[6] "Ethics Training as Taught by Ex Cons: Crime Doesn't Pay," *USA Today*, November 16, 2005, 1B, 2B.

[7] Jeffrey S. Harrison and R. Edward Freeman, "Stakeholders, Social Responsibility, and Performance: Empirical Evidence and Theoretical Perspectives," *Academy of Management Journal*, 1999, vol. 42, no. 5, 479–485. See also David P. Baron, *Business and Its Environment*, 4th ed. (Upper Saddle River, NJ: Prentice Hall, 2003), Chapter 18.

[8] Geoff Colvin, "The 100 Best Companies to Work For 2006," *Fortune*, January 23, 2006, 71–131.

[9] Charles Haddad, "Woe Is WorldCom," *Business Week*, May 6, 2002, 86–90; "Former WorldCom CEO Ebbers Indicted," *USA Today*, March 3, 2004, 1B, 2B; "Ex WorldCom CEO Ebbers Found Guilty," money.cnn.com, March 15, 2005.

[10] http://target.com/target_group/community_giving/index.jhtml, Accessed January 15, 2006.

[11] "As Exxon Pursues African Oil, Charity Becomes Political Issue," *Wall Street Journal*, January 10, 2006, A1, A10.

[12] "Can This Man Save the American Auto Industry?" *Time*, January 30, 2006, 38–48.

[13] William G. Symonds with Geri Smith, "The Tax Games Tyco Played," *Business Week*, July 1, 2002, 40–41. "Tyco Titan Charged with Tax Violations," CBSNews.com (June 4, 2002), at www.cbsnew.com/stories/2002/06/04/national/main511051.shtm; Nicholas Varchaver, "CEOs Under Fire," Fortune.com (December 6, 2002), at www.fortune.com/fortune/ceo/articles/0,15114,442883,00.html; "Kozlowski Gets up to 25 Years," money.cnn.com, September 19, 2005.

[14] Gerald Seib, "What Could Bring 1930s-Style Reform of U.S. Business?" *Wall Street Journal*, July 24, 2002, A1, A8.

[15] "U.S. Suit Alleges Philip Morris Hid Cigarette-Fire, Risk," *Wall Street Journal*, April 23, 2004, A1, A8.

[16] "Price-Fixing Investigations Sweep Chemical Industry," *Wall Street Journal*, June 22, 2004, A1, A6.

[17] "Why Kraft Decided to Ban Some Food Ads to Children," *Wall Street Journal*, October 31, 2005, A1, A13.

[18] Greg Farrell, "Enron Law Firm Called Accounting Practices Creative," *USA Today*, January 2002, 1B.

[19] See Jerald Greenberg and Robert A. Baron, *Behavior in Organizations: Understanding and Managing the Human Side of Work*, 8th ed. (Upper Saddle River, NJ: Prentice Hall, 2003), 410–413.

[20] Cora Daniels, "It's a Living Hell," *Fortune*, April 15, 2002, 367–368.

[21] See Henry R. Cheeseman, *Business Law: Legal, E-Commerce, Ethical, and International Environments*, 5th ed. (Upper Saddle River, NJ: Prentice Hall, 2004), 128–129.

[22] See Michael E. Porter and Mark R. Kramer, "Philanthropy's New Agenda: Doing Well by Doing Good," *Sloan Management Review*, Winter 2000, 7585.

CHAPTER 3

[1] See www.sba.gov.

[2] See www.sba.gov/aboutsba.

[3] Statistical Abstracts of the United States, www.census.gov.csd/mwb.

[4] "A New Generation Re-Writes the Rules," *Wall Street Journal*, May 22, 2002, R4; See also, "Up to the Challenge," *Entrepreneur*, February 2006, 64–67.

[5] Nicholas Stein, "The Renaissance Man of E-Commerce," *Fortune*, February 7, 2000, 181–182.

[6] See Thomas Zimmerer and Norman Scarborough, *Essentials of Entrepreneurship and Small Business*, 4th ed. (Upper Saddle River, NJ: Prentice Hall, 2005).

[7] Ibid.

[8] "In the Know," *Entrepreneur*, January 2006, 90.

[9] "The New Entrepreneurs: Americans Over 50," *USA Today*, January 18, 2005, 1A, 2A.

[10] Statistical Abstracts of the United States, www.census.gov/csd/mwb.

[11] Ibid.

[12] Zimmerer and Scarborough.

[13] See "Keep it Simple," *Entrepreneur*, February 2006, 60–63.

[14] Statistical Abstracts of the United States, www.census.gov/csd/mwb.

[15] Ibid.

[16] Ibid.

[17] "A Little Privacy, Please," *Business Week*, May 24, 2004, 74–75.

[18] "How to Fix Corporate Governance," *Business Week*, May 6, 2002, 68–78.

[19] Matthew Boyle, "The Dirty Half-Dozen: America's Worst Boards, *Fortune*, May 14, 2001, 249–252.

[20] National Center for Employee Ownership, www.nceo.org.

CHAPTER 4

[1] The U.S. Bureau of Economic Analysis, www.bea.gov.
[2] Ricky W. Griffin and Michael W. Pustay, *International Business: A Managerial Perspective*, 5th ed. (Upper Saddle River, NJ: Prentice Hall, 2007).
[3] See Thomas Friedman, *The World Is Flat* (New York: Farrar, Straus, and Giroux, 2005).
[4] Association of Southeast Asian Nations, accessed January 15, 2005, www.aseansec.org/74.htm.
[5] CIA World Fact Book, www.cia.gov.
[6] Bureau of Economic Analysis, www.bea.gov.
[7] See Griffin and Pustay, *International Business: A Managerial Perspective*, 125–127. See also Steven Husted and Michael Melvin, *International Economics*, 5th ed. (Boston: Addison Wesley Longman, 2001), 54–61; and Karl E. Case and Ray C. Fair, *Principles of Economics*, 6th ed. (Upper Saddle River, NJ: Prentice Hall, 2002), 669–677.
[8] This section is based on Michael Porter, *The Competitive Advantage of Nations* (Boston: Addison Wesley Longman, 2001), 54–61; and Case and Fair, *Principles of Economics*, 669–677.
[9] See Lee J. Krajewski and Larry P. Ritzman, *Operations Management: Strategy and Analysis*, 7th ed. (Upper Saddle River, NJ: Prentice Hall, 2005), 109–112.
[10] *Hoover's Handbook of American Business 2006* (Austin, Texas: Hoover's Business Press, 2006), 432–433.
[11] "Fortune Global 500," *Fortune*, July 25, 2005, 119–126.
[12] Bureau of Economic Analysis, "Foreign Direct Investment in the U.S.," July 11, 2001, www.bea.doc.gov/bea/di/di1fdibal.ntm; Progressive Policy Institute, "Foreign Direct Investment Is on the Rise Around the World," July 11, 2001, www.neweconomyindex.org/section1.

CHAPTER 5

[1] Stanley Reed, "Can Scardino Get Pearson Out of This Pickle?" *Business Week*, July 22, 2002, 5052; "The 50 Most Powerful Women in Business," *Fortune*, November 14, 2005.
[2] "Amex's Ken Chenault Talks About Leadership and Integrity," *Leadership and Change*, April 25, 2005.
[3] See Katrina Brooker, "The Pepsi Machine," *Fortune*, February 6, 2006, 68–72.
[4] *Hoover's Handbook of American Business 2006* (Austin, Texas: Hoover's Business Press, 2006).
[5] Ibid.
[6] "At Wal-Mart, Emergence Plan Has Big Payoff," *Wall Street Journal*, September 12, 2005, B1, B3.
[7] "Next Time," *USA Today*, October 4, 2005, 1B, 2B.

CHAPTER 6

[1] Joann S. Lublin, "Place vs. Product: It's Tough to Choose a Management Model," *Wall Street Journal*, June 27, 2001, A1, A4; Joann Muller, "Ford: Why It's Worse Than You Think," *Business Week*, June 25, 2001, 80–841;

"Can This Man Save the American Auto Industry?" *Time*, January 30, 2006, pp. 38–48.
[2] See Amy Wrzesniewski and Jane Dutton, "Crafting a Job: Revisioning Employees as Active Crafters of Their Work," *Academy of Management Review*, 2001, vol. 26, no. 2, 179–201.
[3] Michael E. Raynor and Joseph L. Bower, "Lead From the Center," *Harvard Business Review*, May 2001, 93–102.
[4] "Multi-Tasking: Cost-Reduction Strategy at Case Corp.," Machinery Systems, Inc. (July 20, 2001), at www.machinerysystems.com/RavingFan/CaseCorp.html.
[5] "Wal-Mart Acquires Interspar," Management Ventures (July 20, 2001), at www.mventures.com/news/Key1998/flash98/wmtinters.asp; Kerry Capell et al., "Wal-Mart's Not-So-Secret British Weapon," *Business Week Online* (July 20, 2001), at www.businessweek.com:/2000/00_04/b3665095.htm. Brent Schlender, "Wal-Mart's $288 Billion Meeting," *Fortune*, April 18, 2005, 90–106.
[6] Thomas A. Stewart, "See Jack. See Jack Run," *Fortune*, September 27, 1999, 124–271; Jerry Useem, "America's Most Admired Companies," *Fortune*, March 7, 2005, 67–82.
[7] Leslie P. Willcocks and Robert Plant, "Getting from Bricks to Clicks," *Sloan Management Review*, Spring 2001, 50–60.
[8] "The Office Chart That Really Counts," *Business Week*, February 27, 2006, 48–49.
[9] Carol Loomis, "How the HP Board KO'd Carly," *Fortune*, March 7, 2005, 99–102.

CHAPTER 7

[1] *Our Time: GE Annual Report: 2004* (Fairfield, CT: General Electric Co., 2005), 4–5.
[2] See Terry Hill, *Manufacturing Strategy*, 3rd edition (Boston: Irwin McGraw-Hill, 2000), Chapters 2–4; James A. Fitzsimmons and Mona J. Fitzsimmons, *Service Management*, 4th edition (Boston: Irwin McGraw-Hill, 2004), 46–48.
[3] "Owens Corning Invests in Capacity Expansions," *Toledo Business Journal*, February 1, 2004, 25; "Owens Corning Announces Multi-Million Dollar Investment to Increase Loosefill Insulation Capacity and Meet Demand for More Energy-Efficient Homes," Press Release, January 4, 2006, at http://pressroom.owenscorning.com.
[4] Mark Lander, "Slovakia No Longer a Laggard in Automaking," *nytimes.com* (April 13, 2004), www.nytimes.com/2004/04/13/business/worldbusiness.
[5] "ASQ Glossary of Terms," American Society for Quality (January 17, 2006), www.asq.org/glossary/q.html.
[6] "Savoring Fine Chocolates," January 20, 2006 at www.godiva.com.
[7] Del Jones, "Baldrige Award Honors Record 7 Quality Winners," *USA Today*, November 26, 2003, 6B.
[8] *Tootsie Roll Industries Inc. Annual Report 2003* (Chicago: 2004), 1.
[9] Del Jones, "Baldrige Award Honors Record 7 Quality Winners," *USA Today*, November 26, 2003, 6B.

[10] Dave DeWitte, "Korean-Made Washers, Dryers to Be Sold in U.S. Under Maytag Name," *Knight Ridder Tribune Business News*, February 25, 2004, 1; Nigel F. Maynard, "Made in the USA—For Now," *Builder*, July 2005, 154; "Industrial Brief—Maytag Corp.: More Production Outsourcing is Planned in Bid to Cut Costs," *Wall Street Journal*, March 8, 2005, 1.

CHAPTER 8

[1] Mark Bolino and William Turnley, "Going the Extra Mile: Cultivating and Managing Employee Citizenship Behavior," *Academy of Management Executive*, 2003, vol. 17, no. 3, 60–70.
[2] See Carl Thoresen, Jill Bradly, Paul Bliese, and Joseph Thoresen, "The Big Five Personality Traits and Individual Job Performance," *Journal of Applied Psychology*, 2004, vol. 89, no. 5, 835–853.
[3] See Daniel Goleman, *Emotional Intelligence: Why it Can Matter More Than IQ* (New York: Bantam Books, 1995); see also Kenneth Law, Chi-Sum Wong, and Lynda Song, "The Construct and Criterion Validity of Emotional Intelligence and Its Potential Utility for Management Studies," *Journal of Applied Psychology*, 2004, vol 89, no. 3, 483–596.
[4] Daniel Goleman, "Leadership That Gets Results," *Harvard Business Review*, March–April 2000, 78–90.
[5] See Ricky W. Griffin and Gregory Moorhead, *Organizational Behavior*, 8th ed. (Houghton Mifflin Company: Boston), 2007.
[6] See Daniel Wren, *The History of Management Thought*, 5th ed. (John Wiley & Sons: New York), 2004.
[7] Ibid.
[8] Lyman Porter, Gregory Bigley, and Richard Steers, *Motivation and Work Behavior*, 7th ed. (New York: McGraw-Hill), 2003.
[9] Gary P. Latham, "The Importance of Understanding and Changing Employee Outcome Expectancies for Gaining Commitment to an Organizational Goal," *Personnel Psychology*, 2001, vol. 54, 707–720.
[10] Russ Forrester, "Empowerment: Rejuvenating a Potent Idea," *Academy of Management Executive*, 2002, vol. 14, no. 1, 67–78.
[11] Ricky W. Griffin and Gary C. McMahan, "Motivation Through Job Design," in Jerald Greenberg (ed.), *Organizational Behavior: State of the Science* (New York: Lawrence Erlbaum and Associates, 1994), 23–44
[12] "Working 9-to-5 No Longer," *USA Today*, December 6, 2004, 1B, 2B.

CHAPTER 9

[1] See John Kotter, "What Leaders Really Do," *Harvard Business Review*, December 2001, 85–94.
[2] Ronald Heifetz and Marty Linsky, "A Survival Guide for Leaders," *Harvard Business Review*, June 2002, 65–74.
[3] Frederick Reichheld, "Lead for Loyalty," *Harvard Business Review*, July–August 2001, 76–83.
[4] "Play Hard, Fly Right," *Time, Bonus Section: Inside Business*, June 2002, Y15–Y22.

5 David A. Waldman and Francis J. Yammarino, "CEO Charismatic Leadership: Levels-of-Management and Levels-of-Analysis Effects," *Academy of Management Review*, 1999, vol. 24, no. 2, 266–285.

6 Jane Howell and Boas Shamir, "The Role of Followers in the Charismatic Leadership Process: Relationships and Their Consequences," *Academy of Management Review*, January 2005, 96–112.

7 J. Richard Hackman and Ruth Wageman, "A Theory of Team Coaching," *Academy of Management Review*, April 2005, 269–287.

8 "How Women Lead," *Newsweek*, October 24, 2005, 46–70.

9 "The Best (& Worst) Managers of the Year," *Business Week*, January 10, 2005, 55.

10 Jerry Useem, "Boeing vs. Boeing," *Fortune*, October 2, 2000, 148–160; "Airbus Prepares to 'Bet the Company' As It Builds a Huge New Jet," *Wall Street Journal*, November 3, 1999, A1, A10.

11 "Accommodating the A380," *Wall Street Journal*, November 29, 2005, B1; "Boeing Roars Ahead," *Business Week*, November 7, 2005, 44–45; "Boeing's New Tailwind," *Newsweek*, December 5, 2005, 45.

12 "The Wisdom of Solomon," *Newsweek*, August 17, 1987, 62–63.

13 "Making Decisions in Real Time," *Fortune*, June 26, 2000, 332–334; see also Malcolm Gladwell, *Blink* (New York: Little, Brown, 2005).

14 Charles P. Wallace, "Adidas—Back in the Game," *Fortune*, August 18, 1997, 176–182.

15 Barry M. Staw and Jerry Ross, "Good Money After Bad," *Psychology Today*, February 1988, 30–33; D. Ramona Bobocel and John Meyer, "Escalating Commitment to a Failing Course of Action: Separating the Roles of Choice and Justification," *Journal of Applied Psychology*, vol. 79, 1994, 360–363.

16 Gerry McNamara and Philip Bromiley, "Risk and Return in Organizational Decision Making," *Academy of Management Journal*, vol. 42, 1999, 330–339.

17 See Brian O'Reilly, "What It Takes to Start a Startup," *Fortune*, June 7, 1999, 135–140, for an example.

CHAPTER 10

1 See Luis R. Gómez-Mejía, David B. Balkin, and Robert L. Cardy, *Managing Human Resources*, 4th ed. (Upper Saddle River, NJ: Prentice Hall, 2004), 3–10; see also Angelo DeNisi and Ricky Griffin, *Human Resource Management*, 3rd ed. (Boston: Houghton Mifflin, 2007).

2 See Lathryn Tyler, "Taking E-Learning to the Next Level," *HRMagazine*, February 2005, 56–61.

3 *Hoover's Handbook of Private Companies 2006* (Austin, Texas: Hoover's Business Press, 2006).

4 "Some Employers Offer ID Theft Coverage," *USA Today*, September 12, 2005, 1B.

5 "IBM To Freeze Pension Program," *USA Today*, January 6–8, 2006, p. 1A.

6 See Henry R. Cheeseman, *Business Law: Ethical, International, and E-Commerce Environment*, 5th ed. (Upper Saddle River, NJ: Prentice Hall, 2004), Chapter 41.

7 See Gary Dessler, *Human Resource Management*, 9th ed. (Upper Saddle River, NJ: Prentice Hall, 2003), 31–32.

8 See Henry R. Cheeseman, *Business Law: Ethical, International, and E-Commerce Environment*, 5th ed. (Upper Saddle River, NJ: Prentice Hall, 2004), 806–810; Gary Dessler, *Human Resource Management*, 9th ed. (Upper Saddle River, NJ: Prentice Hall, 2003), 94–99.

CHAPTER 11

1 American Marketing Association, "Marketing Definitions" (November 4, 2005), at www.marketingpower.com/mg-dictionary.php?SearchFor=marketing&Searched=1.

2 See Philip Kotler, *Marketing Management*, 11th ed. (Upper Saddle River, NJ: Prentice Hall, 2003), 76–78.

3 Poonam Khanna, "Hotel Chain Gets Personal with Customers," *Computing Canada*, April 8, 2005, 18.

4 "Top 100 Consumer Magazines 2004," (November 4, 2005), at www.infoplease.com/ipea/A0301522.html.

5 Cecilie Rohwedder and Daniel Michaels, "U.S. Airport Shops Go High-End; Gucci, Hermes, Cartier Open Stores in Domestic Terminals; Best Deals Past Security Gates." *Wall Street Journal (Eastern edition)*, December 20, 2005, D.1; Teena Lyons, "In with the Old. . . in Fashion," *Knight Ridder Tribune Business News*, November 20, 2005, 1.

6 "Financial Cards in Poland," *Euromonitor International*, May 2004, (November 10, 2005), at www.euromonito.com.

7 U.S. Department of Commerce, *Statistical Abstract of the United States: 2004–2005* (Washington, DC: Bureau of the Census, 2005), Tables No. 649, 422, and 756.

8 Ibid., Table No. 718.

9 Ibid., Table No. 416.

10 "Acesulfame K Wins GP Status," *Food Ingredient News*, January 2004, 1.

11 Tom Bachmann, "Another Year, Already?" *Beverage Industry*, January 2003, 6.

12 "Top 100 Global Brands Scoreboard," *BusinessWeek Online* (November 11, 2005), at http://bwnt.businessweek.com/brand/2005.

13 "Product Placement," *Wikipedia, The Free Encyclopedia*, (January, 27, 2006), at http://en.wikipedia.org/wiki/Product_placement; "What is Product Placement?" *Creative Entertainment Services* (January, 27, 2006), at www.acreativegroup.com/ces; Lorne Manly, "When the Ad Turns into the Story Line," *New York Times*, October 2, 2005, Section 3, 1.

14 Judy Strauss, Adel El-Ansary, and Raymond Frost, *E-Marketing*, 5th ed. (Upper Saddle River, NJ: Prentice Hall, 2007)

15 Clive Young, "Grocery Store Wars' Organic Audio," *Pro Sound News*, August 1, 2005, 45.

CHAPTER 12

1 Judy Strauss, Adel El-Ansary, and Raymond Frost, *E-Marketing*, 3rd ed. (Upper Saddle River, NJ: Prentice Hall, 2003), 320–322.

2 Plunkett Research, Ltd., *Retail Industry Statistics: U.S. Retail Industry Overview (2004)*, (June 23, 2005) at www.plunkettresearch.com/retail.

3 American Teleservices Association (May 4, 2004), at www.ataconnect.org; Direct Selling Association (May 4, 2004), at www.dsa.org.

4 Expedia.com (June 23, 2005), at www.expedia.com.

5 Plunkett Research, Ltd., *Retail Industry Statistics: U.S. Retail Industry Overview (2004)*.

6 William J. Dennis, Jr., ed., *NFIB National Small Business Poll*, vol 1, no. 2 (Washington, DC, 2001); "Small Biz Web Sites on the Rise, Yet Many Owners Slow to Embrace the Internet," *Prodigy.com* (April 19, 2000), at www.prodigy.com/pcom/business/content.

7 "Did You Know?" *Catalog News.com* (April 8, 2002), at www.catalog-news.com; Judy Strauss, Adel El-Ansary, Raymond Frost, *E-Marketing*, 140.

8 R. Craig Endicott, "100 Leading Advertisers," *Advertising Age*, June 27, 2005, S-1.

9 "All U.S. Advertising Spending," *Advertising Age* (June 27, 2005), S21.

10 Paul R. LaMonica, "Super Bowl XL's Extra-Large Ad Sales," *CNNMoney.com*, January 3, 2006.

11 "All U.S. Advertising Spending," *Advertising Age* (June 27, 2005), page S21.

12 Ibid.

13 Ibid.

14 Ibid.

15 Ibid.

16 Ibid.

17 Ibid.

18 Associated Press, *MSNBC NEWS*, "New Arrest in Wendy's Finger Case," May 19, 2005.

19 Ron Insana, *USA Today*, "Wendy's Knew from Start Story Was a Hoax," June 6, 2005, 3B.

CHAPTER 13

1 Mike Lazaridis, "Because Someone Had to Stand Up for All Those Frustrated Engineers," *Inc. Magazine*, April 2005, 98; "BlackBerry Subscribers Surge to over Three Million," May 9, 2005, press release, www.blackberry.com/news/press/2005/pr-09_05_2005–01.shtml.

2 "Northrop Grumman Awards International Contracts for F-35 Joint Strike Fighter," *Northrop Grumman News Release* (September 29, 2005) at www.irconnect.com/noc/pages/news_printer.html?=86963&print=1; Faith Keenan and Spencer E. Ante, "The New Teamwork," *BusinessWeek Online*, February 18, 2002.

3 Emily Walzer, "Have it Your Way," *SGB*, vol. 38, no. 1, January 2005, 42.

4 3D Systems, "3D Systems Helps Walter Reed Army Medical Center Rebuild Lives," (July 6, 2005), at www.3dsystems.com.

5 "Wireless Endoscopy—The Camera in a Pill," (August 17, 2005), at www.gihealth.com; "Expanding the Scope of GI," Given Imaging (July 6, 2005), at www.givenimaging.com.

6 www.internetworldstats.com/stats.htm.

7 "An Intranet's Life Cycle," *morebusiness.com* (November 6, 2005), at www.morebusiness.com/getting_started/website/d928247851.brc;

"Calling All Workers," *CIO Magazine* (December 1, 2001), at www.cio.com/archive/120101/rule_ford.html.

[8] See James A. Senn, *Information Technology: Principles, Practices, Opportunities*, 3rd ed. (Upper Saddle River, NJ: Prentice Hall, 2004), 294–97.

[9] *Wal-Mart 2005 Annual Report*, 9.

[10] Paul S. Foote and Malini Krishnamurthi, "Forecasting Using Data Warehousing Model: Wal-Mart's Experience," *The Journal of Business Forecasting Methods & Systems*, Fall 2001, 13–17.

[11] Jerry Adler, "Buried Treasure," *Newsweek*, June 27, 2005, 44–52; Virtual Surfaces Inc., "Scientific Modeling" (July 6, 2005), at www.virtualsurfaces.com.

[12] Alex Leary, "Wi-Fi Cloaks a New Breed of Intruder," *St. Petersburg Times* (July 4, 2005), at www.sptimes.com/2005/07/04/news_pf.

[13] U.S. Department of Justice, "Hacker Sentenced to Prison for Breaking into Lowe's Companies' Computers with Intent to Steal Credit Card Information," (Charlotte, NC: Department of Justice, Western District of North Carolina), December 15, 2004.

[14] Hiawatha Bray, "Music Industry Aims to Send in Radio Cops," *Boston Globe* (November 15, 2004), at www.boston.com/business/technology/articles/2004/11/15/music_industry_aims_to_send_in_radio_cops?mode=PF; "Bush Creates Intellectual Property Czar," *Patent Baristas* (July 28, 2005), at www.patentbaristas.com/archives/000217.php; Howard Paul, "What You Cannot Protect, You Do Not Own," *Sai Global* (January 29, 2004), at www.sai-global.com/newsroom/tgs/2004–02/digital/digital.htm.

[15] For information on spyware see www.webopedia.com/TERM/S/spyware.html.

[16] www.webopedia.com.

[17] "ISP Wins $1 Billion in Spam Suit," *CNET News.com* (December 19, 2004) at http://news.com.com/2102–1028_3–5497211.html?tag-st.util.print; Mike Wendland, "Innocents Suffer in War on Spam," *Detroit Free Press* (July 11, 2003), at www.freep.com/cgi-bin/forms/printerfriendly.pl.

[18] Brad Carlson, "Organizations Face New Federal Records-Destruction Rule," *The Idaho Business Review*, July 25, 2005, 1.

[19] Jason Stein, "Madison, Wis., Company Offers Software that Protects Clients' Information," *The Wisconsin State Journal Distributed by Knight Ridder/Tribune Business News*, July 20, 2005, 1.

CHAPTER 14

[1] Charles T. Horngren et al., *Accounting*, 6th ed. (Upper Saddle River, NJ: Prentice Hall, 2005), Chapter 1.

[2] See Marshall B. Romney and Paul John Steinbart, *Accounting Information Systems*, 9th ed. (Upper Saddle River, NJ: Prentice Hall, 2003), Chapter 1; and Michael L. Werner and Kumen H. Jones, *Introduction to Accounting: A User Perspective* (Upper Saddle River, NJ: Prentice Hall, 2004), Chapter F-2.

[3] See Anthony A. Atkinson, Robert S. Kaplan, and Mark S. Young, *Management Accounting*, 4th ed. (Upper Saddle River, NJ: Prentice Hall, 2004), Chapter 1.

[4] See Walter T. Harrison and Charles T. Horngren, *Financial Accounting*, 5th ed. (Upper Saddle River, NJ: Prentice Hall, 2004), Chapter 1.

[5] See Alvin A. Arens, Mark S. Beasley, and Randal J. Elder, *Auditing and Assurance Services*, 10th ed. (Upper Saddle River, NJ: Prentice Hall, 2003), Chapter 1.

[6] See Horngren et al., *Accounting*, Chapter 1.

[7] Brian W. Wingard, "Careers & Lifestyles," *Pennsylvania CPA Journal*, Spring 2004, 20.

[8] D. Larry Crumbley, Stanley H. Kratchman, and L. Murphy Smith, "Sherlock Holmes and Forensic Accounting," at http://acct.tamu.edu/kratchman/holmes.htm; D. Larry Crumbley, Lester E. Heitger, and G. Stevenson Smith, *Forensic and Investigative Accounting* (Chicago: CCH Incorporated, 2003), 1–3.

[9] Association of Certified Fraud Examiners, at www.acfe.com/Membership/membership.asp.

[10] Christopher Koch, "The Sarbox Conspiracy," *CIO Magazine* (July 1, 2004), at www.cio.com/archive/070104/sarbox.html; Lincoln Spector, "Anonymizer Tool Invites Whistleblowers," *PCWorld.com* (April 24, 2003), at www.pcworld.com/resource/printable/article/0,aid,110413,00.asp.

[11] Form 10K, *2004 Annual Report*, Google, Inc., March 30, 2005.

[12] "SEC Charges Time Warner with Fraud, Aiding and Abetting Frauds by Others, and Violating a Prior Cease-and-Desist Order; CFO, Controller, and Deputy Controller Charged with Causing Reporting Violations," U.S. Securities and Exchange Commission (Washington, DC), March 21, 2005, at www.sec.gov/news/press/ 2005–38.htm; Alec Klein, "Unconventional Transactions Boosted Sales," *Washingtonpost.com*, July 18, 2002, page A01.

[13] Ricky W. Griffin and Ronald J. Ebert, *Business*, 6th ed. (Upper Saddle River, NJ: Prentice Hall, 2002), 521.

[14] Jennifer MacMillan and Emily Sangster, "Ex-Enron Exec to Speak on CSR," *Queen's Journal* (February 15, 2005), at www.queensjournal.ca.

CHAPTER 15

[1] The Federal Reserve (January 2, 2006), at www.federalreserve.gov/releases/h6/current.

[2] Ibid.

[3] Ibid.

[4] *The Nilson Report*, August 2005, at www.nilsonreport.com; Citigroup, at www.citigroup.com.

[5] Federal Deposit Insurance Corporation, "Statistics at a Glance" (March 31, 2004), at www.fdic.gov/bank/statistical/stats.

[6] *Citigroup 2004 Annual Report* (New York: 2005); "National Information Center," Federal Reserve System (June 30, 2005), at http://132.200.33.161/nicSearch/servlet/NICServlet?GRP=TOPINST&REQ=TOPBHC&MODE=RESULT..

[7] The Federal Reserve (August 22, 2005). At www.federalreserve.gov/releases/h15/data/m/prime.

[8] Federal Deposit Insurance Corporation, "Statistics at a Glance" (March 31, 2004), at www.fdic.gov/bank/Index.

[9] "Credit Union Development," National Credit Union Administration (June 14, 2004), at www.ncua.gov.

[10] U.S. Census Bureau, *2003 Statistical Abstract of the United States* (Washington, DC: 2004), No. 1219, at www.census.gov/prod/2004pubs.

[11] "Electronic Funds Transfer" (January 2, 2006), at http//:fms.treas.gov/eft/index.html.

[12] American Bankers Association, "ATM Fact Sheet," *2003 ABA Issue Summary* (June 14, 2004), at www.aba.com/Press1Room/pr_quickfacts.htm.

[13] "Selected Interest Rates," Federal Reserve Statistical Release (December 27, 2005), at www.federalreserve.gov/releases/h15/current.

[14] "U.S. Authorities Fine Arab Bank," *Al Bawaba*, August 18, 2005, 1; Paul R. Osborne, "BSA/AML Compliance Provides Opportunity to Improve Security and Enhance Customer Experience," *ABA Bank Compliance*, July/August 2005, 4.

[15] Rick Rothacker, "Bank Branches Open in N.C. Wal-Marts," *Knight Ridder Tribune Business News*, May 25, 2005, 1.

[16] Susan Ford, "New 'Check 21' Law to do Away with Float," *Toledo Business Journal*, February 1, 2005, 28; Tara Rice, "Implementing Check 21 Act: Potential Risks Facing Banks," *Chicago Fed Letter*, August 2005, 1; Sharon R. Cole, "Expect Checks to Stick Around," *Business Forms, Labels, & Systems*, August 20, 2005, 28.

[17] Geoffrey R. Gerdes, Jack K. Walton II, May X. Liu, and Darrel W. Parke, "Trends in the Use of Payment Systems in the United States," *Federal Reserve Bulletin*, Spring 2005, 180–201.

[18] Estimated from "Statistics for Smart Cards," *ePaynews.com* (September 2, 2005), at www.epaynews.com/statistics/scardststs.html.

CHAPTER 16

[1] *Flow of Funds Accounts of the United States* (Washington, DC: Board of Governors of the Federal Reserve System, December 8, 2005), Table F.212.

[2] Ibid., Tables F.212 and F.213.

[3] Richard Waters, "Battered Dotcom Sector Lifted by Dollars 1.6 Bn Yahoo Purchase," *Financial Times* (London), July 15, 2003, 1.

[4] See Cory Johnson, "The Internet Blue Chip," *The Industry Standard* (August 7, 2001), at www.thestandard.com/article/0,1902,4088,0html; and Chris Nerney "Yahoo!: Bargain or Big Trouble?" *The Internet Stock Report* (August 7, 2001), at www.internetstockreport.com/column/print/0,,530021,00.html. See also "Financial Charts," *Yahoo! Finance* (January 30, 2006), at finance.yahoo.com.

[5] Louise Lee and Lauren Young, "Is Schwab's Latest Come-On Enough?" *Business Week*, June 7, 2004, 44; "Broker Comparison Chart" (February 3, 2006), at www.scottrade.com/brokercomparison/brokercomparison.asp.

[6] Lee and Young, "Is Schwab's Latest Come-On Enough?" 44; Theresa W. Carey, "Online Trading Revives," *Barron's*, February 28, 2005, T6.

[7] See *NYSE Data* (2003) (June 20, 2004), at www.nysedata.com/factbook.

[8] Jerry Putnam, "NYSE's Cheaper Cousin? Archipelago May Revamp Pricing," *Wall Street Letter* (February 7, 2006), at www.InstitutionalInvestor.com; "NYSE Members Overwhelmingly Approve Merger with Archipelago Holdings, Inc., Preliminary Results Indicate," *NYSE News Release* (December 6, 2005), at www.nyse.com

[9] StocksQuest is accessible at http://stocksquest.coe.uga.edu/C001759/stocksquest/mystocks_sample.htm.

[10] "Flow of Funds Accounts of the United States," *Federal Reserve Bulletin* (December 8, 2005), Tables D.3, F.1, and L.106; U.S. Department of the Treasury, Bureau of the Public Debt (January 18, 2006), at www.publicdebt.treas.gov.

[11] "Flow of Funds Accounts of the United States," *Federal Reserve Bulletin* (December 8, 2005), Table F.212.

[12] "Flow of Funds Accounts of the United States," *Federal Reserve Bulletin* (December 8, 2005), Tables L.121, L.122, and L.123.

[13] See Gretchen Morgenson, "Buying on Margin Becomes a Habit," *New York Times*, March 24, 2000, C1, C7; and David Barboza, "Wall Street After Dark," *New York Times*, February 13, 2000, BU1, BU14–BU15.

[14] U.S. Department of Justice, "Joseph P. Nacchio Indicted by Federal Grand Jury: Former Chief Executive Officer of Qwest Communications Charged with Insider Trading, Selling Over $100 Million Stock" (December 20, 2005), at www.usdoj.gov/usao/co/122005Frame1Source1.htm.

APPENDIX III

[1] See Arthur J. Keown, *Personal Finance: Turning Money Into Wealth* (Prentice Hall: Upper Saddle River, NJ, 2004), 600–609.

SOURCE NOTES

CHAPTER 1

What Goes Up. . . Can Go Even Higher!/What Happens When the Well Runs Dry: "Why the World Is One Storm Away From Energy Crisis," *Wall Street Journal*, September 24, 2005, A1, A2; "Prices of Oil Spurts to 42.90 a Barrel," *USA Today*, July 29, 2004, 1B; "Higher and Higher—Again. Gasoline Prices Set a Record," *USA Today*, May 25, 2004, 1B; Brad Foss, "Drivers Pay Price for Imported Gas," Associated Press Wire Story, May 22, 2004; Allan Sloan, "Why $2 Gas Isn't the Real Energy Problem, *Newsweek*, May 24, 2004, 40; "Who Wins and Loses When Gas Prices Skyrocket?" *Time*, May 8, 2006, 28.
Figure 1.2: Adapted from Karl E. Case and Ray C. Fair, *Principles of Economics*, 6th ed., revised (Upper Saddle River, NJ: Prentice Hall, 2002), 47. **Figure 1.3**: Data obtained from U.S Department of Commerce Bureau of Economic Analysis, www.bea.gov/bea/dn/gdplev.xls; U.S Census Bureau, www.census.gov/popest/states/tables/NST-EST2005–01.xls; www.census.gov/popest/archives/1990s/. **Figure 1.4**: © 2006 The Economist Newspaper Ltd. All rights reserved. Reprinted with permission. Further reproduction prohibited. www.economist.com. **Figure 1.5**: Data obtained from U.S Census Bureau, www.census.gov/foreign-trade/balance/c0004.html#2005. **Table 1.2**: U.S. Department of Commerce Bureau of Economic Analysis, January 2006, www.doc.gov.

CHAPTER 2

High Seas Dumping/Royal Flushes: Bill McAllister, "Alaska Still Out Front on Environmental Monitoring," *The Juneau Empire*, May 29, 2004; Marilyn Adams, "Former Carnival Exec Says He Was Fired for Helping Federal Inquiry," *USA Today*, November 8–10, 2003; Michael Connor, "Norwegian Cruise Line Pleads Guilty in Pollution Case," *Reuters*, December 7, 2002; "What Is a Dead Zone?" Oceana Interactive (June 10, 2004), as www.oceana.org/index.cfm?sectionID=11&fuseaction-9#25.
Figure 2.1: Based on Gerald S. Cavanaugh, *American Business Values: With International Perspectives*, 4th ed. (Upper Saddle River, NJ: Prentice Hall, 1998) 71, 84. **Figure 2.2**: David P. Baron, *Business and Its Environment*, 4th ed. (Upper Saddle River, NJ: Prentice Hall, 2003) 768. Entrepreneurship and New Ventures: The Electronic Equivalent of Paper Shredding: Erika Brown, "To Shred and Protect," *Forbes*, November 25, 2002, 114–118; "Omniva Earns Microsoft.net Connected Logo Premium Level Status," *PRNewswire* (October 22, 2002), at www.disappearing.com/news/announcements/02_10_22_dotnet_logo.html; "Tumbleweed Granted New Patent for Electronic Communication," Tumbleweed Communications (November 26, 2002), at www.tumbleweed.com/en/company/news_events/press_releases/2002/pr-1731.html. **Figure 2.4**: Based on Andrew C. Revkin, "Who Cares About a Few Degrees?" *New York Times*, December 12, 1997, F1. **Table 2.1**: The Foundation Center, "Fifty Largest Corporate Foundations by Total Giving," *Researching Philanthropy* (August 12, 2002), at fdncenter.org/research/trends_analysis/top50giving.html.

CHAPTER 3

The Competitor from out of the Blue/How High Can An Airline Fly? "Amid JetBlue's Rapid Ascent, CEO Adopts Big Rivals' Traits," *Wall Street Journal*, August 25, 2005, A1, A6.; Julia Boorstin, "JetBlue's IPO Takes Off," *Fortune*, April 29, 2002, 96–100; Melanie Wells, "Lord of the Skies," *Forbes*, October 14, 2002, 130–138; Paul C. Judge, "How Will Your Company Adapt?" *Fast Company*, February 2003, 105–110. **Figure 3.1**: Data from www.sba.gov, accessed March 6, 2006; and U.S. Department of Commerce, "Statistics About Business Size (Including Small Business) from the U.S. Census Bureau," Statistical Abstract of the United States, at www.census.gov/epcd/www/smallbus.html.
Figure 3.2: Data from U.S. Department of Commerce, "Statistics About Business Size (Including Small Business) from the U.S. Census Bureau," Statistical Abstract of the United States, at www.census.gov/epcd/www/smallbus.html. **Figure 3.3**: Norman M. Scarborough and Thomas W. Zimmerer, *Effective Small Business Management: An Entrepreneurial Approach*, 6th ed. (Upper Saddle River, NJ: Prentice Hall, 2000) 15. Data from Forrester Research and from the U.S. Department of Commerce, www.commerce.gov. **Entrepreneurship and New Ventures: Food for Thought**: "About Us" and "Michael Stark: Kitchen," FreshDirect (November 25, 2002) at www.freshdirect.com; David Kirkpatrick, "The Online Grocer Version 2.0," *Fortune*, November 25, 2002, 84–86; Florence Fabricant, "Fresh Groceries Right off the Assembly Line," *New York Times*, November 6, 2002, 4B; Jane Black, "Can FreshDirect Bring Home the Bacon?" *Business Week*, September 24, 2002, 87–88.

CHAPTER 4

Where Does Management Stand on Beer Breaks?/Mariachi Bands and Other Weapons of the Retail Wars: Andy Serwer, "Wal-Mart: Bruised and Battling," *Fortune*, April 18, 2005, 84–89; 2002 Annual Report, "International Operations," "Wal-Mart International Operations," "Wal-Mart Stores Inc. at a Glance," November 27, 2002, www.walmartstores.com; Amy Tsao, "Will Wal-Mart Take Over the World?" *Business Week*, November 27, 2002, 76–79; Geri Smith, "War of the Superstores," *Business Week*, September 23, 2002, 60; "The 2002 Global 500," *Fortune*, July 8, 2002. **Figure 4.1**: Data from the *CIA World Fact Book*, www.cia.gov/cia/publications/factbook/geos/xx.html.
Table 4.1 Data from the US Census Bureau, www.census.gov/foreign-trade/statistics/highlights/top/top0511.html#imports. **Figure 4.5**: Countries of the World, www.theodora.com/wfb/. **Figure 4.6**: Countries of the World, www.theodora.com/wfb/. **Entrepreneurship and New Ventures: Rolling in the Worldwide Dough**: Ron Lieber, "Give Us This Day Our Global Bread," *Fast Company*, March 2001, 164–167. **Table 4.2** Data from http://money.cnn.com/magazines/fortune/global500/.

CHAPTER 5

The Business of Bagging Customers/The Image Coach: "The Business Week Top 50," *Business Week*, April 4, 2005, 92; "Best Managed Companies in America," *Forbes*, January 10, 2005, 150.; "Coach's Driver Picks Up the Pace," *Business Week*, March 29, 2004, 98–100; Julia Boorstin, "How Coach Got Hot," *Fortune*, October 28, 2003, 131–134; Marilyn Much, "Consumer Research Is His Bag," *Investor's Business Daily*, December 16, 2003; "S&P Stock Picks and Pans: Accumulate Coach," *Business Week*, October 22, 2003. **Entrepreneurship**

and New Ventures: Samuel Adams Makes Headway": "Sam Adams to Expand Cincinnati Brewery," *USA Today*, January 6, 2005; Christopher Edmunds, "Bottom of the Barrel: Boston Beer's Winning Formula," *RealMoney.com* (March 5, 2003), www.thestreet.com/realmoney; Gary Hammel, "Driving Grassroots Growth," *Fortune*, September 4, 2002, 173–87; Ronald Lieber, "Beating the Odds," *Fortune*, March 31, 2002, 82–90. **Figure 5.2**: Based on Thomas L. Wheelen and J. David Hunger, *Strategic Management and Business Policy*, 8th ed. (Upper Saddle River, NJ: Prentice Hall, 2002), 14. **Figure 5.3**: Based on Stephen P. Robbins and Mary Coulter, *Management*, 7th ed. (Upper Saddle River, NJ: Prentice Hall, 2002), 199.

CHAPTER 6

Cooking Up a New Structure/Is There Synergy Between Baked Goods, Shoe Polish, and Underwear? "Sara Lee Net Increases 34%," *Chicago Tribune*, February 3, 2006, B1; *Hoover's Handbook of American Business 2006* (Austin, Texas: Hoover's Business Press, 2006); "Our Brands," Sara Lee (July 3, 2002), at www.saralee.com; Deborah Cohen, "Sara Lee Opens Alternative to Victoria's Secret," *Wall Street Journal*, January 3, 2003, B4; Julie Forster, "Sara Lee: Changing the Recipe— Again," *Business Week*, September 10, 2001, 87–89; "Sara Lee: Looking Shapely," *Business Week*, October 21, 2002, 52.

Entrepreneurship and New Ventures: Making the Grade: *Hoover's Handbook of American Business 2006* (Austin, Texas: Hoover's Business Press, 2006); Brian Dumaine, "How I Delivered the Goods," *Fortune Small Business*, October 2002 (*quote); Charles Haddad, "FedEx: Gaining on the Ground," *Business Week*, December 16, 2002, 126–128; Claudia H. Deutsch, "FedEx Has Hit the Ground Running, but Will Its Legs Tire?" *New York Times*, October 13, 2002, BU7; www. Forbes.com/finance (February 16, 2006).

CHAPTER 7

Keeping Track of German Engineering/ Mercedes Hits the Long Road Back Matt Moore, "Talk of a Change at Mercedes Swirls in Aftermath of Schrempp's Retirement," *Detroit News*, August 1, 2005, at www.detnews.com; Jeremy Van Loon and Dan Stets, "Mercedes, Quality Dropping, Loses Market Share to BMW, Lexus," *Bloomberg*, February 8, 2005, at www.sesh.com/20050209.html; Reuters, "Mercedes May Drop Goal to Top Quality Survey, Chief says," *Detroit News*, May 6, 2005, at www.detnews.com; Doron Levin, "Chrysler Repairman Zetsche Now Must Fix Mercedes," *Bloomberg*, August 8, 2005, at www.bloomberg.com;Chris Isidore, "Mercedes Loses Top Resale Spot," *CNNMoney* (November 10, 2003), at http://cnnmoney. printthis.clickability.com; Alex Taylor III, "Mercedes Hits a Pothole," *Fortune*, October 27, 2003, 140–46; Neal E. Boudette,

"DaimlerChrysler Drops Truck Plant," *Wall Street Journal*, September 24, 2003, A11; Scott Miller and Karen Lundegaard, "An Engineering Icon Slips—Quality Ratings for Mercedes Drop in Several Surveys," *Wall Street Journal*, February 4, 2002, B.1. **Entrepreneurship and New Ventures: One Businessperson's Trash Is Another's New Venture** "Compost Facility Process" (February 8, 2003), at www. jepsonprairieorganics.com; "Food Scraps to Fine Wine," *fashionwindows.com* (January 9, 2003), at (www.fashionwindows.com); "Norcal Waste Systems, Inc.," *Hoover's Online* (February 8, 2003), at www.hoovers.com.

CHAPTER 8

What's the Deal About Work?/Thinking About Work and Pay: "National Cross-Industry Estimates of Employment and Mean Annual Wage for Major Occupational Groups," Bureau of Labor Statistics, November 2004, (October 14, 2005) at www.bls.gov; Daniel Akst, "White-Collar Stress? Stop the Whining," *New York Times*, September 19, 2005, BU6 (quotation); Lisa Belkin, "Take This Job and Hug It," *New York Times*, February 13, 2005, W1. **Figure 8.3**: A. H. Maslow, *Motivation and Personality*, 2nd ed. (Upper Saddle River, NJ: Prentice Hall, 1970). Reprinted by permission of Prentice Hall Inc. **Entrepreneurship and New Ventures: American Girls**: "Company Profile," "Welcome to Pleasant Company," American Girl (June 17, 2003), at www. americangirl.com; Heesun Wee, "Barbie Is Turning Heads on Wall Street Again," *Business Week*, February 9, 2003, 67–69; Julie Sloane, "How We Got Started: Pleasant Rowland," *Fortune Small Business*, October 1, 2002, 110–114; "Our Toys: American Girl," Mattel: The World's Premier Toy Brands (June 20, 2003), at www.mattel.com; Pleasant Rowland, "A New Twist on Timeless Toys," *Fortune Small Business*, October 1, 2002, 85–89.

CHAPTER 9

Bringing the Bounty Back to P&G/ Turning the Tide: "The Best and Worst Managers: A. G. Lafley, Procter & Gamble," *Business Week*, January 10, 2005, 67 (also source of quote); "Follow These Leaders," *Fortune*, December 12, 2005, 25–26; "Who Wants to Be the Boss?" *Fortune*, February 20, 2006, 76–104; "Letter to Shareholders," *Procter & Gamble*, *2002 Annual Report*; "A Healthy Gamble," *Time*, September 16, 2002, 46–48; Katrina Booker, "The Un-CEO," *Fortune*, September 16, 2002, 88–96; Robert Berner, "Procter & Gamble's Renovator-in-Chief," *Business Week*, December 11, 2002, 98–100; Berner. **Entrepreneurship and New Ventures: An Apple a Day:** Steven Berglas, "What You Can Learn from Steve Jobs," www.inc.com; "Apple's Bold Swim Downstream," *Business Week*, January 24, 2006, 32–35; "The Seed of Apple's Innovation," *Business Week*, October 12, 2005, 86–87; Alan Deutschman, *The Second*

Coming of Steve Jobs (New York: Broadway Publishing, 2001); Brent Schlender, "How Big Can Apple Get?" *Fortune*, February 21, 2005, 122–128; Steve Jobs' Magic Kingdom," *Business Week*, February 6, 2006, 62–69 (source of quote). **Table 9.1**: Reprinted with permission of The Free Press, a division of Simon & Schuster Adult Publishing Group, from *A Force of Change: How Leadership Differs From Management* by John P. Kotter. Copyright © 1990 by John P. Kotter, Inc. All rights reserved. **Figure 9.1**: Reprinted by permission of *Harvard Business Review*. Exhibit from 'How to Choose Leadership Patterns' by Robert Tannenbaum & Warren Schmidt, May-June 1973. Copyright © 1973 by the Harvard Business School Publishing Corporation. All rights reserved. Reprinted by permission of *Harvard Business Review*. **Figure 9.2**: Copyright © 1990, by The Regents of the University of California. Reprinted from the *California Management Review*, Vol. 32, No. 2. By the permission of the The Regents. **Figure 9.3**: Ricky W. Griffin, *Management*, 8th ed. (Boston: Houghton Mifflin Company, 2005), 282. Used with permission.

CHAPTER 10

Las Vegas Gambles Online/The Logistics of Hiring en Masse: "While Hiring at Most Firms Chills, Wal-Mart's Heats Up," *USA Today*, August 26, 2003, 3B; "Personnel File," Fast Company, January 2003, 118–122; *Hoover's Handbook of American Business 2006* (Austin: Hoover's Business Press, 2006), 559–560. **Entrepreneurship and New Ventures: The Guru of Fun Takes a Meeting with the V.P. of Buzz**: Eric Wahlgren, "Online Extra: Goodbye, 'Guru of Fun,'" *Business Week*, February 6, 2003, 74–77; Lee Clifford, "You Get Paid to Do What?" *Fortune*, January 20, 2003, 106–108. **Figure 10.3**: *The Wall Street Journal Almanac 1999*, 226. Reprinted by Permission of Dow Jones, Inc., via Copyright Clearance Center Inc. ©1999 Dow Jones and Co., Inc. All rights reserved. **Figure 10.4**: U.S. Department of Labor, Bureau of Labor Statistics, www.aflcio.org/joinaunion/why/ uniondifference/uniondiff11.cfm.

CHAPTER 11

Dell-ivering on Consumer Electronics/Can Dell Shock the Electronics World?: www.dell.com, accessed January 20, 2006; Kevin Maney, "Dell to Dive into Consumer Electronics Market," *USA Today*, September 25, 2003, 1B–2B; David Teather, "Michael Dell Quits as Chief of His Own Company," *The Guardian*, March 5, 2004. **Entrepreneurship and New Ventures: DVDs, as Easy as Netflix.com**: Michael Liedtke, "Netflix 4Q Profit Exceeds Expectations," *BusinessWeek Online* (January 24, 2006), at www.businessweek.com; Michael Liedtke, "Netflix's DVD Rental Pioneer has a Blockbuster Plan," *USA Today*, March 1, 2004, at www.usatoday.com/tech/techinvestor/ 2004 03 01 reed-hastings_x.htm; Lorenza Munoz/*Los Angeles Times*, "Netflix Takes over Wal-Mart Online Movie Rentals, *Detroit News Technology* (May 21, 2005),at www.detnews. com/2005/technology/0505/24/tech-188629.htm. **Figure 11.3**· SAS and all other SAS Institute, Inc. product or service names are registered trademarks or trademarks of SAS Institute, Inc. in the USA and other countries. ® indicates USA registration. Other brand and product names are trademarks of their respective companies. Copyright © 2006. SAS Institute, Inc. Cary, NC, USA. All rights reserved. **Figure 11.4**: Adapted from Jay Heizer and Barry Render, *Operations Management*, 7th ed. (Upper Saddle River, NJ: Prentice Hall, 2004), 157.

CHAPTER 12

The Nostalgia Merchants/Is Nostalgia Just a Fad? "Mitchell & Ness Nostalgia Co. and GenuOne Announce Online Auction Brand Protection Program," GenuOne Press Release (April 19, 2005), at www.genuone.com/G1/ home/Level0/news/Level1/news_releases/ print_script?select_release=Mitchell_Ness_G1; Danielle Knight, "Sniffing out Fakes," *USNews.com* (September 13, 2004), at www.usnews.com/usnews/biztech/articles/ 040913/13eencounter.htm; Alexander Wolff, "Rockin' the Retros," *Sports Illustrated*, December 22, 2003, 46–54; Sean Gregory, "How Old Jerseys Got Hot," *Time* (online edition) (April 7, 2003), at www.time.com/time/ insidebiz/article/0,9171,1101030407–439582,00 **Figure 12.4** William J, Dennis, Jr. ed., *NFIB National Small Business Poll*, vol. 1, no. 2 (Washington, DC: 2001); "Small Biz Web Sites on the Rise, Yet Many Owners Slow to Embrace the Internet," *Prodigy.com* (April 19, 2000), at www.prodigy.com/pcom/business/ business/content. **Figure 12.6** "Top 10 Advertisers in 12 Measured Media," *Advertising Age*, June 27, 2005, S-21. **Entrepreneurship and New Ventures: Capitalizing on the VirTus of Experience**: Dorothy Perin Moore, "Women: Are You Ready to Be Entrepreneurs?" *Business and Economic Review*, January–March 2003, 15; VirTu Inc. (February 2, 2003) at www.virtuinc.com.

CHAPTER 13

Letting Technology Be Your Guide/The Point of Cashing In: Kiosk Marketplace, "Talking Heads—Adding the Human Touch, without the Human" (July 19, 2004), at www.kiosmarketplace.com/research; Erick Schonfeld, "The Wizard of POS," *Business 2.0*, April 2004, 101–10; Michael Gros, *CRN*, August 25, 2003, 93; "No Tools Required for this Work Station," *Computing Canada*, November 14, 2003, 29; Gary Hilson, "Hardware Fit for a King," *Computing Canada*, February 14, 2003, 19; Larry Greenemeier, "Retailers Buy Into Real-Time Business," *InformationWeek*, January 20, 2003, 22.

Entrepreneurship and New Ventures: Upgrading to a Radio Frequency Future: Laurie Sullivan, "Wal-Mart's Way," *Information Week* (September 27, 2004), at www. informationweek.com/shared/ printableArticleSrc.jhtml?articleID=47902662; *Wal-Mart 2005 Annual Report* (Bentonville, Arkansas, 2005); Yen-Hung Chen, "Getting Ready for RFID," *ORMS Today*, June 2004, 30–35; Associated Press, "Smart Tags Moving Fast in Retail," *Columbia Daily Tribune*, September 16, 2004, 2B; John Fontana and Steve Jennings, "RFIDInitiatives— The Race Against Time and Technology," www.quartermaster.army.mil/0qmg/ Professional_Bulletin/2004/Summer04/RFID_ Initiatives_The_Race_Against_Time_an. . . **Figure 13.3**: major modification of diagrams at the Blackberry Web site, modified from Research in Motion Limited, technical images, at www.blackberry. com/images/technical/ bes_exchange_architecture.gif. **Figure 13.4**: Reprint courtesy of International Business Machines Corporation copyright 2006 © International Business Machines Corporation. Reprinted by permission of Paul Huang.

CHAPTER 14

What Numbers Can Be Crunched Offshore?/Accounting Takes a Trip Abroad: Beth Ellyn Rosenthal, "Deloitte Study Discovers 75 Percent of Global Financial Institutions Plan to Outsource Offshore," *BPO Outsourcing Journal*, June 2003, at www.bpo-outsourcing-journal.cm; Lawrence M. Gill, "Questions Loom as Accountants Outsource Work Abroad," *Chicago Lawyer* (Chicago: Law Bulletin Publishing Company, January 26, 2004); "How to Evaluate an Outsourcing Provider and Watch the Bottom Line," *The CPA Journal*, June 2002, 19; Liz Loxton, "Offshoring—Offshore Accounting," *Accountancy*, February 2004, 48; Todd Furniss and Michel Janssen, "Offshore Outsourcing Part 1: The Brand of India," *OutsourcingAsia.com*, April 2003, at www. outsourcing-asia.com; Furniss, "China: The Next Big Wave in Offshore Outsourcing,"; "Cover Feature—Outsourcing the Finance Function—Out with the Count," *Accountancy*, September 1, 2001, 32. **Table 14.1**: Adapted from "CPA Vision Project: 2011 and Beyond" (September 24, 2002), at www.cpavision.org/ final_report; Cynthia Bolt-Lee and Sheila Foster, "The Core Competency Framework: A New Element in the Continuing Call for Accounting Education Change in the United States," *Accounting Education*, vol. 12, issue 1, 2003, 33–47. **Table 14.2**: Executive Summary of the Sarbanes-Oxley Act of 2002 P.L. 107–204," *Conference of State Bank Supervisors*, at www.csbs.org/government/legislative/misc/ 2002_sarbanes-oxley_summary.htm; "Summary of the Sarbanes-Oxley Act of 2002," AICPA, at www.aicpa.org/info/sarbanes_oxley_ summary.htm. **Figure 14.1**: Adapted from Form 10K, *2004 Annual Report*, Google, Inc.,

March 30, 2005. **Figure 14.2**: Adapted from Form 10K, *2004 Annual Report*, Google, Inc., March 30, 2005. **Figure 14.3**: Adapted from Form 10K, *2004 Annual Report*, Google, Inc., March 30, 2005. **Entrepreneurship and New Ventures: How Can You Account for a Good Beer?**: "Brew Tour Update Form," *The Real Beer Page* (February 14, 2003), at www.realbeer.com; "Black Oak Nut Brown Ale," *BeerAdvocate.com* (February 14, 2003), at www.beeradvocate.com; Stephen Beaumont, "Lament for a Brewpub— February 2003," *Stephen Beaumont's World of Beer* (February 14, 2003), at www.worldofbeer.com; "Brewery Profile," *The Bar Towel* (February 14, 2003), at www.bartowel.com/breweries/ blackoak.phtml; John Cooper, "A Pint of Success," *CMA Management*, December 1999/ January 2000, 44–46. **Table 14.3**: AICPA, "Code of Professional Conduct," at www.aicpa.org. **Table 14.4**: "The Corporate Scandal Sheet," *Citizen Works*, August 2004, at www.citizenworks.org/enron/corp-scandal.php; "Largest Health Care Fraud Case in U.S. History Settled," Department of Justice (June 26, 2003), at www.usdoj.gov; "Waste Management, Inc., Founder and Three Other Former Top Officers Settle SEC Fraud Action for $30.8 Million," *U.S. Securities and Exchange Commission, Litigation Release No. 19351*, August 29, 2005, at www.sec.gov/litigation/ litreleases/lr19351.htm; "Kozlowski Is Found Guilty," *TheStreet.com*, June 17, 2005, at www.thestreet.com; "SEC Charges Time Warner with Fraud. . . .," *U.S. Securities and Exchange Commission, Release 2005–38*, March 21, 2005, at www.sec.gov.

CHAPTER 15

Going with the Currency/Taking an Interest in Money: *European Economy*, no. 5, November 28, 2005 (Luxembourg, Economic and Financial Affairs, Europa), at www.europa. eu.int/comm/economy-finance; "European Union Fact Sheet," May 2005 www.dfat. gov.au/geo/fs/eu.pdf; "Business: Tested by the Mighty Euro," *The Economist*, March 20, 2004, 78; G. Thomas Sims, "Tale of Two Recoveries: EU and Tokyo Diverge," *Wall Street Journal*, April 2, 2004, A.7; Justin Lahart, "Is the Euro Too Strong?" *CNNMoney* (January 8, 2004), at http://cnnmoney. com; Jamie McGeever, "Dollar May Gain More Against Euro on ECB Outlook," *Wall Street Journal*, March 29, 2004, C.5. **Figure 15.1**: The Federal Reserve Board (September 1, 2005), at www.federalreserve.gov/ releases/h6/current. **Figure 15.2**: The Federal Reserve Board (August 22, 2005), at www.federalreserve.gov/releases/h15/data/m/ prime. **Figure 15.4**: The Federal Reserve Board (August 23, 2005), at www.federal reserveeducation.org/fed101/structure. **Entrepreneurship and New Ventures: Your Check Is Not in the Mail**: *CheckFree Corporation 2004 Annual Report* (August 29, 2005), at www.checkfree,com; Scott Van Camp, "Know Thy Customer's Customer," *Adweek Magazine's Technology Marketing*, September

2002, 26–28; Jeffrey Kutler, "The Online Finance 40," *Institutional Investor*, March 2002, 144–50; Michael Vizard, "Getting Top Billing," *InfoWorld*, June 24/July 1, 2002, 58; Amalia D. Pathenios, "E-Billing All the Way," *Telephony*, June 25, 2001, 22; CheckFree Corporation (February 17, 2003), at www.checkfree.com; "In the Trench Innovator," *The IndUS Entrepreneurs* (February 17, 2003), at (www.tie-atlanta.org).

CHAPTER 16

Wanna Bet (on a Sure Thing)?/A Strong Case for Regulation: Christine Dugas, "Putnam Ousts CEO in Midst of Fund Probe," *USA Today* (November 3, 2003), at www.usatoday.com/money; "Senators Blast SEC over Mutual Fund Trading Scandal," *USA Today* (November 3, 2003), at www.usatoday.com/money; John Waggoner, Christine Dugas, and Thomas A. Fogarty, "Scandal Outrage Keeps Growing," *USA Today* (November 3, 2003), at www.usatoday.com/money; "NYC Pensions Pull Assets from Putnam," *CNNmoney* (November 4, 2003), at www.cnnmoney.com; "Chairman of Strong Mutual Resigns," *USA Today* (November 3, 2003), at www.usatoday.com/money; "Strong, Firm to Pay $140M in Settlement," *CNNMoney.com* (May 25, 2004), at http://cnnmoney.com; Dan Frost, "Wells Fargo to Buy Strong'sMutual Fund Operations: Purchase of Assets Follows Settlement of Trading Scandal," *San Francisco Chronicle* (May 27, 2004), at www.SFGate.com. **Figure 16.1**: "Yahoo! Inc (YHOO)/Wal-Mart Stores Inc (WMT)," *Quicken.com* (February 2, 2006), at www.quicken.com/investments/charts. **Table 16.1**: Adapted from "World Markets," *StocksQuest: A Global Stock Market Game* (October 21, 2005), at http://investsmart.coe.uga.edu/C001759/world/world_nf.htm. **Figure 16.2**: Carl Beidelman, *The Handbook of International Investing* (Chicago, 1987), 133. **Entrepreneurship and New Ventures: The Personality of a Risk Taker**: Tom Stein, "Every Step You Take, LPs Will Be Watching You," *Venture Capital Journal*, January 1, 2003, 1; Yasmine Chinwala, "U.S. Survey Shows Gender Gap," *eFinancial News* (February 5, 2002), at www.marcusventures.com/financialnews.html; Alison Maitland, "An Idea from the Ladies Room," *FT.com/Financial Times* (February 2, 2003), at www.marcusventures.com/FT.html. **Figure 16.6**: NASDAQ, "Market Performance and Highlights," *Nasdaq.com* (February 2, 2006), at www.nasdaq.com; *Factbook: NYSE*, (February 2, 2006), at www.nysedata.com; U.S. Census Bureau, *Statistical Abstract of the United States 2003* (Washington, DC: 2004), Tables No. 1206 and 1208, at www.census.gov.

APPENDIX III

Figure AIII.6: Charles D. Hodgman, Ed., *Mathematical Tables*, 10th Ed. (Cleveland: Chemical Rubber Publishing Co., 1954). **Figure AIII.8**: State Of California (February 24, 2006), **Figure AIII.11**: Arthur J. Keown, Personal Finance: *Turning Money Into Wealth*, 3rd Ed. (Upper Saddle River, NJ: Prentice Hall, 2004).

CARTOON, PHOTO, AND SCREEN CREDITS

PROLOGUE
Page: xxxv (top): AP Wide World Photos. Page: xxxv (upper middle): Tomas del Amo/PacificStock.com. Page: xxxv (lower middle): AP Wide World Photos. Page: xxxv (bottom): AP Wide World Photos. Page xxxvi: Corbis/Bettmann. Page xxxvii: Courtesy of AND1. Page xxxviii: Maureen Jenkins. Page xxxix: Getty Images, Inc. Page xl: Starbucks Coffee Company. Page xli: AP/Wide World Photos. Page xlii: Alamy Images. Page xliii: AP Wide World Photos.

CHAPTER 1
Page 2/3/27: © Gene Blevins/Corbis. Page 9 (a): Getty Images. Pages 9 (b): © Anthony P. Bolante REUTERS/CORBIS. Page 9 (c): Index Stock Imagery, Inc. Page 12: AP Wide World Photos. Page 26: © JIM YOUNG/Reuters/Corbis.

CHAPTER 2
Page 36/37/63: AP Wide World Photos. Page 40 (left): Getty Images, Inc. Page 40 (right): © Richard Carson/Reuters/Corbis. Page 42: © The New Yorker Collection 1997 Frank Cotham from cartoonbank.com. All Rights Reserved. Page 48: ©Miichael Siluk/The Image Works. Page 49: ©Lionel Derimais/ Visum/The Image Works. Page 53: Getty Images, Inc. Page 56: The Image Works. Page 57: Getty Images/ Time Life Pictures.

CHAPTER 3
Page 72/73/97: © David Butow/CORBIS SABA. Page 78: AP Wide World Photos. Page 82: © The New Yorker Collection 1988 Robert Weber from cartoonbank.com. All Rights Reserved. Page 84: Photodisc/Getty Images. Page 95: AP Wide World Photos.

CHAPTER 4
Page 106/107/131: AP Wide World Photos. Page 110: AP Wide World Photos. Page 111: AP Wide World Photos. Page 123: AP Wide World Photos. Page 128: © The New Yorker Collection 2001 Robert Weber from cartoonbank.com. All Rights Reserved. Page 129: Getty Images, Inc – Liaison.

CHAPTER 5
Page 140/141/167: Churchill & Klehr Photography. Page 143 (a): Newscast US. Page 143 (b): Spencer Platt/Getty Images, Inc. Page 143 (c): AP Wide World Photos. Page 146: CORBIS- NY. Page 149: Kyodo. Page 150: ©

The New Yorker Collection 1993 Mike Twohy from cartoonbank.com. All Rights Reserved. Page 152: Kistone Photography. Page 161: PhotoEdit Inc. Page 163: Corbis/Outline.

CHAPTER 6
Page 174/175/196: PhotoEdit Inc. Page 179: © The New Yorker Collection 1991 Charles Barsotti from cartoonbank.com. All Rights Reserved. Page 181: Steve Jones Photography. Page 183: Vincent Prado.

CHAPTER 7
Page 202/203/226: Peter Arnold, Inc. Page 205 (left): © Kim Kulish/Corbis. Page 205 (right): Getty Images, Inc. Page 208: Masterfile Stock Image Library. Page 220: Chung Sung-Jun/ Getty Image.

CHAPTER 8
Page 236/237/258: Getty Images – PhotoAlto Royalty Free. Page 239: © Jose Luis Pelaez, Inc./CORBIS. Page 253: © The New Yorker Collection 1998 Leo Cullum from cartoonbank.com. All Rights Reserved. Page 254: © JAN PETER KASPER/epa/Corbis. Page 256: James Schnepf Photography, Inc.

CHAPTER 9
Page 264/265/285: Landov LLC. Page 268 (top left): Hulton Archive/Getty Images. Page 268 (top right): Hulton Archive/Getty Images. Page 268 (bottom): Getty Images/Time Life Pictures. Page 271: Getty Images News. Page 272: Getty Images Entertainment. Page 277 (top): AP Wide World Photos. Page 277 (bottom): AP Wide World Photos. Page 283: AP Wide World Photos.

CHAPTER 10
Page 292/293/317: MGM Mirage. Page 299: Taxi/Getty Images. Page 303: Alex Brandon. Page 306: © The New Yorker Collection 1996 Danny Shanahan from cartoonbank.com. All Rights Reserved. Page 310 Joyce Dopkeen/The New York Times.

CHAPTER 11
Page 326/327/352: Courtesy of Dell Inc. Page 332: Ting Shi. Page 333: Getty Images Entertainment. Page 336: Getty Images, Inc. Page 337: © The New Yorker Collection 1992 Bernard Schoenbaum from cartoonbank.com. All Rights Reserved. Page 344: Jill Connelly. Page 348: Heidi Cody. Page 351: www.photos.com/Jupiter Images.

CHAPTER 12
Page 362/363/386: Bill Cramer, Photographer. Page 365: Sean Dungan. Page 369: Corbis/Reuters America LLC. Page 371: JimWest. Page 377: Courtesy of QVC, Inc. Page 348: Tova R. Baruch.

CHAPTER 13
Page 396/397/419: Courtesy of DA Group, plc. Page 399: Courtesy of Blackberry Research in

absenteeism When an employee does not show up for work [240]

absolute advantage The ability to produce something more efficiently than any other country [120]

accommodative stance Approach to social responsibility by which a company, if specifically asked to do so, exceeds legal minimums in its commitments to groups and individuals in its social environment [61]

accountability Obligation employees have to their manager for the successful completion of an assigned task [183]

accounting Comprehensive system for collecting, analyzing, and communicating financial information [428]

accounting equation Assets = Liabilities + Owners' Equity; used by accountants to balance data for the firm's financial transactions at various points in the year [428]

accounting information system (AIS) Organized procedure for identifying, measuring, recording, and retaining financial information for use in accounting statements and management reports [428]

accounts payable (payables) Current liability consisting of bills owed to suppliers, plus wages and taxes due within the coming year [437]

accounts receivable Funds due from customers who have bought on credit [525]

acquisition The purchase of one company by another [96]

activity ratio Financial ratio for evaluating management's efficiency in using a firm's assets [443]

advertising Promotional tool consisting of paid, nonpersonal communication used by an identified sponsor to inform an audience about a product [381]

advertising media Variety of communication devices for carrying a seller's message to potential customers [382]

affirmative action plan Written statement of how the organization intends to actively recruit, hire, and develop members of relevant protected classes [305]

agent Individual or organization acting for and in the name of, another party [541]

aggregate output The total quantity of goods and services produced by an economic system during a given period [19]

anti-virus software Product that protects systems by searching incoming e-mails and data files for "signatures" of known viruses and virus-like characteristics [417]

apparent authority Agent's authority, based on the principal's compliance, to bind a principal to a certain course of action [542]

appellate court Court that reviews case records of trials whose findings have been appealed [538]

assembly line Product layout in which a product moves step by step through a plant on conveyor belts or other equipment until it is completed [214]

asset allocation Relative amount of funds invested in (or allocated to) each of several investment alternatives [505]

asset Any economic resource expected to benefit a firm or an individual who owns it [435]

Association of Southeast Asian Nations (ASEAN) Organization for economic, political, social, and cultural cooperation among Southeast Asian nations [114]

attitudes A person's beliefs and feelings about specific ideas, situations, or people [242]

audit Systematic examination of a company's accounting system to determine whether its financial reports reliably represent its operations [430]

authority Power to make the decisions necessary to complete a task [183]

automated teller machine (ATM) Electronic machine that allows bank customers to conduct account-related activities 24 hours a day, 7 days a week [471]

balance of payments Flow of all money into or out of a country [117]

balance of trade The economic value of all the products that a country exports minus the economic value of all the products it imports [22]

balance sheet Financial statement that supplies detailed information about a firm's assets, liabilities, and owners' equity [436]

banker's acceptance Bank promise, issued for a buyer, to pay a designated firm a specified amount at a future date [470]

bankruptcy Permission granted by the courts to individuals and organizations not to pay some or all of their debts [542]

bargain retailer Retailer carrying a wide range of products at bargain prices [373]

bear market Period of falling stock prices [509]

bearer (coupon) bond Bond requiring the holder to clip and submit a coupon to receive an interest payment [502]

behavioral approach to leadership Focused on determining what behaviors are employed by leaders [269]

benefits Compensation other than wages and salaries [304]

"big five" personality traits Five fundamental personality traits especially relevant to organizations [241]

blue-chip stock Common stock issued by a well-established and respected company with a sound financial history and a stable pattern of dividend payouts [494]

blue-sky laws Laws requiring securities dealers to be licensed and registered with the states in which they do business [514]

board of directors Governing body of a corporation that reports to its shareholders and delegates power to run its day-to-day operations while remaining responsible for sustaining its assets [95]

bond Security through which an issuer promises to pay the buyer a certain amount of money by a specified future date [501]

bonus Individual performance incentive in the form of a special payment made over and above the employee's salary [303]

book value Value of a common stock expressed as total stockholders' equity divided by the number of shares of stock [494]

bookkeeping Recording of accounting transactions [428]

boycott Labor action in which workers refuse to buy the products of a targeted employer [316]

branch office Foreign office set up by an international or multinational firm [126]

brand awareness Extent to which a brand name comes to mind when the consumer considers a particular product category [346]

brand competition Competitive marketing that appeals to consumer perceptions of benefits of products offered by particular companies [332]

brand loyalty Pattern of regular consumer purchasing based on satisfaction with a product [337]

branding Process of using symbols to communicate the qualities of a product made by a particular producer [346]

breakeven analysis For a particular selling price, assessment of the seller's costs versus revenues at various sales volumes [366]

breakeven point Sales volume at which the seller's total revenue from sales equals total costs (variable and fixed) with neither profit nor loss [367]

broker Independent intermediary who matches numerous sellers and buyers as needed, often without knowing in advance who they will be [371]

budget Detailed statement of estimated receipts and expenditures for a future period of time [441]

bull market Period of rising stock prices [509]

business Organization that provides goods or services to earn profits [5]

business continuation agreement Special form of business insurance whereby owners arrange to buy the interests of deceased associates from their heirs [534]

business cycle Short-term pattern of economic expansions and contractions [19]

business ethics Ethical or unethical behaviors by employees in the context of their jobs [39]

business interruption insurance Insurance covering income lost during times when a company is unable to conduct business [534]

business plan Document in which the entrepreneur summarizes her or his business strategy for the proposed new venture and how that strategy will be implemented [80]

business practice law Law or regulation governing business practices in given countries [130]

business process reengineering The rethinking and radical redesign of business processes to improve performance, quality, and productivity [223]

business (competitive) strategy Strategy, at the business-unit or product-line level, focusing on improving a firm's competitive position [157]

cafeteria benefits plan Benefit plan that sets limits on benefits per employee, each of whom may choose from a variety of alternative benefits [304]

capacity Amount of a product that a company can produce under normal conditions [528]

capacity Competence required of individuals entering into a binding contract [212]

capital Funds needed to create and operate a business enterprise [8]

capital gains The earnings, reflecting changes in market value, from buying and selling a share of stock [495]

capital item Expensive, long-lasting, infrequently purchased industrial good, such as a building, or industrial service, such as building maintenance [343]

capital structure Relative mix of a firm's debt and equity financing [529]

capitalism System that sanctions the private ownership of the factors of production and encourages entrepreneurship by offering profits as an incentive [12]

cartel Association of producers whose purpose is to control supply and prices [130]

cash-flow management Management of cash inflows and outflows to ensure adequate funds for purchases and the productive use of excess funds [524]

catalog showroom Bargain retailer in which customers place orders for catalog items to be picked up at on-premises warehouses [373]

centralized organization Organization in which most decision-making authority is held by upper-level management [180]

Certified Fraud Examiner (CFE) Professional designation administered by the Association of Certified Fraud Examiners in recognition of qualifications for a specialty area within forensic accounting [432]

Certified Management Accountant (CMA) Professional designation awarded by the Institute of Management Accountants in recognition of management accounting qualifications [432]

Certified Public Accountant (CPA) Accountant licensed by the state and offering services to the public [429]

chain of command Reporting relationships within a company [174]

charismatic leadership Type of influence based on the leader's personal charisma [272]

check Demand deposit order instructing a bank to pay a given sum to a specified payee [464]

checking account (demand deposit) Bank account funds, owned by the depositor, that may be withdrawn at any time by check or cash [464]

Chief Executive Officer (CEO) Top manager who is responsible for the overall performance of a corporation [95]

classical theory of motivation Theory holding that workers are motivated solely by money [245]

client-server network A common business network in which clients make requests for information or resources and servers provide the services [406]

closely held (private) corporation Corporation whose stock is held by only a few people and is not available for sale to the general public [93]

coalition An informal alliance of individuals or groups formed to achieve a common goal [283]

code of professional conduct The code of ethics for CPAs as maintained and enforced by the AICPA [447]

collateral Borrower-pledged legal asset that may be seized by lenders in case of nonpayment [526]

collective bargaining Process by which labor and management negotiate conditions of employment for union-represented workers [312]

collusion Illegal agreement between two or more companies to commit a wrongful act [55]

commercial bank Company that accepts deposits that it uses to make loans, earn profits, pay interest to depositors, and pay dividends to owners [467]

commercial paper Short-term securities, or notes, containing a borrower's promise to pay [527]

committee and team authority Authority granted to committees or teams involved in a firm's daily operations [185]

common law Body of decisions handed down by courts ruling on individual cases [535]

common stock The most basic form of ownership, including voting rights on major issues, in a company [493]

communism Political system in which the government owns and operates all factors of production [11]

comparative advantage The ability to produce some products more efficiently than others [120]

compensation system Total package of rewards that organizations provide to individuals in return for their labor [301]

compensatory damages Monetary payments intended to redress injury actually suffered because of a tort [539]

competition Vying among businesses for the same resources or customers [16]

competitive product analysis Process by which a company analyzes a competitor's products to identify desirable improvements [222]

compound growth How a sum of money grows by paying interest on the principal of an investment, as well as paying interest on previously earned interest, over several time periods [317]

compulsory arbitration Method of resolving a labor dispute in which both parties are legally required to accept the judgment of a neutral party [317]

computer-aided design (CAD) IS with software that helps knowledge workers design products by simulating them and displaying them in three-dimensional graphics [411]

computer network A group of two or more computers linked together by some form of cabling or by wireless technology to share data or resources, such as a printer [405]

conceptual skills Abilities to think in the abstract, diagnose and analyze different situations, and see beyond the present situation [151]

consideration Any item of value exchanged between parties to create a valid contract [538]

consistency (in quality) A dimension of quality that refers to sameness of product quality from unit to unit [214]

consumer behavior Study of the decision process by which people buy and consume products [337]

consumer goods Physical products purchased by consumers for personal use [329]

Consumer Price Index (CPI) A measure of the prices of typical products purchased by consumers living in urban areas [24]

consumerism Form of social activism dedicated to protecting the rights of consumers in their dealings with businesses [54]

contingency planning Identifying aspects of a business or its environment that might entail changes in strategy [160]

contingent worker Employee hired on something other than a full-time basis to supplement an organization's permanent workforce [311]

contract Agreement between two or more parties enforceable in court [538]

controller Person who manages all of a firm's accounting activities (chief accounting officer) [429]

controlling Management process of monitoring an organization's performance to ensure that it is meeting its goals [146]

convenience good/convenience service Inexpensive good or service purchased and consumed rapidly and regularly [342]

convenience store Retail store offering easy accessibility, extended hours, and fast service [373]

cooperative Form of ownership in which a group of sole proprietorships and/or partnerships agree to work together for common benefits [91]

copyright Exclusive ownership right belonging to the creator of a book, article, design, illustration, photo, film, or musical work [541]

core competencies for accounting The combination of skills, technology, and knowledge that will be necessary for the future CPA [431]

corporate bond Bond issued by a company as a source of long-term funding [502]

corporate culture The shared experiences, stories, beliefs, and norms that characterize an organization [161]

corporate governance Roles of shareholders, directors, and other managers in corporate decision making and accountability [94]

corporate strategy Strategy for determining the firm's overall attitude toward growth and the way it will manage its businesses or product lines [156]

corporation Business that is legally considered an entity separate from its owners and is liable for its own debts; owners' liability extends to the limits of their investments [92]

cost of goods sold Costs of obtaining materials for making the products sold by a firm during the year [439]

cost-of-living adjustment (COLA) Labor contract clause tying future raises to changes in consumer purchasing power [314]

cost of revenues Costs that a company incurs to obtain revenues from other companies [438]

cost-oriented pricing Pricing that considers the firm's desire to make a profit and its need to cover production costs [366]

counterproductive behaviors Behaviors that detract from organizational performance [240]

coupon Sales promotion technique in which a certificate is issued entitling the buyer to a reduced price [384]

creative selling Personal selling task in which salespeople try to persuade buyers to purchase products by providing information about their benefits [384]

credit union Nonprofit, cooperative financial institution owned and run by its members, usually employees of a particular organization [469]

crisis management Organization's methods for dealing with emergencies [160]

currency (cash) Government-issued paper money and metal coins [464]

current asset Asset that can or will be converted into cash within a year [436]

current liability Debt that must be paid within one year [437]

current ratio Financial ratio for measuring a company's ability to pay current debts out of current assets [444]

customer departmentalization Dividing an organization to offer products and meet needs for identifiable cutomers groups [178]

cybermall Collection of virtual storefronts (business Web sites) representing a variety of products and product lines on the Internet [384]

data Raw facts and figures that, by themselves, may not have much meaning [408]

data mining The application of electronic technologies for searching, sifting, and reorganizing pools of data to uncover useful information [410]

data warehousing The collection, storage, and retrieval of data in electronic files [410]

debenture Unsecured bond for which no specific property is pledged as security [503]

debit card Plastic card that allows an individual to transfer money between accounts [479]

debt financing Long-term borrowing from sources outside a company [527]

debt A company's total liabilities [445]

decentralized organization Organization in which a great deal of decision-making authority is delegated to levels of management at points below the top [181]

decision making Choosing one alternative from among several options [280]

decision-making skills Skills in defining problems and selecting the best courses of action [151]

decision support system (DSS) Interactive system that creates virtual business models for a particular kind of decision and tests them with different data to see how they respond [412]

deductible An amount of the loss that the insured must absorb prior to reimbursement [532]

defensive stance Approach to social responsibility by which a company meets only minimum legal requirements in its commitments to groups and individuals in its social environment [60]

delegation Process through which a manager allocates work to subordinates [183]

demand The willingness and ability of buyers to purchase a good or service [13]

demand and supply schedule Assessment of the relationships among different levels of demand and supply at different price levels [14]

demand curve Graph showing how many units of a product will be demanded (bought) at different prices [14]

demographic variables Characteristics of populations that may be considered in developing a segmentation strategy [335]

department store Large product-line retailer characterized by organization into specialized departments [373]

departmentalization Process of grouping jobs into logical units [177]

depreciation Accounting method for distributing the cost of an asset over its useful life [437]

depression A prolonged and deep recession [26]

deregulation Elimination of rules that restrict business activity [536]

detailed schedule A schedule showing daily work assignments with start and stop times for assigned jobs [216]

direct channel Distribution channel in which a product travels from producer to consumer without intermediaries [370]

direct-response retailing Form of nonstore retailing by direct interaction with customers to inform them of products and to receive sales orders [374]

direct selling Form of nonstore retailing typified by door-to-door sales [374]

discount Price reduction offered as an incentive to purchase [369]

discount house Bargain retailer that generates large sales volume by offering goods at substantial price reductions [373]

discount rate Interest rate at which member banks can borrow money from the Fed [476]

distribution Part of the marketing mix concerned with getting products from producers to consumers [334]

distribution channel Network of interdependent companies through which a product passes from producer to end user [370]

distribution mix The combination of distribution channels by which a firm gets its products to end users [370]

diversification Purchase of several different kinds of investments rather than just one [505]

divestiture Strategy whereby a firm sells one or more of its business units [96]

dividend A payment to shareholders, on a per share basis, out of the company's earnings [493]

division Department that resembles a separate business in that it produces and markets its own products [186]

divisional structure Organizational structure in which corporate divisions operate as autonomous businesses under the larger corporate umbrella [186]

domestic business environment The environment in which a firm conducts its operations and derives its revenues [7]

double taxation Situation in which taxes may be payable both by a corporation on its profits and by shareholders on dividend incomes [93]

Dow Jones Industrial Average (DJIA) Market index based on the prices of 30 of the largest industrial firms listed on the NYSE [509]

dumping Practice of selling a product abroad for less than the cost of production [130]

e-cash Electronic money that moves between consumers and businesses via digital electronic transmissions [480]

e-catalog Nonstore retailing in which the Internet is used to display products [375]

e-commerce The use of the Internet and other electronic means for retailing and business-to-business transactions [398]

e-intermediary Internet distribution channel member that assists in delivering products to customers or that collects information about various sellers to be presented to consumers [375]

earnings per share Profitability ratio measuring the net profit that the company earns for each share of outstanding stock [445]

economic environment Relevant conditions that exist in the economic system in which a company operates [8]

economic indicator A statistic that helps assess the performance of an economy [18]

economic strike Strike usually triggered by stalemate over one or more mandatory bargaining items [316]

economic system Nation's system for allocating its resources among its citizens [8]

electronic conferencing IT that allows groups of people to communicate simultaneously from various locations via e-mail, phone, or video [405]

electronic funds transfer (EFT) Communication of fund-transfer information over wire, cable, or microwave [471]

electronic retailing Nonstore retailing in which information about the seller's products and services is connected to consumers' computers, allowing consumers to receive the information and purchase the products in the home [375]

electronic storefront Commercial Web site in which customers gather information about products, buying opportunities, placing orders, and paying for purchases [376]

embargo Government order banning exportation and/or importation of a particular product or all products from a particular country [129]

eminent domain Principle that the government may claim private land for public use by buying it at a fair price [541]

emotional intelligence (emotional quotient, EQ) The extent to which people are self-aware, can manage their emotions, can motivate themselves, express empathy for others, and possess social skills [242]

emotional motives Reasons for purchasing a product that are based on nonobjective factors [339]

employee behavior The pattern of actions by the members of an organization that directly or indirectly influences the organization's effectiveness [238]

employee-focused leader behavior Leader behavior focusing on satisfaction, motivation, and well-being of employees [269]

employee information system (skills inventory) Computerized system containing information on each employee's education, skills, work experiences, and career aspirations [296]

employee stock ownership plan (ESOP) Arrangement in which a corporation holds its own stock in trust for its employees, who gradually receive ownership of the stock and control its voting rights [96]

employment at will Principle, increasingly modified by legislation and judicial decision, that organizations should be able to retain or dismiss employees at their discretion [307]

encryption system Software that assigns an e-mail message to a unique code number (digital fingerprint) for each computer so only that computer, not others, can open and read the message [418]

entrepreneur Individual who accepts both the risks and the opportunities involved in creating and operating a new business venture [9]

entrepreneurship The process of seeking businesses opportunities under conditions of risk. [79]

environmental analysis Process of scanning the business environment for threats and opportunities [158]

equal employment opportunity Legally mandated nondiscrimination in employment on the basis of race, creed, sex, or national origin [305]

Equal Employment Opportunity Commission (EEOC) Federal agency enforcing several discrimination-related laws [305]

equity financing Use of common stock and/or retained earnings to raise long-term funding [528]

equity theory Theory of motivation holding that people evaluate their treatment by the organization relative to the treatment of others [249]

escalation of commitment Condition in which a decision maker becoming so committed to a course of action that she or he stays with it even when it appears to have been wrong [284]

ethical behavior Behavior conforming to generally accepted social norms concerning beneficial and harmful actions [39]

ethical leadership Leader behaviors that reflect high ethical standards [278]

ethics Beliefs about what is right and wrong or good and bad in actions that affect others [38]

euro A common currency shared among most of the members of the European Union (excluding Denmark, Sweden, and the United Kingdom) [119]

European Union (EU) Agreement among major Western European nations to eliminate or make uniform most trade barriers affecting group members [113]

exchange rate Rate at which the currency of one nation can be exchanged for the currency of another nation [119]

expectancy theory Theory of motivation holding that people are motivated to work toward rewards that they want and that they believe they have a reasonable chance of obtaining [249]

expense item Industrial product purchased and consumed rapidly and regularly for daily operations [342]

export Product made or grown domestically but shipped and sold abroad [109]

exporter Firm that distributes and sells products to one or more foreign countries [124]

express authority Agent's authority, derived from written agreement, to bind a principal to a certain course of action [541]

express warranty Warranty whose terms are specifically stated by the seller [542]

external environment Everything outside an organization's boundaries that might affect it [6]

external recruiting Attracting persons outside the organization to apply for jobs [298]

extranet A system that allows outsiders limited access to a firm's internal information network [405]

factors of production Resources used in the production of goods and services—labor, capital, entrepreneurs, physical resources, and information resources [8]

factory outlet Bargain retailer owned by the manufacturer whose products it sells [373]

federal deposit insurance corporation (FDIC) Federal agency that guarantees the safety of deposits up to $100,000 in the financial institutions that it insures [472]

federal reserve system (The Fed) Central bank of the United States, which acts as the government's bank, serves member commercial banks, and controls the nation's money supply [473]

finance (corporate finance) Activities concerned with determining a firm's long-term investments, obtaining the funds to pay for them, conducting the firm's everyday financial activities, and managing the firm's risks [523]

finance company Nondeposit institution that specializes in making loans to businesses and consumers [469]

financial accounting Field of accounting concerned with external users of a company's financial information [429]

financial manager Manager responsible for planning and controlling the acquisition and dispersal of a firm's financial resources [523]

financial plan A firm's strategies for reaching some future financial position [524]

financial planning Process of looking at one's current financial condition, identifying one's goals, and anticipating requirements for meeting those goals [546]

financial statement Any of several types of reports summarizing a company's financial status to stakeholders and to aid in managerial decision making [436]

firewall Security system with special software or hardware devices designed to keep computers safe from hackers [416]

first-line manager Manager responsible for supervising the work of employees [148]

fiscal policies Policies used by a government regarding how it collects and spends revenue [26]

fixed asset Asset with long-term use or value, such as land, buildings, and equipment [437]

fixed cost Cost that is incurred regardless of the quantity of a product produced or sold [366]

flat organizational structure Characteristic of decentralized companies with relatively few layers of management [181]

flextime programs Method of increasing job satisfaction by allowing workers to adjust work schedules on a daily or weekly basis [256]

float Total amount of checks written but not yet cleared through the Fed [476]

follow-up Operations control activity for ensuring that production decisions are being implemented [219]

foreign direct investment (FDI) Arrangement in which a firm buys or establishes tangible assets in another country [126]

forensic accounting The practice of accounting for legal purposes [432]

franchise Arrangement in which a buyer (franchisee) purchases the right to sell the good or service of the seller (franchiser) [82]

full disclosure Guideline that financial statements should not include just numbers but should also furnish management's interpretations and explanations of those numbers [443]

functional departmentalization Dividing an organization according to groups' functions or activities [178]

functional strategy Strategy by which managers in specific areas decide how best to achieve corporate goals through productivity [157]

functional structure Organization structure in which authority is determined by the relationships between group functions and activities [185]

gainsharing plan Incentive plan that rewards groups for productivity improvements [304]

general (active) partner Partner who actively manages a firm and who has unlimited liability for its debts [91]

General Agreement on Tariffs and Trade (GATT) International trade agreement to encourage the multilateral reduction or elimination of trade barriers [114]

general partnership Business with two or more owners who share in both the operation of the firm and the financial responsibility for its debts [90]

generally accepted accounting principles (GAAP) Accounting guidelines that govern the content and form of financial reports [430]

geographic departmentalization Dividing an organization according to the areas of the country or the world served by a business [179]

geographic variables Geographical units that may be considered in developing a segmentation strategy [335]

global business environment The international forces that affect a business [7]

globalization Process by which the world economy is becoming a single interdependent system [108]

goal Objective that a business hopes and plans to achieve [154]

goods operations (goods production) Activities producing tangible products, such as radios, newspapers, buses, and textbooks [204]

goodwill Amount paid for an existing business above the value of its other assets [437]

government bond Bond issued by the federal government [502]

grapevine Informal communication network that runs through an organization [193]

gross domestic product (GDP) Total value of all goods and services produced within a given period by a national economy through domestic factors of production [20]

gross national product (GNP) Total value of all goods and services produced by a national economy within a given period regardless of where the factors of production are located [20]

gross profit A preliminary, quick-to-calculate profit figure calculated from the firm's revenues minus its cost of revenues (the direct costs of getting the revenues) [439]

hacker Cybercriminal who gains unauthorized access to a computer or network, either to steal information, money, or property or to tamper with data [414]

hardware The physical components of a computer network, such as keyboards, monitors, system units, and printers [407]

Hawthorne effect Tendency for productivity to increase when workers believe they are receiving special attention from management [246]

hierarchy of human needs model Theory of motivation describing five levels of human needs and arguing that basic needs must be fulfilled before people work to satisfy higher-level needs [247]

high-contact system Level of customer contact in which the customer is part of the system during service delivery [208]

hostile work environment Form of sexual harassment deriving from off-color jokes, lewd comments, and so forth [307]

human relations skills Skills in understanding and getting along with people [150]

human resource management (HRM) Set of organizational activities directed at attracting, developing, and maintaining an effective workforce [294]

identity theft Unauthorized stealing of personal information (such as social security number and address) to get loans, credit cards, or other monetary benefits by impersonating the victim [414]

implied authority Agent's authority, derived from business custom, to bind a principal to a certain course of action [542]

implied warranty Warranty, dictated by law, based on the principle that products should fulfill advertised promises and serve the purposes for which they are manufactured and sold [542]

import Product made or grown abroad but sold domestically [109]

importer Firm that buys products in foreign markets and then imports them for resale in its home country [124]

incentive program Special compensation program designed to motivate high performance [303]

income statement (profit-and-loss statement) Financial statement listing a firm's annual revenues and expenses so that a bottom line shows annual profit or loss [438]

independent agent Foreign individual or organization that agrees to represent an exporter's interests [125]

individual differences Personal attributes that vary from one person to another [240]

individual retirement account (IRA) Tax-deferred pension fund that wage earners set up to supplement retirement funds [470]

industrial goods Physical products purchased by companies to produce other products [329]

industrial market Organizational market consisting of firms that buy goods that are either converted into products or used during production [339]

inflation Occurs when widespread prices increases occur throughout an economic system [24]

informal organization Network, unrelated to the firm's formal authority structure, of everyday social interactions among company employees [192]

information The meaningful, useful interpretation of data [408]

information resources Data and other information used by businesses [10]

information system (IS) A system that uses IT resources to convert data into information and to collect, process, and transmit that information for use in decision making [408]

information systems managers Managers who operate the systems used for gathering, organizing, and distributing information [409]

information technology (IT) The various appliances and devices for creating, storing, exchanging, and using information in diverse modes, including visual images, voice, multimedia, and business data [398]

initial public offering (IPO) The first sale of a company's stock to the general public [497]

insider trading Illegal practice of using special knowledge about a firm for profit or gain [59]

institutional investor Large investor, such as a mutual fund or a pension fund, that purchases large blocks of corporate stock [96]

institutional market Organizational market consisting of such nongovernmental buyers of goods and services as hospitals, churches, museums, and charitable organizations [339]

insurance company Nondeposit institution that invests funds collected as premiums charged for insurance coverage [469]

insurance policy A formal agreement to pay the policyholder a specified amount in the event of certain losses [532]

insurance premium   Fee paid to an insurance company by a policyholder for insurance coverage [532]

intangible asset   Nonphysical asset, such as a patent or trademark, that has economic value in the form of expected benefit [437]

intangible personal property   Property that cannot be seen but that exists by virtue of written documentation [540]

intellectual property   A product of the mind—something produced by the intellect, with great expenditure of human effort—that has commercial value [415]

intellectual property   Property created through a person's creative activities [540]

intentional tort   Tort resulting from the deliberate actions of a party [539]

interactive marketing   Nonstore retailing that uses a Web site to provide real-time sales and customer service [376]

intermediary   Individual or firm that helps to distribute a product [370]

intermediate goal   Goal set for a period of one to five years into the future [156]

internal recruiting   Considering present employees as candidates for openings [298]

international competition   Competitive marketing of domestic products against foreign products [333]

international firm   Firm that conducts a significant portion of its business in foreign countries [124]

international monetary fund (IMF)   U.N. agency consisting of about 150 nations that have combined resources to promote stable exchange rates, provide temporary short-term loans, and serve other purposes [481]

international organizational structures   Approaches to organizational structure developed in response to the need to manufacture, purchase, and sell in global markets [188]

Internet   A gigantic system of interconnected computers; more than 100 million computers in over 100 countries [404]

intranet   An organization's private network of internally linked Web sites accessible only to employees [405]

intrapreneuring   Process of creating and maintaining the innovation and flexibility of a small-business environment within the confines of a large organization [193]

intuition   An innate belief about something, often without conscious consideration [283]

inventory   Materials and goods that are held by a company that it will sell within the year [525]

inventory control   Receiving, storing, handling, and counting of all raw materials, partly finished goods, and finished goods [219]

investment bank   Financial institution engaged in issuing and reselling new securities [493]

involuntary bankruptcy   Bankruptcy proceedings initiated by the creditors of an indebted individual or organization [543]

ISO 14000   Certification program attesting to the fact that a factory, laboratory, or office has improved its environmental performance [223]

ISO 9000   Program certifying that a factory, laboratory, or office has met the quality management standards set by the International Organization for Standardization [223]

job analysis   Systematic analysis of jobs within an organization [295]

job description   Description of the duties and responsibilities of a job, its working conditions, and the tools, materials, equipment, and information used to perform it [295]

job enrichment   Method of increasing job satisfaction by adding one or more motivating factors to job activities [255]

job redesign   Method of increasing job satisfaction by designing a more satisfactory fit between workers and their jobs [255]

job satisfaction   Degree of enjoyment that people derive from performing their jobs [243]

job specialization   The process of identifying the specific jobs that need to be done and designating the people who will perform them [176]

job specification   Description of the skills, abilities, and other credentials and qualifications required by a job [295]

joint venture   Strategic alliance in which the collaboration involves joint ownership of the new venture [96]

just-in-time (JIT) production   A type of lean production system that brings together all materials at the precise time they are required at each production stage [219]

key person insurance   Special form of business insurance designed to offset expenses entailed by the loss of key employees [534]

knowledge information system   Information system that supports knowledge workers by providing resources to create, store, use, and transmit new knowledge for useful applications [411]

knowledge workers   Employees who are of value because of the knowledge they possess [309]

labor (human resources)   Physical and mental capabilities of people as they contribute to economic production [8]

labor relations   Process of dealing with employees who are represented by a union [312]

labor union   Group of individuals working together to achieve shared job-related goals, such as higher pay, shorter working hours, more job security, greater benefits, or better working conditions [311]

law of demand   Principle that buyers will purchase (demand) more of a product as its price drops and less as its price increases [14]

law of supply   Principle that producers will offer (supply) more of a product for sale as its price rises and less as its price drops [14]

laws   Codified rules of behavior enforced by a society [535]

leadership   Process of motivating others to work to meet specific objectives [266]

leadership neutralizers   Factors that may render leader behaviors ineffective [274]

leadership substitutes   Individual, task, and organizational characteristics that tend to outweigh the need for a leader to initiate or direct employee performance [274]

leading Management process of guiding and motivating employees to meet an organization's objectives [145]

lean production system A Production system designed for smooth production flows that avoid inefficiencies, eliminate unnecessary inventories, and continuously improve production processes [219]

letter of credit Bank promise, issued for a buyer, to pay a designated firm a certain amount of money if specified conditions are met [470]

leverage Ability to finance an investment through borrowed funds [445]

liability Debt owed by a firm to an outside organization or individual [435]

liability insurance Insurance covering losses resulting from damage to people or property when the insured party is judged liable [533]

licensed brand Brand-name product for whose name the seller has purchased the right from an organization or individual [347]

licensing arrangement Arrangement in which firms choose foreign individuals or organizations to manufacture or market their products in another country [125]

limit order Order authorizing the purchase of a stock only if its price is equal to or less than a specified amount [511]

limited liability Legal principle holding investors liable for a firm's debts only to the limits of their personal investments in it [93]

Limited Liability Corporation (LLC) Hybrid of a publicly held corporation and a partnership in which owners are taxed as partners but enjoy the benefits of limited liability [94]

limited partner Partner who does not share in a firm's management and is liable for its debts only to the limits of said partner's investment [91]

limited partnership Type of partnership consisting of limited partners and a general (or managing) partner [91]

line authority Organizational structure in which authority flows in a direct chain of command from the top of the company to the bottom [184]

line department Department directly linked to the production and sales of a specific product [184]

line of credit Standing arrangement in which a lender agrees to make available a specified amount of funds upon the borrower's request [527]

liquidity Ease with which an asset can be converted into cash [436]

load fund Mutual fund in which investors are charged sales commissions when they buy in or sell out [503]

local area network (LAN) Computers that are linked in a small area, such as all of a firm's computers within a single building [406]

local content law Law requiring that products sold in a particular country be at least partly made there [130]

lockout Management tactic whereby workers are denied access to the employer's workplace [316]

long-term expenditures Purchases of fixed assets [525]

long-term goal Goal set for an extended time, typically five years or more into the future [156]

long-term liability Debt that is not due for at least one year [438]

low-contact system Level of customer contact in which the customer need not be part of the system to receive the service [208]

M-1 Measure of the money supply that includes only the most liquid (spendable) forms of money [464]

M-2 Measure of the money supply that includes all the components of M-1 plus the forms of money that can be easily converted into spendable forms [464]

M-3 Measure of the money supply that includes all the components of M-2 plus less liquid deposits of large institutional depositors [466]

mail order (catalog marketing) Form of nonstore retailing in which customers place orders for catalog merchandise received through the mail [374]

make-to-order operations Activities for one-of-a-kind or custom-made production [208]

make-to-stock operations Activities for producing standardized products for mass consumption [208]

management Process of planning, organizing, leading, and controlling an organization's resources to achieve its goals [144]

management accountant Private accountant who provides financial services to support managers in various business activities within a firm [432]

management advisory services Assistance provided by CPA firms in areas such as financial planning, information systems design, and other areas of concern for client firms [430]

management by objectives (MBO) Set of procedures involving both managers and subordinates in setting goals and evaluating progress [252]

management information system (MIS) Computer system that supports managers by providing information—reports, schedules, plans, and budgets—that can be used for making decisions [412]

managerial (management) accounting Field of accounting that serves internal users of a company's financial information [429]

managerial ethics Standards of behavior that guide individual managers in their work [40]

margin Percentage of the total sales price that a buyer must put up to place an order for buying stock [512]

market Mechanism for exchange between buyers and sellers of a particular good or service [11]

market appreciation The change in market values for a share of stock at two points in time [496]

market economy Economy in which individuals control production and allocation decisions through supply and demand [11]

market index Summary of price trends in a specific industry and/or the stock market as a whole [509]

market order Order to buy or sell a security at the market price prevailing at the time the order is placed [511]

market price (equilibrium price) Profit-maximizing price at which the quantity of goods demanded and the quantity of goods supplied are equal [14]

market segmentation   Process of dividing a market into categories of customer types [335]

market share   A company's percentage of the total industry's sales for a specific product [365]

market value   Current price of a share of stock in the stock market [493]

marketing   A set of processes for creating, communicating, and delivering value to customers and for managing customer relationships in ways that benefit the organization and its stakeholders [328]

marketing manager   Manager who plans and implements the marketing activities that result in the transfer of products from producer to consumer [333]

marketing mix   The combination of product, pricing, promotion, and distribution strategies used to market products [333]

marketing plan   Detailed strategy for focusing marketing efforts on consumer needs and wants [333]

markup   Amount added to an item's cost to sell it at a profit [366]

mass-customization   Although companies produce in large volumes, each unit features the unique options the customer prefers [401]

master limited partnership   Form of ownership that sells shares to investors who receive profits and that pays taxes on income from profits [91]

master production schedule   Schedule showing which products will be produced, and when, in upcoming time periods [216]

materials management   Planning, organizing, and controlling the flow of materials from sources of supply through distribution of finished goods [219]

matrix structure   Organizational structure created by superimposing one form of structure onto another [188]

media mix   Combination of advertising media chosen to carry a message about a product [382]

mediation   Method of resolving a labor dispute in which a third party suggests, but does not impose, a settlement [316]

merger   The union of two corporations to form a new corporation [96]

merit salary system   Individual incentive linking compensation to performance in nonsales jobs [303]

middle manager   Manager responsible for implementing the strategies and working toward the goals set by top managers [148]

mission statement   Organization's statement of how it will achieve its purpose in the environment in which it conducts its business [155]

missionary selling   Personal selling task in which salespeople promote their firms and products rather than try to close sales [384]

mixed market economy   Economic system featuring characteristics of both planned and market economies [12]

monetary policies   Policies used by a government to control the size of its money supply [476]

monetary policy   Management of the nation's economic growth by managing the money supply and interest rates [26]

money   Any object that is portable, divisible, durable, and stable and that serves as a medium of exchange, a store of value, and a measure of worth [463]

money market mutual fund   Fund of short-term, low-risk financial securities purchased with the pooled assets of investor-owners [465]

monopolistic competition   Market or industry characterized by numerous buyers and relatively numerous sellers trying to differentiate their products from those of competitors [17]

monopoly   Market or industry in which there is only one producer, which can therefore set the prices of its products [17]

mortgage loan   Loan secured by property being purchased [573]

motivation   The set of forces that cause people to behave in certain ways [245]

multinational (or transnational) corporation   Form of corporation spanning national boundaries [94]

multinational firm   Firm that designs, produces, and markets products in many nations [124]

municipal bond   Bond issued by a state or local government [502]

mutual fund   Company that pools cash investments from individuals and organizations to purchase a portfolio of stocks, bonds, and other securities [503]

mutual savings bank   Financial institution whose depositors are owners sharing in its profits [469]

NASDAQ Composite Index   Value-weighted market index that includes all NASDAQ-listed companies, both domestic and foreign [510]

National Association of Securities Dealers (NASD)   The largest private-sector, securities-regulation organization in the world [512]

National Association of Securities Dealers Automated Quotation (NASDAQ) system   World's oldest electronic stock market consisting of dealers who buy and sell securities over a network of electronic communications [499]

national brand   Brand-name product produced by, widely distributed by, and carrying the name of a manufacturer [347]

national competitive advantage   International competitive advantage stemming from a combination of factor conditions, demand conditions, related and supporting industries, and firm strategies, structures, and rivalries [120]

national debt   The amount of money the government owes its creditors [23]

natural monopoly   Industry in which one company can most efficiently supply all needed goods or services [18]

negligence   Conduct falling below legal standards for protecting others against unreasonable risk [539]

net asset value (NAV)   Current market value of one share [509]

net income (net profit, net earnings)   Gross profit minus operating expenses and income taxes [439]

no-load fund   Mutual fund in which investors pay no sales commissions when they buy in or sell out [503]

nominal GDP   Gross domestic product (GDP) measured in current dollars or with all components valued at current prices [20]

North American Free Trade Agreement (NAFTA) Agreement to gradually eliminate tariffs and other trade barriers among the United States, Canada, and Mexico [112]

obstructionist stance Approach to social responsibility that involves doing as little as possible and may involve attempts to deny or cover up violations [60]

Occupational Safety and Health Act of 1970 (OSHA) Federal law setting and enforcing guidelines for protecting workers from unsafe conditions and potential health hazards in the workplace [306]

odd-even pricing Psychological pricing tactic based on the premise that customers prefer prices not stated in even dollar amounts [369]

odd lot Fraction of a round lot [512]

officers Top management team of a corporation [95]

offshoring The practice of outsourcing to foreign countries [124]

off-the-job training Training conducted in a controlled environment away from the work site [300]

oligopoly Market or industry characterized by a handful of (generally large) sellers with the power to influence the prices of their products [17]

on-the-job training Training, sometimes informal, conducted while an employee is at work [300]

open-book credit Form of trade credit in which sellers ship merchandise on faith that payment will be forthcoming [542]

open-market operations The Fed's sales and purchases of securities in the open market [476]

operating expenses Costs, other than the cost of revenues, incurred in producing a good or service [439]

operating income Gross profit minus operating expenses [439]

operational plan Plan setting short-term targets for daily, weekly, or monthly performance [159]

operations Activities involved in making products—goods and services—for customers [204]

operations (production) management Systematic direction and control of the processes that transform resources into finished products that create value for and provide benefits to customers [205]

operations (production) managers Managers responsible for ensuring that operations processes create value and provide benefits to customers [205]

operations capability An activity or process that production does especially well with high proficiency [210]

operations control Process of monitoring production performance by comparing results with plans and taking corrective action when needed [219]

operations process Set of methods and technologies used to produce a good or a service [207]

order fulfillment All activities involved in completing a sales transaction, beginning with making the sale and ending with on-time delivery to the customer [378]

order processing Personal selling task in which salespeople receive orders and see to their handling and delivery [384]

organization chart Diagram depicting a company's structure and showing employees where they fit into its operations [174]

organizational analysis Process of analyzing a firm's strengths and weaknesses [158]

organizational citizenship Positive behaviors that do not directly contribute to the bottom line [239]

organizational commitment An individual's identification with the organization and its mission [243]

organizational stakeholders Those groups, individuals, and organizations that are directly affected by the practices of an organization and who therefore have a stake in its performance [46]

organizational structure Specification of the jobs to be done within an organization and the ways in which they relate to one another [174]

organizing Management process of determining how best to arrange an organization's resources and activities into a coherent structure [145]

outsourcing The practice of paying suppliers and distributors to perform certain business processes or to provide needed materials or services [123]

over-the-counter (OTC) market Organization of securities dealers formed to trade stock outside the formal institutional setting of the organized stock exchanges [499]

owners' equity Amount of money that owners would receive if they sold all of a firm's assets and paid all of its liabilities [435]

packaging Physical container in which a product is sold, advertised, or protected [348]

paid-in capital Money that is invested in a company by its owners [438]

par value Face value of a share of stock, set by the issuing company's board of directors [493]

participative management and empowerment Method of increasing job satisfaction by giving employees a voice in the management of their jobs and the company [253]

patent Exclusive legal right to use and license a manufactured item or substance, manufacturing process, or object design [541]

pay for performance (or variable pay) Individual incentive that rewards a manager for especially productive output [303]

pay-for-knowledge plan Incentive plan to encourage employees to learn new skills or become proficient at different jobs [304]

penetration pricing Setting an initially low price to establish a new product in the market [368]

pension fund Nondeposit pool of funds managed to provide retirement income for its members [469]

perfect competition Market or industry characterized by numerous small firms producing an identical product [16]

performance (in quality) A dimension of quality that refers to how well a product does what it is supposed to do [214]

performance appraisal Evaluation of an employee's job performance in order to determine the degree to which the employee is performing effectively [301]

performance behaviors The total set of work-related behaviors that the organization expects employees to display [239]

personal net worth Value of one's total assets minus one's total liabilities (debts) [546]

personal selling Promotional tool in which a salesperson communicates one-to-one with potential customers [383]

personality The relatively stable set of psychological attributes that distinguish one person from another [240]

person-job fit The extent to which a person's contributions and the organization's inducements match one another [244]

PERT chart Production schedule specifying the sequence of activities, time requirements, and critical path for performing the steps in a project [217]

physical distribution Activities needed to move a product efficiently from manufacturer to consumer [377]

physical resources Tangible items organizations use in the conduct of their businesses [10]

picketing Labor action in which workers publicize their grievances at the entrance to an employer's facility [316]

planned economy Economy that relies on a centralized government to control all or most factors of production and to make all or most production and allocation decisions [11]

planning Management process of determining what an organization needs to do and how best to get it done [144]

pledging accounts receivable Using accounts receivable as loan collateral [526]

point-of-sale (POS) display Sales promotion technique in which product displays are located in certain areas to stimulate purchase or to provide information on a product [384]

point-of-sale (POS) terminal Electronic device that allows customers to pay for retail purchases with debit cards [480]

political-legal environment The relationship between business and government [7]

portfolio The combined holdings of all the financial assets of any company or individual [503]

positioning Process of establishing an identifiable product image in the minds of consumers [380]

positive reinforcement Reward that follows desired behaviors [251]

preferred stock Stock shares that have preference, or priority, over common shares when dividends are distributed [495]

premium Sales promotion technique in which offers of free or reduced-price items are used to stimulate purchases [384]

pricing Process of determining what a company will receive in exchange for its products [364]

price-earnings ratio Current price of a stock divided by the firm's current annual earnings per share [508]

price lining Setting a limited number of prices for certain categories of products [369]

price skimming Setting an initially high price to cover new product costs and generate a profit [368]

pricing objectives Goals that sellers hope to attain in pricing products for sale [364]

primary securities market Market in which new stocks and bonds are bought and sold [492]

prime rate Interest rate available to a bank's most creditworthy customers [468]

principal Individual or organization authorizing an agent to act on its behalf [541]

private accountant Salaried accountant hired by a business to carry out its day-to-day financial activities [431]

private brand (private label) Brand-name product that a wholesaler or retailer has commissioned from a manufacturer [348]

private enterprise Economic system that allows individuals to pursue their own interests without undue governmental restriction [15]

private warehouse Warehouse owned by and providing storage for a single company [377]

privatization Process of converting government enterprises into privately owned companies [12]

proactive stance Approach to social responsibility by which a company actively seeks opportunities to contribute to the well-being of groups and individuals in its social environment [61]

process departmentalization Dividing an organization according to production processes used to create a good or service [178]

process layout Physical arrangement of production activities that groups equipment and people according to function [213]

product Good, service, or idea that is marketed to fill consumer needs and wants [333]

product departmentalization Dividing an organization according to specific products or services being created [178]

product differentiation Creation of a product feature or product image that differs enough from existing products to attract consumers [333]

product feature Tangible and intangible qualities that a company builds into a product [341]

product layout Physical arrangement of production activities designed to make one type of product in a fixed sequence according to its production requirements [214]

product liability Tort in which a company is responsible for injuries caused by its products [540]

product life cycle (PLC) Series of stages in a product's commercial life [345]

product line Group of products that are closely related because they function in a similar manner or are sold to the same customer group who will use them in similar ways [343]

product mix Group of products that a firm makes available for sale [343]

product placement A promotional tactic for brand exposure in which characters in television, film, music, magazines, or video games use a real product that is visible to viewers [346]

productivity A measure of economic growth that compares how much a system produces with the resources needed to produce it [21]

professional corporation Form of ownership allowing professionals to take advantage of corporate benefits while granting them limited business liability and unlimited professional liability [94]

profit center Separate company unit responsible for its own costs and profits [177]

profits Difference between a business's revenues and its expenses [5]

profitability ratio Financial ratio for measuring a firm's potential earnings [443]

profit-sharing plan Incentive plan for distributing bonuses to employees when company profits rise above a certain level [303]

program trading Large purchase or sale of a group of stocks, often triggered by computerized trading programs that can be launched without human supervision or control [513]

promissory note A formal, written promise to pay [526]

promotion Aspect of the marketing mix concerned with the most effective techniques for communicating information about and selling a product [380]

promotional mix Combination of tools used to promote a product [380]

property Anything of value to which a person or business has sole right of ownership [540]

property insurance Insurance covering losses resulting from physical damage to or loss of the insured's real estate or personal property [534]

prospectus Registration statement filed with the SEC before the issuance of a new security [514]

protected class Set of individuals who by nature of one or more common characteristics is protected under the law from discrimination on the basis of that characteristic [305]

protectionism Practice of protecting domestic business against foreign competition [129]

psychographic variables Consumer characteristics, such as lifestyles, opinions, interests, and attitudes, that may be considered in developing a segmentation strategy [336]

psychological contract Set of expectations held by an employee concerning what he or she will contribute to an organization (referred to as contributions) and what the organization will in return provide the employee (referred to as inducements) [243]

psychological pricing Pricing tactic that takes advantage of the fact that consumers do not always respond rationally to stated prices [369]

public relations Company-influenced information directed at building goodwill with the public or dealing with unfavorable events [385]

public warehouse Independently owned and operated warehouse that stores goods for many firms [377]

publicity Promotional tool in which information about a company, a product, or an event is transmitted by the general mass media to attract public attention [385]

publicly held (or public) corporation Corporation whose stock is widely held and available for sale to the general public [93]

punishment Unpleasant consequences of an undesireable behavior [251]

punitive damages Fines imposed over and above any actual losses suffered by a plaintiff [539]

purchasing Acquisition of the materials and services that a firm needs to produce its products [219]

purchasing power parity The principle that exchange rates are set so that the prices of similar products in different countries are about the same [20]

pure risk Risk involving only the possibility of loss or no loss [531]

quality The combination of characteristics of a product or service that bear on its ability to satisfy stated or implied needs [214]

quality control Taking action to ensure that operations produce products that meet specific quality standards [220]

quality improvement team TQM tool in which collaborative groups of employees from various work areas work together to improve quality by solving commonly shared production problems [222]

quality ownership Principle of total quality management that holds that quality belongs to each person who creates it while performing a job [221]

quid pro quo harassment Form of sexual harassment in which sexual favors are requested in return for job-related benefits [307]

quota Restriction on the number of products of a certain type that can be imported into a country [127]

rational motives Reasons for purchasing a product that are based on a logical evaluation of product attributes [338]

real GDP Gross domestic product (GDP) adjusted to account for changes in currency values and price changes [20]

recession A period during which aggregate output, as measured by GDP, declines [26]

recruiting Process of attracting qualified persons to apply for jobs an organization is seeking to fill [297]

registered bond Bond bearing the name of the holder and registered with the issuing company [502]

regulatory (administrative) law Law made by the authority of administrative agencies [536]

relationship marketing Marketing strategy that emphasizes lasting relationships with customers and suppliers [330]

replacement chart List of each management position, who occupies it, how long that person will likely stay in the job, and who is qualified as a replacement [296]

reseller market Organizational market consisting of intermediaries that buy and resell finished goods [339]

reserve requirement Percentage of its deposits that a bank must hold in cash or on deposit with the Fed [476]

responsibility Duty to perform an assigned task [183]

retailer Intermediary who sells products directly to consumers [370]

retained earnings Earnings retained by a firm for its use rather than paid out as dividends [438]

revenue recognition Formal recording and reporting of revenues at the appropriate time [442]

revenues Funds that flow into a business from the sale of goods or services [438]

revolving credit agreement Arrangement in which a lender agrees to make funds available on demand and on a continuing basis [527]

risk Uncertainty about future events [531]

risk avoidance Practice of avoiding risk by declining or ceasing to participate in an activity [532]

risk control Practice of minimizing the frequency or severity of losses from risky activities [532]

risk management Process of conserving the firm's earning power and assets by reducing the threat of losses due to uncontrollable events [531]

risk propensity Extent to which a decision maker is willing to gamble when making a decision [284]

risk retention Practice of covering a firm's losses with its own funds [532]

risk-return relationship The principle that safer investments tend to offer lower returns, while riskier investments tend to offer higher returns [504]

risk transfer Practice of transferring a firm's risk to another firm [532]

Roth IRA Provision allowing individual retirement savings with tax-free accumulated earnings [559]

round lot Purchase or sale of stock in units of 100 shares [512]

S corporation Hybrid of a closely held corporation and a partnership, organized and operated like a corporation but treated as a partnership for tax purposes [94]

salary Compensation in the form of money paid for discharging the responsibilities of a job [301]

sales agent Independent intermediary who generally deals in the related product lines of a few producers and forms long-term relationships to represent those producers and meet the needs of steady customers [371]

sales promotion Short-term promotional activity designed to encourage consumer buying, industrial sales, or cooperation from distributors [384]

Sarbanes-Oxley Act of 2002 (Sarbox) Enactment of federal regulations to restore public trust in accounting practices by imposing new requirements on financial activities in publicly traded corporations [433]

savings and loan association (S&L) Financial institution accepting deposits and making loans primarily for home mortgages [468]

secondary securities market Market in which existing stocks and bonds are traded [493]

secured bond Bond backed by pledges of assets to the bond holders [502]

secured loan Loan for which the borrower must provide collateral [526]

securities Stocks, bonds, and mutual funds representing secured, or asset-based, claims by investors against issuers [492]

Securities and Exchange Commission (SEC) Federal agency that administers U.S. securities laws to protect the investing public and maintain smoothly functioning markets [493]

securities investment dealer (broker) Finanial institution that buys and sells stocks and bonds both for investors and for its own accounts [469]

securities markets The markets in which stocks and bonds are sold [492]

selective credit controls The Fed's authority to set both margin requirements for consumer stock purchases and credit rules for other consumer purchases [477]

service operations (service production) Activities producing intangible and tangible products, such as entertainment, transportation, and education [204]

services Products having nonphysical features, such as time, expertise, or an activity that can be purchased [329]

sexual harassment Making unwelcome sexual advances in the workplace [306]

shopping agent (e-agent) E-intermediary (middleman) in the Internet distribution channel that assists users in finding products and prices but that does not take possession of products [375]

shopping good/shopping service Moderately expensive, infrequently purchased good or service [342]

short sale Stock sale in which an investor borrows securities from a broker to be sold and then replaced at a specified future date [512]

short-term (operating) expenditures Payments incurred regularly in a firm's everyday business activities [524]

short-term goal Goal set for the very near future [156]

short-term solvency ratio Financial ratio for measuring a company's ability to pay immediate debts [444]

shortage Situation in which quantity demanded exceeds quantity supplied [14]

situational approach to leadership Assumes that appropriate leader behavior varies from one situation to another [270]

small business Independently owned business that has relatively little influence in its market [74]

Small Business Administration (SBA) Government agency charged with assisting small businesses [74]

Small Business Development Center (SBDC) SBA program designed to consolidate information from various disciplines and make it available to small businesses [84]

small-business investment company (SBIC) Government-regulated investment company that borrows money from the SBA to invest in or lend to a small business [83]

smart card Credit-card-size plastic card with an embedded computer chip that can be programmed with electronic money [480]

social audit Systematic analysis of a firm's success in using funds earmarked for meeting its social responsibility goals [62]

social responsibility The attempt of a business to balance its commitments to groups and individuals in its environment, including customers, other businesses, employees, investors, and local communities [46]

socialism Planned economic system in which the government owns and operates only selected major sources of production [12]

sociocultural environment The customs, mores, values, and demographic characteristics of the society in which an organization functions [8]

software Programs that tell the computer's hardware what resources to use and how [408]

sole proprietorship Business owned and usually operated by one person who is responsible for all of its debts [90]

solvency ratio Financial ratio, either short- or long-term, for estimating the borrower's ability to repay debt [443]

spam Junk e-mail sent to a mailing list or a newsgroup [416]

span of control Number of people supervised by one manager [182]

specialty good/specialty service Expensive, rarely purchased good or service [342]

specialty store Retail store carrying one product line or category of related products [373]

speculative risk Risk involving the possibility of gain or loss [531]

speed to market Strategy of introducing new products to respond quickly to customer or market changes [344]

spin-off Strategy of setting up one or more corporate units as new, independent corporations [96]

spyware Program unknowingly downloaded by users that monitors their computer activities, gathering e-mail addresses, credit card numbers, and other information that it transmits to someone outside the host system [416]

stability Condition in which the amount of money available in an economic system and the quantity of goods and services produced in it are growing at about the same rate [24]

stabilization policy Government economic policy intended to smooth out fluctuations in output and unemployment and to stabilize prices [27]

staff authority Authority based on expertise that usually involves counseling and advising line managers [184]

staff members Advisers and counselors who help line departments in making decisions but who do not have the authority to make final decisions [184]

staff schedule Assigned working times in upcoming days for each employee on each work shift [217]

Standard & Poor's Composite Index Market index based on the performance of 400 industrial firms, 40 utilities, 40 financial institutions, and 20 transportation companies [510]

standard of living The total quantity and quality of goods and services people can purchase with the currency used in their economic system [19]

statement of cash flows Financial statement describing a firm's yearly cash receipts and cash payments [440]

statutory law Law created by constitutions or by federal, state, or local legislative acts [536]

stock A portion of ownership of a corporation [493]

stock broker Individual or organization who receives and executes buy-and-sell orders on behalf of other people in return for commissions [496]

stock exchange Organization of individuals formed to provide an institutional setting in which stock can be traded [496]

stockholder (or shareholder) Owner of shares of stock in a corporation [95]

stop order Order authorizing the sale of a stock if its price falls to or below a specified level [511]

strategic alliance Arrangement (also called joint venture) in which a company finds a foreign partner to contribute approximately half of the resources needed to establish and operate a new business in the partner's country [126]

strategic alliance Strategy in which two or more organizations collaborate on a project for mutual gain [96]

strategic goal Goal derived directly from a firm's mission statement [157]

strategic leadership Leader's ability to understand the complexities of both the organization and its environment and to lead change in the organization so as to enhance its competitiveness [277]

strategic management Process of helping an organization maintain an effective alignment with its environment [153]

strategic plan Plan reflecting decisions about resource allocations, company priorities, and steps needed to meet strategic goals [159]

strategy Broad set of organizational plans for implementing the decisions made for achieving organizational goals [154]

strategy formulation Creation of a broad program for defining and meeting an organization's goals [157]

strict product liability Principle that liability can result not from a producer's negligence but from a defect in the product itself [540]

strike Labor action in which employees temporarily walk off the job and refuse to work [316]

strikebreaker Worker hired as a permanent or temporary replacement for a striking employee [316]

subsidy Government payment to help a domestic business compete with foreign firms [129]

substitute product Product that is dissimilar from those of competitors but that can fulfill the same need [332]

supermarket Large product-line retailer offering a variety of food and food-related items in specialized departments [373]

supplier selection Process of finding and choosing suppliers from whom to buy [219]

supply The willingness and ability of producers to offer a good or service for sale [14]

supply chain (value chain) Flow of information, materials, and services that starts with raw-materials suppliers and continues adding value through other stages in the network of firms until the product reaches the end customer [224]

supply chain management (SCM) Principle of looking at the supply chain as a whole to improve the overall flow through the system [225]

supply curve Graph showing how many units of a product will be supplied (offered for sale) at different prices [14]

surplus Situation in which quantity supplied exceeds quantity demanded [14]

SWOT analysis Identification and analysis of organizational strengths and weaknesses and environmental opportunities and threats as part of strategy formulation [158]

sympathy strike (secondary strike) Strike in which one union strikes to support action initiated by another [316]

syndicated selling E-commerce practice whereby a Web site offers other Web sites commissions for referring customers [375]

tactical plan Generally short-term plan concerned with implementing specific aspects of a company's strategic plans [159]

tall organizational structure Characteristic of centralized companies with multiple layers of management [181]

tangible personal property Any movable item that can be owned, bought, sold, or leased [540]

tangible real property Land and anything attached to it [540]

target market Group of people that has similar wants and needs and that can be expected to show interest in the same products [335]

tariff Tax levied on imported products [129]

task-focused leader behavior Leader behavior focusing on how tasks should be performed in order to meet certain goals and to achieve certain performance standards [269]

tax services Assistance provided by CPAs for tax preparation and tax planning [430]

technical skills Skills needed to perform specialized tasks [150]

technological environment All the ways by which firms create value for their constituents [7]

telecommuting Form of flextime that allows people to perform some or all of a job away from standard office settings [256]

telemarketing Form of nonstore retailing in which the telephone is used to sell directly to consumers [374]

tender offer Offer to buy shares made by a prospective buyer directly to a target corporation's shareholders, who then make individual decisions about whether to sell [93]

Theory X Theory of motivation holding that people are naturally lazy and uncooperative [246]

Theory Y Theory of motivation holding that people are naturally energetic, growth-oriented, self-motivated, and interested in being productive [246]

time deposit Bank funds that have a fixed term of time to maturity and cannot be withdrawn earlier or transferred by check [465]

time management skills Skills associated with the productive use of time [151]

time value of money Principle that invested money grows by earning interest or yielding some other form of return [548]

top manager Manager responsible for a firm's overall performance and effectiveness [147]

tort Civil injury to people, property, or reputation for which compensation must be paid [539]

Total Quality Management (TQM) The sum of all activities involved in getting high-quality goods and services into the marketplace [221]

trade credit Granting of credit by one firm to another [526]

trade deficit Situation in which a country's imports exceed its exports, creating a negative balance of trade [116]

trade show Sales promotion technique in which various members of an industry gather to display, demonstrate, and sell products [384]

trade surplus Situation in which a country's exports exceed its imports, creating a positive balance of trade [116]

trademark Exclusive legal right to use a brand name or symbol [541]

traditional Individual Retirement Account (IRA) Provision allowing individual tax-deferred retirement savings [575]

trait approach to leadership Focused on identifying the essential traits that distinguished leaders [268]

transactional leadership Comparable to management, it involves routine, regimented activities [271]

transformational leadership The set of abilities that allows a leader to

recognize the need for change, to create a vision to guide that change, and to execute the change effectively [271]

transportation Activities in transporting resources to the producer and finished goods to customers [219]

trial court General court that hears cases not specifically assigned to another court [537]

trust services Bank management on behalf of an individual to manage an estate, investments, or other assets [470]

turnover Annual percentage of an organization's workforce that leaves and must be replaced [240]

two-factor theory Theory of motivation holding that job satisfaction depends on two factors, hygiene and motivation [248]

unemployment The level of joblessness among people actively seeking work in an economic system [25]

unethical behavior Behavior that does not conform to generally accepted social norms concerning beneficial and harmful actions [39]

Uniform Commercial Code (UCC) Body of standardized laws governing the rights of buyers and sellers in transactions [542]

unlimited liability Legal principle holding owners responsible for paying off all debts of a business [90]

unsecured loan Loan for which collateral is not required [526]

utility Ability of a product to satisfy a human want or need [205]

value Relative comparison of a product's benefits versus its costs [328]

value-added analysis Process of evaluating all work activities, materials flows, and paperwork to determine the value that they add for customers [222]

value package Product marketed as a bundle of value-adding attributes, including reasonable cost [341]

variable cost Cost that changes with the quantity of a product produced or sold [366]

venture capital company Group of small investors who invest money in companies with rapid growth potential [83]

vestibule training Off-the-job training conducted in a simulated environment [301]

video marketing Nonstore retailing to consumers via home television [376]

viral marketing A promotional method that relies on word of mouth and the Internet to spread information like a "virus" from person-to-person about products and ideas [347]

virtual leadership Leadership in settings where leaders and followers interact electronically rather than in face-to-face settings [278]

voluntary arbitration Method of resolving a labor dispute in which both parties agree to submit to the judgment of a neutral party [317]

voluntary bankruptcy Bankruptcy proceedings initiated by an indebted individual or organization [543]

VSAT satellite communications A network of geographically dispersed transmitter-receivers (transceivers) that send signals to and receive signals from a satellite, exchanging voice, video, and data transmissions [405]

wage reopener clause Clause allowing wage rates to be renegotiated during the life of a labor contract [314]

wages Compensation in the form of money paid for time worked [301]

warehousing Physical distribution operation concerned with the storage of goods [377]

warehousing Storage of incoming materials for production and finished goods for distribution to customers [219]

warranty Seller's promise to stand by its products or services if a problem occurs after the sale [542]

whistle-blower Employee who detects and tries to put an end to a company's unethical, illegal, or socially irresponsible actions by publicizing them [58]

wholesale club Bargain retailer offering large discounts on brand-name merchandise to customers who have paid annual membership fees [373]

wholesaler Intermediary who sells products to other businesses for resale to final consumers [370]

wide area network (WAN) Computers that are linked over long distances through telephone lines, microwave signals, or satellite communications [406]

Wi-Fi Short for wireless fidelity; a wireless local area network [407]

wildcat strike Strike that is unauthorized by the strikers' union [316]

wireless local area network A local area network with wireless access points for PC users [407]

wireless wide area network (WWAN) A network that uses airborne electronic signals instead of wires to link computers and electronic devices over long distances [407]

work sharing (job sharing) Method of increasing job satisfaction by allowing two or more people to share a single full-time job [255]

work slowdown Labor action in which workers perform jobs at a slower than normal pace [316]

work team Groups of operating employees who are empowered to plan and organize their own work and to perform that work with a minimum of supervision [185]

workers' compensation coverage Coverage provided by a firm to employees for medical expenses, loss of wages, and rehabilitation costs resulting from job-related injuries or disease [534]

workers' compensation insurance Legally required insurance for compensating workers injured on the job [304]

workforce diversity The range of workers' attitudes, values, beliefs, and behaviors that differ by gender, race, age, ethnicity, physical ability, and other relevant characteristics [308]

working capital Difference between a firm's current assets and current liabilities [525]

World Bank U.N. agency that provides a limited scope of financial services, such as funding improvements in underdeveloped countries [481]

World Trade Organization (WTO) Organization through which member nations negotiate trading agreements and resolve disputes about trade policies and practices [114]

World Wide Web A standardized code for accessing information and transmitting data over the Internet; the common language that allows information sharing on the Internet [404]